Handbook of Education Politics and Policy

This revised edition of the *Handbook of Education Politics and Policy* presents the latest research and theory on the most important topics within the field of the politics of education. Well-known scholars in the fields of school leadership, politics, policy, law, finance, and educational reform examine the institutional backdrop to our educational system, the political behaviors and cultural influences operating within schools, and the ideological and philosophical positions that frame discussions of educational equity and reform.

In its second edition, this comprehensive handbook has been updated to capture recent developments in the politics of education, including Race to the Top and the Common Core State Standards, and to address the changing role politics plays in shaping and influencing school policy and reform. Detailed discussions of key topics touch upon important themes in educational politics and help leaders understand issues of innovation, teacher evaluation, tensions between state and federal lawmakers over new reforms and testing, and how to increase student achievement. Chapter authors also provide suggestions for improving the political behaviors of key educational groups and individuals with the hope that an understanding of political goals, governance processes, and policy outcomes may contribute to ongoing school reform.

Bruce S. Cooper is a retired Professor of Educational Leadership in the Fordham University Graduate School of Education, USA.

James G. Cibulka is President of the Council for the Accreditation of Educator Preparation (CAEP) and former Dean of the College of Education at the University of Kentucky, USA.

Lance D. Fusarelli is Professor of Educational Leadership and Educational Policy at North Carolina State University, USA.

Handbook of Education Politics and Policy

Second Edition

Edited by
Bruce S. Cooper, James G. Cibulka,
and Lance D. Fusarelli

Routledge
Taylor & Francis Group

NEW YORK AND LONDON

Second edition published 2015
by Routledge
711 Third Avenue, New York, NY 10017

and by Routledge
2 Park Square, Milton Park, Abingdon, Oxon, OX14 4RN

Routledge is an imprint of the Taylor & Francis Group, an informa business.

© 2015 Taylor & Francis

First edition published by Routledge 2008

Library of Congress Cataloging-in-Publication Data
Handbook of education politics and policy / edited by Bruce S. Cooper, James G. Cibulka, and Lance D. Fusarelli. —
    Second edition.
        pages cm
    Includes bibliographical references and index.
    1. Education and state—United States—Handbooks, manuals, etc.   2. Education—Political aspects—United States—
Handbooks, manuals, etc.   I. Cooper, Bruce S.   II. Cibulka, James G.   III. Fusarelli, Lance D. (Lance Darin), 1966–
    LC89.H24 2015
    379.73—dc23
    2014010601

ISBN: 978-0-415-66042-6 (hbk)
ISBN: 978-0-415-66044-0 (pbk)
ISBN: 978-0-203-07410-7 (ebk)

Typeset in Minion
by Apex CoVantage, LLC

Printed and bound in the United States of America
by Edwards Brothers Malloy

CONTENTS

Preface: Constants and Changes in the Politics of Education by Bruce S. Cooper,
James G. Cibulka, and Lance D. Fusarelli   vii

Part I   **THE INSTITUTIONAL CONTEXT OF EDUCATIONAL
               POLITICS**   1

Chapter 1   Beyond Pluralistic Patterns of Power: Research on
               the Micropolitics of Schools   3
               BETTY MALEN AND MELISSA VINCENT COCHRAN (WITH UPDATED REFERENCES
               BY ANCHALA SOBRIN)

Chapter 2   Hitting a Moving Target: How Politics Determines the Changing
               Roles of Superintendents and School Boards   37
               THOMAS ALSBURY

Chapter 3   Advocates and Partners for Education Excellence: A 21st-Century
               Role for Mayors   62
               FREDERICK S. EDELSTEIN

Chapter 4   Understanding Education Policy Making and Policy Change in
               the American States: Learning from Contemporary Policy Theory 86
               MICHAEL K. McLENDON, LORA COHEN-VOGEL, AND JOHN WACHEN

Chapter 5   Political Cultures in Education: Emerging Perspectives   118
               KAREN SEASHORE LOUIS, KAREN FEBEY, AND MOLLY F. GORDON

Chapter 6   Judicial Impact on Education Politics and Policies   148
               MARTHA McCARTHY

Chapter 7   The Politics of School Finance in the New Normal Era   166
               BRUCE D. BAKER AND PRESTON C. GREEN

Chapter 8   Federal Education Policy from Reagan to Obama: Convergence,
             Divergence, and "Control"   189
             LANCE D. FUSARELLI AND BONNIE C. FUSARELLI

Chapter 9   Federalism, Equity, and Accountability in Education   211
             KENNETH K. WONG

Part II   INTEREST GROUPS, ACTIVISTS, ENTREPRENEURS, AND
             EDUCATION REFORM   229

Chapter 10   Binders of Women and the Blinders of Men: Feminism
             and the Politics of Education   231
             CATHERINE MARSHALL, LOIS ANDRE-BECHELY, AND BROOKE MIDKIFF

Chapter 11   Religious Faith and Policy in Public Education: A Political and
             Historical Analysis of the Christian Right in American Schooling   267
             NATHAN R. MYERS AND JAMES G. CIBULKA

Chapter 12   Respecting Religion and Culture in Schools: An International
             Overview   284
             CHARLES L. GLENN

Chapter 13   The Politics of Entrepreneurship and Innovation   304
             MICHAEL Q. McSHANE AND FREDERICK M. HESS

Chapter 14   The Ideological and Political Landscape of School Choice
             Advocacy   322
             JANELLE SCOTT, CHRISTOPHER LUBIENSKI, AND ELIZABETH DeBRAY

Chapter 15   The Collective Politics of Teacher Unionism   343
             BRUCE S. COOPER

Chapter 16   Outliers: Political Forces in Gifted and Special Education   365
             FRANCES R. SPIELHAGEN, ELISSA F. BROWN, AND CLAIRE E. HUGHES

Chapter 17   A New Kind of Integrated Education   384
             PAUL GREEN

Chapter 18   Interest Groups Revisited   411
             TAMARA YOUNG, CATHERINE DiMARTINO, AND BRIAN BOGGS

Contributors   425
Index   431

PREFACE

CONSTANTS AND CHANGES IN THE POLITICS OF EDUCATION

Welcome to the revised, second edition of the *Handbook of Education Politics and Policy,*
originally released in 2008. The need for a revised edition was driven by the growing
interest in and recognition of the critical (if sometimes unpleasant) role education politics plays in shaping and influencing school policy and educational reform.

In fact, judging from well-publicized conflicts among school boards over student reas-
signment and community schools, within state legislatures over vouchers, and between
state and federal lawmakers over the Common Core and the imposition of reforms
brought about through Race to the Top funding, one might argue that the politics in
education is growing increasingly partisan and contentious.

These conflicts and changes led to this revised second edition of the *Handbook.* While
some of the politics have remained consistent, others have changed in new and somewhat unpredictable directions. For example, urban regime theory, institutional agility,
urban leadership praxis, and the politics of coordinated social services have been deem-
phasized in the revised *Handbook,* while emerging areas of aggressive federal involvement in education reform, policy entrepreneurship and innovation, special education,
and international education receive far more extensive treatment in these new chapters.

In addition, all the remaining chapters in the original edition have been extensively
updated to capture recent developments in the politics of education. The original edition was broken into three separate parts, including Section I on federal, state, and local
politics; Section II on interest groups and institutions; and Section III on the politics of
equity and excellence. The revised edition is more tightly organized into two sections:
Part I, the institutional context of education politics; and Part II on interest groups,
activists, entrepreneurs, and education reform.

THE INSTITUTIONAL CONTEXT OF EDUCATION POLITICS

Part I of the revised edition begins with the critically important area of the micropolitics of education—teacher-to-teacher politics, teacher-to-principal politics, and related

building-level politics. We then examine politics at the district level, particularly between superintendents and local boards of education. Often, board turnover leads to superintendent turnover, policy churn, and leadership instability.

For example, Wake County (Raleigh), North Carolina, home to the 15th largest school district in the country, has had four superintendents in seven years (one retired, one resigned as a result of board turnover, and another was fired after even more board turnover). Politics at the local level often involves enduring conflicts between parents, teachers, school leaders, and the communities they serve. These constants often apply equally well to rural, suburban, or urban school districts.

We then move to politics at the municipal (mayoral) and state levels. Mayoral control remains a contentious issue and state legislatures have stimulated a great deal of discussion about the politics of education as they have initiated reforms such as merit pay, the elimination of teacher tenure, teacher personnel appraisal and value-added systems, and school vouchers. These reforms have triggered an enormous amount of politicking about education at the state level, with a class action lawsuit recently filed when the North Carolina legislature (under unified Republican control) passed a statewide voucher plan.

Moving from the states to the larger U.S. political context, the next two chapters discuss the intense politics surrounding school law and finance, specifically the role of the courts in these areas. This again reflects one of the constants in the politics of education—arguing over who is entitled to get what type of educational provision, at what cost, and who will pay for it. These are fundamental, enduring issues in the politics of education that reflect fundamental differences in value preferences and belief systems.

The final two chapters in Part I of the *Handbook* address an old, yet in many ways, a fundamentally new federal role in education reform. These two chapters explore how a succession of U.S. "education presidents" has left their imprint on education politics and policies, and how the growth of federal power and control over local education is reshaping educational politics in profound and as yet undetermined ways.

The first part of this book, therefore, explores the "contexts" in which education policy is made and by whom. Chapter 1 is by Betty Malen and Melissa Vincent Cochran and explores the important theories and practices of "micropolitics" of education, which to them are complex and often underdeveloped, as they involve, for example, "the space from community politics to classroom and corridor dynamics, employ various theoretical orientations, focus on different units of analysis, encompass a maze of loosely defined formal and informal arenas, and address an array of salient topics and prevalent policy issues."

Yet we know that politics is often personal and that good leaders understand their colleagues and can work with them well. In fact, all relationships in organizations are political in some sense, as educators, politicians, parents, and citizens all try to influence schools in their organizations, staffing, programs, and outcomes.

Efforts to change school structures and controls, as with charter schools, also alter the micropolitics of education, as smaller, more autonomous schools still require management, funding, leadership, and organization, whether on a large or small scale, and vary state to state, place to place. Microanalysis is a useful tool as we look at individual schools and organizations and at teacher and parent involvement. And as more people are getting involved (e.g., parents, teachers, citizens, foundations, and other funding agencies) the interactions are best understood, as Malen and Vincent Cochran explain, at the micropolitical level.

As this chapter found, others are aware of this level of analysis, as Blasé and Blasé explain: "Now, more than ever before, school reform efforts require that principals and teachers work together collaboratively to solve educational problems" (2004, p. 266). And to update the chapter, Anchala Sobrin reviewed current literature on micropolitics of education, appended to the end of Chapter 1, and found that Webb asserts that "micro-political studies formalize the concept of power as a binary relationship between the concepts of authority and influence" (2007, p. 127).

Chapter 2 by Thomas Alsbury explores the role changes and relationships between school superintendents and the board of education that hired and supervises them. He then explains the political theories of governance (by school boards) and management (by superintendents), culminating, for example, in the Iowa Lighthouse Project, that

> found that more effective schools with higher student achievement could be developed through a leadership partnership between the board and the superintendent. In these districts, unique team approaches were employed including role negotiation, shared training, shared goals development, joint accountability measures, policy development, and alignment of superintendent hiring focus, job expectations, and evaluation criteria.

Building on these concepts, Alsbury goes on to question whether public education is a "democratically run" local operation or a larger state and national operation that's integrated into a larger, less local system and process. And the important relationship between the local school superintendent and school board is yet another concern because superintendents were initially hired in education to be the board's secretary, not an independent education professional. Kowalski (2008) has described superintendents as evolving from (1) teacher-scholar (1865 to 1910), (2) manager (1910 to 1930), (3) democratic leader (1930 to mid-1950), (4) applied social scientist (mid-1950 to 1980), and (5) communicator (1980 to present).

And Alsbury concludes that despite the changes, particularly in larger cities, in the role and relationships of school boards to superintendents, we need to continue to examine local settings, locations, and outcomes to learn how school boards and their executives can improve our schools. He ends by saying that: "school governance embodies a wide and varying contextual tapestry that will continue to challenge and alter a static and homogenous description of the changing roles of superintendents and school board members."

Chapter 3 by Frederick S. Edelstein examines the role of city mayors (and similarly county executives) as both partners and advocates for education quality. First, since the first edition of this *Handbook* was published in 2008, mayors of many cities have matured in their views of education in their cities and towns; in fact, many have moved from being outsiders to insiders in the education policy process, as these leaders take the "bully pulpit" in voicing their opinions and choices in local education. Edelstein characterizes these leaders as "advocates" for schools, using various cities and towns—and their mayors—as examples, using Cleveland, New York City, and the Los Angeles Unified School District.

As Edelstein explains, "Mayors believe that their leadership and involvement can assist school districts to be more transparent, efficient, and accountable, as well as provide better coordination of services with other agencies that affect the lives of children and families." Importantly, he points out that most notice and publicity are given to mayors who "take over" schools, while we can also learn much from those who use influence and ideas to help schools improve, while building community and business support for improving local urban schools across the United States. Edelstein acknowledges that the role of mayors is changing in education, as they are more engaging, influential, and important to reform in their local schools and the quality of urban life for the whole community.

Chapter 4 by Michael K. McLendon, Lora Cohen-Vogel, and John Wachen looks at education politics from the perspective of the 50 states, as the states' roles have changed and increased in importance and activeness. The authors explain summarily that "In K-12 education, we noted, states had adopted new curriculum standards, embarked on innovative teacher certification regimens, established new assessment and accountability regimes, experimented with incentives programs linking teacher compensation with student performance, litigated hundreds of school finance lawsuits, and witnessed the ascendancy and retreat—and re-ascendance—of countless other 'reform' initiatives at the local, state, and national levels."

Their chapter covers the states' role at both the higher and K-12 (lower) levels of education, and compares the two levels. Little research, the authors found, has compared the competition by state between higher and K-12 education, and between states as they vie for attention, resources, and political support. How do states vary in adopting and changing policies that affect schools and universities? Pressures rise as more states implement new policies and programs, as Chapter 4 explores and explains.

Chapter 5 by Karen Seashore Louis, Karen Febey, and Molly F. Gordon examines the "political culture" that is rising across the education landscape at both the state and national levels for higher and K-12 education. In fact, states are now changing their education in light of national trends and pressures. The authors explore Race to the Top and No Child Left Behind, both key federal programs. They explain that the Obama administration is creating "an historic moment in American education . . . that offers bold incentives to states willing to spur systemic reform" (www.whitehouse.gov/issues/education/k-12/race-to-the-top).

This chapter uses North Carolina as a place to study state-local relationships, and finds that "Overall, the North Carolina schools did not talk about a need for local-level autonomy in crafting policies to fit the context of their school or district, even when they expressed a desire for more influence in the state policy process." And in Nebraska, the authors find, prevalence of the "individualist culture" showed that while local educators were in favor of accountability, they also valued and stressed local beliefs and practices in schools, based on local student needs and learning styles.

But higher education was different, as schools had a financial and practical interest in students doing well and repaying their college loans. More research on higher education policies and standards is called for, as Chapter 5 indicates, comparing and contrasting higher and "lower" education, in its accountability, policy making, and outcomes. By using the lens of "political culture," we can begin to grasp the "linkages among state-level policies, stakeholder involvement in the policy process, and teachers' and principals' interpretations of these policies in the classroom," as Louis, Febey, and Gordon suggest at the end of this useful chapter.

Martha McCarthy in Chapter 6 moves to the judicial role in education policy making, as issues in education, often not easily solved, end up in court, usually the federal judiciary. As this chapter explains, "The impact of the courts, particularly the federal judiciary, on education policies and politics has evoked interest and critique for the past several decades." Based on the principle of "separation of powers," this chapter explores and explains the judicial role (Section III of the U.S. Constitution and many state constitutions), in comparison to the legislative and executive branches that govern our schools. The courts interpret the laws, not make them, as McCarthy explains, and are accountable to the law, not to an electorate or political party (and judges often serve for life).

This chapter treats cases like *Brown* (1954) on racial desegregation and *Engle v. Vitale* (1963) on school prayer that have shaped key policies and practices in our schools. And Martha McCarthy reminds us that the courts are usually the "last resort" in politics, and that school leaders, teachers, and school boards still make and enact school policies and go to court only when they feel they have no choice. For "going to court" over education problems and issues is still a big step and needs to be observed, researched, and analyzed regularly.

Chapter 7, coauthored by Bruce D. Baker and Preston C. Green, explores the key role of politics and finance in education, for who pays, how much, and drawn (e.g., taxed) from whom are certainly hot political issues. Money matters, to tax providers and school users and educators. We learn that money matters now more than ever, as 26 states are cutting funding for schools on a per-pupil basis, when Baker and Green report that: "Three states—Arizona, Alabama, and Oklahoma—each have reduced per-pupil funding to K-12 schools by more than 20 percent. (These figures, like all the comparisons in this chapter, are in inflation-adjusted dollars and focus on the primary form of state aid to local schools.)"

And the role of financing is distinct, as societies "invest" in their children at different levels and in different ways. Money matters, and Baker and Green show us how. As Baker explains elsewhere:

> Sustained improvements to the level and distribution of funding across local public school districts can lead to improvements in the level and distribution of student outcomes. While money alone may not be the answer, more equitable and adequate allocation of financial inputs to schooling provide a necessary underlying condition for improving the equity and adequacy of outcomes. The available evidence suggests that appropriate combinations of more adequate funding with more accountability for its use may be most promising. (Baker, 2012, p. 18)

Thus funds, as shown in Chapter 7, are related to the quality of resources, programs, and outcomes.

Chapter 8 by Lance D. Fusarelli and Bonnie C. Fusarelli traces the role and impact of U.S. presidents, ranging from Ronald Reagan (1981–1989) to our current leader, Barack Obama (2009 to present), and explores how these leaders have and are influencing education at the national, state, and local levels, a movement often termed "federalization": as we are "one nation, under God, with liberty and justice for all."

Starting with the early 1980s, this chapter traces the rising role of education in American life and politics; this chapter links our quality of life and economic well-being to our schools when the Fusarellis write: "Concerned by this lack of economic competitiveness, big business became a major player in pushing for system-wide, school-based accountability by linking reform to international economic competition (Jackson & Cibulka, 1992)."

When the federal government got involved, national leaders put together the levels of government and found them more "tightly coupled" than previously believed, starting with the idea that presidents can mount the "bully pulpit" and call attention to problems of equity, quality, and outcomes for all. And this interesting chapter even looks at the effects of left- and right-wing politics, and how presidents and their party can influence school policies, programs, and outcomes.

Even the lingo has changed, as presidents and other leaders now talk about a Race to the Top (RTTT), the Common Core State Standards (CCSS), and changes in the evaluation of teachers. Earlier presidents hardly ever mentioned teachers, much less classroom practices and outcomes. Although Chapter 8 explains that we don't (yet) have true "national standards" for the 14,000 plus school districts, the Common Core State Standards are moving us in that direction—national associations of school superintendents and state governors are getting strong support from President Obama and other groups. These national leaders are pushing ideas, according to Lance Fusarelli and Bonnie Fusarelli, to use "merit pay" to recognize and push school classroom instruction and attainment.

Thus, an ever-widening "circle of control" is occurring, "inserting" the federal government into state and local school policies and outcomes, more now than ever. Thus, we see "the limitations imposed by constitutional design can be overcome" (Fusarelli & Cooper, 2009, p. 263), as education becomes an important national concern, a policy area, that is more open to federal regulations.

In Chapter 9, Kenneth K. Wong puts the pieces all together, looking at federalism, equity, and accountability—the *setting* (called "federalism"), the *values* (e.g., "equity"), and *process* (through "accountability"), in that order. Wong describes the three levels of education (federal, state, local, and now even school) as in constant flux, depending on the regime in Washington, DC, the leadership in the states, and local control, where money and power come together.

Wong believes that we need all the levels, and that the federal level is most vulnerable as education becomes more local and state controlled. But he argues at the end of his chapter that keeping federal investments in education alive has four key benefits to education across the 50 states and 14,000 or so districts: (1) investing in a national data system that is both reliable and comprehensive; (2) providing a national detailed view of what works in every community; (3) the importance of national-presidential leadership and influence for school improvement, rather than having each community get stuck in its own rut; (4) coordination among agencies and departments, beyond just education. As Wong explains toward the end of his chapter:

> Currently, federal appropriations in key education and related services are managed by more than a dozen federal agencies. In addition to the Department of Education, these agencies include Agriculture, Defense, Health and Human Services, Homeland Security, Interior, Justice, Labor, Veteran Affairs, Appalachian Regional Commission, National Endowment for the Arts, National Endowment for the Humanities, and National Science Foundation.

With so many groups, Wong ends his chapter with a call for a continued investment in education and education research, to give us a national view of what works and to what extent across the whole country. Intergovernmentalism must work if U.S. schools are to benefit and work for all children, regardless of background, ability, language or race, *or location,* as Wong explains.

INTEREST GROUPS, ACTIVISTS, ENTREPRENEURS, AND EDUCATION REFORM

The second part of the new *Handbook* examines the dizzying array of interest groups, activists, entrepreneurs, and think tanks that increasingly play key roles in shaping education politics. The authors of each of the first four chapters of this part explore the role that ideas, ideologies, and culture play in mobilizing political interests.

In Chapter 10, Catherine Marshall, Lois Andre-Bechely, and Brooke Midkiff address gender issues in the politics of education. They illustrate how a feminist perspective illuminates many education controversies such as single-sex schooling, school violence, educational attainment by females, women's employment opportunities in superintendencies, and many other issues.

While the authors chronicle the progress that has been made for females in recent decades on a variety of fronts, they also present a mixed picture on representation, attainment, and outcomes. The chapter ends with a discussion of vulnerabilities as well as promising directions. Some trends push in both directions. Social media, for example, have not only facilitated organizing around feminist causes, but also exacerbated a focus on intergroup relations, which can work against gender equality.

In Chapter 11, Nathan R. Myers and James G. Cibulka examine the evolving role of the Christian right in education politics. While they trace its influence to 19th-century conflicts over religion in public education, they distinguish the "New Fundamentalism" that has emerged since the 1970s from its forebearers. The Christian right is no longer exclusively Protestant, is activist in its use of media, direct marketing, and other mobilizing strategies, and has forged a close alliance with the national Republican Party. Still, the movement's members represent an aging demographic, leadership turnover, and a growing diversity of perspectives, including competition from Tea Party priorities, all of which threaten its future influence in national politics and state and local education politics more broadly.

Myers and Cibulka argue that the Christian right's political gains on education issues have been mixed and remain secondary to sexuality and family issues for them. They foresee a continuing potential for political influence in the short term, providing the movement manages its challenges adroitly, but question the Christian right's ability over the long term to shape a political agenda to achieve its aims rather than repeat its tendency merely to react to societal trends it abhors.

In Chapter 12, Charles L. Glenn provides an international overview of the role that religion and culture play in education policy and politics and how these factors have evolved in different national contexts. Among the factors that influence how nations respect religion and culture are the role of ethnic minorities, native cultures, and immigrants, as well as the role of language. Issues of racial segregation also come into play. Glenn shows how today there has been "a mixing together of what had been distinct conflicts over religion and culture."

He argues that even in countries that respect more than one religion, the legal and constitutional frameworks in education carry different consequences. Glenn extols the virtues of freedom of choice as promoting social capital and illustrates this in different contexts, including the historic role of Catholic schooling in the United States. In short, this chapter helps place the U.S. approach to separating church and state in a comparative international context.

In Chapter 13 Michael Q. McShane and Frederick M. Hess analyze how current institutional frameworks in education impede innovation and its handmaiden, entrepreneurship. The current system, they argue, produces lots of innovation but little systemic change. They review entrepreneurship as a potential "disruptive change" that can drive needed innovation to improve educational opportunities for children who have been ill served by the present system, can improve the quality of educators, and create better education tools and services. They review barriers to entrepreneurship such as politics, attitudes, beliefs, and habits, as well as formal ones enshrined in laws, rules, and regulations.

While McShane and Hess assert that professional authority and entrepreneurship are not fundamentally at odds, they do distinguish between two competing worldviews—bureaucracy and professionalism on the one side and the alternative that "accepts the risk that some new ventures will fail so as to address a larger risk . . . staid mediocrity." It is clear that McShane and Hess embrace the latter worldview and the education politics that flow from that embrace.

A View from the Top

The last five chapters of this *Handbook* apply a political and policy lens to different but related topics that will prove useful as we analyze them. Each is different, but they all provide insight into the politics of education and how the field informs theory and practice. Here's a listing of the chapter numbers, authors, and themes, which will be elaborated on in this introduction.

In Chapter 14 by Janelle Scott, Christopher Lubienski, and Elizabeth DeBray, the authors "revisit" the role and importance of interest groups in education, like other political areas. While important, before this handbook, first and second editions, these groups, associations, organizations, and even individuals were not well studied and understood in education. Yet what could be more important to more people than education, which involves more than 55 million children and 5 million teachers and other professionals daily, not to mention parents and grandparents who nurture the kids?

This chapter acknowledges the prior insights of Opfer, Young, and Fusarelli, in "Politics of Interest: Interest Groups and Advocacy Coalitions in American Education" in the previous edition of the *Handbook* (2008), moving beyond their arguments from our first edition of this *Handbook* while also looking at politics in fields other than education. Scott, Lubienski, and DeBray provide valuable knowledge of what the interest groups are and how they are important in lobbying and helping school boards and other key leaders win election.

What could be more central and critical to an active democracy than working to change and improve our schools? In an important way, Chapter 14 opens the way for other chapters in this edition of the *Handbook* that follow it. Certainly, students and their families of all levels, incomes, races, and types are affected by classroom teachers, which are dependent in many cases on their unions to get them decent pay and benefits.

Bruce S. Cooper, in Chapter 15, looks at employee-employer politics, with the important, changing role of unions (e.g., American Federation of Teachers and the National Education Association), which have gained power and influence in policy making at all levels of government, particularly the state and local jurisdictions. The AFT and NEA even attempted to merge, to become a single, more powerful force in setting policies and determining pay and benefits. While the AFT, led by Al Shanker, voted "YES," the NEA at the New Orleans football arena voted "NO."

But this chapter also discusses the antiunion movements in several states, as politicians attempt to withdraw the right to bargain and strike. As President Obama commented about such movements in Michigan, "They have everything to do with politics. What they're really talking about is giving you the right to work for less money" (Davey, 2012, p. 1). Karl Marx would understand this effort, we think.

In Chapter 16, Frances R. Spielhagen, Elissa F. Brown, and Claire E. Hughes move from teacher politics to the twin concerns for gifted and disabled children and the politics of these key groups. While much research has been done on high- and low-ability children, few analyses are available comparing the politics of kids of all backgrounds and levels. For as President John F. Kennedy explained, "Not every child has an equal talent or an equal ability or equal motivation; but children have the equal right to develop their talent, their ability, and their motivation."

This chapter explores the politics of educating all children, without sacrificing any students, based on their backgrounds, needs, or abilities (and disabilities) and how we as a nation within our schools help some without shortchanging others—equity at work. Does meeting the needs of *all children* lead to ignoring the exceptional ones?

Chapter 17 by Paul Green explores and explains the newest policies of school integration, based on race. It appears, as analyzed in this chapter, that public education in states likes Kentucky and Washington are reinterpreting the *Brown* (1954) decision: that assigning children to school based on race was no longer unconstitutional. In fact, Green warns that this movement away from integration was also an effort to make our schools *apartheid*. He also warns us that retreating from desegregation, much less integration, will have a terrible effect on our children and society.

Green argues, in fact, that "regional versus local planning is also required to link housing, school, and employment, as well as political and cultural opportunities, to spread accountability throughout entire metropolitan areas." Thus, in this chapter, we learn that integration of life, society, and schools go together, "integrally."

And in Chapter 18, Tamara V. Young, Catherine DiMartino, and Brian Boggs revisit the important role of "interest groups" that are key to any understanding of politics in any field. Thus these five chapters are a nearly perfect circle, starting with "interest group" analysis in Chapter 14, and ending with Chapter 18 on similar issues. We hope that these analyses help everyone to understand politics and policies and how various groups and processes affect the schooling of our children.

FEARLESS FORECASTS

Given the changes in the politics of education since the original edition of the *Handbook* came out six years ago, we offer some intrepid forecasts of political battles over education policy and reform in the coming decade. First, we forecast continuing conflict between the federal role and state and local responsibilities. It is not clear whether this playbook will continue to evolve in new ways or persist largely as it is framed at present.

Second, we anticipate continuing political challenges to established bureaucratic institutions and funding patterns, as well as to established professional autonomy and authority, largely from advocates of market choice and innovation. Third, we see growing political mobilization to challenge social and educational inequality and its impact on educational opportunities and outcomes, with implications for educational service delivery and resource allocations.

Fourth, we believe debates over testing, its expenditures and impacts on children, teaching, and schools will expand in the coming decade as will debate over efforts to rate and evaluate teachers and schools within the United States and in international contexts for global competitiveness. Finally, we see the continued proliferation of groups mobilizing around ideas, ideologies, and interests. And battles over educational policy and reform now include diverse areas: for example, merit pay, teacher evaluation, Common Core, testing and accountability, and expanded school choice, are heating up in the coming decades. And this book anticipates and elaborates them in the following sections and chapters.

Bruce S. Cooper, James G. Cibulka,
and Lance D. Fusarelli

REFERENCES

Baker, B. D. (2012). Revisiting the age-old question: Does money matter in education? *Albert Shanker Institute*.

Blasé, J., & Blasé, J. (2004). The dark side of school leadership: Implications for administrator preparation. *Leadership & Policy in Schools, 3*(4), 245–273.

Brown v. the Board of Education. (1954).

Davey, M. (2012). Michigan governor signs law limiting unions. *New York Times:nytimes.com/2012/12/12/us/protesters-rally-over-michigan-union-limits-plan.html?*

Fusarelli, B. C., & Cooper, B. S. (2009). *The rising state: How state power is transforming our nation's schools*. Albany, NY: State University of New York Press.

Jackson, B. L., & Cibulka, J. G. (1992). Leadership turnover and business mobilization: The changing political ecology of urban school systems. In J. G. Cibulka, R. J. Reed, & K. K. Wong (Eds.), *The politics of urban education in the United States* (pp. 71–86). Washington, DC: Falmer Press.

Kowalski, T. J. (2008). School reform, civic engagement, and school board leadership. In T. L. Alsbury (Ed.), *The future of school boards governance: Relevancy and revelation* (pp. 225–246). Lanham, MD: Rowman & Littlefield.

Opfer, V. D., Young, T. V., & Fusarelli, L. D. (2008). Politics of interest: Interest groups and advocacy coalitions in American education. In B. S. Cooper, J. G. Cibulka, & L. D. Fusarelli (Eds.), *Handbook of education politics and policy* (pp. 195–216). New York: Routledge.

Webb, T. P. (2008). Re-mapping power in educational micropolitics. *Critical Studies in Education, 49*(2), 127–142.

Part I
The Institutional Context of Educational Politics

1

BEYOND PLURALISTIC PATTERNS OF POWER

Research on the Micropolitics of Schools

Betty Malen and Melissa Vincent Cochran
with updated references by Anchala Sobrin

The micropolitics of schools is an evolving but arguably underdeveloped field of study (Blasé & Anderson, 1995; Scribner, Aleman, & Maxy, 2003). Its conceptual boundaries and distinctive features remain elusive and contested. Its empirical foundation is broad in scope but uneven in quality. For example, studies span the space from community politics to classroom and corridor dynamics, employ various theoretical orientations, focus on different units of analysis, encompass a maze of loosely defined formal and informal arenas, and address an array of salient topics and prevalent policy issues. Some studies unpack the dynamic, power-based, and interest-driven processes through which conflict is regulated and make clear the basis of judgments rendered; others do not. Some studies explain how and why cases were selected; others do not. Some studies support broader generalizations; others are more "existence proofs." These attributes of the field confound the prospects for developing an exhaustive, integrated, and definitive review of literature on the micropolitics of schools. Thus we adopt more modest aims.

PURPOSE AND PERSPECTIVE

We seek to update and extend the findings of an earlier review of research on the micropolitics of schools that focused on "mapping the multiple dimensions of power relations in school polities" (Malen, 1995, p. 147). The power relations emphasis was, at the time, a unifying theme in the empirical and theoretical literature on the micropolitics of schools (Bacharach & Mundell, 1993; Ball, 1987; Blasé, 1991, Bowles, 1989; Hoyle, 1986). It remains a unifying construct in the broader politics of education field (Malen, 2001b), as well as in the parent discipline. As Hochschild writes, "That . . . power would unify otherwise disparate articles is hardly surprising; if our discipline [political science] has any center toward which its many peripheries gravitate, it is the study of power in all of its many manifestations" (2005, p. 213).

Although power is a core element and a unifying component of political analysis, the early review (Malen, 1995) noted that studies draw on different conceptions of power

3

and its companion terms, authority, influence, and control. Some employ "pluralist" views that concentrate on the overt manifestations of power evidenced by influence (or noninfluence) on visible, contentious, and consequential decisions. Others draw on "elitist" views that expose the more covert expressions of power apparent in the suppression of dissent, the confinement of agendas to "safe" issues, the management of symbols, and the "suffocation . . . [of] . . . demands for change in the existing allocation of benefits and privileges" (Bacharach & Baratz, 1970, p. 44). Still others draw on "radical" or "critical" views that delve into the more opaque "third face" of power and derive inferences on how power relations shape aspirations and define interests through subtle but presumably detectable processes of socialization/indoctrination that elude the awareness of individuals who succumb to them but may be evident to the analyst who searches for them (Gaventa, 1980; Lukes, 1974). All these views have their advocates and critics (Clegg, 1989; Geary, 1992). All these views are reflected in studies of the "micropolitics" of schools.

We draw on this multidimensional view of power to anchor our review of research on select but significant aspects of the micropolitics of schools. Because this field of study has not arrived at a consensus definition of "micropolitics," we adopt a general and inclusive construction. In our view, micropolitical perspectives characterize schools as mini political systems, nested in multilevel governmental structures that set the authoritative parameters for the play of power at the site level. Confronted by multiple, competing demands, chronic resource shortages, unclear technologies, uncertain supports, critical public service responsibilities, and value-laden issues, schools face difficult and divisive allocative choices. Like actors in any political systems, actors at the site level manage the endemic conflict and make the distributional choices through processes that pivot on power exercised in various ways in various arenas (Malen, 1995). With others, we maintain that micropolitical perspectives cast schools as "arenas of struggle" (Ball, 1987; Blasé, 1991) where actors use their power to advance their interests and ideals; where conflict, competition, cooperation, compromise, and co-optation coexist; and where both public and private transactions shape organizational priorities, processes, and outcomes. Always conditioned and often constrained by broad institutional, economic, and sociocultural forces, these actor relationships, interactions, and exchanges, and their impact on the distribution of valued outcomes, become the foci of study.

We analyze adult relationships, namely the professional-patron, principal-teacher, and teacher-teacher interactions that occur in select formal and informal arenas in public school systems in the United States because they provide telling glimpses into the micropolitics of schools.[1] We synthesize information on the sources of tension, the patterns of politics, and the outcomes of transactions in those arenas. Although most definitions of micropolitics direct attention to "those activities and strategies used by organizational participants to influence decisions that allocate scarce but valued resources within the organization" (Johnson, 2001, p. 119), scholars recognize that context situates and mediates the play of power in organizations generally and in schools more specifically (e.g., Bacharach & Mundell, 1993; Townsend, 1990). Therefore, we highlight policy developments that condition the play of power at the school site to set the stage for our analysis of key aspects of politics within U.S. public schools.

Our analysis is based on studies identified through a search for research-based articles that directly address the micropolitics of schools, for articles that might enable us to draw inferences about power relationships in school contexts even though the term "micropolitics" is not used in the text, and for articles that examine the manner in which policy developments in the broader context may affect the autonomy of schools and the discretion afforded site actors.[2] We began our search with major refereed journals dating from 1992–2006, and then expanded it to include citations uncovered during that process as well as other books and research reports that addressed the major themes we were uncovering.[3] While we located and reviewed more than 200 articles and more than 75 additional works, we do not cite all the sources we consulted. Rather we use citations selectively, to illustrate the major themes we uncovered in the literature and to highlight disconfirming as well as confirming evidence regarding the observations and interpretations we set forth. Because much of the research takes the form of case studies, we underscore that the political dynamics we describe are not necessarily typical of the dynamics found in the vast universe of U.S. public schools. We draw on this research to generate insights, not to make definitive claims, about the micropolitics of schools and how the broader policy context may be shaping those dynamics.

THE POLICY CONTEXT

Our analysis suggests that the broad policy context may be affecting the micropolitics of schools by narrowing the parameters for influence at the site level,[4] by creating alternative organizational forms, and by injecting more "external" actors into the governance, management, and operation of schools. We discuss each of these developments in turn.

Narrowing Parameters for Influence at the School Level

The initial review of literature (Malen, 1995) alluded to the modest degrees of discretion afforded site actors, given resource constraints, the "web of rules" governing site decision making, and the weak design of the various policies that were advanced to ensure that site actors had considerable (and additional) decision-making authority. This review reinforces that observation, and then argues that site autonomy has been constrained even more, by the packages of federal, state, and local policies that further circumscribe the power, limit the discretion, and restrict the influence of site actors.

The unfulfilled promise of greater discretion. Reforms aimed at "empowering" schools and the people who worked in them became prominent in the mid- to late 1980s with countless calls for site-based management councils, school-level budgeting and decision making, school improvement teams, advisory committees, and other structural arrangements that presumably would grant site actors the autonomy and the authority required to reform their schools (Bauch & Goldring, 1998; Ingersoll, 2003: Malen & Muncey, 2000). Several lines of evidence suggest that, to date, the promise of greater discretion has been largely unfulfilled.

First, the scope of "new" authority delegated to schools is still modest and temporary. Save for settings that permitted school councils to hire and fire their principals, we found little evidence of a fundamental expansion of decision-making authority in any, let alone all the critical areas of budget, personnel, and instructional programs (Croninger & Malen, 2002; Handler, 1998; Odden & Busch, 1998; Summers & Johnson, 1996). Moreover, it has become clear that whatever "new authority" was decentralized could be re-centralized (Leithwood & Menzies, 1998; Shipps, 1998; Shipps, Kahne, & Smylie, 1999). Thus site actors do not appear to have more extensive or more dependable degrees of freedom (Malen & Muncey, 2000).

Second, resource constraints and the "web of rules" embedded in the broader system continue to restrict site autonomy. Oftentimes site actors are empowered to manage budget cuts, not to initiate program improvements (Croninger & Malen, 2002; Fine, 1993; Handler, 1998). While some state governments have tried to relax rules and regulations for "high-performing" schools or to engage in various forms of "differential regulation," these exemptions have not operated to significantly enhance site autonomy (Fuhrman & Elmore, 1995). On the contrary, they may further limit autonomy because these policies remind schools that states can deploy the punishment of a takeover as well as the reward of regulatory relief (Malen & Muncey, 2000). Whether other forms of deregulation such as charter schools, choice plans, and for-profit educational management arrangements will enhance the discretion afforded site actors remains an open, empirical question (Crawford & Forsythe, 2004; Johnson & Landman, 2000; Mintrom, 2001). But for "traditional" public schools, and particularly for low-performing schools, rule and resource constraints still limit the autonomy of site actors (Malen & Muncey, 2000; Sipple et al., 2004; Timar, 2004).

Third, the responsibilities of site actors have intensified, in part because policy packages exacted a price (stronger accountability for the promise of greater autonomy) and in part because policy rhetoric located the blame for low performance squarely on schools (Elmore, 2002; Malen et al., 2002). Schools have been given additional assignments, such as developing school improvement plans, implementing curricular frameworks, incorporating new testing procedures, adapting to various "external partners," and otherwise "demonstrating" that they are meeting the terms of more stringent "results-based" accountability systems. These responsibilities have come in addition to, not in lieu of, other demands and obligations (Anagnostopoulos, 2003; Booher-Jennings, 2005; Mintrop, 2004; Sunderman, 2001; Wong & Anagnostopoulos, 1998).

In short, for site actors, various "empowerment" reforms resulted in a substantial increase in responsibility but not a commensurate increase in authority, a dependable increase in relevant resources, or a meaningful measure of relief from the sets of regulations and obligations that guide and govern what site actors may and must do. While "empowering" reforms did little to expand and much to limit the latitude of site actors, other initiatives, launched primarily at the state level and reinforced by federal legislation and district reaction, further constrained the autonomy of site actors (Anagnostopoulos, 2005; Conley, 2003; Timar, 2004). Recognizing that data are limited,[5] we point to the standards and high-stakes accountability policies to illustrate that observation.

The stark reality of stricter accountability. During the 1980s and 1990s states intensified their efforts to control schools. Under the auspices of stronger accountability and coherent policy, states stepped up their efforts (a) to articulate curriculum content through various requirements, frameworks, and tests; (b) to define school programs through mandates that make schools select programs for at-risk students from a fairly short list of state-approved options, and, in so doing, to regulate the professional development that school staffs receive; and (c) to issue public sanctions ranging from public listing of "low-performing schools" to focused state interventions or full-scale reconstitution, privatization, or takeovers (Ladd, 1996; Malen, 2003). While not all states have been equally active in all domains of education, generally speaking, states appear to be coupling policy instruments in potent ways and asserting unprecedented levels of control over schools (Conley, 2003; Malen, 2003; Neuman-Sheldon, 2006; Timar, 2004).

Over the past decade, the federal government also stepped up efforts to control public schools with its rhetorical press for "results-based" accountability and its formal endorsement of graduated but stringent sanctions for schools that fail to meet the requirements of No Child Left Behind. While federal policies have been contested, they represent a renewed effort to influence the core of schooling (Cohn, 2005; McDonnell, 2005; Superfine, 2005). Likewise, districts in some settings have generated initiatives and developed responses that may limit the latitude of site actors (Anagnostopoulos, 2003; Booher-Jennings, 2005; Ogawa, Sandholtz, & Scribner, 2003; Sunderman, 2001; Wong & Anagnostopoulos, 1998).

A small but growing body of evidence indicates that these policies are changing (for better or worse) the content of curriculum (Dorgan, 2004; Firestone, Fitz, & Broadfoot, 1999; Firestone, Mayrowetz, & Fairman, 1998; Sandholtz et al., 2004; Trujillo, 2005), the pace if not the pedagogy of instruction (Dorgan, 2004; Finkelstein et al., 2000; McNeil, 2000; Swanson & Stevenson, 2002), and the allocation of time and personnel (Dorgan, 2004; Stetcher & Barron, 1999; Wong & Anagnostopoulos, 1998). In some cases schools "pull resources away from the most needy students . . . [in order to concentrate] on students most likely to improve school-wide achievement test scores" (Sunderman, 2001, p. 526; see also Booher-Jennings, 2005; Diamond & Spillane, 2004; Elmore, 2002; Neuman-Sheldon, 2006). Although the evidence is not as extensive, it appears that these policies are changing other important aspects of schooling, such as: the nature of professional development (Fairman & Firestone, 2001; Firestone et al., 1999); the substance and structure of site-level school improvement deliberations (Finkelstein et al., 2000; Maxcy & Nguyên, 2006); the nature and attractiveness of teachers' work (Anagnostopoulos, 2005; Dorgan, 2004; Finkelstein et al., 2000; Swanson & Stevenson, 2002); conceptions of the primary purposes of schooling; views of the appropriate roles of governmental units (Malen & Muncey, 2000); and views of what counts as good teaching (Booher-Jennings, 2005). Although the effects vary depending on the severity of the stakes attached to accountability systems and, at times, the level of schooling, survey and case study data suggest that standards and accountability policies are limiting the autonomy of site-level actors (Dorgan, 2004; Finkelstein et al., 2000; Pedulla et al., 2003).

While external policies are not the only factor shaping what site actors do, and while site responses vary (Grant, 2001; Pedulla et al., 2003; Zancanella, 1992), the developments highlighted here suggest that school-level actors may not be in a position to evade, remake, or rebuff directives from afar as readily as they have in the past (Cohen & Spillane, 1992; Hill, 2001; Kirp & Driver, 1995; Rossman & Wilson, 1996; Schon, 1981). Rather, it appears that through various combinations of symbols, sanctions, rules, regulations, and exhortations, the broader system has exerted considerable control over the agenda of public schools, rewritten the rules of the game, and created what Mazzoni terms "a new set of givens" that restrict the range of options open to and the degree of discretion available to site actors (Malen & Muncey, 2000).

While it appears that these policy developments may be marginalizing site actors, we are reminded that "reforms that appear to be centralizing control over schools might well serve to promote local democratic practice" (Mintrom, 2001, p. 638). For example, standards and accountability policies have the potential to produce information that attentive publics or what Gamson (1960) terms "potential partisans" might use to press for school reforms that they view as key (Cibulka, 1991; Mintrom, 2001). More drastic measures, such as the creation or imposition of new organizational forms or "top-down takeovers of schools," might "clear new spaces for democratic practice to emerge" (Mintrom, 2001, p. 638). Thus, these new organizational forms along with other changes in the policy landscape hold important implications for our understanding of the micropolitics of schools.

Generating Alternative Organizational Forms

Charter schools along with other alternative organizational forms have gained prominence over the past decade (Mintrom, 2001; Wasley et al., 2000). The policies governing charter schools and their profiles vary considerably within and across states (Manno et al., 1998). Generally speaking, however, these schools are freed from select constraints and afforded opportunities to recruit "like-minded staff," to control their budgets, to select curricula, and to recruit students (Bulkley & Hicks, 2005; Johnson & Landman, 2000, p. 102; Loveless & Jasin, 1998). Often relatively small, these schools may engender a different political dynamic because school staffs are likely to be more homogeneous and because parents and educators choose to be part of the organization. Because some charter schools are run by private, for-profit companies and some traditional public schools are being turned over to private, for-profit education management companies (a trend that may accelerate if sanctions for chronically low-performing schools are enforced), we have yet another class of organizations to explore as we try to understand more fully the micropolitics of schools. Although data on the micropolitics of charter schools, privately managed schools, reconstituted schools (Hess, 2003; Malen et al., 2002), various versions of autonomous small schools (Wasley et al., 2000), and other alternative organizational forms are thin, we incorporate insights from studies that illuminate the political dynamics in these new arenas.

Injecting New Organizational Actors

Largely as a result of more stringent accountability pressures and local capacity constraints, some schools, notably low-performing schools, are developing or are being required to develop various partnerships with external organizations or to work more closely with various networks that offer assistance and support (Hess, 2003; Honig, 2004; Smith & Wohlstetter, 2001; Weschler & Friedrich, 1997; Wohlstetter et al., 2003). At times these arrangements inject new actors like monitoring teams, instructional coaches, after-school programmers, and organizational consultants into the school and alter the size and composition of school-based leadership teams (Camburn, Rowan, & Taylor, 2003; Datnow & Castellano, 2001; Wong & Anagnostopoulos, 1998). Because data regarding how these new players affect the micropolitics of the school are limited, this potentially important development gets short shrift in this review.

PROFESSIONAL-PATRON TRANSACTIONS IN FORMAL AND INFORMAL ARENAS

Principals, teachers, parents, and community residents interact in formal arenas, such as program-specific advisory committees, school-wide improvement teams, and school-based governing boards. These long-standing avenues for citizen engagement are rooted in ideals of local, democratic control, criticisms of unresponsive bureaucratic systems, and issues surrounding the quality and fairness of educational programs and services. As such, they provide a strong starting point for uncovering the micropolitics of schools.

Ironically, we have "surprisingly few accounts of how deliberations actually occur on the ground" (Fung, 2004, p. 133). But surveys of participants' responses, summaries of case study findings, and several more detailed accounts of professional-patron dynamics help unpack the play of power in these formal arenas. Anecdotal references to private exchanges and several more detailed accounts of professional-patron relationships suggest how power may be exercised in informal arenas.

Sources of Tension

Consistent with the findings of the initial review (Malen, 1995), professional-parent tensions still center on who has the legitimate right to decide policy and whether the school has provided appropriate and equitable educational services to various groups of students within the school. Because professionals realize that, at any time, their constituents can level criticisms that threaten the stability and legitimacy of the school (Greenfield, 1995; Johnson & Fauske, 2000; Malen, 1995), anxieties about the school's ability to withstand scrutiny and to contain conflicts rooted in divergent views of appropriate and equitable policies, programs, and services are ever-present. These enduring tensions are brokered through patterns of politics that reveal the capacity of professionals and select parents to gain, at least momentarily, a relative power advantage.

Patterns of Politics in Formal Arenas

The patterns of politics in formal arenas range from exchanges that avoid and suppress conflict to those that inflame and expand it. We begin with the avoidance/suppression patterns that protect established interests because they are the most pronounced in the literature.

Avoiding/suppressing conflict—Protecting established interests. Much of the early literature on site-based councils documents that the underlying tensions between professionals and parents are managed and minimized through ceremonial exchanges that avert conflict and reinforce traditional patterns of power wherein professionals control school policy and instructional programs and parents provide support. More recent research indicates that "strong professional control remains intact regardless of the extent of parental empowerment at the school site" for many of the schools that are part of Chicago's relatively ambitious effort to grant parents real power in school governance (Wong, 1994, p. 174; see also Bryk et al., 1998; Hess, 1996, 1999c; Lewis & Nakagawa, 1995), as well as for schools located in other settings (Bauch & Goldring, 1998; Croninger & Malen, 2002; Leithwood, Jantzi, & Steinbach, 1999).

Even though school councils have not redistributed power in substantial and durable ways, they do appear to serve important political functions. Repeated references to council topics as "trivial," council functions as "rubberstamping" decisions made elsewhere, and council processes as "manufacturing consent" (Seitsinger & Zera, 2002, p. 352) or as "socializing parents" into submissive roles as "trustees of the status quo" (Nakagawa, 2000; Seitsinger & Zera, 2002, p. 340) suggest that councils may serve as fairly effective mechanisms for suppressing conflict. The councils may operate to co-opt parental concerns, to deflect criticisms of schools (Anderson, 1998; Croninger & Malen, 2002; Lewis & Nakagawa, 1995), and to diffuse the influence of parents "who wish to say something about the pattern of resource inequities [or uneven accomplishments] across schools" (Shipps, 1997, p. 103). These and other features and functions of parental participation in site-based governance bodies indicate that opportunities for meaningful participation in school governance may be rare, especially for parents of children from low-income, minority, and migrant populations (Croninger & Malen, 2002; Hess, 1996; Lopez, Scribner, & Mahitivanichcha, 2001).

Even more troubling is evidence suggesting that "participatory reforms" may not only curb the ability of parents to voice their concerns but also divert attention from the life circumstances that must be addressed before parents can be involved in school governance (Lopez et al., 2001) and from the underlying sources of educational inequities (Anderson, 1998). They may do so by putting the focus on innocuous topics, organizational "tinkerings," and symbolic reassurances that "mean little when neither leadership nor revenue is there to meet the challenges of poverty and racism" (Lewis & Nakagawa, 1995, p. 173).

As noted elsewhere (Malen, 1995), the avoidance/suppression of conflict and the exclusion of interests pattern of politics are produced by a combination of factors, such as the principal's capacity to control the agenda and the information flow, and at times the composition of the council; the willingness of teachers to align with the principal to protect what they view as professional prerogatives; the ability of professionals to reroute contentious issues to more private subcommittees; and the reluctance of parents to challenge these dynamics. These patterns are further reinforced by ingrained norms surrounding the topics that can be raised and the degree of disagreement allowed, the formal powers granted site council members, the availability of resources to assist and support the work of council members, and by the broader forces of race, ethnicity, and economics that converge to structure access and influence in our educational and social systems.

Managing conflict—Acknowledging diverse interests. At times, professionals and parents engage in council exchanges that appear to be more open, deliberative, and representative. In fact, about one-third of the elementary schools in Chicago exhibited signs of this pattern (Bryk et al., 1998). While a few additional "existence proofs" are present in the literature (Murray & Grant, 1995), an in-depth analysis of what researchers termed "strong sites" in Chicago is particularly instructive (Fung, 2004). Although the author concedes that patterns of participation uncovered were not equal or ideal, the analysis illustrates how site-based governance councils can foster "the inclusion of disadvantaged residents," civic engagement in education, and meaningful changes in local schools (Fung, 2004, p. 226).

A critical factor in this dynamic seems to be the alignment of parents with civic associations and activist organizations that monitor the implementation of participatory structures, mobilize parents and community residents, enhance their capacity to advocate through training and technical assistance, and provide "ordinary parents and residents the confidence and presence of mind to deal as equals with the street-level public servants in forums such as . . . LSC [local school council] sessions" (Fung, 2004, p. 229). Even when these alignments are present, however, the evidence suggests that parents often approve decisions made by others and that professionals perpetuate a clear division of labor that keeps important decisions about school policy, curriculum, and pedagogy beyond the reach of parental influence. For example, in these cases, professionals often "took the lead in formulating school proposals and developing strategies to implement them, and then sought the approval and sometimes active contribution of lay participants to execute those strategies . . . lay persons served primarily as monitors and supporters rather than as fully equal innovators" (Fung, 2004, p. 143).

Studies of efforts to organize communities so that residents can become effective advocates for school reform tend to corroborate these findings (Fine, 1993; Gold, Simon, & Brown, 2005).[6] Even with support from external actors, parents in general and low-income parents in particular find it hard to break the power advantage that professionals, most notably principals, often hold (Fine, 1993; Horvat, Weininger, & Lareau, 2003; Lewis & Nakagawa, 1995). Although principals are constrained by cross-cutting demands, governmental regulations, and community expectations, they can, by virtue of their positions as gatekeepers, filter demands and structure relationships in ways that minimize and marginalize some external influences. As Baum put it, "A community organization's chances of influencing a school depend greatly on a principal's interest in having the school influenced ... community organizations may influence schools when interventions leave basic academic policies and practices untouched" (Baum, 2003, pp. 258–259).

Likewise, studies of various partnerships between schools and community organizations illustrate that principals are able to compartmentalize initiatives, regulate communications, structure work relationships, and otherwise exert considerable control over the degree to which these initiatives affect school priorities and practices (Kahne et al., 2001; Smylie et al., 1994). Principals appear to be a key factor in determining whether these partnerships provide ad hoc support for existing arrangements or whether they operate to significantly alter organizational roles, relationships, and responsibilities (Croninger & Malen, 2002; Sanders & Harvey, 2002). Generally speaking, studies of both large-scale initiatives and more localized efforts suggest that community partnerships are not dependable mechanisms for engendering more inclusive forms of governance or meaningful levels of parent influence on school policies, priorities, and practices (Croninger & Malen, 2002; Gerry, 1999; Riehl, 2000; Smrekar & Mawhinney, 1999; White & Wehlage, 1995).

At times, principals and professionals "reach out" to parents and related constituencies in an apparent effort to cultivate parental participation and community engagement by creating new arenas for educators, students, and patrons to come together to discuss educational concerns (Amatea & Vandiver, 2004; Cate, Vaughn, & O'Hair, 2006) or by mobilizing parents and residents to support some action (Giles et al., 2005). However meritorious the new forms of parent conferences and community engagement may be, these initiatives tend to confine parental involvement to areas that professionals deem appropriate. For example, professionals invite parents to be involved in their children's education and to mobilize around student safety issues in the school's immediate environment. Such gestures may cultivate good will, enable professionals and patrons to identify shared interests, and engender some improvements in social relationships and environmental safety. But these overtures do not challenge existing patterns of power in school governance.

Whether professionals can retain this degree of control over the micropolitics of schools in the alternative organizational forms that are being promulgated is an open, empirical question. For example, parents in choice schools may be more likely than non-choice parents to report that they can influence educational policies and priorities in their schools (Smrekar & Goldring, 1999; Yu & Taylor, 1997); but evidence that they actually do so directly is thin. For example, few choice parents serve on governance councils or advisory boards or participate in formal decision-making arenas (Yu & Taylor, 1997). Moreover, the kind of parent involvement encouraged in choice and charter schools appears to embrace the "serve and support" norms and to reflect the class bias found in invitations that professionals extend to parents in more traditional public schools (Becker, Nakagawa, & Corwin, 1997; Croninger & Malen, 2002). However, some parents—notably middle- and upper middle-class white parents who comprise a "local elite"—may be able to exercise influence indirectly and informally, through a host of strategies including but not limited to threats to withdraw their children from the school (Lipman, 1997; Wells & Serna, 1996) or threats to expand the scope of conflict beyond the formal boundaries of the school.

Mobilizing conflict—Activating interests. Interactions between professionals and patrons are not confined to measured exchanges. At times conflict escalates and erupts. The formal arenas are unable to contain the conflict as parents and community residents link up with each other and, with broader networks, adopt more confrontational tactics, ignite the deep divisions that exist within and among groups, and otherwise alter power relationships in the schools by taking the political battle beyond the calm arenas of the individual school to the volatile amphitheaters of public protests and "street brawls" (Schattschneider, 1960). Parents are inclined to mobilize when events (e.g., desegregation plans, curricular changes, schools closures) signal that their core values have been violated and that the school is not taking their concerns seriously or responding appropriately (Apple, 1996; Malen, 2006; Zimmerman, 2002). In the current context, efforts to promote the rights of gay and lesbian students, to distribute condoms in secondary schools, or to make clinical services and daycare centers part of the school program have evoked evangelical responses, public protests, school boycotts, and other confrontational tactics that can alter, at least temporarily, the relative power of patrons (Sharp, 1999).

To be sure, not all eruptions take on adversarial forms. Community activism may be instigated or embraced by professionals who want to alter the system through public but peaceful demonstrations that dramatize shared interests and collective commitments. Perhaps because these and other scope-expansion dynamics are so unpredictable and so unnerving, professionals generally seek to keep conflict in the orbit of the organization. That aim is accomplished, not only through the formal structures, but also through informal exchanges that apparently operate to preempt conflict and to preserve the existing balance of power.

Patterns of Politics in Informal Arenas

References to middle-class and upper middle-class advantage are prevalent in critiques of school systems and in characterizations of the micropolitics of schools, but the dynamic processes through which these advantages are procured are not well documented.[7] We rely on a few of the more detailed accounts to illustrate how these informal exchanges reinforce patterns of power and privilege evident in the broader society.

Avoiding/containing conflict—Protecting established interests. In the initial review (Malen, 1995), principals surfaced as key actors whose primary political function was to prevent or to contain conflict through public reassurances that the school is in good hands, through the selective application and enforcement of school policies, and through other private compacts with middle-class and upper middle-class parents who might expand the scope of conflict or exercise the exit option if their preferences are not accommodated. The more recent literature affirms that the middle-class and upper middle-class parents still have the edge, not just because school personnel may make private deals, but because administrators and teachers anticipate their interests and adjust accordingly (Brantlinger, 2003). One adjustment involves confining agendas to safe issues. For example, Lipman (1997) documents how teacher work groups confined their conversations to nonthreatening issues and effectively shut down those who tried to raise challenging issues, especially regarding racial disparities in school practices, in part because they, like the principal, anticipated intense parental reactions and feared that "powerful White parents would withdraw their support—and their children from public schools" (Lipman, 1997, p. 31). Another adjustment involves scaling back reforms like de-tracking that call into question the entitlements that children of the "local elites" have traditionally received (Wells & Serna, 1996). Such accommodations may appease parents who reputedly have the power to affect the careers of school employees, to alter the composition of the student population, and to undercut the legitimacy of the system by withdrawing their children and their support from the school (Wells & Serna, 1996).

The pattern of middle-class advantage in the micropolitics of schools is produced in part by "middle-class networks" that encourage parents to confront the school and provide resources that parents can use to challenge the expertise and the authority of professional educators (Horvat, Weininger, & Lareau, 2004). Described as "uniquely able to mobilize the information, expertise or authority needed to contest the judgments of schools officials" (Horvat et al., 2004, p. 319), these networks command attention and accommodation. The middle-class advantage is also perpetuated by the willingness of professionals to accede to their demands, by the inability of other parents to offset their resource advantages, by the norms of conflict containment that exist in school systems, and by the broader societal scripts that frame middle-class demands as "entitlements" that educators are expected to protect (Wells & Serna, 1996).

Whether these patterns of power will hold sway in the new organizational forms that are becoming more prevalent remains to be seen (Bauch & Goldring, 1995; Schneider & Buckley, 2002). The evidence indicates that the threat of exit, when leveled by middle-class parents or "local elites" may help these parents gain leverage in the schools they presently attend. Whether these parents maintain comparable leverage in the micropolitics in alternative "choice" and charter sites is not clear. We suspect that leverage in those sites may be contingent on the number of students waiting to enter and on the characteristics of parents threatening to exit the school.

Mobilizing conflict—Recognizing broader interests. Many parents "enter the contested sphere of public education typically with neither resources nor power. They are usually not welcomed by the schools, to the critical and serious work of rethinking educational structures and practices" (Fine, 1993, p. 682; see also Eccles & Harold, 1993; Nakagawa, 2000). Like other less powerful individuals and groups in society, these parents may require infrastructures of support and assistance so their chances of getting a favorable hearing can be improved (Fine, 1993; Walker, 1991). Some argue that choice options and charter schools would empower parents who have little power in the current system; others disagree (Andre-Bechely, 2005; Fine, 1993). At this time, the data are not available to settle this debate. What can be said is that the manner and degree to which parents acquire influence in schools are contingent on many factors, including but not limited to the norms and features of the school itself. Studies of the power dynamics in new organizational forms might help us understand more fully how institutional arrangements shape the exercise and the distribution of power among parents and professionals.

Outcomes of Professional-Patron Interactions

Professional and patron exchanges in formal and informal arenas beget mixed reviews that closely resemble those noted in the initial review (Malen, 1995).

Formal Arenas. Across studies, professionals continue to express appreciation for the support parents provide on site councils and concerns about the time invested and the stress generated when parents raise issues or make demands in areas that fall outside the accepted domains for parent "input." Likewise, parents continue to express appreciation for the intrinsic awards that can accompany participation (e.g., a sense of belonging, a sense of importance, new knowledge about school programs and operations) and concerns about the time commitment and the "token" involvement (Lewis & Nakagawa, 1995; Ryan et al., 1997; Seitsinger & Zera, 2002). Assessments that go beyond the impact of these arrangements on the participants suggest that school councils may stimulate marginal adjustments in school operations, but these changes, in and of themselves, do little to alter school performance or the distribution of educational gains (Heck, Brandon, & Wang, 2001; Lewis & Nakagawa, 1995, p. 126; Robertson, Wohlstetter, & Mohrman, 1995). While encouraging signs are present in some settings (Bryk, Hill, & Shipps, 1999; Designs for Change, 2005; Ryan et al., 1997), the literature reveals "an awesome gap between the rhetoric and the reality of SBM's [site-based management's] contribution to student growth" (Leithwood & Menzies, 1998, p. 23; see also Finkelstein & Tritter, 1999; Smylie, Lazarus, & Brownlee-Conyers, 1996; Summers & Johnson, 1995).

Some have tried to reconcile these competing assessments by looking to Chicago's experiment with "democratic localism" because it is the most thoroughly documented study of a broad effort to alter the relative power of professionals and patrons on site-based governance councils and to use that change in governance as a force for improving students' educational opportunities and academic accomplishments. According to Bryk and colleagues (1998), roughly one-third of Chicago's underperforming elementary schools developed strong patterns of participation and made noticeable improvements in the organization of teachers' work, the quality of instruction, and the relationships between parents and other local actors (Bryk, 1999). Despite these changes, initial analyses of Chicago's governance reforms found achievement gains to be negligible across the district and modest in most schools, including those schools with active local councils (Hess, 1996), in part because fiscal shortfalls meant schools had to use their resources to maintain basic operations, not launch new initiatives (Hess, 1999c).

Subsequent efforts to sort out the possible achievement efforts underscore the difficulty of linking achievement gains to this reform not only because measurement is highly problematic, but also because gains are unstable across years, vary by subject, and may be attributed to a host of factors that go well beyond local school council activities (Hess, 1999a, 1999b, 1999c). Nonetheless, studies using fairly sophisticated techniques and controls for student mobility show greater gains in achievement than earlier studies and these gains appear to be strongest in schools with active local councils and supportive principals who have adopted school improvement plans that address professional development, social relationships, and student achievement (Bryk, 1999). A recent analysis of reform initiatives in Chicago's elementary schools maintains that "144 inner city Chicago elementary schools," all of which were low-performing in 1990, "have shown 15 years of substantial sustained achievement gains" in reading (Designs for Change, 2005, p. i). Like other studies (Hess, 1999b), this analysis attributes student achievement gains to a combination of effective practices, including but not limited to local councils that carry out their formal responsibilities, organize politically to lobby the district, and select "strong but inclusive" principals who seek broad participation in decision making, monitor school operations, develop faculty capacity, and foster trust among professionals, parents, and community residents.

Informal arenas. Evidence of the impact of informal exchanges between professionals and parents remains thin. The private deals may be a source of frustration and resentment for educators, particularly if those agreements violate their conceptions of sound educational practice and fair treatment (Malen, 1995). They also may placate the demands of select parents in ways that are unfair to less vocal or powerful constituencies (Brantlinger, 2003; Lipman, 1997; Wells & Serna, 1996). The most obvious effects may be to "maintain smooth operations by deflecting fundamental challenges to those operations" (Bryk et al., 1993, p. 7) and to reinforce existing patterns of power and privilege (Rollow & Bryk, 1993a).

PRINCIPAL-TEACHER INTERACTIONS IN FORMAL AND INFORMAL ARENAS

Principals and teachers interact in an array of formal arenas, often referred to as "professional communities" or classified as forms of "organic management" (Miller & Rowan, 2006). Various structures, such as site-based management councils; school improvement teams; leadership councils; grade-level, department, or school-within-a-school teams; teacher leader or mentor teacher positions; and peer review committees purportedly enable teachers to influence aspects of organizational life long considered the prerogative of principals. These diverse arrangements typically seek to create quasi-administrative roles for select teachers, introduce status differences into an otherwise egalitarian teaching profession, and cast leadership as a shared but zero-sum phenomenon. These micro arenas have been the subject of studies that yield different portraits of their dynamics and contested propositions about their effects.

A smaller body of literature examines principal and teacher interactions in a variety of collaborative groups, also referred to as professional learning communities or "distributed leadership" configurations (Spillane, 2006). Although these initiatives are introduced in traditional hierarchically organized schools, they bow to the egalitarian norms of teaching, mute status differences, and place no fixed cap on who may be viewed as a leader in the school. Some of these studies examine how principals and teachers interact in settings that deliberately assemble a small, "like-minded" faculty and staff in a relatively flat organizational form designed to mute status and ideological differences and preempt competition for a limited number of formal, teacher leadership positions. In all these varied organizational contexts, principals and teachers also engage in informal exchanges. Many allude to the political nature of these "everyday interactions," but few array their dynamics (for exceptions, see Blasé, 1991; Blasé & Anderson, 1995; Blasé & Blasé, 1999).

Sources of Tension

Consistent with the findings of the initial review (Malen, 1995), this review affirms that principal-teacher tensions still center on who has the legitimate right to make decisions about budget, personnel, programs, and services; who has the right to regulate classroom practice; who has the right to determine school-wide policy; and who has the right to control the academic and social functions of schools (Ingersoll, 2003). This review also indicates that high-stakes accountability systems may be intensifying these endemic tensions between principals and teachers. For example, in some schools, accountability pressures sharpen the principal-teacher divide over what counts as appropriate supervision and regulation of classroom instruction; what subjects really matter; who is responsible for the sanctions imposed on schools; and what remedies, if any, should be enacted (Anagnostopoulos, 2003; Booher-Jennings, 2005; Finkelstein et al., 2000; Maxcy & Nguyên, 2006; Mintrop, 2004). In some schools, accountability provisions alter the size and composition of leadership teams (Camburn et al., 2003), inject new actors into the work lives of principals and teachers, and otherwise alter the interests and alignments that play out in schools (Datnow, 2000; Datnow & Castellano, 2001; Hess, 2003; Sunderman, 2001; Wong & Anagnostopoulos, 1998). Methods of dealing with the long-standing tensions and the current accountability pressures undoubtedly unfold in unique and nuanced ways, but several broad patterns are evident in the literature.

Patterns of Politics in Formal Arenas

The patterns of politics in formal arenas vary across settings. We begin with the conflict avoidance/suppression pattern that legitimates principals' power because this pattern is the most pronounced in the literature.

Avoiding/suppressing conflict—Legitimating principals' power. Like the initial review (Malen, 1995), this review indicates that principals and teachers continue to manage the various tensions they experience through cordial, ceremonial exchanges that affirm the power of the principal. For example, studies report that teachers still view participatory decision-making structures as "empty gestures" that do little if anything to alter power relations in schools (Brooks, Scribner, & Eferakorho, 2004, p. 258), and as readily available mechanisms for legitimating decisions made elsewhere (Wall & Rhinehart, 1998). Studies document that principals are still inclined to allow input but to curb influence (Bredeson, 1993; Bryk et al., 1998; Somech, 2005a, 2005b; Weiss, 1993). They do so by strategically managing if not effectively controlling the schools' agendas, information flow, work assignments, personnel evaluations, and professional development opportunities (Anderson & Shirley, 1995; Copland, 2003; Riehl, 1998); by handpicking members of leadership teams (Datnow & Castellano, 2001); by shaping the norms of interaction (Riehl, 1998; Uline, Tschannen-Moran, & Perez, 2003) and the meaning of initiatives (Coburn, 2005); by supporting or sanctioning teachers in public meetings or private conversations (Blasé & Blasé, 2002a, 2002b; Booher-Jennings, 2005; Copland, 2003; Uline et al., 2003); by defining the givens in key decision situations (Datnow, 2000); and by overturning collaborative decisions by not implementing them. Studies also reveal the pronounced tendency of teachers to "self-censor" (Weiss, 1993, p. 89), to be "deferential" (Riehl, 1998, p. 119), to form "a society of the silent" that refrains from expressing controversial views (Schempp, Sparkes, & Templin, 1993, p. 468) that might get them labeled as a troublemaker or jeopardize their relationships with administrators and teachers.

To be clear, teachers may exert influence in subtle ways because principals at times anticipate teacher resistance and adjust accordingly (Datnow & Castellano, 2001). For example, principals may select initiatives that involve only minor changes in instructional practices or organizational routines (Datnow, 2000), modify initiatives to make them more palatable to teachers, or keep initiatives vague and flexible enough to preempt or to minimize conflict (Brooks et al., 2004; Datnow & Castellano, 2001; Smylie et al., 1994). In addition, principals may work to cultivate support as well as to temper resistance through strategies associated with "facilitative power" (Goldman, Dunlap, & Conley, 1993) and collegial styles of play (Blasé & Blasé, 1999, 2002; Copland, 2003). The broader point to be made, however, is that despite participatory structures and various "empowering" reforms, teachers typically exert relatively modest influence vis-à-vis principals on key aspects of the organizations in which they carry out their work.

An exceptionally fine-grained and conceptually sound analysis of the distribution of power and control in schools gives credence to that claim. Drawing on national survey data and case study findings, Ingersoll uncovers "a steep hierarchy of organizational control within schools across the nation" (2003, p. 83). Principals sit at the top of that hierarchy when it comes to issues regarding personnel, budget, teacher assignments, school discipline, and student placements in classes and programs. Teachers exercise some influence on curriculum and related academic matters, but principals exercise considerable control over the key resources on which teachers are dependent and over key policies and issues that directly affect the jobs of teachers"[8] (Ingersoll, 2003, pp. 126–127). Thus, principals, like other managers, have "a range of inducements, rewards, and punishments with which they can control employees" (Ingersoll, 2003, p. 126). That leverage does not go unnoticed by teachers who recognize the potential costs and consequences of taking on the principal and accede to the principal's preferences. A prevalent theme in studies of principal-teacher interactions in various committee, conference, and council structures is that teachers are inclined to take their cues from the principal, to limit their involvement to areas the principal deems appropriate, and to display deference to administrative authority (Goldstein, 2003; Riehl, 1998; Waite, 1993). But this pattern is not universal.

Expressing conflict—Evoking teacher influence. Like the initial review (Malen, 1995), this review uncovered instances where teachers voiced concerns through union-backed grievance processes (Finkelstein et al., 2000; Malen, 2001a) and mobilized to check the principal's capacity to control policy decisions and to override the principal's initiatives (Johnson & Pajares, 1996; Maxcy & Nguyên, 2006; Murray & Grant, 1995). We found references to teachers who align with principals around shared interests (Blasé & Blasé, 1999; Reitzug, 1994) and engage in more democratic and more critical deliberations (Cate et al., 2006; Uline et al., 2003). We also found examples of principals who adopted a more collegial style of play (Blasé & Anderson, 1995; Blasé & Blasé, 1999, 2002; Bryk, Camburn, & Louis, 1999; Scribner, Hager, & Warne, 2002). But these apparent exceptions and "existence proofs" do not override the prior claim. Even in these cases, teachers often operated within the boundaries set by principals. Their ability to exert influence on school policies, priorities, and practices is highly contingent on what their principals permitted or encouraged them to do (Ingersoll, 2003; Mangin, 2005; Weiss, 1993). The preponderance of evidence from studies in established public schools indicates that site actors exert influence within a fairly narrow band of discretion and that within those increasingly circumscribed parameters, principals tend to hold the relative power advantage.

Preempting conflict—Creating like-minded groups. Some of the alternative organizational forms being advanced rely on the idea of "like-mindedness" as a mechanism to preempt conflict among professionals in schools. For example, some autonomous small schools, pilot schools, charter schools, and privately managed schools seek to recruit principals and teachers who agree on key issues such as the primary purpose of schools and the process of teaching and learning (Bulkley & Hicks, 2005; Holland, 2002; Johnson & Landman, 2000; Reisner et al., 2003; SRI International & American Institutes for

Research, 2003). The degree to which teachers have influence over school-wide decisions and instructional programs varies in these new organizational settings. In some new autonomous small schools, teachers report having more voice in reform efforts (Holland, 2002), more opportunities for leadership (Sporte, Kahne, & Correa, 2004), and greater influence on decision making generally (Swanson & Stevenson, 2002). However, other studies report that teachers have diminished opportunities to exert influence and experience greater risks if they seek to influence school policies and practices because they may not have the due-process, grievance, and related employment protections embedded in union contracts (Johnson & Landman, 2000) or the reserves required to withstand the intense conformity pressures (Johnson & Landman, 2000; Neufeld & Levy, 2004). In essence, those who disagree may be forced to depart (Bulkley & Hicks, 2005). Thus, teacher influence may occur within an ideologically circumscribed zone of acceptance that pre-structures the content, intensity, and outcome of disputes among teachers as well as between principals and teachers.

Patterns of Politics in Informal Arenas

The patterns of politics in informal arenas reflect the pronounced tendency to avoid or suppress conflict. We illustrate this dominant pattern and the exceptions to it.

Avoiding/suppressing conflict—Reinforcing traditional patterns of power. Drawing largely on the pioneering work of Blasé (1988) and Ball (1987), the initial review (Malen, 1995) highlighted an array of control strategies that principals may employ in their informal interactions with teachers. For example, principals may confine conversations to safe issues, consult with teachers selectively and ritualistically to preempt or co-opt resistance, grant favors to dispel criticism and engender loyalty, and otherwise stifle the expression of dissent. These strategies along with other more intense control tactics are evident in the more current research (Blasé & Blasé, 2002a, 2002b). For example, Blasé and Blasé (2002a) argue that given their positional assets, principals can create and perpetuate a "culture of fear" wherein they may intimidate, mistreat, and abuse teachers without retaliation (Blasé & Blasé, 2002a). As the researchers explain, "teachers victimized by abusive principals seldom had viable opportunities for redress . . . teachers rarely complained to district-level administrators because they expected 'no help' and because they 'feared' reprisals" (Blasé & Blasé, 2002a, p. 715). In these settings, victimized teachers found it difficult to transfer for many reasons, including fear of damaging recommendations, self-doubt, fatigue, and other debilitating feelings that accompany abuse (Blasé & Blasé, 2002a).

Again, drawing largely on the pioneering work of Blasé (1988), the initial review (Malen, 1995) highlighted protective strategies that teachers use to insulate themselves from the social and professional sanctions they may receive from principals and peers and promotional strategies that teachers use to advance their views and values. It also uncovered "preparatory strategies" (Malen, 1995) that teachers employ to accumulate resources that might be converted to influence at a later time. These strategies are still evident in the literature. Teachers continue to protect themselves by quietly disregarding directives, by deliberately "retreating" to their classrooms, or by tacitly limiting their interactions to a small cadre of trusted colleagues (Finkelstein et al., 2000; Malen, 2000). They continue to promote their interests by voicing concerns diplomatically and obliquely (Blasé & Blasé, 2002b; Riehl, 1998) and to prepare themselves to exert influence by acquiring expertise, taking on special projects, and assisting other teachers (Little, 1995; Mangin, 2005).

The major change we found in this review is that the tacit mutual noninterference pacts (Malen, 1995) wherein principals purchase unfettered control over school policies by assuring teachers that they will not interfere in their classrooms may be harder to uphold in the current policy context. It appears that high-stakes accountability policies and pressures may be prompting districts to apply more pressure on principals and principals to apply more pressure on teachers to adjust the content and pace of instruction (Anagnostopoulos, 2003; Finkelstein et al., 2000), to demonstrate that they are in compliance with the broader system's curricular priorities and schedules (Diamond & Spillane, 2004), and to work with district-approved external partners to alter their instructional practices (Anagnostopoulos, 2003; Wong & Anagnostopoulos, 1998). To be sure, teachers still have ingenious ways to resist what they perceive as unwarranted interference in their classrooms and unwarranted attacks on professional autonomy and to create the appearance that they are complying with the expectations voiced by the principal, the monitoring teams, and/or the external consultant who may be part of the school polity (Anagnostopoulos, 2003; Diamond & Spillane, 2004; Finkelstein et al., 2000). But a primary source of power—the ability to veto directives by closing the classroom door—is being challenged, at least in some settings (Anagnostopoulos, 2003).

Whether principals and teachers can continue to manage these pressures through the cordial and ceremonial interactions and measured exchanges noted here is hard to determine. At present, it appears teachers cope with these tensions individually as opposed to collectively. They may file a grievance or express concerns among a small group of trusted colleagues, but they have not banded together in organized resistance. The response tends to be, to expand Hirschman's (1970) typology, exit or "retreat" rather than voice or loyalty (Finkelstein et al., 2000; Malen, 2001a).

Managing/embracing conflict—Reconfiguring power relations. As was the case in the initial review, we found references to principal-teacher interactions that were marked by efforts to recognize diverse views, blur hierarchical distinctions, and modify if not equalize the balance of power between principals and teachers (Blasé & Blasé, 1999; Cate et al., 2006; Henkin & Dee, 2001; Reitzug, 1994). We also found references to principals as supportive agents who fostered teachers' professional growth and development (Blasé & Blasé, 1999), helped teachers deal with the dual demands of classroom instruction and committee service (Scribner et al., 2002), and otherwise enabled teachers to carry out their work (Mangin, 2005). However valuable these more cordial and collegial interactions may be, we found little evidence that such exchanges altered patterns of power between principals and teachers (Ingersoll, 2003).

Outcomes of Principal-Teacher Interactions
Formal Arenas. Principal-teacher interactions in formal arenas continue to get mixed reviews on multiple dimensions of interest (Harris, 2005; York-Barr & Duke, 2004). For example, some studies indicate that teachers prefer to focus on "instructional" rather than "institutional" responsibilities (Bakkenes, de Brabander, & Imants, 1999). Others document the frustration teachers experience when they can't influence the broad organizational policies that shape the conditions under which they carry out their work and identify teachers' lack of control over their work environments as a major factor affecting teacher retention (Ingersoll, 2003; Smith & Rowley, 2005; Stockyard & Lehman, 2004), particularly in high-stakes accountability environments (Malen et al., 2002; Malen & Rice, 2004; Mintrop, 2004). Some studies suggest that various participatory

arrangements enhance commitment to the organization and foster innovation (Somech, 2005a, 2005b). Others point to overload and burnout (Smylie et al., 1996) as major risks if not inevitable outcomes for both principals and teachers. Some studies document that teacher participation in decision making has little impact on services rendered to students (Jenkins et al., 1994) or on select areas of student achievement (Heck et al., 2001) while others suggest that when shared decision-making forums focus on curriculum, assessment, and instruction, teacher pedagogy and student performance may improve substantially (Marks & Printy, 2003).

Because levels of teacher influence, satisfaction, and frustration vary within and across sites, the emerging consensus seems to be that participatory structures of one form or another may be necessary but not sufficient to realize classroom effects and to precipitate major changes in organizational performance (Marks & Louis, 1999). A recent, relatively sophisticated analysis of national databases makes the point. Various participatory structures and leadership styles do not appear to be "a particularly powerful determinant of student achievement" at either the elementary or the secondary level (Miller & Rowan, 2006, p. 219), though they "might have effects on student achievement when other conditions are present" (Miller & Rowan, 2006, p. 245). Scholars have employed prominent theories of organizational effectiveness and comparative studies of participatory structures like site-based management in an effort to clarify the conditions under which these arrangements might lead to instructional innovation and organizational improvement (Robertson et al., 1995), but a consensus on these conditions is not yet evident in the literature.

Informal Arenas. Principal-teacher interactions in informal arenas also continue to get mixed reviews. As one might expect, the control strategies, particularly in their more abusive forms, have debilitating effects on teacher engagement, satisfaction, and well-being (Blasé & Blasé, 2002a, 2002b). The more respectful, collegial styles of play can foster teacher commitment and enhance their individual, if not their collective, performance. Consistent with the findings of the initial review (Malen, 1995), the "politics" of principal-teacher interactions is a source of stress for principals; particularly in high-stakes accountability environments where their job security can become a real issue (Finkelstein et al., 2000). In terms of organizational effects, it appears that informal exchanges between principals and teachers operate to reinforce conventional roles and relationships and to make organizational change, for better or worse, an incremental if not an incidental outcome.

TEACHER-TEACHER INTERACTIONS IN FORMAL AND INFORMAL ARENAS

Teachers interact in a variety of formal and informal settings. The formal structures, often termed "professional learning communities," presumably create opportunities for teachers to work collaboratively to improve their practice and to improve student outcomes. Configurations of teacher community include whole-school arrangements (Achinstein, 2002b; Bryk et al., 1999; Giles & Hargreaves, 2006; Louis & Marks, 1998; Louis, Marks, & Kruse, 1996; Scribner et al., 2002; Westheimer, 1999); grade-level or cross-grade groups; (Supovitz, 2002); subject-based clusters at the secondary level (Grossman, Wineburg, & Woolworth, 2001; Little, 2003); and interdisciplinary schools-with-a-school teams at middle schools and high schools (Muncey & McQuillan, 1996; Pounder, 1999).

Participation in these communities may be voluntary (Bryk et al., 1999) or it may be a required component of school reform initiatives (Supovitz, 2002). Whatever their configuration, these formal "communities" and the informal conversations and "everyday interactions" (Blasé, 1991) are "arenas of struggle" (Ball, 1987) and outlets for exploring the micropolitics of schools (Ball, 1987; Blasé, 1991). While these arenas were not included in the initial review (Malen, 1995), they clearly warrant attention, particularly given the move to frame leadership as a horizontal as well as a hierarchical phenomenon and to redefine the scope and target of teacher influence through policies that encourage teachers to focus on instructional as opposed to broad organizational issues and to focus their influence on teachers' practice rather than organizational policy.

Sources of Tension

Historically, teachers have worked in egalitarian communities where organizational status differences were virtually nonexistent save for a few early, intermittent experiments with differentiated staffing. In the 1980s and 1990s, with the advent of formal teacher leadership posts designed to increase teacher influence in administrative functions, curriculum development, and staff development (Cobb et al., 2003), teacher roles and relationships became what Little (1995) termed "contested ground." Conflicts over what teacher leaders could and should do as well as conflicts between teachers who did and did not assume leadership positions surfaced (Harris, 2005; Little, 1995; Smylie, 1992). In response to these contested roles, new visions of teacher roles that emphasize inclusiveness emerged. Although schools still create formal leadership positions for a handful of teachers, they also form professional communities to encourage all teachers to exercise instructional leadership and to improve student learning.

Despite efforts to temper the "contested ground," tensions among teachers persist. In schools that continue to differentiate teachers' roles, we find tensions between those who hold formal leadership positions and those who do not (Little, 1995; Mangin, 2005; Muncey & McQuillan, 1996). In schools that organize around teams responsible for a subset of students, we find tensions within and across those groupings (Crow & Pounder, 2000; Kruse & Louis, 1997; Muncey & McQuillan, 1996; Pounder, 1999). In schools where leadership opportunities are distributed across all or nearly all teachers and in settings that hire "like-minded staff," we also find evidence of tensions among teachers (Bulkley & Hicks, 2005; Johnson & Landman, 2000). In short, none of the organizational structures and arrangements in schools eliminate teacher-teacher conflicts. To be sure, the school's history, structure, and culture shape the modes of interaction among members of that organization (Grossman et al., 2001; Little, 2003; Scribner et al., 1999), and the school's principal can affect how teachers interact with one another (Blasé & Anderson, 1995; Blasé & Blasé, 2002a, 2002b; Coburn, 2001; Kardos et al., 2001). But when teachers come together to work together, conflict is inevitable.

For example, teachers may not agree on the appropriate balance between their desire for autonomy and the pressure to adopt preferred group practices or to accept organizational priorities that may not align with their individual views and values (Grossman et al., 2001; Scribner et al., 2002; Uline & Berkowitz, 2000). Teachers may not agree about the relative importance of subject-based versus interdisciplinary instruction (Uline & Berkowitz, 2000) and pedagogical versus content knowledge (Grossman et al., 2001; Scribner et al., 2002). Teachers may have different views regarding the appropriate balance between the demands of their classrooms and the demands of their new roles, particularly when those new roles challenge the norms of privacy, equality, and cordiality that are so pronounced in schools (Neufeld & Levy, 2004; Sporte et al., 2004; Uline & Berkowitz, 2000). Teachers may have different views regarding how various teams or communities in the school should relate to each other or to the school as a whole (Conley, Fauske, & Pounder, 2004; Kruse & Louis, 1997). At times veteran and novice teachers hold competing conceptions of what counts as quality teaching, what constitutes appropriate professional conduct, and which teachers are in the best position to determine those matters (Datnow, 2000; Grossman et al., 2001). These and other divisions may be intensified in high-stakes accountability environments where pressures to standardize instruction and to blame select teachers for problematic organizational performance may be especially pronounced (Booher-Jennings, 2005; Finkelstein et al., 2000; Giles & Hargreaves, 2006; Malen et al., 2002; Maxcy & Nguyên, 2006).

Because few studies focus explicitly on micropolitical dimensions of professional community, we rely heavily on exploratory case studies that examine how teachers deal with the "essential tension" (Grossman et al., 2001) between pedagogical and subject matter knowledge and between individual autonomy and organizational obligation[9] and how they cope with peer conflicts. We augment those detailed accounts with other writings on how teachers interact.

Patterns of Politics in Formal Arenas

Generally speaking, teachers manage the tensions by avoiding conflict and suppressing dissent or by embracing conflict and drawing on the diverse views and values of the group to scrutinize their work.[10] We begin with the first pattern because it is the most prevalent in the literature (Achinstein, 2002a, 2002b; Gitlin, 1999; Westheimer, 1998).

Avoiding/suppressing conflict—Affirming established interests. When groups of teachers initially come together to form a professional community, they tend to "play community" (Grossman et al., 2001); in other words, members behave as if everyone holds the same beliefs and agrees on all issues. In part because in organizations "the benign 'tyranny of peers' can substitute for the benign 'tyranny of managers,' with conformity pressures as strong and sanctions for deviance as impelling" (Kanter, 1982, p. 1–27), teachers are reluctant to challenge one another's ideas. They are inclined to keep agendas on safe issues, such as how teachers might share materials and help each other do what they are presently doing. Conversations typically focus on supporting rather than altering current practice (Mangin, 2005), on accepting rather than inspecting the assumptions that undergird how teachers carry out their responsibilities and how schools structure educational opportunities (Giles & Hargreaves, 2006; Gitlin, 1999; Lipman, 1997). In this pseudo-community, as some term it, teachers may voice concerns in private conversations with select individuals but group processes and pressures operate to silence dissent when teachers assemble to engage in collaborative work. As one researcher describes it, teachers "outface" and disengage from opportunities to learn from each other (Coburn, 2001). They also relinquish opportunities to look beyond their own individual practices to examine the assumptions embedded in instructional programs, student groupings, resource allocations, and other organizational practices that shape the quality and equity of educational experiences available to students within the school (Lipman, 1997). In essence, teachers "effect a compromise, one in which all members get to behave and teach in ways most pleasing to their individual styles at the expense of delving into issues that touch on deeply held convictions" (Kruse & Louis, 1997, p. 280).

Embracing conflict—Challenging established interests. A second pattern of interaction is one in which community and conflict form what Achinstein calls an "unexpected marriage" wherein the community "explores divergent beliefs and practices of the community; acknowledges and owns responsibilities for conflicts that may result; opens the borders to diverse members and perspectives; and, at times, questions the organization's premises to change them" (2002b, p. 447). Teachers confront differences publicly. They discuss issues openly among one another and take into account diverse perspectives and points of view. "Typically, the principal resists the temptation to push politics underground and hands conflict back to the faculty to resolve" (Achinstein, 2002b, p. 436). Teachers and administrators alike develop protocols for school-wide decision making, seize opportunities for critical reflection, and assume responsibility for creating a trusting culture where teachers are more willing to express alternate viewpoints and to critique both classroom and organizational practices.

Patterns of Politics in Informal Arenas

In informal, teacher-teacher exchanges, teachers tend to rely on the same types of protective, promotional, and preparatory strategies they use in dealing with their principal. They shield themselves from criticisms and sanctions by maintaining a cordial demeanor, adhering to the tacit mutual noninterference pacts, avoiding difficult, divisive issues, "retreating" (Malen, 2001a) to the classroom, or confining their conversations to a small group of teachers who hold similar views (Coburn, 2001; Grossman et al., 2001; Malen, 2001a). They may try to influence their colleagues through fairly delicate and diplomatic exchanges wherein they downplay their accomplishments, bring resources back to colleagues, and establish, albeit in a self-effacing fashion, that "they have something worthwhile to say" (Hatch, White, & Faigenbaum, 2005, p. 1028).

Outcomes of Teacher-Teacher Interactions

Formal Arenas. Teacher-teacher interactions have individual, group, and organizational effects (Achinstein, 2002b; Little, 2003). They are a source of frustration and satisfaction as well as a source of stress and support for the individuals involved (Achinstein, 2002a, 2002b). While various teacher teams and collaboratives may be a mechanism through which teachers exercise greater influence on how students are grouped for instruction, how instructional time is allocated, and how the social and academic aspects of schooling are carried out (Pounder, 1999), they do not necessarily operate that way. Each pattern along the continuum (from avoiding/suppressing to embracing conflict) has multiple consequences that we briefly summarize and arguably oversimplify.

Generally speaking, in professional communities where conflict is avoided or suppressed, teachers make modifications required to maintain organizational stability. As a result, the core values and norms of the organization are not questioned. Organizational theorists define this outcome as single-loop learning (Argyris & Schon, 1996) and posit that when group dynamics place the premium on group agreement rather than critical inspection, the prospects for major changes in the organization are sharply diminished (Achinstein, 2002b). In professional communities where conflict is embraced, individuals may gain new perspectives, learn to inquire about their practice, and benefit from the ideas that get aired and shared (Hatch et al., 2005). Groups that embrace conflict tend to be more willing to alter their instructional practice (Achinstein, 2002b; Grossman et al., 2001), to challenge existing organizational arrangements, and to engage in the "double-loop learning" required to make and sustain fundamental changes in organizational purposes, operations, and outcomes (Argyris & Schon, 1996).

Informal Arenas. The outcomes of informal interactions among teachers are not well documented. We know that teachers can impose painful social sanctions on their peers and that they can offer essential personal and professional support to some if not all of their colleagues (Blasé & Anderson, 1995; Datnow & Castellano, 2001; Finkelstein et al., 2000; Malen, 2001a). In terms of broader, organizational effects, it appears that informal interactions among teachers operate to maintain rather than alter conventional practices in classrooms and in schools (Blasé & Anderson, 1995; Coburn, 2001). Indeed, studies of teacher interactions in both formal and informal arenas raise "important questions about assumptions that empowering teachers will facilitate school-based change . . . Although teacher involvement and professional collaboration may be indispensable . . . without . . . a willingness to challenge existing power relations, there is little cause for optimism that teacher participation in reform will significantly alter the marginalization of low-income students of color in schools" (Lipman, 1997, p. 33).

OBSERVATIONS ON THE MICROPOLITICS OF SCHOOLS

This updated review of the literature warrants several more general observations about the phenomenon of interest and about the nature of research on this important dimension of schools.

First, in some respects, little has changed. The basic patterns of politics and power identified in the initial literature review are still prominent in the more recent research on the micropolitics of schools. Generally speaking, professionals have the relative power advantage vis-à-vis parents, particularly in formal decision-making arenas; principals hold the relative power advantage vis-à-vis teachers in both formal and informal arenas. Insofar as parents, or more precisely select, middle-class and upper middle-class parents gain leverage, they do so primarily through private agreements that reflect and reinforce their privileged position in the broader society and through tacit or explicit threats of exit that prompt professionals to accommodate their interests as a way to protect the legitimacy of the school. Insofar as teachers exert influence, they tend to do so within the boundaries set by the principal. These basic patterns have persisted, despite an array of participatory decision-making initiatives purportedly designed to grant parents and teachers significant influence on significant issues. They also are evident in the new organizational forms that are developing and in sites where external actors are part of the scene. In short, the patterns we found are durable features of the micropolitics of schools. In the research we consulted, the ever-present tendency to avoid, suppress, or contain conflict and to protect established interests trumped opportunities for more diverse interests to be expressed, embraced, and accommodated. In some cases, a more open, inviting pattern of politics seemed to be brewing and in other instances a more confrontational dynamic surfaced. But the prevalent patterns of politics in formal and informal arenas indicate the balance of power within schools has remained remarkably constant. And, as one might expect, these patterns reflect the distribution of power in the hierarchy of school organizations and in the economic and sociocultural divides that structure access and influence in the broader society.

Second, although we discovered little change in the balance of power among site actors, we uncovered considerable change in the rules of the game. Developments in the policy context have reduced the discretion afforded site actors and narrowed the domains in which they may exercise influence. Be it through endemic resource constraints, tighter regulations, stricter accountability measures, "innovative" initiatives that prompt teachers to target the practice of their peers rather than the policies of the school, or participatory structures that foster the suppression rather than the expression of critical views, policy decisions made outside the school are shaping the politics in the school. To be sure, both longitudinal and comparative studies are required to gauge more precisely how actions taken at higher levels of the systems are permeating, if not dominating the micropolitics of schools. But the available research suggests that macro-forces may be controlling the agenda, limiting the latitude, restricting the scope of influence, and otherwise circumscribing the power of site actors. If these findings hold, the macro-forces in the policy environment may be among the most critical factors affecting the micropolitics in schools.

Third, research in the field is moving beyond pluralist perspectives on power. Most of the studies we reviewed challenged pluralist assumptions regarding the ability of diverse groups to gain access, to mobilize support, and to exert influence on authorities in the system. Most of the research also affirmed assumptions associated with elitist perspectives on power. The tendency to confine agendas to safe issues and to silence demands for changes in existing patterns of power and privilege was pronounced in professional-patron, principal-teacher, and teacher-teacher interactions. Studies that unveil these more subtle processes have added to our understanding of the second face of power. We have a stronger sense of how powerful actors can suppress conflict, instill conformity, and censor criticism and why less powerful players succumb to the insidious pressures imposed on them. While research is cutting deeper into the second face of power, the third face of power remains largely unexamined, perhaps because it is so very difficult to get at it. Attempts to study this more psychological, cognitive-cultural dimension of power confront a host of conceptual and empirical problems that some scholars have addressed by incorporating ethnographic methods, investing a great deal of time at the site of study, and generating exceptionally detailed descriptions of these more obscure aspects of power and politics (see, for example, Gaventa, 1980). Given the prevalence of the more covert and murky manifestations of power, scholars who focus on the micropolitics of schools may have to make comparable investments to display, more fully explicitly and systematically, how all the faces of power might be manifest in schools.

Finally, research on the micropolitics of schools tends to emphasize process but slight outcomes. Like the initial review of literature (Malen, 1995), this review indicates that research focuses on how power is unequally allocated, strategically protected, and, at times, creatively mobilized in school settings. As a result, we know a good bit about political processes in formal arenas and how those processes measure up to the ideals of equitable access, authentic participation, and democratic deliberation. We also know something about the impact of political processes in formal arenas on the principals, teachers, and parents who interact in these settings. For example, both case studies and surveys depict their levels of anxiety, frustration, satisfaction, and alienation. However, we know much less about the impact of political interactions in informal arenas and still less about the relationship between political dynamics and educational outcomes. Some scholars have worked to trace the impact of various patterns of politics and power on teachers' sense of efficacy and effectiveness. Others have linked different patterns of politics and power to profiles of student performance. Despite these contributions, our knowledge of how the micropolitics of schools affects the core technology of schools, the quality of teaching and learning, and the production and distribution of educational gains is more limited than it needs to be. Moving beyond the process emphasis and beyond the pluralist perspectives on power should enable us to develop a deeper understanding of the relationship between micropolitical processes, power dynamics, and educational outcomes.

NOTES

1. Unfortunately, we do not include an analysis of adult-student or student-student interactions even though these exchanges may affect students' identities, aspirations, and attachments to the school policy. Nor do we address studies carried out in international contexts, even though some of the most interesting theoretical work on the micropolitics of schools is based on research conducted outside the United States (e.g., Ball, 1987).

2. This strategy is in keeping with the strategy Blasé and Blasé (2002a, 2002b) outlined in their review of literature on the micropolitics of instructional supervision.

3. For example, we included topics like school restructuring, school reform, site-based management, shared decision making, teacher leadership, distributed leadership, instructional leadership, transformational leadership, professional learning communities, teaching teams, principal-teacher and teacher-teacher relationships, parent and community involvement, and school-level responses to testing mandates, standards-based reforms, deregulation, and reconstitution. We searched *Education Evaluation and Policy Analysis, Educational Administration Quarterly, Educational Policy, American Educational Research Journal, American Journal of Education, Review of Educational Research, Teachers College Record, Educational Researcher, Journal of School Leadership, Leadership and Policy in Schools, American Journal of Education,* and *Journal of Education.*

4. With others, we recognize that when compared to schools in many other countries, U.S. schools are more decentralized (Ingersoll, 2003). Our point is that policy developments at broader levels of the system and most especially at the state level translate into less autonomy than U.S. schools have traditionally been granted (Conley, 2003; Malen, 2003; Sipple, Killeen, & Monk, 2004).

5. For example, studies of the implementation and impact of these initiatives rely on surveys that tap educators' perceptions of these reforms and case studies carried out in select states, districts, and sites. Both forms of research track the impact of state accountability policies on select aspects of schooling, such as instruction in a specific subject (e.g., mathematics) or a single curricular unit and the use of Title I funds. As a result, we do not yet have a comprehensive, comparative, and longitudinal database.

6. In addition, that finding is consistent with broader literatures on the role that various activist, reform-oriented organizations can play in developing the infrastructures required to mobilize "perennially neglected" communities who lack the financial, social, and cultural capital required to mount a real challenge to existing patterns of power and privilege (Malen, 2001b; Walker, 1991).

7. The processes are difficult to document because the exchanges occur in private conversations between professionals and parents and because the resultant compromises could be viewed as favored treatment of select groups. Moreover, professionals anticipate parental and community reactions and adjust in ways that preempt the expression of discontent and render accommodations less visible (Brantlinger, 2003; Lipman, 1997).

8. As Ingersoll notes, "The 'perks' that principals typically control include the distribution of physical space; the determination of each faculty member's schedule, teaching assignments and course load; the assignment of non-teaching duties; and the control of the portion of the budget devoted to such things as field trips, projects, and professional development conferences"(p. 126).

9. Grossman and her colleagues argue that efforts to improve teachers' content knowledge compete with efforts to improve pedagogy as a means of increasing student learning. Some teachers believe the individual's pursuit of content knowledge runs counter to the goal of professional collaboration, particularly in devising student-centered curriculum (Scribner et al., 2002). Others see the importance of being life-long learners and maintain that this orientation can improve teaching (Grossman et al., 2001). A second major tension within the teacher community is the degree to which individual autonomy should or should not have precedence over organizational goals, priorities, and compacts. Maintaining both a sense of "I-ness" (individual autonomy and development) and "we-ness" (shared identity) in community is a real challenge for individual teachers and for groups of teachers (Scribner et al., 2002).

10. These patterns could be viewed as end points on a continuum of more nuanced responses to conflict management. At one end of this continuum is the avoidance stance, where conflict is reluctantly recognized and

quickly absorbed or deflected to maintain a unified and stable community (Achinstein, 2002b). By ignoring or suppressing dissent, the group maintains a sense of harmony. The other end of the spectrum embraces conflict. Differences are acknowledged and reflected on in order to bring about systematic change. Dissent is encouraged, valued, and incorporated in deliberations. These responses to conflict form boundaries that delineate membership in the community and dictate who is included and who is pushed to the outside. When diverse points of view are encouraged, the community falls along the inclusive side of the continuum. However, when those with different viewpoints are quieted, the politics of border negotiation falls to the exclusive side (Achinstein, 2002b).

REFERENCES

Achinstein, B. (2002a). *Community, diversity and conflict among schoolteachers: The ties that blind.* New York: Teachers College Press.

Achinstein, B. (2002b). Conflict amid community: The micropolitics of teacher collaboration. *Teachers College Record, 104*(3), 421–455.

Amatea, E. S., & Vandiver, F. (2004). Best practices: Expanding the school leadership team—Using counselors to facilitate teacher collaboration with families. *Journal of School Leadership, 14*(3), 327–344.

Anagnostopoulos, D. (2003). The new accountability, student failure, and teachers' work in urban high schools. *Educational Policy, 17*(3), 291–316.

Anderson, G. L. (1998). Toward authentic participation: Deconstructing the discourses of participatory reforms in education. *American Educational Research Journal, 35*(4), 571–603.

Anderson, L. W., & Shirley, J. R. (1995). High school principals and school reform: Lessons learned from a statewide study of project re: learning *Educational Administration Quarterly, 31*(3), 405–423.

Andre-Bechely, L. (2005). Public school choice at the intersection of voluntary integration and not-so-good neighborhood schools: Lessons from parents' experiences. *Educational Administration Quarterly, 41*(2), 267–305.

Apple, M. W. (1996). *Cultural politics and education.* New York: Teachers College Press.

Argyris, C., & Schon, D. (1996). *Organizational Learning II.* Reading, MA: Addison-Wesley Publishing Company.

Armor, D. J. (1995). *Forced justice: School desegregation and the law.* New York: Oxford University Press.

Bacharach, P., & Baratz, M. S. (1970). *Power and poverty.* New York: Oxford University Press.

Bacharach, S. B., & Mundell, B. L. (1993). Organizational politics in schools: Micro, macro, and logics of action. *Educational Administration Quarterly, 29*(4), 423–452.

Bakkenes, I., de Brabander, C., & Imants, J. (1999). Teacher isolation and communication network analysis in primary schools. *Educational Administration Quarterly, 35*(2), 166–202.

Ball, S. J. (1987). *The micro-politics of the school.* London, Great Britain Methuen & Co.

Bauch, P. A., & Goldring, E. B. (1995). Parent involvement and school responsiveness: Facilitating the home-school connection in schools of choice. *Educational Evaluation and Policy Analysis, 17*(1), 1–21.

Bauch, P. A., & Goldring, E. B. (1998). Parent-teacher participation in the context of school governance. *Peabody Journal of Education, 73*(1), 15–35.

Baum, H. S. (2003). *Community action for school reform.* Albany: State University of New York Press.

Becker, H., Nakagawa, K., & Corwin, R. G. (1997). Parent involvement contracts in California's charter schools: Strategy for educational improvement or method of exclusion? *Teachers College Record, 98*(3), 511–536.

Björk, L., & Blasé, J. (2009). The micropolitics of school district decentralization. *Educational Assessment, Evaluation & Accountability, 21*(3), 195–208.

Blasé, J. (1988). The politics of favoritism: A qualitative analysis of the teachers' perspective. *Educational Administration Quarterly, 24,* 152–177.

Blasé, J. (Ed.). (1991). *The politics of life in schools: Power, conflict and cooperation.* Newbury Park, CA: Sage.

Blasé, J., & Anderson, G. (1995). *The micropolitics of educational leadership: From control to empowerment.* New York: Teachers College Press.

Blasé, J., & Blasé, J. (1999). Principals' instructional leadership and teacher development: Teachers' perspectives. *Educational Administration Quarterly, 35*(3), 349–378.

Blasé, J., & Blasé, J. (2002a). The dark side of leadership: Teacher perspectives of principal mistreatment. *Educational Administration Quarterly, 38*(5), 671–727.

Blasé, J., & Blasé, J. (2002b). The micropolitics of instructional supervision: A call for research. *Educational Administration Quarterly, 38*(1), 6–44.

Blasé, J., & Blasé, J. (2004). The dark side of school leadership: Implications for administrator preparation. *Leadership & Policy in Schools, 3*(4), 245–273.

Booher-Jennings, J. (2005). Below the bubble: "Educational triage" and the Texas accountability system. *American Educational Research Journal, 42*(2), 231–268.

Bowles, B. D. (1989). Gaining support for change: The politics of strategic leadership. In J. J. Mauriel (Ed.), *Strategic leadership for schools* (pp. 163–210). San Francisco, CA: Jossey-Bass.

Brantlinger, E. (2003). *Dividing classes: How the middle class negotiates and rationalizes school advantage.* New York: RoutledgeFalmer.

Bredeson, P. V. (1993). Letting go of outlived professional identities: A study of role transition and role strain for principals in restructured schools. *Educational Administration Quarterly, 29*(1), 34–68.

Brooks, J. S., Scribner, J. P., & Eferakorho, J. (2004). Teacher leadership in the context of whole school reform. *Journal of School Leadership, 14*(3), 242–265.

Brosky, D. (2011). Micropolitics in the school: Teacher leaders' use of political skill and influence tactics. *The International Journal of Educational Leadership Preparation, 6*(1), 1–11.

Bryk, A. S., Camburn, E., & Louis, K. S. (1999). Professional community in Chicago elementary schools: Facilitating factors and organizational consequences. *Educational Administration Quarterly, 35*(5), 751–781.

Bryk, A. S. (1999). Policy lessons from Chicago's experience with decentralization. In D. Ravitch (Ed.), *Brookings papers on educational policy* (pp. 67–99). Washington, DC: Brookings Institution.

Bryk, A. S., Hill, P., & Shipps, D. (1999). *Improving school-community connections: Moving toward a system of community schools.* Baltimore, MD: Annie E. Casey Foundation.

Bryk, A. S., Lee, V. E., & Holland, P. B. (1993). *Catholic schools and the common good.* Cambridge, MA: Harvard University Press.

Bryk, A. S., Sebring, P. B., Kerbow, K., Rollow, S., & Easton, J. Q. (1998). *Charting Chicago school reform: Democratic localism as a lever for change.* Boulder, CO: Westview Press.

Bulkley, K. E., & Hicks, J. (2005). Managing community: Professional community in charter schools operated by educational management organizations. *Educational Administration Quarterly, 41*(2), 306–348.

Caffyn, R. (2010). Enabling long-term effective school leadership: Nine ways to understand and utilize micropolitics in international schools. *International Schools Journal, 29*(2), 50–59.

Camburn, E., Rowan, B., & Taylor, J. E. (2003). Distributed leadership in schools: The case of elementary schools adopting comprehensive school reform models. *Educational Evaluation and Policy Analysis, 25*(4), 347–373.

Caruso, L. F. (2013). The micropolitics of educational change experienced by novice public middle school principals. *NASSP Bulletin, 97*(3), 218–252.

Cate, J. M., Vaughn, C. A., & O'Hair, M. J. (2006). A 17-year case study of an elementary school's journey: From traditional school to learning community to democratic school community. *Journal of School Leadership, 16*(1), 86–111.

Cibulka, J. G. (1991). Educational reforms: Performance information and political power. In S. H. Fuhrman & B. Malen (Eds.), *The politics of curriculum and testing: The 1990 yearbook of the Politics of Education Association.* London: Falmer Press.

Clegg, S. R. (1989). *Frameworks of power.* Newbury Park, CA: Sage.

Cobb, P., McClain, K., Lamberg, T. D. S., & Dean, C. (2003). Situating teachers' instructional practices in the institutional setting of the school and district. *Educational Researcher, 32*(6), 13–24.

Coburn, C. E. (2001). Collective sensemaking about reading: How teachers mediate reading policy in their professional communities. *Educational Evaluation and Policy Analysis, 23*(2), 145–170.

Coburn, C. E. (2005). Shaping teacher sensemaking: School leaders and the enactment of reading policy. *Educational Policy, 19*(3), 476–509.

Cohen, D. K., & Spillane, J. P. (1992). Policy and practice: The relations between governance and instruction. *Review of Research in Education, 18*(1), 3–49.

Cohn, C. A. (2005). NCLB implementation challenges: The local superintendent's view. *Peabody Journal of Education, 80*(2), 156–169.

Conley, D. T. (2003). *Who governs our schools? Changing roles and responsibilities.* New York: Teachers College Press.

Conley, S., Fauske, J., & Pounder, D. G. (2004). Teacher work group effectiveness. *Educational Administration Quarterly, 40*(5), 663–703.

Copland, M. A. (2003). Leadership of inquiry: Building and sustaining capacity for school improvement. *Educational Evaluation and Policy Analysis, 25*(4), 375–395.

Crawford, J. R., & Forsyth, P. B. (2004). Teacher empowerment and charter schools. *Journal of School Leadership, 14*(1), 62–84.

Croninger, R., & Malen, B. (2002). The role of school governance in the creation of school community. In K. Leithwood & P. Hallinger (Eds.), *Second international handbook of educational leadership and administration* (pp. 281–320). Dordrecht: Kluwer Academic Publishers.

Crow, G. M., & Pounder, D. G. (2000). Interdisciplinary teaching teams: Context, design, and process. *Educational Administration Quarterly, 36*(2), 216–254.

Datnow, A. (2000). Power and politics in the adoption of school reform models. *Educational Evaluation and Policy Analysis, 22*(4), 357–374.

Datnow, A., & Castellano, M. (2001). Managing and guiding school reform: Leadership in success for all schools. *Educational Administration Quarterly, 37*(2), 219–249.

Designs for Change. (2005). *The big picture: School-initiated reforms, centrally initiated reforms and elementary school achievement in Chicago (1990 to 2005).* Chicago, IL: Designs for Change.

Diamond, J. B., & Spillane, J. P. (2004). High-stakes accountability in urban elementary schools: Challenging or reproducing inequality? *Teachers College Record, 106*(6), 1145–1176.

Dorgan, K. (2004). A year in the life of an elementary school: One school's experiences in meeting new mathematics standards. *Teachers College Record, 106*(6), 1203–1228.

Eccles, J. S., & Harold, R. D. (1993). Parent-school involvement during the early adolescent years. *Teachers College Record, 94*(3), 568–587.

Eilertsen, T., Gustafson, N., & Salo, P. (2008). Action research and the micropolitics in schools. *Educational Action Research, 16*(3), 295–308.

Elmore, R. F. (2002). *Bridging the gap between standards and achievement: The imperative for professional development in education.* Washington, DC: Albert Shanker Institute.

Fairman, J. C., & Firestone, W. F. (2001). The district role in state assessment policy: An exploratory study. In S. H. Fuhrman (Ed.), *From the capital to the classroom: Standards-based reform in the states* (pp. 124–147). Chicago, IL: National Society for the Study of Education.

Fine, M. (1993). Parent involvement: Reflections on parents, power, and urban public schools. *Teachers College Record, 94*(4), 682–729.

Finkelstein, B., Malen, B., Muncey, D. E., Rice, J. K., Croninger, R. G., Briggs, L., et al. (2000). *Caught in contradictions: The first two years of a school reconstitution initiative.* College Park: Department of Education Policy and Leadership, University of Maryland.

Finkelstein, N. D., & Tritter, J. Q. (1999). *Managing education or managing money? Findings from Great Britain and the United States on the partial implementation of site-based management.* Paper presented at the annual meeting of the American Educational Research Association, Montreal, Canada.

Firestone, W., Mayrowetz, D., & Fairman, J. (1998). Performance-based assessment and instructional change: The effects of testing in Maine and Maryland. *Educational Evaluation and Policy Analysis, 20*(2), 95–113.

Firestone, W. F., Fitz, J., & Broadfoot, P. (1999). Power, learning and legitimation: Assessment implementation across levels in the United States and the United Kingdom. *American Educational Research Journal, 36*(4), 759–793.

Fuhrman, S. H., & Elmore, R. F. (1995). Ruling out rules: The evolution of deregulation in state education policy. *Teachers College Record, 97*(2), 279–309.

Fung, A. (2004). *Empowered participation: Reinventing urban democracy.* Princeton, NJ: Princeton University Press.

Gamson, W. A. (1960). *Power and discontent.* Homewood, IL: Dorsey Press.

Gaventa, J. (1980). *Power and powerlessness: Quiescence and rebellion in an Appalachian valley.* Oxford: Clarendon Press.

Geary, L. S. (1992). *Review of the literature [on the meaning and measurement of power] and explication of the conceptual framework [for examining political processes], in L. S. Geary, The policymaking process resulting in fiscal policy for special education in Utah, doctoral dissertation.* University of Utah, Salt Lake City, UT.

Gerry, M. (1999). Service integration and beyond: Implications for lawyers and their training. In J. P. Heubert (Ed.), *Law and school reform: Six strategies for promoting educational equity* (pp. 204–305). New Haven, CT: Yale University Press.

Giles, C., & Hargreaves, A. (2006). The sustainability of innovative schools as learning organizations and professional learning communities during standardized reform. *Educational Administration Quarterly, 42*(1), 124–156.

Giles, C., Johnson, L., Brooks, S., & Jacobson, S. L. (2005). Building bridges, building community: Transformational leadership in a challenging urban context. *Journal of School Leadership, 15*(5), 519–545.

Gitlin, A. (1999). Collaboration and progressive school reform. *Educational Policy, 13*(5), 630–658.

Gold, E., Simon, E., & Brown, C. (2005). A new conception of parent engagement: Community organizing for school reform. In F. W. English (Ed.), *The SAGE handbook of educational leadership: Advances in theory, research and practice* (pp. 237–268). Thousand Oaks, CA: Sage.

Goldman, P., Dunlap, D. M., & Conley, D. T. (1993). Facilitative power and nonstandardized solutions in school site restructuring. *Educational Administration Quarterly, 29*(1), 69–92.

Goldstein, J. (2003). Making sense of distributed leadership: The case of peer assistance and review. *Educational Evaluation and Policy Analysis, 26*(2), 173–197.

Grant, S. G. (2001). An uncertain lever: Exploring the influence of state-level testing in New York State on teaching social studies. *Teachers College Record, 103*(3), 398–426.

Greenfield Jr., W. D. (1995). Toward a theory of school administration: The centrality of leadership. *Educational Administration Quarterly, 31*(1), 61–85.

Grossman, P., Wineburg, S., & Woolworth, S. (2001). Toward a theory of teacher community. *Teachers College Record, 103*(6), 942–1012.

Handler, J. F. (1998). Chicago school reform: Enablement or empowerment? *The Good Society, 8*(2), 9–14.

Hargreaves, A. (1994). *Changing teachers, changing times: Teachers' work and culture in the postmodern age.* New York: Teachers College Press.

Harris, A. (2005). Teacher leadership: More than just a feel-good factor? *Leadership and Policy in Schools, 4*(3), 201–220.

Hatch, T., White, M. E., & Faigenbaum, D. (2005). Expertise, credibility, and influence: How teachers can influence policy, advance research, and improve performance. *Teachers College Record, 107*(5), 1004–1035.

Heck, R. H., Brandon, P. R., & Wang, J. (2001). Implementing site-managed educational changes: Examining levels of implementation and effect. *Educational Policy, 15*(2), 302–322.

Henkin, A. B., & Dee, J. D. (2001). The power of trust: Teams and collective action in self-managed schools. *Journal of School Leadership, 11*(1), 48–62.

Hess, G. A. (1996). *Implementing reform: Stories of stability and change in 14 schools.* Chicago, IL: The Chicago Panel on School Policy.

Hess, G. A. (1999a). Community participation or control? From New York to Chicago. *Theory into Practice, 38*(4), 217–224.

Hess, G. A. (1999b). Expectations, opportunity, capacity, and will: The four essential components of Chicago school reform. *Educational Policy, 13*(4), 494–517.

Hess, G. A. (1999c). Understanding achievement (and other) changes under Chicago school reform. *Educational Evaluation and Policy Analysis, 21*(1), 67–83.

Hess, G. A. (2003). Reconstitution–three years later: Monitoring the effect of sanctions on Chicago high schools. *Education and Urban Society, 35*(3), 300–327.

Hill, H. C. (2001). Policy is not enough: Language and the interpretation of state standards. *American Educational Research Journal, 38*(2), 289–320.

Hirschman, A. O. (1970). *Exit, voice and loyalty.* Cambridge, MA: Harvard University Press.

Hochschild, J. L. (2005). Editor's note: Introduction and comments. *Perspectives on Politics, 3*(2), 213–214.

Holland, N. E. (2002). *Small schools making big changes: The importance of professional communities in school reform.* Paper presented at the Annual Meeting of the National Association of African American Studies, the National Association of Hispanic and Latino Studies, the National Association of Native American Studies, and the National Association of Asian Studies, Houston, TX.

Honig, M. I. (2004). Where's the "up" in bottom-up reform? *Educational Policy, 18*(4), 527–561.

Horvat, E. M., Weininger, E. B., & Lareau, A. (2003). From social ties to social capital: Class differences in the relations between schools and parent networks. *American Educational Research Journal, 40*(2), 319–352.

Hoyle, E. (1986). *The politics of school management.* London: Hodder and Stoughton.

Iannaccone, L. (1975). *Education policy systems: A guide for educational administrators.* Fort Lauderdale, FL: Nova University Press.

Ingersoll, R. M. (2003). *Who controls teachers' work?* Cambridge, MA: Harvard University Press.

Jenkins, J. R., Ronk, J., Schrag, J. A., Rude, G. G., & Stowitschek, C. (1994). Effects of using school-based participatory decision making to improve services for low-performing students. *Elementary School Journal, 94*(3), 357–372.

Jester, T. E. (2005). Transfer of standards-based education in rural Alaska: An analysis of the politics of educational transfer in the Tikishla school district. *Teachers College Record, 107*(4), 862–893.

Johnson, B. L. J. (2001). Micropolitical dynamics of education interests: A view from within. *Educational Policy, 15*(1), 115–134.

Johnson, B. L. J. (2003). Those nagging headaches: Perennial ideas and tensions in the politics of the education field. *Educational Administration Quarterly, 39*(1), 41–67.

Johnson, B. L. J., & Fauske, J. R. (2000). Principals and the political economy of environmental enactment. *Educational Administration Quarterly, 36*(2), 159–185.

Johnson, M. J., & Pajares, F. (1996). When shared decision making works: A 3-year longitudinal study. *American Educational Research Journal, 33*(3), 599–627.

Johnson, S. M., & Landman, J. (2000). "Sometimes bureaucracy has its charms": The working conditions of teachers in deregulated schools. *Teachers College Record, 102*(1), 85–124.

Kahne, J., O'Brien, J., Brown, A., & Quinn, T. (2001). Leveraging social capital and school improvement: The case of a school network and a comprehensive community initiative in Chicago. *Educational Administration Quarterly, 37*(4), 429–461.

Kanter, R. M. (1982). Dilemmas of managing participation. *Organizational Dynamics, 11*(1), 5–27.

Kardos, S. M., Johnson, S. M., Peske, H. G., Kauffman, D., & Liu, E. (2001). Counting on colleagues: New teachers encounter the professional cultures of their schools. *Educational Administration Quarterly, 37*(296–321).

Kirp, D. L., & Driver, C. E. (1995). The aspirations of systemic reform meet the realities of localism. *Educational Administration Quarterly, 31*(4), 589–612.

Kruse, S. D., & Louis, K. S. (1997). Teacher teaming in middle schools: Dilemmas for a schoolwide community. *Educational Administration Quarterly, 33*(3), 261–289.

Ladd, H. (1996). *Holding schools accountable: Performance-based reform in education.* Washington, DC: Brookings Institution.

Lee, V. E., Smith, J. B., & Cioci, M. (1993). Teachers and principals: Gender-related perceptions of leadership and power in secondary schools. *Educational Evaluation and Policy Analysis, 15*(2), 153–180.

Leithwood, K., Jantzi, D., & Steinbach, R. (1999). Do school councils matter? *Educational Policy, 13*(4), 476–493.

Leithwood, K., & Menzies, T. (1998). Forms and effects of school-based management: A review. *Educational Policy, 12*, 325–346.

Lewis, D. A., & Nakagawa, K. (1995). *Race and educational reform in the American metropolis: A study of school decentralization.* Albany: State University of New York Press.

Linn, R. L. (2003). Accountability: Responsibility and reasonable expectations. *Educational Researcher, 32*(7), 3–13.

Linn, R. L., Baker, E. L., & Betebenner, D. W. (2002). Accountability systems: Implications of requirements of the No Child Left Behind Act of 2001. *Educational Researcher, 31*(6), 3–16.

Lipman, P. (1997). Restructuring in context: A case study of teacher participation and the dynamics of ideology, race, and power. *American Educational Research Journal, 34*(1), 3–37.

Little, J. W. (1995). Contested ground: The basis of teacher leadership in two restructuring high schools. *The Elementary School Journal, 96*(1), 47–63.

Little, J. W. (2003). Inside teacher community: Representations of classroom practice. *Teachers College Record, 105*(6), 913–945.

Lopez, G. R., Scribner, J. D., & Mahitivanichcha, K. (2001). Redefining parental involvement: Lessons from high-performing migrant-impacted schools. *American Educational Research Journal, 38*(2), 253–288.

Louis, K. S., Febey, K., & Schroeder, R. (2005). State-mandated accountability in high schools: Teachers' interpretations of a new era. *Educational Evaluation and Policy Analysis, 27*(2), 177–204.

Louis, K. S., & Marks, H. M. (1998). Does professional community affect the classroom? Teachers' work and student experiences in restructuring schools. *American Journal of Education, 106*(4), 532–575.

Louis, K. S., Marks, H. M., & Kruse, S. (1996). Teachers' professional community in restructuring schools. *American Educational Research Journal, 33*(4), 757–798.

Loveless, T. (1998). Uneasy allies: The evolving relationship of school and site. *Educational Evaluation and Policy Analysis, 20*(1), 1–8.

Loveless, T., & Jasin, C. (1998). Starting from scratch: Political and organizational challenges facing charter schools. *Educational Administration Quarterly, 34*(1), 9–30.

Lukes, S. (1974). *Power: A radical view.* London: Macmillan.

Malen, B. (1995). The micropolitics of education: Mapping the multiple dimensions of power relations in school politics. In J. D. Scribner & D. H. Layton (Eds.), *Politics of Education Association Yearbook* (Vol. 9, pp. 147–167). New York, NY: Taylor & Francis.

Malen, B. (2001a). *Fostering exit, voice or loyalty: The multiple effects of reconstitution.* Paper presented at the annual meeting of the American Education Finance Association, Cincinnati, OH.

Malen, B. (2001b). Generating interest in interest groups. *Educational Policy, 15*(1), 168–186.

Malen, B. (2003). Tightening the grip? The impact of state activism on local school systems. *Educational Policy, 17*(2), 195–216.

Malen, B. (2005). Educational leaders as policy analysts. In F. W. English (Ed.), *The SAGE handbook of educational leadership* (pp. 191–215). Thousand Oaks, CA: Sage.

Malen, B. (2006). Revisiting policy implementation as a political phenomenon: The case of reconstitution policies. In M. I. Honig (Ed.), *New directions in policy implementation: Confronting complexity.* Albany: State University of New York Press.

Malen, B., Croninger, R., Muncey, D., & Redmond-Jones, D. (2002). Reconstituting schools: "Testing" the "theory of action." *Educational Evaluation and Policy Analysis, 24*(2), 113–132.

Malen, B., & Muncey, D. (2000). Creating "a new set of givens"? The impact of state activism on school autonomy. In N. D. Theobald & B. Malen (Eds.), *Balancing local control and state responsibility for education* (pp. 199–244). Larchmont, NY: Eye on Education.

Malen, B., & Rice, J. K. (2004). A framework for assessing the impact of education reforms on school capacity: Insights from studies of high-stakes accountability initiatives. *Educational Policy, 18*(5), 631–660.

Mangin, M. M. (2005). Distributed leadership and the culture of schools: Teacher leaders' strategies for gaining access to classrooms *Journal of School Leadership, 15*(4), 456–484.

Manno, B., Finn, C., Bierlein, L., & Vanourek, G. (1998). How charter schools are different: Lessons and implications from a national study. *Phi Delta Kappan 79*(7), 488–498.

Marks, H. M., & Louis, K. S. (1999). Teacher empowerment and the capacity for organizational learning. *Educational Administration Quarterly, 35*(5), 707–750.

Marks, H. M., & Printy, S. M. (2003). Principal leadership and school performance: An integration of transformational and instructional leadership. *Educational Administration Quarterly, 39*(3), 370–397.

Maxcy, B. D., & Nguyên, T. S. o. n. T. (2006). The politics of distributing leadership: Reconsidering leadership distribution in two Texas elementary schools. *Educational Policy, 20*(1), 163–196.

McDonnell, L. M. (2005). No child left behind and the federal role in education: Evolution or revolution? *Peabody Journal of Education, 80*(2), 19–38.

McGough, D. J. (2003). Leaders as learners: An inquiry into the formation and transformation of principals' professional perspectives. *Educational Evaluation and Policy Analysis, 25*(4), 449–471.

McNeil, L. M. (2000). *Contradictions of school reform: Educational costs of standardized testing*. New York: Routledge.

Meyer, M. J., Macmillan, R. B., & Northfield, S. K. (2011). Principal succession and the micropolitics of educators in schools: Some incidental results from a larger study. *Canadian Journal of Educational Administration and Policy, 117*, 1–26.

Miller, R. J., & Rowan, B. (2006). Effects of organic management on student achievement. *American Educational Research Journal, 43*(2), 219–256.

Mintrom, M. (2001). Educational governance and democratic practice. *Educational Policy, 15*(5), 615–643.

Mintrop, H. (2004). *Schools on probation: How accountability works (and doesn't work)*. New York: Teachers College Press.

Muncey, D. E., & McQuillan, P. J. (1996). *Reform & resistance in schools and classrooms: An ethnographic view of the Coalition of Essential Schools*. New Haven, CT: Yale University Press.

Murray, C. E., & Grant, G. (1995). *The normative structure of a successful experiment in shared decision making*. Paper presented at the annual meeting of the American Educational Research Association, San Francisco, CA.

Nakagawa, K. (2000). Unthreading the ties that bind: Questioning the discourse of parent involvement. *Educational Policy, 14*(4), 443–472.

Neufeld, B., & Levy, A. (2004). *Baseline report: High school renewal in Boston*. Cambridge, MA.

Neuman-Sheldon, B. (2006). *Building on state reform: Maryland school restructuring*. Washington, DC: Center on Education Policy.

Oakes, J. (1985). *Keeping track: How schools structure inequality*. New Haven, CT: Yale University Press.

Oakes, J., Quartz, K. H., Ryan, S., & Lipton, M. (2000). *Becoming good American schools: The struggle for civic virtue in education reform*. San Francisco, CA: Jossey-Bass.

Odden, A., & Busch, C. (1998). *Financing schools for high performance: Strategies for improving the use of educational resources*. San Francisco, CA: Jossey-Bass.

Ogawa, R. T., Sandholtz, J. H., & Scribner, S. P. (2003). The substantive and symbolic consequences of a district's standards-based curriculum. *American Educational Research Journal, 40*(1), 147–176.

Pedulla, J. J., Abrams, L. M., Madaus, G. F., Russell, M. K., Ramos, M. A., & Miao, J. (2003). *Perceived effects of state-mandated testing programs on teaching and learning: Findings from a national survey of teachers*. Boston, MA: Lynch School of Education, Boston College.

Pounder, D. (1999). Teacher teams: Exploring job characteristics and work-related outcomes of work group enhancement. *Educational Administration Quarterly, 35*(3), 317–348.

Reisner, E. R., Rubenstein, M. C., Johnson, M. L., & Fabiano, L. (2003). *Evaluation of the new century high schools initiative: Report on program implementation in the first year*. Washington, DC.

Reitzug, U. C. (1994). Case study of empowering principal behavior. *American Educational Research Journal, 31*(2), 283–307.

Rex, L. A., & Nelson, M. C. (2004). How teachers' professional identities position high-stakes test preparation in their classrooms. *Teachers College Record, 106*(6), 1288–1331.

Rice, J. K., & Malen, B. (2003). The human costs of education reform: The case of school reconstitution. *Educational Administration Quarterly, 39*(5), 635–666.

Riehl, C. (1998). We gather together: Work, discourse, and constitutive social action in elementary school faculty meetings. *Educational Administration Quarterly, 34*(1), 91–125.

Riehl, C. (2000). The principal's role in creating inclusive schools for diverse students: A review of normative, empirical, and critical literature on the practice of educational administration. *Review of Educational Research, 70*(1), 55–82.

Robertson, P. J., Wohlstetter, P., & Mohrman, S. A. (1995). Generating curriculum and instructional innovations through school-based management. *Educational Administration Quarterly, 31*(3), 375–404.

Rollow, S. G., & Bryk, A. S. (1993). Democratic politics and school improvement: The potential of Chicago school reform. In C. Marshall (Ed.), *The new politics of race and gender* (pp. 97–106). New York: Falmer Press.

Rossman, G. B., & Wilson, B. L. (1996). Context, courses, and the curriculum: Local responses to state policy reform. *Educational Policy, 10*(3), 399–421.

Rusch, E. A. (2005). Institutional barriers to organizational learning in school systems: The power of silence. *Educational Administration Quarterly, 41*(1), 83–120.

Ryan, S., Bryk, A. S., Lopez, G., Williams, K. P., & Luppescu, S. (1997). *Charting reform: LSCs – local leadership at work.* Chicago, IL: Consortium on Chicago School Research.

Saito, E., & Atencio, M. (2013). A conceptual discussion of lesson study from a micro-political perspective: Implications for teacher development and pupil learning. *Teaching & Teacher Education, 31*, 87–95.

Sanders, M. G., & Harvey, A. (2002). Beyond the school walls: A case study of principal leadership for school-community collaboration. *Teachers College Record, 104*(7), 1345–1368.

Sandholtz, J. H., Ogawa, R. T., & Scribner, S. P. (2004). Standards gaps: Unintended consequences of local standards-based reform. *Teachers College Record, 106*(6), 1177–1202.

Schattschneider, E. E. (1960). *The semi-sovereign people.* New York: Holt, Rinehart and Winston.

Schempp, P. G., Sparkes, A. C., & Templin, T. J. (1993). The micropolitics of teacher induction. *American Educational Research Journal, 30*(3), 447–472.

Schneider, M., & Buckley, J. (2002). What do parents want from schools? Evidence from the Internet. *Educational Evaluation and Policy Analysis, 24*(2), 133–144.

Schon, D. (1981). A review of the federal role in curriculum development, 1950–1980. *Educational Evaluation and Policy Analysis, 5*(1), 55–61.

Scribner, J. D., Aleman, E., & Maxy, B. (2003). Emergence of the politics of education field: Making sense of the messy center. *Educational Administration Quarterly, 39*(1), 10–40.

Scribner, J. P., Cockrell, K. S., Cockrell, D. H., & Valentine, J. W. (1999). Creating professional communities in schools through organizational learning: An evaluation of a school improvement process. *Educational Administration Quarterly, 35*(1), 130–160.

Scribner, J. P., Hager, D. R., & Warne, T. R. (2002). The paradox of professional community: Tales from two high schools. *Educational Administration Quarterly, 38*(1), 45–76.

Seitsinger, R. M., & Zera, D. A. (2002). The demise of parent involvement in school governance. *Journal of School Leadership, 12*(4), 340–367.

Sharp, E. B. (Ed.). (1999). *Culture ways and local politics.* Lawrence: University Press of Kansas.

Shipps, D. (1997). The invisible hand: Big business and Chicago school reform. *Teachers College Record, 99*(1), 73–116.

Shipps, D. (1998). Corporate influence on Chicago school reform. In C. N. Stone (Ed.), *Changing urban education* (pp. 161–183). Lawrence: University Press of Kansas.

Shipps, D., Kahne, J., & Smylie, M. A. (1999). The politics of urban school reform: Legitimacy, city growth, and school improvement in Chicago. *Educational Policy, 13*(4), 518–545.

Silva, D. Y., Gimbert, B., & Nolan, J. (2000). Sliding the doors: Locking and unlocking possibilities for teacher leadership. *Teachers College Record, 102*(4), 779–804.

Sipple, J., Killeen, K., & Monk, D. H. (2004). Adoption and adaptation: School district responses to state imposed learning and graduation requirements. *Educational Evaluation and Policy Analysis, 26*(2), 143–168.

Smith, A. K., & Wohlstetter, P. (2001). Reform through school networks: A new kind of authority and accountability. *Educational Policy, 15*(4), 499–519.

Smith, T. M., & Rowley, K. J. (2005). Enhancing commitment or tightening control: The function of teacher professional development in an era of accountability. *Educational Policy, 19*(1), 126–154.

Smrekar, C., & Goldring, E. (1999). *School choice in urban America: Magnet schools and the pursuit of equity.* New York: Teachers College Press.

Smrekar, C., & Mawhinney, H. (1999). Integrated services: Challenges in linking schools, families, and communities. In J. Murphy & K. S. Louis (Eds.), *Handbook of research on educational administration* (2nd ed., pp. 443–461). San Francisco, CA: Jossey-Bass.

Smylie, M. A. (1992). Teacher participation in school decision making: Assessing the willingness to participate. *Educational Evaluation and Policy Analysis, 14*(1), 53–67.

Smylie, M. A., Crowson, R. L., Chou, V., & Levin, R. A. (1994). The principal and community-school connections in Chicago's radical reform. *Educational Administration Quarterly, 30*(3), 342–364.

Smylie, M. A., Lazarus, V., & Brownlee-Conyers, J. (1996). Instructional outcomes of school-based participative decision making. *Educational Evaluation and Policy Analysis 18*(3), 181–198.

Somech, A. (2005a). Directive versus participative leadership: Two complementary approaches to managing school effectiveness. *Educational Administration Quarterly, 41*(5), 777–800.

Somech, A. (2005b). Teachers' personal and team empowerment and their relations to organizational outcomes: Contradictory or compatible constructs? *Educational Administration Quarterly, 41*(2), 237–266.

Song, M., & Miskel, C. G. (2005). Who are the influentials? A cross-state social network analysis of the reading policy domain. *Educational Administration Quarterly, 41*(1), 7–48.

Spillane, J. P. (2002). Local theories of teacher change: The pedagogy of district policies and programs. *Teachers College Record, 104*(3), 377–420.

Spillane, J. P. (2003). Educational leadership. *Educational Evaluation and Policy Analysis, 25*(4), 343–346.

Spillane, J. P. (2006). *Distributed leadership.* San Francisco, CA: Jossey-Bass.

Spillane, J. P., Diamond, J. B., Burch, P., Hallett, T., Jita, L., & Zoltners, J. (2002). Managing in the middle: School leaders and the enactment of accountability policy. *Educational Policy, 16*(5), 731–762.

Spillane, J. P., & Orlina, E. C. (2005). Investigating leadership practice: Exploring the entailments of taking a distributed perspective. *Leadership and Policy in Schools, 4*(3), 157–176.

Spillane, J. P., & Thompson, C. L. (1997). Reconstructing conceptions of local capacity: The local education agency's capacity for ambitious instructional reform. *Educational Evaluation and Policy Analysis, 19*(2), 185–203.

Sporte, S., Kahne, J., & Correa, M. (2004). *Notes from the ground: Teachers, principals, and students' perspectives on the Chicago High School Redesign Initiative, year two.* Chicago, IL.

SRI International, & American Institutes for Research. (2003). *High time for high school reform: Early findings from the evaluation of the national school district and network grants program.* Menlo Park, CA.

Stein, M. K. (2003). Leadership content knowledge. *Educational Evaluation and Policy Analysis, 25*(4), 423–448.

Stetcher, B. M., & Barron, S. (1999). *Test-based accountability: The perverse consequences of milepost testing.* Paper presented at the Annual Conference of the American Educational Research Association, Montreal, Canada.

Stockyard, J., & Lehman, M. B. (2004). Influences on the satisfaction and retention of 1st year teachers: The importance of effective school management. *Educational Administration Quarterly, 40*(5), 742–771.

Summers, A. A., & Johnson, A. W. (1995). Doubts about decentralized decisions. *The School Administrator, 52,* 24–32.

Summers, A. A., & Johnson, A. W. (1996). The effects of school-based management plans. In E. A. Hanushek & D. W. Jorgenson (Eds.), *Improving America's schools: The role of incentives* (pp. 75–96). Washington, DC: National Academy Press.

Sunderman, G. L. (2001). Accountability mandates and the implementation of Title I schoolwide programs: A comparison of three urban districts. *Educational Administration Quarterly, 37*(4), 503–532.

Superfine, B. M. (2005). The politics of accountability: The rise and fall of Goals 2000. *American Journal of Education, 112*(1), 10–43.

Supovitz, J. A. (2002). Developing communities of instructional practice. *Teachers College Record, 104*(8), 1591–1626.

Swanson, C. B., & Stevenson, D. L. (2002). Standards-based reform in practice: Evidence on state policy and classroom instruction from the NAEP state assessments. *Educational Evaluation and Policy Analysis, 24*(1), 1–27.

Timar, T. B. (2004). School governance and oversight in California: Shaping the landscape of equity and adequacy. *Teachers College Record, 106*(11), 2057–2080.

Townsend, R. G. (1990). Toward a broader micropolitics of schools. *Curriculum Inquiry 20*(2), 205–225.

Trujillo, A. (2005). Politics, school philosophy, and language policy: The case of Crystal City schools. *Educational Policy, 19*(4), 621–654.

Uline, C. L., & Berkowitz, J. M. (2000). Transforming school culture through teaching teams. *Journal of School Leadership, 10*(5), 416–444.

Uline, C. L., Tschannen-Moran, M., & Perez, L. (2003). Constructive conflict: How controversy can contribute to school improvement. *Teachers College Record, 105*(5), 782–816.

Waite, D. (1993). Teachers in conference: A qualitative study of teacher-supervisor face-to-face interactions. *American Educational Research Journal, 30*(4), 675–702.

Walker, J. L. J. (1991). *Mobilizing interest groups in America: Patrons, professions, and social movements.* Ann Arbor: The University of Michigan Press.

Wall, R., & Rinehart, J. S. (1998). School based decisionmaking and the empowerment of secondary school teachers. *Journal of School Leadership, 8*(1), 49–64.

Wallach, C. A., Lambert, M. B., Copland, M., & Lowry, L. K. (2005). *Distributing leadership: Moving from high school hierarchy to shared responsibility.* Seattle, WA.

Wasley, P., Fine, M., Gladden, M., Holland, N. E., King, S. P., Mosak, E., et al. (2000). *Small schools: Great strides.* New York: Bank Street College of Education.

Webb, T. P. (2008). Re-mapping power in educational micropolitics. *Critical Studies in Education, 49*(2), 127–142.

Wechsler, M. E., & Friedrich, L. D. (1997). The role of mediating organizations for school reform: Independent agents or district dependents? *Journal of Education Policy, 12*(5), 385–401.

Weiss, C. H. (1993). Shared decision-making about what? A comparison of schools with and without teacher participation. *Teachers College Record, 95*(1), 69–92.

Wells, A. S., & Serna, I. (1996). The politics of culture: Understanding local political resistance to detracking in racially mixed schools. *Harvard Educational Review, 66*(1), 93–118.

Westheimer, J. (1998). *Among schoolteachers: Community, individuality, and ideology in teachers' work.* New York: Teachers College Press.

Westheimer, J. (1999). Communities and consequences: An inquiry into ideology and practice in teachers' professional work. *Educational Administration Quarterly, 35*(1), 71–105.

White, J. A., & Wehlage, G. (1995). Community collaboration: If it is such a good idea, why is it so hard to do? *Educational Evaluation and Policy Analysis, 17*, 23–38.

Wohlstetter, P., Malloy, C. L., Chau, D., & Pohlemus, J. L. (2003). Improving schools through networks: A new approach to urban school reform. *Educational Policy, 17*(4), 399–430.

Wong, K. K. (1994). Linking governance reform to schooling opportunities for the disadvantaged. *Educational Administration Quarterly, 30*(2), 153–177.

Wong, K. K., & Anagnostopoulos, D. (1998). Can integrated governance reconstruct teaching? Lessons learned from two low-performing Chicago high schools. *Educational Policy, 12*(1), 31–47.

York-Barr, J., & Duke, K. (2004). What do we know about teacher leadership? Findings from two decades of scholarship. *Review of Educational Research, 74*(3), 255–316.

Yu, C. M., & Taylor, W. L. (1997). *Difficult choices: Do magnet schools serve children in need?* Washington, DC: Citizen's Commission on Civil Rights.

Zancanella, D. (1992). The influence of state-mandated testing on teachers of literature. *Educational Evaluation and Policy Analysis, 14*(3), 283–295.

Zimmerman, J. (2002). *Whose America? Culture wars in the public schools.* Cambridge, MA: Harvard University Press.

ADDENDUM TO CHAPTER 1

Anchala Sobrin (Fordham University, 2013)

Given below are details of recently published research on micropolitics in education since the original version of this chapter was first published, written as a brief update to supplement this micropolitics chapter. For example, Eilertsen, Gustafson, and Salo discuss the impact of action research on the micropolitics in schools. They present different aspects and expressions of micropolitics, focusing particularly on initiatives to and engagement with action research. They indicate that action research "heightens teachers' awareness of power relationships between teachers and their pupils but not among themselves or in consideration to their relationship to head-teachers" (2008, p. 297). They conclude that "micro-political tensions and challenges ought to be addressed and dealt with during action research" (p. 306).

Caffyn writes on micropolitics in international school leadership, stating that "micro-politics is often seen as a negative aspect of school management"; however, "a knowledge of these complex and difficult areas of school life is essential to international school leadership" (2010, p. 50). Caffyn concludes: "Leaders and those involved with leadership and management . . . should have knowledge and expertise . . . not just about academic concerns, but social and emotional so as to empower, support and direct both staff and clientele forward" (p. 56).

Björk and Blasé write about the micropolitics of school district decentralization, looking at a district where the "superintendent's success at implementation of district-wide decentralization policies is related to the nature and structure of micropolitics at the middle management level of the organization" (2009, p. 195).

Findings suggest that "the micro-politics of district middle management limited the superintendent's capacity to collect evaluation information on implementation of new policies, programs, and practices as well as interfered with his ability to take corrective action at administrative, school board and community levels" (p. 208).

They conclude that "our understanding of the micropolitical process at the school district middle management level is in a nascent stage of development. . . . Micro-politics of middle management helps to explain the 'implementation gap' and illuminate political issues that superintendents face in implementing district educational reform initiatives" (p. 206).

Likewise, Blasé and Blasé discuss the misuse of power by school principals resulting in mistreatment of teachers, stating that educational leadership programs "have failed to address the destructive problem of principal mistreatment of teachers" (2004, p. 265).

They conclude: "Now, more than ever before, school reform efforts require that principals and teachers work together collaboratively to solve educational problems" (p. 266) and assert the need for knowledge of micropolitical systems within the schools to build trust in their schools and develop their schools into a "powerful community of learners willing to take responsibility for and capable of success" (p. 266).

Webb asserts that "micro-political studies formalize the concept of power as a binary relationship between the concepts of authority and influence" (2008, p. 127). He examines power as a concept that operates "covertly and pantopically," discusses forms of power that are not easily observed or not observed at all, and concludes that "mapping stealth forms of power . . . reaffirms the importance of political action in schools. . . . From this, a 'new' politics is born from which to address equity and, perhaps democratic, concerns in public schools micro-politically" (p. 139). Micropolitics has continued to be an important perspective in analyzing school operations, or politics, as this update explains.

REFERENCES

Björk, L., & Blasé, J. (2009). The micropolitics of school district decentralization. *Educational Assessment, Evaluation & Accountability, 21*(3), 195–208.

Blasé, J., & Blasé, J. (2004). The dark side of school leadership: Implications for administrator preparation. *Leadership & Policy in Schools, 3*(4), 245–273.

Caffyn, R. (2010). Enabling long-term effective school leadership: Nine ways to understand and utilize micropolitics in international schools. *International Schools Journal, 29*(2), 50–59.

Eilertsen, T., Gustafson, N., & Salo, P. (2008). Action research and the micropolitics in schools. *Educational Action Research, 16*(3), 295–308.

Webb, T. P. (2008). Re-mapping power in educational micropolitics. *Critical Studies in Education, 49*(2), 127–142.

2

HITTING A MOVING TARGET

How Politics Determines the Changing Roles of Superintendents and School Boards

Thomas Alsbury

Schools and school governance structures began and have continued to be a seemingly paradoxical combination of the active exercise of politics and the declaration of its apolitical purity. Some researchers observe that board members believe that education "is too important to become a political affair and that school board members are trustees for, and not representatives of, the public"(Lutz, 1977, p. 4); however, most agree that politics and policy are extrinsically linked (Hanson, 2003; Keedy & Björk, 2003; Kirst, 2008; Wirt & Kirst, 2001).

Historically, the essential value of the public school was to educate the masses and thus enable democracy—an undeniably political purpose (Alsbury, 2009, 2011; Glickman, 1993; Mountford & Alsbury, 2012). This lay governance in our local public system had its beginnings in township committees in New England as early as 1647 where education of the citizenry was included amongst their responsibilities. As the population of the communities grew, these township committees evolved into an autonomous school committee with elected members, the precursor of present-day school boards (Griffiths, 1966; Kirst, 2008; Mountford, 2008).

As larger cities developed, managing the schools became increasingly difficult. School committees appointed superintendents to assume responsibility for the increasing clerical and management functions. By the early 1890s, all major cities had superintendents, and the stage was set for what became a sparring match between school board members and superintendents over who would run the schools and what role each would play.

Central to this balancing of authority is what Kowalski (2004, 2008) described as a tension between the need for the professional knowledge of superintendents and the democratic political influence of lay board members.

These local school boards were to provide the means by which segments in each community have a representative voice in how schools will educate their children. In principle, school boards were to provide public credibility, stewardship, and direction to local education as well as a political vehicle for the citizenry to exercise authority over the schools. However, a counter-aristocratic ideology has been warring against the

American model of school governance since its inception. "Aristocrats condemn democracy because they believe it subjects the wise to the rule of the foolish" (Glickman, 1993, p. 13). In the context of school governance, an emerging professional superintendency provided the vehicle for the application of expert knowledge to schools and challenged the foundational notion of school board authority. Today, this aristocratic condemnation of local democracy has reemerged, embodied in a new school governance construct called integrated governance being promoted by proponents who believe centralized control limits "competing interests by consolidating decision making" (Wong & Shen, 2008, p. 223). Proponents go on to note, "The school system is integrated into broader municipal governance, allowing for citywide interests to prevail over parochial ones" (p. 323). The elimination of stakeholder voices appears to be the primary, albeit taciturn, goal of mayoral takeover; efficiency trumps diversity and collaboration.

HISTORICAL ROLES

The attempt to understand and balance superintendent and school board roles of power and authority began early. In fact, by 1890 major cities were experiencing power struggles between school boards and superintendents, making the position tenuous and unstable (Knezevich, 1984). Because superintendents were initially hired to perform clerical and supervisory duties, like writing uniform courses of study for multiple buildings and evaluating class instruction for quality (Spring, 1994), boards maintained control and superintendents acted as board servants or what Callahan (1962) called the *teacher-scholar* role. In fact, Kowalski (2006) initially chronicled the historical transition of the superintendency through five roles: (1) teacher-scholar (1865 to 1910), (2) manager (1910 to 1930), (3) democratic leader (1930 to mid-1950), (4) applied social scientist (mid-1950 to 1980), and (5) communicator (1980 to present). School board roles influenced and reacted to shifting superintendent roles, the two transitioning in concert and often conflicting with each other.

A brief review of these role transitions is instructive in demonstrating how the political environments changed superintendent and board roles over time. Many present-day researchers believe that while these roles changed in their level of prominence over time, current superintendents and school board members still enact all of these role attributes to some extent (Cuban, 1976; Keedy & Björk, 2003; Kowalski, 2006, 2008). In fact, the understanding and balance of these roles still dominate the debate among school governance theorists and frustrate school board members and superintendent practitioners.

Shifting Roles
As mentioned earlier, the first superintendent role was that of *teacher-scholar*. During this role era, superintendents provided instructional oversight while school board members performed legislative and executive functions, often assuming day-to-day managerial responsibilities (Kowalski, 2006). It should also be remembered that until around 1932, most non-urban school districts operated without the need of a superintendent. At this time, the school board member to student ratio was approximately 1 to 46, representing more than 172,000 mostly one-room schoolhouses (Zeigler, Jennings, & Peak, 1974). Therefore, the political and demographic realities in this era seemed to make the school board members' predominance in school governance nearly absolute. However, in urban centers, it would not take long for the superintendent role of *teacher-scholar* to

be challenged. By 1895, the Draper report urged school boards to delegate authority to superintendents to employ teachers, supervise instruction, and manage finances (Callahan, 1962).

This marked the introduction of the idea of distinguishing between a policy development role for the board and a policy implementation role for the superintendent (Zeigler et al., 1974), similar to what many believe is the current primary role distinction. The fledgling American School Board Association renounced the report, arguing that superintendents were not trained or experienced in management. In fact, superintendents at this time were mostly teachers selected by boards for political purposes, as personal favors, or as promising instructional experts, not because of leadership or management experience or potential (Kowalski, 2003).

School board roles also shifted over time between what some researchers describe as *elite* (trustee) or *arena* (delegate) governance roles and behaviors (Bailey, 1965; Kowalski, 2008). Elite boards tend to take little input from the public, working outside of the public forum to ensure unanimity in the public board meetings, and believing that their election has given them the mandate to make decisions based on their own personal agendas and belief systems. Conversely, arena boards seek multiple and constant public input, value open debate, and believe that they should make decisions based on their constituents' wishes even when they conflict with their own. During this era, the elite board member role of trustee predominated and authority rested almost exclusively with the school board.

By 1910, the industrial revolution, the growth of urban school districts, and the success of hierarchical systems in business and industry transformed school structures and the role of the superintendent to that of *manager* (Kowalski & Brunner, 2005; Lutz, 1996; Tyack & Hansot, 1982). The transition was fueled not only by the belief that new theories of scientific management could improve the efficiency of schools (Norton et al., 1996; Tyack, 1972), but was aided by a burgeoning educational administration profession. School administration courses and a hierarchical separation between administration and teaching emerged during this time (Callahan, 1962; Cubberley, 1924). However, some school board members opposed this development as did city managers and council members who feared a power shift and a loss of control (Callahan, 1962; Glass, 2003).

In this era in particular, the confusion and conflict between authority roles are evident. Researchers writing about the battle of roles during this time display widely diverse interpretations. Callahan's (1962) Thesis of Vulnerability characterized superintendents as self-protective pawns of their employers, lacking courage and conviction, while others suggest that they were either political pragmatists (Burroughs, 1974; Tyack, 1972) or opportunists (Thomas & Moran, 1992), responding to the political and social realities of the day and protecting their growing power bases.

It appears that the interpretation of role shift during this era depends on viewing the change through either the superintendent or the school board lens. For the school board member, and other political pundits, focused on maintaining control of schools by the locally elected citizenry, the advancement of power and authority of the superintendent through the professionalization of the position was a deleterious turn of events to be opposed. For superintendents, it was an opportunity to advance their role to a more prestigious level above the teaching staff, providing much-needed educational expertise to the management of the school system, and diminishing the inefficiencies of local political influences that were sometimes not in the best interests of students.

By 1930, economic and political forces changed the superintendent role. Important to these was the Great Depression, which had raised serious doubt about the success of the business management movement and intensified criticism from progressive educators arguing for more democratic and grassroots managing of educational systems (Hanson, 2003; Hoy & Miskel, 2005). The apparent failure of hierarchical management approaches in industry diminished public support for increasing the superintendent's authority in school governance (Kowalski, 1999). This sentiment was also supported by proponents of the core tenets of local citizen control and what was called "democratic schooling" (Counts, 1927; VanTil, 1971), which focused on student and teacher needs and relegated administrators to resource acquisition.

In keeping with this role transition, superintendents were forced to engage with their communities in a new way. While politically active superintendents had been considered unprofessional (Björk & Lindle, 2001; Kowalski, 1995), scarce resources forced them to compete for dwindling funds in an attempt to maintain a competitive edge over city managers who were fighting to provide other public services. Proponents of the day encouraged superintendents to "mobilize the educational resources from communities" (Melby, 1955, p. 250), also leading to a combination of a shift back to increased school board authority, while pushing superintendents into an unfamiliar political role that has been described as *democratic statesman* (Kowalski, 2006) and *political strategist* (Björk & Gurley, 2003). This era marked the emergence of the superintendent and board as political activists, responsible for realizing community support for public schools (Howlett, 1993). This political role would continue to grow and intensify to the present day, although Kowalski and Keedy (2003) indicate that the transformation was more philosophical than substantive at the time.

The next identified role shift occurred from the mid-1950s to the 1980s and called on superintendents to function in the role of *applied social scientist* (Callahan, 1964). This role shift was caused by the emergence of the practical applications of social science theory, postwar beliefs that democratic leadership was too idealistic, and an increasing criticism of public education (Callahan, 1964). Also present was a push to establish school administration as a separate and legitimate academic discipline (Culbertson, 1981) fueled by significant graduate study funding from the Kellogg Foundation. This development prompted superintendents to use social sciences to address larger societal problems (Kellogg Foundation, 1961). In addition, the development of systems theory emphasized the importance for superintendents to shift from a focus on internal operations to external legal, political, social, and economic influences (Getzels, 1977).

Superintendents started studying theory and looking for normative standards leading to effective schools (Johnson & Fusarelli, 2003). Simultaneously, increased pressure by special interest groups to influence school decision making pressed school boards to return to a more politicized role (Danzberger & Usdan, 1994). These shifts acted to increase the professionalism of the role of superintendent and force superintendents more squarely into community political roles. At the same time, school boards were being pressured to focus back on the demands of citizen groups and away from influence of professional administrators within the school system. This conflict of roles further intensified the tension between the importance of the professional knowledge of the superintendent and the grassroots and democratic political governance of school boards (Kowalski, 2004; Wirt & Kirst, 2001, 2005).

The next role transition, as conceptualized by Kowalski (2001), was that of the superintendent as *communicator*. This role was brought on by the national shift, after 1980, from an industrial to an information age (Drucker, 1999), and was further fueled by a national reform movement and the belief that change could only be sustained by an in-school/in-district, cultural transformation (Chance & Björk, 2004; Fullan, 1996; Murphy, 1991; Schlechty, 1997). Current superintendents were taught that stakeholder buy-in was critical to successful reform efforts (Kowalski, 1997), making the superintendent's ability to communicate effectively for the purpose of influencing and leading diverse and varied, external and internal constituents critical. This final role further propelled superintendents into a political role in the community.

From the 2000s to the present, superintendents and board roles have become more a conflagration than clearly defined parts. The most recent addition is the role of *civic engagement* (Kowalski, 2008, p. 235). This role, closely tied to communicator, is described as a form of deliberative democracy through a more direct intervention in school improvement planning and implementation. In fact, centralizing responsibility for student achievement gains to the superintendent and school board was a trend that has expanded even beyond local boards to state and national controls.

CONTEMPORARY SUPERINTENDENT ROLE

While superintendent and school board roles have ebbed and flowed in prominence through history, each has contributed to the present-day amalgam, with none of the historical roles being completely relinquished. Today the *teacher-scholar* role is still evident in the debate over whether superintendents should come from an educational background and whether they should focus on being instructional leaders. Some suggest that the position is not unique from general administration (Broad Foundation & Fordham Institute, 2003; Hess, 2002, 2008), and school leaders can be drawn from any background or profession. In fact, today, most superintendents come from a teaching position, following the teacher-scholar role set in the 1860s (Elmore, 2000; Murphy, 2002; Negroni, 2000). Recent studies show that superintendents have always exercised an indirect but significant influence on instructional effectiveness even when focused on management tasks (Bredeson, 1996; Morgan & Petersen, 2002; Petersen, 2002; Petersen & Barnett, 2003); however, there are calls for more direct superintendent involvement in instructional reform (Fullan, 2006).

The role of *manager* is also still evident today (Glass, 2003; Kowalski, 1995). In fact, the 1980s brought on a renewed push to infuse business theory and techniques into educational leadership training programs and school operations. In addition, the primary debate over the past decade has centered on the balance of management versus leadership (Kowalski, 1995) in school administrative practice. Currently, researchers are bringing the same debate into the arena of how school boards govern (Kowalski, 2008; LaMonte, Delagardelle, & VanderZyl, 2005; Mountford & Alsbury, 2012; Stringfield, 2008).

Turning to the role of *political strategist* or *democratic leader*, today most observers agree that school politics and policy are extrinsically linked (Hanson, 2003; Keedy & Björk, 2003; Wirt & Kirst, 2001, 2005). Finally, the role of *applied social scientist* continues to be critical and is fueled by demands for district-wide school reform and accountability (Fullan, 2006), a call for superintendents and boards to transform district culture toward greater social justice and activism (Fusarelli & Fusarelli, 2005), and the increasing demands to use data to legitimize and direct decision making (McCaw & Watkins, 2007; Park & Datnow, 2009).

The ability to combine and apply these various role demands within unique district contexts presents a complicated and perhaps impossible challenge, especially considering that the superintendent is constantly thwarted by internal culture that may often be antithetical to either good instructional practice or political acuity (Alsbury, 2008c; Fullan, 2006). Thus, the challenge of balancing professionalism and external local political control continues.

CONTEMPORARY SCHOOL BOARD ROLE

When discussing school board roles, the current issue is focused on whether school board governance in practice is effective in representing the public interest, and whether school boards should be more directly responsible for leading school improvement efforts (Walser, 2009). While different views evolved over time regarding the primary purpose of school boards (Campbell & Greene, 1994; Eadie, 2003; Kowalski, 2006; Sarason, 1997; Schlechty, 1992; Simon, 1986), most agree that the historically traditional purpose of reflecting the community vision for education in a democracy is still relevant (Alsbury, 2011; Kowalski, 2006; Mountford & Alsbury, 2012).

Since the 1990s, and some argue throughout their history, school boards have been criticized as ineffective and irrelevant in effectively leading schools and school reform, responding to community demands, or providing a representative voice reflective of community diversity, particularly in urban areas (Alsbury, 2011; Fusarelli & Fusarelli, 2005; Wong & Shen, 2008). In fact, Secretary of the U.S. Department of Education Chester Finn said, "School boards are an aberration, an anachronism, an educational sinkhole" (as cited in Kowalski, 2006, p. 124). Today, many (68%) superintendents believe that boards need to be restructured or replaced (Glass, 2001; Glass & Franceschini, 2007).

This criticism is caused by, amongst other things, a continuing confusion by superintendents, school board members, and the public as to their roles in school governance today. For example, while community special interest groups and the public in general expect more voice in shaping school policy and procedure, most board members (87%) don't believe they need to behave based on the wishes of the public and view themselves as *trustees* rather than *delegates* of the citizenry (Kowalski, 2006, 2008). In the past, this role functioned well because local elite leaders, who were elected onto the school board or influenced the school board, generally reflected the majority opinions and values of the community (Wirt & Kirst, 2001). However, when teacher unions became a political force in board elections after the 1970s, coupled with the simultaneous increase in community ideological plurality and diversity and a decline in general community involvement in school boards, local special interest group politics increased (Moe, 2001), focused more on protectionism.

While boards continued to function in an elite fashion, the change in the community and the accompanying lack of open and frequent communication caused an increasing gap between community values and desires and boards' perception of such. This led Kowalski (2008) to call for the role of the school board to shift to a focus on civic engagement and two-way, open communication. This change would require boards to take on a *facilitative* role, requiring school boards to include the public in decision making.

Currently, most boards serve either in an *instrumental* role, where boards enforce rules, or in a *representative* role, where communication with the public is optional.

Various theorists described these resulting governance patterns, concluding that board systems were no longer democratic (Zeigler et al., 1974), infrequently democratic (Wirt & Kirst, 2001), or largely democratic (Lutz & Iannaccone, 1978). Although differing in their conclusions, all these theorists focused their primary arguments on to what extent boards fairly represent their communities.

Issues of Representation

Similar to studies of city councils and other publicly elected officials, the early studies of school boards tended to categorize boards into dichotomous groups based on the degree to which they were considered representative of and/or responsive to their constituent populations. These categories took various names but were similar in the conceptual description of board members as either more politically or professionally oriented toward their representative responsibilities.

Based on studies of city councils in the mid-1960s that described elite and arena councils, Gresson (1976) conducted some of the early research on school boards from these two perspectives described earlier in this chapter. Researchers following this example (Kowalski, 2008; Lutz, 1980; Lutz & Gresson, 1980) argued that elite or trustee boards relied heavily on the superintendent, sought consensus, and rejected the notion of representing specific constituencies as opposed to the arena or delegate boards that relied less on the superintendent, frequently had split vote decisions, and deliberately represented specific segments of the community.

Tucker and Zeigler (1980) described boards as either hierarchical or bargaining. The hierarchical boards deferred to the decision-making authority of the superintendent and then served as the communication link between the superintendent and the public. The bargaining boards, on the other hand, reflected both the recommendations of the superintendent and the preferences of the community. Kowalski (2008) describes board members as either trustees of the public interest or representatives/delegates of specific groups. Trustee board members emphasized a reliance on the superintendent while delegate members emphasized accountability to their constituents. According to Greene (1992), the distinctions among these different views of representation were whether board members view themselves as part of a technical/political process and respond to the demands of parent and community groups, as part of a professional process and defer to the expertise of the superintendent and other school professionals, or some combination of the two and negotiate district policies that accommodate the needs of both the professionals and the community. Greene concluded that the majority of school boards operate under the professional orientation, a finding supported by current national surveys of school board members (Hess & Meeks, 2010; Mountford et al., 2012). Mountford and colleagues' (2012) findings support the professional orientation of most boards, indicating superintendents as most influencing board member decisions and parents and community as a minimal influence.

In addition, 100 percent of board members reported high levels of confidence in information received from their superintendent with only 28 percent reporting high confidence in information received from the community. On the other hand, studies from the 1990s to today illustrate board members' interest in taking more responsibility in key areas of schooling (Kirst, 2008; LaMonte et al., 2005). In addition, Lutz (1980) argued that most school board members try to come to decisions that are equally good for everyone: a conclusion supported by current studies that board consensus and local reform efforts hold the most hope for school improvement (Mountford et al., 2012; Stringfield, 2008; Townsend et al., 2007).

However, Lutz (1977) and Glass and Franceschini (2007) noted that despite the public's press for more arena board behavior, board members continue to seek consensus in private, to avoid public conflict and the public debate of controversial issues. Further, community culture pressures boards to act in an elite fashion. Boards that have prolonged debates in public, attempt to represent multiple viewpoints, entertain special interests, and experience split votes on educational issues are viewed as disorganized, lacking leadership, and ineffective, and are often pressured to return to an elite style of governance or face replacement at election time (Walser, 2009). Indeed, board members currently report that special interest groups do not significantly influence board decision making, but board members serve as a civic duty for the overall development of students (Alsbury, 2008; Mountford & Alsbury, 2012; Mountford et al., 2012).

Since the 1980s, board members believed their role was to be supportive in nature and function as a policy approval body rather than taking a more active role in instructional improvements. Typical duties used to be restricted to approving the budget, dealing with constituents, generating revenue, and keeping the public "at bay" around politically sensitive issues. However, recent studies of effective school boards have suggested the need for a more dynamic leadership role. Resnick (1999) identified ten fundamentals of good board operations: (a) setting the vision, (b) focusing on student achievement, (c) providing a structure for success, (d) advocating for education, (e) involving the community, (f) accounting for results, (g) empowering the staff, (h) setting policy, (i) collaborating with other agencies, and (j) committing to continuous improvement.

More recently, Delagardelle (2008) distinguished a difference between effective and ineffective school boards based on five main conditions: (a) setting clear expectations for measurable outcomes, (b) ensure conditions for success, (c) build the collective will of staff and community, (d) time to learn together as a board, and (e) accountability for themselves and the staff to reach instructional goals. Walser (2009) suggested that effective school boards must change their role from overseers to leaders of instruction. These fundamental operations are consistent with other models that have attempted to describe school board functions for more effective board leadership (Goodman et al., 1997 Land, 2002; Smoley, 1999).

However, despite the encouraging findings that shifting a school board role includes a greater understanding of and responsibility for curriculum and instructional leadership, other researchers maintain a traditional policy approval role for school boards (Quinn & Dawson, 2011). Unfortunately, most school boards have ignored researched-based governance models and still embrace a business style of CEO/policy board model of governance (Carver & Carver, 1997), promoted by powerful and well-funded organizations like the Broad Foundation. As a result, operations on most school boards have remained stable, and the outcomes of schooling (student achievement results) have not improved (Delagardelle, 2008; Grissmer et al., 2000; LaMonte et al., 2005).

Today, the main reason for board frustration and community criticism is likely a tension between two different perspectives on the role of board members. Some board members believe that their role should be restricted to a policy development focus, with the superintendent acting as the professional administrator of the school program. However, many in the community and on the school board still see the superintendent as a political appointee and believe that "personal interests, common sense, and their own wisdom should trump a superintendent's recommendations" (Kowalski, 2006, p. 137). This latter role description reflects the 1860s concept of the superintendent as an anti-professional, domesticated public servant of the board (Kowalski, 2004).

Issues of Board Representativeness

Early criticisms of school boards' ability to represent their communities as truly democratic bodies (Wirt & Kirst, 2006) were buoyed by criticisms that board members did not resemble their communities demographically or politically. The most recent studies of board members show marked representativeness among school boards nationally. Mountford and Alsbury (2012) and Hess and Meeks (2010) found that board members now are comprised of 44 percent women, more than double other politically elected bodies like Congress at 17 percent (Hess & Meeks, 2010). Likewise, representation of African Americans on school boards is nearly 12 percent nationally and 22 percent in more diverse urban districts; much more representative than in the federal government, with about 9 percent and 1 percent African American representation in the U.S. House and Senate, respectively (Hess & Meeks, 2010).

On the topic of representative governance, some argue that because of low voter turnout for school board elections, school boards do not adequately represent the citizenry (Wirt & Kirst, 2005. In fact, proponents of centralizing school governance to mayors Wong & Shen note "mayoral elections, with higher voter participation, actually enhance democracy in the sense that more voters participate" (2008, p. 325). They go on to argue that a higher and broader vote makes "mayoral elections less susceptible to the influential groups that are overrepresented in school board elections" (p. 325). However, several key points are missed in this argument. First, while mayoral election turnout is higher, voter decisions are spread thin over broad mayoral issues from taxes to city services. The inability to vote based solely on their satisfaction of school leadership diminishes direct influence over school leadership.

Second, while school board election turnout is about 20 percent overall compared to national election turnouts of around 50 percent, parents with children in schools currently represent approximately 25 percent of the total electorate. Thus, perhaps a higher percentage of citizens with children in the schools are participating in school board elections when compared to the overall public in general elections. Third, voter turnout for school board elections increases dramatically when there are issues of community dissatisfaction with the school (Alsbury, 2003). In fact, research indicates that school board members are regularly defeated in school elections by citizens demanding a change in their schools. Alsbury (2003) found that, on average, 30 percent of the school board members turned over in every biennial election, representing a majority vote turnover on boards and the subsequent removal of the superintendent in 74 percent of the districts over the course of his seven-year study.

These findings take on particular relevance when realizing that high politically motivated board turnover and the subsequent superintendent turnover lead to a decrease in student achievement (Alsbury, 2008b). In addition, Alsbury (2003) and Glass (2008) noted that superintendents and board member roles begin to shift as a result of these turnover events, predicated by political protectionism and self-interest on part of both superintendents and board members.

INFLUENCES ON CURRENT SUPERINTENDENT
AND BOARD ROLES

Current research indicates that superintendent and school board roles are influenced mainly by (a) a general loss of confidence in institutions and leaders, (b) an increase in special interest group activism, (c) more expectations from the public for involvement in policy decision making, (d) a growing cultural, ideological, and values divide in local communities, and (e) a shift to centrist policy making coupled with a simultaneous devolution to distributed leadership and shared decision making (Björk, 2008; Björk & Gurley, 2005; Björk & Lindle, 2001; Cibulka, 1999; Keedy & Björk, 2003; Petersen & Fusarelli, 2008). These influences have led to what Petersen and Fusarelli (2008) and Walser (2009) describe as confusion in role clarification, ambiguous expectations, and ill-defined authority between boards and superintendents. Other researchers, like Norton and colleagues (1996), state the problem more simply, pointing to overlapping job responsibilities as the main issue.

As early as 1899 Dewey posited that increasing immigration would lead to cultural pluralism and the need for a more democratic approach to determine the purpose of education. At the time, Dewey believed that this change was occurring, a trend also evident today and similarly influencing superintendent and board roles in both eras. In addition, Kowalski (2006) pointed to several economic changes, including the loss of unskilled jobs and the advent of a global economy, increasing the push for centralized education reforms evident in the 1960s and in the 1990s. Dewey also catalogues several recent social and demographic shifts including: (a) an increase in the ethnic population, bringing with it increased ideological diversity; (b) an increase in poverty without the luxury of high-paying minimal-skills jobs; (c) the rise in the private schooling of the upper classes; (d) an increase in the political power of older individuals without children in school (Jenks & Philips, 1998); (e) an increase in single-parent families (Glass, 2004); (f) a decrease in the time parents spend with their children (Hewlett, 1991); (g) an increase in the reliance on schools as social agencies (Duncan, 1992); (h) an increase in antisocial behaviors through violence in the media (Pride, 2002); and (i) the diminished role and participation in community civic/service organizations calling on more reliance on schools for things like character education (Schwartz, 1996). These and other societal changes led Kowalski (2006) to argue that the purpose of schooling was no longer commonly agreed on by the citizenry. In fact, some believe a battle exists between whether schools should be focused on excellence or equity, confusing superintendents and board members trying to set a focus for schooling supported by their communities.

This confusion was supported by Mountford and colleagues (2012) and Hess and Meeks (2010) in national surveys of school board members who indicate that the purpose of schooling is mainly to "help students fulfill their potential" and "prepare students for a satisfying and productive life." These results belie the current focus of national policy leaders who suggest schools are for preparing students for college or the high-tech workforce.

DEMANDS ON SUPERINTENDENTS AND
SCHOOL BOARD MEMBERS

Today, superintendents and boards are being asked to do an ever-lengthening list of tasks for an ever-increasing list of diverse stakeholders. One proposed list of duties for superintendents and boards asks them to: (a) focus on student achievement and quality of instruction, (b) use data, (c) develop a targeted and phased focus on student improvement, (d) invest in instructional leadership, (e) emphasize teamwork and professional community, (f) improve the board/superintendent relationship, (g) improve district culture, and (h) enhance professional development for teachers (Leithwood, Fullan, & Watson, 2003).

Superintendents are also being asked to increase their political leadership skills and build consensus with multiple, diverse stakeholders (Björk, 2008; Björk & Lindle, 2001) and to develop collaborative cultures, buy-in, flexibility, and professional learning communities (Delagardelle, 2008; Mountford, 2008; Walser, 2009). Superintendents tend to be more pragmatic, citing their greatest problems as a lack of finances, assessing learner outcomes, pressures of state accountability, new teaching strategies, and changing curriculum priorities (Glass & Franceschini, 2007; Hess & Meeks, 2010; Mountford et al., 2012).

While demands have increased, challenges to the superintendency have as well. Superintendent instability is cited as a major obstacle to maintaining positive school board relationships and developing a mutual understanding of roles (Glass, 2008; Mountford, 2008; Natkin et al., 2002). Superintendent instability and high turnover are noted as particular problems in urban (Carter & Cunningham, 1997; Glass, 1992, 2008; Glass & Franceschini, 2007; Hess, 2008; Kowalski, 1995) and rural (Chance & Capps, 1990; Eaton & Sharp, 1996; Ramirez & Guzman, 1999) districts, while practicing superintendents seem to be less satisfied, citing job insecurity, interference by special interests in policy development (Glass, 2008; Petersen & Fusarelli, 2008), and conflicts with board members (Alsbury, 2004; Metzger, 1997) as reasons for wanting to leave the position.

In fact, superintendent instability and vulnerability to firing on the whim of locally elected boards led Wisener (1996) to suggest that superintendents may make most of their decisions based on self-preservation. Glass suggested, "sometimes the easiest solution to solve conflict or excuse low test scores is to fire a scapegoat superintendent and hire a private-sector contractor" (2008, p. 305). Alsbury argued that superintendents' longevity in highly political local school environments was based mostly on "avoiding change and reform in an effort to curry peace, diminish conflict, and keep their list of enemies as short as possible" (2008, p. 253).

Clearly, political influence and demands on superintendents and boards have made the importance of a clear understanding of roles critical to the effective operations of schools, especially in a pluralistic and diverse environment. Role negotiation is tightly linked to positive superintendent/board relationships and effective communications. In fact, improved organizational effectiveness is most influenced by developing and nurturing a quality superintendent/board relationship (Björk, 2008; Björk & Keedy, 2001; Petersen & Fusarelli, 2008).

SCHOOL BOARD AND SUPERINTENDENT RELATIONSHIP

School board and superintendent relationship studies have been numerous (Allison, Allison, & McHenry, 1995; Hess & Meeks, 2010; Mountford, 2008; Petersen & Fusarelli, 2008; Walser, 2009), with most concluding that a positive board/superintendent interaction is the single most important factor to successful governance of a district (Björk, 2008; Kowalski, 2008; Mountford, 2008; Petersen & Fusarelli, 2008; Smoley, 1999; Stringfield, 2008; Walser, 2009). In fact, when this relationship is strained, programs fail, morale is weakened, mistrust builds, board members form politically controlling subgroups, and long-term goal setting becomes impossible (Delagardelle, 2008; Norton et al., 1996). Both boards and superintendents recognize the importance of a good relationship to effective leadership and superintendent success (Glass, 2008; Kowalski, 2008; Mountford, 2008).

Studies indicate that poor communication is a major obstacle to a positive school board/superintendent relationship (Delagardelle, 2008; Smoley, 1999; Walser, 2009). Peterson and Short (2002) further noted that communication skill, and the resulting quality of the superintendent/school board president relationship, influenced school board decision making more than any other factor. Kowalski (2005) concluded that the superintendent's new role should be characterized as expert communicator.

However, the American Association of School Administrator's (AASA) five-year survey showed that most superintendents (62%) spend three hours or less per week in direct communication with board members (Glass & Franceschini, 2007) and board members complained that they had little or no contact with their superintendent outside of the board meeting (Glass, 1993; Glass & Franceschini, 2007). Some blamed superintendent communication problems on an autonomous leadership style (Blumberg & Blumberg, 1985; Kowalski, 1995), shaped by particular role perceptions.

For example, superintendents who viewed themselves as the sole school expert and decision maker and saw the board's role as policy making and community buffer did not keep members informed, wanted things their own way, took no suggestions from the board, got mad if challenged, tried to intimidate, withheld important information, and did not give clear answers (Grady & Bryant, 1991; Norton et al., 1996). In fact, 30 percent of superintendents view their school boards as unqualified to lead the district (Glass & Franceschini, 2007).

Role Incongruity

Previously, we discussed how the school board role of maintaining local influence and being directed by community voice can have negative effects on effective school governance. Cassel (1999), for example, found that problems arose when boards functioned primarily in a democratic, political role. In these districts, superintendents would make recommendations that, they believed, would have led to improved instructional quality and student achievement; however, the board, lacking expertise and functioning to satisfy political interests, disagreed and reversed those decisions (Glass & Franceschini, 2007). Because superintendents are vulnerable to firing by the board, they often do not insist that boards choose educational over political efficacy (Glass, 2008; Metzger, 1997; Zirkel, 1997). In another study, Glass (2001) and Glass and Franceschini (2007) found that although boards approved superintendent recommendations 90 percent of the time, superintendents often reported gathering learning preferences of individual board members and modifying recommendations to less effective compromises in order to get approval (Lashway, 2002). Forty percent of the 2000 AASA Superintendent of the Year winners reported having decisions unadvisedly overturned by their boards (Chan, Pool, & Strickland, 2001).

In a recent study, Alsbury and Whitaker (2007) interviewed superintendent focus groups from several states as part of the Voices III national study (Acker-Hocevar & Ivory, 2006) and found that role incongruity was a key concern of superintendents. In one example, school board members, principals, and teachers seemed to gravitate toward "turf protection" of their own agenda, building, or classroom and failed to understand

and/or practice what was best for all students. One superintendent, representing many in the study, lamented:

> If I'm really honest, I don't see board members looking at the big picture and making a decision because it's the best thing to do for kids. I think that they get sidetracked by agendas, and by different community groups that get their attention. I also see the same thing with all the staff . . . principals get very building minded . . . and teachers are out to protect their classroom, so I think that sometimes they lose sight of why decisions are made for the good of the whole and for the good of all kids.

These superintendents also seemed to argue for more administrative decision-making power and less "democratic" voice from the community or board. Other superintendents in the study relayed that often they avoid communicating broadly with community constituents and some board members who, while representing a majority community opinion, do not speak for minority voices. One superintendent noted:

> I think what is best for students isn't always what other people think is best. I want to begin a K-12 foreign language program and I know I'm going to get a lot of grief because that foreign language is Spanish and some members of the community will ask, why are we doing that because the kids need to speak English.

These situations tend to prompt many superintendents to view broadening communications, distributing leadership, and sharing decision making as not only time-consuming but potentially harmful to educational and equitable advancement. These pressures cause superintendents to favor elite board roles that are more focused on broad policy making and functioning as a buffer between unprofessional community opinion and school operations.

In fact, because of the potential incongruity between the role communities want their board members to play and the role that is viewed as most politically effective and efficient, often superintendents and board members engage in closed-door, one-on-one negotiations and conflict resolution to be able to offer a unified façade in public board meetings. Board members, who already know the eventual outcome of a board vote, will still challenge ideas and engage in discussion in the public meeting so as not to be labeled a "rubber stamp" board by the voting public (Kowalski, 2008). Eadie (2003), in fact, encourages the use of this approach to maintain trust amongst the public and provide for a more stable political environment, which he believes promotes superintendent and board longevity and school effectiveness.

Power Struggles

Mountford and Brunner (2001) and Mountford (2008) found a lack of cohesion among school board and superintendents as a result of differing conceptions and uses of power. These researchers characterized the collaborative and appropriate use of *power with* versus the divisive use of *power over*, as a disruptor of positive and effective school board/superintendent relationships. Other researchers have similarly found the power struggles within the board and between the board and superintendent are common and counterproductive (Boyd, 1975; Kowalski, 1995, 2008).

In the past, it was believed most school board members ran for office because of a sense of civic duty. While Alsbury (2004, 2008b) found that this motivation is still predominate for board members in small and medium-sized rural districts, it may no longer be the case in urban districts where board members approach their role with political aspirations and single-agenda interests. Mountford (2008) noted that board members interested in exerting control, rather than seeking input and the common good, often created turbulent intra-board relationships.

McCarty and Ramsey (1971) developed a model with four types of community power structures that influenced the orientation and function of the local school boards: (a) dominated structures with a few individuals possessing most of the power resulting in dominated boards; (b) factional structures with power distributed among community factions and competing agendas resulting in board members representing major factions; (c) pluralistic structures where power was dispersed among coalitions that temporarily formed around specific issues resulting in issue-oriented boards; and (d) inert structures where community power is rarely exercised in relation to public schools resulting in boards that routinely approved administrative recommendations (Kowalski, 2006). In recent studies, Glass and Franceschini (2007) and Mountford and colleagues (2012) found that board members and superintendents reported findings consistent with those of McCarty and Ramsey. Specifically, they learned that the majority of schools operate in the dominated and factional power structure, while most superintendents identified their primary role as a professional advisor (47.7%) or a dominant decision maker (49.5%); these roles were considered incongruent for districts using those power structures.

Who Makes the Decisions?

Several research efforts surfacing in the 1960s and 1970s and continuing to the present have focused on the relationship between the superintendent and the school board and asked questions related to who controls whom. Several early studies (Kerr, 1964; Smith, 1974) confirmed that boards deferred to the judgments and values of the school professionals and, therefore, were controlled by them. Other researchers during this time (Cistone, 1977) challenged these results and provided evidence that board members, over the course of their tenure, reported a decreasing expectation in the administrative role related to the division of labor and responsibility between the board and the superintendent.

An even different twist on the control issue surfaced with the publication of the Zeigler and Jennings (1974) *Governing American Schools* study. Their inquiry into the interaction between the school board and the superintendent, as a measure of the democratic principles playing out in school governance, concluded that board opposition to the superintendent and board dependence on the superintendent for educational information varied significantly depending on the size of the school district. This study was later confirmed by Glass (2003) and Cox-Buteau (2005), who found differences in superintendent responsibility and expectation based on district size.

Specifically, superintendents in smaller districts were expected to be competent in personnel and fiscal matters while leaders in larger districts were favored for visionary skill. Interestingly, all superintendents were expected to be good communicators and to maintain positive school board/superintendent relations (Alsbury, 2008a; Glass & Franceschini, 2007; Hess & Meeks, 2010). These studies, with both conflicting and congruent observations, supported the generalization that much of the confusion about roles and responsibilities of governing boards grows out of a desire for two distinctively different categories of representative behavior: being a trustee of the public interest or a delegate of specific group or individual interests.

RETURNING TO OUR ROOTS?

In the ultimate historical school governance recycling, some urban cities, like Boston, Chicago, Cleveland, and New York, have reverted to organizational approaches of the 1850s, when almost every mayor had direct authority over education. Mayoral-appointed school boards in Boston began in 1991 and in New York in 2002. In both these cities, the school boards have been reduced to an advisory committee with no superintendent and who serves at the will of the mayor. In New York, the mayor can and, some believe, has removed school board members who did not agree with a policy on student promotion (Wirt & Kirst, 2006).

Wong and Shen (2003, 2008) indicate that mayoral and state takeover of school districts, and the accompanying dissolution or decline in the power of the school board and superintendent, increased dramatically during a three-year period between 1995 and 1997 and have continued to escalate during the 2000s. Prior to 1995, most takeovers were based on financial reasons; however, takeovers since have been predominately pursued because of real or perceived academic and management failure.

While mayoral takeovers did occur infrequently in the 1960s to 1980s, most mayors hesitated to seize any real operational control from elected board members and superintendents who remained in place. Currently, however, mayors are being reminded that their cities' economic growth and development are affected by schools, not to mention their reelection chances. A report by Edelstein (2006), funded through the affluent Bill & Melinda Gates Foundation and the U.S. Conference of Mayors, has recently developed an action guide for mayoral leadership and involvement in education. All mayors are now being encouraged to influence the school governance system in profound ways, gauging their intrusiveness on their city's unique needs, the level of community dissatisfaction in their school system, and potential political backlash.

Between 1988 and 2003, mayoral and state takeovers have occurred in no fewer than 40 cities (Wong & Shen, 2003), fueled by the perception of failing student achievement, political conflict, inexperienced teaching staff, low expectations for students, lack of a demanding curriculum, lack of instructional coherence, and poor management (Edelstein, 2006). In Edelstein's report, mayors are encouraged seriously to consider involvement in school system operations, teaching and learning, budget, and school governance, including school board and superintendent selection. Since 2003, mayoral takeovers have declined, and numerous cities have returned to elected school boards with fewer than 20 cities currently under mayoral control (Education Commission of the States, 2011).

While mayoral takeovers have generally led to efficiencies in budgeting, support programs, supplies, and facilities, through management integration, the promise of improved student achievement has not been realized. In a study of the 14 comprehensive state and mayoral takeovers since 1988, Wong and Shen (2003, 2008) found ambiguous achievement trends with each district exhibiting simultaneous improvement and decline after the takeover. Generally, however, they concluded that mayoral takeovers (a) improved student achievement in the elementary grades, (b) helped the lowest-achieving schools, and (c) lowered per pupil costs. These takeovers, strongly promoted by the business community, included the infusion of non-teacher administrators into management, and stressed the need to run schools more like a business. These student achievement gains, albeit mixed, will likely fuel more interest in alternative governance structures that do not include elected school boards and/or superintendents.

Opponents of mayoral control and appointed school boards assert that these actions result in a loss of democracy. When appointed, advisory school boards are not elected from a particular geographic region of a city and thus will not be able to represent a grassroots constituency as readily. In fact, one study indicated that board members elected from subdistricts changed their role and behavior and were more attentive to the needs of a particular section of the city (Danzberger, Kirst, & Usdan, 1992; Glass, 2008). Because cities tended to be geographically divided by ethnicity and socioeconomic differences, subregional and elected school board members produced a better overall representation of the city and the citizenry.

While the return to appointed school boards and mayoral takeovers in the 1990s appeared to be a new development, it is arguably little more than a return of the superintendent to the nonprofessional *teacher-scholar* role, the governing board to an elite group, and the predominance of the industrial business model of management popular in the 1920s and outlined earlier in this chapter. This latest trend is viewed by opponents as threatening further to turn schools into service agencies and not publicly responsive, publicly run organizations. Proponents argue that mayoral-run schools respond more favorably to public demands by eliminating external political pressure from minority groups that have hamstrung superintendents and boards from program implementation, and internal organizational structures and power brokering designed more to maintain the adults' comfort than to advance the students' achievement (Wirt & Kirst, 2006).

However, opponents argue that centralizing the governance of schooling is inequitable and undemocratic (Alsbury, 2009, 2011; Mountford & Alsbury, 2012). Lutz and Iannaccone noted that education being governed by locally elected school boards was not only unique to American democracy but also represented the "crucible of democracy." They also believe that local school elections in America provide the "closest example of democracy for the American people" (2008, p. 5). The scant opportunity for citizens to exercise local democratic control is diminished further with the movement to mayoral governance of local schools. Alsbury (personal communication, 2013), during a debate at the NSBA National Federal Relations Network conference, noted, "When local boards run schools, parents and community members can stroll down to their local school and have a voice in how their school is being run. Remove that access and we diminish the voices of citizens, especially the underrepresented."

Finally, early policy theorists suggested that attempts to try to change an organizational structure as basic as those found in school districts only leads to permutations of the original institution (DiMaggio, Paul, & Powell, 1983). They would predict that schools led by mayors will probably end up operating in much the same manner as schools run by school boards and superintendents. Mayoral and city government politics, power brokering, corruption, inefficiencies, and mismanagement are no less likely to occur than in district central offices and may be more likely. Aside from some improvements in management issues like providing integrated fiscal, transportation, food service, facility, and purchasing operations, mayoral takeovers have not yet resulted in promises of transforming teaching and instruction or improving student learning.

Indeed, much of what is written on school boards by mayoral takeover and charter school proponents suggests that most school board members serve mainly to advance single or hidden agendas. However, research findings consistently report only 5 percent of board members are motivated to school board service for political reasons (Alsbury, 2003; Hess & Meeks, 2010; Mountford, 2008) and corruption by school board members occurs with much less frequency than in higher political offices (Hess, 2008; Mountford, 2008). In fact, research shows that school board members are motivated for school board service to improve schools and learning and/or community involvement (Alsbury, 2008; Hess & Meeks, 2010; Mountford & Alsbury, 2012).

FUTURE RESEARCH DIRECTIONS

From a research perspective, the shift of attention from school to district- and state-level reform efforts (Fullan, 2006), the emergence of mayoral and state takeovers, and studies that demonstrate the effectiveness of school board–led district reform (Delagardelle, 2008; Joyce, Delagardelle, & Wolf, 2001) speak to a need for a shift in future research to the effectiveness of systemic reform efforts. Researchers need to explore new and more integrative governance approaches and their effects on instructional quality and student achievement gains. Research questions should also include whether the practice of particular superintendent and/or school board roles influences district performance. In addition, research methods need to include those that allow for the consideration of the unique contextual realities within small, medium, and large districts as well as those in rural and urban settings.

A renewed interest in research in the area of school boards, in general, is necessary. Currently, very few studies exist on school boards and school board members, and little attention is given to their role in influencing superintendents, school policy, instructional quality, and student achievement. Ultimately, researchers need to explore governance by including the perspective of student benefits rather than designs that only examine economic efficiencies, shifts of power among stakeholders, or political game playing. Only by adopting a more student-centered lens will researchers begin to shed light on the commonly held belief that superintendents and boards are isolated from and irrelevant to the real business of schooling.

CONCLUSIONS AND IMPLICATIONS

While superintendent and school board member roles have shifted over time, and environments have changed including shifting community demographics, centrist accountability directives, and community values pluralism, roles have been enacted with little change. This stagnation can best be understood by a review of the historical, political, and social forces influencing board and superintendent roles and realizing that conflicting accountability systems have always been part of the landscape for these school leaders.

Iterative Role Cycles

One example of a return to a previous role involves the *teacher-scholar* role of the 1890s. Today, a demand for this role has returned in a slightly modified format where school leaders are being called on to focus on instructional quality and the production of educational outcomes. As in this return to a focus on instruction, some believe that superintendent roles have shifted in iterative cycles, rather than an evolutionary one (Kowalski, 2008; Petersen, 1999; Petersen & Fusarelli, 2008; Sumbramani & Henderson, 1996). The main differences in role enactment over time may be found less in the role demands than in the external context wherein they exist.

Role Shift Ambiguity

Bredeson and Kose (2005) argued that an intensified work load for superintendent and board members including high public visibility, unpredictable school finances, greater demands through judicial rulings, and state/federal legislative mandates for increased student achievement outcomes has resulted in role overload. In addition, external pressure comes from an accountability shift from the local to the state level (Timar, 2003).

However, while some researchers see this as a call for a clear change in how superintendents lead schools (Glass, 2008; Wong & Shen, 2008), others point to tensions between various accountability systems and stakeholders within those systems that cause role shift ambiguity. Goldring, Crowson, and Berk (2003) discuss six types of accountability systems: bureaucratic, legal, professional, political, moral, and market. For when superintendents and board members are looking for a clear role to play, they often find conflicting messages from these various accountability systems. For example, the professional system may call for superintendents to be collaborators, while the bureaucratic system calls for them to make quick and efficient decisions that favor internal stakeholders. Likewise, legal accountability demands from federal legislation (like No Child Left Behind) may call for test score increases while moral demands may call for flexibility for special education students.

Similarly, market accountability from parents may press schools to ensure lower academic pressures and to increase affective, holistic experiences in the fine arts and athletics, while state accountability systems often demand test improvement and the decline of these "extracurricular" programs. This likely explains why superintendents and school board members are reporting putting instructional improvement and shared decision making as a top priority but in actual practice are spending about the same amount of time on these matters as before federal and state accountability legislation was passed (Glass & Franceschini, 2007; Hess & Meeks, 2010; Mountford et al., 2012).

Political Strategist Role

This might best be understood by Björk and Gurley's (2005) description of the superintendent as political strategist. They have pointed to Cuban's belief that superintendent and board roles have "waxed and waned as time passed, yet none disappeared. They competed; they were durable" (1976, p. 21). Cuban believed that multiple roles existed simultaneously and that superintendents would utilize each role or roles as the specific context dictated. Because school board and superintendent roles are extrinsically linked, I would argue that board members behaved similarly both in the past and today. This result is especially evident as we compare the superintendent and board role enactments in current urban versus small school districts as described earlier. Even today no single role is played by the board and superintendent. Björk and Gurley (2005) also point out the problem of macropolitics versus micropolitics, variable interest group typology and activity between communities, and over time to suggest that superintendents and boards have really always functioned as political strategists. Recognizing the changing national and local contexts of schools calls on superintendents and school boards to have the political acuity to recognize and understand these changes and the skill to work within an environment that is unique for its rapid change.

Communicator

Practicing superintendents and board members must be proficient in working collaboratively and strategically with internal and external groups, using a social systems perspective (Chance & Björk, 2004; Kowalski, 2008). Schlechty (1997) asserted that systemic thinking requires us to accept that we work in irrational and chaotic organizations, led most readily by understanding how and why people behave the way they do, determining what they need to learn and how. Once this is determined, the primary tool and influencer both inside and outside the organization—among and between students, teachers, administrators, board members, and the community—is communication.

Kowalski (2005) asserts that the current school reform movement demonstrates that relationship-enhancing communication rather than top-down dicta is necessary for advancing educational agendas. Others agree that effective communication influences culture and productivity (Morgan & Petersen, 2002; Petersen & Short, 2002); and while the influence of communication of superintendents and school board members has not been studied adequately (Kowalski & Keedy, 2003; Mountford, 2008), the importance of focusing on the role of *communicator* seems important and necessary (Kowalski & Keedy, 2003; Mountford, 2008; Stringfield, 2008).

Moving from Roles to Role

The implications for practicing superintendents and school board members in terms of separate and clear role clarification remain elusive. Rapidly changing demographics, political and social pluralism, contextual effects on micropolitics, and community needs dictate either a more amorphous shifting role or perhaps moving from the idea of two separate and complementary roles to a single shared role. This idea is described by Kowalski (2006), who suggests that board members must focus on transforming schools, based on community interest, but filtered through student need and professional, educational expertise. Likewise, superintendents must understand that educational reform, to be successful, must be applied through a political context.

A recent study (Delagardelle, 2008), the Iowa Lighthouse Project, found that more effective schools with higher student achievement could be developed through a leadership partnership between the board and the superintendent. In these districts, unique team approaches were employed including role negotiation, shared training, shared goals development, joint accountability measures, policy development, and alignment of superintendent hiring focus, job expectations, and evaluation criteria. This activity led superintendent/school board teams to focus on and enact instructional improvement within these districts, solidifying some traditional roles, exchanging others, modifying and negotiating roles in unique ways while maintaining professional protections for superintendents.

As with other areas, the answer in the search for standardized roles for school board members and superintendents may be most readily found within the political and social context of each individual school district. The importance of context to the role of the superintendent and school board member becomes pronounced when comparing small rural town superintendent and school board members to those in the large urban city. From the threat of mayoral takeovers and political stair stepping in the city, to driving the bus and having a town hall meeting at the grocery store in the small town, school governance embodies a wide and varying contextual tapestry that will continue to challenge and alter a static and homogenous description of the changing roles of superintendents and school board members.

REFERENCES

Acker-Hocevar, M., & Ivory, G. (2006). *Update on Voices III: Focus groups under way and plans and thoughts about the future. UCEA Review, 48*(1), 22–24.

Allison, D. J., Allison, P. A., & McHenry, H. A. (1995). Chiefs and chairs: Effective working relationships between effective CEOs and boards of education chairpersons. In K. Leithwood (Ed.), *Effective school district leadership: Transforming politics into education* (pp. 33–50). New York: State University of New York Press.

Alsbury, T. L. (2003). Superintendent and school board member turnover: Political versus apolitical turnover as a critical variable in the application of the Dissatisfaction Theory. *Educational Administration Quarterly, 39*(5), 667–698.

Alsbury, T. L. (2004). Does school board turnover matter? Revisiting critical variables in the dissatisfaction theory of American democracy. *International Journal of Leadership in Education, 7*(4), 357–377.

Alsbury, T. L. (2007). Needing to be reelected. In G. Ivory & M. Acker-Hocevar (Eds.), *Successful school board leadership: Lessons from superintendents* (pp. 164–184). Lanham, MD: Rowman & Littlefield.

Alsbury, T. L. (2008a). School board politics and student achievement. In T. L. Alsbury (Ed.), *The future of school boards governance: Relevancy and revelation* (pp. 247–272). Lanham, MD: Rowman & Littlefield.

Alsbury, T. L. (2008b). School board member and superintendent turnover and the influence on student achievement: An application of the dissatisfaction theory. *Leadership & Policy in Schools, 7*(2), 202–229.

Alsbury, T. L. (2008c). The crucible of reform: The search for systemic leadership. In B. Depres (Ed.), *System thinkers in action: A field guide for effective change leadership in education* (pp. 77–108). Lanham, MD: Rowman & Littlefield.

Alsbury, T. L. (2009, June 25). Mayoral takeover cools the crucible of democracy. *Teacher College Record, Invited Commentary.*

Alsbury, T. L. (2011). Should the K-12 organizational structure of schools in the U.S. be changed dramatically? In C. Russo (Ed.), *Debating issues in American education.* Thousand Oaks, CA: Sage.

Alsbury, T. L., & Whitaker, K. S. (2007). Voices of superintendents: Accountability, students, and democratic voice. *Journal of Educational Administration, 45*(2), 157–174.

Alsbury, T. L., & Whitaker, K. S. (2012). *Pressure of outside forces, stress, and finding balance.* In W. Place, M. A. Acker-Hocevar, J. Ballenger, A. W. Place, & G. Ivory (Eds.), *Snapshots of school leadership in the 21st century: Perils and promises of leading for social justice, school improvement, and democratic community* (UCEA Leadership Series) [Chapter 9]. Charlotte, NC: Information Age.

Alvey, D. T., & Underwood, K. E. (1985). When boards and superintendents clash, it's over the balance of school power. *American School Board Journal, 172*(10), 21.

Bailey, F. G. (1965). Decisions by consensus in councils and committees. In M. Banton (Ed.), Political systems and the distribution of power. London: Taveslock.

Blumberg, A., & Blumberg, P. (1985). *The school superintendent: Living with conflict.* New York, NY: Teachers College.

Björk, L. (2008). Leading in an era of change: The micropolitics of superintendent-board relations. In T. L. Alsbury (Ed.), *The future of school boards governance: Relevancy and revelation* (pp. 61–80). Lanham, MD: Rowman & Littlefield.

Björk, L., & Gurley, K. (2003). Superintendents as transformative leaders: Schools as learning communities and communities of learners. *Journal of Thought, 38*(4), 37–78.

Björk, L., & Gurley, K. (2005). Superintendent as educational statesman. In L. Björk & T. Kowalski (Eds.), *The contemporary superintendent: Preparation, practice and development* (pp. 163–186). Thousand Oaks, CA: Corwin Press.

Björk, L., & Keedy, J. (2001). Politics and the superintendency in the USA: Restructuring in-service education. *Journal of In-Service Education, 27*(2) 275–302.

Björk, L., & Lindle, J. C. (2001). Superintendents and interest groups. *Educational Policy, 15*(1) 76–91.

Boyd, W. L. (1975). School board-administrative staff relationships. In P. Cistone (Ed.), *Understanding school boards: Problems and prospects. A National School Board Association Study.* Toronto and London: Lexington Books.

Bredeson, P. V. (1996). Superintendents' role in curriculum development and instructional leadership: Instructional visionaries, collaborators, supporters, and delegators. *Journal of School Leadership, 6*(3), 2243–2264.

Bredeson, P. V., & Kose, B. (2005, April). *School superintendents as instructional leaders: Responses to a decade of education reform 1994–2003.* Paper presented at the Annual American Educational Research Association Conference, Montreal, Canada.

Broad Foundation & Thomas B. Fordham Institute. (2003). *Better leaders for America's schools: A manifesto.* Los Angeles: Authors.

Burroughs, W. A. (1974). *Cities and schools in the gilded age.* Port Washington, NY: Kennikat.

Callahan, R. E. (1962). *Education and the cult of efficiency: A study of the social forces that have shaped the administration of public schools.* Chicago: University of Chicago Press.

Callahan, R. E. (1964). *The superintendent of schools: An historical analysis. Final report of project S-212.* Washington, DC: U.S. Office of Education, Department of Health, Education, and Welfare.

Campbell, D. W., & Greene, D. (1994). Defining the leadership role of school boards in the 21st century. *Phi Delta Kappan, 75*(5), 391.

Carter, G. R., & Cunningham, W. G. (1997). *The American school superintendent.* San Francisco, CA: Jossey-Bass.

Carver, J., & Carver, M. (1997). *Reinventing your board.* San Francisco, CA: Jossey-Bass.

Cassel, R. N. (1999). The American academy of school psychology offers promise for school problems and a nation at risk. *Education, 119*(4), 584–587.

Chan, T. C., Pool, H., & Strickland, J. S. (2001, November). *Who's in charge around here?* Paper presented at the annual meeting of the Southern Regional Council on Educational Administration, Jacksonville, FL.

Chance, P. L., & Björk, L. (2004). The social dimension of public relations. In T. J. Kowalski (Ed.), *Public relations in schools* (3rd ed., pp. 125–150). Upper Saddle River, NJ: Merrill, Prentice Hall.

Chance, E., & Capps, J. L. (1990, October). *Administrator stability in rural schools: The school board factor.* Paper Presented at the Annual Conference of the National Rural Education Association, Colorado Springs, CO.

Cibulka, J. G. (1999). Ideological lenses for interpreting political and economic changes affecting schooling. In J. Murphy & K. S. Lewis (Eds.), *The handbook of research on educational administration: A project of the American Educational Research Association* (2nd ed., pp. 163–182). San Francisco: Jossey-Bass.

Cistone, P. J. (1977). The socialization of school board members. *Educational Administration Quarterly, 13*(2), 19–33.

Cistone, P. J. (2008). School board research: A retrospective. In T. L. Alsbury (Ed.), *The future of school boards governance: Relevancy and revelation* (pp. 25–36). Lanham, MD: Rowman & Littlefield.

Counts, G. S. (1927). *The social composition of boards of education.* Chicago: University of Chicago Press.

Cox-Buteau, B. S. (2005). *School governance in New Hampshire: Revisiting a study of school board-superintendent relations in small rural school districts* (Doctoral dissertation, University of New Hampshire, 2005) (UMI No. 3169080).

Cuban, L. (1976). *Urban school chiefs under fire.* Chicago: University of Chicago Press.

Cubberley, E. P. (1924). *Public school administration.* Boston, MA: Houghton Mifflin.

Culbertson, J. A. (1981). Antecedents of the theory movement. *Educational Administration Quarterly, 17*(1), 25_/47.

Danzberger, J. P., Kirst, M. W., & Usdan, M. D. (1992). *Governing public schools: New times new requirements.* Washington, DC: The Institute for Educational Leadership.

Danzberger, J. P., & Usdan, M. D. (1994). Local education governance: Perspectives on the problems and strategies for change. *Phi Delta Kappan, 75*(5), 366.

Delagardelle, M. L. (2008). The Lighthouse inquiry: Examining the role of school board leadership in the improvement of student achievement. In T. L. Alsbury (Ed.) The future of school board governance: Relevancy and revelation [pp. 191-224]. Lanham, MD: Rowman & Littlefield.

Dexter, R., & Ruff, W. (2008). Challenge: Fostering student achievement. In G. Ivory & M. Acker-Hocevar (Eds.), *Successful school board leadership: Lessons from superintendents* (pp. 52–66). Lanham, MD: Rowman & Littlefield.

DiMaggio, P. J., & Powell, W. W. (1983). The iron cage revisited: Institutional isomorphism and collective rationality in organizational fields. *American Sociological Review, 48*(2), 147-60.

Drucker, P. F. (1999). *Management challenges for the 21st century.* New York: HarperCollins.

Duncan, C. P. (1992). Parental support in schools and changing family structure. *NASSP Bulletin, 76*(543), 10–14.

Eadie, D. (2003). *Eight keys to an extraordinary board-superintendent partnership.* Lanham, MD: Scarecrow Education.

Eaton, W. E., & Sharp, W. L. (1996). Involuntary turnover among small-town superintendents. *Peabody Journal of Education, 71*(2), 78–85.

Edelstein, F. (2006). *Mayoral leadership and involvement: An action guide for success.* Washington, DC: U.S. Conference of Mayors.

Education Commission of the States. (2011). ECS state notes: Local school boards. Retrieved February 9, 2013 from http://mb2.ecs.org/reports/Report.aspx?id=170.

Elmore, R. F. (2000). *Building a new structure for school leadership.* Washington, DC: The Albert Shanker Institute.

Fullan, M. G. (1996). Turning systemic thinking on its head. *Phi Delta Kappan, 77*(6), 420–423.

Fullan, M. G. (2006). *Turnaround leadership.* San Francisco, CA: Jossey-Bass.

Fusarelli, B. C., & Fusarelli, L. D. (2005). Reconceptualizing the superintendency: Superintendents as applied social scientists and social activists. In L. G. Björk & T. J. Kowalski (Eds.), *The contemporary superintendent: Preparation, practice, and development* (pp. 187–206). Thousand Oaks, CA: Corwin Press.

Gerstl-Pepin, C. I. (2007). Challenge: Mandates and micropolitics. In G. Ivory & M. Acker-Hocevar (Eds.), *Successful school board leadership: Lessons from superintendents* (pp. 135–148). Lanham, MD: Rowman & Littlefield.

Getzels, J. W. (1977). Educational administration twenty years later, 1954–1974. In L. Cunningham, W. Hack, & R. Nystrand (Eds.), *Educational administration: The developing decades* (pp. 3–24). Berkeley, CA: McCutchan.

Glass, T. E. (1992). *The 1992 study of American school superintendency.* Arlington, VA: American Association of School Administrators.

Glass, T. E. (1993). Point and counterpoint: What is the context of what might be? In D. Carter, T. Glass, & S. Hord (Eds.), *Selecting, preparing and developing the school district superintendent.* London: Falmer Press.

Glass, T. E. (2001). *Superintendent leaders look at the superintendency, school boards and reform* (Commissioned Issue Paper). Denver, CO: Education Commission of the States.

Glass, T. E. (2003). *The superintendency: A managerial imperative?* Paper presented at the annual meeting of the American Educational Research Association, Chicago.

Glass, T. E. (2004). Changes in society and schools. In T. J. Kowalski (Ed.), *Public relations in schools* (3rd ed., pp. 30–46). Upper Saddle River, NJ: Merrill, Prentice-Hall.

Glass, T. E. (2008). Elected versus appointed boards. In T. L. Alsbury (Ed.), *The future of school boards governance: Relevancy and revelation* (pp. 295–318). Lanham, MD: Rowman & Littlefield.

Glass, T. E., & Franceschini, L. A. (2007). *The 2006 study of the state of the American school superintendency: A mid-decade study.* Lanham, MD: Rowman & Littlefield.

Glickman, C. D. (1993). *Renewing America's schools: A guide for school-based action.* San Francisco, CA: Jossey-Bass.

Goldring, E., Crowson, R., Laird, D., & Berk, R. (2003). Transition leadership in a shifting policy environment. *Educational Evaluation and Policy Analysis, 25*(4), 473–488.

Goodman, R. H., Fulbright, L., & Zimmerman, W. Jr. (1997). *Getting there from here: School board-superintendent collaboration: Creating a school governance team capable of raising student achievement.* Arlington, VA: New England School Development Council.

Grady, M. L., & Bryant, M. T. (1991). School board turmoil and superintendent turnover: What pushes them to the brink? *School Administrator, 48*(2), 19.

Greene, K. R. (1992). Models of school board policy-making. *Educational Administration Quarterly, 28*(2), 220–236.

Gresson, A. D. (1976). *External-internal mandates and elite-arena behavior of local school boards.* Doctoral dissertation, Pennsylvania State University.

Griffiths, D. E. (1966). *The school superintendent.* New York: The Discourse for Applied Research in Education.

Grissmer, D., Flanagan, A., Kawata, J., & Williamson, S. (2000). *Improving student achievement: What state NAEP test scores tell us.* Arlington, VA: RAND Corporation.

Hanson, E. M. (2003). *Educational administration and organizational behavior* (5th ed.). Boston, MA: Allyn & Bacon.

Hess, F. M. (2002). *School boards at the dawn of the 21st century: Conditions and challenges of district governance.* Alexandria, VA: National School Boards Association.

Hess, F. M. (2008). Money, interest groups, and school board elections. In T. L. Alsbury (Ed.), *The future of school boards governance: Relevancy and revelation* (pp. 137–154). Lanham, MD: Rowman & Littlefield.

Hess, F. M., & Meeks, O. (2010). School boards circa 2010: Governance in the accountability era. Report by the National School Boards Foundation, the Thomas B. Fordham Institute, and the Iowa School Boards Foundation.

Hewlett, S. A. (1991). *When the bough breaks: The cost of neglecting our children.* New York: Basic Books.

Howlett, P. (1993). The politics of school leaders, past and future. *Education Digest, 58*(9), 18–21.

Hoy, W. K., & Miskel, C. G. (2005). *Educational administration: Theory, research, and practice* (8th ed.). New York: McGraw-Hill.

Jenks, C., & Phillips, M. (1998). Black-white test score gap: Introduction. In C. Jenks & M. Phillips (Eds.), *The black-white test score gap* (pp. 1–54). Washington DC: Brookings Institution Press.

Johnson, B. C., & Fusarelli, L. D. (2003, April). *Superintendent as social scientist.* Paper presented at the annual meeting of the American Educational Research Association, Chicago, IL.

Joyce, B., Delagardelle, M. L., & Wolf, J. (2001, April). *The lighthouse inquiry: School board/superintendent team behaviors in school districts with extreme differences in student achievement.* Paper presented at the annual meeting of the American Educational Research Association, Seattle, WA.

Keedy, J., & Björk, L. (2003). Who will lead? Examining the superintendent shortage. *Journal of School Leadership, 13*(3), 256–263.

Kellogg Foundation. (1961). *Toward improved school administration: A decade of professional effort to heighten administrative understanding and skills.* Battle Creek, MI: Kellogg Foundation.

Kerr, N. D. (1964). The school board as an agency of legitimation. *Sociology of Education, 38*(1), 34–59.

Kirst, M. W. (2008). The evolving role of school boards: Retrospect and prospect. In T. L. Alsbury (Ed.), *The future of school boards governance: Relevancy and revelation* (pp. 37–60). Lanham, MD: Rowman & Littlefield.

Knezevich, S. (1984). *Administration of public education: A sourcebook for the leadership and management of educational institutions* (4th ed.). New York: Harper and Row.

Kowalski, T. J. (1995). *Keepers of the flame: Contemporary urban superintendents.* Thousand Oaks, CA: Corwin.

Kowalski, T. J. (1997). School reform, community education, and the problem of institutional culture. *Community Education Journal, 25*(3-4), 5-8.

Kowalski, T. J. (1999). *The school superintendent: Theory, practice, and cases.* Upper Saddle River, NJ: Merrill, Prentice Hall.

Kowalski, T. J. (2001). The future of local school governance: Implications for board members and superintendents. In C. Brunner & L. Björk (Eds.), *The new superintendency* (pp. 183–201). Oxford, UK: JAI, Elsevier Science.

Kowalski, T. J. (2003). *Contemporary school administration: An introduction* (2nd ed.). Boston, MA: Allyn & Bacon.

Kowalski, T. J. (2004). School public relations: A new agenda. In T. J. Kowalski (Ed.), *Public relations in schools* (3rd ed., pp. 3–29). Upper Saddle River, NJ: Merrill, Prentice Hall.

Kowalski, T. (2005). Evolution of the school district superintendent position. In L. Björk & T. J. Kowalski (Eds.), *School district superintendents: Role expectations, professional preparation, development and licensing.* Thousand Oaks, CA: Corwin Press.

Kowalski, T. J. (2006). *The school superintendent: Theory, practice, and cases* (2nd ed.). Thousand Oaks, CA: Sage.

Kowalski, T. J. (2008). School reform, civic engagement, and school board leadership. In T. L. Alsbury (Ed.), *The future of school boards governance: Relevancy and revelation* (pp. 225–246). Lanham, MD: Rowman & Littlefield.

Kowalski, T. J., & Brunner, C. C. (2005). The school district superintendent. In F. English (Ed.), *The handbook of educational leadership* (pp. 147–167). Thousand Oaks, CA: Corwin Press.

Kowalski, T. J., & Keedy, J. (2003, November). *Superintendent as communicator: Implications for professional preparation and licensing.* Paper presented at the annual conference of the University Council for Educational Administration, Portland, OR.

Kowalski, T., & Reitzug, R. (1993). *Contemporary school administration: An introduction.* New York: Longman.

Kruse, S., & Louis, K. S. (1995, Spring). Teacher teams: Opportunities and dilemmas. *Brief to Principals,* 11.

LaMonte, H., Delagardelle, M. L., & VanderZyl, T. (2005). *The lighthouse project: Past, present, and future.* Iowa School Boards Foundation, Des Moines.

Land, D. (2002). *Local school boards under review: An examination of the literature on their role and effectiveness in relation to students' achievement.* Washington, DC: Johns Hopkins University.

Lashway, L. (2002). *Developing instructional leaders.* Eugene, OR: ERIC Clearinghouse on Educational Management. (ERIC Document Reproduction Service No. ED 466023).

Leithwood, K., Fullan, M., & Watson, N. (2003). What should be the boundaries of the schools we need? *Education Canada, 43*(1), 12–15.

Lutz, F. W. (1977, April). *Elite-arena council behavior and school boards.* Paper presented at the annual American Educational Research Association Conference, New York City.

Lutz, F. W. (1980). Local school board decision-making: A political-anthropological analysis. *Education and Urban Society, 12*(4), 452.

Lutz, F. W. (1996). Viability of the vulnerability thesis. *Peabody Journal of Education, 71*(2), 96–109.

Lutz, F. W., & Gresson, A. (1980). Local school boards as political councils. *Educational Studies, 11*(2), 125.

Lutz, F., & Iannaccone, L. (1978). *Public participation in local school districts: The dissatisfaction theory of American democracy.* Lexington, MA: Lexington Books.

Lutz, F., & Iannaccone, L. (2008). The dissatisfaction theory of American democracy. In T. L. Alsbury (Ed.), *The future of school boards governance: Relevancy and revelation* (pp. 3–24). Lanham, MD: Rowman & Littlefield.

McCarty, D. J., & Ramsey, C. E. (1971). *The school managers: Power and conflict in American public education.* Westport, CT: Greenwood.

McCaw, D., & Watkins, S. (2007). *Accountability for results: The realities of data-driven decision making.* Lanham, MD: Rowman & Littlefield.

Melby, E. O. (1955). *Administering community education.* Englewood Cliffs, NJ: Prentice Hall.

Metzger, C. (1997). Involuntary turnover of superintendents. *Thrust for Educational Leadership, 26,* 20–22.

Moe, T. M. (2001). A union by any other name. *Education Next, 1*(3), 40–45.

Morgan, C. L., & Petersen, G. J. (2002). The role of the district superintendent in leading academically successful school districts. In B. S. Cooper & L. D. Fusarelli (Eds.), *The promises and perils facing today's school superintendent* (pp. 175–196). Lanham, MD: Scarecrow Education.

Mountford, M. (2008). Historical and current tensions among board-superintendent teams: Symptoms or causes? In T. L. Alsbury (Ed.), *The future of school boards governance: Relevancy and revelation* (pp. 81–114). Lanham, MD: Rowman & Littlefield.

Mountford, M. E., & Alsbury, T. L. (2012). School boards: Nobody does it better. *UCEA Review, 52*(3), 11–13.

Mountford, M., Alsbury, T. L., Johannson, O., Risku, M., Paulsen, J., Townsend, T. (2012, October). *The future of school board governance: Improving educational governance structures through an international comparative study.* Paper presented at the annual convention of the University Council for Educational Administration, Denver, CO.

Mountford, M., & Brunner, C. C. (2001, November). *Superintendents and school board members: Conceptions of power and decision-making.* Paper presented at the annual meeting of the University Council for Educational Administration, Cincinnati, OH.

Murphy, J. (1991). *Restructuring schools.* New York: Teachers College Press.

Murphy, J. (2002). Reculturing the profession of educational leadership: New blueprints. In J. Murphy (Ed.), *The educational leadership challenge: Redefining leadership for the 21st century* (pp. 65–82). Chicago: University of Chicago Press.

Natkin, G. L., Cooper, B., Fusarelli, L., Alborano, J., Padilla, A., & Ghosh, S. (2002). Myth of the revolving door superintendency. *School Administrator, 59*(5), 28–31.

Negroni, P. (2000). A radical role for superintendents. *School Administrator, 57*(8), 16–19.

Norton, M. S., Webb, L. D., Dlugosh, L. L., & Sybouts, W. (1996). *The school superintendency: New responsibilities, new leadership.* Boston, MA: Allyn & Bacon.

Park, V., & Datnow, A. (2009). Co-constructing distributive leadership: District and school connections in data-driven decision-making. *School Leadership & Management, 29*(5), 477–494.

Petersen, G. J. (2002). Singing the same tune: Principals' and school board members' perceptions of the superintendent's role in curricular and instructional leadership. *Journal of Educational Administration, 40*(2), 158–171.

Petersen, G. J., & Barnett, B. G. (2003, April). *The superintendent as instructional leader: History, evolution, and future of the role.* Paper presented at the annual meeting of the American Educational Research Association, Chicago, IL.

Petersen, G. J., & Fusarelli, L. D. (2008). Systemic leadership amidst turbulence: Superintendent-school board relations under pressure. In T. L. Alsbury (Ed.), *The future of school boards governance: Relevancy and revelation* (pp. 115–136). Lanham, MD: Rowman & Littlefield.

Petersen, G. J., & Short, P. M. (2002). An examination of school board presidents' perceptions of their superintendent's interpersonal communication competence and board decision making. *Journal of School Leadership, 12*(4), 411–436.

Peterson, M. R. (1999). *Superintendent competencies for continued employment as perceived by Louisiana public school superintendents and board presidents.* Unpublished doctoral dissertation. University of Southern Mississippi, Hattiesburg.

Pride, R. A. (2002). How critical events rather than performance trends shape public evaluations of the schools. *The Urban Review, 34*(2), 159–178.

Quinn, R., & Dawson, L. J. (2011). Good governance is a choice: A way to re-create your board the right way. Lanham, MD: Rowman & Littlefield.

Ramirez, A., & Guzman, N. (1999, October). *The rural school district superintendency: A Colorado perspective.* Paper presented at the annual conference of the National Rural Education Association, Colorado Springs, CO.

Resnick, M. S. (1999). *Effective school governance: A look at today's practice and tomorrow's promise.* Denver, CO: Education Commission of the States.

Ruff, W., & Dexter, R. (2008). Success strategy: Base decisions on data. In G. Ivory & M. Acker-Hocevar (Eds.), *Successful school board leadership: Lessons from superintendents* (pp. 67–82). Lanham, MD: Rowman & Littlefield.

Saatcioglu, A., Moore, S., Sargut, G., & Bajaj, A. (2011). The role of school board social capital in district governance: Effects on financial and academic outcomes. *Leadership and Policy in Schools, 10*(1), 1–42.

Sarason, S. B. (1997). *How schools might be governed and why.* New York: Teachers College Press.

Schlechty, P. C. (1992). Deciding the fate of local control. *American School Board Journal, 178*(11), 27–29.

Schlechty, P. C. (1997). *Inventing better schools.* San Francisco. CA: Jossey-Bass.

Schwartz, W. (1996). *An overview of strategies to reduce school violence.* East Lansing, MI: National Center for Research on Teacher Learning. (ERIC Document Reproduction Service No. ED410321).

Simon, T. R. (Ed.). (1986). *Fundamentals of school board membership.* Trenton: New Jersey School Boards Association.

Smith, M. P. (1974). Elite theory and policy analysis: The politics of education in suburbia. *Journal of Politics, 36,* 1006–1032.

Smoley, E. R. (1999). *Effective school boards: Strategies for improving board performance.* San Francisco, CA: Jossey-Bass.

Spring, J. H. (1994). *The American school, 1642–1993* (3rd ed.). New York: McGraw-Hill.

Stringfield, S. (2008). School boards and raising student outcomes: Reflections (confessions?) of a former urban school board member. In T. L. Alsbury (Ed.), *The future of school boards governance: Relevancy and revelation* (pp. 273–294). Lanham, MD: Rowman & Littlefield.

Subramani, M. R., & Henderson, J. C. (1996). *Gaps that matter: The influence of perspectives on IS service quality.* Retrieved at http://hsb.baylor.edu/ramsower/ais.ac.96/papers/GAPFINN2.htm.

Thomas, W. B., & Moran, K. J. (1992). Reconsidering the power of the superintendent in the Progressive Period. *American School Board Journal, 29*(1), 22–50.

Timar, T. B. (2003). The "new accountability" and school governance in California. *Peabody Journal of Education, 78*(4), 177–200.

Townsend, R. S., Johnston, G. L., Gross, G. E., Lynch, P., Garcy, L., Roberts, B., & Novotney, P. B. (2007). *Effective school board practices: Strategies for developing and maintaining good relationships with your board.* Thousand Oaks, CA: Corwin Press.

Tucker, H. J., & Zeigler, L. H. (1980). *Professionals and the public: Attitudes, communication, and response in school districts.* New York, NY: Longman.

Tyack, D. (1972). The One Best System: An historical analysis. In H. Walberg & A. Kopan (Eds.), *Rethinking urban education* (pp. 231–246). San Francisco, CA: Jossey-Bass.

Tyack, D., & Hansot, E. (1982). Hard times, hard choices: The case for coherence in public school leadership. *Phi Delta Kappan, 63*(8), 511–515.

U.S. Department of Education National Center for Education Statistics. (2003). *Digest of Education Statistics.* Washington, DC: NCES.

VanTil, W. (1971). Prologue: Is progressive education obsolete? In W. VanTil (Ed.), *Curriculum: Quest for relevance* (pp. 9–17). Boston, MA: Houghton-Mifflin.

Walser, N. (2009). *The essential school board book: Better governance in the age of accountability.* Cambridge, MA: Harvard Education Press.

Wirt, F. M., & Kirst, M. W. (2001). *The political dynamics of American education* (2nd ed.). Richmond, CA: McCutchan.

Wirt, F. M., & Kirst, M. W. (2005). *The political dynamics of American education* (3rd ed.). Richmond, CA: McCutchan.

Wisener, B. F. (1996). Influence of Callahan's Vulnerability Thesis on thought and practice in educational administration, 1962–1992. *Peabody Journal of Education, 71*(2), 41–63.

Wong, K. K., & Shen, F. X. (2003). Measuring the effectiveness of city and state takeover as a school reform strategy. *Peabody Journal of Education, 78*(4), 89–119.

Wong, K. K., & Shen, F. X. (2008). Education mayors and big-city school boards: New directions, new evidence. In T. L. Alsbury (Ed.), *The future of school boards governance: Relevancy and revelation* (pp. 319–356). Lanham, MD: Rowman & Littlefield.

Zeigler, L. H., Jennings, M. K., & Peak, G. W. (1974). *Governing American schools: Political interaction in local school districts.* North Scituate, MA: Duxbury Press.

Zirkel, P. A. (1997). Who's the boss? *Phi Delta Kappan, 79,* 165–166.

3

ADVOCATES AND PARTNERS FOR EDUCATION EXCELLENCE

A 21st-Century Role for Mayors
Frederick S. Edelstein

INTRODUCTION

In the five years since "The Evolving Political Role of Urban Mayors in Education" chapter was published in the *Handbook of Education Politics and Policy,* mayors are seeing their role in education from a slightly different perspective. Their understanding of the importance of education to their community and its economy has matured, and most have adjusted their approach to be participants, advocates, and partners in the education reform process. Mayors are no longer outsiders looking in, but are insiders engaged and often using their bully pulpits as advocates for change. It should also be stated that other locally elected leaders such as county executives have also taken an interest in a role in education.

The public discussion is less about "takeover or control," although there is still interest among some mayors. Now, the conversation is more about how mayors can be advocates for improving education in their city, town, or community and take an active role in the change process. The importance of mayoral leadership and involvement rose to a new level when Secretary of Education Arne Duncan, speaking before a gathering of mayors and superintendents in March 2009, urged the mayors to assume greater responsibility for improving public education. Secretary Duncan took the position that mayors can provide steady and strong leadership to raise performance in schools.

These remarks are another indication of the growing interest in mayoral accountability in a climate of declining public confidence in America's education system (Wong & Farris, 2011, p. 215). Duncan has participated in four consecutive winter meetings of the U.S. Conference of Mayors at which he discussed education issues and indicated his willingness to have one-on-one conversations with attending mayors.

Mayors are now more focused on what they can do within their communities as a partner, and connect the variety of services and issues including education, health care, social services, workforce development, environment, juvenile justice, and the city's economy. Thus, the coordination and possibly control of these functions becomes the role of the local general purpose government (a city or county) (Henig, 2013).

The range of roles of what mayors can do and how they are engaged has not changed significantly. What has evolved is their effort to improve communication and messaging, explain and show by example how they will be engaged, and connect issues and services. During the past five years Sacramento Mayor Kevin Johnson, the current president of the U.S. Conference of Mayors, has made education a priority both during his presidency and prior to that by leading an effort to increase mayoral involvement in education. Since being elected mayor and becoming active in the conference he has made an ongoing effort to explain to mayors the variety of roles that they can have in education at all levels, especially at the local level. Much of his campaign is based on the strategies and examples included in the U.S. Conference of Mayors' action guide entitled "Mayoral Leadership and Involvement in Education" (U.S. Conference of Mayors, 2006), which was developed and written by Frederick (Fritz) Edelstein during his tenure at the conference. The action guide's mayoral examples have been updated, but the strategies and suggested types of involvement are the same in newest published version of the guide.

The depth and breadth of involvement by mayors in urban, suburban, and rural cities and towns have expanded as a result of a better practical understanding of the complexness of education and related issues, and how they are linked within their community. Kenneth Wong (2011), in an article entitled "Redesigning Urban Districts in the USA," discusses the redrawing of boundaries between the school system and other major local institutions, and cites this change as a reform strategy. Wong attributes this change in part to mayoral involvement in education. Jeff Henig's new book, *The End of Exceptionalism in American Education* (2013), discusses education as part of general purpose government rather than as a separate entity or governmental function as it is currently. Thus, education becomes subsumed within city government rather than its own governmental entity.

The 1990s started a new wave of interest in education by mayors, beginning with the mayoral taking responsibility for and control of the Boston Public Schools, as well as Mayor Richard Daley's new responsibility for the Chicago Public Schools (now under the control of Mayor Rahm Emanuel). This was followed in 2001 by New York City Mayor Michael Bloomberg's control of his city's schools with the approval of the state legislature, and later, Washington, DC. In 2007, Mayor Adrian Fenty received authority from the city council to take over the responsibility for the District of Columbia's public schools (now under Mayor Vincent Gray).

Other efforts for a more active mayoral role in education during this period included St. Louis Mayor Francis Slay's initiating the establishment of charter schools, and Los Angeles Mayor Antonio Villaraigosa's establishment of 40 mini school districts within the city after he failed to take over the city's schools. In February 2012, Cleveland (Ohio) Mayor Frank Jackson's proposal to the governor and state legislature to make changes to his city's schools was successful.

In late 2012, Columbus (Ohio) Mayor Michael Coleman became more engaged in his local district as a result of a school system scandal on data manipulation. He formed a special commission (with the support of Ohio's governor and the local business community) to review and recommend the restructuring of the Columbus school system. The commission's final report recommended increasing the mayor's role in education and the state's legislature passed legislation that institutionalized the recommendations of the commission. The recommendations have the support of the business community, education associations, and the governor.

Mayors in several other cities have discussed and considered mayoral control and expanded involvement including the cities of Bridgeport (Connecticut), Indianapolis, Milwaukee, Newark (New Jersey), Sacramento, St. Paul, and Minneapolis. So far, none has taken control, but are fully engaged.

Also, numerous mayors of smaller cities and communities have become engaged in the education reform conversation and process such as Davenport (Iowa) Mayor Dave Gluba, Pembroke Pines (Florida) Mayor Frank Ortis, Syracuse (New York) Mayor Stephanie Miner, and Welch (West Virginia) Mayor Reba Honaker.

However, mayoral control of school systems is not a universal trend. Regardless of the approach or level of interest, the basic rationale mayors use to have control of their local school systems is quite consistent. In Chicago, Cleveland, Boston, Philadelphia, Trenton, Providence, Hartford, New Haven, New York City, and Washington, DC the fundamental rationale has been accountability for the use of public dollars and the impact of education on the community as a whole. Other mayors use the same rationale as they move to increase their role in education, but not to control the public schools.

Mayors believe that their leadership and involvement can assist school districts to be more transparent, efficient, and accountable, as well as provide better coordination of services with other agencies that affect the lives of children and families. These efforts can result in improved student achievement, increased graduation rates, and improved level of skills needed to transition to postsecondary education or the world of work. More important, mayors understand that increased educational attainment is critical to maintaining a city's economic viability and is essential to attract new jobs and business. In Wong and Farris' discussion of regime theory, they provide another reason for a mayoral role in education. "The mayor is expected to engage other key stakeholders, he or she is uniquely positioned to overcome power fragmentation, to raise system performance and strengthen public confidence" (2011, p. 220).

HISTORICAL CONTEXT

The present-day view that mayoral involvement in education can produce positive outcomes represents a marked departure from the past. At the turn of the 20th century—the last period when mayors had significant authority over public schools—the effects were not good. At that time, mayoral involvement in education was associated with widespread cronyism, corruption, and the predominance of adult interests over the interests of students. It was this situation that ultimately led reformers to replace mayoral control of education with a system in which public schools were overseen by local school boards and professional educators.

This chapter describes the growth and evolution of mayoral involvement and role in public education, and analyzes how it differs from the mayoral role more than a century ago. It is clear that the standards-based accountability movement in education, as well as the emergence of education as a high priority for voters, has resulted in the development of a form of electoral currency that creates political incentives for mayors to take a greater role in the management of their school districts or become involved in the issue given its impact on the city's economic well-being and how it is viewed as viable, robust, and healthy.

The passage of the federal No Child Left Behind Act (NCLB) in 2001 increased awareness and understanding of educational achievement and related outcome data, increased federal, state, and philanthropic support for educational improvement and change, and encouraged numerous reports and research studies that support linking social, family, and children's services to improve a student's opportunity for success in school and life. NCLB coupled with the historic effort by the National Governors' Association and the Council of Chief State School Officers to create and establish the Common Core of State Standards Initiative were instrumental in defining excellence, common sets of skills and knowledge, and a uniformity for education standards in the nation, which never before had a common set of standards. Both the statute and the initiative coupled with President Obama's education initiatives (Race to the Top and i3, which support common assessments) have contributed greatly to changing mayors' views as to whether they should become involved in the affairs of their cities' school systems and what they can do to effect change or at least be a part of the process (Kirst & Edelstein, 2006).

This chapter also discusses the continuing shift in how mayors see their leadership role and education's relationship to other key local government issues. Before the new wave of mayoral interest in education in the 1990s, very few mayors sought a role in public education because it was largely viewed as separate from the rest of the city's political and business life. Some mayors steer clear of their cities' schools to this day. But in many other places, mayors have found that they can use the bully pulpit as the chief elected official of the city to raise concerns about the quality of the education system, promote bond and tax levy efforts linking education to workforce development and key social services, and even question and criticize the local school board and superintendent. Prior to the 1990s, such actions were rare. The sea change here is the notion that local general purpose government has a role in education (Henig, 2013; Usdan, 2013).

Five mayors who took an interest in education and became actively engaged in local education efforts are now serving as governors and three as lieutenant governors. They have taken their mayoral experience and interest and moved it to the state. The five governors are Colorado Governor John Hickenlooper (former mayor of Denver), Kentucky Governor William Haslam (former mayor of Knoxville), Connecticut Governor Dannel Malloy (former mayor of Stamford), California Governor Jerry Brown (former mayor of Oakland), and North Carolina Governor Pat McCrory (former mayor of Charlotte). Three former mayors, who were engaged in local education reform, serve as lieutenant governors: Gavin Newsom in California (former mayor of San Francisco), Jerry Abramson in Kentucky (former mayor of Louisville), and Robert Duffy in New York (former mayor of Rochester).

THE LITERATURE ON MAYORS AND EDUCATION

The literature on mayoral leadership and involvement is not extensive. Over the past 15 years more has been written on the topic because of the increased interest among mayors and policy makers. Most recently, the focus has been on the results of mayoral control, especially the New York City effort. Studies and analyses of the mayoral role in education have been undertaken by a variety of scholars including Michael Kirst, David Tyack, Larry Cuban, Mike Usdan, Kenneth Wong, Paul Hill, Jeff Henig, Wilbur Rich, Warren Simmons, Sarah Reckhow, Fritz Edelstein, and Clarence Stone. Some of the work includes Cuban and Usdan, 2003; Henig and Rich, 2003; Hill, 2005; Kirst, 2002; Kirst and Bulkley, 2003; Kirst and Wirt, 2005; Usdan, 1994, 2005, 2013; Wong, 2005, 2011; Wong and Shen, 2003a, 2003b; Wong and Farris, 2011; Simmons, 2005; Edelstein and LaRock,

2003; Henig, 2013; and Reckhow, 2013. Their research and writing, and the work of organizations such as the Annenberg Institute for School Reform at Brown University, the U.S. Conference of Mayors, and the National League of Cities, have established the primary body of research and information on the mayoral role in education.

Works of particular note that draw on the earlier scholarship in the politics of education include Jeff Henig and Wilbur Rich's edited work *Mayors in the Middle: Politics, Race, and Mayoral Control of Urban Schools* (2003); Larry Cuban and Mike Usdan, *Powerful Reforms with Shallow Roots* (2003); an *Education Week* commentary by Fritz Edelstein and J. D. LaRock, "Takeovers or Toeholds? Mayors Don't Need to Run Schools to Make Them Better" (2003); Fritz Edelstein's monograph for the U.S. Conference of Mayors, *Mayoral Leadership and Involvement in Education: An Action Guide for Success* (2006); his "The Evolving Political Role of Urban Mayors in Education" (2008); and the National League of Cities' *Improving Public Schools: Action Kit for Municipal Leaders* (2002).

The growth of interest in this topic was reflected in the summer 2006 issue of the *Harvard Educational Review*, which focused on the mayoral role in education through a series of articles by Michael Kirst and Fritz Edelstein, Mike Usdan, Kenneth Wong, Paul Hill, and Warren Simmons. Clearly, this topic will continue to spark scholarship because of its continued political saliency and as mayors try new and different approaches to being engaged at the local, state, and national levels.

Of the more recent work, Kenneth Wong in 2011 in an article on redrawing boundary lines of relationships entitled "Redesigning Urban Districts in the USA," and Wong and Farris' chapter in *Shaping Education Policy: Power and Process* entitled "Redrawing Institutional Boundaries" broaden the discussion of mayoral leadership roles. Two books published in 2013 that include discussions of the evolving mayoral role and what may influence that role are Jeff Henig's *The End of Exceptionalism in American Education*, and Sarah Reckhow's *Follow the Money: How Foundation Dollars Change Public School Politics.*

Much of the press, writing, and research have focused on takeover—not the change in the type of involvement mayors have undertaken. Takeover is still the "sexy" subject in part because it has taken place in the largest urban centers. Gone mostly unnoticed have been the fundamental change efforts by mayors, which are making a difference in the success of schools and students, and having an impact on the community as a whole.

ESTABLISHING THE MAYOR'S ROLE

Mayoral takeovers of school systems usually generate the most public attention, and much of the recent research has focused on mayoral control in New York City and Chicago. However, most mayors merely want to increase their working relationship with the public schools, not assume responsibility for their day-to-day management. The political and geographic configuration of school systems and local government often poses an obstacle to an increased mayoral role, particularly for large cities that are located in a county-based system of government, such as in Maryland, North Carolina, and Florida, and sporadically in other states like Virginia and Georgia (Edelstein et al., 2005).

In some cities, several public school systems are located within a city's limits, so mayoral control would not be practical or realistic. This exists in such cities as San Jose, Houston, Mobile, Dallas, San Antonio, Fresno, Indianapolis, and Omaha. A rare instance is when the city school system may be larger than the city limits. This is the case with the

Los Angeles Unified School District (LAUSD), which encompasses more than 20 cities within its boundaries. When Los Angeles Mayor Antonio Villaraigosa sought in 2006 to initiate a takeover of LAUSD, this structural challenge posed a serious obstacle to the mayor's takeover plan. In the end, he was allowed to control a mini-district within LAUSD and within the confines of the city's boundaries.

In cities without such structural constraints, one can find mayors with some degree of control over or direct involvement with the public schools. Not all of these are recent. Several mayoral "control" arrangements are the result of long-standing governmental changes that occurred many years ago. Some of these are a result of the tradition of local governance by the town hall meeting. In cities such as Providence (Rhode Island), New Haven (Connecticut), Trenton (New Jersey), Hartford (Connecticut), and Oakland (California), the mayor selects either all or some of the members of the school board, and at times serves on it in an official or ex-officio capacity.

In Cleveland, the mayor has responsibility for selecting the school board; then the board selects the superintendent, but the mayor has no say in the budget development process. The mayor of Cleveland received responsibility for the city's public school system in 1998. In 2012, as a result of poor school performance, the district, the governor, and the state legislature agreed to a proposal made by the mayor and school superintendent with business community support to increase the mayoral role in an effort to improve the school system's performance and options for students.

The Cleveland process to select a school board includes an application, interview, and vetting to develop a slate of candidates. The slate is presented to the mayor and selections are made from the list. A similar approach is used in Providence. This process differs from that used in some of the "takeover cities," including Boston, Chicago, and New York, where the mayor directly appoints the school superintendent and all or most of the school board members. In Philadelphia, the mayor and the governor select the school board as set out in state law. Because Washington, DC is considered for the purposes of education both a city and a state, the takeover legislation created only an elected state board because a local board would be redundant. Under the current state statute, the New York City mayor and borough presidents select members of a policy board. With the election of Mayor de Blasio nothing has changed even though during the campaign he made several statements about changing the current structure. There was a review of this structure because the state statute is up for reauthorization after Mayor Bloomberg's third term (Liu, 2013).

Why have mayors become more involved in local public education? As stated several times earlier in this chapter, the standards and accountability movement in public education has played a significant role as has the access to quality data and the use of technology to provide greater transparency. As part of the U.S. Department of Education's Race to the Top Initiative, winning states are required to have districts provide individual student data to the state and to parents. Learning about and understanding student performance is easier and expected. Trying to hide poor performance or graduation data can only get administrators into trouble.

In 2012, Ohio's state education agency uncovered the manipulation of test and attendance data in several school systems. This included Columbus and forced the retirement of the school superintendent at the end of the 2012–2013 school year. A state investigation emboldened Columbus Mayor Michael Coleman and the community to increase their involvement and oversight and force a top-to-bottom examination of the district.

Mayor Coleman became visibly engaged in education. Up to this point during his tenure as mayor, Coleman's involvement was at arm's length except for managing and funding the city's after-school program. Coleman became enraged and frustrated over the school board's lack of cooperation, but not enough to want to ask for the power to take over the schools. He considered how he might replace or change the school board, but rejected that approach. The mayor's efforts have the support of Governor Kasich and the state legislature.

In 2013, as a result of the school system's problems that had come to light, the mayor along with business leaders created a citywide commission to determine how to improve the school system's management, organization, and delivery of education. Although the school board asked for the mayor's participation in the search for and selection of a new superintendent, it never followed through on this request. The search continued even after the mayor asked that it be delayed until the commission made its recommendations for improvements. Then, Mayor Coleman stated he would not support any permanent successor to Superintendent Gene Harris. Coleman insisted that the board name an interim school superintendent, and he stated that the board was "on a path toward failure" if it didn't heed his advice. This furthered the schism between the elected board and the mayor, business, and other political leaders as well as many in the community. The board eventually did suspend the search given legislation written by the state legislature and later hired an interim superintendent, Dan Good.

The interim superintendent now meets weekly with Mayor Coleman, a welcome sign that two of the community's top leaders are pulling together on behalf of a public asset in dire need of support: the city schools. An indication of the importance of the mayor was that Good's first meeting the first day on the job was with Coleman. Mayor Coleman's inclination to stick with the leadership role he took on has been very encouraging and novel. Ohio law separates the governance of school districts from that of cities, villages, and townships, and historically, Columbus mayors have had little role in schools. But these aren't ordinary times.

The city, by contrast, has been excellently managed by Coleman and is thriving. That's why Coleman's decision to create a Columbus Education Commission and to invite top civic and academic leaders to participate was so valuable.

Similar data manipulations occurred in several smaller Ohio school districts. It is not clear if other community elected officials will take similar action, as has the mayor in Columbus. Clearly this indicates that mayors understand the need for quality education systems and transparency.

Many school systems have found themselves with significant funding deficits in recent years. Chicago Mayor Rahm Emanuel has had to be involved in significant budget cuts, school closures, and a reduction in the teaching force. The most unique mayoral action has come in Philadelphia. The school system had a $50 million deficit that threatened opening school on time. Mayor Michael Nutter fought with the state to obtain the necessary funds, but the governor balked because he felt there had not been the management reforms necessary to provide the additional funds. So Mayor Nutter decided to issue $50 million in general purpose bonds to cover the costs to open school on time. This is a perfect example of general purpose government becoming involved in education for the good of the city. Mayor Nutter was both an advocate for and partner with the school system.

Mayor Nutter recognized the importance of education at the beginning of his tenure. The mayor has had a long-standing working relationship with the school system, in part because he selects members of the school board along with the governor. He has an education advisor who is very proactive. And he established within City Hall an office to assist high school students in gaining access to postsecondary education including advice on student aid, college applications, and the academic rigor needed to pursue postsecondary education. It is probably the first office of this kind in the country within a mayor' office.

The disaggregation of data, as required in NCLB, has pointed out shortcomings in performance in many schools for various selected student populations. This policy required by NCLB has assisted mayors and others to understand and address the needs of underperforming schools and students, and provide additional supportive services. With this information several mayors have strengthened their efforts and increased programs including expanded learning time and longer school days (Peterson, 2013).

Mayors clearly understand and identify with the concept of accountability. Numerous public opinion polls have indicated that the public holds mayors accountable for education whether they have formal responsibility for the schools or they don't. Polls also indicate that voters consider the quality of education one of the most important issues facing their communities, and one of the most important factors that local voters consider in choosing whether to reelect a mayor. This public—and electoral—sentiment has impelled mayors to take a more active role in education. By rejecting increases to real estate taxes or the issuing of new bonds to fund education and/or school construction, voters also have indicated numerous times in various cities that they are not willing to continue to write a blank check to the local school system without corresponding results. Such negative votes translate into citizens saying they want more accountability for the funds school systems receive. Most recently this has manifested itself with "parent triggers" that enable parents to change the management and organization of individual schools that are not performing.

Several mayors have suggested that they can provide the back office functions of a school system more efficiently and effectively than school boards or educators. As many educators would agree, the core business of education is teaching and learning—not managing lunchrooms, information technology, bus systems, payroll, human resources, legal services, grounds maintenance, facilities management, and school construction and modernization. As such, many mayors have decided to take on these functions when making their first foray into school system affairs.

For example, when Dannel Malloy was mayor of Stamford, Connecticut (prior to becoming governor), he made a cost-effective decision that the city would manage information technology support and purchasing for the school system, as well as payroll and maintenance. Savings were returned to the school system. In St. Petersburg, Florida, then Mayor Rick Baker worked out an arrangement with the county school superintendent for the city parks and recreation department to take care of school grounds maintenance for schools that are adjacent to city parks. Similarly, in Nashville during Mayor Bill Purcell's tenure, he helped add parks to school grounds as a community and school asset.

In several cities, mayors have become deeply involved in teacher contract negotiations, given their skill and experience in collective bargaining and understanding the long-term budget implications of compensation package increases. Shortly after taking control over the Chicago school system in 1995, Mayor Richard Daley moved quickly to soothe strained relations between the city's teacher union and the school district, leading to the ratification of a new contract after months of stalemate. This occurred again in

2012 under Mayor Rahm Emanuel, who forced a variety of issues to be included in the contract negotiations, in which he was fully engaged. These included a longer school day, a longer school year, and teacher evaluation components. Emanuel was a champion for all of these and won each one.

In 2003, Denver Mayor John Hickenlooper (now Colorado governor) became involved in negotiating and then promoting a new pay-for-performance teacher contract, Pro Comp, that has since received widespread public support. We will be seeing more and more of this level and type of involvement in cities and smaller communities because mayors understand the direct relationship between education and a city's quality of life, including economic well-being.

In 2011, then New Haven (Connecticut) Mayor John DeStefano was involved in the teacher contract negotiations. In the end, U.S. Secretary of Education Arne Duncan applauded the new contract as a landmark in education for how it was structured and the compensation component, as well as the cooperation between the teachers' union, district, and the mayor. Mayor DeStefano has also been a champion for early learning and early childhood programs in the city.

As Hill (2006) noted, before mayors get involved in public education, they must be prepared to address the complicated accounting and financial management issues of the school district. Both the public and some local education professionals are concerned about school budgets and tracking how funds are spent in schools and classrooms. Some school systems have more than one accounting system, which makes efforts to increase financial transparency difficult. If there is to be true accountability and transparency, then one set of books that covers the city as well as the schools would clearly be preferable to separate accounting systems.

Mayor Daley made budget transparency and fiscal management key priorities when he took over the Chicago public schools in 1995. Tracking education dollars within school districts has become a very important issue as legal challenges continue over the ways states fund local districts and how local districts allocate funds to individual schools. It is expected in the coming years that there will be more school finance cases as a result of inequitable funding formulas in states.

The most notable cases were in New York and New Jersey. Other states are now being confronted with similar court decisions. Mayors in all types of communities are a part of the discussion, especially in New Jersey. Also as school and city/county budgets come under greater fiscal pressures, we may see consolidations of budgets as well as increased budget transparency. Consolidated education and local government budgets exist when the city and education system are co-terminus.

MAYORS, EDUCATION, AND WRAP-AROUND SERVICES

Another key reason for mayors' increased interest in public education is their growing perception that education should be linked with other human and social services that the city provides. Most mayors—and educators—agree that teachers cannot attend to the needs of all children by themselves. Thus, mayors are increasingly collaborating with school systems to provide a more comprehensive and strategic approach to ensure that children are ready to learn and be successful in school.

In 1993 Louisville Mayor Jerry Abramson (now Kentucky's lieutenant governor) established the first "Neighborhood Place," a program that links education and related social services for children and families. There are now eight such programs across Louisville and Jefferson County. Louisville's current mayor, Greg Fisher, has continued this effort and has expanded his education efforts. In 2004, under the leadership of Mayor Greg Nickels, Seattle revised its "Family and Education Levy" to fund activities that focus on closing the achievement gap and investing in student health services through school-based health centers in the city's public comprehensive high schools. In New York City, then Mayor Michael Bloomberg collaborated with the Children's Aid Society to locate social services and health clinics in several schools in the Bronx, as an initial step to integrate school and social services as part of his "Children First" education reform plan. The city has also been supportive of the Harlem Children's Zone.

In Washington, DC, then Mayor Adrian Fenty adopted a similar approach in his 2007 legislative proposal to change the governance structure of that city's public schools. The legislation created a committee within his cabinet of all the departments and agencies responsible for child-related services and provides services to children as they attend school. This policy and practice has been continued under Mayor Vincent Gray, who chaired the city council when Fenty was mayor. There will be a new mayor in January 2015 who will also be a former council member, and we shall see if the policy and practice continues.

Mayors recognize the need to coordinate education and social services as a critical component in reducing the achievement gap, ensuring that students are ready to learn, increasing graduation rates, preparing students for postsecondary education and the world of work, and meeting many low-income students' basic physical and mental health needs.

One of the best examples is in Metro Nashville. First under Mayor Bill Purcell and now under Mayor Karl Dean, they have made a full-court press to improve the schools and related services. Mayor Dean was the first mayor in the nation to hold a dropout prevention conference and this has remained a high priority. Other mayors have joined the national effort to increase high school graduation rates because they understand the economic impact of having a trained and skilled workforce.

Dropout prevention and increasing high school graduation rates are a new hot issue on mayors' agendas. Over the past four years, mayors from across the country have partnered with school systems and the America's Promise campaign to develop strategies and initiatives to address this national problem. Dr. Robert Balfanz, a researcher at Johns Hopkins University, coined the phrase "dropout factories" to describe and identify the group of high schools with the lowest graduation rates. This effort has become a national campaign that includes an initiative to increase high school graduation rates by the president and Education Secretary Arne Duncan. The number of high schools has been reduced during the past two years, and mayors have been instrumental in raising the issue and participating in local interventions.

In rural McDowell County, West Virginia (population 22,000), an interesting and unique initiative is currently under way with the full support of the county board and other locally elected officials including Welch Mayor Reba Honaker. The American Federation of Teachers is a full partner in this effort along with the state of West Virginia and an additional 110 organizations, businesses, and individuals. This is a true example of blending educational needs with related services. Mayor Honaker is engaged in everything, both inside and outside her jurisdiction because of the importance of the effort. She is everywhere.

A critical shortage of teachers exists in McDowell county as well as housing for them. The Welch mayor is creating housing through the renovation of abandoned buildings in her city to create a teachers' village. Also, given that this is a mountainous area without much flat land, parking is a problem. So the city is creating parking for the teachers. Mayor Honaker has made the library into a community-learning center to address adult literacy needs. Hunger and drug addiction are two big problems. Forty-six percent of the students live in homes where a parent has had a drug abuse problem and 72 percent of the homes have no working adult. Nine deaths a month are attributed to narcotics. The mayor and other leaders are trying to change the culture, keep students in school, recruit quality teachers, and be creative in the change process, including engaging the county community in the conversation.

EXTENDED LEARNING TIME OPPORTUNITIES

In many cities—especially those where mayors have selective involvement in public education—mayors provide the funding to support after-school and extended learning time programs. They commit millions of dollars in city budgets to fund these year-around efforts.

Similar to their motivation for integrating education and social and related services, mayors have become involved in supporting after-school and extended learning opportunities because they understand that children and teenagers who have nothing to do when school lets out can get into trouble.

Two of the simplest interventions have been substantive after-school and extended day or year programs that combine academic with social and athletic activities. This modest investment has paid off significantly in the cities where it has been implemented. Mayors in Columbus, St. Paul, Nashville, Charlotte, Louisville, San Jose, Albuquerque, Akron, St. Louis, Trenton, Providence, and many other cities are the primary funders of after-school and extended day programs. Sometimes they are responsible for managing the programs; in other cases, the funding goes directly to the school system. Mayors are always raising funds to sustain and make these programs successful and ensure they address the needs of more children for a longer part of the year.

A compendium entitled *Expanding Minds and Opportunities: Leveraging the Power of Afterschool and Summer Learning for Student Success,* edited by Terry K. Peterson, PhD, was published in February 2013. It is the seminal work on after-school and extended learning time. The book features studies, reports, and commentaries by more than 100 thought leaders, including community leaders, elected officials, educators, researchers, advocates, and other prominent authors. One such piece is by St. Paul Mayor Chris Coleman, who writes about the importance of after-school programs to the city of St. Paul and his role in this effort—another example of general purpose government being engaged in education and the mayor being both partner and advocate.

Also, the Ford Foundation announced in 2013 the Time (Time for Innovation Matters in Education) Collaborative, which is a joint venture with the National Center on Time and Learning. It funds projects in select public schools and communities in Colorado, Connecticut, Massachusetts, New York, and Tennessee to expand and redesign their school calendars starting in 2013 in an effort to radically improve learning for tens of thousands of students. The Ford Foundation has committed $3 million a year over three years in support of these state efforts. Three of the states (Colorado, Connecticut, and

Tennessee) have governors who previously served as a mayor. The governors attribute their interest and eagerness to participate and their understanding of the importance of this effort to their experience and lessons learned as mayors.

EDUCATION AND ECONOMIC DEVELOPMENT

By the 1980s, many cities found themselves in economic doldrums or in actual decline. Cities were losing jobs and population, with little new economic investments being made. Since then, many mayors have argued that low-performing schools and the inability of public school systems to prepare students with the skills needed to be successful in the workforce are among the root causes of this decline. Despite changes in industry and the elimination of manufacturing jobs, mayors point out the need for new types of jobs in the economic pipeline. However, many mayors have found it difficult to get the local education system to react to the changing job environment.

Since the 1960s, mayors have been advocates for and cared deeply about workforce development and job training. Most programs have either been under mayoral or county government control. In 1993, one of the first pieces of legislation President Bill Clinton proposed to Congress was a novel school-to-work program, which required a partnership of the federal Departments of Education and Labor. Although the program no longer exists, it started a new era of cooperation and set the tone for enhanced working relationships between city and education leaders. More efforts have followed at the local level (Edelstein, 2008).

The Elementary and Secondary Education Act (ESEA) was reauthorized twice during the Clinton administration. It included accountability, reform, and curriculum and standards alignment requirements that provided a policy foundation and framework for the NCLB. ESEA has yet to be reauthorized since the passage of NCLB, but the Obama administration has tinkered with the legislation through directives, policy guidance, waivers, and new initiatives such as Race to the Top. New reauthorization bills were introduced in the House and Senate in June 2013. The likelihood that reauthorization will occur is not promising prior to the 2014 mid-term elections and those results may effect efforts to reauthorize the legislation in the 114th Congress prior to the 2016 presidential election. Currently the proposals in the House and Senate are significantly different in substance and approach.

These mayoral efforts in education have coincided with a rebuilding of many of urban centers, because of an increase in federal investments. Mayors were invigorated, and found themselves with an opportunity to begin economic development projects to revive the vitality of their cities only to find themselves strapped for budget dollars when the recession hit in 2008.

Mayors continue to view the quality of education provided in their public schools as a stumbling block. Clearly there is a need for them to become more engaged in public education. But many mayors wonder how to undertake this challenge because they do not have legal responsibility for the schools. This interest and awareness have taken place at the same time as discussions focus on the need to align school curricula and needed skills, defining skills for the 21st-century workplace, and the inclusion of community/technical colleges as part of a workforce development strategy.

First, with private industry councils and now workforce investment boards, mayors in partnership with business and industry have an opportunity to be more engaged in, and have a say about, the content and objectives of public education as one examines career and college readiness. This provides an opportunity for mayors to take their first step or foray in the world of education or expand their existing involvement. Too often mayors have been slow to speak out on education, in part because it was forbidden territory as an outgrowth of the changes first initiated in the early 20th century. Today, education is no longer a foreign or forbidden issue. In fact, such efforts are more often expected, especially now that there is acceptance to include in the discussion of 21st-century job skills and educational skills.

In 2011, the National Governors' Association and the Council of Chief State School Officers were the catalysts for the development of the Common Core State Standards. This effort was a major undertaking and political statement. The U.S. Conference of Mayors passed a resolution endorsing the Common Core because it understood the implications of and relationship to workforce skills, quality education, and high standards for all students.

During the first term of the Obama administration, the Departments of Education and Labor partnered in making grants for college and career readiness, for workforce and technical training development, and to community colleges to strengthen workforce skills in communities. These efforts were often coordinated with the U.S. Conference of Mayors Workforce Development Council comprised of the workforce directors in most major cities across the country. This cooperation continues during the administration's second term.

THE MATURING OF MAYORAL LEADERSHIP AND INVOLVEMENT

In the late 1960s, New York City Mayor John Lindsay and Detroit Mayor Jerome Cavanaugh were the first urban mayors to speak out about the relationship between education and a city's economic viability. Neither sought control of their schools, but they did begin a public discourse about a mayoral role in education.

In the wake of Boston's struggle with school desegregation in the 1970s, the city's mayor, Kevin White, made an effort to take over the schools by asking the Massachusetts state legislature to give him the authority to do so. Some 20 years later, Mayor Thomas Menino oversaw the full takeover of the Boston Public Schools by the city government, which was followed by Mayor Daley's takeover of the Chicago schools in 1995. This was the beginning of a broader movement supporting an enhanced mayoral role in education (Edelstein, 2006; Kirst & Edelstein, 2006). In both Boston and Chicago, mayors pushed for a greater role because they saw poorly managed school systems that were not being held accountable, and became frustrated with the failure of their schools to educate students.

Several other mayors followed once the precedent had been set. Not all of the efforts were drastic mayoral takeovers, but they were based on the same principles: to improve the quality of education provided to students; increase transparency in such areas as accounting; and improve the school system's management. Today, mayors are no longer asking if they can be involved, but how and what can they do as part of their role as the chief elected official of the city.

Mayoral involvement in education has taken both formal and informal approaches. The takeovers that have been discussed represent the formal approach. In several other cities, mayors have a formal role as a result of long-standing statutory changes, and other cities have created arrangements for mayoral involvement that do not involve takeovers.

The formal and informal roles take many different forms that are primarily shaped by individual mayoral interests, personality, unique issues, and the needs of the city and school system. Henig and Rich (2003), Cuban and Usdan (2003), Hill (2005), Kirst (2002a, 2002b), Kirst and Bulkley (2003), Kirst and Wirt, (2005), Henig (2013), Wong (2011), and Reckhow (2013) all provide descriptions of the political evolution of the mayoral role.

Henig and Rich (2003) wrote several case studies of what transpired in the cities of Baltimore, Detroit, and Cleveland when the mayors in these cities sought to increase their involvement in public education. A shortcoming of many of these case studies is that in most of the cities discussed, mayoral involvement had not yet been institutionalized, so when the mayor changed, often the mayor's role in education changed, too. Only a few cities have what one might describe as "a mayor for life." In these instances, the political and mayoral roles are significantly different from cities that have term limits, where a mayor seeks higher office or moves on to a career outside public service or where the mayor is defeated for reelection. There are few cases when the mantle was passed that level of involvement and commitment did not change. Two examples are Chicago and Nashville.

Mayor Richard Daley of Chicago was elected in 1989 and served until 2012. Thomas Menino of Boston was elected in 1993 and served as mayor until 2014. Their tenures in office are much longer than those of typical U.S. mayors. But the long-term mayor of Charleston, South Carolina (Mayor Joseph Riley) has shown a major commitment to education. Mayor Riley has a more informal relationship with education issues in his city, but it is very strong because of his passion for the issue and his longevity in office. Mayor Riley is the longest-serving urban mayor in the nation and is considered the "dean of mayors." He will end his tenure at the end of 2014.

In Harrisburg, Pennsylvania, then Mayor Stephen J. Reed was deeply involved in local education issues for years. Mayor Reed, like his counterparts in Chicago and Boston, had control over the Harrisburg schools, which was granted in 2000 when the Pennsylvania state legislature approved a mayoral takeover as part of a larger education reform bill. Reed was very engaged in public education, seeing it as one of the cornerstones in the revitalization of Harrisburg. He met with the school superintendent weekly to chart the education course for the city. Now, the current mayor of Harrisburg does not have that authority over the schools in part because of the academic improvements by the district. Daley and Menino became involved because education was essential for the vitality and growth of their cities and because, in their view, a good system would project an image of quality for their cities.

Another long-serving mayor who has increased his involvement in public education is Akron Mayor Donald Plusquellic. Although he has no formal education role, without his leadership and novel approach to funding school construction Akron would not have been able to receive school construction funds from the state. When a local bond referendum failed, Mayor Plusquellic stepped in because he recognized an opportunity to make schools joint-use facilities and "community assets." The schools would become a resource for the whole city, not just students. Residents would have access to auditoriums, libraries, and recreation facilities. Mayor Plusquellic accomplished this by using the city's municipal bond allocation to provide the matching funds, thus mandating a joint-use strategy. The mayor has a place at the table for planning the new schools and has an ongoing dialogue with the school system.

Plusquellic further showed his interest in education through his involvement with a statewide effort, the Ohio Mayors' Education Roundtable. Created in 2003 as a means for mayors from Ohio's eight largest cities to discuss local and state education issues, the Roundtable evolved into a group that included mayors from the state's 21 largest cities, the chief state school officer, and the governor's education advisor. The focus of the group from mid-2004 to 2006 was school finance reform. Plusquellic's commitment, along with the involvement of Columbus Mayor Michael Coleman, Dayton Mayor Rhine McLin, Springfield Mayor Warren Copeland, and other mayors from across the state led an ongoing dialogue about education in the state. Mayoral staff also played an important role in shaping policy documents along with a working group comprised of education stakeholder organizations. All of the state's education stakeholder groups were a part of the discussion and development of the ballot initiative, but the conversation would not have taken place without the mayors' involvement (Edelstein, 2008).

In 2007, a California Mayors' Education Roundtable was created comprised of mayors from the state's largest cities and continues today. One of its first acts was to write a vision statement signed by the mayors. California Governor Arnold Schwarzenegger met with the Roundtable mayors in March 2008 to find ways to work together on several key education issues including dropout prevention and linkage of youth services as well as funding. This effort continued in 2013 with Jerry Brown (a former mayor) as governor under the leadership of Sacramento Mayor Kevin Johnson. Also, Mayor Johnson has engaged U.S. Secretary of Education Arne Duncan in regularly scheduled conference calls with mayors from across the country on education issues and how they can be effective in their communities.

In 2012, Cleveland Mayor Frank Jackson announced a new reform proposal in partnership with Cleveland Public School head Eric Gordon. The plan would rely heavily on charter schools and a portfolio management approach. Also, there would be a focus on improving student achievement in existing schools and enhancing teacher classroom skills. He had the support of Governor Kasich and the state legislature, as well as business, philanthropic, and community groups (Henig, 2013, p. 151). In 2013, a similar legislative effort began to provide new authority to Columbus Mayor Michael Coleman, including charter school authorization. And Mayor Nutter's effort in Philadelphia is a further indication of how far mayors have come in understanding the importance of education to a city's vitality, economic development, and stability.

EXPANDING MAYORAL LEADERSHIP AND INVOLVEMENT

As the number of mayors involved in education continues to grow because of the saliency and local nature of the topic, mayors are adopting unique approaches and strategies that others have not used before. For example, in 2006, Miami's mayor, Manuel Diaz, had a compact with Dade County schools superintendent Rudy Crew that focused on the mayor's involvement with Crew concerning the schools located in the city of Miami. Also, the compact specifies a plan for the creation of new schools in the city to meet the specific interests and needs of Miami's diverse community, and lays out the ways the mayor will be involved in the planning and implementation of new schools.

Using a more informal approach, St. Petersburg Mayor Rick Baker had a verbal agreement with the Pinellas County school superintendent to work together on education issues. Baker has initiated a number of new programs for the 40 public schools located in his city, including a mentoring initiative, a scholarship program, and a schoolyard maintenance effort coordinated by the city's parks department. Before taking such actions, however, Baker consulted with the superintendent.

Although these two Florida mayors were the elected leaders of the largest cities in their respective counties and provide the largest number of students to their respective public school systems, they could not have more formal roles in public education because the school systems in their cities are county based, and not contiguous with the cities' boundaries. However, the mayors were committed to education because they understood its importance to their cities' future economic growth. This commitment manifested itself in a strategy that is focused on improving the schools, lives, and opportunities for students and the city as a whole.

Recently elected mayors in several cities are in the midst of or have worked to define their relationships with local school system leaders, such as Charlotte Mayor Anthony Foxx (now U.S. Secretary of Transportation), Louisville Mayor Greg Fisher, Sacramento Mayor Kevin Johnson, Hartford Mayor Pedro Segarra, San Jose Mayor Chuck Reed, Jacksonville Mayor Alvin Brown, Denver Mayor Michael Hancock (chairs the U.S. Conference of Mayors K-12 Task Force), and Providence Mayor Angel Taveras. Other longer-serving mayors are strengthening their efforts to be engaged in education, such as Des Moines Mayor Frank Cownie, St. Louis Mayor Francis Slay, Columbus Mayor Michael Coleman, Newark Mayor Corey Booker, Bridgeport Mayor Bill Finch, Long Beach Mayor Bob Foster, St. Paul Mayor Chris Coleman, Davenport Mayor Bill Gluba, and Dallas Mayor Mike Rawlings.

GENERAL TRENDS

The mayor is the only locally elected official who can bring the community together to raise an issue or solve a crisis. Mayors are responsible for general purpose government; they are the CEO (Henig, 2012). Mayors organize and call town meetings, orchestrate the discussion on education issues, utilize the bully pulpit to take a position, and promote a specific initiative or strategy that will benefit the schools and the community. One example is mayoral support of local school bond issues and levies. Another is supporting the expansion of early learning opportunities. In most cases, a mayor's support and involvement are tantamount to passage by the voters or initiating a new program.

Increasingly, mayors are signaling the importance of public education as part of their portfolio by expanding the number of staff assigned the issue at City Hall. Some mayors have formally established offices within city government focused on education and related issues, and others have added high-level appointees whose responsibilities include these topics. The mayors of Philadelphia, St. Paul, District of Columbia, Louisville, Los Angeles, New York City, St. Louis, Newark, Orlando, Indianapolis, Providence, San Francisco, Fresno, Chicago, Boston, San Jose, Akron, New Haven, Bridgeport, Baltimore, Albuquerque, Nashville, Columbus, Charlotte, Denver, Salt Lake City, Ft. Worth, Jacksonville (Florida), and many more have a cabinet-level position or senior-level appointees working on education and related issues.

Still others have taken more novel approaches, going so far as to use the power of the mayor's office to establish new schools outside the traditional school system. For example, the former mayor of Indianapolis, Bart Peterson, sought and received the authority to approve charter schools, making him the only mayor in the nation with such power.

(Peterson's successor, Mayor Greg Ballard, retains this authority and created the position of deputy mayor for education.) Peterson exercised this authority by creating a new charter school system in Indianapolis under the aegis of the mayor's office. Under the leadership of David Harris (who created and now runs The Mind Trust), the division gained local and national attention for its rigorous review of applications, strong accountability, and reporting requirements for all charter schools under the mayor's authority, and the ongoing quality of the charter schools that have been authorized.

In 2006, the mayor and the city of Indianapolis won an award for public-sector innovation and creativity from Harvard University's Kennedy School of Government for these efforts, and Mayor Peterson formalized the arrangement further by establishing a specific division in the mayor's office to manage the charter school program. Numerous mayors and city officials, educators, and others have visited Indianapolis to learn more about how the mayor obtained and implemented this authority.

Several mayors have expressed interest in obtaining similar authority in an effort to shake up their school systems or provide an alternative after unsuccessful efforts to work with local school boards and school systems. The mayors realize that charter schools are not a panacea for the problems of their cities' schools. However, they do believe charter schools can provide an opportunity to bring about change through public education and one that they can have an influential role in shaping without wading too far into the traditional school system's affairs.

In March 2013, Prince Georges (Maryland) County Executive Rushern Baker III proposed that he takeover control of the county school system. The countywide district has had a series of violent episodes in schools, poor academic performance, and a high turnover of the county school superintendent during the past several years. His proposal was modified by the state's legislature. In the end he was given the power to select the school superintendent and four members of the county school board including the chair and vice chair. The board has a total of 13 members so he did not get total control over the school system, but does have say in its governance and management. On June 1, 2013, Baker appointed the new school board chair and vice chair, and a new superintendent was selected prior to the 2013–2014 school year. He is one of the first, if not the first, county executive to have this state-legislated role in education. States and mayors have, but there is no known history of a county executive.

Numerous mayors of cities and smaller towns, especially in the Northeast, have had a formal role in education. They have had no need to seek more innovative ways of getting involved, as in Indianapolis. These formal responsibilities include appointing school board members, selecting school superintendents, and oversight and passage of school budgets. This long-standing involvement is particularly pronounced in localities in New England as an outgrowth of their "town meeting" tradition of local government. In these communities it is common for mayors to appoint school board members, sit on the school board as a member or ex officio, and even at times help select the superintendent. These examples are rarely mentioned when there is an outcry against a strong and formal mayoral role, especially in takeover situations. However, in communities such as New Haven and West Haven, Connecticut; Providence, Rhode Island; Chicopee, Massachusetts; Trenton and East Orange, New Jersey; and many other smaller communities, the mayor either selects members of the school board or has a seat on the board. In Hartford, Connecticut Mayor Pedro Segarra selects a majority of his school board (Edelstein, 2008).

Former New Haven Mayor John DeStefano stated on numerous occasions that he believes that serving on the school board is one of the most rewarding things he does as mayor. He led the recent effort to redefine and restructure the teacher contract (described earlier) and has been a major proponent for expanding early childhood educational opportunities in New Haven schools. It is too early to tell how the working relationship is going between newly elected Mayor Toni Harp and New Haven's new superintendent, Garth Harries.

Providence Mayor Angel Taveras (now running for governor) and his predecessor, David Cicilline (now a member of Congress), used their office's long-standing responsibility over education to promote the modernization of school buildings, which they believe will help carry forward larger-scale neighborhood redevelopment efforts in the city. With the mayor's support, Providence has led the effort to promote "smaller learning communities" in public education, community schools, and extended learning time. And they support small schools, including The Met—a nationally recognized alternative high school developed by Big Picture Learning. In addition, Mayor Cicilline led a statewide campaign for school finance reform. Providence's mayor also appoints the school board, helps select the school superintendent, and has oversight authority with the city council for the school system's budget.

Mayors also look for new opportunities for involvement. College and career readiness and college access are two areas where mayors have begun to exert their involvement. Philadelphia Mayor Michael Nutter has established in City Hall as part of the mayor's office a college access office to be of assistance to any student who wants help in finding postsecondary education opportunities and learn more about what it takes, courses and costs, to go to school beyond high school. The office also provides information on student financial assistance for postsecondary education. His education advisor, Lori Shorr, has been instrumental in setting up this office. Soon we will see better linkages between college access, career opportunities, and job skill programs.

Each of these and other examples indicate how mayors have embraced education as an issue in which they can be involved. This engagement is in part a result of the broader portfolio, which exposes them "to different ways of thinking about education and to different ways of implementing government power" (Henig, 2013, p. 77).

THE PERILS AND CONSEQUENCES

Mayoral involvement and leadership in education are not always a smooth road or rosy scenario. These efforts can create tension or be effective only for a short while and then be nullified. One prominent example occurred in the late 1990s, when Los Angeles Mayor Richard Riordan pushed a slate of mayor-backed candidates for the school board and won the majority. By the next election, he lost the majority as a result of an effort by the local teachers' union to unseat his candidates. Mayor Riordan made education reform a major priority, which included recruiting former Colorado governor Roy Romer to become the Los Angeles Urban School District (LAUSD) superintendent. Romer has retired as superintendent after having served three different mayors.

Los Angeles' former mayor Antonio Villaraigosa lobbied the state legislature in 2006 to change the governance structure of LAUSD so the mayor would have more control. The effort resulted in a jumbled piece of legislation often characterized as the "bill of 100 compromises." In the end, the mayor was allowed to have control over a small number of schools as a demonstration district. Romer was vocally opposed to the mayor's efforts, but Villaraigosa had the support of former Mayor Riordan to change the education governance structure. Ultimately, Villaraigosa's efforts were undone when the school board successfully challenged his takeover legislation in court on state constitutional grounds. Despite this defeat, Villaraigosa sought new ways to maintain a role in school system affairs (Danzberger, Kirst, & Usdan, 1992; Hess, 1998). He worked with the city's new school superintendent, John Deasy, and met with members of the LAUSD school board. In subsequent school board elections he has supported slates of candidates, but not always winning a majority of the seats. It is a wait and see what Los Angeles' new mayor, Gil Garcetti, will be doing in education.

The experience of St. Louis Mayor Francis Slay offers another cautionary tale. From the beginning of his first term in 2001 (in 2013 he was elected to his fourth term as mayor), Slay felt as mayor that he needed to become more engaged in the city's low-performing school system—a sea change from previous mayors' views. Almost from the beginning, political shock waves reverberated in the city. The outgoing school superintendent, not a favorite of the mayor, announced at his last school board meeting in 2003 that the district was facing a staggering and unexpected budget deficit.

Mayor Slay worked with the existing school board and the business community and hired a business takeover firm, Alvarez and Marsal, to fix management and accounting systems of the school system and ensure they were in order, and establish fiscal responsibility. The process took one year, and during that period the mayor became even more active in education. He supported a slate of school board candidates that won and gained a majority on the board. The new board began to initiate reforms in consultation with the mayor and his staff. In addition, the mayor worked with the board to select a new school superintendent, Creg Williams, who had worked for Paul Vallas, the former CEO of the Chicago and Philadelphia public schools as well as New Orleans and currently the interim superintendent in Bridgeport, Connecticut. Hopes rose for stability, continuity, and a comprehensive approach to improving the schools. Unfortunately, in 2006, the results of the next school board election defeated the mayor's candidates and the majority (Wong & Shen, 2003b).

As a result of the school board election, Mayor Slay requested that the state take over the system because of the rash action by the school board and the continued poor academic performance of the district. The state department of education created an independent commission to review the St. Louis public schools. Its report recommended that the state take over the district until 2011 and turn oversight of the schools to a three-member board. The state implemented the recommendation. Oversight panel members continue to be selected by Mayor Slay, the state's school superintendent, and the chair of the city council. Mayor Slay got in part what he wanted, but still does not see things changing or moving quickly enough. The school system's problems are still not being solved. Nor is there a permanent governance structure to bring stability to the system in the near future (Edelstein, 2008).

Also, Mayor Slay did not let his frustration with the public school system stop his interest and involvement in education. He has been actively involved in supporting the establishment of quality charter schools in the city. And when these schools are not successful, he has supported the withdrawal of their charter. The first charters began to appear during the 2008–2009 school year.

Leadership of the school system in many of the mayoral-controlled districts can be a perilous journey. Several educators have seen their star fall hard during their tenure as the head of a district. In 2012, Jean-Claude Brizard was handpicked to lead the Chicago public schools by Mayor Rahm Emanuel. However, he became a casualty of the teacher's strike just three weeks after the mayor negotiated a new teacher contract later that year. The mayor replaced Brizard with Barbara Byrd Bennett, former superintendent of Cleveland (Ohio), which had semi-mayoral control. Similarly, in New York City, Cathy Black, who succeeded Joel Klein, found her tenure as chancellor very short lived and was replaced by Mayor Michael Bloomberg with former deputy mayor Dennis Walcott. Now, recently elected Mayor Bill de Blasio selected Carmen Farina, who is former New York City Schools administrator. In Washington, DC, when Mayor Fenty was defeated for reelection by Vincent Gray, Mayor Gray replaced Michelle Rhee, who had a two-year tenure with Kaya Henderson as chancellor of the DC public schools. Ms. Henderson had worked for Ms. Rhee so the transition was easier. DC has a mayoral election in the Fall 2014, that will elect a new mayor. One candidate has already committed to keep Kaya Henderson as chancellor, and the other candidate has yet to take a position and currently chairs the city council's education committee.

PASSING THE TORCH

A number of mayors have forged partnerships with their superintendents to assist in improving learning environments and support cooperative programs, supplemental educational activities, coordinating services, and the general importance of education. One of the best examples of this occurred in Nashville, Tennessee, under Bill Purcell, the mayor from 2002 to 2007. Purcell believed strongly in spotlighting education through the use of the mayor's bully pulpit, and sponsored a "First Day of School" rally at the beginning of each school year. This included a major event in the city's municipal arena that drew thousands of people, including thousands of parents who were attending the first day of class with their children. It eventually became so popular that others attended from communities outside the county.

In addition, the mayor instituted a policy that city and county workers could take the morning of the first day of school off to escort their children to school. Soon after, local business leaders followed suit. Furthermore, the mayor developed youth councils to provide a voice for students and encouraged them to speak out about their schools. Finally, the mayor worked closely with the county's school superintendent to develop a strong after-school program that is credited with helping to raise test scores.

The mayor did not run for reelection in 2007, causing many to wonder whether the next mayor would sustain Purcell's commitment to education. However, by establishing a pattern and legacy of mayoral involvement through the efforts described earlier, Nashville's current mayor, Karl Dean, has continued the tradition of support for the school system. "Alignment Nashville," a metro-wide coalition of the 260 nongovernment organizations focused solely on improving education, has played a key role in sustaining this involvement (Hill, Campbell, & Harvey, 2000; Hill & Celio, 1998; Payzant, 2005; Sharrat & Fullan, 2005; Simmons, 2005; Smith, 2005).

The coalition has four committees that include the leadership of the school system, local government, independent agencies, business, and other organizations and focuses on addressing the priority needs of pre-kindergarteners, kindergarten through middle school students, high school students, and students beyond high school, including those in need of workforce development and job training services. True to Purcell's pattern of influencing the public education from the outside, the groups in the coalition work together, rather than each trying to get to do something with the school district or inside schools. Because of Alignment Nashville's continuing work, as well as the efforts of Mayor Purcell, the coalition has been able to make educational change an institution-alized priority and keep its eyes on the prize—a quality education for every child in the school system.

Mayor Dean has furthered that tradition by hosting the first communitywide summit on dropouts in the nation in 2011. He has also been active in all aspects of education and working closely with the Race to the Top reforms in the state.

The question of whether mayoral involvement can be sustained after an activist mayor leaves office was also posed in Long Beach, California when Beverly O'Neill, a three-term mayor, retired from office in 2006. One of O'Neill's major legacies was her involvement in education. As mayor, she created a citywide partnership with all of the city's education leaders, including the school superintendent, community college and university presi-dents, and business leaders. This partnership created an important city dialogue that led to increased cooperation between the members of the city's education community and the support of innovative programs and approaches that improved the Long Beach Uni-fied School District's academic performance, which culminated in the district's receipt of the prestigious Broad Prize for Urban Education in 2004. O'Neill's successor, Bob Foster, was one of the business leaders who participated in O'Neill's citywide partnership.

Mayor Foster continued the tradition, commitment, and belief that education is a key driver of success, vitality, and economic growth in the city. In his first year as mayor, he helped create a new school with superintendent Chris Steinhauser, and they plan more partnerships. He has just finished his second term, and we will see if the successor, Rob-ert Garcia, keeps up the tradition.

In other cities like San Francisco, Fresno, Syracuse, Bridgeport, St. Paul, Providence, Chicago, Charlotte, Dallas, Denver, and Louisville, mayors who were elected more recently are all continuing the tradition of increased mayoral involvement in education established by their predecessors. This is another indication that education is here to stay as an issue in which mayors can be engaged, involved, vocal, and proactive. In many respects mayoral leadership, involvement, and advocacy in education are expected by the voters and have become an institutionalized role.

CONCLUSION

No major mayoral takeovers of public school systems have occurred during the past five years. There has been a significant rise in mayoral interest, involvement, and engage-ment in education at the local, state, and federal levels. Education is now a topic that has become a part of mayors' talking points and policy discussions. Mayors have become very familiar with the multitude of education issues confronting their communities and the nation, and articulate about how education is directly connected to other city issues that affect growth, economic stability, workforce skills, and social services.

During the past several years, mayors have been aware of and engaged in the discus-sions concerning the stability of their public school systems, districts' capacity to meet the new Common Core standards, a state's Race to the Top requirements, teacher evaluation and retention, recruitment and contract issues, charter schools, choice vouchers, budget and data transparency, school safety including bullying, technology, and a myriad of other education and related issues. They have not shied away from participating in all of these discussions, decisions, or solutions. Mayors have built a comfort zone over the past five years that has emboldened them to be a part of the solution and not avoid being engaged.

Some scholars, experts, and policy wonks have called for more takeovers by mayors because they see education as an integral part of general purpose local government. They include Chester A. Finn, Jr. of the Thomas Fordham Institute, Frederick Hess of the American Enterprise Institute, and U.S. Secretary of Education Arne Duncan. Several mayors have expressed interest in having the responsibility but none have been able to secure state approval to take the step. These include the mayors of Bridgeport, Milwaukee, Indianapolis, St. Paul, and Sacramento.

One can expect efforts by mayors to assume formal control of their cities' school systems to continue on an episodic basis and when the conditions permit. More likely, however, mayors will continue to be more actively engaged in education in various ways depending the saliency or urgency of the issue; how quickly a school system responds to making the changes necessary to meet the educational needs of its students; the requirements of federal and state education statutes; community calls for improvements; and the increased needs of the city to link education and related services. Mayors have made the connection between quality education and the economic well-being of their city. This can only mean that education will continue to be a part of a mayor's agenda and interest since a city's future and vitality will in part be influenced by the quality of his education system's graduates.

Mayors are politicians, and public support is critical to any decision that they make, especially one that changes the governing landscape in the city. But mayors are also risk takers once they weigh the political consequences.

Clearly, mayors are more comfortable making education part of their portfolio in some shape or form. They definitely want to expand their partnership with the school system, and find ways to work jointly whenever possible. Given current budget constraints for both cities and schools, mayors and school systems may find ways to jointly purchase services and equipment to reduce costs and get more favorable pricing. We will also be seeing more mayors and locally elected officials testifying on behalf of or in support of their school districts at the state and federal levels, which would be unheard of only a few years ago. Mayors have become advocates for education because quality education benefits the community.

Research on mayors and education has focused too much on takeovers and the outcomes of this strategy. These studies have not addressed the impact of mayoral leadership and involvement through the informal engagements that change policy, practice, and programs; change a community's commitment to the public schools; establish an initiative that forces changes in behavior; make services that keep students in school more efficient; or one of many other improvements. This focus for research should be encouraged rather than what seems to be "sexy" but is more mundane and likely to make a long-term difference. We need to learn more of these influences and impact on school systems, students, teachers, related services, and the community.

In the end we have seen a change in the landscape. Mayors are becoming more engaged, visible, and vocal when it comes to education. These efforts are only the beginning. Citizens can expect their visible involvement more and more.

The ice has been broken and the tradition has been started. No longer are mayoral interest and advocacy taboo. Mayors' engagement is expected and even required in some cities, as people get used to mayoral education involvement. The case has been made for the connection between education, city/county services, and improving the quality of life for the whole community.

REFERENCES

Borut, D., Bryant, A., & Houston, P. (2005, September 26). Conflict or consensus? Why collaboration between cities and schools is the key to reform. *Nation's Cities Weekly, 28,* 9.

Cooper, B. S., Cibulka, J. G., & Fusarelli, L. D. (Eds.). (2008). *Handbook of education politics and policy.* New York: Routledge.

Cuban, L., & Usdan, M. (2003). *Powerful reforms with shallow roots.* New York: Teachers College Press.

Danzberger, J., Kirst, M., & Usdan, M. (1992). *Governing public schools.* Washington, DC: Institute for Educational Leadership.

Edelstein, F. (2006). *Mayoral leadership and involvement in education: An action guide for success.* Washington, DC: U.S. Conference of Mayors.

Edelstein, F. (2008). The evolving political role of urban mayors in education. In B. S. Cooper, J. G. Cibulka, & L. D. Fusarelli (Eds.), *Handbook of education politics and policy* (pp. 179–191). New York: Routledge.

Edelstein, F., & LaRock, J. D. (2003, October 1). Takeovers or toeholds? Mayors don't need to run the schools to make them better. *Education Week, 34,* 44.

Edelstein, F., Lesure, D., Fraga, L., Kirst, M., Woolfalk, K., & Elis, R. (2005). *Profiles of cities and schools: Defining future relationships between mayors and school systems.* Unpublished report for the Broad Foundation.

Henig, Jeffrey R. (2013). *The end of exceptionalism in American education: The changing politics of school reform.* Cambridge, MA: Harvard University Press.

Henig, J., & Rich, W. (Eds.). (2003). *Mayors in the middle: Politics, race, and mayoral control of urban schools.* Princeton, NJ: Princeton University Press.

Hess, F. M. (1998). *Spinning wheels: The politics of urban school reform.* Washington, DC: Brookings Institution Press.

Hill, P. T. (2006). Getting hold of district finances: A make or break issue for mayoral involvement in education. *Harvard Educational Review 76,* no. 2, 178–89.

Hill, P. T., Campbell, C., & Harvey, J. (2000). *It takes a city: Getting serious about urban school reform.* Washington, DC: Brookings Institution Press.

Hill, P. T., & Celio, M. B. (1998). *Fixing urban schools.* Washington, DC: Brookings Institution Press.

Kirst, M. W. (2002a). *Alternative mayoral roles in education.* Unpublished paper, Stanford University, Stanford, CA.

Kirst, M. W. (2002b). *Mayoral influence, new regimes, and public school governance.* Philadelphia: Consortium for Policy Research in Education.

Kirst, M., & Bulkley, K. (2003). Mayoral takeover: The different directions taken in different cities. In J. Cibulka & W. Boyd (Eds.), *A race against time: The crisis in urban schooling* (pp. 93–108). Westport, CT: Praeger.

Kirst, M., & Edelstein, F. (Summer 2006). The maturing mayoral role in education. *Harvard Education Review,* 152–163.

Kirst, M. W., & Wirt, F. (2005). *The political dynamics of American education.* Berkeley, CA: McCutchan.

Liu, John C. (January 2013). *No more rubber stamps: Reforming New York City's Panel of Education Policy.* Unpublished draft report. New York City Comptroller, New York.

National League of Cities. (2002). *Improving public schools: Action kit for municipal leaders.* Washington, DC: Author.

Payzant, T. W. (Fall 2005). *Continuous improvement: Sustaining education reform long enough to make a difference.* Voices in Urban Education Reform. Providence, RI: Annenberg Institute for School Reform, Brown University.

Peterson, Terry K. (Ed.) (2013). *Expanding minds and opportunities: Leveraging the power of afterschool and summer learning for student success.* Washington, DC: Collaborative Communications Group.

Reckhow, Sarah. (2013). *Follow the money.* New York: Oxford University Press.

School Communities That Work: A National Task Force Report on the Future of Urban Districts. (2002). Providence, RI: Annenberg Institute for School Reform, Brown University.

Sharrat, L., & Fullan, M. (Fall 2005). *The school district that did the right things right.* Voices in Urban Education Reform. Providence, RI: Annenberg Institute for School Reform, Brown University.

Simmons, W. (2005). *District reform action guide.* Unpublished paper, Annenberg Institute for School Reform, Brown University.

Smith, H. (2005). Using community assets to build an "education system." *Voices in Urban Education Reform, 7,* 25–35.

Stone, C., Henig, J., Jones, B., & Pierannunzi, C. (2001). *Building civic capacity: The politics of reforming urban schools.* Lawrence: University Press of Kansas.

Tyack, D. (1974). *The one best system: A history of American urban education.* Cambridge, MA: Harvard University Press.

U.S. Conference of Mayors (2006). *Mayoral leadership and involvement in education: An action guide for success.* Washington, DC: Author.

Usdan, M. D. (1994). The relationship between school boards and general-purpose government. *Phi Delta Kappan, 75,* 374–378.

Usdan, M. D. (2005). *Mayors and public education: The case for greater involvement.* Unpublished paper. Institute for Educational Leadership, Washington, DC.

Usdan, M. D. (2013). Schooling the mayors. *Phi Delta Kappan, 94,* 80.

Wong, K. K. (2005). *The political dynamics of mayoral engagement in public education.* Unpublished paper, Brown University.

Wong, K. K. (2011). Redesigning urban districts in the USA: Mayoral accountability and the diverse provider model. *Education Management, Administration & Leadership Journal, 39*(4), 486–500.

Wong, K. K., & Farris, E. (2011). Governance in urban school systems: Redrawing institutional boundaries. In D. Mitchell, R. Crowson, & D. Shipps (Eds.), *Shaping education policy: Power and process* (pp. 215–237). New York: Routledge.

Wong, K. K., & Shen, F. (2003a). Big city mayors and school governance reform: The case of school district takeover. *Peabody Journal of Education, 78*(1), 5–32.

Wong, K. K., & Shen, F. (2003b). Measuring the effectiveness of city and state takeover as a school reform strategy. *Peabody Journal of Education, 78,* 89–119.

4

UNDERSTANDING EDUCATION POLICY MAKING AND POLICY CHANGE IN THE AMERICAN STATES

Learning from Contemporary Policy Theory

Michael K. McLendon, Lora Cohen-Vogel, and John Wachen

Writing only a few short years ago, two of this chapter's authors commented on the vast policy changes that seemed to have engulfed America's K-12 and higher education sectors since the mid-1980s (McLendon & Cohen-Vogel, 2008). In K-12 education, we noted, states had adopted new curriculum standards, embarked on innovative teacher certification regimens, established new assessment and accountability regimes, experimented with incentives programs linking teacher compensation with student performance, litigated hundreds of school finance lawsuits, and witnessed the ascendancy and retreat—and re-ascendance—of countless other "reform" initiatives at the local, state, and national levels.

In higher education, the evidence at the time seemed equally compelling that the period between 1980 and 2005 had been one of dramatic change on the state policy landscape. State governments had experimented with a raft of new financing schemes for postsecondary education, including college savings plans, prepaid tuition programs, and broad-based, merit-scholarship programs, such as the immensely popular HOPE scholarship program, begun in Georgia in the early 1980s and in operation today in 13 other states (Cohen-Vogel & Ingle, 2007; Doyle, 2006).

States also had experimented with newer governance and accountability regimes. During this period, for example, states witnessed the emergence of "charter colleges" and the adoption and spread of performance-funding mandates in higher education that, for the first time, tied relatively small amounts of public funding to the performance of colleges and universities (McLendon, Hearn, & Deaton, 2006; Zumeta, 2001). Adding to the era's volatility, state spending on higher education had begun to decline relative to student enrollments, per capita wealth, and the size of state budgets. Together, these and other developments led some observers to surmise the arrival on the scene of a "privatization" movement in public higher education. In reflecting on the nature of these and other state policy trends in education, we declared: "Rarely have students of education policy lived in times more dynamic than the current one" (McLendon & Cohen-Vogel, 2008).

Writing today, we find the pace of state policy change in education, if anything, having accelerated, rather than slowed. To the list of noteworthy developments that seem to be reshaping the policy climate for K-12 and higher education, one can add the following: (1) implementation of the Common Core State Standards for Mathematics and English Language Arts, which "define the knowledge and skills students should gain throughout their K–12 education in order to graduate high school prepared to succeed in entry-level careers, introductory academic college courses, and workforce training programs" (CCSSI, n.d., para. 5); (NGA/CCSSO, 2010); (2) ongoing activity—and controversy—stemming from waivers exempting states from requirements of the No Child Left Behind legislation; (3) the embrace by at least 32 states of a college completion agenda for higher education that pledges the states and their colleges to implement action plans through which they aim to achieve significant increases in graduation rates at both two-year and four-year campuses; and (4) the arrival on the scene of "Performance Funding 2.0," whereby some states (e.g., Tennessee) have redirected their *entire* appropriation for higher education to institutions on the basis of performance, rather than student enrollments, as had been the case since the rapid expansion of public higher education in the 1950s and 1960s.

Despite the clear importance of these and other recent fluctuations in state policy for education, scholarly understanding of the forces shaping educational policy change in the American states remains woefully underdeveloped. What factors propel states to undertake the policy reforms they do, when they do? Is it variation in the sociodemographic or economic development patterns of the states that accounts for across-state differences in state education policies? Or does "politics," in the sense of institutional political actors, such as interest groups, legislative leadership and design, partisanship, and election cycles, more fully explain patterns in state policy change for education? To what extent does competition or emulation between and among states, rather than sociopolitical conditions within individual states, help drive these changes? How do problems gain attention, solutions emerge, and issue agendas take shape before state governments?

To what extent do beliefs, values, ideas, and interests matter in the determination of education policy outcomes? How, precisely, do education policies change? If rationalism and incrementalism have lost the paradigmatic power they once enjoyed, how can the vast policy changes in education of the past three decades best be explained? What are the implications for effective policy advocacy of these different ways of conceptualizing change? Scholarship traditionally has paid too little systematic attention to these kinds of questions.

Notably lagging in the research literature are efforts aimed toward building, elaborating, and testing theories of state policy making and policy change for education.[1] Conversely, however, the study of public policy formation in political science has undergone a renaissance over the past 30 years. A number of factors have spurred this disciplinary development, including (1) a recognition of the growing influence of the states as important policy actors in America's federal system, (2) a growing awareness both of the limitations inherent in existing theories of policy making and of the need for better explanations,[2] (3) a revival in the study of political institutions and of how they undergo institutional change, and (4) a resurgent interest in the study of public policy, in particular (March & Olsen, 1989; Olsen, 2001; Rockman, 1994; Sabatier, 1999).

Out of these distinct yet reinforcing developments emerged new theorizing about the processes of policy change and, equally important, renewed thinking about the nature of governmental institutions. Importantly, these developments also have produced a sizeable body of conceptual and empirical scholarship that researchers can use in helping address unanswered questions about state policy change in the K-12 and higher education arenas.

In the remainder of this chapter, we examine the suitability of four contemporary policy theories for helping organize and stimulate future research on state policy making and policy change in K-12 and higher education. We used several criteria for selection of the frameworks presented in this chapter. First, we sought theories that conceptualize policy making at the *systemic policy level,* rather than at the micro-level of individual actors. Second, we searched for theories that explicitly address the problem of *change* in large policy systems.

Finally, we sought *theories* that have garnered widespread attention in noneducation policy domains. These criteria led us to select the multiple-streams framework (Kingdon, 1984, 1995), the punctuated equilibrium framework (Baumgartner & Jones, 1991, 1993; True et al., 1999, 2007), the advocacy coalition framework (Jenkins-Smith & Sabatier, 1994; Sabatier, 1988; Sabatier & Jenkins-Smith, 1993), and the policy innovation and diffusion framework (Berry, 1994; Berry & Berry, 1990, 1992; Gray, 1994; Mintrom, 1997; Walker, 1969).

In the following section, we distill the central tenets and examine the conceptual and empirical traditions associated with each of these four theoretical frameworks. We also identify key works that have applied or elaborated each theory since its original formulation. In the concluding section of this chapter, we assess the prospects for each framework's application in future research on educational policy making and policy change.

THEORIES OF PUBLIC POLICY CHANGE: MULTIPLE STREAMS, PUNCTUATED EQUILIBRIUM, ADVOCACY COALITION, AND POLICY INNOVATION AND DIFFUSION[3]

Multiple-Streams (Revised Garbage Can) Framework

Developed 30 years ago, John Kingdon's (1984, 1994, 1995) multiple-streams model[4] today remains both an influential and well-cited contemporary policy theory, if also one lacking systematic elaboration. The model seeks to explain change in the *issue agenda* of the U.S. national government—that is, how and why some issues gain prominence before policy makers, while other issues do not. In Kingdon's own words: "How do subjects come to officials' attention? How are the alternatives from which they choose generated? How is the governmental agenda set? Why does an idea's time come when it does?" (1984, p. vii).

Through the use of case studies and a panel design consisting of 247 interviews with policy makers over a four-year period in the domains of transportation and health, he developed a counter-conventional explanation for the rise of issues on the government's agenda. Indeed, Kingdon's explanation for policy change is distinctive in at least three respects: (1) its focus on the predecision processes of policy formation; (2) its reliance on perspectives from organization sciences and behavior as a basis for conceptualizing change in public policy; and (3) its portrayal of policy formation as both preternaturally dynamic and idiosyncratic.

An initially distinctive feature of the multiple-streams model is its concern with the predecision processes of policy making termed *agenda setting* (i.e., how issues initially come to be *issues*), which can be viewed as distinct from policy choice (i.e., authoritative enactments) or from the carrying out of authoritative decisions (i.e., implementation). By the time Kingdon developed his framework, scholars had already observed that control of the policy agenda confers important advantages in shaping policy outcomes; Cobb and Elder's (1983) work is noteworthy in this regard. Yet Kingdon was among the first to theorize on the *processes* resulting in agenda change, rather than describe the factors contributing to agenda status, alone.

The model's second distinctive feature is its heavy reliance on theory and research in a then-emerging facet of organizational studies known as "garbage can decision making." Scholars of Congress had long used a variety of organization-theoretic lenses in their study of the institution (e.g., Cooper, 1977; Polsby & Schickler, 2002), but Kingdon built explicitly on an emerging conception of complex organizations—garbage can decision making—that emphasized the highly contingent nature of decision making in organizations beset by ambiguity.

Drawing on the garbage can model of organizational choice popularized by Cohen, March, and Olsen (1972), Kingdon conceptualized the federal government as an "organized anarchy," attributing to it many of the same organizational properties that Cohen and colleagues had first assigned to universities in their landmark study of decision making in those institutions. The key organizational properties included problematic preferences, unclear means, and fluid participation. Adapting these ideas to fit the conditions of the federal government (rather than the modern research university), Kingdon then portrayed agenda setting as a process wherein ambiguity runs rampant, problems and solutions remain only loosely tethered, and participants drift from one decision venue (e.g., a committee hearing or a floor vote) to another, often with little predictability.

Kingdon's analogizing of the federal government to that of an organized anarchy enabled him to portray agenda setting as highly dynamic, although not to such an extent that elements of order cannot also be seen. This tension between dynamism and order indeed constitutes the model's third distinctive feature. The multiple-streams framework postulates a highly contingent set of processes and relationships whereby problems, ideas (potential solutions), and politics flow independently through government, combining only occasionally with choice opportunities to propel issues onto the national policy agenda.

Multiple streams retains much of the spirit of March and colleagues' original garbage can conceptualization, in that it characterizes agenda setting as considerably fluid, capricious even. Yet Kingdon's revised framework also differs from the original garbage can model in important ways, mainly as seen in its depiction of the role that order and structure can play in developments at the level of the individual streams of activity. Kingdon observed: "we . . . find our emphasis being placed more on the 'organized' than the 'anarchy,' as we discover structures and patterns in the processes [of agenda setting]" (1984, p. 86). Thus, the discussion that follows focuses on the model's two main constituent components: a set of more or less organized, individual "streams" of policy activity and a set of more or less anarchic processes involving the convergence of those streams at the level of the macro-system.

The multiple-streams framework views the federal government as an arena through which three "streams" of separate albeit concurrent activity flows. The *problem stream* consists of certain conditions that policy makers have chosen to interpret as problems. The *policy stream* consists of the ideas or "solutions" specialists have developed over time in various policy communities. Last, the *political stream* consists of both routine and unplanned changes occurring on the political landscape, such as public opinion, electoral turnover, and interest group politics. These three streams—of problems, policies, and politics—flow through the governmental system, Kingdon argues, largely independent of one another, and each in accordance with its own set of internal rules. As a consequence, change in any given stream may occur independently of change in the other streams.

With respect to the *problem* stream, the ways policy makers learn about certain social conditions or issues can help to determine when a condition becomes elevated to the status of *a problem*. There are three mechanisms that may lead officials to interpret a condition as a problem: indicators, focusing events, or feedback. With respect to problem definition, officials tend to convert conditions into problems in three ways: conditions that violate important values may be transformed into problems; conditions become problems by comparison with relevant units; and conditions become problems through their classification into one category rather than another. Policy advocates attend closely to the merits of their arguments, thus one finds at work here many aspects of the traditional problem-solving model of decision making, including the use of a variety of analytic techniques, such as benefit-cost calculations and modeling of different forms, in an effort by advocates to build a persuasive, rational case for the importance of a given problem.

Policies, or potential solutions to problems policy makers have chosen to acknowledge, develop in ways analogous to that of biological natural selection, Kingdon asserts. Specialists working in policy communities develop and experiment with ideas, which then "float" in and around government in a sort of "policy primeval soup," bumping into one another over time to form combinations, recombinations, and mutations. One finds incrementalism at work here, in the development of solutions within policy communities. One also finds some degree of rationalism, inasmuch as policy makers may use certain decision criteria (e.g., technical feasibility, value congruence, and anticipation of future constraints) when selecting some ideas for survival and some others for extinction.

Third, Kingdon describes the forces that can "soften up" the *political* system for change, thus enabling issues to move onto the governmental agenda. Developments in this stream can be either predictable or unforeseen. Predictable changes sometimes include the cyclical turnover in office holding by elected officials that stems from regularized elections. Unforeseen changes can result from political scandal, sudden shifts in public opinion, or economic perturbations. Interest groups usually play a crucial role in mobilizing support for or against certain policy ideas.

How, then, do agendas change, if, as the preceding discussion suggests, the identification of problems, the generation of policy solutions, and the march of politics proceed largely independently of one another? According to Kingdon's formulation, an issue gains the serious attention of policy makers only when the three separate streams of activity conjoin with a decision opportunity. This "coupling" of the otherwise semiautonomous streams represents the single most significant feature of the model.

Streams may converge when a window of opportunity opens and "policy entrepreneurs" mobilize attention around their pet problems or push their pet solutions. Because problems and solutions are only weakly tethered one to another in the governmental garbage can, much variability exists in the ways entrepreneurs link *particular* problems, solutions, and political conditions. According to Kingdon, entrepreneurs "lie in wait in and around government with their solutions [already] in hand," waiting for problems to "float by to which they can attach their solutions, waiting for a development in the political stream they can use to their advantage" (1984, p. 165). What emerges on the national policy agenda, therefore, can be viewed as a product of the mix of metaphorical "trash" that is already floating in the individual streams of the governmental garbage can at the precise moment at which a policy entrepreneur successfully marries the separate flows of activity. Some considerable degree of pattern can be found in the forces that guide developments at the level of the individual streams, whereas arbitrariness and unpredictability characterize the manner in which these streams converge, catapulting issues onto the government's decision agenda.

In summarizing the complexity of the forces at work in his model, Kingdon (in a close paraphrase of Cohen, March, & Olsen, 1972) characterized agenda setting at the U.S. national level as a collection of choices looking for issues, problems looking for decision situations in which they can be aired, solutions looking for problems to which they might credibly provide an answer, and politicians looking for pet problems or policies with which they may advance their careers.

This distinctive feature of the multiple-streams framework—an emphasis placed on contingency, rather than certainty; volatility, instead of stableness—broke with dominant conceptions about the nature of policy formation in the United States. Whereas the "muddling through" of policy *incrementalism* (Lindblom, 1965) comfortably rested on the bedrocks of gradualism and marginal adjustment, Kingdon's model envisioned a policy climate preternaturally prone to rapid, sometimes unpredictable, changes.

Likewise, the multiple-streams framework also challenged the precepts of rationalism, by rejecting both the linearity and strict, means-end hierarchies of the rational-comprehensive approach to policy formation. After all, in the universe of the metaphorical garbage can, any problem, under the right conditions, can become "the right solution" for the issue at hand—sometimes, solutions indeed may precede the problems to which they eventually will become attached (McLendon, 2003a).

Since its publication, the multiple-streams framework has been lauded on a number of grounds. Some observers have praised Kingdon's efforts as having helped upend the prominence of so-called black-box models of policy formation of the kind David Easton's (1965) work popularized. To these parties, Kingdon's scholarship is noteworthy in the degree that it endeavors to explain the processes of policy *conversion* (e.g., Zahariadis, 1999), rather than merely describe the inputs and outputs of policy systems. Additionally, the multiple-streams framework received acclaim for its use of an eclectic, rigorous set of research methods in pursuit of shedding light on a phenomenon (i.e., agenda setting) widely regarded as patently messy. King (1994), for example, extolled Kingdon for his having deployed an innovative research design of panel interviews, policy histories, and case studies, alongside a sophisticated system of content coding for data analysis.

Criticisms of the multiple-streams model likewise exist. For example, some observers have questioned whether the purportedly separate streams of problems, policies, and politics could operate more *interdependently* than independently, thus rendering the model conceptually unworkable (e.g., Robinson & Eller, 2010). Second, the lack of precision in explaining how "policy windows" open, operate, and close leaves an essential component of the framework poorly articulated. Finally, some scholars argue that the framework is more a descriptive device than a predictive one, limiting its usefulness overall (e.g., Durant & Diehl, 1989; King, 1994; Mucciaroni, 1992; Sabatier, 1991; Zahariadis, 1999). In a series of subsequent writings, Kingdon (1994, 1995) responded to a number of these stated concerns.

Another problem, however, has long persisted. Although the multiple-streams model remains one of the most widely cited policy theories in existence—indeed, it influenced the development of other contemporary theories, such as *punctuated equilibrium* and *advocacy coalition*, discussed later in this chapter—too little research has systematically evaluated the model's external validity. This incongruence, between the apparent popularity of Kingdon's formulation and the frequency with which it has been systematically studied, could be attributable to the model's innate complexity or, as some critics contend, to its imprecision; multiple streams provides too few testable propositions, these observers claim.

A modest number of studies have examined the framework's explanatory power at both the U.S. national and state levels. Analysts have applied the framework in the arenas of health care policy, environmental policy, and national defense policy (e.g., Blaukenau, 2001; Durant & Diehl, 1989; Kamieniecki, 2000; Kawar, 1989; Lindquist et al., 2010; Oliver, 1991). The multiple-streams framework has also been studied systematically in research on policy development internationally, particularly in Western Europe and the European Union (e.g., Ackrill & Kay, 2011; Peters, 1994; Pollack, 1997; Zahariadis & Allen, 1995).

Scholarly treatment of the multiple-streams framework in the fields of education and higher education has grown in recent years. McLendon (2003a) first systematically evaluated the applicability of the framework (in tandem with other theories) for higher education with his comparative-state analysis of governance reforms for postsecondary education. A series of like analyses followed, each entailing interviews, document analysis, and case studies of the formation of state-level policy change for higher education (e.g., Larson, 2004; Leslie & Berdahl, 2008; Leslie & Novak, 2003; Mills, 2007; Ness, 2008, 2010; Ness & Minestra, 2009, 2010; Protopsaltis, 2004). Across these studies, of which many examined the formation of policy agendas to reorganize statewide governance of higher education, one finds discernible evidence of the multiple-streams model's explanatory power, even when competing explanations are rigorously considered.

Ness' (e.g., 2008, 2010; Ness and Minestra, 2009, 2010) research program stands as a particularly insightful undertaking. With large numbers of elite interviews, Ness applied the multiple-streams model to cases of policy formation surrounding governments' decisions to establish broad-based, merit aid programs in a handful of (mainly Southern) states. His findings suggest the usefulness of the multiple-streams approach in explaining the programs' emergence; yet they also point to the need for further conceptual elaboration, principally around the operation of policy windows and the role of research and information in helping shape state policy behavior.

Several analysts of K-12 education policy making also have found the framework capable of explaining state policy change in that sector (e.g., McDermott, 2005; Portz, 1996; Stout & Stevens, 2000). McDermott's (2005) analysis of the adoption in Massachusetts of policies providing for alternative certification and pay incentives for teachers is one such example.

Punctuated Equilibrium Framework

"Punctuated equilibrium" has become a widely recognized phrase in the years since paleontologists Niles Eldredge and Stephen Jay Gould coined it (1972). With it, Eldredge and Gould challenged the Darwinian model of phyletic gradualism that had dominated evolutionary theory throughout much of the 20th century. Rather, punctuated equilibrium—known hereafter as "PE"—portrays evolutionary change as taking place over long periods of "stasis," during which species remain virtually unchanged, punctuated by relatively brief periods of intense change when new species are introduced, old ones die out, and existing ones undergo sudden transformations. In his massive text on evolutionary theory, Gould writes: "Punctuated equilibrium addresses the origin and deployment of species in geological time. . . . As a central proposition, [it] holds that the great majority of species . . . originate in geological moments (punctuations) and then persist in stasis throughout their long durations" (2002, pp. 765–766).

In the 1990s, ideas similar to these emerged in political science as a way theorists and analysts sought to explain policy change in American governmental systems. Scholars had grown increasingly dissatisfied with incrementalism, then the leading paradigm for understanding policy making in democratic systems (Prindle, 2012). In the place of policy or budgetary incrementalism, some analysts turned instead to notions such as those found in PE, ones better suited, it seemed, to explain the simultaneous influence of stability and change in public policy formation in the United States (Kelly, 1984). Indeed, PE now stands as one of political science's leading models of policy change, a development attributable largely to the pioneering work of Frank Baumgartner and Bryan Jones (1991, 1993).

Baumgartner and Jones contend that many areas of U.S. policy making exhibit long periods of "relative gridlock" interspersed by brief episodes of "dramatic change" (1991, p. 1). Drawing on the case of civilian nuclear policy in the post–World War II era, they argue that public attention at any given moment tends to focus narrowly on one aspect of an issue to the exclusion of others, but that, over time, public attention can shift from "virtual euphoria" (over a particular policy image) to "an equally one-sided preoccupation with negative aspects of the same policy or industry" (Baumgartner & Jones, 1991, p. 1046). Their punctuated equilibrium formulation seeks to account for this phenomenon and for the manner in which it unfolds.

The PE model contends that policies tend to be processed quietly within "policy subsystems," but occasionally attract considerable attention when struggles are played out on the "macropolitical" agenda. Periods of equilibrium in policy making are those spans in time when issues become captured by a subsystem of policy actors and issue experts and "policy monopolies" take hold. Periods of disequilibrium, by contrast, occur when policy monopolies are challenged or overthrown and issues are thrust into the macropolitical arena. At the heart of PE's explanation of this process reside the twin notions of policy *venues* and *images* and their intersection.

A policy monopoly consists of a "definable institutional structure," a venue in which advocacy and conflict over the policy occurs, and a "powerful supporting image." Venues exist in many forms and can include, for example, federal agencies, state and local authorities, interest groups, professional associations, the open market, and various other institutions. When a venue involves government, it is known as a policy subsystem. Policy subsystems tend to be closed, dominated by small groups of issue specialists in the government bureaucracy, congressional committees and subcommittees, and interest groups that operate away from the public eye. Over time, policy subsystems, when reinforced with a powerful supporting image, can evolve into policy monopolies. Such monopolies tend to induce only support among those involved, or indifference by those not involved. Once established, policy monopolies can endure for long periods of time, decades even.

Only when issues move from isolated policy subsystems arenas into the macropolitical arena can large-scale policy change occur, write Baumgartner and Jones (1993). Precisely how does such change happen? The "venue shopping" efforts of strategically minded political actors play a crucial role.

Because the American political system is replete with policy venues, disadvantaged issue advocates may find multiple sites at which to attempt to gain (or regain) control of a policy. These advocates "shop" for new venues in which political actors and governmental institutions different than those that currently monopolize an issue can claim jurisdiction over the issue. Advocates do so by formulating new ways of understanding old problems. As policy images become redefined, new participants are drawn to the emerging debate, thus different venues surface as legitimate arenas for issue deliberation. Soon, macropolitical institutions begin to intervene as national institutions "grapple with [the issue] and with each other in an effort to resolve the new 'hot' issue" (True, Jones, & Baumgartner, 1999, p. 102).

These processes also can become reinforcing: "as venues change, images may change as well; as the image of a policy changes, venue changes [also] become more likely" (Baumgartner & Jones, 1991, pp. 1046–1047). These shifts in policy image and policy venue result in the disintegration of an existing policy monopoly; policy ownership begins to change hands. Substantial bursts of new policy activity follow and, over time, the system returns to a steady state, as interests that had been marginalized become newly institutionalized, a development that can result in a policy's re-monopolization.

Since the mid-1990s, researchers have applied PE to a variety of political phenomena across a number of substantive policy domains. For example, in an application of the theory to voting and elections, Kelly (1994) draws comparisons between the PE cycle and eras of divided government in the United States. He reasons that the American political cycle, consisting of stasis that occasionally is interrupted by "compressed periods of rapid transformation" surrounding presidential elections, essentially adheres to the principles of PE. He describes several notable punctuations in American political history, ranging from the Jacksonian period (1824) to the New Deal era (1930–1932). Changes in the nature of divided government, Kelly concludes, occur very much in line with the principles of PE.

The domain in which punctuated equilibrium has been applied most frequently is that of public finance and budgeting. Policy scholars have studied many aspects of governmental budgeting using the PE framework (e.g., Breunig, Koski, & Mortensen, 2010; Ryu, 2009; True, Jones, & Baumgartner, 2007). One reason for this seems to be that scholars have access to high-quality data on budgeting at the national, state, and local levels of American government (Breunig & Koski, 2012).

For instance, in an application of PE to public-sector economics, Jordan (2003) examined the model's suitability for explaining variation in local government budget expenditures. She points to the many opportunities for nonincremental change that exist within local government budgeting as evidence of "punctuations" in the arena. She further draws a connection between the observed rhythm of the budget process and the hypothesized nature of policy change as embodied in punctuated equilibrium, concluding that the model indeed affords a firm theoretical foundation for large budget shifts.

In a more recent application, Breunig and Koski (2012) extend PE to state-level spending, analyzing state expenditures across all 50 states in specific budgetary categories (e.g., education, highways, parks) from 1984 to 2009. The authors used the descriptive statistic, L-kurtosis, to assess the magnitude of "punctuations" in state budgets. The statistic is particularly well suited for this purpose, they claim, because it measures the extent to which distributions possess the "high peaks," "narrow shoulders," and "fat tails" indicative of patterns in which incremental budgetary changes occasionally undergo larger-than-expected increases—that is, punctuations.[5] The authors find significant variation in the degree of punctuation in state spending overall, as well as in spending by budgetary category. For instance, education spending exhibited the least amount of punctuation in state spending among the ten budget categories examined. Breunig and Koski argue that the observed fluctuations across budget categories may result from variation in the levels of attention policy makers pay to a given issue or issue domain. Expenditures for categories with a high level of perceived importance (and which are, in some cases, federally mandated) are less likely to see fluctuations than budget categories with less universal support, the authors surmise.

In a recent flourish of research activity around PE, *Policy Studies Journal* in 2012 published a collection of papers examining the theory and its application to policy development both in the United States and internationally. Included in the collection are an event history analysis of the role of media attention on policy formation (Wolfe, 2012); a conceptual exploration of PE's potential in accounting for the spread of policy innovations (Boushey, 2012); a historical analysis of presidential issue attention and presidential policy tools, using PE as an explanatory lens (Larsen-Price, 2012); a historical analysis of agricultural policy, examining media attention, pre-legislative activity, and committee hearings dealing with agriculture from the 1930s to 2000, in an effort to explain the discriminatory practices of the USDA against African American farmers (Worsham & Stores, 2012); a content analysis of shifts in the policy agenda of the European Council from 1975 to 2010 (Alexandrova, Carammia, & Timmermans, 2012); and a historical analysis of policy punctuations in the United Kingdom (John & Bevan, 2012). Indeed, applications of PE to policy making in non-U.S. policy settings, particularly in the European Union and in Western European nations, have grown in number over the past decade.

Research on PE's application to educational policy making, however, trails that in other policy domains, although a few such analyses exist. In a series of applications of PE to education policy formation, Miskel and colleagues (Sims & Miskel, 2001, 2003) find strong support for the PE framework in explaining the emergence of children and adult literacy policies at the U.S. national level. Using content analysis, these authors measured changes in the images of literacy conveyed by various national media, and tracked the introduction of major reading legislation across policy venues at the national level over a period of nearly 30 years. They interpret their findings as lending support for one key tenet of PE: as policy images change, advocates attempt to find new policy venues that are more suitable to their desired ends, and the locus of policy activity within a given policy domain shifts accordingly.

Robinson (2004) utilized PE in analyzing instructional spending per pupil among schools of varying levels of bureaucratization. He found that more bureaucratized school systems do a better job in adjusting their expenditures to fiscal realities than do less bureaucratic ones, possibly because bureaucracy enhances the acquisition and processing of information. Additionally, he concluded that the cycle of expenditure management in schools bears a strong resemblance to the vicissitudes of the PE cycle.

In an application of PE to school choice policy development, Lacireno-Paquet and Holyoke examined the evolution of charter school policies in Michigan and Washington, DC. The authors argue that charter school policy is an instance of punctuated equilibrium because "it was a sign of new interest groups, such as the business community and conservative interests, emerging and achieving a powerful foothold in education policy," as well as a new conception of public education (2007, p. 189).

The authors seek to determine if policy reforms that result from punctuations endure or if there is evidence of resistance and reversion. The authors find that in Michigan, where there were two strong sides in the debate, the policy was limited in its scope and application. Conversely, in Washington, where there was substantially less resistance to the policy punctuation, the new policy became more encompassing, and flourishes.

Fewer applications of PE can be found in the research literature on higher education (e.g., McLendon, 2001; Orr-Bement, 2002). In one rigorous undertaking, Orr-Bement (2002) applied the Baumgartner and Jones framework in analyzing legislative decision making for higher education in the state of Washington. She deployed content analysis in examining some 3,600 bills passed by the Washington state legislature between 1977 and 1998, of which 346 bills pertained to higher education. Her analysis of the trend data yielded strong support for the PE model: higher education legislation during the period exhibited patterns of stability, punctuated by brief bursts of change, as legislative attention shifted from higher education to other issues. Rigorous applications of PE to higher education policy formation, however, remain rare.

Advocacy Coalition Framework

The advocacy coalition framework (ACF) is a model of the policy process that focuses on the interactions of competing advocacy coalitions within policy subsystems. Introduced by Paul Sabatier and Hank Jenkins-Smith in the late 1980s, the ACF is a framework for examining learning and change that occurs within a policy subsystem over a relatively long period of time, usually a decade or more (Jenkins-Smith & Sabatier, 1994; Sabatier, 1988; Sabatier & Jenkins-Smith, 1993). In the years since its initial formulation, the ACF has undergone extensive modification and revision, and today includes several important additions to the original theory (Sabatier & Weible, 2007; Weible, Sabatier, & McQueen, 2009).

Three core elements of the ACF model are policy subsystems, a three-tiered belief system, and advocacy coalitions. First, policy subsystems, organized around particular policy problems, are the prime unit of analysis within the ACF model. The model assumes that policy actors must specialize within a policy subsystem in order to understand the complexities of a topic and produce change. The behavior of actors within subsystems is affected by two sets of external factors in the broader political environment: stable factors, such as fundamental values and constitutional structures, which influence the constraints and resources of subsystem actors; and dynamic factors, such as public opinion and socioeconomic conditions, which are susceptible to substantial change and therefore are important for bringing about policy change within a subsystem (Sabatier & Weible, 2007).

Second is an embedded assumption within the ACF that beliefs drive political behavior. Indeed, among major contemporary policy theories, the ACF places the heaviest emphasis on the values and belief structures of policy makers. The theory identifies a three-tiered hierarchical structure of beliefs: deep core beliefs, policy core beliefs, and secondary beliefs. At the highest level are deep core beliefs, which are the broadest and most stable in the system. Deep core beliefs involve "very general normative and onto-logical assumptions about human nature" (Sabatier & Weible, 2007, p. 194).

Next in the hierarchy are policy core beliefs, which are applications of deep core beliefs to a policy subsystem. The final level consists of secondary beliefs, which are narrower in scope than policy core beliefs and more susceptible to change than either deep core or policy core beliefs. According to ACF theorists, beliefs interact with information in important ways to create policy change. Specifically, policy actors' beliefs serve as filters of received information. Information supporting actors' beliefs is more readily incor-porated into the body of knowledge held by members of a coalition than information contradicting those beliefs, which is resisted. In some few instances, information can also alter actors' beliefs.

Finally, within a policy subsystem, policy actors attempt to achieve their policy objec-tives by seeking allies that have similar policy core beliefs. By creating networks and sharing resources with these allies, policy actors increase the likelihood of success in achieving their policy goals. When these policy actors engage in some degree of coor-dinated, collaborative work toward a policy objective, they are said to have formed an *advocacy coalition.*

Advocacy coalitions often comprise members from diverse stakeholder groups, including elected officials, interest group leaders, researchers, journalists, and others from governmental and private organizations (Jenkins-Smith & Sabatier, 1994). An advocacy coalition mobilizes resources and information to translate its beliefs into pol-icy designs. A policy subsystem will usually consist of a dominant advocacy coalition and one or more minority coalitions.

In an analysis of after-school programming policies in urban school districts, for example, Brecher, Brazill, Weitzman, and Silver (2010) identified two advocacy coalitions within an after-school programming subsystem that formed based on different policy core beliefs about the goal of these programs: an academic coalition that believed in and advocated for programs emphasizing academic achievement and a developmental coali-tion that believed in and advocated for programs promoting holistic youth development.

According to the ACF, policy participants are influenced to form coalitions in response to "the devil shift," a term used to describe policy participants' tendency to perceive oppo-nents as stronger and more threatening than they actually are. As a result of the devil shift, policy participants will perceive their adversaries as more influential in the policy subsystem and themselves as less influential, which leads to efforts to collaborate and pool resources with potential allies. The devil shift argument also hypothesizes that the amount of exaggeration of adversary influence is correlated with ideological distance. In other words, opponents with very different beliefs are likely to perceive adversaries as more "devilish" than adversaries whose beliefs are not as far apart (Sabatier, Hunter, & McLaughlin, 1987). Policy change occurs within a policy subsystem when coalitions of actors with similar beliefs succeed in translating these beliefs into policies.

In addition to policy subsystems, the hierarchical belief system, and advocacy coa-litions, the ACF model postulates four paths to belief and policy change. Two of these paths were described as part of the original theory: (1) policy-oriented learning and (2) shocks external to the policy subsystem (Sabatier & Jenkins-Smith, 1993). Two more paths were added in a later theoretical revision: (3) shocks internal to the policy sub-system and (4) negotiated agreements (Sabatier & Weible, 2007). Theorists contend that these four paths vary in their ability to change beliefs. Policy-oriented learning, for example, is more likely to change secondary beliefs than deep core beliefs or policy core beliefs. External and internal shocks, on the other hand, may alter policy core beliefs.

The ACF was originally applied to environmental and energy policy in the United States, and the majority of subsequent ACF applications have been focused in these areas. In a review of applications of the ACF, however, Weible, Sabatier, and McQueen (2009) observe that in the years since it was introduced, the ACF has been applied to social, economic, and health policy areas. As is the case with other theories we have surveyed, the theory has also gradually been applied to policy making outside the United States, particularly in Europe.

The ACF is now firmly established as a valid research program. Analysts have applied the ACF to various policy domains, including drug policy, water policy, nuclear policy, forest policy, land use, and health care (Sabatier & Weible, 2007). As we noted, there have also been several theoretical revisions since the framework was first introduced (Jones & Jenkins-Smith, 2009; Sabatier & Jenkins-Smith, 1999; Sabatier & Weible, 2007) and the framework remains a subject of considerable debate. Additionally, although one assumption of the ACF is that research on policy subsystems and policy change should take a long-term perspective of a decade or more, the ACF has been applied to a range of time perspectives, from one year or less (Henry, 2011; Matti & Sandstrom, 2011) to 200 years (Albright, 2011).

Critics have argued that the ACF does not adequately address potentially conflicting individual interests within a coalition (Schlager & Blomquist, 1996); that the framework's assumptions may not be applicable to political systems outside the United States, including less democratic societies and developing countries (Sabatier & Weible, 2007); and that the framework does not provide sufficient evidence that policy participants with shared beliefs actually do form coalitions in which actors coordinate their behavior (Schlager, 1995). Sabatier and colleagues have responded to these criticisms in subsequent modifications to the framework.

The ACF's application to educational policy making has been limited. One application of the ACF to education policy studied the networks present in the school reform movement in Oakland, California (Ansell, Reckhow, & Kelly, 2009). The authors interviewed school district stakeholders and employed social network analysis to identify challenges to building coalitions in urban education policy. They found that a highly centralized, cohesive group of actors in the district formed a strong advocacy coalition with shared beliefs about school reform.

Yet this coalition did not include many key district stakeholders, whose beliefs did not fully align with the coalition, thus threatening the ability of the coalition to achieve and sustain policy change. They note that narrow coalitions, which are likely to have greater homogeneity in beliefs than broader coalitions, may not be broad enough to bring about policy change and argue that outreach and agenda expansion strategies may expand coalition support.

In another application of the ACF to education policy, Mintrom and Vergari (1996) studied education policy change in Michigan. The authors examined the 1993 abolition of local property taxes as a source of school funding. Using the ACF model, the authors identified a dominant coalition with the core belief that the established system of public education could adequately address existing problems in education and, therefore, sought to maintain the status quo.

Conversely, a minority coalition consisting of members of the business community and grassroots organizations had a core belief that the established system could not adequately address problems in education and that market-based reforms—notably, legislation enabling charter schools—were needed. The funding crisis, an external shock to the school reform policy subsystem, provided the minority coalition with a path to policy change. The authors conclude that the ACF is a useful framework for understanding the process of educational policy change.

In an application to higher education policy making, Beverwijk, Goedegebuure, and Huisman (2008) studied policy change in the Mozambican higher education system. By analyzing policy developments over a ten-year period, the authors sought to determine the applicability of the ACF to developing countries. The authors used participant observations, interviews, and document analysis to study policy change between 1993 and 2003 and found that major policy change in the higher education subsystem occurred more frequently than is predicted by the ACF. The authors conclude that the ACF needs to be refined to adequately account for the process of policy change in developing countries. Detailed analyses of the ACF, as applied to policy change for higher education in the United States, are few.

Policy Innovation and Diffusion Theory

The policy innovation and diffusion framework is the most widely studied, tested, and elaborated of the four policy theories we survey. Indeed, today it stands as a leading framework for studying policy change across many substantive domains. Both the conceptual underpinnings and empirical applications of policy innovation and diffusion (PID) have improved with time, although questions—and criticisms—linger with respect to the model's internal coherence. Unlike some of the other areas of contemporary policy theory, PID researchers have extensively applied the framework in the domain of education policy.

A convention long ago emerged in political science (and in numerous policy fields), defining a policy *innovation* as a policy that is new to the jurisdiction adopting it, without regard to the number of other states that may already have adopted the policy (Berry & Berry, 1990; Gray, 1994; Walker, 1969). In so doing, innovation is differentiated from *invention*, or the process through which original policy ideas are conceived. Innovation *diffusion* is the process by which a public policy or program (an innovation) spreads among the members of a social system, most frequently understood to mean the governments of the 50 American states (McLendon, 2003b), although a large volume of literature has arisen around the study of policy innovation and diffusion at other levels of U.S. government (e.g., Clarke et al., 1999; Samuels & Glantz, 1991) and in across-national contexts (e.g., Collier & Messick, 1975; Dolowitz & Marsh, 1996).

Much of the theory and research that exists on policy innovation and diffusion has its origins in the fields of anthropology, rural sociology, and mass communications. Indeed, diffusion studies in those fields constitute the oldest of the diffusion research traditions. Beginning in the 1920s, scholars in these areas mainly used participant observation to study the transfer of technological innovations. The early work emphasized the importance of culture on the success and the rate of diffusion within and across adopting units. Since that time, diffusion research itself has spread to virtually every other discipline and field within the social sciences, and beyond. The distinguishing feature of much of the scholarship conducted in the political and policy sciences is the focus on governments as units of analysis and on sources of variation (across both space and time) in governments' adoption of new policies and programs.

Since political scientist Jack Walker's pioneering work in 1969, interest and research on state policy innovation have exploded, although certain methodological improvements of the past 20 years have vastly improved the empirical foundations of this line of scholarship. Historically, researchers pursued two distinct tracks of scholarship into state policy innovation and diffusion, one focusing on *intrastate* determinants of the phenomenon and a second explanation examining *interstate* determinants. Since the early 1990s, a third, synthetic approach, which combines elements of the earlier models, has emerged as paradigmatic.

The *internal determinants* explanation argues that state governments innovate when their political, economic, and social environments are favorable (Gray, 1994). Researchers have found that adoption is generally faster among (1) larger, wealthier states; (2) among states with more electoral competition, higher turnover in political office, and more professionalized legislatures; and (3) among states with more urban and educated citizenries (Berry & Berry, 1990; Morgan & Watson, 1991; Walker, 1969). A critical assumption of this type of model is that states influence one another's policy behaviors in negligible ways.

By contrast, *interstate diffusion* explanations view policy innovation as intrinsically intergovernmental in nature; policies arise because states emulate the policy behaviors of their neighbors or peers (McLendon, 2003b, p. 113). Most such models treat geographically proximate neighbors as ones being likely to exert the strongest influence on a neighbor's policy behavior. In his landmark 1969 study, Walker documented regional patterns in policy adoption, characterizing state policy making as a "system of emulation" (p. 898) of regional, bellwether states. In his factor analyses of the adoption of more than 100 policies over time, certain states in each region of the United States emerged as opinion leaders. Once these opinion leaders adopted a new policy or program, Walker contended, other states in the region follow suit. Indeed, some states appeared to have copied, word for word, legislation adopted in a nearby state—typographical errors and all (Walker, 1969). Walker's early work, particularly his account of the underlying forces he believed had prompted states to emulate one another's policies, left a deep imprint on the direction of future research.

A third, synthetic approach arose largely from the work of William Berry and Frances Stokes Berry, whose studies in the early 1990s of the adoption and spread of new state lotteries and taxes (Berry & Berry, 1990, 1992, respectively) helped unite the two earlier, separate traditions. As pure models, Frances Stokes Berry later observed, "internal determinants explanations and diffusion explanations are deficient" because each model employed "single-explanation" methodologies shown to detect effects, when, in fact, none existed (1994, p. 443).

In their analyses of factors influencing state adoption of lotteries and new taxes Berry and Berry utilized a methodology newer to the social sciences—event history analysis (EHA), a regression-like technique applied to panel data. In studies using EHA, the dependent variable typically is dichotomous; in the context of the Berrys' research, for example, the outcome variable was whether a state adopted a new lottery or a new tax in a given year. The independent variables in EHA studies can include indicators of certain hypothesized influences, such as a state's sociodemographic (e.g., race/ethnicity, population distribution), economic (e.g., wealth, unemployment levels, etc.), and political (e.g., partisanship, electoral competition, ideology) composition. Crucially, the EHA can also include a variable indicating the past policy behavior of a state's neighbors, thereby accounting for the pressures on a given state to adopt other states' existing policies (i.e., diffusion).

The two early EHA studies by Berry and Berry netted a number of interesting findings, particularly with respect to the influence of state-to-state diffusion. In their study of state lotteries, Berry and Berry concluded that if the "fiscal health [of a state] remains moderate and it is an election year, the effect of previously adopting neighbors on the likelihood of adoption is stronger" (1990, p. 420). Their analysis of tax innovations yielded similar evidence of both internal and diffusion influences on policy adoption (Berry & Berry, 1992). In that study, a tax hike was found to be more likely among states with longer periods between elections, among ones where there existed a fiscal crisis, and among ones whose neighbors recently had increased taxes. Overall, these early studies seemed to suggest that the policy behaviors of bordering states, rather than noncontiguous ones, had exerted a stronger effect on the likelihood of a state innovating.

Why, precisely, policy makers in a given state might be influenced by the policy choices of those in other states remains a contested question. Several explanations exist. Two of the most common ones point to economic competition and policy learning (Berry & Baybeck, 2006; Boehmke & Witmer, 2004; Walker, 1969).

According to the first rationale, state policy makers make policy choices to gain an economic advantage or avoid a disadvantage over other states (Dye, 1990; Ingle, Cohen-Vogel, & Hughes, 2007; Walker, 1969). During this process of competition, officials may "feel pressure to enact a policy that exists elsewhere because it affects their state's relative attractiveness" (Karch, 2007, p. 55). Specifically, states may compete for private investment because it promises to bring more jobs and tax revenue (Bailey & Rom, 2004; Berry & Baybeck, 2005; Saiz & Clarke, 2013). Additionally, states may compete to repel "undesirables." Peterson and Rom (1990); Berry, Fording, and Hanson (2003); and Allard and Danziger (2000), for example, speak of a "race to the bottom" in state welfare policy making. According to Karch, "the logic here is straightforward: If a state has more generous welfare programs than its neighbor, it may attract welfare recipients from that neighbor. As a result, the adoption of more stringent welfare-related policies in one state can cause its neighbors to follow suit"(2007, p. 62).

According to the second rationale, state officials take cues from one another in an attempt to simplify the range of alternatives from which they can choose. Such cue taking, what Mooney and Lee (1995) called "policy learning," reduces political risk by turning to solutions that have proven successful somewhere else (Simon, 1997). Policy learning among the American states has been found to be facilitated by supra-state organizations (e.g., the Council of State Governments) and networks (Balla, 2001; Cohen-Vogel et al., 2008; Ingle et al., 2007).

Indeed, a key component of the mission statements of various national organizations is the diffusion of information to policy makers, something these organizations do by publishing reports and hosting conferences that encourage the development and strengthening of professional networks (Karch, 2007; Rich, 2004). Policy entrepreneurs also serve as information conduits and facilitate the learning process (Mintrom & Vergari, 1996).

In the view of those who take a policy learning approach, very few states are willing to adopt a new policy in the first years of diffusion because they have not yet had the time to learn about the consequences of such a decision. How then do we explain cases of rapid diffusion? Recently, one study investigated instances where policies diffuse very rapidly rather than in the familiar S-shaped pattern that can easily be reconciled with a policy learning explanation. Nicholson-Crotty analyzed 57 policies, finding evidence that policy characteristics may help explain the likelihood of rapid diffusion. In particular, the author showed that "the salience and complexity of an issue condition lawmakers' willingness to discount long-term consequences in favor of short-term electoral gain and, thus, to forgo policy learning in favor of immediate adoption" (2009, p. 192). Other studies, including one of states' adoption of the Common Core State Standards, show that rapid diffusion can also be conditioned by federal fiscal incentives, especially in lean budget years (Allen, Pettus, & Haider-Markel, 2004; LaVenia, Cohen-Vogel, & Lang, 2011).

Other scholars too have suggested that a policy learning explanation may oversimplify the reasons for state policy adoption. Volden, Ting, and Carpenter, for example, argue that much of the research seen as evidence of policy diffusion "could have arisen through independent actions of states that confront common problems at about the same time and only learn from their own experiences" (2008, p. 329). In short, many of the policy phenomena held up as examples of policy learning may in fact simply reflect the individual decisions of independent adopters. The authors do not suggest "that policy learning is absent from the decision-making processes of politicians and bureaucrats" but, instead, that scholars should redirect their "efforts toward providing evidence that distinguishes between policy diffusion and myopic choice" (p. 327). They call for studies that "focus on policy success, on conditional patterns of policy maintenance and longevity, on policy abandonment, and on free-riding behavior" (p. 329).

Several other critiques of the policy innovation and diffusion framework have surfaced, among them concerns that the research is limited because it (1) focuses on the correlates of policy *adoption,* while ignoring other stages in the policy life cycle, and (2) emphasizes a positive regional effect, whereas, in fact, empirical evidence for diffusion is questionable (McLendon, Hearn, & Deaton, 2006; Mintrom & Vergari, 1998; Mooney, 2001). With respect to the former criticism, it is indeed the case that state policy diffusion research traditionally has focused on factors leading states to adopt altogether new policies (i.e., enactment), rather than on forces shaping problem identification, agenda formation, implementation, or policy termination.

Two efforts intended to remedy this limitation bear mentioning. Through interviews with state policy makers, Cohen-Vogel and Ingle (2007) concluded that the influence of neighboring states is most pronounced during the agenda setting and proposal formulation stages, and least pronounced during the adoption stage. Cohen-Vogel and Ingle found evidence that policy entrepreneurs, working across state lines, attempt to build awareness about problems and then link those problems with particular solutions. The authors found little to suggest that policy makers in nearby states borrowed political strategies from one another in an effort to build support (or opposition) for a given policy.

A study by Mintrom and Vergari (1998) also examined diffusion pressures at various stages of the policy-making process with respect to charter school legislation. In exploring the role that policy networks—and policy entrepreneurs within them—play in the diffusion of policy innovations, the authors found that external networks of advocates from other states increased the likelihood of legislative consideration, yet did not affect the likelihood of legislative approval. External networks can be a source of new ideas, but may lose significance as state policy makers attempt to secure legislative approval. To ensure approval, policy makers instead turn inward and rely on their own knowledge of local context and intrastate politics.

Another critique of policy diffusion research contends that state policy scholars have emphasized a positive diffusion effect, even though evidence for such an effect is mixed (e.g., Lutz, 1987; Mooney, 2001). In fact, Mooney (2001) reported that only half of the 24 EHA models reported in studies of state policy diffusion and published during the 1990s in top-tier political science journals contained positively and statistically significant coefficients indicating a regional diffusion effect. Mooney attributes, in part, the positive bias to methodological flaws in much of the early EHA modeling. By failing to account for temporal dependence, many early models of state policy innovation and diffusion produced spurious diffusion results.

Methodological improvements since that time—including the use of annual dummy and time-trend variables, the introduction of spline techniques, and, most important, increasing use of the Cox Proportional Hazards model—have corrected for these early design flaws. With these recent methodological improvements, event history analysis has become the dominant analytic approach for use in studying policy innovation and diffusion in the states (e.g., Box-Steffensmeier & Jones, 2004; McLendon et al., 2006).

Only recently has a robust research program focusing on state-level policy innovation and diffusion arisen in the arena of state education policy.[6] Most of the works on K-12 education, launched in the wake of the frenzied school reform movement in the United States, examine the conditions that are associated with the introduction of school choice initiatives in the states (Karch, 2010; Mintrom, 1997; Mintrom & Vergari, 1998; Wong & Langevin, 2006; Wong & Shen, 2002). For example, Wong and Langevin (2006) conducted an event history analysis of the influence of social, economic, political, and interstate diffusion factors on state passage of charter school laws. They found statistically significant evidence for the influence of partisan gubernatorial control (Republican), classroom spending (negative), minority legislative representation (positive), and the percentage of private school enrollments in states (positive). They found, however, no evidence of a diffusion effect.

As noted, Mintrom (1997) melded event history analysis with surveys of state officials to ascertain the influence of "policy entrepreneurs" in the spread of school choice policies. Mintrom found the likelihood of adoption of these initiatives to be higher in states with the following characteristics: larger percentages of students enrolled in private schools; looming statewide elections; weaker unions; and poorer student test score performance, relative to national norms. He also found adoption more likely in states where policy entrepreneurs had helped facilitate passage of the laws. In addition to these within-state factors, Mintrom found evidence of state-to-state diffusion: states with a larger proportion of neighbors that had already adopted a given policy were more likely themselves to adopt.

Research into policy innovation and diffusion in higher education evolved later than it did in the field of K-12 education studies, yet has recently gained strong momentum. Hearn and Griswold's (1994) study was one of the first systematic empirical works to delve into the influences on state-level policy innovation in postsecondary education. These analysts used multivariate regression and a cross-sectional research design to test a variety of hypotheses, which they had distilled mainly from the field of organization theory, about state policy innovation in such areas as college savings bonds and prepaid tuition plans, mandated assessments of undergraduate students, and alternative licensure for K-12 teachers.

Hearn and Griswold found evidence indicating that governance structure, along with population size, levels of wealth and postsecondary enrollment, and regional variation, appears to influence a state's propensity to innovate, although the relationships varied across the six polities the authors studied and the directions of the patterns were not always consistent with the hypotheses.

The longest-sustained line of scholarship around policy innovation and diffusion in higher education—that by McLendon and colleagues—adheres closely to the conceptual scaffolding of Walker (1969), Berry and Berry (1990), and other political scientists. This line of work has relied primarily on EHA in analyzing the rise and spread of new state policies in the areas of postsecondary accountability, governance, and finance (e.g., Doyle, McLendon, & Hearn, 2010; Hearn, McLendon, & Lacy, 2013; Hearn, McLendon, & Mokher, 2008; McLendon, Deaton, & Hearn, 2007; McLendon et al., 2006; McLendon, Heller, & Young 2005; Mokher & McLendon, 2009).

For example, in the field's first application of EHA to state policy adoption in higher education, McLendon, Hearn, and Deaton (2006) found Republican legislative strength and centralized governance structures for postsecondary education to have exerted a statistically significant influence on the probability of state adoption of new performance funding policies. Hearn, McLendon, and Mokher (2008) deployed EHA in analyzing passage of state student unit-record systems, while Mokher and McLendon (2009) conducted an EHA study into the determinants of state adoption of dual-enrollment programs.

A series of studies by Cohen-Vogel and colleagues has used qualitative approaches to explore the mechanisms of policy diffusion, interviewing policy makers and other policy "elites" about the adoption of merit-based funding programs in higher education (e.g., Cohen-Vogel et al., 2008; Cohen-Vogel & Ingle, 2007; Ingle et al., 2007). They found evidence for what they termed the "3 Cs" of diffusion—that convenience, coalitions, and competition among states for high-performing students explained whether and when a state adopted a merit aid program.

VIEWING FUTURE RESEARCH ON EDUCATION POLICY CHANGE THROUGH THE FOUR LENSES

Although a subfield devoted to the analysis of politics and public policy long ago arose in the K-12 research arena, and one such has recently emerged in higher education studies, too little research has analyzed education policy making and policy change in the American states. In this chapter's final section, we explore how each of the four policy theories can be productively deployed in shedding new research light onto state policy making for K-12 and higher education.

Viewing K-12 and Higher Education Policy Change through a Multiple-Streams Lens

Thirty years since its emergence in the political science literature, the multiple-streams framework remains a highly distinctive explanation of policy change. By inviting the analyst to conceptualize governmental decision making as subject to the same forces as arise in organizational "garbage cans," the multiple-streams framework has challenged once conventional assumptions that policy change in education necessarily must unfold incrementally or rationally. Instead, the multiple-streams model focuses the analyst's attention on occasional intersections of presumably unrelated—or, only marginally related—sets of developments, involving (1) the availability of solutions at a given moment, (2) policy makers' awareness of problems, and (3) political contingency.

The multiple-streams framework contends that education policy change is most likely to occur when policy solutions already in the open become linked with problems of emergent concern to politicians during moments of political volatility. Many different policy ideas can serve as "answers" to different kinds of problems, even those the problem was never intended to address—the only requirement being that a potential solution must satisfy an entrepreneur's parochial interests. Because of this residual randomness, virtually any solution can become bound up with a given problem; almost anything, the model contends, can conceivably be related to almost anything else—and in unexpected ways.

Despite the growing number of studies that have applied multiple streams in K-12 and higher education policy settings, questions persist about the model and its utility. For example, it remains unclear why policy windows open at the times they do. Precisely what combination of factors and actors "converge" to enable the opening of policy windows of opportunity? And how do policy windows in the education domain function differently than political windows of the kind Kingdon conceptualized, occurring in other policy domains?

Additionally, how does the content of a possible solution influence the solution's credibility, when policy entrepreneurs make choices among different (indeed competing) alternatives? To paraphrase Kingdon on this point, what are the criteria that elevate some of the available solutions up out of the "primeval policy soup" of the education community, while consigning others to continued floating? In what specific ways do policy entrepreneurs facilitate education policy change? Scant research has inventoried, much less elucidated, the roles entrepreneurs play in defining educational problems, identifying solutions, and positioning issues on the state policy agenda.

How and where do interest groups fit in? Kingdon's original formulation viewed interest groups as serving primarily to "soften up" the political system. Might not the roles of interest groups in state-level agenda setting differ from those of groups operating at the national level? In the states, the advent of term limits for elected officials, the waxing influence of national policy organizations (e.g., Complete College America) and large foundations (e.g., Gates and Lumina Foundations), and the emergence of issues of substantial technical complexity (e.g., value-added modeling in K-12 education or performance-based funding for higher education) may well be undermining the policy independence of elected officials, rendering them more reliant on outside groups (e.g., such as those listed earlier, as well as think tanks) at all stages of the policy process, particularly agenda setting. Each of the questions raised here represents gaps in our understanding of the multiple-streams model, and signals interesting conceptual directions for future research.

Future research into education policy change using the multiple-streams lens would stand to benefit from several methods-related improvements. First, greater sophistication in study designs is needed. Multiple-streams scholarship on K-12 and higher education policy making has relied almost exclusively on case studies, whether of a single-case or a comparative-case design. This approach has yielded valuable perspectives, but other designs are warranted, now that descriptive and conceptual insights have accumulated. For instance, by studying multiple episodes in a given state over time, analysts could better assess the dynamics underpinning the opening and closing of policy windows under consistently similar structural conditions (e.g., demographic, economic development, and political patterns), yet meaningfully dissimilar contextual ones (e.g., across reform initiatives).

A greater diversity of data collection techniques also is warranted. To date, most research has utilized interviews and document analysis. Mintrom's (1997) study of the rise of charter school legislation in the states, however, points to the value of other kinds of data. He used mail surveys of state education experts, asking them to identify specific individuals who had advanced charter school proposals in their states (i.e., policy entrepreneurs) and to rate the importance of certain actions these individual had taken. Case studies are appealing, because they permit analysts to combine eclectic modes of in-depth field research (e.g., in-depth interviews, archival data, observations, etc.). Integrating insights derived from interviews and document analysis with ones gleaned from surveys conducted across a large number of states, however, would enable analysts to build richly textured accounts of how policy entrepreneurship (or other facets of the model) plays out episodically, while also gauging the range and prevalence of such phenomena in the education policy domain across state varied contexts.

Viewing K-12 and Higher Education Policy Change through a Punctuated Equilibrium Lens

The punctuated equilibrium framework holds considerable promise as a lens through which to understand education policy making and policy change in the states. By describing the conditions under which (1) issues become defined and, later, redefined, (2) policy agendas become institutionalized, and (3) prevailing policy images and venues become challenged and, in time, overturned, the PE framework provides both a plausible rationale for the rise and fall of education policies over time and conceptual and analytical constructs with which to study the phenomena. Future research could draw on the PE model in a number of ways.

First, analysts could study how the personal electoral interests of state legislators influence the transition in education policy from periods of stasis to ones of punctuation. To date, little research in the education arena has empirically assessed the relationship between legislators' electoral interests and their policy behaviors. By analyzing data on bill sponsorship, committee and floor votes, and bill sponsors' party affiliations and district characteristics, researchers could better discern how legislators' electoral interests shape policy changes over time (McLendon, Mokher, & Doyle, 2009).

Second, the PE framework points to the value of future research into policy venues. The existence of multiple policy venues is a foundational component of the PE framework because individuals and interests that are excluded from a policy monopoly must have other venues to which they can appeal. How do education reformers in the states bypass existing policy monopolies and how do alternative venues pay off in terms of advocacy success? One such alternative venue appears to be the statewide ballot, an arena of growing, if ill-understood, significance in education policy making (McLendon & Eddings, 2002). How do education advocates make strategic use of the availability of alternative policy venues when seeking to challenge existing monopolies from which they are disenfranchised?

Third, tracking the agenda status of education reform legislation across both chambers of state legislatures, rather than aggregating data for the legislature as a whole, would enable analysts to assess the relative suitability of upper and lower chambers of statehouses as venues for different kinds of education reform initiatives. Fourth, adding information on committee deliberations and floor debates would enable analysts to assess how advocates use political rhetoric and technical information in advancing policy change. Finally, with respect to research design, collecting information on bills introduced in a number of states, rather than data on bills enacted in a single state alone, would allow analysts to draw even stronger inferences about the conditions under which education reforms advance onto and recede from the agenda.

The data requirements the PE model imposes on analysts can be quite burdensome, however. Collecting, organizing, and coding trend data on media coverage of education reforms in the states—the conventional approach in the PE literature for assessing the stability of policy images over time—presents significant challenges. This kind of challenge has been made easier in recent years by the continued enhancement of searchable, electronic databases of newspaper coverage in each of the states. Analyzing change in policy venues is even more formidable an undertaking. For research at the national level, the Policy Agendas Project, a data archive that is publicly available at the University of Texas at Austin, now stands as an important data resource. At the Web sites (www. policyagendas.org), one can find archived historical data on the U.S. budget; House and Senate committee hearings of the U.S. Congress; executive orders; Gallup Poll information; State of the Union addresses; Supreme Court cases; *New York Times* Index Data; and data on public laws passed since the 1940s.

No such comparable data sets exist at the state level, thus necessitating of analysts extensive archival work in one or more states of interest. Whereas, in many states complete bill information from the early 1990s forward is available online, elsewhere the record is incomplete. For instance, the format for reporting bill information in a given state may change over time, limiting comparisons. Alternatively, the record may cover only a brief span of time or omit particular years of interest.

Yet the strategy of selecting a small number of states, chosen for their theoretical importance, and concentrating attention on publicly available data sources within them seems feasible. Notwithstanding the challenges in collecting bill histories from state legislative databases, state departments of education and statewide coordinating and governing boards for higher education in most cases serve as good data repositories for archival information on various policy initiatives.

A few databanks hosted by national policy organizations, such as the State Higher Education Executive Officers Association (SHEEO), the National Center for Higher Education Management Systems (NCHEMS), the Education Commission of the States (ECS), and the National Conference on State Legislatures (NCSL), also provide key information on the governance patterns of the states and of their education systems. When combined with governors' annual state-of-the-state addresses, executive budget notes, and indicators of state political systems derived from other reliable archives, these data provide the necessary information for testing key tenets of the PE framework and for elaborating new conceptions distinctively tailored to studying education policy change in the states.

Viewing K-12 and Higher Education Policy Change through an Advocacy Coalition Lens

The advocacy coalition framework points analysts of education policy making and policy change in several prospectively important directions, each distinctive to the model. First, the ACF focuses the attention of analysts on the belief systems of members of coalitions and how changes in beliefs over time influence changes in public policy. This emphasis on beliefs is particularly useful in the context of studying K-12 education policy because of the deep, long-standing differences among members of the education policy domain in their views over the proper role of government in American schooling. In a school choice policy coalition, for example, deep core beliefs about the fundamental value of freedom or equality would be expected to shape policy core beliefs about the proper role of governments and markets in education and secondary beliefs addressing details such as resource allocations for school choice policies.

How do these differences in belief structures shape coalition formation, coalition maintenance, the choice of coalition strategy, and, eventually, policy change involving other deeply contested issues in education, such as debates surrounding teacher professionalism and performance? Although scant advocacy coalition research exists in the domain of higher education, growing debate in that sector over the proper role of for-profit postsecondary providers, the future of public subsidies for state colleges and universities, the productivity of faculty, the value of the research enterprise, and the relative merits of the liberal arts and of vocational preparation, signals the potential value of the ACF as a lens for understanding policy change in the sector. In each of these areas, differences in beliefs among policy actors seem to be playing an important role in intensifying policy debates in the states. Application of the ACF in clarifying how these purported differences in beliefs indeed are shaping policy changes at the state level would be a useful direction for future research.

A second possible contribution of the ACF involves its focus on the role of scientific and technical information in the policy process. Rigorous scientific studies on the effects of policies and policy interventions—for example, on such hotly debated matters as teacher effectiveness, student performance, college affordability, and student financial aid—are more readily available to members of the education policy domain today than at any previous time. The use of education research among state policy makers, however, is not very well understood (Ness, 2010). There is a large and growing market in the states for technical analysis of education policies and interventions, but as yet little systematic understanding of the ways technical information *is* (rather than should be) used in defining the magnitude and parameters of problems, their causes, and their likely impacts (Sabatier & Jenkins-Smith, 1999).

How do coalitions in the education domain use research and other technical information to organize their efforts, adhere their members more closely to the coalition's policy objectives, and influence the behavior of governmental authorities? How does the availability, credibility, and perceived quality of education research influence coalitions' choices of "guidance instruments" when seeking to influence the behavior of governments? How do public and elite perceptions about the adequacy of governmental decisions, in turn, influence the strategic choices coalitions make, and the role research and technical information plays in these choices? These are illustrative questions of the kind that could productively frame future research into education policy change.

Clearly, one finds limitations in applying the ACF to state education policy making. Neither the original nor revised models account as fully as they should for the processes by which policies indeed change. Additionally, there is a significant question in this model involving data collection requirements.

Although a clear conceptual and analytical advantage to the ACF is its focus on an expanded set of policy subsystem actors, to include officials from all levels of government, as well as consultants, researchers, and members of the media, the data burdens associated with obtaining meaningful information from all of these parties, and perhaps doing so across states in an effort to generalize findings, could prove prohibitive for analysts. The use of creative research designs, therefore, perhaps to involve surveys of different actors in the education domains of a large number of states, combined with an in-depth analysis of the ACF in only a few states, would enable researchers to apply the framework in educational settings, under reasonable expectations with respect to resources and timing.

Viewing K-12 and Higher Education Policy Change through an Innovation and Diffusion Lens

The distinctive value of the policy innovation and diffusion lens resides in its ability to incorporate into a single analytic formulation indicators of both "intrastate" and "interstate" factors hypothesized as likely to influence a state's adoption of a new education policy or program. Whereas some other contemporary models of public policy formation attend only tangentially to the intergovernmental dimensions of policy adoption, the PID framework expressly seeks to account for them—conceptually and empirically. In so doing, the PID model enables analysts to ascertain the independent influence on policy adoption of factors such as demographic, social, economic, political, and structural conditions within states and pressures arising between and among states. With the important methodological advances of the past decade, PID designs that utilize event history analysis now can produce highly reliable and efficient estimates of the effects of such hypothesized factors on the probability of a state's adopting an education change or reform *at a given moment in time.*

Because innovation and diffusion researchers seek to examine patterns in policy adoption across states and over time, studies applying the framework require data sets possessing both temporal and spatial dimensions. Most such analyses call for the use of panel data sets, incorporating indicators of the states (both internal characteristics of states and indicators of state-to-state policy influence) over time; the state-year, in these studies, serves as the primary unit of analysis. In the K-12 arena, Mintrom (1997) and Wong and Shen (2002) created early data sets of this kind. In an effort to study innovation and diffusion of state policies for higher education, McLendon and colleagues (e.g., Hearn et al., 2013; McLendon et al., 2007; McLendon et al., 2006; Mokher & McLendon, 2009) built event history data sets that include several hundred indicators of the states and their higher education systems spanning a period of almost 40 years. Other analysts have built similar data sets (e.g., Doyle, 2006; Doyle et al., 2010).

Creating and maintaining state-level event history data sets of the kind needed for PID studies of the factors driving education policy change requires the assembling and cleaning of data from a variety of primary and secondary sources. Analysts often compile data for the dependent variable(s)—that is, state adoption decisions—from online databases of state statutes and legislative bill histories. Occasionally, secondary sources, such as policy organizations (e.g., Education Commission of the States or National Conference of State Legislatures) and state boards of education will have systematically reported on dates of adoption for certain education policies enacted in the states.

In many studies, data for most of the state-level independent variables are drawn from a variety of reliable secondary sources, such as the Bureau of Economic Analysis (e.g., data on per capita income), the Inter-University Consortium for Political and Social Research (e.g., political ideology scores of state governments and citizenries), or the National Conference on State Legislatures (e.g., aspects of legislative design). Data on party strength in state legislatures often is taken from data sets publicly available, such as the online archive of the *State Politics and Policy Quarterly* (http://academic.udayton.edu/sppq-TPR/index.htm) or from the Council of State Governments. Increasingly, researchers have begun developing unique indicators of certain hypothesized influences of state education policy, including, for example, ones on the representational attributes of state legislators (e.g., McLendon, Mokher, & Flores, 2011).

The conceptualization, coding, and analysis of *diffusion* in these studies represent a critical set of decisions for PID researchers. Traditionally, the diffusion variable included in longitudinal analyses of state adoption of new policies or programs represents some measure of the number (or percentage) of states that had already adopted an innovation at the time a given state adopted one. The higher the number (or percentage) of previous adopters, the greater the presumed diffusion pressure on a given state to follow suit. The important question, therefore, involves the proper defining of a social community of states among which the policy is likely to have spread. Taking cue from Walker (1969) and the early work of the Berrys (1990, 1992), many studies have defined this community of influence as residing strongest among geographically proximate states, usually contiguous neighbors. Alternative specifications of diffusion can also be modeled. For instance, fixed-region models assume that state officials will be inclined to emulate educational policies of states within their region; analysts following this convention, therefore, will include the number (or percentage) of states from the region that already had adopted the policy or program by the year a given policy is adopted.

While these specifications of diffusion may seem straightforward, other approaches entail greater complexity. For example, when studying education policies, why would analysts presume that new policies and programs should diffuse along regional lines, when regionalism in American public policy matters less today than at any previous time in the nation's history? While regional influences may still exert some pressure on states, communication channels within and among education policy communities today tend to be fashioned along national lines, through professional associations, such as the Council of Chief State School Officers (CCSSO), the Educational Commission of the States (ECS), the State Higher Education Executive Officers Association (SHEEO), the National Conference of State Legislatures (NCSL), the National Governors Association (AGB), and through any number of other organizations that view their role as working to diffuse educational reforms and "best practices" nationally.

Clearly, professional associations built along strong regional ties, including the Western Interstate Commission on Higher Education (WICHE), the Southern Regional Education Board (SREB), and others among the higher education regional "compacts," still play an important role in disseminating ideas and information about postsecondary education. Yet the trend increasingly has been toward national communication channels and interactions among state officials. Future research on education policy making and policy change using the PID framework must better account for these developments in its modeling efforts.

CONCLUSION

Public policy for education in the United States today exhibits as much volatility as that at any moment in the nation's history. Understanding education policy making and policy change in the states may grow more important still, as the states and the federal government continue rethinking—and redesigning—the nation's education landscape.

Indeed, as we draft our conclusion, President Barack Obama has announced a historic series of proposals that would fundamentally overhaul the role of the federal government in higher education, an arena historically dominated by the separate states. Among other things, the administration's proposals, for the first time, would (1) establish a new ratings system for colleges and universities, whereby campuses would be evaluated based on the performance of their graduates, (2) link federal student aid allocations to these outcomes at the campus level, and (3) toughen requirements on students receiving federal student aid. Although, at present, the prospects of congressional passage of these proposals seem unlikely, the announcement caps years of growing public frustration over questions around accountability and affordability in higher education, and signals the lengths to which both federal and state governments in the United States have been willing to go in altering the nation's educational landscape. As we noted at the chapter's outset, this shift also includes numerous other recent policy changes in both K-12 and higher education, including new and different ways of holding education publicly accountable, governing schools and campuses, financing education, promoting coordination and competition, compensating faculty and leaders, staffing systems and schools, and measuring learning and the many other outcomes of schooling.

In this context of frenetic change, systematic and rigorous scholarship around education policy formation in the states can serve at least two valuable purposes. First, *theorizing* about education policy making—meaning formulating propositions, empirically assaying relationships, and elaborating extant understandings—is useful in its own right because doing so is a foundational step in the field's awareness of how the world it purports to understand, indeed, works. Although scholarship around education policy change can demonstrate noteworthy advances over the past decade, overall, the knowledge base remains thin and piecemeal. Much more research is needed.

Second, policy theory can and should improve policy advocacy and practice. Understanding better how policy systems work, and the conditions under which policy systems change, can enhance advocates' success in affecting change in desired ways—and in forestalling change in undesired ones. Multiple streams, punctuated equilibrium, advocacy coalition, and policy innovation and diffusion afford valuable lenses through which to improve the field's theoretical and applied-policy foundations, at a time when the political, financial, and symbolic stakes for the nation's K-12 and higher education systems have never been greater.

NOTES

1. Of course, there have been notable exceptions. Mazzoni (1991) and Fowler's (1994) policy-arenas model of state education reform and Mawhinney's (1993) application of advocacy-coalition theory in the context of Canadian education reform stand as such. As described in this chapter, the field's understanding also has improved as a result of very recent scholarship.
2. One development in this vein was growing criticism of the so-called stages heuristic as a causal theory of the policy process. The stages model of policy making has been criticized as depicting the process as overly linear, when in fact the various "stages" are often compressed or skipped and lacking in terms of identifying the

mechanisms or actors that drive a policy idea from one stage to the next. Sabatier, in particular, has argued that the model tends to focus on processes within individual stages rather than across them and therefore has not developed an adequate causal theory of the policy process (Sabatier, 1986, 1991).

3. In our discussion of three of the four frameworks (i.e., multiple streams, punctuated equilibrium, and policy innovation and diffusion), we draw on several of our previously published writings on the topic, notably McLendon and Cohen-Vogel (2008), Cohen-Vogel and McLendon (2008), and McLendon (2003a, 2003b, 2003c).

4. Although Kingdon initially termed his framework the "revised garbage can" model, in homage to its conceptual origins in the literature on "garbage can" decision making in organizations, subsequent analysts increasingly referred to Kingdon's formulation as the "multiple-streams" framework. We follow this convention.

5. For additional description of the statistical tools used to assess these budgetary data, see Breunig and Jones (2011).

6. The first diffusion studies in the field of education, those conducted in the 1950s by researchers at Teachers College, had as their primary concern the extent to which local control and educational spending led to school and district innovativeness (e.g., Gray, 1973). Later research focused on the teacher as the unit of analysis, and examined the diffusion of ideas and practices within schools (Rogers, 2003). Another vein of research in K-12 and postsecondary education has focused on technology adoption among classroom teachers and college faculty (Straub, 2009; Tabata & Johnsrud, 2008; Williams van Rooij, 2009).

REFERENCES

Ackrill, R., & Kay, A. (2011). Multiple streams in EU policy-making: The case of the 2005 sugar reform. *Journal of European Public Policy, 18*(1), 72–89.

Albright, E. A. (2011). Policy change and learning in response to extreme flood events in Hungary: An advocacy coalition approach. *Policy Studies Journal, 39*(3), 485–511.

Alexandrova, P., Carammia, M., & Timmermans, A. (2012). Policy punctuations and issue diversity on the European Council agenda. *Policy Studies Journal, 40*(1), 69–88.

Allard, S. W., & Danziger, S. (2000). Welfare magnets: Myth or reality? *Journal of Politics, 62*, 350–68.

Allen, M. D., Pettus, C., & Haider-Markel, D. (2004). Making the national local: Specifying the conditions for national government influence on state policymaking. *State Politics and Policy Quarterly, 4*, 318–344.

Ansell, C., Reckhow, S., & Kelly, A. (2009). How to reform a reform coalition: Outreach, agenda expansion, and brokerage in urban school reform. *Policy Studies Journal, 37*(4), 717–743.

Bailey, M. A., & Rom, M. C. (2004). A wider race: Interstate competition across health and welfare programs. *Journal of Politics, 66*, 326–347.

Balla, S. J. (2001). Interstate professional associations and the diffusion of policy innovations. *American Politics Research, 29*, 221–245.

Baumgartner, F. R., & Jones, B. D. (1991). Agenda dynamics and policy subsystems. *Journal of Politics, 53*, 1044–1074.

Baumgartner, F. R., & Jones, B. D. (1993). *Agendas and instability in American politics.* Chicago, IL: University of Chicago Press.

Beck, N., Katz, J. N., & Tucker, R. (1998). Taking time seriously: Time series-cross-section analysis with a binary dependent variable. *American Journal of Political Science, 42*, 1260–1288.

Berry, F. S. (1994). Sizing up state policy innovation research. *Policy Studies Journal, 22*(3), 442–456.

Berry, F. S., & Baybeck, B. (2005). Using geographic information systems to study interstate competition. *American Political Science Review, 99*(4), 505–519.

Berry, F. S., & Berry, W. D. (1990). State lottery adoptions as policy innovations: An event history analysis. *American Political Science Review, 84*(2), 395–416.

Berry, F. S., & Berry, W. D. (1992). Tax innovation in the states: Capitalizing on political opportunity. *American Journal of Political Science, 36*(3), 715–742.

Berry, F. S., & Berry, W. D. (1994). The politics of tax increases in the states. *American Journal of Political Science, 52*(1), 167–196.

Berry, F. S., & Berry, W. D. (1999). Innovation and diffusion models in policy research. In P. Sabatier (Ed.), *Theories of the policy process.* Boulder, CO: Westview Press.

Berry, F. S., & Berry, W. D. (2007). Innovation and diffusion models in policy research. In P. Sabatier (Ed.) (2nd ed.). *Theories of the policy process.* Boulder, CO: Westview Press.

Berry, W. D., Fording, R. C., & Hanson, R. (2003). Reassessing the "race to the bottom" in state welfare policy. *Journal of Politics, 65*, 327–349.

Beverwijk, J., Goedegebuure, L., & Huisman, J. (2008). Policy change in nascent subsystems: Mozambican higher education policy 1993–2003. *Policy Sciences, 41*(4), 357–377.

Blaukenau, J. (2001). The fate of national health insurance in Canada and the United States: A multiple-streams explanation. *Policy Studies Journal, 29*(1), 38–55.

Boehmke, F. J., & Witmer, R. (2004). Disentangling diffusion: The effects of social learning and economic competition on state policy innovation and expansion. *Political Research Quarterly, 57,* 39–51.

Box-Steffensmeier, J., & Jones, B. (2004). *Event history modeling.* Cambridge: Cambridge University Press.

Boushey, G. (2012). Punctuated equilibrium theory and the diffusion of innovations. *Policy Studies Journal, 40*(1), 127–146.

Brecher, C., Brazill, C., Weitzman, B. C., & Silver, D. (2010). Understanding the political context of "new" policy issues: The use of the advocacy coalition framework in the case of expanded after-school programs. *Journal of Public Administration Research and Theory, 20*(2), 335–355.

Breunig, C., & Jones, B. D. (2011). Stochastic process methods with an application to budgetary data. *Political Analysis, 19*(1), 103–117.

Breunig, C., & Koski, C. (2012). The tortoise or the hare? Incrementalism, punctuations, and their consequences. *Policy Studies Journal, 40*(1), 45–67.

Breunig, C., Koski, C., & Mortensen, P. (2010). Stability and punctuations in public spending: A comparative study of budget functions. *Journal of Public Administration Research and Theory, 20*(3), 703–722.

Clarke, H., Wilson, M., Cummings, M., & Hyland, A. (1999). The campaign to enact New York City's Smoke-Free Air Act. *Journal of Public Health Management Practice, 5,* 1–13.

Cobb, R. W., & Elder, C. D. (1983). *Participation in American politics: The dynamics of agenda building.* Baltimore, MD: Johns Hopkins University Press.

Cohen, M., March, J., & Olsen, J. (1972). A garbage can model of organizational choice. *Administrative Sciences Quarterly, 17,* 1–25.

Cohen-Vogel, L., & Ingle, K. (2007). When neighbors matter most: Innovation, diffusion and state policy adoption in tertiary education. *Journal of Education Policy, 22*(3), 241–262.

Cohen-Vogel, L., Ingle, K., Albee, A., & Spence, M. (2008). The "spread" of merit-based college aid: Politics, policy consortia and interstate competition. *Educational Policy, 22*(3), 339–362.

Cohen-Vogel, L., & McLendon, M. K. (2008). New approaches to unanswered questions about federal involvement in education. In D. Plank, G. Sykes, & B. Schneider (Eds.), *AERA handbook on education policy research* (pp. 42–90). Hillsdale, NJ: Lawrence Erlbaum & Associates.

Collier, D., & Messick, R. E. (1975). Prerequisites versus diffusion: Testing explanations of social security adoption. *American Political Science Review, 69,* 1299–1315.

Cooper, J. (1977). Congress in organizational perspective. In L. Dodd & B. Oppenheimer (Eds.), *Congress reconsidered* (pp. 140–163). New York: Praeger.

DeBray-Pelot, E. H., Lubienski, C. A., & Scott, J. T. (2007). The institutional landscape of interest group politics and school choice. *Peabody Journal of Education, 82*(2–3), 204–230.

Dolowitz, D., & Marsh, D. (1996). Who learns from whom: A review of the policy transfer literature. *Political Studies, 44,* 343–357.

Doyle, W. R. (2006). Adoption of merit-based student grant programs: An event history analysis. *Educational Evaluation and Policy Analysis, 28*(3), 259–285.

Doyle, W. R., McLendon, M. K., & Hearn, J. C. (2010). Why states adopted prepaid tuition and college savings programs: An event history analysis. *Research in Higher Education, 51*(7).

Durant, R. F., & Diehl, P. F. (1989). Agendas, alternatives, and public policy: Lessons from the U.S. foreign policy arena. *Journal of Public Policy, 9*(1), 179–205.

Dye, T. R. (1990). *American federalism: Competition among governments.* Lexington, MA: Lexington Books.

Easton, D. (1953). *The political system.* New York: A. Knopf.

Easton, D. (1965). *A systems analysis of political life.* New York: Wiley.

Eldredge, N., & Gould, S. J. (1972). Punctuated equilibria: An alternative to phyletic gradualism. In T. Schopf (Ed.), *Models in paleobiology.* San Francisco: Freeman.

Fowler, F. C. (1994). Education reform comes to Ohio: An application of Mazzoni's arena models. *Educational Evaluation and Policy Analysis, 16*(3), 335–350.

Glick, H. R., & Hays, S. P. (1991). Innovation and reinvention in state policymaking: Theory and the evolution of living will laws. *Journal of Politics, 53*(3), 835–850.

Grattet, R., Jenness, V., & Curry, T. R. (1998). Innovation and diffusion in U.S. hate crime law. *American Sociological Review, 63,* 286–307.

Gray, V. (1973). Innovation in the states: A diffusion study. *American Political Science Review, 67*(4), 1174–1185.

Gray, V. (1994). Competition, emulation, and policy innovation. In L. Dodd & C. Jillson (Eds.), *New perspectives on American politics.* Washington, DC: Congressional Quarterly Press.

Hearn, J. C. (1993). The paradox of growth in federal aid for college students: 1965–1990. In J. C. Smart (Ed.), *Higher education: Handbook of theory and research, volume IX* (pp. 94–153). New York: Agathon.

Hearn, J. C., & Griswold, C. P. (1994). State-level centralization and policy innovation in U.S. postsecondary education. *Educational Evaluation and Policy Analysis, 16*(2), 161–190.

Hearn, J. C., McLendon, M. K., & Lacy, T. A. (2013). State-funded "eminent scholars" programs: University faculty recruitment as an emerging policy instrument. *The Journal of Higher Education, 84*(5), 601–639.

Hearn, J. C., McLendon, M. K., & Mokher, C. (2008). Accounting for student success: An empirical analysis of the origins and spread of state student unit-record systems. *Research in Higher Education, 50*(1), 665–683.

Henry, A. D. (2011). Ideology, power and the structure of policy networks. *Policy Studies Journal, 39*(3), 361–383.

Holyoke, T., Henig, J. R., Brown, H., & Lacireno-Paquet, N. (2009). Policy dynamics and the evolution of state charter school laws. *Policy Sciences, 42*(1), 33–55.

Ingle, K., Cohen-Vogel, L., & Hughes, R. (2007). The public policy process among Southeastern states: Elaborating theories of regional adoption and hold-out behavior. *Policy Studies Journal, 36*(1), 607–628.

Jenkins-Smith, H., & Sabatier, P. A. (1993). The study of public policy processes. In P. A. Sabatier & H. Jenkins-Smith (Eds.), *Policy change and learning: An advocacy coalition approach* (pp. 1–12). Boulder, CO: Westview Press.

Jenkins-Smith, H. C., & Sabatier, P. A. (1994). Evaluating the advocacy coalition framework. *Journal of Public Policy, 14*(2), 175–203.

John, P., & Bevan, S. (2012). What are policy punctuations? Large changes in the legislative agenda of the UK government, 1911–2008. *Policy Studies Journal, 40*(1), 89–108.

Jones, M. D., & Jenkins-Smith, H. C. (2009). Trans-subsystem dynamics: Policy topography, mass opinion, and policy change. *Policy Studies Journal, 37*(1), 37–58.

Jordan, M. M. (2003). Punctuations and agendas: A new look at local government budget expenditures. *Journal of Policy Analysis and Management, 22*(3), 345.

Kamieniecki, S. (2000). Testing alternative theories of agenda setting. *Policy Studies Journal 28*(1), 176–189.

Karch, A. (2007). Emerging issues and future directions in state policy diffusion research. *State Politics & Policy Quarterly, 7*(1), 54–80.

Kawar, A. (1989). Issue definition, democratic participation, and genetic engineering. *Policy Studies Journal, 17*(4), 719–744.

Kelly, S. Q. (1994). Punctuated change and the era of divided government. In L. Dodd & C. Jillson (Eds.), *New perspectives on American politics* (pp. 162–190). Washington, DC: Congressional Quarterly Press.

King, D. C. (1994). John Kingdon as an agenda item. *Policy Currents, 4*(3), 17–20.

Kingdon, J. W. (1984). *Agendas, alternatives, and public policies.* Boston, MA: Little, Brown.

Kingdon, J. W. (1994). Agendas, ideas, and policy change. In L. Dodd & C. Jillson (Eds.), *New perspectives on American politics* (pp. 215–229). Washington, DC: Congressional Quarterly Press.

Kingdon, J. W. (1995). *Agendas, alternatives, and public policies* (2nd ed.). New York: HarperCollins.

Lacireno-Paquet, N., & Holyoke, T. T. (2007). Moving forward or sliding backward: The evolution of charter school policies in Michigan and the District of Columbia. *Educational Policy, 21*(1), 185–214.

Larson, T .E. (2004). Decentralization in U.S. public higher education: A comparative study of New Jersey, Illinois, and Arkansas. Paper presented at the annual meeting of the Association for the Study of Higher Education. Kansas City, MO, November 3, 2004.

Larsen-Price, H. A. (2012). The right tool for the job: The canalization of presidential policy attention by policy instrument. *Policy Studies Journal, 40*(1), 147–168.

LaVenia, M., Cohen-Vogel, L., & Lang, L. (2011). The Common Core State Standards initiative: An event history analysis of state policy adoption. Paper presented at the annual meeting of the Association for Education Finance and Policy. Seattle, WA.

Leslie, D. W., & Berdahl, R. O. (2008). The politics of restructuring in Virginia: A case study. *Review of Higher Education, 31*(3), 309–328.

Leslie, D. W., & Novak, R. J. (2003). Substance vs. politics: Through the dark mirror of governance reform. *Educational Policy, 17*(1), 98–120.

Lindblom, C. E. (1959). The science of "muddling through." *Public Administration Review, 19*(2), 79–88.

Lindblom, C. E. (1965). *The intelligence of democracy: Decision making through mutual adjustment.* New York: Free Press.

Lindblom, C. E. (1968). *The policymaking process.* Englewood Cliffs, NJ: Prentice Hall.

Lindquist, E., Liu. X., Vedlitz, A., & Vincent, K. (2010). Understanding local policymaking: Policy elites' perceptions of local agenda setting and alternative policy selection. *Policy Studies Journal, 38*(1), 69–91.

March, J., & Olsen, J. P. (1989). *Rediscovering institutions: The organizational basis of politics.* New York: Free Press.

Matti, S., & Sandstrom, A. (2011). The rationale determining advocacy coalitions: Examining coordination networks and corresponding beliefs. *Policy Studies Journal, 39*(3), 385–410.

Mawhinney, H. B. (1993). An advocacy-coalition approach to change in Canadian education. In P. Sabatier & H. C. Jenkins-Smith (Eds.), *Policy change and learning: An advocacy coalition approach* (pp. 59–82). Boulder, CO: Westview Press.

Mazzoni, T. (1991). Analyzing state school policymaking: An arena model. *Educational Evaluation and Policy Analysis, 13*(2), 115–138.

McDermott, K. (2005). In MINT condition? The politics of alternative certification and pay incentives for teachers in Massachusetts. *Educational Policy, 19*(1), 44–62.

McLendon, M. K. (2003a). Setting the governmental agenda for state decentralization of higher education. *Journal of Higher Education, 74*(5), 479–516.

McLendon, M. K. (2003b). State governance reform of higher education: Patterns, trends, and theories of the public policy process. In J. Smart (Ed.), *Higher education: Handbook of theory and research* (Volume XVIII) (pp. 57–143). London: Kluwer.

McLendon, M. K. (2003c). The politics of higher education: Toward an expanded research agenda. *Educational Policy, 17*(1), 165–191.

McLendon, M. K., & Cohen-Vogel, L. (2008). Understanding education policy change in the American states: Lessons from contemporary political science. In B. S. Cooper, J. G. Cibulka, & L. D. Fusarelli (Eds.), *Handbook of education politics and policy* (1st ed.) (pp. 66–112). Washington, DC: Lawrence Erlbaum & Associates.

McLendon, M. K., Deaton, R., & Hearn, J. C. (2007). The enactment of state-level governance reforms for higher education: A test of the political-instability hypothesis. *The Journal of Higher Education, 78*(6), 645–675.

McLendon, M. K., & A. S. Eddings. (2002). Direct democracy and higher education: The state ballot as an instrument of higher education policymaking. *Educational Policy, 16*(1), 193–218.

McLendon, M. K., Hearn, J. C., & Deaton, R. (2006). Called to account: Analyzing the origins and spread of state performance-accountability policies for higher education. *Educational Evaluation and Policy Analysis, 28*(1), 1–24.

McLendon, M. K., Heller, D. E., & Young, S. P. (2005). State postsecondary education policy innovation: Politics, competition, and the interstate migration of policy ideas. *Journal of Higher Education, 76*(4), 363–400.

McLendon, M. K., Mokher, C. G, & Doyle, W. (2009). Privileging public research universities: The political economy of state appropriations to higher education. *Journal of Education Finance, 34*(4), 372–401.

McLendon, M.K., C. Mokher, & S.M. Flores. (2011). Legislative agenda-setting for in-state resident tuition policies: Immigration, representation, and educational access. *American Journal of Education, 117*(4), 563–602.

Mills, M. (2007). Stories of politics and policy: Florida's higher education governance reorganization. *The Journal of Higher Education, 78*(2), 162–187.

Mintrom, M. (1997). Policy entrepreneurs and the diffusion of innovation. *American Journal of Political Science, 41*, 738–770.

Mintrom, M. (2000). *Policy entrepreneurs and school choice.* Washington, DC: Georgetown University Press.

Mintrom, M., & Vergari, S. (1996). Advocacy coalitions, policy entrepreneurs, and policy change. *Policy Studies Journal, 24*(3), 420–434.

Mintrom, M., & Vergari, S. (1998). Policy networks and innovation diffusion: The case of state education reforms. *The Journal of Politics, 60*(1), 126–148.

Mokher, C., & McLendon, M. K. (2009). Uniting secondary and postsecondary education: An event history analysis of state adoption of dual enrollment policies. *American Journal of Education, 115*(2), 249–277.

Mooney, C. Z. (2001). Modeling regional effects on state policy diffusion. *Political Research Quarterly, 54*(1), 103–124.

Mooney, C. Z., & Lee, M. H. (1995). Legislating morality in the American states: The case of pre-Roe abortion regulation reform. *American Journal of Political Science, 39*(3), 599–627.

Morgan, D. R., & Watson, S. S. (1991). Political culture, political systems characteristics, and public policies among the American states. *Publius, 21*(2), 31–43.

Mucciaroni, G. (1992). The garbage can model and the study of policy making: A critique. *Polity, 24*(3), 460–482.

Ness, E. (2008). *Merit aid and the politics of education.* New York: Routledge.

Ness, E. (2010). The politics of determining Merit Aid eligibility criteria: An analysis of the policy process. *Journal of Higher Education, 81*(1), 33–60.

Ness, E., & Mistretta, M. A. (2009a). Merit aid in North Carolina: A case study of a non-event. *Educational Policy, 24*(5), 703–734.

Ness, E., & Mistretta, M. A. (2009b). Policy adoption in North Carolina and Tennessee: A comparative case study of lottery beneficiaries. *Review of Higher Education, 32*(4), 489–514.

Nice, D. C. (1994). *Policy innovation in state government.* Ames: Iowa State University Press.

Nicholson-Crotty, S. (2009). The politics of diffusion: Public policy in the American states. *The Journal of Politics, 71*(1), 192–205.

Oliver, T. R. (1991). Health care market reform in Congress: The uncertain path from proposal to policy. *Political Science Quarterly, 106*(3), 453–477.

Olsen, J. P. (2001). Garbage cans, new institutionalism, and the study of politics. *The American Political Science Review, 95*(1), 191–198.

Orr-Bement, D. M. (2002, November 21). A theoretical perspective of the state policy process for higher education policy decisions. Paper presented at the annual meeting of the Association for the Study of Higher Education, Sacramento, CA.

Perry, J. L., & Kraemer, K. L. (1979). *Technological innovation in American local governments: The case of computing.* New York: Pergamon Press.

Peters, G. (1994). Agenda setting in the European Community. *Journal of European Public Policy, 1*(3), 9–26.

Peterson, P. E., & Rom, M. C. (1990). *Welfare magnets.* Washington, DC: Brookings Institution.

Pollack, M. A. (1997). Delegation, agency, and agenda setting in the European Community. *International Organization, 51*(1), 99–134.

Polsby, N., & Schickler, E. (2002). Landmarks in the study of Congress since 1945. *Annual Review of Political Science, 5,* 333–367.

Portz, J. (1996). Problem definitions and policy agendas: Shaping the educational agenda in Boston. *Policy Studies Journal, 24*(3), 371–386.

Prindle, D. F. (2012). Importing concepts from biology into political science: The case of punctuated equilibrium. *Policy Studies Journal, 40*(1), 21–44.

Protopsaltis, S. (2004). Political and policy dynamics of higher education governance and finance reform: The shaping of the first college voucher system. Paper presented at the annual meeting of the Association for the Study of Higher Education. Kansas City, MO, November 3, 2004.

Rich, A. (2004). *Think tanks, public policy, and the politics of expertise.* Cambridge, UK: Cambridge University Press.

Robertson, D. B., & Waltman, J. L. (1993). The politics of policy borrowing. In D. Finegold, L. McFarland, & W. Richardson (Eds.), *Something borrowed, something learned.* Washington, DC: Brookings Institution.

Robinson, S. E., & Eller, W. S. (2010). Participation in policy streams: Testing the separation of problems and solutions in subnational policy systems. *Policy Studies Journal, 38*(2), 199–215.

Rockman, B. (1994). The new institutionalism and the old institutions. In L. Dodd, and C. Jillson (eds.), *New Perspectives on American Politics.* Washington, DC: Congressional Quarterly Press.

Rogers, E. M. (2003). *Diffusion of innovations.* New York: Free Press.

Ryu, J. E. (2009). Exploring the factors for budget stability and punctuations: A preliminary analysis of state government sub-functional expenditures. *Policy Studies Journal, 37*(3), 457–473.

Sabatier, P. A. (1986). Top-down and bottom-up approaches to implementation research: A critical analysis and suggested synthesis. *Journal of Public Policy, 6*(1), 21–48.

Sabatier, P. A. (1988). An advocacy coalition model of policy change and the role of policy oriented learning therein. *Policy Sciences, 21*(2–3), 129–168.

Sabatier, P. A. (1991). Toward better theories of the policy process. *PS: Political Science and Politics, 24*(2), 147–156.

Sabatier, P., Hunter, S., & McLaughlin, S. (1987). The devil shift: Perceptions and misperceptions of opponents. *Western Political Quarterly, 40*(3), 51–73.

Sabatier, P. A., & Jenkins-Smith, H. C. (1993). *Policy change and learning: An advocacy coalition approach.* Boulder, CO: Westview Press.

Sabatier, P. A., & Jenkins-Smith, H. C. (1999). The advocacy coalition framework: An assessment. In P. Sabatier (Ed.), *Theories of the policy process* (pp. 117–166). Boulder, CO: Westview Press.

Sabatier, P. A., & Weible, C. M. (2007). The advocacy coalition framework: Innovations and clarifications. In P. Sabatier (Ed.), *Theories of the policy process* (2nd ed.) (pp. 189–220). Boulder, CO: Westview Press.

Saiz, M., & Clarke, S. E. (2013). Economic development and infrastructure policy. In V. Gray, R. L. Hanson, & T. Kousser (Eds.), *Politics in the American states: A comparative analysis,* (10th ed.) (pp. 501–532). Washington, DC: Congressional Quarterly Press.

Samuels, B., & Glantz, S. A. (1991). The politics of local tobacco control. *JAMA, 266*(15), 2110–2117.

Savage, R. L. (1985). Diffusion research traditions and the spread of policy innovations in a federal system. *Publius, 15,* 1–27.

Schlager, E. (1995). Policymaking and collective action: Defining coalitions within the advocacy coalition framework. *Policy Sciences, 28*(3), 243–270.

Schlager, E., & Blomquist, W. (1996). A comparison of three emerging theories of the policy process. *Political Research Quarterly, 49*(3), 651–672.

Simon, H. A. (1997). *Administrative behavior* (4th ed.). New York: Free Press.

Sims, C. H., & Miskel, C. G. (2001). The punctuated equilibrium of national reading policy: Literacy's changing images and venues. Paper presented at the annual meeting of the American Educational Research Association, Seattle, WA.

Sims, C. H., & Miskel, C. G. (2003). The punctuated equilibrium of national reading policy: Literacy's changing images and venues. In W. Hoy & C. G. Miskel (Eds.), *Studies in leading and organizing schools* (pp. 1–26). Greenwich, CT: Information Age.

Soule, S., & Earl, J. (2001). The enactment of state-level hate crime law in the United States: Intrastate and interstate factors. *Sociological Perspectives, 44*(3), 281–305.

Stout, K., & Stevens, B. (2000). The case of the failed diversity rule: A multiple streams analysis. *Educational Evaluation and Policy Analysis, 22*(4), 341–355.

Straub, E. T. (2009). Understanding technology adoption: Theory and future directions for informal learning. *Review of Educational Research, 79*(2), 625–649.

True, J. L., Jones, B. D., & Baumgartner, F. R. (1999). Punctuated-equilibrium theory. In P. A. Sabatier (Ed.), *Theories of the Policy Process* (pp. 97–115). Boulder, CO: Westview Press.

True, J. L., Jones, B. D., & Baumgartner, F. R. (2007). Punctuated-equilibrium theory: Explaining stability and change in public policymaking. In P. Sabatier (Ed.), *Theories of the policy process* (2nd ed.) (pp. 155–187). Boulder, CO: Westview Press.

Vergari, S. (2007). The politics of charter schools. *Educational Policy, 21*(1), 15–39.

Volden, C., Ting, M., & Carpenter, D. (2008). A formal model of learning and policy diffusion. *The American Political Science Review, 102*(3), 319–332.

Walker, J. L. (1969). The diffusion of innovations among the American states. *American Political Science Review, 67*, 1174–1185.

Weible, C. M., Sabatier, P. A., & McQueen, K. (2009). Themes and variations: Taking stock of the advocacy coalition framework. *Policy Studies Journal, 37*(1), 121–140.

Weir, M. (1992). Ideas and the politics of bounded innovation. In S. Steinmo, K. Thelin, & F. Longsthreth (Eds.), *Structuring politics: Historical institutionalism in comparative analysis* (pp. 188–216). Cambridge: Cambridge University Press.

Williams van Rooij, S. (2009). Adopting open-source software applications in U.S. higher education: A cross-disciplinary review of the literature. *Review of Educational Research, 79*(2), 682–701.

Wolfe, M. (2012). Putting on the brakes or pressing on the gas? Media attention and the speed of policymaking. *Policy Studies Journal, 40*(1), 109–126.

Wong, K. K., & Langevin, W. E. (2006). "Policy Expansion of School Choice in the States." Working paper, National Center on School Choice, Nashville, TN.

Wong, K. K., & Shen, F. X. (2002). Politics of state-led reform in education: Market competition and electoral dynamics. *Educational Policy, 16*, 161–192.

Worsham, J., & Stores, C. (2012). Pet sounds: Subsystems, regimes, policy punctuations, and the neglect of African American farmers, 1935–2006. *Policy Studies Journal, 40*(1), 169–190.

Zahariadis, N. (1999). Ambiguity, time, and multiple streams. In P. A. Sabatier (Ed.), *Theories of the policy process* (pp. 73–96). Boulder, CO: Westview Press.

Zahariadis, N., & Allen, C. S. (1995). Ideas, networks, and policy streams: Privatization in Britain and Germany. *Policy Studies Review, 14*(1), 71–88.

Zumeta, W. (2001). Public policy and higher education accountability: Lessons from the past for the new millennium. In D. Heller (Ed.), *Access, affordability, and accountability* (pp. 155–197). Baltimore, MD: Johns Hopkins University Press.

5

POLITICAL CULTURES IN EDUCATION

Emerging Perspectives

Karen Seashore Louis, Karen Febey, and Molly F. Gordon

INTRODUCTION

In 2008 we published a chapter in the first edition of this handbook that examined how political culture affects the development of K-12 educational policies at state and local levels. In that analysis, we focused on how the expanding role of the state as a key actor in educational policy has increased over the past few decades (Clune, 1987; Reeves, 1990; Timar & Kirp, 1988), and included data about how local districts and schools reacted to state policies. Since then we have expanded our examination of political cultures, considering additional in-depth analysis of states within the United States, differences between countries within the European Union, and some of the differences between the K-12 and higher education sectors. This chapter therefore represents both a deepening and an extension of the ideas developed in the previous contribution, but with a stronger focus on state and national political cultures.

As we began our exploration of state political cultures, we drew on the accumulating evidence that the role of the state as a key actor in educational policy had increased (Clune, 1987; Reeves, 1990; Timar & Kirp, 1988). States are still active in policy making, although they are required to respond to an increasingly active national educational agenda, which includes both requirements (such as those in the No Child Left Behind Act of 2001, www2.ed.gov/policy/elsec/leg/esea02) and programs, included in the Race to the Top funding for states, which the Obama administration claimed to be "a historic moment in American education . . . that offers bold incentives to states willing to spur systemic reform" (www.whitehouse.gov/issues/education/k-12/race-to-the-top). Government policies that pressed for the design and implementation of a U.S. educational system that diminishes variability between states have also been recently reinforced by initiatives from other sources. According to a Web site sponsored by the Council of Chief State School Officers and the National Governors Association, the press for a "Common Core" curriculum in English/language arts and mathematics:

> is state-led, and has support from across the country, including CCSSO, the NGA Center, Achieve, Inc, ACT, the College Board, the National Association of State Boards

of Education, the Alliance for Excellent Education, the Hunt Institute, the National Parent Teacher Association, the State Higher Education Executive Officers, the American Association of School Administrators, and the Business Roundtable. (www. corestandards.org/)

Similar efforts are taking place in higher education, with increasing calls for national accountability standards, measurement of what students have learned during their undergraduate careers, and more careful monitoring of faculty performance.

If one were to believe the national media coverage of these initiatives, the muscular state policy presence of the 1980s and 1990s has been significantly diminished in favor of uniformity in structure, content, delivery, and accountability. This metanarrative of an unstoppable march toward national standards and practices is reinforced by international bodies, such as the OECD, which have been strong advocates for international benchmarking, standards, and curriculum (Schleicher, 2009).

The narrative of a reduced role for states has another side, however. In this chapter we will argue that below the simple charts that show how many states have adopted "Common Core" there are still significant differences in the way educational policies are enacted at subnational levels in the United States. And, in spite of the national conversations about international standards among European countries (where the OECD and other international organizations are more influential), significant differences remain in how the hot topics of standards and accountability are enacted.

In addition, we will argue that states vary greatly in the types of policies enacted, but most reports on differences among states have continued to be largely descriptive, such as the annual *Education Week* reviews of state educational reform and progress, which accord most states a low grade (*Education Week,* 2012). Some analyses look in more detail at the effects of different policy and/or accountability systems on student outcomes (Baker & Friedman-Nimz, 2004; Hanushek & Raymond, 2005; Jellison Holmes et al., 2010; Roch & Howard, 2008; Smith, 2007; Teitelbaum, 2003; Warren, Jenkins, & Kulick, 2006), but most of these studies do not analyze the details of different policy frameworks.[1]

Even less attention has been paid to how state political cultures affect the manner in which educational accountability policies are enacted and the assumptions on which they are based. Many high-quality studies that describe the interaction between a policy and student outcomes tend to focus on a single state (Heilig & Darling-Hammond, 2008; Ladd & Lauen, 2010; Mintrop & Trujillo, 2007). Comparative research about the relationship between policies and student outcomes is emerging from international studies (Akiba, LeTendre, & Scribner, 2007; Schnepf, 2007; Werfhorst & Mijs, 2010), but much of the analytic work is still in single-country studies. In addition, at least one international analysis suggests that differences in formal policies explain less of the variance in the outcomes of schooling than accumulated traditions and expectations (Goos et al., 2013), which leads us to the topic of political culture and how it affects educational policy making.

We rely on the traditional definition of political culture as enduring political attitudes and behaviors associated with groups that live in a defined geographical context (Elazar, 1970; Lieske, 1993). According to this definition, political cultures can be distinguished from party affiliations ("red state, blue state") or particular views on or reactions to a current issue. Although temporary interruptions in public attitudes may occur around hot topics, such as gay marriage or welfare reform, these issues usually have a limited long-term impact on the more deeply embedded assumptions about "what we believe and how things work around here."

A political culture perspective leads to the presumption that, although governments are responding to broad international shifts in expectations about the accountability of educational institutions, a state's interpretations of and assumptions about specific policies and practices to support accountability usually reflect its unique culture makeup and other historical circumstances. To illuminate the usefulness of this perspective, we pose the following questions:

1. How do distinctive political cultures at the state level help to explain the unfolding of states' K-12 educational accountability and standards policies?
2. Do state political cultures affect the policies and practices of local districts?
3. Does a state political culture framework apply equally well to the K-12 and higher education sectors?

WHAT WE KNOW

We will briefly review two concepts that are central to our investigation: political culture and state policy formation.

Political Culture[2]

Political culture is a multidimensional concept subsuming the collective cognitions, values, and emotional commitments that regulate the pressures felt by elected and appointed politicians (Patterson, 1968). Political decisions result from the exercise of power and influence, but decision outcomes, particularly in the case of complex policies, are not usually predicted by knowing which actors have the most money or the largest elected majority. Rather, political culture constrains the way actors make collective and individual political decisions (Berezin, 1997). Political culture is more than the aggregation of individual preferences and values; rather, it emerges from both individual and group efforts and ability "to make those preferences publicly common" (Chilton, 1988, p. 430). In other words, it reflects the accumulated history of public discourse and repeated actions, and expressed preferences of groups are critical elements of the context in which public policy decisions are made.

States' political cultures have developed from religious-social-political predispositions of ethnic and religious groups, combined with geographical migration patterns (Johnson, 1976; Lowery & Sigelman, 1982). Political scientists point to openness, rationalism, decentralism, and egalitarianism of social relations as key cultural features that distinguish states' cultures (Herzik, 1985). Each of these elements has a corresponding pattern of political behavior. For example, in more open political cultures, the general public has substantial influence in determining the nature of government structures and political processes, while more closed political cultures have stringent requirements for participation that may lessen the public's interest and influence. The long-term effects of culture may not be visible in every legislative session because no government is entirely consistent. However, these effects may become apparent over longer periods of time.

Within political systems, culture is embedded in relationships and shared values among groups, which become the backdrop of public preferences for behaviors and beliefs (Wirt, Mitchell, & Marshall, 1988) and in explaining decision outcomes (Berezin, 1997). A state's political culture may make a significant contribution to predicting political party identification and ideological preferences more so than its demographic characteristics (Erikson, McIver, & Wright, 1987). This distinctive political culture is often agreed on by most of the state's citizens, including those who are outside the state's dominant religious, ethnic, or social traditions (Cook, Jelen, & Wilcox, 1993).

Research that focused on U.S. regional and state political cultures and their effects reached a peak in the middle 1980s. Since that time, the concept has become less prominent as a theme in both political science and education. Most research is derived from Elazar's (1970) initial classification of states into three categories: traditionalistic, moralistic, and individualistic (see also Elazar, 1980) and can be summarized as follows:

Traditionalistic political cultures are characterized by elite dominance of the political system, with little grassroots-level participation. States characterized as traditionalistic have comparatively less policy innovation, democratic political participation, and interparty competition. Government's purpose is to maintain social and economic hierarchy and is limited to basic functions related to public safety and order. (Elazar, 1984)

Moralistic political cultures emphasize the role of government in maintaining the common welfare, and emphasize economic equality more than other states. Popular participation in the political process is viewed as a way of airing a variety of opinions and is considered an obligation of citizenship. Decentralization is the means through which the government seeks to increase this participation. Moralistic states also tend to be less tolerant of political corruption. (Elazar, 1984; Fitzpatrick & Hero, 1988)

Individualistic political cultures emphasize an economic, practical orientation toward government. The role of government is limited, but popular participation through strong political parties is encouraged because of the emphasis on a competitive environment. Also in individualistic states, private concerns often trump public concerns, so government corruption is more likely to be tolerated. (Elazar, 1970)

Elazar's three types are controversial but have been supported by studies that show their value as predictors of state policy decision outcomes (Cook et al., 1993; Erikson et al., 1987; Norrander, 2000). For example, a content analysis of school laws in the 1970s found no direct correlation between the state's level of centralization and the amount it spends on schools. This analysis was linked to Elazar's cultures as it showed that state education expenditures do not seem to influence the state's level of centralization (Wirt, 1980). A further study found that cultural indicators and the state's level of liberalism and affluence can be "policy predictors" of state and local expenditures, especially in the Southern region of the United States. This finding is related to Elazar's framework, as the Southern states are largely considered to have a traditionalistic political culture (Morgan & Wilson, 1990).

More recently, another study examined state administrative culture by measuring school principals' responses to five dimensions of leadership in states that covered all three of Elazar's political culture types. When comparing the rankings of states on those dimensions, traditionalistic states, or those with the greatest amount of centralization, ranked the highest, while moralistic states, or those with the least amount of centralization, ranked the lowest (Wirt & Krug, 2001).

Some research suggests more than three political culture types, but the identified subtypes are largely consistent with Elazar's conceptualizations (Johnson, 1976; Lieske, 1993). A meta-analysis of more than 100 articles found support for the framework in the majority of studies (cited in Koven & Mausolff, 2002). One recent study found that high-stakes graduation exams were more likely to be used in states that allocate less money per pupil than the national average, have more centralized governments, and are located in the South, which are also characteristics of states with traditionalistic political cultures (Amrein & Berliner, 2002). Of the 18 states ranked as having the highest K-12 testing stakes, 11 were classified as having a traditionalistic political culture and only one had a moralistic culture.

While many school improvement and reform efforts are shaped or dictated by state policy, less is known about how these initiatives affect schools, even though school-based studies suggest significant variation in the ways that schools respond to reforms (Allison & Hargreaves, 2008; Louis, Febey, & Schroeder, 2005; Rossman & Wilson, 1996; Sipple, Killeen, & Monk, 2004).

Political Culture and Formulation of Educational Policy

In the United States, individual states bear the responsibility for developing most significant social policies, even when they do so within federal guidelines (Reeves, 1990). Even the No Child Left Behind (NCLB) Act acknowledges the central role of the states in setting standards and designing their own accountability systems (Sunderman, 2003), and the more recent federal initiatives such as Race to the Top also presume that the states will change policies in areas such as teacher and principal evaluation and school choice. NCLB foreshadowed a more formal, national regulatory system, but because school funding is local and state based, federal influence is likely to remain contested for the foreseeable future. In other words, the state is, historically, the locus in which educational policy is played out (Timar & Kirp, 1988), and state political activism is increasing, along with vocal resistance among both politicians/policy advocates (Scott, 2012) and scholars (Ravitch, 2012) to the national standards and accountability movement. It is beyond the scope of this chapter to consider how current debates over national state control will emerge, but there is reason to believe that states may be, at minimum, ambivalent about giving up their constitutional right to separateness in education (Gass & Stergios, 2013; Strauss, 2013).[3]

States exercise both direct and indirect influences on school districts and schools. Direct influence comes through legitimate rules that are based on accumulated legislative and court actions (Roch & Howard, 2008); indirect influence emerges as part of cultural constraints and shared assumptions that have also accumulated over long periods of time (Marshall, Mitchell, & Wirt, 1986; Timar & Kirp, 1988). However, although both the cultural and legal/legislative systems are designed for stability, stakeholders show little agreement on the proper state role in education when confronting a high demand for reform. States are, for example, expected to lead standard setting for student achievement and curricular content and monitor school quality, while also simplifying regulations for running schools and promoting site-based management and citizen participation (Elmore & Fuhrman, 1995; Louis, 1998; Swanson & Stevenson, 2002), but recent reviews of school reform efforts suggest that states' capacity to carry out the expected role is variable, as is states' ability to finance significant reform efforts (Gottfried et al., 2011; Mehan, 2013). As states attempt to enact policies and mechanisms to affect education, political culture will play a role in determining how they balance conflicting expectations and policies, and whether the development of capacity to exercise leadership in school reform is a priority. State-specific studies have continued to show that political culture and accumulated history help to predict both the dynamics and outcomes of legislation (Mazzoni, 1993; Sacken & Medina, 1990).

In addition to political culture, state educational policy making and activism are affected by legislative politics, structural limitations, economic constraints, and legal context (Roch & Howard, 2008; Wong, 1989). States have, therefore, struggled to find the appropriate policy mechanisms to influence teaching and learning—the core of educational policy, but also the most difficult and resistant to change from outside the school. Because of political and economic pressures, policy makers often use a narrow range of policy mechanisms (mandates and incentives) because they are most likely to produce positive, short-term results (Rossman & Wilson, 1996), although they also narrow and constrain professional flexibility at the school level (Olsen & Sexton, 2009). Longer-term strategies such as capacity building and systems change are less common, partly because they are slow to demonstrate significant impacts (Datnow et al., 2003; Elmore & Fuhrman, 1995; Gross, Booker, & Goldhaber, 2009).

Regardless of the type of policy mechanisms that states use to develop and implement educational policy, the primary values driving policies are *efficiency* (detailed procedures for school authorities to abide by); *equity*—redistribution of resources for those lacking them; *quality*—standards of excellence (Garms, Guthrie, & Pierce, 1978); and *choice*—the range of options available (Marshall et al., 1986). There are distinct differences in the ways that those values are manifested in state educational policy makers' actions and school laws (Marshall, Mitchell, & Wirt, 1989).

A recent study of U.S. states (Louis et al., 2008) expanded on the values driving policies by combining frameworks of political culture dimensions, level and type of stakeholder involvement, and policy levers to analyze differences in states' educational policies for leadership and accountability. The seven states in this study (Indiana, Mississippi, Missouri, Nebraska, New Mexico, Oregon, and Texas) differed and were similar in complex ways: Political culture clearly was a factor in all, and accounted for differences as well as similarities. In the next two sections of this chapter, we explore the impact of political culture on the development of state educational policy and provide illustrations of schools' responses to policy in two states.

ILLUSTRATIVE CASES OF POLITICAL CULTURE

To investigate state political cultures, we use case descriptions of North Carolina and Nebraska.[4] Our focus is on the evolution of states' policies both before and after the implementation of NCLB, which allows us to analyze the development during a period characterized by greater federal activity. These states' educational policies differ greatly when examining their approaches to reform, especially standards and assessments, and can be explained partly by using Elazar's culture types.[5] For example, one study developed a scale where 1 was considered highly moralistic and 9 was considered highly traditionalistic: Nebraska had a score of 3.6 and North Carolina an 8.5 (Sharkansky, 1969). Another study used an index to rank states and subcultures with respect to the openness of their governmental structures and political processes on a scale that ranged from 1 to 19. Nebraska received a score of 12, while North Carolina scored an 8 (Herzik, 1985).

Thus, we began with the assumption that the two states represent genuinely different political cultures that we examine for differences in policy development, policy type, and local-level reactions to policies.

Data and Methods

We provided an overview of the states' educational policy climate by outlining key historical events and policies in their evolution of accountability and school improvement initiatives. In doing so, we also looked for the roles and perspectives of different stakeholders during the development and implementation of the policies. Our primary sources of information on the states' policies came from the states' departments of education, dissertations, periodicals, scholarly journals, and personal communications. In both states, we also interviewed staff members in two school districts in each state over a three-year period, while documentary updates and member checking continued through early 2013.[6]

When analyzing the data, we began by identifying key state activities and actors, and then looked for how their effects were manifested in policy, and subsequently in the schools. The advantage of this technique is that it involves finding critical incidents believed to be influenced by the state policy, then looking back at the policies to find possible connections (Elmore, 1979). In addition, we looked beyond a single-level organizational analysis (focusing on one level as the "locus" of culture) to a multiple-variable and relationship analysis that allowed us to consider how states' political culture is manifested from the state level down to the individual level in schools. Examining multiple variables and relationships allowed us to determine how cultural components are interrelated at different levels, thus allowing culture to be the moderating variable (Dansereau & Alutto, 1990).

We started data collection in North Carolina in 2000, when it was already considered a "high accountability" state. Data collection began in Nebraska in 2003, when it had no statewide accountability system at all (based on accountability components each state had before the 2001 reauthorization of ESEA). Thus, based on the consistency of these scholars with Elazar and with our own interviews and document analyses, we also conceptualize North Carolina and Nebraska as Elazar did.

The choice of these two states from a larger sample of nine was also based on several purposive criteria. First, they are both moderately sized states that are characterized by smaller urban areas, small towns, and significant rural agricultural populations. Neither has a mega city: Omaha is the largest city in Nebraska, with a population of slightly less than half a million, and Charlotte is the largest in North Carolina, with a population of just more than 730,000.[7]

State Characteristics that Affect Political Culture

We will first provide a brief overview of each state's relevant history, and then discuss the intersection between political culture and educational policy making.

North Carolina. The history of North Carolina is intertwined with the region that includes most of the original Southern states in which the plantation system, with large agricultural holdings and slave labor, dominated the eastern part of the state, while small farms characterized the more mountainous western part. Early residents (before and during the 18th century) came from all over Northern Europe, but later waves of southern and central European immigration largely passed the state by. After the Civil War, the economy evolved to focus on tobacco, but other crops are also important, as is the furniture and textile industry. The outmigration of blacks starting in the 1930s has left a population that is predominantly white (68%), but with a substantial and increasing black population (22%) and a very rapid increase in Hispanics (approximately 8.5%).[8] Increasingly, however, the state's economy is focused on the development of the financial and high tech industries. The once poor state is now one of the most economically vibrant in the southeastern part of the country (Fleer, 1994).

Economic gains have not been accompanied by educational progress to the same degree. Many of those who move to North Carolina to work in the new industries are highly educated, but the graduation rates of North Carolina residents are still well below the national average for white students (64% compared to 76%) as well as Hispanics (44% compared to 55%). (Black and Asian graduation rates are about the same as the national average, at 50% and 76%.)[9] Those who graduate from high school are as likely to attend college as are students in other states, but those who do not make it through high school are left behind. Spending on primary and secondary education is below the national average. Most of the funding for education comes from the state: Only 38 percent is provided through local property or other taxes, and state policies are far-reaching, including teacher salary scales and textbook options.

The most apparent political characteristic of North Carolina is the fluid boundaries between political parties and the lack of a dominant perspective. The most recent election, like those in many states, resulted in a significant shift to the right in state elected positions. However, Barack Obama carried the state in 2010, and historically state elected officials come from both parties, and represent both traditional and more progressive perspectives within each party.

Nebraska. Nebraska's history cannot be separated from its engagement with Midwestern populist movements, which fostered a strong concern for the rights of farmers and other small business people operating under harsh economic conditions (Ostler, 1992). Although there was some diversity among the original immigrants, Nebraska remains one of the least diverse states, with more than 85 percent of the population reported as white. Although the United States as a whole has encountered a surge in immigrant populations, less than 6 percent of Nebraskans are foreign born.

Politics in Nebraska has always revolved around farming. While the Populist Party was a major force in the state, it faded in the late 1890s, replaced by the dominance of a strong Republican Party. Nebraska retained a focus on progressive policies, however, and was an early proponent of child protection and food safety laws. Nebraskans have a long tendency to be fiercely independent, resisting excessive intrusion of the state and federal governments into local decision making. It is the only state to have a small (49 representatives) nonpartisan unicameral legislature that meets briefly;[10] some analysts have observed that legislature leadership structures are deliberately weak (Comer, 1980).

These features of Nebraska history are interwoven with the educational system. The state spends an average of approximately $10,000 per student per year (just slightly below the national average) and 57 percent of that comes from local property taxes. Most school districts are small or medium-sized—there are only three in the state that enroll more than 10,000 students.[11] Nebraska has traditionally placed a relatively high value on education. Nebraska students tend to do relatively well on the National Assessment of State Progress tests: For example, only two states (Massachusetts and Connecticut) scored significantly higher in reading for fourth graders (nine-year-olds), while they were not significantly different from other higher-scoring states among eighth graders (13-year-olds). In addition, it has one of the highest high school graduation rates (87%), and an above average proportion of college-aged youths are enrolled in higher education (57%, as contrasted with 46% nationally).[12] Students in poverty performed relatively better than for the country as a whole (NCES, 2002), while black students were half as likely to graduate from high school as white students.

A Comparison of State Political Cultures and Educational Policy

Elazar (1980) argues that states' political culture is deeply affected by their history. In this section, we elaborate on the brief descriptions and link each state's context to the way educational policies are made. We focus, in particular, on the different approaches taken to the national/international movement to increase standards and accountability in education.

North Carolina – Political Culture. As noted earlier, based on Elazar's (1970) assessment of three predominant political cultures in the United States, North Carolina is generally regarded as traditional, but later authors have noted that there are a few progressive strands. Overall, North Carolina is considered semi-open and centralized because the concentration of power and influence is primarily with the governor's office and the general assembly, but there are a few avenues for the public to get involved and exert their influence. Historically, the governor's office has been the dominant political player in the educational arena, with the general assembly/legislature a close second. North Carolina has a long history of rationalism, most notably in its gradual movement toward a comprehensive state accountability framework well before the passage of NCLB. Efficiency and egalitarianism have taken a back seat to quality in the state, although the state has been forced by the court system to address inequality and by fiscal restraints to be more efficient. Overall, North Carolina state policy makers have used mandates to implement educational policies, while building capacity and focusing on systems change as policy levers.

How Education Policy Is Made in North Carolina. Influence over education policy in North Carolina is concentrated in the governor's office and the governor's presence is felt in almost every educational policy-making arena. For example, the governor has the authority to appoint people to the state board of education, the state standards and accountability committee, and the education cabinet. The governor is also able to appoint four people to the only independent advocacy-oriented education group with influence, the Public School Forum. Although the governor elects members to serve on the state board of education, the general assembly has authority over educational policy decisions and has historically micromanaged the state board of education. Education has been a top priority for governors of North Carolina for a long time. Between 1993 and 2013, governors were from the Democratic Party, and education was a policy priority for all of them.[13] The most recently elected governor, Republican Pat McCrory, is also leading the policy discussions, although his focus is on slowing increases in K-12 education spending. Although the specific policy initiatives have changed because of a change in parties, the dominance of the gubernatorial voice is still clear.

Besides the governor, the North Carolina Department of Public Instruction is the agency charged with implementing state public school laws, policies, and procedures. In addition, the public elects a state superintendent to the state board of education, but this position generally has not held real statutory authority or power within educational policy circles, although there are recent efforts to change this. Thus, educational policy making in the state of North Carolina primarily is a top-down process, but with lot of influence exerted by prominent outside stakeholders.

The main avenue for broader external stakeholder involvement in North Carolina is through the Public School Forum, an advocacy group for K-12 public education comprised of about 64 members. The Forum was initiated by two members of the state legislature with a grant from a prominent local foundation to foster long-term strategic thinking by bringing political and business figures as well as parents and community stakeholders interested in public education together to advocate for a joint agenda. Most of the people who serve on the Forum are very influential in the state; about one-third are business members, one-third elected or appointed officials, and one-third educators such as the head of the teachers' union, the state superintendent, and the president of the community colleges. On the makeup of the Forum board, the executive director said, "it's a nice combination as a board because there are checks and balances there." Every other year, the Forum investigates a major educational issue and builds support for its subsequent agenda.

The legislature and the public look to the Forum to provide the "real story" of what is happening in North Carolina schools, and overall the members tend to collaborate with one another and work well together focusing on broad policy systems changes. While there is currently considerable discussion among conservative populists about eliminating the Common Core curriculum (which North Carolina adopted early), there is already pressure building from the business community and within the Forum to keep it in place.

Standards and Accountability Policies in North Carolina. North Carolina has a long history of accountability policies dating back to 1977 when the governor's office required all high school students to pass a competency test to graduate from high school. By 1983, the Department of Public Instruction required students to take part in state accountability tests for reading, writing, and math, and in 1985 the general assembly made the first move toward a statewide comprehensive and rational curriculum framework. Toward the end of that decade, the general assembly passed the School Improvement Accountability Act, which restructured leadership and responsibility for accountability in schools, and in 1990, the state began to provide school report cards based on the state tests. The ABCs of Public Education, passed by the general assembly in 1996, established an accountability plan that included a school growth model that systematically measured students' yearly academic progress on the state curriculum. In addition, the ABCs delineated five strategic goals set by the state board of education and the Public School Forum including: (1) high student performance; (2) healthy students in safe, orderly, and caring schools; (3) quality teachers, administrators, and staff; (4) strong family, community, and business support; and (5) effective and efficient operations. By the time NCLB was passed in 2001, the only difference it made in the North Carolina education system was that the test data had to be disaggregated by student groups. Otherwise, efforts for testing and standards were already well under way in the state.

Although decision-making power in North Carolina is centralized and governor driven, the accountability policies have given school districts some flexibility. For example, the School Improvement and Accountability Act of 1989 increased the authority and capacity of school districts to address local needs to improve student achievement. This act also decreased the size and power of the state board of education and reallocated funding to the local level. The ABCs policy also increased local control and accountabil-ity for student achievement by requiring each individual school to set its own achieve-ment goals and targets for student improvement. Funds again were diverted from the Department of Public Instruction to local school districts for professional development use and other needs. Thus, while policy making remains centralized, the state began to gradually decentralize by encouraging local districts to create their own local school improvement practices that fit their contexts and situations.

By 2008, the North Carolina State Board of Education adopted a policy called the "Framework for Change: The Next Generation of Assessments and Accountability" in an attempt to modernize the state's previous standards and assessment system. Because of this, the state began implementing a new statewide curriculum, testing, and accountabil-ity model in the 2012–2013 school year, based on the Common Core. Even though the state has been long committed to a statewide standards and accountability framework, funding issues have forced the state to focus on saving money. Recently, for example, the state has rolled back some previous accountability requirements because of fiscal con-cerns and the state's economic downturn. Funding problems have also led the govern-ment to focus more on efficiency, including elimination of the end of high school exams to save funds, and a recent proposal to eliminate teacher tenure. In addition, in early 2011 the governor signed a bill eliminating statewide testing except for tests required under NCLB.

Additional Elements of Political Culture in North Carolina. North Carolina state officials prioritized quality through their efforts to recruit and retain high-quality teachers from inside and outside of the state and through various leadership development efforts. More specifically, the legislature passed the Excellent Schools Act in 1997, which increased state teacher salaries to the national average while also increasing teacher accountability. At the same time, the state began providing incentives to strong teachers while changing laws to make it easier to get rid of poor teachers, and the current governor has proposed eliminating teacher tenure. In addition to seeking to improve teacher quality, North Car-olina also began recruiting and retaining quality administrators through a state leader-ship development program and a principal fellows program, in collaboration with local university partners.

Although North Carolina emphasized teacher and leadership quality, the state histor-ically has not focused on egalitarianism, especially in the area of funding formulas and how they relate to equal opportunity of education. In 1994, a lawsuit was filed against the state by groups in five of the low-wealth rural counties, and the suit was upheld in 2005 after an appeal by the state. The court ruled that the state's funding of public schools was unconstitutional and that it had to work to improve equity and quality in these high-poverty counties. By 2012, however, the state was still among the most regressive in its funding distributions (Baker, Sciarra, & Farrie, 2012). The last formal vestiges of racial segregation were eliminated under court order, but funding disparities associated with race/ethnicity remain.

In contrast, the state has placed more emphasis on providing students and parents a variety of educational options. North Carolina has supported choice policies for several years, beginning in 1996 when legislation was passed to support the creation of charter schools. The state has a mandated maximum of 100 charter schools, but discussions have occurred about whether to lift the cap. The National Alliance for Charter Schools rates the effectiveness of this form of choice in each state, and ranks North Carolina 32 out of 50, noting that the cap, funding, accountability, and governance issues need attention.[14] The most recent budget also provides funding to allow low-income children to attend private schools (while cutting other educational funding).

In sum, North Carolina's response to the federal push for increased standards and accountability was to continue to mandate statewide testing at certain ages and to maintain its high-quality rigorous standards, while decentralizing slightly and attending to quality. With a long history of rational and comprehensive policies, state policy makers have encouraged continuous improvement at the local level, thus increasing their capacity to handle all of the system changes. The state faces significant funding challenges that have slowed the years of a nuanced approach to accountability. Like in many states, there are concerns about the change in assessments that accompanies the implementation of the Common Core curriculum.[15]

Nebraska Political Culture

In contrast to North Carolina, Nebraska historically has exhibited a minimal state policy presence in education, maintaining a strong emphasis on local control and decentralized decision-making processes. The state has an open policy-making process, with several avenues for both internal and external stakeholders to exert their influence and provide input on educational ideas. The state of Nebraska had standards in place by 1997 and assessment regulations by 1999, but until recently allowed districts to create their own standards and assessments as long as they aligned with the state standards. The political culture of the state is "individualistic" (Elazar, 1970, 1984) in the sense that the state gives districts as much autonomy and local control as possible while still maintaining compliance with state and federal policies.

For many years Nebraskan state leaders resisted mandating that districts adopt wholesale statewide standards and testing, but in 2009 finally set in motion an implementation plan for a statewide accountability framework. The state has not focused on egalitarianism but lawsuits forced the state to take a closer look at equity and its public education funding formula. However, overall the state is neither particularly regressive nor progressive in terms of steering funds toward low-income districts (Baker et al., 2012). Efficiency and choice have also taken a back seat to quality, especially while the state focused on maintaining decentralized, but rigorous, standards and assessments across multiple districts. Nebraskan state policy makers were reluctant to change their system until pressures from the federal government became too pervasive, and in 2012 earned a "grade" of D+ from *Education Week*'s Quality Counts report for their accountability efforts (in contrast to North Carolina's unsurprising A) (*Education Week*, 2012). Because of its commitment to local control, the state has not used inducements as a policy lever, but it does have a history of building capacity by training administrators and teachers in how to create and use locally designed assessments.

How Education Policy Is Made in Nebraska. Educational policy making in Nebraska is an open process and there are several avenues for public participation and input. Although education is listed as a top priority in the governor's office, fiscal concerns over the cost of education usually take precedence over other educational issues. The unicameral legislature has also focused primarily on fiscal issues. Thus, educational initiatives and policies unrelated to financing are usually addressed by the elected state board of education and the commissioner of education, but with broad public input. The state board and the commissioner have regular "policy forums" where they elicit input and have discussions and open dialogues over education policy issues. For the policy forums, the board and commissioner take ideas out into the community around the state and have conversations with administrators, school board members, teachers, and parents. The Nebraska State Department of Education also has ongoing communication with the education community through regular workshops and by providing information to the public about current education initiatives. For example, the state department of education hired a group to conduct focus groups to gauge the public's reaction to one proposed education initiative and to build grassroots public support.

While the state board of education and the commissioner have a lot of policy influence, the Nebraska State Education Association, a teachers' union, and a group of superintendents around the state also have significant say in how educational policies get translated and implemented into local school contexts.[16] In addition, Nebraska has a system of independent intermediate education service units to provide resources and help individual school districts implement policies. The business community and the chamber of commerce regularly exercise influence, but tend to only look at efficiency and take a hard no-taxes line when it comes to funding. Raising property taxes to pay for education is a major issue in the state and most oppose it (although the end result is an average level of funding compared to other states). Because the state has a long history of local control, most educational decision making is decentralized with power given to local school districts to make the best decisions for their communities.

Standards and Accountability Policies in Nebraska. The federal push for comprehensive statewide standards and accountability model had a greater impact on Nebraska than on other states because of its long-standing commitment to decentralized decision making and local control. Prior to NCLB, Nebraska had developed model standards and testing, but districts were expected to adapt them to their local contexts. District standards were reviewed at the state level to determine whether they were of equal or greater rigor than state standards, but individual districts determined what standards were important and designed (or chose) assessments that fit their standards.

Although reluctant to mandate the details of an accountability system, the state recognized in 1997 that it needed a statewide effort to improve student achievement across all educational sectors. The Nebraska P-16 Initiative coordinated educational efforts across Nebraskan systems through an alignment of curriculum documents in English and language arts, mathematics, and world languages. By 1999, Nebraska instituted the Educational Quality Accountability Act, which required assessment of student learning and the regular reporting of student performance by each school district. With this act, the state board adopted an assessment and reporting plan, which began with statewide writing assessments. For the other subject areas, however, districts could either adopt the state's assessments or create their own. Like district-created standards, locally constructed assessments were reviewed by the state department of education and independent assessment experts to ensure their rigor. The amount of time and effort districts put into creating their own standards and assessments varied, but most spent significant amounts of time and resources in the process.

The Education Quality and Accountability Act was amended in 2000 to establish general procedures for implementing standards and assessments and to require districts to report student achievement. The School-based Teacher-led Assessment and Reporting System (STARS) required districts to adopt measurable quality academic standards and to report the results of all local assessments on a building-level basis to the state. By the time NCLB was made into law in 2001, the state, with leadership from the commissioner of education, fought hard to keep local control even though the federal government was pushing states to centralize their standards and accountability systems. The commissioner of education at the time, Doug Christensen, was successful in getting the Nebraska model approved as a legitimate alternative. In this sense, the impact of the federal policy was not perceived as dramatic. But for many districts, the change was difficult and time consuming as they "tweaked" their standards and assessments to conform to NCLB. The political culture of Nebraska is evident, also, in the inclination of districts to distinguish themselves by creating standards that went above and beyond state expectations. It was considered an extra mark of quality when a district established standards that exceeded state standards.

The state continued to fight with the federal Department of Education over the Nebraska model. One sticking point with the federal legislation was that the state could not properly comply with the annual yearly progress reporting mandate because it had multiple locally designed assessments rather than a single statewide assessment. In 2005, the legislature and commissioner of education adopted the Creating Essential Educational Opportunities for All Children Act, which set aside funds for teacher mentoring programs and for teacher time to work on local assessments. By 2009, however, the Nebraskan legislature caved in to federal demands after years of pressure and proposed the Nebraska State Accountability Framework, a statewide assessment system that outlined a plan to test students in reading, writing, math, and science using the same assessment across the state. Because of the shift the commissioner of education, who fought hard to keep standards and assessments local, resigned his post. State education leaders continue to struggle to make sense of these changes in the context of their commitment to local control, including a general lack of interest in adopting the Common Core curriculum. Some even argue that Nebraska state law prevents consideration of Common Core because it requires the Department of Education to work with Nebraska educators to develop any state curriculum.[17]

Additional Elements of Political Culture in Nebraska. Besides fighting so hard to keep the standards and accountability movement in local hands, the most contentious issue in Nebraska is financing public education. The legislature provides state and local aid to schools but, as mentioned earlier, legislators' main concern is balancing the budget and being fiscally responsible. This has raised issues of equal educational opportunity that pit urban (generally wealthier) and rural districts (often less wealthy because of federally managed land trusts) against each other. Because of the economic downturn in the state and throughout the country, Nebraskan legislators have tried to cut funding to schools in an equitable manner.[18]

In an effort to create more equity and efficiency in rural communities, state and business leaders have pushed to consolidate small districts. This process has been contentious because it butts up against the idea of local control of education. Both the governor's office and groups of small rural districts oppose the move, arguing that combining smaller districts would not save state money. School finance reform is largely off the table.

Finally, school choice in Nebraska has not been a policy priority. Although legislation was introduced for charter schools and school voucher programs in 1998 and 1999, these issues did not make it out of the House committee. A more recent bill that would have allowed charter schools only in Omaha also failed.

In sum, Nebraska has an open political culture with ample room for participation at every level of policy making. The state's first response to the national narrative about state accountability was to ignore it in favor of the traditional investment in local control. Teachers and administrators within local districts spent a significant amount of time and effort creating their own accountability systems that reflected their unique communities, with evidence of state leaders working to build capacity through the regional intermediate service units that provided local teachers and others with assessment training. The reaction to how this local control worked in practice revealed a political culture that values collaboration as well as individualism. The state still largely ignores issues of inequality and efficiency, nor is choice a state priority.[19] The dominant belief seems to be that the state should reach consensus about what needs to be done, and then let everyone go and carry that out in their own way.

Comparing Political Culture, Policy Levers, and Their Consequences. The differences in the political cultures of North Carolina and Nebraska appear more evident than their similarities, whether looking at how each state responded to federal legislation to create accountability systems or each state's response to the economic exigencies that have faced both in recent years.

North Carolina, on the one hand, was one of the first states to develop a statewide accountability system that included state curriculum standards, testing, and rewards and sanctions years before NCLB was enacted. Driven by centralized gubernatorial policies and groups that are appointed by the governor, policies have been developed over a long period of time in a comprehensive and rational way, while being updated and amended slightly over the years to include Common Core. Nebraska, in contrast, was the last state to agree to a statewide testing and standards model, two years after the implementation of NCLB, and then only because of external pressure. Although this new development has forced the state to centralize its accountability framework, it has not changed the political culture of the state, which still favors local control and decentralized decision making. While both states use mandates to implement their accountability policies, the Nebraskan way of mandating is much less heavy-handed than North Carolina's and invariably involves consultation before, during, and after the passage of a new piece of legislation. The one new contribution of NCLB was the impetus to develop a statewide student information system and a push to disaggregate data by groups to look for and address achievement gaps.

Despite trends that favor a new public management model of education with a distinct focus on cost-effectiveness and efficient operations, neither of the two states that we analyzed for this chapter has put much time or energy into making sure their systems are efficient. Although business communities in both states lobby to keep taxes low, few, if any, policy levers have been used to make efficiency a state priority. Each of the two states has approached efficiency in different ways. In North Carolina, the Forum proposed to address efficiency by eliminating bureaucracy in state-level jobs; Nebraska's business community, on the other hand, has focused exclusively on keeping taxes in the state low.

In Nebraska, concerns about quality improvement and building capacity are also long-standing, but the political culture of individualism is evident in the push to maintain local involvement in defining and measuring educational quality even when doing so required an elaborate (and cumbersome) process to determine how each district's accountability systems measured up on a quality scale. Resources in Nebraska were diverted to help individual school districts train teachers and administrators in how to create and administer high-quality standards and assessments because doing so was new for Nebraskan teachers. Quality in North Carolina, in contrast, takes on a different, more traditional form, with state leaders at the top charged with maintaining a rigorous system of standards and testing, and state leaders mandating all districts implement the statewide policies. Preserving quality in North Carolina also meant putting policies into place to help retain and recruit high-quality teachers and administrators—but not at the cost of giving them more professional autonomy.

Both states are considered open systems, but Nebraska is much more open to external stakeholder influences in the policy-making process than North Carolina. The state board of education and the commissioner of education have built regular contact with school personnel and the public into the policy-making process, with state leaders going out into the community to gather input during each phase of the policy development process. In comparison, there is only one real avenue for stakeholders to influence education policy in North Carolina, and that is through the Public School Forum, which is stocked with business, government, and school-level elites, with fewer teacher, parent, or interested community member voices.[20] The two states are the most similar in how they have handled and dealt with issues of funding and equity, with both states experiencing a rural and urban divide. The lawsuits in each state challenge the existing funding formulas by arguing that because the states do not distribute resources in an equitable fashion, districts, especially rural ones, are unable to provide quality educational opportunities for all students. Both lawsuits have resulted in attempts by state officials to redistribute funds more equitably, but these are constrained by weak economies.

Are states becoming more alike because of the accountability movement? The answer to this question is both yes and no. On the one hand, both states now have statewide accountability systems with standards and assessments in each of the core subject areas. In addition, each state prepares and distributes annual student report cards so that parents and the larger public can see the results of the assessments and follow student progress. As a result of the accountability movement, each state has also had to confront achievement gaps between white students and students of color and between students in high- and low-income communities.

Despite these similarities, the political cultures of the two states have resulted in two very different approaches to accountability. The superficial similarity in some accountability structures belies the basic differences, which are largely consistent with the classification of these two states as "traditional" and "individualistic" (Elazar, 1970; Herzik, 1985). In the educational arena, this difference is nowhere more prominent than in the choices that the states have made—and continue to make—about promoting common standards for all schools, and monitoring outcomes based on those standards. Our findings are consistent with the observations of political scientists that national trends may hide the prominence of local interest groups (Wolak et al., 2002), and suggest that differences in educational political culture are deeper than in many other areas, which are more affected by cross-state fissures around religion and social values (Layman & Carmines, 1997).

DOES STATE POLITICAL CULTURE MAKE A DIFFERENCE? A BOTTOM-UP VIEW[21]

Our study included investigations of local responses to state policy initiatives, which suggest that, while federal policies are relevant, both district and school-based educators are more responsive to state initiatives, including their interpretations of federal policies

(Louis & Robinson, 2012; Louis, Thomas, & Anderson, 2010). To illustrate, we look at local perspectives from North Carolina and Nebraska.

North Carolina: State Accountability Is "Part of the Water"

River District[22] regards itself as the vanguard of accountability, and many teachers and administrators believe that state standards are based, in part, on what they were already doing. River District's perception of itself as the vanguard of accountability was evident in West Patterson and Wrigley High schools, both of which had systematic means of collecting and using data, as mandated by the state, to determine overall performance and to develop the schools' annual improvement plan. A primary piece of the accountability-based data was the results on the end of course (EOC) exams. The school district disaggregated EOC test results by competency to provide teachers with information on how to focus their efforts with successive groups of students. Teachers believed that the data were an effective method of feedback to gear instruction toward students on the weak end of the competencies.

The schools' principals and teachers worked together by analyzing data and forming data utilization plans to align their instruction with students' EOC results. Teachers and administrators did not, however, rely solely on EOC data to form a comprehensive view of school, teachers, and student performance. They argued to use multiple indicators to demonstrate students' competencies in a subject if they were unable to pass an EOC test. Both schools also surveyed their teachers, parents, and students about the schools' climate, programs, and staff efficacy as a means to plan curricular improvements and show teachers and community members how their high school ranked in comparison to others in North Carolina.

Maple Grove Elementary, in contrast to the two high schools, is a small school serving families on the edge of financial meltdown. Although the school does relatively well on North Carolina state tests, the principal describes this as a challenge. The district is home to a military base, which contributes to high turnover of families and teachers. In spite of the poverty rate, the principal and teachers generally support the standards and accountability systems set in place in the state.

The principal combines a strong emphasis on social justice for her poor students and families with a high level of expectations for teachers and students and emphasizes preparing children to break through the cycle of poverty in which their families have become mired. When she became principal, she "counseled out" teachers who did not accept her dual emphasis on standards and caring. Her focus is on getting consensus around big goals, and then providing teachers with "a very long leash so to speak. If they are doing what is in the best interest of children, and it follows along with our school vision, then . . . I almost always find the funding for it." Teachers agree.

The district and school administrators are critical of the state's inequitable funding system and their inability to have a voice in the debates. However, they work hard to create a profile of success within the state system, and to find unique ways of adapting funding and programs to their students, and speak positively of the inducements (additional funding) that accrue to schools that are making progress. The school professionals do not see significant inconsistency between what external agencies (state and district) are looking for in education, and what they are working toward in the school.

Although in her position for only five years, the principal radiates a sense that the environment—private funders, state agencies, and the district office—is a source of energy for change rather than an impediment. While she quibbled with a few aspects of the state's accountability system and the way it meshes with NCLB, she sees, for the most part, that the testing and disaggregation of data have been helpful because they keep people's eyes on the need to raise student achievement.

Nebraska: Maintaining Localism in a Rural and Medium-Sized Setting

In Nebraska our focus will be on district as well as school responses because state policy initiatives gave the former increasing responsibility for implementing accountability.

Midwest District, in a medium-sized city, was fortunate because the development of district standards involved the participation of hundreds of teachers at all levels.[23] When the state standards and accountability legislation were changed, the district found it relatively easy to demonstrate that its standards exceeded those of the state, so teachers were generally positive about the standards and saw them as "locally owned."

Even with the large degree of local control and teacher participation, the shift to a more district-centered school system created tensions. Student assessments were created primarily by a team of experts at the district level and then adjusted to fit NCLB requirements. In one sense, the accountability system was well under way but teachers perceived district-developed assessments as an intrusion as well as time-consuming. To many, the push for standards has changed the way that schools view districts as well as the way districts interact with the state. A large number of teachers engaged with the development process, but they were handpicked and final decisions were made by curriculum specialists and outside consultants. In order to allay some of the school (principal and teacher) concerns about the burdens of tracking student progress the district provided simplified recording tools. Nevertheless, there seems to be an underlying consensus that the state is over-assessing students and many expressed concern over the recent centralizing shift and state pressure.

Johnston Public Schools (JPS) is the most rural of the districts discussed in this chapter, and serves a population that is relatively affluent and predominantly white.[24] The administrative team consisted of the superintendent and three principals. The staff is stable and teachers are experienced and well educated (60% hold MA degrees). Recent reductions in state funding resulted in the consolidation of the elementary and middle schools, the loss of several teachers, and the elimination of a curriculum director position in the district office. The community complained, but failed to pass an override tax levy.

JPS students perform well overall; district priorities were focused on deeper student learning and better education for the bottom quartile. State reviews of the JPS-developed assessments have always been glowing, and school professionals believed that they had developed the system in collaboration with the state. A dominant view was that accountability policies were here to stay, and that the responsibility of local educators was to constructively engage with state policies and their implementation. Not surprising, they have volunteered as a pilot district for state initiatives, and have supported participation of district educators on state-sponsored curriculum and assessment work groups.

JPS administrators believed that current standards and accountability policies were contributing to a refocusing on teacher responsibility for student learning outcomes and related teaching methods rather than on coverage of the curriculum. They claimed that local initiatives were not just a response to state directions, but often emerged in concert with those directions. Teachers also believe that the state trusts them to provide high-quality education and gives them the responsibility to initiate programs and to respond to locally sensitive indicators (such as ACT scores).

Comparison of Local Responses

Teachers and administrators in the local schools that we studied are proud of their educational policy history: The North Carolina teachers we interviewed point with satisfaction to the progress that their state has made over a short period of time in improving educational quality; Nebraskans relish their state's role as a policy outlier around continued reliance on local input and control. While there are some concerns that the state's policies make it difficult for Nebraska to qualify for current federal incentive funding (which assumes a more consistent state role), the price is viewed as relatively small compared to preserving state traditions.[25]

In other words, as the tide of accountability swept across the United States, much has changed but much has also stayed the same, both at the state level and in the schools. The simultaneous presence of stability and change is, in our view, one of the major justifications for reemphasizing the analysis of state political cultures. Although as policy analysts we can be swayed by the seemingly endless calls for reform and can turn our attention to studying the impacts of these initiatives in schools, we also recognize that states mediate the way these broad change forces affect schools and teachers. Furthermore, the way they are mediated, at least over the long haul, is apparently consistent with historical preferences and modes of operating that are rooted not just in the past few decades, but in at least a century of experience.

STATE POLITICAL CULTURES: WHAT ABOUT HIGHER EDUCATION?

This chapter has laid out an argument for the continuing relevance of state political cultures in determining both how educational policies are made and the nature of the policies themselves. These arguments develop a counternarrative to the dominant assumption that the pressures of globalization and a newly muscular federal government have overwhelmed the local voice in shaping K-12 education. We do not, however, wish to end this chapter with the simple conclusion that states are consistently powerful actors in the educational policy environment.

When we began to apply a state political culture lens to the related sector of public higher education, it quickly became clear that state political cultures explain less about institutional choices and system characteristics and practices than in public schools. Indeed, with few exceptions, research in higher education rarely examines state policy differences, except at a superficial descriptive level. We initially found this surprising because the state pressures on higher education to be more accountable and to be more responsive to political priorities emerged at nearly the same time as the accountability movement in the K-12 sector, and have been persistent (at least for state-funded systems) for many years (McLendon, Hearn, & Deaton, 2006; Stein, 1979). To understand the limits of a political culture perspective, we felt that it was important to examine why political cultures may have less impact on the higher education systems that politicians and the public often regard as the jewels of their state. We examine a number of factors that may help to account for the difference in effects, including funding patterns, institutional structures, and the source of accountability pressures.

Funding: Varied Sources Reduce State Influence

The influence of states' political cultures on higher education can be seen most clearly in the funding of higher education, which is from direct legislative appropriations to higher education in the form of subsidies, grants, tuition waivers, loans, work study, and loan forgiveness (Doyle, Delaney, & Naughton, 2008). While declining in recent years, higher education is often the largest discretionary expense in states' budgets (NASBO, 2006, as cited in Layzell, 2007). Legislatures' direct appropriations reflect decisions about state support and whether financial aid awarded to students is based on financial need or merit.

Factors other than political culture appear to determine how states make their decisions about higher education funding. In theory, states classified as moralistic emphasize correcting inequalities and improving citizen well-being through government aid and programs. Again, in theory, this should extend to higher education, which is generally viewed as an important public good. However, even a cursory examination of state funding patterns in the 1980s (before the general trend toward declining state support for higher education) suggests that moralistic states such as Oregon do not necessarily invest more money in higher education than states with traditionalistic or individualistic policy cultures (Layzell & Lyddon, 1990, pp. 22–23). Some traditionalistic and individualistic states invested heavily in higher education (Wyoming and North Carolina) while others were low in the allocation of income-adjusted funding (Connecticut, Illinois, and Florida).

The potential for state influence through targeting funding is, if anything, eroding. State funding for higher education is increasingly a smaller proportion of higher education budgets in all states, and provides lower per-student support (SHEEO, 2012). Other sources, including the federal government and increased tuition, represent a clear uptick as the main source of funding in all but a handful of states. While the amount that a higher education institution receives from federal sources can vary greatly depending on the source of funding (federal student loans, research funds), institutional type (public/private/proprietary; research-intensive or two-year career schools), it plays a major role in attracting students, staff, and administrators and in setting the institution's research and development agenda.

In sum, federal money talks in higher education in ways that are less apparent in K-12, where, even under the greatly expanded funding available from the Obama administration, it provides only 8.3 percent. A point that is often overlooked is that K-12 federal funding, although relatively small, is allocated to and managed by the state, while federal funding for higher education goes primarily to the institution, either directly (grants) or indirectly (through student loans that create tuition). Thus, the role of the state in determining how most of the money is spent is minimized.

A Market-Driven Model

Federal funding creates a market-driven system that is less local than in the elementary and secondary sectors. The Department of Education, through its Office of Federal Student Aid, provides approximately $194 billion a year to individual students in grants, work-study funds, tax benefits, and low-interest student loans.[26] In addition, it administers more than 60 programs aimed at increasing access to higher education through its Office of Postsecondary Education. The Department of Defense also allocates about $500 million in tuition reimbursement to institutions through the Military

Tuition Assistance Program and the GI Bill, which is provided to eligible service members and veterans. While most students attend higher education within their state, they are free to take their loans to any institution, including private colleges and universities. (This is, of course, what some choice theorists dream of in K-12 education, but there are additional market constraints in primary and secondary education due to children's age and dependence on parents.)

Institutions also receive significant funding from private corporations, special interest groups, and nonprofits, which helps to shape their agendas. For instance, the Gates Foundation's Postsecondary Success Strategy funds institutions to develop strategies for innovative practices that can increase low-income students' completion rates.[27] Overall, the 50 top foundations gave more than $1.5 billion to higher education institutions in 2010.[28]

Institutional System Differences

The reason that higher education is less sensitive to the political culture of the states in which its institutions are located is, in part, because of the very diverse sources of funding that we have emphasized. However, it is also, in part, because of historical factors, which have created a very robust private sector, national recruitment of students among more prestigious institutions, and huge variation in institutional types (Tolbert, 1985).

For example, while most states look at their largest universities as representatives of the state (and these institutions often receive nearly half of all of the state higher education allocation), they are also the least responsive to state policy oversight, largely because of research funding over which states have little or no control. Much of that funding comes from the National Science Foundation, which provides about $7 billion in nonmedical basic research at universities and the National Institutes of Health, which funds $31 billion in medical and scientific research—the majority of which goes to universities, medical schools, and other research institutions, and determines how faculty members will spend their time and how institutions determine future strategies for success.[29] Defense-related research also provides nearly a billion dollars in grants and contracts to universities.

In addition, in many states the private sector in higher education is more robust than in K-12. In 2009, according to the National Center for Educational Statistics, approximately 12 million students were enrolled in state-funded degree-granting institutions; nearly 6 million were enrolled in private institutions.[30] In contrast, enrollment in private schools in K-12 was approximately 11 percent in 2008, but appears to be declining.[31] State policies have limited direct effect in the private sector.

Standards-Based Accountability: A Weak Tool for Change

States, federal agencies, and other organizations that provide funding to institutions hold institutions accountable for using the funds in a judicious manner by requiring regular reporting, standards that must be met, and evaluations of their activities—all with the purpose of ensuring appropriate and effective use of funds.

Since the early 1990s, many states have held institutions of higher education accountable for outcomes in areas such as retention and graduation rates, licensure test scores, transfer rates, and research productivity rather than on inputs and financial audits—as had been done in the past (Harnisch, 2011). In 2013, 12 states (including Ohio, Tennessee, Indiana, and Texas) already tied some funding to performance indicators, while most of the others were transitioning to some performance funding or discussing it.[32] All states provide the public stakeholders with information about performance.

Because states determine how exactly performance is measured (and in the process have developed varying ways of doing so), they hoped that these policy levers could bring about changes in institutional performance. However, none of the different types of performance-based accountability is associated with significant changes in performance, nor are there differences between states with and without performance-based accountability (Dougherty & Reddy, 2011). Instead, changes in performance can largely be attributed to institutional characteristics (which are associated with other sources of funding), over which state policies have limited effect (Shin, 2010).

The federal government's use of different forms of performance-based accountability, on the other hand, has teeth, but limited impact on internal decision making. Accreditation serves as a quality assurance mechanism to ensure that fraudulent institutions do not receive any funds, a concern that is reinforced through a variety of additional reporting requirements.[33] None of these requirements, however, define student learning or evaluate student outcomes (Gillen, Bennett, & Vetter, 2010).[34] The Department of Education also uses required performance reporting through its Integrated Postsecondary Data System (IPEDS), which requires institutions to report revenue and expenses; percentage of students receiving federal, state, and institutional financial aid; graduation rates; and degrees conferred.[35] This reporting is not, however, directly tied to any funding and is used primarily by legislators, legislative staff, and other policy makers.

But other agencies that have no financial clout also have a direct impact on institutions of higher education. For instance, *U.S. News and World Report* uses indicators such as freshman acceptance rates, retention rates, and six-year graduation rates to release its yearly rankings of the top colleges and universities in the United States.[36] Institutions are becoming increasingly competitive with one another to maintain or improve their rankings to the point where some universities have admitted to submitting false information (Jaschik, 2013) and recent research has found that each one-point increase in ranking in the report equates to a 1 to 2 percent increase in applicants (Luca & Smith, 2011). It is unclear if the increases in rankings also mean that institutions have improved the quality of education provided to students and the research that they conduct.

DISCUSSION

This chapter just begins to explore the significance of state political culture in shaping the way schools and higher education institutions are expected to respond to emerging public expectations. One point is clear: Specific leaders and short-term targeted policies at the state level appear to have limited long-term impacts on both primary/secondary and higher education. If we are to understand how *schools* respond to the zeitgeist of reform, we must move our analysis toward a better understanding of state political cultures that have a lively and continuing impact on the future directions of our educational system. In contrast, if we wish to understand how *institutions of higher education* improve or decline in quality, we can easily locate historic policy initiatives (the Morrill Act, the GI Bill, the establishment of two-year colleges) that have changed the system significantly, but it is much more difficult to find evidence that policy tweaking at the state or federal levels has much impact. Nevertheless, we can begin to gather some insights related to the questions that we posed at the beginning.

1. How do distinctive political cultures at the state level help to explain the unfolding of states' K-12 educational accountability and standards policies?

Scholars argue that American political behavior has become increasingly nationalized and cannot be primarily attributed to states' political cultures (Cook et al., 1993). Alternative views are that behavior is mediated by personal values, beliefs, and underlying assumptions (Koven & Mausolff, 2002). We, however, argue that it is possible to trace the development of accountability policies using Elazar's framework of state policy types. When comparing Elazar's state-level traditionalistic and individualistic political cultures, we found that political culture plays a significant role in explaining states' educational accountability and standards policies. North Carolina's educational policy-making history is largely consistent with Elazar's conceptions of it as a traditionalistic state: Decision-making authority was centralized with its elites and policy innovation confined largely to mandates and incentives to support increased testing and accountability. Nebraska's policy route to educational accountability, in contrast, is aligned with Elazar's conceptions as an individualistic state: educational policies were designed to empower local-level stakeholders and promote local innovation.[37]

2. Do state political cultures affect the policies and practices of local districts and schools?

To what extent do different assumptions and interpretations of educational policies at the state level filter down to the local level that can be explained by distinctive political cultures? The North Carolina schools in our study displayed characteristics consistent with the traditionalistic political culture, which provided a contrast to the individualistic political culture. State-level policy makers had mandated a set of consistent processes and mechanisms for teachers to interpret and use data from the state's accountability framework that were visible in the interviews with teachers and administrators in the schools as they discussed how their pedagogies and curricula were much aligned with state standards. Alignment was also reflected in the use of testing data to steer many schoolwide and districtwide decisions. Overall, the North Carolina schools did not talk about a need for local-level autonomy in crafting policies to fit the context of their schools or districts, even when they expressed a desire for more influence in the state policy process.

In the Nebraska schools in our study, the individualistic culture was apparent through the concentrated preference of teachers and administrators for autonomy. Those at the school and district levels were not opposed to accountability through testing; they believed that they should be the ones to determine the standards and type of testing against which their students would be measured. In addition, they emphasized the importance of their professional knowledge, which included increasing expertise in assessment and curriculum development, but also in their understanding of their students and how they learned.

3. Does a state political culture framework apply equally well to the K-12 and higher education sectors?

Higher education has a wider array of federal and nongovernmental stakeholders involved in its funding, direction, and accountability, which mediates the influence of state-level political culture. Even the lack of clear, long-term system effects of state funding policies suggests that the system is not designed to be easily changed through the state policy process. Therefore, it is not possible to consider higher education culture in the context of the state where it is located, but rather as influenced more by research agendas at the federal, for-profit, and NGO levels; by federal policies for data reporting as a form of accountability, and by the accreditation bodies.

At the same time, the extent to which existing federal entities and other organizations have an impact on institutional decisions is unclear. High-stakes accountability in the form of performance funding may have little to do with spurring the institution to make systemic changes; rather, it may be more a matter of institutions educating their students on the importance of repaying their loans and teaching them financial management skills. For accreditation, institutions have to meet certain criteria of quality and demonstrate a plan for continuous improvement if they fall short, but whether accreditation stimulates significant internal change is not clear.[38]

Future Research Directions

Although there is considerable general debate in the higher education literature about how proposed accountability indicators will be applied, we found limited research about how state policies influence colleges and universities. The few studies that we identified point to a weaker connection between state policies and institutional responses. In contrast, our comparative cases point to enduring features of political culture that mediate other national or globalizing policy messages. Both of these simple conclusions reveal that there is much more that needs to be known about the way political culture affects education. We consequently propose ideas for further research about the intersections between states' educational policies and political cultures.

Most of the higher education research that we located was conducted in larger research-intensive institutions, which are less sensitive to state funding and have more nonlocal stakeholders than MA-granting four-year and two-year institutions. We suggest that there is room for more investigations of political culture that focus on understudied institutional types. Given current policy emphasis on increasing the links between high schools and colleges, as well as proposed policies in many states tying funding to retention and graduation, between-state comparisons on how higher education accountability policies are developed, implemented, and affect institutional decisions could be more fruitful than those that we uncovered.

In contrast, as noted earlier, the U.S. elementary and secondary education system has undergone an adjustment in educational policy-making authority, which has shifted from the local level to the state level (with a federal presence looming in the background). With this shift, the state has the role of crafting policies that both satisfy federal requirements and align with existing state resources and needs, and at least one study suggests that this has placed great pressure not on elected policy makers, but on state education agencies that are responsible for adjudicating between state and federal expectations (Thomas, 2012). In the context of NCLB, federal policy makers provide states with the authority to interpret and implement the law, which states do in the context of their political cultures, and there is clearly a need to add to the very thin knowledge that exists about state educational agencies, as opposed to elected or appointed officials.

As state policy makers engage in this process of interpretation and implementation, teachers and principals do the same in a way that is generally aligned with their states' political cultures, as well as their district and school cultures. Most of the research on how changing policy contexts affect teachers has emphasized the role of the district. However, less is known about how exactly the different political cultures manifest themselves at all levels in the policy process, and how different actors (such as professional associations) affect those responses.

Also, little is known about how specific actors (e.g., governors, influential legislators) and organizations (e.g., professional associations, nonprofits) at the school, district, and state levels influence and are influenced by their state's political culture. It would be informative to research systematically how those stakeholders and organizations serve as mediators of federal, state, and local policies, all within their respective state contexts.

It is therefore essential to move beyond descriptive reports of state policy differences by using the lens of political culture to interpret the types of policies states use, stakeholder groups involved, and the specific mechanisms or policy levers employed as states comply with NCLB and enact other policies to aid in educational reform. Additional research on states' different political cultures will ultimately allow for a more comprehensive understanding of the linkages among state-level policies, stakeholder involvement in the policy process, and teachers' and principals' interpretations of these policies in the classroom.

NOTES

1. One exception is a recent analysis of the development of systemic policies in Massachusetts in the *New York Times* (Chang, 2013).
2. Much of the review of political culture research draws on Febey and Louis (2008), largely because relatively little additional work has been done other than our own work, which will be covered later in this chapter. Our focus is on U.S. political culture at the state level, and ignores the U.S. national political culture, which is best reflected in other policy arenas such as foreign policy, and which is regarded as largely individualistic and contentious (Merelman, Streich, & Martin, 1998).
3. See Malen (2003) for an earlier analysis of increasing state activism.
4. The case description of North Carolina has been substantially changed from that published in Febey and Louis (2008) based on additional data collection and analysis. Both the North Carolina and Nebraska cases were analyzed in Gordon and Louis (2012).
5. We do not address the question of whether Elazar's classification remains useful. While our analysis gives primary attention to political culture, more research will help to clarify whether there are (semi)permanent clusters of states that exhibit political cultures that are sufficiently similar to have predictive or explanatory value.
6. For more details about methods, see Louis and colleagues (2010).
7. The 2010 census lists them as the 42nd and 17th largest cities, respectively.
8. http://quickfacts.census.gov/qfd/states/37000.html.
9. www.all4ed.org/files/NorthCarolina.pdf
10. Unofficially, the Republican Party dominates among the elected senators.
11. Figures are derived from U.S. Census Bureau (2011).
12. http://trends.collegeboard.org/education_pays/report_findings/indicator/CollegeEnrollment_Rates_by_State; www.all4ed.org/files/Nebraska.pdf
13. The current governor, Pat McCrory, was a conservative candidate in a state that has traditionally been "middle of the road." Because his tenure has been brief, it is too early to speculate on how specific educational policies will change. However, there is no evidence that his education agenda directly challenges preexisting initiatives in K-12 education, although the lt. governor has suggested that he is opposed to the Common Core curriculum.
14. http://charterlaws.publiccharters.org/charterlaws/state/NC
15. www.morganton.com/news/education/article_7122d182-0ff1-11e3-b093-001a4bcf6878.html
16. http://eagnews.org/a-dominant-union-in-conservative-country-how-the-nebraska-teachers-union-quietly-dominates-education-policy/
17. http://lexch.com/news/local/common-core-education-standards-stall-in-nebraska/article_6914a22c-d518-11e2-9a82-001a4bcf887a.html
18. Nebraska's funding is inequitable between districts because of its reliance on property taxes. The inequity is not, however, regressive in the sense that it results in lower funding available to districts with low personal wealth (Baker et al., 2012). Thus, Nebraska earns a low grade on funding equity from *Education Week's*

Quality Counts, but an average (slightly progressive) grade from Baker and colleagues, where the focus is on redistribution between districts with different family wealth.

19. The other states with no charter law are Alabama, Kentucky, Montana, North Dakota, South Dakota, Vermont, and West Virginia. (www.charterschoolsearch.com/schoolsbyState.cfm).

20. The populist conservative Tea Party movement appears to be active in both states, but has not substantially challenged the political culture assumptions about centralization (NC) or decentralization (NE) in education. In North Carolina, the focus has been on opposing Common Core (which is viewed as a nonnative takeover). In Nebraska, there is no easily available evidence that education is a focus of local meetings.

21. All names are pseudonyms.

22. The River District case draws on Febey and Louis (2008), but is consistent with additional cases conducted in high schools in the state at a later time.

23. Midwest District is analyzed in more detail in Gordon (2010).

24. A more extensive analysis of the Johnson City school's response to state policies may be found in Louis, Thomas, and Anderson (2010).

25. Nebraska submitted Race to the Top proposals in both rounds, but scored poorly.

26. (http://febp.newamerica.net/background-analysis/federal-higher-education-programs-overview

27. www.gatesfoundation.org/What-We-Do/US-Program/Postsecondary-Success

28. www.grantspace.org

29. www.nsf.gov/about/; www.nih.gov/about/budget.htm; www.military.com/; http://gibill.va.gov/

30. http://nces.ed.gov/programs/digest/d11/tables/dt11_206.asp

31. http://nces.ed.gov/programs/projections/projections2020/tables/table_01.asp

32. www.ncsl.org/issues-research/educ/performance-funding.aspx

33. One requirement is that each institution with students who received federal student loans must report their cohort default rate. Institutions must meet the standard of below an average of 25 percent for three years or below 40 percent for one year. www2.ed.gov/offices/OSFAP/defaultmanagement/index.html.

34. Another type of performance funding is the requirement for career colleges, which include most for-profit programs and certificate programs, to meet at least one of the following conditions to qualify for federal student aid: (1) a minimum of 35 percent of former students who took out federal student loans are in repayment status; (2) the estimated annual loan payment of graduates is less than 30 percent of their discretionary income; or (3) the estimated annual loan payment does not exceed 12 percent of their income (www.ed.gov/news/press-releases/gainful-employment-regulations).

35. http://nces.ed.gov/ipeds/sdc/

36. www.colleges.usnews.rankingsandreviews.com/best-colleges/rankings/national-universities/data

37. The previous version of this chapter included two states that conform to Elazar's "moralistic" template (Iowa and Minnesota) (Febey & Louis, 2008).

38. One study by McLendon, Hearn, & Deaton (2006) provides insight about the effects of institutional transparency, indicating that while respondents believed that "sunshine laws" increased public confidence, the data do not demonstrate a link between confidence and actual operations.

REFERENCES

Akiba, M., LeTendre, G. K., & Scribner, J. P. (2007). Teacher quality, opportunity gap, and national achievement in 46 countries. *Educational Researcher, 36*(7), 369–387.

Allison, S., & Hargreaves, A. (2008). Student diversity and secondary school change in a context of increasingly standardized reform. *American Educational Research Journal, 45*(4), 913–945.

Amrein, A. L., & Berliner, D. C. (2002). High-stakes testing, uncertainty, and student learning. *Education Policy Analysis Archives, 10*(18).

Baker, B. D., & Friedman-Nimz, R. (2004). State policies and equal opportunity: The example of gifted education. *Educational Evaluation and Policy Analysis, 26*(1), 39–64.

Baker, B. D., Sciarra, D., & Farrier, D. (2012). *Is school funding fair? A national report card.* Rutgers, NJ: Rutgers Graduate School of Education.

Berezin, M. (1997). Politics and culture: A less fissured terrain. *Annual Review of Sociology, 23,* 361–383.

Carnoy, M., & Loeb, S. (2002). Does external accountability affect student outcomes? A cross-state analysis. *Educational Evaluation and Policy Analysis, 24*(4), 305–331.

Chang, K. (2013, September 3). "One State Had a Plan and Saw It Through." *New York Times,* D1, D8.

Chilton, S. (1988). Defining political culture. *The Western Political Quarterly, 41*(3), 419–445.

Clune, W. H. (1987). Institutional choice as a theoretical framework for research on educational policy. *Educational Evaluation and Policy Analysis, 9*(2), 117–132.

Comer, J. C. (1980). The Nebraska nonpartisan legislature: An evaluation. *State & Local Government Review, 12*(3), 98–102.

Cook, E. A., Jelen, T. G., & Wilcox, C. (1993). State political cultures and public opinion about abortion. *Political Research Quarterly, 46*(4), 771–781.

Dansereau, F., & Alutto, J. A. (1990). Level of analysis issues in climate and culture research. In B. Schneider (Ed.), *Organizational climate and culture* (pp. 153–192). San Francisco, CA: Jossey-Bass.

Datnow, A., Borman, G. D., Stringfield, S., Overman, L. T., & Castellano, M. (2003). Comprehensive school reform in culturally and linguistically diverse contexts: Implementation and outcomes from a four-year study. *Educational Evaluation and Policy Analysis, 25*(2), 143–170.

Dougherty, K., & Reddy, V. (2011). *The impacts of state performance funding systems on higher education institutions: Research literature review and policy recommendations.* New York: Community College Research Center, Teachers College.

Doyle, W. R., Delaney, J. A., & Naughton, B. A. (2008). Public institutional aid and state policy: Compensation or compliance? *Research in Higher Education, 50*(5), 502–523.

Education Week. (2012). *Quality counts 2012: The global challenge.* www.edweek.org/ew/toc/2012/01/12/index.html.

Elazar, D. (1970). *Cities of the prairie.* New York: Basic.

Elazar, D. (1980). Political culture on the plains. *The Western Historical Quarterly, 11*(3), 261–283.

Elazar, D. (1984). *American federalism: A view from the states.* New York: Harper & Row.

Elmore, R. F. (1979). Backward mapping: Implementation research and policy decisions. *Political Science Quarterly, 94*(4), 601–619.

Elmore, R. F., & Fuhrman, S. (1995). Opportunity-to-learn standards and the state role in education. *Teachers College Record, 96*(3), 432–457.

Erikson, R. S., McIver, J. P., & Wright, G. C., Jr. (1987). State political culture and public opinion. *The American Political Science Review, 81*(3), 797–814.

Febey, K., & Louis, K. S. (2008). Perspectives on political cultures in three states. In B. Cooper, J. Cibulka, & L. D. Fusarelli (Eds.), *Handbook of educational policy research* (pp. 52–72). New York: Routledge.

Fitzpatrick, J. L., & Hero, R. E. (1988). Political culture and political characteristics of the American states: A consideration of some old and new questions. *The Western Political Quarterly, 41*(1), 145–153.

Fleer, J. D. (1994). *North Carolina government and politics.* Lincoln: University of Nebraska Press.

Garms, W. I., Guthrie, J., & Pierce, J. (1978). *School finance: The economics and politics of public education.* New York: Prentice Hall.

Gass, J., & Stergios, J. (2013). The beginning of Common Core's trouble. www.weeklystandard.com/blogs/beginning-common-cores-trouble_731923.html.

Gillen, A., Bennett, D. L., & Vetter, R. (2010). The inmates running the asylum? An analysis of higher education accreditation. Center for College Affordability and Productivity. www.centerforcollegeaffordability.org/uploads/Accreditation.pdf.

Goos, M., Schreier, B. M., Knipprath, H. M. E., Fraine, B. D., Damme, J. V., & Trautwein, U. (2013). How can cross-country differences in the practice of grade retention be explained? A closer look at national educational policy factors. *Comparative Education Review, 57*(1), 54–84.

Gordon, M. F. (2010). Bringing parent and community engagement back into the education reform spotlight: A comparative case study. (Order No. 3398307, University of Minnesota) *ProQuest Dissertations and Theses,* 211.

Gordon, M. F., & Louis, K. S. (2012). North Carolina and Nebraska: Two states, two policy cultures, two outcomes. In K. S. Louis & B. A. M. van Velzen (Eds.), *Educational policy in an international context.* New York: Palgrave Macmillan.

Gottfried, M. A., Stecher, B. A., Hoover, M., & Cross, A. B. (2011). *Federal and state roles and capacity for improving schools.* Santa Monica, CA: Rand Corporation.

Gross, B., Booker, T. K., & Goldhaber, D. (2009). Boosting student achievement: The effect of comprehensive school reform on student achievement. *Educational Evaluation and Policy Analysis, 31*(2), 111–126.

Hanushek, E. A., & Raymond, M. E. (2005). Does school accountability lead to improved student performance? *Journal of Policy Analysis and Management, 24*(2), 297–327.

Harnisch, T. (2011). Performance-based funding: A re-emerging strategy in public higher education financing *Policy Matters.* Washington, DC: American Association of Colleges and Universities.

Heilig, J. V., & Darling-Hammond, L. (2008). Accountability Texas-style: The progress and learning of urban minority students in a high-stakes testing context. *Educational Evaluation and Policy Analysis, 30*(2), 75–110.

Herzik, E. B. (1985). The legal-formal structuring of state politics: A cultural explanation. *The Western Political Quarterly, 38*(3), 413–423.

Jaschik, S. (2013, February 6). Can you verify that? Inside higher ed. www.insidehighered.com/news/2013/02/06/wake-reports-false-data-us-news-considers-new-way-promote-accuracy.

Jellison Holmes, J., Richards, M. P., Jimerson, J. B., & Cohen, R. W. (2010). Assessing the effects of high school exit examinations. *Review of Educational Research, 80*(4), 476–526.

Johnson, C. A. (1976). Political culture in American states: Elazar's formulation examined. *American Journal of Political Science, 20*(3), 491–509.

Koven, S., & Mausolff, C. (2002). The influence of political culture on state budgets. *American Review of Public Administration, 32*(1), 66–77.

Ladd, H. F., & Lauen, D. L. (2010). Status versus growth: The distributional effects of school accountability policies. *Journal of Policy Analysis and Management, 29*(3), 426–450.

Layman, G. C., & Carmines, E. G. (1997). Cultural conflict in American politics: Religious traditionalism, postmaterialism, and U.S. political behavior. *The Journal of Politics, 59*(3), 751–777.

Layzell, D. T. (2007). State higher education funding models: An assessment of current and emerging approaches. *Journal of Education Finance, 33*(1), 1–19.

Layzell, D. T., & Lyddon, J. W. (1990). *Budgeting for higher education at the state level: Enigma, paradox, and ritual. ASHE-ERIC Higher Education Report 4, 1990* (Vol. 4). Washington, DC: George Washington University.

Lieske, J. (1993). Regional subcultures of the United States. *The Journal of Politics, 55*(4), 888–913.

Louis, K. S. (1998). A light feeling of chaos: Educational reform and policy in the United States. *Daedalus, 127*(4), 13–40.

Louis, K. S., Febey, K., Gordon, M., & Thomas, E. (2008). Does state leadership matter? An analysis of three states. *Educational Administration Quarterly, 44*(4), 562–592.

Louis, K. S., Febey, K., & Schroeder, R. (2005). State-mandated accountability in high schools: Teachers' interpretations of a new era. *Educational Evaluation and Policy Analysis, 27*(2), 177–204.

Louis, K. S., Leithwood, K., Wahlstrom, K., Anderson, S. A., & Michlin, M. (2010). *Learning from leadership: Investigating the links to improved student learning: Final report of research findings.* New York: Wallace Foundation.

Louis, K. S., & Robinson, V. (2012). External mandates and instructional leadership: Principals as mediating agents. *Journal of Educational Administration, 50*(5), 629–665.

Louis, K. S., Thomas, E., & Anderson, S. (2010). How do states influence leadership in small districts? *Educational Policy and Leadership, 9*(3), 328–366.

Lowery, D., & Sigelman, L. (1982). Political culture and state public policy: The missing link. *The Western Political Quarterly, 35*(3), 376–384.

Luca, M., & Smith, J. (2011). Salience in quality disclosure: Evidence from the U.S. News college rankings. www.hbs.edu/research/pdf/12–014.pdf.

McLendon, M. K., Hearn, J. C., & Deaton, R. (2006). Called to account: Analyzing the origins and spread of state performance-accountability policies for higher education. *Educational Evaluation and Policy Analysis, 28*(1), 1–24

Malen, B. (2003). Tightening the grip? The impact of state activism on local school systems. *Educational Policy, 17*(2), 195–216.

Marshall, C., Mitchell, D., & Wirt, F. (1986). The context of state-level policy formation. *Educational Evaluation and Policy Analysis, 8*(4), 347–378.

Marshall, C., Mitchell, D., & Wirt, F. (1989). *Culture and education policy in the American states.* New York: Falmer.

Mazzoni, T. L. (1993). The changing politics of state education policy making: A 20-year Minnesota perspective. *Educational Evaluation and Policy Analysis, 15*(4), 357–379.

McLendon, M. K., Hearn, J. D., & Deaton. R. (2006) Called to account: Analyzing the origins and spread of state performance-accountability policies for higher education. *Educational Evaluation and Policy Analysis, 28*(1), 1–24.

Mehan, H. (2013). The changing but underrealized roles of state education agencies in school reform. *Journal for Students Placed At Risk, 10*(1), 140–146.

Merelman, R. M., Streich, G., & Martin, P. (1998). Unity and diversity in American political culture: An exploratory study of the national conversation on American pluralism and identity. *Political Psychology, 19*(4), 781–807.

Mintrop, H., & Trujillo, T. (2007). The practical relevance of accountability systems for school improvement: A descriptive analysis of California schools. *Educational Evaluation and Policy Analysis, 29*(4), 319–352.

Morgan, D. R., & Wilson, L. A. (1990). Diversity in the American states: Updating the Sullivan Index. *Publius, 20*(1), 71–81.

NCES. (2002). *State reading 2002: Nebraska.* Washington, DC: National Center for Educational Statistics. http://nces.ed.gov/nationsreportcard/pdf/stt2002/2003526NE.pdf.

Norrander, B. (2000). The multi-layered impact of public opinion on capital punishment implementation in the American states. *Political Research Quarterly, 53*(4), 771–793.

Olsen, B., & Sexton, D. (2009). Threat rigidity, school reform, and how teachers view their work inside current education policy contexts. *American Educational Research Journal, 46*(1), 9–44.

Ostler, J. (1992). Why the populist party was strong in Kansas and Nebraska but weak in Iowa. *The Western Historical Quarterly, 23*(4), 451–474.

Patterson, S. C. (1968). The political cultures of the American states. *The Journal of Politics, 30*(1), 187–209.

Ravitch, D. (2012, June 7). Do our public schools threaten national security? *New York Review of Books.*

Reeves, M. M. (1990). The states as polities: Reformed, reinvigorated, resourceful. *The Annals of the American Academy of Political and Social Science, 509,* 83–93.

Roberts, N. C., & King, P. J. (1996). *Transforming public policy.* San Francisco, CA: Jossey-Bass.

Roch, C. H., & Howard, R. M. (2008). State policy innovation in perspective: Courts, legislatures, and education finance reform. *Political Research Quarterly, 61*(2), 333–344.

Rossman, G. B., & Wilson, B. L. (1996). Context, courses, and the curriculum: Local responses to state policy reform. *Educational Policy, 10*(3), 399–421.

Sacken, D. M., & Medina, M., Jr. (1990). Investigating the context of state-level policy formation: A case study of Arizona's bilingual education legislation. *Educational Evaluation and Policy Analysis, 12*(4), 389–402.

Schleicher, A. (2009). Securing quality and equity in education: Results from PISA. *Prospects, 39*(NA), 251–263.

Schnepf, S. V. (2007). Immigrants' educational disadvantage: An examination across ten countries and three surveys. *Journal of Population Economics, 20*(3), 527–545.

Scott, D. (2012, February 29). ESEA reauthorization passes house. www.governing.com/news/federal/gov-esea-reauthorization-passes-house-committee.html.

Sharkansky, I. (1969). The utility of Elazar's political culture: A research note. *Polity, 2,* 66–83.

SHEEO. (2012). Higher education finance: FY 2011. Boulder, CO: State Higher Education Executive Officers.

Shin, J. C. (2010). Impacts of performance-based accountability on institutional performance in the U.S. *Higher Education, 60*(1), 47–68.

Sipple, J. W., Killeen, K., & Monk, D. H. (2004). Adoption and adaptation: School district responses to state imposed learning and graduation requirements. *Educational Evaluation and Policy Analysis, 26*(2), 143–168.

Smith, R. (1993). Beyond Tocqueville, Myrdal, and Hartz: The multiple traditions in America. *The American Political Science Review, 87*(3), 549–566.

Smith, T. M. (2007). How do state-level induction and standards-based reform policies affect induction experiences and turnover among new teachers? *American Journal of Education, 113*(2), 273–309.

Stein, R. H. (1979). Impact of federal intervention on higher education. *Research in Higher Education, 10*(1), 71–82.

Strauss, V. (2013). Resistance to Common Core standards growing. www.washingtonpost.com/blogs/answer-sheet/wp/2013/02/26/resistance-to-common-core-standards-growing/.

Sunderman, G. (2003). Federal-state relationships and the implementation of No Child Left Behind: First impressions. *PEA Bulletin, 28*(1), 1–13.

Swanson, C. B., & Stevenson, D. L. (2002). Standards-based reform in practice: Evidence on state policy and classroom instruction from the NAEP state assessments. *Educational Evaluation and Policy Analysis, 24*(1), 1–27.

Teitelbaum, P. (2003). The influence of high school graduation requirement policies in mathematics and science on student course-taking patterns and achievement. *Educational Evaluation and Policy Analysis, 25*(1), 31–57.

Thomas, E. J. M. (2012). *New federalism and state leadership: The changing role of state education agencies (SEAs) as quality assurance bureaus.* (Order No. 3498581, University of Minnesota). ProQuest Dissertations and Theses, 193. http://login.ezproxy.lib.umn.edu/login?url=http://search.proquest.com/docview/926962769?accountid=14586. (926962769).

Timar, T. B., & Kirp, D. L. (1988). State efforts to reform schools: Treading between a regulatory swamp and an English garden. *Educational Evaluation and Policy Analysis, 10*(2), 75–88.

Tolbert, P. S. (1985). Institutional environments and resource dependence: Sources of administrative structure in institutions of higher education. *Administrative Science Quarterly, 30*(1), 1–13.

U.S. Census Bureau. (2011). *Public education finances: 2009* (G09-ASPEF). Washington, DC: U.S. Government Printing Office. www2.census.gov/govs/school/09f33pub.pdf.

Warren, J. R., Jenkins, K. N., & Kulick, R. B. (2006). High school exit examinations and state-level completion and GED rates, 1975 through 2002. *Educational Evaluation and Policy Analysis, 28*(2), 131–152.

Werfhorst, H. G. V. D., & Mijs, J. J. B. (2010). Achievement inequality and the institutional structure of educational systems: A comparative perspective. *Annual Review of Sociology, 36,* 407–428.

Winders, B. (1999). The roller coaster of class conflict: Class segments, mass mobilization, and voter turnout in the U.S., 1840–1996. *Social Forces, 77*(3), 833–862.

Wirt, F. M. (1980). Does control follow the dollar? Value analysis, school policy, and state-local linkages. *Publius, 10*(2), 24–47.

Wirt, F. M., & Krug, S. (2001). National and state cultural influences on principals' administration of local schools. *Publius, 31*(2), 81–98.

Wirt, F., Mitchell, D., & Marshall, C. (1988). Culture and education policy: Analyzing values in state policy systems. *Educational Evaluation and Policy Analysis, 10*(4), 271–284.

Wolak, J., Newmark, A. J., McNoldy, T., Lowery, D., & Gray, V. (2002). Much of politics is still local: Multi-state lobbying in state interest communities. *Legislative Studies Quarterly, 27*(4), 527–555.

Wong, K. K. (1989). Fiscal support for education in American states: The "parity-to-dominance" view examined. *American Journal of Education, 97*(4), 329–357.

6

JUDICIAL IMPACT ON EDUCATION POLITICS AND POLICIES

Martha McCarthy

> It would be far better indeed for these great social and political problems to be resolved in the political arena by other branches of government . . . but these are social and political problems which seem at times to defy resolution. In such situations, under our system, the judiciary must bear a hand and accept its responsibility to assist in the solution where constitutional rights hang in the balance. (*Hobson v. Hansen*, 1967, p. 517)

The impact of the courts, particularly the federal judiciary, on education policies and politics has evoked interest and critique for the past several decades. This chapter explores the complexities of the judiciary's influence, including arguments of those who support and lament the judiciary being actively involved in public education. Following an overview of the role of the courts in general, this chapter addresses historical trends in education litigation. The next section explores the interplay and tension across branches and levels of government, with particular attention to legislative, judicial, and administrative exchanges and state versus federal courts.

OVERVIEW OF THE JUDICIAL ROLE

A distinctive feature of our system of government is the separation of powers among the legislative, judicial, and executive branches of government.[1] Checks and balances are designed to ensure that no governmental branch becomes too powerful. The judiciary's role is to resolve disputes (see Article III of the U.S. Constitution and corresponding state constitutions). Courts cannot initiate rulings on their own simply because they are aware of unlawful practices, such as a public school's suspension of students without procedural safeguards. The judiciary is confined to reviewing cases initiated by parties with standing to bring suit. In resolving controversies, courts are called on to interpret constitutional and statutory provisions and to apply legal principles or create new principles as constitutional and statutory interpretations change over time.

Being the final arbiter of the federal Constitution, the U.S. Supreme Court decides what constitutional provisions mean; the only way to challenge the Court's interpretations is to amend the U.S. Constitution. Kagan has asserted that the most important "form of judicial policymaking in the United States arises from the courts' . . . authority to hold legislative statutes and executive branch decisions and actions unconstitutional" (2004, p. 21). The Court's judicial influence through its interpretive powers takes on additional significance considering that many Supreme Court decisions are five to four. It is sobering to realize that one justice can determine the outcome, which may restrict or expand constitutional rights.

Unlike legislators, who are elected and answerable to the electorate, federal judges are appointed for life. It is often said that federal courts are thus removed from politics and more likely to act independently than legislative bodies or even state courts, where many judges are still elected. We like to think of justices as objectively interpreting the law, but that is not always the case. Judges are human beings with biases and political leanings, and they are not immune to social and political pressures (Caldarone, Canes-Wrone, & Clark, 2009). Presidents nominate individuals to become federal judges in part because of their political orientation. Studies of the voting behavior of justices show a correlation, but not as strong as one might expect, along party lines of the presidents who named them to the bench (see Lax & Rader, 2010; Lloyd, 1995; Rowland & Carp, 1996; Scherer, 2001). Over time, some federal judges, including a few Supreme Court justices, have delivered opinions that are not in line with their earlier political orientation. Public schools definitely have been influenced by decisions delivered during the tenure of Chief Justice Earl Warren (1953–1969), who voted quite differently than President Eisenhower anticipated on key issues, including school desegregation.

Reliance on Precedent

In resolving disputes, courts apply precedents established in previous decisions in their efforts to maintain consistency in the law on a given issue. School authorities, therefore, can feel somewhat confident in relying on judicially created principles when they are developing school policies. Yet interpretations of the prior decisions change as they are applied by courts in new situations, even though the earlier decisions are not often overturned.

For example, in 1969 the Supreme Court interpreted the First Amendment as affording public school students the right to express their ideological views in public schools as long as their expression did not disrupt the educational process or interfere with the rights of others (*Tinker v. Des Moines*, 1969). Subsequently, the Court narrowed, but did not overturn, the *Tinker* principle, giving school personnel more discretion to curtail lewd and vulgar student comments (*Bethel School District v. Fraser*, 1986), speech appearing to represent the school (*Hazelwood School District v. Kuhlmeier*, 1988), and expression promoting unlawful behavior (*Morse v. Frederick*, 2007). Even though *Tinker's* reach has been narrowed in terms of in-school speech (Kozlowski, 2011), the disruption standard continues to be applied by the federal judiciary in assessing constitutional protection of students' electronic expression that originates off school grounds. Most courts have ruled that only if the electronic expression threatens a disruption of the work of the school can it be curtailed or the basis for disciplinary action (see *Doninger v. Niehoff*, 2011; *J.S. v. Blue Mountain School District*, 2012; *Layshock v. Hermitage School District*, 2012).

In some instances, however, instead of distinguishing or limiting the reach of its precedents, the U.S. Supreme Court has directly overturned its previous decisions, reasoning that its prior interpretations were wrong. The most noteworthy example is the Supreme

Court's invalidation of racial segregation in public schools (*Brown v. Board of Education,* 1954), overturning the "separate, but equal" interpretation of the Fourteenth Amendment's Equal Protection Clause that had been precedent for more than 50 years (*Plessy v. Ferguson,* 1896). Also, the Court in *West Virginia State Board v. Barnette* (1943) ruled that public schools cannot require students to pledge their allegiance to the American flag, overturning a precedent established only three years earlier (*Minersville School District v. Gobitis,* 1940).

Importance of Judicially Created Criteria or Tests

Although courts do not make laws as legislative bodies do, they influence the law by exercising their interpretive powers. The Supreme Court often develops tests to assess whether a particular constitutional or statutory provision has been abridged, and some of these tests have become almost as significant as the constitutional or statutory provisions in determining whether challenged practices will be upheld or struck down. In short, the judicially created test that is selected can determine the fate of a given school practice.

Perhaps the best illustration of the importance of judicial tests pertains to the Equal Protection Clause of the Fourteenth Amendment. In the 1950s and 1960s, the Supreme Court under Chief Justice Earl Warren seemed committed to expanding individual rights, and accordingly created *strict scrutiny analysis* to assess equal protection claims. Using this test, a challenged governmental classification will be struck down if it creates a suspect classification or affects a fundamental right and is not justified by a compelling governmental interest and narrowly tailored to achieve that interest. Because legislative acts rarely can satisfy the strict scrutiny standard, the critical factor is whether the Court determines that a suspect class or fundamental right is at stake. If so, the legislative action is invalidated. The Court established in the mid-20th century that race and national origin are suspect classes and the rights to vote in state elections and to interstate travel are fundamental rights (see Dayton, 2012).

It appeared that the Court might expand the list of suspect classes and fundamental rights, but the more conservative Supreme Court under Chief Justice Warren Burger (1969–1986) put the brakes on applying strict scrutiny beyond race and national origin cases (see Webb, McCarthy, & Thomas, 1988). The Supreme Court ruled five to four in 1973 that because education is not mentioned in the U.S. Constitution, it is not a fundamental right that would cause legislative acts affecting this interest to be subjected to strict judicial scrutiny (*San Antonio Independent School District v. Rodriguez,* 1973). If one more justice had joined the dissenters, all contested education laws, policies, and practices could have been subjected to strict scrutiny, necessitating a compelling governmental justification to uphold challenged classifications affecting education. In *Rodriguez,* the Court also ruled that wealth is not a suspect class, declining to apply the highest level of scrutiny to federal constitutional challenges to school finance systems. In 1974, the Supreme Court also lacked one vote to elevate sex to a suspect class that would trigger strict scrutiny of governmental classifications based on sex (*Frontiero v. Richardson,* 1973).

While the strict scrutiny standard still is used in claims of racial discrimination, in assessing other classifications, federal courts are now more likely to apply an intermediate standard that requires an important justification to advance a significant government goal or the lenient rational basis test that requires the challenged classification to have only a rational relationship to a legitimate government goal. It is easier for governmental action to satisfy these tests than to meet strict judicial scrutiny. Clearly, the judicial assessment of the nature of the classification and interest involved determines how the Court will apply the Equal Protection Clause.

Desegregation cases also illustrate the importance of judicial tests. After much inaction in desegregating schools to comply with the *Brown v. Board of Education* (1954) decision, the Supreme Court in the late 1960s announced that school districts in states with school segregation by law in 1954 had an *affirmative duty* to take whatever steps were needed to convert segregated dual school systems to unitary systems (*Green v. County School Board*, 1968). Thus, simply removing barriers (e.g., state laws) to school integration was not sufficient; desegregation efforts would be assessed based on their effectiveness in integrating schools. All school district decisions would be evaluated in light of whether this affirmative duty was fulfilled; it was not enough for districts to be neutral in terms of school segregation. Application of this stringent standard in desegregation cases resulted in a number of school districts being under court supervision, some for several decades, as their efforts to fulfill their affirmative duty were found lacking (McCarthy, Cambron-McCabe, & Eckes, 2014).

However, the Supreme Court began relaxing its position in the early 1990s, holding that judicial supervision will be relinquished if schools boards have complied with desegregation orders in *good faith* and eliminated the vestiges of past discrimination *to the extent practicable* (see *Board of Education v. Dowell*, 1991; *Freeman v. Pitts*, 1992). By applying these standards, numerous school districts were able to achieve unitary status and be released from judicial supervision.

Whereas under an affirmative duty, school districts had to consider race in assigning students, more recently the Court seems to be favoring neutral policies, holding that considering race in assigning students where school districts are not under judicial desegregation orders abridges the Equal Protection Clause of the Fourteenth Amendment (*Parents Involved v. Seattle School District*, 2007). The change in judicial standards applied has had a significant impact on who prevails in desegregation litigation and has served as a deterrent to litigation (Zirkel & Johnson, 2011). In 2013, the Supreme Court emphasized that the use of race in admitting students to public education institutions must be assessed using strict judicial scrutiny (*Fisher v. University of Texas*, 2013).

Also illustrative of the importance of judicial tests is the church/state arena. In the early 1970s, the Supreme Court developed a stringent tripartite test, referred to as the *Lemon* test, which requires governmental action to have a secular purpose, neither advance nor impede religion, and avoid excessive governmental entanglement with religion to satisfy the Establishment Clause (*Lemon v. Kurtzman*, 1971). Using this test, the Supreme Court invalidated a number of religious activities in public schools and various forms of state aid to nonpublic schools (see McCarthy et al., 2014). Despite negative reactions to the elimination of school-sponsored devotionals, the Court's rulings have influenced school practices (Alley, 1996; Dolbeare & Hammond, 1971; Muir, 1967). But when a majority of the justices became dissatisfied with the stringent *Lemon* test, the Court devised additional standards, such as the endorsement test (requiring challenged governmental action to have a purpose or effect of endorsing or disapproving religion to be struck down), under which many types of governmental aid to nonpublic schools and devotional expression in public schools have been allowed (see *Good News Club v. Milford Central School*, 2001; McCarthy et al., 2014; *Zelman v. Simon-Harris*, 2002).

Deciding which test to apply can be significant in determining case outcomes, as these examples portray. Over time, these standards or tests have been modified or sometimes dropped and replaced with new tests, reflecting changes in the composition of the Supreme Court.

Sanctions and Incentives

Judicial pronouncements do not implement themselves, and the ultimate impact of judicial decisions is determined by how others respond to them. Often the degree of compliance depends on how intensely people feel about the topic, their attitudes toward the judiciary, and their sentiments regarding the consequences of complying or not complying with the court rulings (Canon & Johnson, 1999; Dunn & West, 2009).

Among sanctions, courts can issue injunctions that direct parties to do something or to not do something (Rebell & Block, 1982), such as requiring a school district to implement a desegregation plan or to refrain from conducting blanket suspicionless personal student searches. Also, if courts find legislative acts in violation of state or federal constitutional provisions, the judiciary can instruct legislative bodies to remedy the constitutional defects identified. For example, when state courts have invalidated school finance systems as not adequately funding the basic education guaranteed by their state constitutions, legislatures have been judicially required to revise their school funding schemes (Baker & Welner, 2011; Hess, 2006; Springer, Liu, & Guthrie, 2009; Tang, 2011).

Although major judicial decisions do alter policies and practices, including those in public schools, judicial sanctions are weak compared with those available to the other branches of government. In contrast to the meager judicial arsenal, the legislative branch can impose various punitive measures, such as withholding funds from schools that do not comply with legislative mandates. Legislatures also can provide incentives, including financial awards to schools that adhere to specific guidelines. Baum has asserted that "courts lack some very important legal powers; . . . the judiciary does not control the sword or the purse" (1980, p. 561).

However, the federal judiciary in the past several decades has expanded its impact on government action by interpreting the reach of the first provision of the Civil Rights Act of 1871 (codified as 42 U.S.C., Section 1983), which was enacted to protect African Americans following the Civil War. In the 1960s, federal courts started broadly interpreting this law as providing a damages remedy against persons (including school officials and school districts) acting on behalf of the state who are found guilty of violating clearly established federally protected rights (see Alexander & Alexander, 2012). This development has been important in the school context because it has encouraged students, parents, and teachers to challenge school policies, thus greatly increasing the amount of school litigation. The possibility of getting large monetary awards for the violation of federal rights provides a far more powerful incentive to initiate lawsuits than does an order for the school to stop a specific practice.

In addition to Section 1983 suits, the Supreme Court has interpreted other federal laws as authorizing damage awards. To illustrate, after the Court ruled that individuals can sue school districts under Title IX of the Education Amendments of 1972 for alleged sexual harassment (*Franklin v. Gwinnett Public Schools*, 1992), the number of sexual harassment claims against school districts increased significantly. Presumably this growth was due to the monetary incentive to sue, because it is unlikely that the number of actual incidents of harassment suddenly escalated.

Supreme Court decisions also can dampen subsequent litigation. For example, the Supreme Court ruled in 2002 that there is no private right to bring suit for violations of the Family Educational Rights and Privacy Act (FERPA) (*Gonzaga University v. Doe,* 2002). Because Congress was not explicit in identifying such a right, the remedy for a FERPA violation is for the U.S. Department of Education to withhold funds from school districts that are not in compliance with the law's provisions. If the Supreme Court had concluded instead that there is a private right to sue under FERPA, this would have stimulated litigation by aggrieved parents who may not be inclined to seek a remedy of withholding federal funds from their children's school.

Also, Supreme Court rulings have provided a disincentive for parents to bring some lawsuits against school districts in special education disputes. The Court ruled in 2005 that the party challenging individualized education programs for students with disabilities has the burden of proof; the burden is not automatically placed on the school district (*Schaffer v. Weast,* 2005). The following year, the Court held that parents who win in challenging programs provided for their children cannot seek reimbursement from school districts for funds spent on the services of experts to support their claims (*Arlington Central v. Murphy,* 2006). If these Supreme Court decisions had gone the other way, they would have stimulated special education litigation, which already is outpacing litigation in other areas of school law (Lupini & Zirkel, 2003; Zirkel & Johnson, 2011).

In resolving school disputes by applying legal principles, the judiciary has the potential to influence many aspects of public education in significant ways. As discussed later, the judicial impact on education has fluctuated over time and across substantive areas.

HISTORICAL TRENDS IN EDUCATION LITIGATION

It is important to remember that significant education litigation primarily "is a phenomenon of the second half of the twentieth century" (West & Dunn, 2009, p. 4). Traditionally, judicial decisions seemed to have little impact on public schools, and they rarely triggered volatile political responses. *Local control* was the guiding principle, and most political controversies were between local boards of education and professional educators (Kirp, 1986). Courts primarily dealt with student injury cases and contract disputes that were resolved on the basis of state law (Hogan, 1985; Kirp & Jensen, 1986). The federal judiciary rarely addressed social issues "that challenged fundamental aspects of the U.S. educational system" (Superfine, 2010, p. 111).

School law began to change in the mid-20th century when the Supreme Court extended constitutional protection to vulnerable groups, requiring desegregation of public schools and protecting the rights of racial minorities in other arenas. It is not a coincidence that the Education Law Association was established in 1954 shortly after the landmark *Brown v. Board of Education* desegregation decision was rendered.[2] Most legal analysts agree that *Brown* was the single most important Supreme Court decision affecting education politics, policies, and practices. This litigation launched a paradigm change in judicial intervention in school controversies beyond school segregation by drawing attention to discriminatory practices based on characteristics such as sex, national origin, and disabilities and to inequities across school districts in resources, programs, and facilities. Prior to the Supreme Court's *Brown* decision in 1954, fewer than 400 education cases had been initiated in federal courts (Hogan, 1985). *Brown* "put the courts centrally in the education policy business" (Kirp, 1986, p. 1).

The amount of federal litigation involving public schools was fairly stable from 1920 until the 1940s. Then, the number of federal education cases more than quadrupled from 1940 through the 1970s (Dunn & West, 2009; Zirkel & Johnson, 2011). Indeed, in less than 15 years—between 1967 and 1981—the number of school cases doubled (Tyack & Benavot, 1985). Several factors contributed to this growth in school litigation, such as the civil rights movement, the Supreme Court's expansive interpretation of constitutionally protected individual rights, anti–Vietnam War sentiment, environmentalism, and feminism (Miller & Barnes, 2004).

Also, the growth of public interest groups, such as groups advocating on behalf of individuals with disabilities and conservative citizen groups, provided an impetus for legal challenges to government policies (Dunn & West, 2009). Judicial opinions influenced school practices not only substantively, such as invalidating arbitrary constraints on free expression rights, but also procedurally in that courts required procedural safeguards to ensure fundamental fairness in placement, disciplinary, and dismissal decisions (see McCarthy et al., 2014).

According to Cunningham, at all levels of government in the 1970s "the executive and legislative branches appeared to be less and less able to respond to challenges to the traditional expectations for educational management and governance," and courts were called on to resolve disputes with increasing frequency (1978, p. xi). Civil rights activists appreciated the social changes instigated by the courts when other institutions were not willing, or perhaps able, to address important societal concerns. They viewed the federal courts as an important check on majority rule when the majority supported discriminatory practices.

Others, however, perceived the federal courts as increasingly going beyond their legitimate role (see Hess, 2006). Critics feared that the movement of life-appointed judges into the policy-making realm could "atrophy the sense of responsibility of citizens and elected representatives alike in making fundamental political decisions" (Rebell & Block, 1982, p. 6).

Increasing criticism of the judicial influence on school policies and practices accompanied the expanding role of the courts in the education domain. The judiciary was criticized in the 1970s for assuming a dominant role not only in dispute resolution but also in education policy development and administration, domains that traditionally belonged to other branches of government (Cunningham, 1978; Nystrand & Staub, 1978). Much of the concern focused on judicial decisions that eroded local control of schools, with federal courts allegedly functioning as a "super board of education" (Fischer, 1989, p. 699). Noting the "remarkable expansion of judicial participation in the implementation of public policy" in the 1960s and 1970s, Diver concluded that plaintiffs increasingly were asking courts to go beyond identifying discrete violations "to effect systemic reform of entire institutions or programs" (1979, p. 44). Many educators, instead of welcoming judicial involvement to clarify protected rights, lamented the constraints placed on their activities and began viewing the courts as their adversaries. And often fears of the law or of being sued were more confining than the laws themselves (Hess & Fusarelli, 2009).

Yet one should not assume that the federal courts generally wanted to play an influential role in determining school policies. The Supreme Court has declared on several occasions that educational policy is an area "in which this Court's lack of specialized knowledge and experience counsels against premature interference with the informed judgments made at the state and local levels" (*San Antonio Independent School District v.*

Rodriguez, 1973, p. 42). Federal courts often have voiced regret that they have to resolve controversies that should be handled elsewhere (*Epperson v. Arkansas,* 1968), and they attempt to uphold challenged public school policies and practices if possible.

The dramatic growth in education litigation, especially cases dealing with civil rights, started to level off in the 1980s, but the number of school cases remained at a high level.[3] During this decade, the amount of education litigation declined a little overall, but the amount of state cases increased slightly over the prior decade (Zirkel & Johnson, 2011), so the biggest decline was in federal litigation.

In the aftermath of the U.S. Department of Education disseminating *A Nation at Risk* (National Commission on Excellence in Education, 1983), states became more assertive in enacting education reform measures, and education assumed a higher priority on federal and state political agendas. State statutes became more prescriptive as to accountability measures, components of the curriculum, student assessment, and a host of other topics, and many of these provisions have generated legal challenges.

Also, federal laws guaranteeing the procedural and substantive rights of children with disabilities stimulated a large amount of litigation. More recently, the 600-page No Child Left Behind (NCLB) Act of 2001 placed additional responsibilities on public schools and spawned numerous legal controversies, including lawsuits challenging the federal government's authority to impose programmatic and accountability requirements on schools without adequately funding the mandates (Daniel, 2006; McCarthy et al., 2014).

Reports on the volume of school litigation during the past 15 years have been somewhat mixed. Zirkel declared in the late 1990s that the "supposed explosion in educational litigation is a matter of the past" and "we are moving down the other side of the mountain of judicial activism in school affairs" (1997, p. 349). Lupini and Zirkel (2003) reported a gradual decline in school litigation during the 1990s. In contrast, Redfield (2003) found that the burgeoning school legislation at the federal and state levels nurtured a steady increase in school litigation through the turn of the century. And Zirkel and Johnson reported in 2011 that school litigation increased significantly in the first decade of the 21st century, surpassing the volume of education cases documented in the 1970s. However, these researchers reported that the balance between federal and state cases had shifted somewhat, with more federal cases (45% of the total) documented than in any prior decade (Zirkel & Johnson, 2011). While fluctuations may be ahead, a retreat to the level of judicial deference in school cases that characterized the first half of the 20th century is not possible. And without question, advocacy groups are becoming increasingly assertive in influencing school policies and challenging practices, which ensures continued litigation (Sawchuk, 2012).

Most analysts agree that the litigation trends are not evenly distributed across issue areas. For example, the number of desegregation cases has declined significantly since the 1960s and 1970s, whereas cases pertaining to special education have continued to increase (Zirkel & Lyons, 2011). Case outcomes reflect some differences during the past few decades as well. Zirkel in the late 1990s recognized the "pendulum shift" that had occurred, with the federal courts moving away from their "former student-friendly orientation" toward support for the public school's authority to govern student conduct (1998, p. 242). But more recently, students have prevailed in some significant cases pertaining to search and seizure (*Safford Unified School District v. Redding,* 2009) and electronic expression (*Layshock v. Hermitage School District,* 2011; McCarthy et al., 2014). Thus, a steady trend is not as apparent as it seemed to be a decade or so ago.

Criticisms of the judicial impact on public schools have continued and currently emanate from both conservative and liberal camps (West & Dunn, 2009). Some conservative critics still lament the judicial inroads on majority rule. Hess has asserted that state court rulings invalidating school funding systems "are part of a broader strategy to use courts to win victories on spending and government expansion that proponents have been unable to win at the ballot box" (2006, p. 3).

The criticisms are not confined to judicial mandates that place demands on the government. Some liberal policy makers recently have complained about "conservative judicial activism" evident in many Supreme Court decisions, such as those limiting the application of civil rights laws to state employees (Biskupic, 1999; *Board of Trustees v. Garrett*, 2001) and restricting constitutional protection of public employees' free speech rights (see *Garcetti v. Ceballos*, 2006; McCarthy, 2006). The cycles of liberal and conservative judicial activism in part reflect changing societal sentiments in this regard.

INTERPLAY AND TENSION AMONG BRANCHES
AND LEVELS OF GOVERNMENT

The various branches of government and levels of policy making are complicated, making it difficult to understand the "tangled web of interactions" (Miller & Barnes, 2004, p. 3). The checks and balances across the executive, legislative, and judicial branches include inherent tensions, and both cooperative and discordant interactions have been evident in connection with public education.

Judicial, Legislative, and Executive Exchanges

The courts can stimulate or discourage legislative and executive activity, depending on whether challenged provisions are invalidated, upheld, or possibly misinterpreted. If the Supreme Court strikes down a law as violating the U.S. Constitution, theoretically a national standard is established. Congress and state legislatures cannot adopt provisions that conflict with the Supreme Court's decision. The only recourse is to amend the Constitution. However, legislative bodies can introduce new legislation in an effort to satisfy the Court while still achieving their initial goals.[4] In the 1970s when the Supreme Court struck down a series of laws to provide public funds to private, primarily religious, schools, state legislatures immediately adopted slightly altered statutes in hopes that the revised provisions would be upheld by the federal judiciary, and some of these measures in fact received judicial endorsement (see Alexander & Alexander, 2012).

A more recent example of legislative/judicial interplay involves state efforts to place restrictions on illegal immigration. Although these laws do not specifically bar the education of such students at public expense, which Texas was not allowed to do in *Plyler v. Doe* (1982), the Alabama law required identification of undocumented students. This requirement was viewed as a deterrent for these children to enroll in public schools, and in 2012, the Eleventh Circuit blocked implementation of the provision as violating the equal protection rights of the affected children (*United States v. Alabama*, 2012). A few months earlier, the Supreme Court struck down several parts of the Arizona immigration law as intruding on the federal government's responsibilities to regulate immigration but upheld the provision allowing police officers to verify the immigration status of those arrested (*Arizona v. United States*, 2012). The Arizona law has no student identification provision, and whether states can require public schools to identify undocumented students has not yet been addressed by the Supreme Court. However, given the Supreme Court's interpretation of the U.S. Constitution in *Plyler,* such children clearly cannot be denied a public education.

In contrast to the Supreme Court striking down a state law as conflicting with the U.S. Constitution, which leaves states no discretion in that regard, when the Court rejects a constitutional challenge to a legislative act, states still have latitude to impose limitations. To illustrate, after the Supreme Court in 1977 found no federal constitutional violation in the use of corporal punishment in public schools (*Ingraham v. Wright,* 1977), this topic received a great deal of attention in state legislative forums. At the time of the *Ingraham* decision, only one state placed restrictions on the use of corporal punishment in public education. Since *Ingraham,* more than half of the states have enacted legislation that bans this disciplinary technique in public schools. And in the absence of state legislation, numerous school districts have placed restrictions on using corporal punishment (McCarthy et al., 2014).

Legislatures can also respond when the courts *misinterpret* congressional intent in civil rights laws (designed to implement federal constitutional provisions) or federal funding laws (enacted pursuant to congressional spending powers). If the judiciary misinterprets a federal law, Congress can amend the law in question to clarify its meaning, which has happened on a number of occasions. For example, the Supreme Court in 1976 held that Title VII of the Civil Rights Act of 1964 excluded pregnancy-related disabilities from its protection of employees against sex discrimination (*General Electric v. Gilbert,* 1976), and Congress responded by amending Title VII in 1978, specifically prohibiting employers from discriminating against employees on the basis of pregnancy. Similarly, when the Supreme Court interpreted the Individuals with Disabilities Education Act as precluding the award of attorneys' fees to successful plaintiffs (*Smith v. Robinson,* 1984), Congress amended the law to authorize the award of such fees. Between 1967 and 1990, Congress nullified 121 Supreme Court decisions by amending the laws in question (Baum, 1998), but only a handful of them pertained to education.

Sometimes, however, Congress does not amend a law, even though its enforcement has differed from the Supreme Court's interpretation. As discussed previously, after the Supreme Court interpreted FERPA as precluding a private right to bring suit (*Gonzaga University v. Doe,* 2002), the law was not amended to authorize such a right. The remedy for a FERPA violation is the withdrawal of federal aid from the noncomplying institution. If Congress had responded to the Supreme Court's decision by amending the law to provide an individual remedy, the volume of FERPA litigation undoubtedly would have increased significantly because of the possibility of receiving monetary damages.

Legislators, local policy makers, and school administrators at times may *encourage* lawsuits to avoid taking stands on politically sensitive issues. Graber has noted that "mainstream politicians may facilitate judicial policymaking in part because they have good reason to believe that the courts will announce those policies they privately favor but cannot openly endorse without endangering their political support" (1993, p. 43). Policy makers often have not wanted to take unpopular positions publicly, but have welcomed judicially mandated school policy changes in connection with desegregation, special education services, student discipline, and religious influences in public schools. Superintendents at times have viewed lawyers as their allies in affecting school reform (Hess & Fusarelli, 2009). This development has been especially evident in the church/state arena, as these issues generate strong emotional and political responses. Under such circumstances, judicial policy making can serve "the reigning coalition and party system by insulating the elected branches of government from divisive issues" (Miller & Barnes, 2004, p. 4).

The historical developments regarding programs for English language learners (ELLs) offer a good example of the interplay, involvement, and tension among all three branches of government. In the 1960s, the federal government provided some funds to assist ELLs, but it was not until the Supreme Court's decision in *Lau v. Nichols* (1974) that national attention focused on this topic. The Court interpreted the protection against national origin discrimination included in Title VI of the Civil Rights Act of 1964 as obligating public school districts to give ELLs special assistance, but the Court did not stipulate what specific assistance schools had to provide. The same year as *Lau*, Congress enacted the Equal Educational Opportunities Act (EEOA), requiring public school systems to develop appropriate programs for students with limited English proficiency. Following the Supreme Court's decision, the former U.S. Department of Health, Education, and Welfare issued advisory guidelines, *The Lau Remedies*, outlining various approaches school districts could use to provide equal educational opportunities for these students. *The Lau Remedies* were controversial and led to a range of interpretations across school districts. Also, some lower courts ruled that ELLs were entitled to bilingual/bicultural education, whereas others held that the provision of compensatory programs was sufficient to address their language needs (Brisk, 1998). The U.S. Department of Education responded that it would issue more specific regulations to clarify some of the ambiguities, but this effort became politicized and was abandoned during the Reagan administration (see Kirp & Jensen, 1986). The federal government ultimately gave states more flexibility to determine the types of assistance school districts must provide ELLs, and current federal guidelines do not advocate a particular program of instruction for these students. But controversy continues over the Department of Education's directive for ELLs to take the same reading tests as those given to native English speakers to determine whether schools are making adequate yearly progress in compliance with NCLB (Glod, 2007).

Lower courts in the past decade have issued a range of decisions regarding the rights of ELLs, and some states, such as California, have adopted measures requiring "nearly all" classroom instruction to be in English (McCarthy et al., 2014). The Supreme Court in *Horne v. Flores* (2009) held that states and local educational authorities have latitude in determining which programs and techniques they will implement to meet their federal statutory obligations. In this case, the Court instructed the lower court to assess whether changed conditions now satisfied the EEOA, declining to enjoin Arizona's program for ELLs simply because funding had not increased.

This activity pertaining to ELLs reflects the interactions among the branches of government and at times the blurring of their designated roles. The Supreme Court drew national attention to this issue and established the principle that these students were entitled to special assistance in public schools. The topic, however, became very political, involving the legislative and executive branches as well as the courts.

Federal and State Courts

Because education is a state function, one is not surprised that education litigation takes place primarily in state courts. The most widely publicized decisions, however, usually are federal cases that involve individual rights or establish national standards regarding the legality of specific school practices.

As noted, if the Supreme Court *invalidates* a school practice under the U.S. Constitution, such as segregated schools, state courts cannot offer a contrary interpretation, asserting that the practice satisfies state law. But if the Supreme Court *allows* a particular practice under the U.S. Constitution, such as drug testing public school students who participate in extracurricular activities (*Board of Education v. Earls,* 2002), the practice still may not satisfy state constitutional provisions. A permissive Supreme Court ruling often stimulates challenges in state courts under state law as has been evident with challenges to school funding systems and voucher programs.

For example, after the Supreme Court rejected a Fourteenth Amendment Equal Protection Clause challenge to the Texas school funding system in *San Antonio Independent School District v. Rodriguez* (1973), challenges under state constitutional provisions ensued. Starting with the widely publicized California Supreme Court decision, *Serrano v. Priest* (1971), invalidating the California school finance system because of its inequities, about four-fifths of the states have experienced school finance litigation (Hess, 2006; Tang, 2011). And the outcomes in these cases have been mixed. Some state courts have mirrored the U.S. Supreme Court's interpretation of the U.S. Constitution in their interpretations of state provisions, even though all state constitutions address education unlike the U.S. Constitution's silence in this regard. Other state courts have invalidated school funding systems under their state constitutions' education clauses or equal protection provisions (see Dayton, Dupre, & Kiracofe, 2004; Springer et al., 2009; Tang, 2011).

When school funding systems are invalidated, legislative action is stimulated and perhaps required to respond to the judicial decisions. Often the revised system is again challenged, generating another round of litigation as the sequence is repeated. A few states have experienced multiple state supreme court decisions pertaining to their school funding systems (see Sergiovanni et al., 2004; Tang, 2011). The most recent wave of state school finance cases has involved claims that funding systems are not providing the adequate education to which all children are entitled under state constitutional provisions that obligate the legislature to provide for a system of free public schools. State courts in general seem more receptive to these adequacy claims than they were to former challenges to inequities in state funding schemes, but the scoreboard remains mixed (see Baker & Welner, 2011; Dayton et al., 2004; Hess, 2006; Sergiovanni et al., 2004; Springer et al., 2009).

Legal activity pertaining to state-supported tax credit programs and voucher systems to fund education also illustrates the interplay between federal and state courts. The Supreme Court resolved the First Amendment Establishment Clause question in *Zelman v. Simmons-Harris* (2002), upholding the Cleveland scholarship program that allows disadvantaged students to use public funds for private education. Even though almost all participants used the vouchers to attend religious schools, the Supreme Court ruled that the program was part of a religiously neutral initiative to provide choices to families in Cleveland and thus satisfied the Establishment Clause (McCarthy, 2007).

More recently, in 2011, the Supreme Court rejected a challenge to Arizona's tax benefit program allowing citizens to claim a tax credit for contributions to private student tuition organizations (STOs) that provide scholarships for students to attend private schools (*Arizona Christian School Tuition Organization v. Winn,* 2011). The Supreme Court concluded that taxpayers did not have standing to raise an Establishment Clause challenge to the program because they did not show a connection between the alleged injury and improper state conduct; the taxpayers contributing to STOs are spending their own money rather than tax funds the state has already collected. Even though the vast majority of the STOs are religiously affiliated and can restrict their scholarships to particular sectarian schools, the Court considered STOs to be *private*, not *government*, entities. Thus, the Court suggested that state-created tax relief programs involving such private entities to distribute the scholarship funds to religious school students will not likely be vulnerable to Establishment Clause challenges.

However, simply because the Establishment Clause permits state-funded vouchers to be used in religious schools and scholarship programs for private school tuition does not mean that religious schools have a constitutional right to receive state funds if other nonpublic schools receive them (see *Locke v. Davey*, 2004). Thus, similar to challenges to state school funding systems, the legality of voucher systems and tax credit programs for private school scholarships will be determined primarily by state courts and may depend somewhat on the predispositions of the respective state courts in interpreting their state constitutional provisions. In short, the U.S. Constitution does not preclude the adoption of voucher plans that allow religious schools to participate, but such plans may run afoul of state law.

The Milwaukee and Cleveland programs have been endorsed by state courts (*Jackson v. Benson*, 1998; *Simmons-Harris v. Goff*, 1999), but some other programs have not fared well when challenged under state education clauses or state prohibitions on the use of public funds for religious purposes. The Florida Supreme Court, for example, relied on the state constitution's education clause, similar to provisions in many other states, to invalidate the statewide voucher program for students attending public schools rated as deficient. The court reasoned that the Florida voucher program unconstitutionally diverted public funds into separate, nonuniform, private systems that compete with and reduce funds for public education (*Bush v. Holmes*, 2006). The Colorado Supreme Court also invalidated a pilot voucher program for low-income students attending low-performing schools, concluding that the program violated the "local control" clause of the state constitution by taking away districts' discretion in spending funds for instruction (*Owens v. Colorado Congress*, 2004). In addition, the exclusion of religious schools from tuition reimbursement programs for high school students in districts that do not operate public high schools has been upheld in Maine and Vermont (*Anderson v. Durham*, 2006; *Chittenden Town School District v. Department of Education*, 1999; *Eulitt v. Maine Department of Education*, 2004).

In 2013, the Louisiana Supreme Court struck down the state voucher system as unconstitutionally diverting public school funds to private schools (*Louisiana Federation of Teachers v. Louisiana*, 2013), and a New Hampshire appeals court invalidated a tuition tax credit program under the constitutional prohibition on state aid to religious schools and institutions (*Duncan v. New Hampshire*, 2013). But also in 2013, the Indiana Supreme Court upheld the most liberal state voucher program adopted to date, rejecting claims under the state's education clause as well as the constitutional prohibitions on compelled support of religion and state support of religious institutions (*Meredith v. Pence*, 2013). And a Colorado appeals court upheld a school district's voucher program, finding no violation of various constitutional provisions and the state's school funding law (*Taxpayers for Public Education v. Douglas County School District*, 2013). Although the trend since 2000 seemed to be for state high courts to strike down voucher systems based on state constitutional grounds, the 2013 rulings are mixed.

States continue to consider voucher plans and programs to give taxpayers and businesses tax credits for contributions to private school scholarships. Since 2010, voucher bills have been introduced in a majority of the states, and as noted, Indiana has adopted the most comprehensive program, with relaxed eligibility criteria for students to use state funds to attend private schools (Banchero, 2012; Indiana Department of Education, 2012). In addition to state initiatives, the federal government is funding a voucher program for low-income students to attend private schools in Washington, DC (Pershing, 2012).

The legality of voucher plans and tax credits for private school tuition will depend primarily on state courts' interpretations of state constitutional provisions. Indeed, instead of a national policy, we soon may have 50 standards regarding the legality of these initiatives. And if such measures to enhance parental choice result in a substantial increase in the number of children attending private schools, this could have a significant impact on support for public education in our nation.

Even though school litigation has grown at a faster pace in federal courts than in state courts since the turn of the century (Zirkel & Johnson, 2011), state education cases remain important on many topics. And state courts currently are dominant in connection with state legislation to fund public and private schools and to provide educational choices for parents.

A FINAL WORD

Landmark school law decisions, such as *Brown* (1954) and the school prayer cases in the early 1960s (*Engel v. Vitale*, 1962; *School District of Abington Township v. Schempp*, 1963), established the constitutional framework and stimulated political activities that ultimately changed the educational landscape and altered the judicial influence in public schools (Johnson, 1967; Kirp & Jensen, 1986). The Supreme Court's *Rodriguez* (1973) ruling also significantly affected public education by *not* considering education a fundamental right under the U.S. Constitution and shifting challenges to school funding systems to state courts (Sergiovanni et al., 2004). Court decisions are critically important because they can stimulate political action, bringing specific policy issues into the national spotlight (Fleming, Bohte, & Wood, 1997). Judicial rulings increase awareness of legal rights and play a significant role in developing discussion frameworks that can mobilize the citizenry (McCann, 1994). Wilhelm (2009) has asserted that the liberal or conservative ideological leanings of state courts can influence the nature of school policies that are adopted.

It must be kept in mind, however, that many legislative acts, school board policies, and local school rules are never challenged in court. These measures have a greater daily impact on school activities than do court decisions. And if school actions are challenged, courts are reluctant to interfere with judgments of school boards and educators; the judiciary will do so only if protected rights are implicated.

Thus, educators—not courts or legislatures—must usually determine what actions are reasonable and just (Bull & McCarthy, 1995). If educators abdicate this responsibility or act arbitrarily or unfairly, their actions can elicit legal challenges. Teachers and school leaders can prevent some legal controversies by understanding established law and acting in a manner that respects the rights of others. It is unfortunate that educators' distrust of federal courts, which started during the rapid growth of federal litigation several decades ago, is still prevalent today. School personnel often view judicial decisions as imposing external constraints and unreasonable barriers on their roles, rather than protecting minority interests and facilitating educators' ability to make fair decisions and perform their jobs effectively. When judicial interpretations are contrary to the will of the majority, such rulings can generate harsh criticism (Hess, 2006). Mistrust of the courts and criticism of the judiciary's influence on school policies and practices remain widespread (West & Dunn, 2009).

Despite the large volume of education cases each year, the judicial impact on education policies and politics has not recently been examined to the same extent it was investigated in the 1970s and early 1980s. The enhanced judicial role was a hot topic during the 1970s because this development was new, but now the courts' impact on education politics and policies is not eliciting as much interest and concern. Perhaps we have simply grown accustomed to the judiciary taking an active role in shaping educational policies and stimulating political reactions, with educators and policy makers now resigned that their decisions and policies may be challenged in court.

With the recent upswing in litigation to the highest level ever reached, which is particularly pronounced for federal litigation (Zirkel & Johnson, 2011), there is a continuing need for analysis of judicial interpretations and dispute resolution. Considering the dearth of recent research on the judicial impact in education, studies on this topic seem long overdue. Such research might reveal whether the judicial influence on educational policies is confined to its interpretive role or at times is usurping the legislative function. Studies also might clarify whether judicial decisions involving schools are serving to protect vulnerable minorities against majority rule (Nader & Hirsch, 2004) or simply reinforcing majoritarian sentiments (Rosenberg, 1991).

The appropriate judicial role in education remains controversial, and myths regarding the extent of the judicial impact will continue to be perpetuated in the absence of data to refute them (Zirkel, 2005). One certainty is that we will not return to the pre-1960s level of judicial involvement in education. Governmental and individual interests will continue to clash in the school context, and courts will be called on to resolve these disputes and in doing so will influence educational policies and practices. Perhaps if educators can gain a better understanding of the law and the legitimate judicial role, this knowledge may alleviate their suspicions of judicial intervention and their fears that the scales of justice are tipped against them.

NOTES

1. While the legislative branch is charged with making laws, the executive branch with enforcing the laws, and the judicial branch with interpreting the laws, these roles are not always as distinct as envisioned. When the New Deal elevated executive power in the 1930s, some thought the courts might become weak in dealing with administrative agencies, as has been true in Great Britain, but this has not happened in the United States. Melnick has attributed the strength of the judiciary to "the traditional American distrust of bureaucracy and insistence upon having a 'day in court'" (2004, p. 90).

2. The Education Law Association was originally called the National Organization on Legal Problems of Education. A group of attorneys and educators correctly predicted that the *Brown* decision was launching a new era in school law and that public education in our nation would never be quite the same.

3. Given the volume of education litigation, in the early 1980s West Publishing Company launched a reporter, *Education Law Reporter,* devoted solely to education cases and commentary.

4. One of the best examples of the interplay and tension across branches of government is the abortion topic. For a discussion of the political responses to *Roe v. Wade* (1973), see Canon and Johnson (1999).

REFERENCES

Alexander, K., & Alexander, M. D. (2012). *American public school law* (8th ed.). Belmont, CA: Wadsworth Cengage Learning.

Alley, R. (1996). *Without a prayer: Religious expression in public schools.* Amherst, NY: Prometheus Books.

Anderson v. Town of Durham, 895 A.2d 944 (Me. 2006), *cert. denied,* 127 S. Ct. 661 (2006).

Arizona v. United States, 132 S. Ct. 2492 (2012).

Arizona Christian School Tuition Organization v. Winn, 131 S. Ct. 1436 (2011).

Arlington Central School District v. Murphy, 126 S. Ct. 2455 (2006).

Baker, B., & Welner, K. (2011). School finance and courts: Does reform matter, and how can we tell? *Teachers College Record, 113,* 2374–2414.

Banchero, S. (2012, April). School vouchers gain ground. *Wall Street Journal,* http://online.wsj.com/article/SB1000 14240527023036240045773381316097 45296.html.

Baum, L. (1980). The influence of legislatures and appellate courts over the policy implementation process. *Policy Studies Journal, 8,* 560–574.

Baum, L. (1998). *American courts: Process and policy* (4th ed.). Boston, MA: Houghton Mifflin.

Bethel School District v. Fraser, 478 U.S. 675 (1986).

Biskupic, J. (1999, March 31). Rehnquist asks Congress to clear judiciary funding. *Washington Post,* A27.

Board of Education v. Dowell, 498 U.S. 237 (1991).

Board of Education v. Earls, 536 U.S. 822 (2002).

Board of Trustees v. Garrett, 531 U.S. 356 (2001).

Brisk, M. E. (1998). *Bilingual education: From compensatory to quality schooling.* Mahwah, NJ: Lawrence Erlbaum Associates.

Brown v. Board of Education of Topeka, 347 U.S. 483 (1954).

Bull, B., & McCarthy, M. (1995). Reflections on the knowledge base in law and ethics for educational leaders. *Educational Administration Quarterly, 31,* 613–631.

Bush v. Holmes, 919 So. 2d 392 (Fla. 2006).

Caldarone, R., Canes-Wrone, B., & Clark, T. (2009). Partisan labels and democratic accountability: An analysis of state supreme court abortion decisions. *Journal of Politics, 71,* 560–573.

Canon, B. C., & Johnson, C. A. (1999). *Judicial policies: Implementation and impact* (2nd ed.). Washington, DC: Congressional Quarterly Press.

Chittenden Town Sch. Dist. v. Dep't of Educ., 738 A.2d 539 (Vt. 1999).

Cunningham, L. L. (1978). Foreword. In C. P. Hooker (Ed.), *The courts and education: The seventy-seventh yearbook of the national society for the study of education, part I* (pp. xi–xix). Chicago, IL: University of Chicago Press.

Daniel, P. T. K. (2006). No Child Left Behind: The balm of Gilead has arrived in American education. *Education Law Reporter, 206,* 791–814.

Dayton, J. (2012). *Education law: Principles, policies, and practice.* Athens, GA: Wisdom Builders.

Dayton, J., Dupre, A., & Kiracofe, C. (2004). Education finance litigation: A review of recent state high court decisions and their likely impact on future litigation. *Education Law Reporter, 186,* 1–14.

Diver, C. (1979). The judge as political powerbroker: Superintending structural changes in public institutions. *Virginia Law Review, 65,* 43–106.

Dolbeare, K., & Hammond, P. (1971). *The school prayer decisions: From court policy to local practice.* Chicago, IL: University of Chicago Press.

Doninger v. Niehoff, 642 F.3d 334 (2d Cir. 2011), *cert. denied,* 132 S. Ct. 499 (2011).

Duncan v. New Hampshire, No. 219–2012-CV-00121 (N.H. Super. Ct. Jan. 11, 2013).

Dunn, J. M., & West, M. R. (Eds.). (2009). *From schoolhouse to courthouse: The judiciary's role in American education.* Washington, DC: Thomas B. Fordham Institute, Brookings Institution.

Engel v. Vitale, 370 U.S. 421 (1962).

Epperson v. Arkansas, 393 U.S. 114 (1968).

Eulitt v. Maine Department of Education, 386 F.3d 344 (1st Cir. 2004).

Fischer, L. (1989). When courts play school board: Judicial activism in education. *Education Law Reporter, 51,* 693–709.

Fisher v. University of Texas, 133 S. Ct. 2411 (2013).

Fleming, R. B., Bohte, J., & Wood, B. D. (1997). One voice among many: The Supreme Court's influence on attentiveness to issues in the United States, 1947–1992. *American Journal of Political Science, 41,* 1224–1250.

Franklin v. Gwinnett County Public Schools, 503 U.S. 60 (1992).

Freeman v. Pitts, 503 U.S. 467 (1992).

Frontiero v. Richardson, 411 U.S. 677 (1973).

Garcetti v. Ceballos, 126 S. Ct. 1951 (2006).

General Electric Company v. Gilbert, 429 U.S. 125 (1976).

Glod, M. (2007, February 1). Va. is urged to obey "No Child" on reading test. *Washington Post,* B01.

Gonzaga University v. Doe, 536 U.S. 273 (2002).

Good News Club v. Milford Central School, 533 U.S. 98 (2001).

Graber, M. (1993). The nonmajoritarian difficulty: Legislative deference to the judiciary. *Studies in American Political Development, 7,* 35–73.

Green v. County School Board, 391 U.S. 430 (1968).

Hazelwood School District v. Kuhlmeier, 484 U.S. 260 (1988).

Hess, F. (2006, July/August). When unaccountable courts meet dysfunctional schools. *The American Enterprise Education Fairy Tales*, www.taemag.com/issues/issueID.185/toc.asp.

Hess, F., & Fusarelli, L. (2009). School superintendents and the law: Cages of their own design? In J. M. Dunn & M. R. West (Eds.), *From schoolhouse to courthouse: The judiciary's role in American education* (pp. 49–70). Washington, DC: Thomas B. Fordham Institute, Brookings Institution.

Hobson v. Hansen, 269 F. Supp. 401 (D.D.C. 1967).

Hogan, J. C. (1985). *The schools, the courts, and the public interest* (2nd ed.). Lexington, MA: D. C. Heath.

Horne v. Flores, 557 U.S. 433 (2009).

Indiana Department of Education (2012). *Indiana's school voucher program*, www.myschoolvoucher.com/welcome.aspx.

Ingraham v. Wright, 430 U.S. 651 (1977).

Jackson v. Benson, 578 N.W.2d 602 (Wis. 1998).

Johnson, R. (1967). *The dynamics of compliance*. Evanston, IL: Northwestern University Press.

J.S. v. Blue Mountain School District, 650 F.3d 915 (3d Cir. 2011), *cert. denied*, 132 S. Ct. 1097 (2012).

Kagan, R. A. (2004). American courts and the policy dialogue. In M. Miller & J. Barnes (Eds.), *Making policy, making law* (pp. 13–34). Washington, DC: Georgetown University Press.

Kirp, D. L. (1986). Introduction: The fourth R: Reading, writing, 'rithmetic—and rules. In D. L. Kirp & D. N. Jensen (Eds.), *School days, rule days: The legalization and regulation of education* (pp. 1–17). Philadelphia, PA: Falmer Press.

Kirp, D. L., & Jensen, D. N. (Eds.). (1986). *School days, rule days: The legalization and regulation of education*. Philadelphia, PA: Falmer Press.

Kozlowski, D. (2011). Toothless *Tinker*: The continued erosion of student speech rights. *Journalism & Mass Communication Quarterly, 88*, 352–373.

Lau v. Nichols, 414 U.S. 563 (1974).

Lax, J., & Rader, K. (2010). Legal constraints on Supreme Court decision making: Do jurisprudential regimes exist? *Journal of Politics, 72*, 273–284.

Layshock v. Hermitage School District, 650 F.3d 205 (3d Cir. 2011), *cert. denied*, 132 S. Ct. 1097 (2012).

Lemon v. Kurtzman, 411 U.S. 192 (1971).

Lloyd, R. D. (1995). Separating partisanship from party in judicial research: Reapportionment in the U.S. district courts. *American Political Science Review, 89*, 413–420.

Locke v. Davey, 540 U.S. 712 (2004).

Louisiana Federation of Teachers v. State, Nos. 2013-CA-0120, 2013-CA-0232, 2013-CA-0350, 2013 WL 1878913 (La. May 7, 2013).

Lupini, W., & Zirkel, P. (2003). An outcomes analysis of education litigation. *Education Policy, 17*, 257–279.

McCann, M. (1994). *Rights at work: Pay equity reform and the politics of legal mobilization*. Chicago, IL: University of Chicago Press.

McCarthy, M. (2006). *Garcetti v. Ceballos:* Another hurdle for public employees. *Education Law Reporter, 210*, 867–884.

McCarthy, M. (2007). Determining the legality of school vouchers: Are state courts the new venue? *Journal of Education Finance, 32*, 351–372.

McCarthy, M., Cambron-McCabe, N., & Eckes, S. (2014). *Public school law: Teachers' and students' rights* (7th ed.). Boston, MA: Pearson.

Melnick, R. S. (2004). Courts and agencies. In M. C. Miller & J. Barnes (Eds.), *Making policy, making law* (pp. 89–104). Washington, DC: Georgetown University Press.

Meredith v. Pence, 984 N.E.2d 1213 (Ind. 2013).

Miller, M. C., & Barnes, J. (Eds.). (2004). *Making policy, making law*. Washington, DC: Georgetown University Press.

Minersville School District v. Gobitis, 310 U.S. 586 (1940).

Morse v. Frederick, 551 U.S. 393 (2007).

Muir, W. K. (1967). *Prayer in the public schools: Law and attitude change*. Chicago. IL: University of Chicago Press.

Nader, R., & Hirsch, A. (2004). Making eminent domain humane. *Villanova Law Review, 49*, 207–232.

National Commission on Excellence in Education. (1983). *A nation at risk: The imperative for educational reform: A report to the nation and the secretary of education*. Washington, DC: U.S. Department of Education.

Nystrand, R. O., & Staub, F. (1978). The courts as educational policy makers. In C. P. Hooker (Ed.), *The courts and education: The seventy-seventh yearbook of the national society for the study of education, part I.* (pp. 27–53). Chicago, IL: University of Chicago Press.

Owens v. Colorado Congress, 92 P.3d 933 (Colo. 2004).

Parents Involved in Community Schools v. Seattle School District, No. 1, and *McFarland v. Jefferson County Public Schools,* 551 U.S. 701 (2007).

Pershing, B. (2012, June 18). *D.C. school vouchers program supporters strike deal with White House,* www.washingtonpost.com/blogs/dc-wire/post/dc-school-voucher-program-supporters-strike-deal-with-white-house/2012/06/18/gJQAV8WVlV_blog.html.

Plessy v. Ferguson, 163 U.S. 537 (1896).

Plyler v. Doe, 457 U.S. 202 (1982).

Rebell, M. A., & Block, A. R. (1982). *Educational policy and making the courts: An empirical study of judicial activism.* Chicago, IL: University of Chicago Press.

Redfield, S. E. (2003). The convergence of education and law: A new class of educators and lawyers. *Indiana Law Review, 36,* 609–642.

Roe v. Wade, 410 U.S. 959 (1973).

Rosenberg, G. N. (1991). *The hollow hope: Can courts bring about social change?* Chicago, IL: University of Chicago Press.

Rowland, C. K., & Carp, R. A. (1996). *Politics and judgment in federal district courts.* Lawrence: University Press of Kansas.

Safford Unified School District v. Redding, 557 U.S. 364 (2009).

San Antonio Independent School District v. Rodriguez, 411 U.S. 1 (1973).

Sawchuk, S. (2012, May 23). Advocacy groups target local politics, *Education Week,* 1, 13.

Schaffer v. Weast, 126 S. Ct. 528 (2005).

Scherer, N. (2001). Who drives the ideological makeup of the lower federal courts in a divided government? *Law & Society Review, 35,* 191–219.

School District of Abington Township v. Schempp, 374 U.S. 203 (1963).

Sergiovanni, T. J., Kelleher, P., McCarthy, M., & Wirt, F. M. (2004). *Educational governance and administration* (5th ed.). Boston, MA: Allyn and Bacon.

Serrano v. Priest I, 487 P.2d 1241 (Cal. 1971).

Simmons-Harris v. Goff, 711 N.E.2d 203 (Ohio 1999).

Smith v. Robinson, 468 U.S. 992 (1984).

Springer, M., Liu, K., & Guthrie, J. (2009). The impact of school finance litigation on resource distribution: A comparison of court-mandated equity and adequacy reforms. *Education Economics, 17,* 421–444.

Superfine, B. (2010). Court-driven reform and equal educational opportunity: Centralization, decentralization, and the shifting judicial role. *Review of Educational Research, 80,* 108–137.

Tang, A. (2011). Broken systems, broken duties: A new theory for school finance litigation. *Marquette Law Review, 94,* 1195–1239.

Taxpayers for Public Education v. Douglas County School District, Nos. 11CA1856 & 11CA18, 2013 WL 791140 (Colo. App. Ct. Feb. 28, 2013).

Tinker v. Des Moines Independent School District, 393 U.S. 503 (1969).

Tyack, D., & Benavot, A. (1985). Courts and public schools: Education litigation in historical perspective. *Law and Society Review, 19,* 339–80.

United States v. Alabama, 691 F.3d 1269 (11th Cir. 2012).

Webb, L. D., McCarthy, M., & Thomas, S. (1988). *Financing elementary and secondary education,* chapter 11. Columbus, OH: Merrill.

West, M. R., & Dunn, J. M. (2009). The Supreme Court as school board revisited. In J. M. Dunn & M. R. West (Eds.), *From schoolhouse to courthouse: The judiciary's role in American education* (pp. 3–16). Washington, DC: Thomas B. Fordham Institute, Brookings Institution.

West Virginia State Board of Education v. Barnette, 319 U.S. 624 (1943).

Wilhelm, T. (2009). Strange bedfellows: The policy consequences of legislative-judicial relations in the American states. *American Politics Research, 37,* 3–29.

Zelman v. Simmons-Harris, 536 U.S. 639 (2002).

Zirkel, P. (1997). The "explosion" in education litigation: An update. *Education Law Reporter, 114,* 341–351.

Zirkel, P. (1998). National trends in education litigation: Supreme Court decisions concerning students. *Journal of Law and Education, 27,* 235–245.

Zirkel, P. (2005). The paralyzing fear of education litigation. *The State Education Standard, 6*(2), 43–44.

Zirkel, P., & Johnson, B. (2011). The "explosion" in education litigation: An updated analysis. *Education Law Reporter, 265,* 1–8.

Zirkel, P., & Lyons, C. (2011). Restraining the use of restraints for students with disabilities: An empirical analysis of the case law. *Connecticut Public Interest Law Journal, 10,* 323–354.

7

THE POLITICS OF SCHOOL FINANCE IN THE NEW NORMAL ERA

Bruce D. Baker and Preston C. Green

INTRODUCTION

The great recession of 2008 ushered in the "new normal" era of school finance. According to the Center on Budget and Policy Priorities, in 2012–2013, local public school districts continued to face substantial cuts to state aid because of the impact of the great recession. Oliff, Mai, and Leachman summarize:

- Twenty-six states are providing less funding per student to local school districts in the new school year than they provided a year ago. These funding cuts have been modest, but, in many states, they come on top of severe cuts made in previous years.
- Some states are beginning to restore their school funding over the past year, but those restorations are, for the most part, far from sufficient to make up for cuts in past years. For example, Florida is increasing school funding by $273 per pupil this year. But that is not nearly enough to offset the state's $569 per-pupil cut over the previous four years.
- As a result, school funding remains well below prerecession levels. Thirty-five states are providing less funding per student than they did five years ago.
- Seventeen states have cut per-student funding by more than 10 percent from 2008 levels.
- Three states—Arizona, Alabama, and Oklahoma—each have reduced per-pupil funding to K-12 schools by more than 20 percent. (These figures, like all the comparisons in this chapter, are in inflation-adjusted dollars and focus on the primary form of state aid to local schools.) (2012, p. 1)

The great recession has coincided with an evolving political rhetoric, years in the making, regarding the value of providing equitable and adequate funding for local public school districts. From the bully pulpit of the U.S. Department of Education, Secretary of Education Arne Duncan declared the great recession the start of the "new normal" era for public schooling, one in which public school districts must learn to do more with less, and should view the recession as an opportunity, not a threat.

166

My message is that this challenge can, and should be, embraced as an opportunity to make dramatic improvements. I believe enormous opportunities for improving the productivity of our education system lie ahead if we are smart, innovative, and courageous in rethinking the status quo.

It's time to stop treating the problem of educational productivity as a grinding, eat-your-broccoli exercise. It's time to start treating it as an opportunity for innovation and accelerating progress. (Duncan, 2010, p. 1)

Other major public figures including Bill Gates also seized the opportunity to declare that improved efficiency, not more money, is the answer to the woes of the American education system:

Over the last four decades, the per-student cost of running our K-12 schools has more than doubled, while our student achievement has remained flat, and other countries have raced ahead. The same pattern holds for higher education. Spending has climbed, but our percentage of college graduates has dropped compared to other countries. (Gates, 2011)

The echo chamber has amplified throughout the recession, and the message drifted toward the logical conclusion that the level and distribution of funding provided to schools is, in fact, largely irrelevant: that money simply doesn't matter.

At the state level, where the primary responsibility for financing public schools lies, this rhetoric has been particularly bold. Florida Governor Rick Scott, in justifying his recent cuts to the state's education budget, remarked:

We're spending a lot of money on education, and when you look at the results, it's not great. (*Orlando Sentinel,* October 11, 2011)

In his 2011 "State of the State" address, New York Governor Andrew Cuomo declared:

Not only do we spend too much, but we get too little in return. We spend more money on education than any state in the nation and we are number 34 in terms of results. (Cuomo, 2011)

And in an interview with New Jersey's Governor Chris Christie, the *Wall Street Journal* reported:

According to Mr. Christie, New Jersey taxpayers are spending $22,000 per student in the Newark school system, yet less than a third of these students graduate, proving that more money isn't the answer to better performance. (Freeman, 2010)

Political certainty regarding the unimportance of money for schools and the need for schools to "tighten their belts" is frequently grounded in misrepresentations of total spending growth and test score trends at the national level over the past 30 years, like those Gates presented to support his claim (Baker, 2012; Baker & Welner, 2011a). The typical storyline is that spending per pupil has increased dramatically and pupil-to-teacher ratios have declined, at the same time that scores on national assessments have stagnated, and scores on international assessments have fallen behind the rest of the developed world (Gates, 2011). The conclusion: we're spending more and more, and not getting results, so it's clear that money doesn't make a difference.

Logically, to the extent that having more money would not possibly improve schooling quality, then reductions in funding cannot possibly be harmful. And thus we enter a modern era of school finance policy where cutting funding is not merely an unfortunate "new normal" but in fact is characterized as progressive, productive, and efficient.

In this chapter, we begin with an overview of the traditional goals of state school finance systems, as they have evolved over the past several decades. Next, we summarize recent national reports evaluating the equity and adequacy of state school finance systems, noting that the American education system remains as 51 distinct entities when it comes to financing of public education. Next, we review evidence of the recent retreat from equity in select states and reductions of funding especially to districts serving higher concentrations of children in poverty. We also explore causes of persistent inequities and inadequacies in select states. We conclude with a review of pervasive political arguments regarding state school finance systems that often thwart progress toward funding equity and adequacy objectives.

EQUITY, ADEQUACY, AND STATE AID FORMULAS

In this section, we discuss the role of state school finance systems in advancing equity and adequacy objectives. By a "state school finance system," we mean the set of rules, regulations, and policies that combine state aid with local resources to fund schools to meet a given educational goal—usually having at least something to do with improving equity and adequacy of resources for the children of the state. Within that system are various streams of state aid as well as policies regulating local property taxation. Further, there may be additional local income taxes or county-level tax revenues distributed to school systems. As mathematical equations, state aid formulas include numerous constants and variables, each of which is the product of political deliberation, and each of which changes who wins or loses when it comes to state aid. We refer to each politically determined formula factor as a "policy lever." Similarly, local and intermediate tax policies include a multitude of policy levers, such as tax limits, definitions of property types, valuation methods, and exemptions. In short, a multitude of policy levers influence the distribution of state aid, county-level intermediate resources, and the raising of revenues from local taxes.

Modern state school finance formulas—aid distribution formulas—strive to achieve two simultaneous objectives:

- Accounting for differences in the costs of achieving equal educational opportunity across schools and districts;
- Accounting for differences in the ability of local public school districts to cover those costs.

A local district's ability to raise revenues often is a function of local taxable property wealth and/or the incomes of local residents.

Figure 7.1 provides an illustration of how state and local revenues combine in an "ideal" finance system to fund per-pupil spending. In this system, state aid compensates

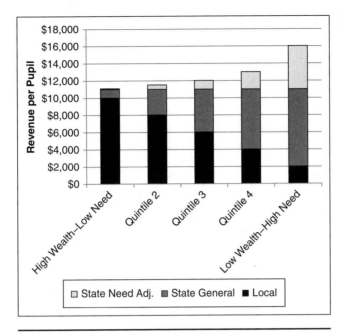

Figure 7.1 Hypothetical Need and Cost Adjusted, Wealth Equalized Foundation Aid Formula

Source: U.S. Census Bureau Fiscal Survey of Local Governments (2007–09), Public Elementary and Secondary School Finances & U.S. Census Bureau Small Area Income and Poverty Estimates (2007–09)

for differences in local capacity to raise revenues and provides more revenues to districts with greater educational needs, which may be directly and indirectly related to local poverty. Thus, revenues differ by poverty concentration with high-poverty districts typically raising less in local revenues and receiving more state aid, and low-poverty districts raising more in local revenues and relying less on state assistance. Also, the typical low-poverty district raises most of its revenues from local taxes on property. To the extent that state aid depends on local fiscal capacity, this illustration makes the simplified assumption that districts with weaker revenue-raising capacity also tend to be higher-poverty districts. While this is not uniformly true—consider a high-poverty urban district with a large commercial property tax base—generally a correlation exists between the two. Districts may receive a small share of general state aid if the total cost of providing equal educational opportunity exceeds the local resources raised with a fair tax rate.

Overall, the balance of state and local revenue in our hypothetical case is progressive. In Figure 7.1, general state aid is used to achieve equality of dollar inputs across districts with varying fiscal capacity, and need-based aid is used to adjust for varying costs of achieving equal educational opportunity. In practice, how general and need-based aid is integrated into school funding systems varies across states. Many states use multipliers or *weights* in their general aid formula to target more aid to children with greater needs. Other states use separate *categorical* allocations for specific programs, services, or student populations, while still others use a combination of weights and categorical funding. Yet despite these progressive aspirations or intentions of many funding formulas, as we show, things don't always turn out as one might expect or how the state aid formulas intend.

EQUITY AND ADEQUACY IN THE MODERN ERA

In this section, we summarize the current condition of state school finance systems. Beginning in 2010, the Education Law Center of New Jersey released a new national school funding fairness report.[1] That report characterizes state school finance systems in terms of their relative level of overall support for schools (both fiscal effort and funding level) and in terms of the *fairness* of the distribution of that funding. Fairness in the report is conceptualized in terms of the progressiveness or regressiveness of total state and local revenue per pupil with respect to child poverty concentrations.

Progressive: Total state and local revenue per pupil is systematically higher in local public school districts with higher poverty concentrations (controlling for differences in competitive wage variation, economies of scale, and population sparsity)
  Neutral: Total state and local revenue per pupil is not systematically different between local public school districts with higher and lower poverty rates (controlling for differences in competitive wage variation, economies of scale, and population sparsity)
  Regressive: Total state and local revenue per pupil is systematically lower in local public school districts with higher poverty concentrations (controlling for differences in competitive wage variation, economies of scale, and population sparsity)

Importantly, inequities and inadequacies, while separate school finance concepts, are interconnected in important practical ways (Baker & Green, 2008). One might assert, for example, that even though high-poverty New York State districts have fewer resources than lower-poverty New York State districts, they have more total state and local revenues than even lower-poverty districts in other states, including their neighbor to the south, Pennsylvania. Thus, despite having less than their surrounding more affluent neighbors, they clearly have enough to get the job done. The problem with this assertion is that the majority of cost pressures involved in providing adequate educational services are local or regional. It might be less expensive, for example, to provide adequate educational programs and services in New York City and lower-income surrounding districts if not for the high labor costs stimulated by the spending behavior of far more affluent Westchester County districts, most of which can also provide more desirable working conditions. The spending behaviors of these surrounding districts necessarily influence the costs for all. Specifically, they affect the ability of districts to pay a competitive wage to recruit and retain quality teachers, the largest driver of school district expense.

Further, students graduating from local public school districts in the same region must compete with each other for access to postsecondary education and employment. Those growing up in impoverished neighborhoods already face a substantial uphill challenge, one that can be moderated by the provision of targeted interventions both in their communities and in their schools. Those targeted interventions, which include early childhood education and reduced class sizes, among other things, cost money. If the money isn't there, the interventions won't be there either.

SCHOOL FUNDING FAIRNESS AND EFFORT

Table 7.1 draws on the National Report Card on School Funding Fairness, listing states that have *progressive, neutral,* and *regressive* overall funding. Note that several states maintain school funding systems where state and local school revenue remains systematically lower in school districts serving high-poverty populations. Table 7.1 also organizes states by the

Table 7.1 Funding Fairness and Effort across States

Effort / Fairness	Progressive	Neutral	Regressive
High Effort	New Jersey Ohio	Indiana Kansas Maryland New Mexico South Carolina Vermont West Virginia Arkansas Connecticut Georgia Rhode Island Wisconsin	Michigan New York Pennsylvania New Hampshire
Medium Effort	Massachusetts Minnesota	Iowa Kentucky Mississippi Montana Nebraska	Alabama Idaho Texas Illinois
Low Effort	Utah South Dakota	Arizona California Delaware Louisiana Oklahoma Oregon Tennessee Washington	Maine Missouri Virginia Colorado Florida North Carolina Nevada North Dakota

level of effort they put into funding their education systems, where effort is measured as the share of state level gross domestic product spent (state and local) on elementary and secondary schools. New Jersey and Ohio are relatively high-effort states, where on average, districts serving high-poverty populations receive additional resources. By contrast, Missouri, Colorado, Virginia, and Florida are among those states where high-poverty districts receive systematically fewer resources, and where relatively low state effort is applied.

THE GREAT RECESSION BACKSLIDE

Findings from Table 7.1 are drawn from models estimated using data from 2007–2008 to 2009–2010 and thus do not necessarily capture the onset of the "new normal" period. Figure 7.2 takes a look at two progressive and two regressive states from 2005 to 2011. Figure 7.2 reports the trendlines for the relationship between state and local revenue per pupil and child poverty concentrations across local public school districts within these states. As explained earlier, a downward sloping trendline, from left to right, represents regressiveness whereas an upward trendline is progressive. In Pennsylvania, from 2005 to 2007, the trendline shifted upward (not inflation adjusted), meaning that total revenue increased, but regressiveness remained constant. From 2007 to 2009, potentially as a result of funding reforms adopted in 2008, the trendline became less regressive (right-hand side rises). But, by 2011, the system had backslid, with the average level remaining relatively unchanged (not inflation adjusted) but funding in higher-poverty districts declining while revenue in lower-poverty districts continued to rise. The story is similar in New York State.

Ohio and New Jersey, two historically progressively financed states, have seen backsliding of funding fairness. Ohio slid upward from 2005 to 2007, then shifted to even

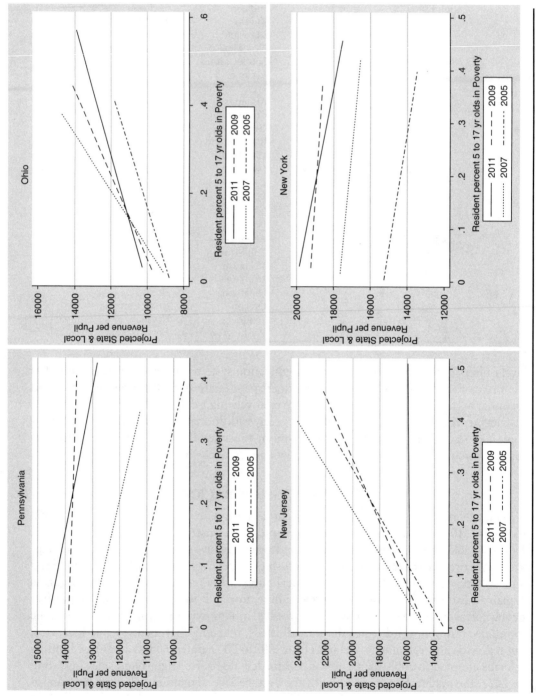

Figure 7.2 Fairness Profiles of Select States

greater progressiveness. But between 2009 and 2011, Ohio saw significant backsliding of state and local revenue for high-poverty districts. The backslide in New Jersey had already begun between 2007 and 2009. By 2011, New Jersey, which had been among the most progressively funded in the nation appears to be backsliding toward neutral funding. Additional years of data will make clearer whether these effects are temporary or permanent. Whether in regressive or progressive states, what is clear is that lower-poverty districts have been harmed much less by the recession's effects. In progressive states, high-poverty districts have lost the funding edge they need to provide necessary supplemental programs, supports and services, and/or the wage premiums needed to recruit and retain teachers, compared to their lower-poverty neighbors. Lower-poverty districts by comparison have remained relatively untouched.

MODERN POLITICS OF STATE AID FORMULAS

The 1990s ushered in what some might consider the "empirical era" of school funding; an era is characterized by a shift in attention from achieving equitable distribution of dollar inputs to schooling, to a focus on providing minimally adequate funding (Clune, 1994). The shift from equity to adequacy objectives, which was to eventually be argued in state courts across the nation, led to numerous attempts to (a) define educational adequacy both in terms of the programs and services that should be available to all children and in terms of the outcomes children should be able to achieve, and (b) estimate the costs of providing those programs and services and/or the costs of achieving the identified outcomes across children and settings (Baker, Taylor, & Vedlitz, 2005). However, no empirical method or evidence can ever fully overcome the politics of state legislatures determining how billions of dollars will ultimately be distributed across their various constituents.

In this section, we provide illustrations of how state policy makers have, in this new era of empiricism, hidden behind a veneer of empirical validity in their efforts simply to preserve what is and has always been. Next, we provide a brief overview of persistent features of state school finance systems referred to as *stealth inequalities* in a recent report from the Center for American Progress (Baker & Corcoran, 2012).

CREATING A VENEER OF EMPIRICAL VALIDITY

Over the past two decades in particular, states and advocacy groups have engaged with greater frequency in attempting to define the amount of funding that would be necessary for achieving adequate educational outcomes. One might characterize the period as one of the rise of empiricism in school finance, which coincided with a shift in litigation strategies from emphasis on funding equity to emphasis on funding adequacy—specifically whether funding was adequate either to provide specific programs and services or to achieve specific measured educational outcomes. In some cases, states have adopted their empirical strategy in response to judicial orders that the legislature comply with a state constitutional mandate for the provision of an adequate education. In other cases, states have proactively set out to validate spending targets they know they can already meet (or have already been met), to claim *school finance reform* political victory.

Prior to this new "empirical era," total state budgets would be set based on political preferences of governors and legislators regarding state tax policy and the revenues expected to be produced by the state tax system. Revenue projections, based on politically palatable tax policy, divided by the numbers of children to be served, generated the average per-pupil amount of available aid. And then the tug of war over shifting distributions toward one constituency and thus away from another ensued. The biggest difference between the two approaches is that now, state policy makers are more likely to justify the amount through an "empirically valid" estimate of the funding needed for children to achieve adequate outcomes.

Baker, Taylor, and Vedlitz (2005) provide an explanation of early gaming of estimates of the costs of providing an adequate education in Illinois and Ohio in the 1990s.

Augenblick and colleagues provide multiple cost estimates for Illinois based on different outcome standards, using single or multiple years of data and including some or all outcome standards. The higher of the two figures in Table 7.5 represents the average expenditures of Illinois school districts which, using 1999–2000 data, had 83% of students meeting or exceeding the standard for improvement over time. The lower of the two figures is based on the average expenditure of districts which, using 2000 data only, had 67% of pupils meet or exceed the standards, and 50% meeting standards on all tests.

Similar issues exist in a series of successful schools cost estimates produced in Ohio a year earlier. In Ohio, however, estimates were derived and proposed amidst the political process, with various constituents picking and choosing their data years and outcome measures to yield the desired result. Two Ohio estimates are provided in the table, but multiple estimates were actually prepared based on different subsets of districts meeting different outcome standards. The Governor's office chose 43 districts meeting 20 of 27 1999 standards, the Senate selected 122 districts meeting 17 of 18 1996 standards, the House chose 45 districts meeting all 18 original standards in 1999, and the House again in an amended bill used 127 districts meeting 17 of 18 1996 standards in 1996 and 20 of 27 standards in 1999. (Baker et al., 2005, p. 15)

Put simply, legislators in Ohio backed into outcome standards to identify that subset of school districts that on average were spending what the state was willing to spend within its current budget.

New York's Numbers Game

More recent school finance reforms in New York State reveal that similar games persist. In response to court order in *Campaign for Fiscal Equity v. State* (2006), the legislature adopted a foundation aid formula to be phased in from 2007 to 2011 where the basic funding level in that formula would be set as follows:

The Foundation Amount is the cost of providing general education services. It is measured by determining instructional costs of districts that are performing well. (NYSED, Primer on State Aid, 2011–2012)

The state defined "performing well" as a standard of 80 percent of children scoring proficient or higher on state assessments, a performance level marginally lower than the statewide mean at the time.

In constructing their baseline cost estimates, state officials adopted a handful of additional steps to ensure a politically palatable, low, basic cost estimate. First, state officials chose only to consider the average spending of those districts that were both "performing

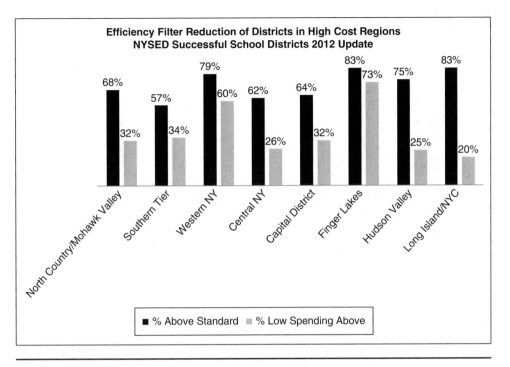

Figure 7.3 Influence of Efficiency Filter on Spending Estimates in NY State

Note: [1] Tabulated based on RCI as reported in DBSAD1, 3-29-12, N(MI0123) 03 REGIONAL COST INDEX (RCI), using data set with RCI mergedinto NYSED FARU District Fiscal Profiles (http://www.oms.nysed.gov/faru/Profiles/profiles_cover.html) 2007 to 2011
[2] Based on "successful district" classification as presented in Excel Workbook used for 2012 Successful Schools Update analysis.
[3] Based on "low spending district" classification as presented in Excel Workbook used for 2012 Successful Schools Update analysis.

well" and in the lower half of spending among those performing well. By taking this step, nearly all districts in the higher-cost regions of the state are excluded and thus have limited effect on the basic cost estimate. The effect of this exclusion is shown in Figure 7.3. Instead, basic costs for districts statewide are measured largely against the average spending of districts lying somewhere in the triangle between Ithaca, Buffalo, and Syracuse. Spending behavior of these districts has little relevance to costs of providing adequate education in and around New York City.

Another step in the process further deflates basic cost estimates. Instead of adopting a comprehensive measure of annual operating expenditures, the state chose a pruned "general instructional spending" figure. Figure 7.4 summarizes differences between the state-selected partial, general operating expenditure figure, and a more comprehensive figure of general education spending per pupil by region. In particular, the pruned general instructional spending figure was substantively lower than the state's approved operating expense figure for downstate districts.

The combined (a) setting of a low outcome bar, (b) filtered exclusion of districts in higher-cost regions of the state, and (c) selection of a partial spending figure rather than a more comprehensive one guaranteed a more politically palatable minimum cost estimate, while still providing a veneer of empirical validity. Despite taking such care to generate such a low estimate of adequate spending undergirding the state foundation aid formula, in recent years, the state has failed to come even close to funding the targets established by the formula—providing less than half of the target levels of aid required for many of the state's highest-need districts.

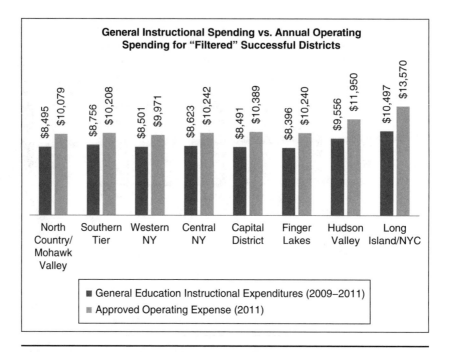

Figure 7.4 Influence of Selected General Expense Figure on Foundation Spending Level

Note: [1] Based on "successful district" classification as presented in Excel Workbook used for 2012 Successful Schools Update analysis. [2] Based on "low spending district" classification as presented in Excel Workbook used for 2012 Successful Schools Update analysis. [3] General Expenditure as presented in Excel Workbook used for 2012 Successful Schools Update analysis divided by enrollment(not adjusted for low income students). [4] File DBSAC1, 3-29-12, M(WM0006) 00 2010-11 AOE/TAPU FOR EXP

Rhode Island's Numbers Game

Perhaps most ludicrous of all is the Rhode Island public officials' attempt to validate empirically their selected spending levels for recent school finance reforms. Rhode Island's school finance reforms gained significant attention among policy think tanks as a model of proactive political collaboration leading to progressive, empirically based but elegantly simple reform (Wong, 2013). As described in official documents, the basic funding level for the Rhode Island formula is set as follows:

(1) The core instruction amount shall be an amount equal to a statewide per pupil core instruction amount as established by the department of elementary and secondary education, derived from the average of northeast regional expenditure data for the states of Rhode Island, Massachusetts, Connecticut, and New Hampshire from the National Center for Education Statistics (NCES) that will adequately fund the student instructional needs as described in the basic education program and multiplied by the district average daily membership as defined in section 16–7-22. (RIDE, 2010)

As articulated by State Education Commissioner Deborah Gist:

Our core instructional amount was based on national research, using data from the NCES, is sufficient to fund the requirements of the Rhode Island Basic Education

Program, and it in no way focused on states with low per-pupil expenditures. In fact, we looked particularly carefully at our neighboring states, which have some of the highest per-pupil expenditures in the nation, and we included only those states that have an organizational structure and staffing patterns similar to ours. (Gist, 2010)

Several points here are worthy of note.

a) Like New York officials, Rhode Island officials chose to focus on a reduced spending figure—core instructional spending—rather than a complete current operating spending figure.
b) Average core spending of other states is hardly to be considered "national research" and average spending based on national data sources in other states is hardly indicative of what might be required to achieve Rhode Island's required outcomes unless the state's outcomes are also contingent on standards set in other states.
c) The data used to set funding targets for school year 2010–2011 and beyond come from several years prior.
d) New Hampshire is not a neighboring state of Rhode Island.

Table 7.2 shows the effect of including New Hampshire among Rhode Island's "neighbors" when calculating the basic spending levels. Spending in New Hampshire is substantively lower than in Massachusetts or Connecticut, and thus brings down the average. Notably, spending in Vermont, which is much higher than in New Hampshire, is not included. Vermont might be excluded from the analysis on the basis of its more sparse population and large number of very small districts. But western Massachusetts is similar in this regard, as is northern New Hampshire. There appears little justification, other than to lower the average, for including New Hampshire among Rhode Island's neighbors in this analysis.

Eventually, in accordance with their "analyses," Rhode Island officials proposed a foundation level for 2010–2011 and beyond to be set at $8,295 (RIDE, 2010; Wong, 2013). Notably, however, the average spending in Connecticut, Massachusetts, and New Hampshire, which most closely approximates that figure, comes from 2006–2007. Further, the 2007–2008 Rhode Island average core instructional spending per pupil was already more than $8,500, and a more comprehensive measure of current operating spending per pupil exceeded $13,000 per pupil.

Table 7.2 Effect of Including/Excluding New Hampshire from Mean Spending Calculations

Year	Rhode Island Current Spending	Rhode Island Core Spending	Connecticut	Massachusetts	New Hampshire	Avg. with New Hampshire	Avg. without New Hampshire
2006	$11,769	$7,466	$8,106	$7,978	$6,626	$7,828	$7,922
2007	$12,612	$7,964	$8,314	$8,492	$7,026	$8,259	$8,425
2008	$13,539	$8,551	$8,877	$9,013	$7,640	$8,806	$8,962

Data Source: U.S. Census Fiscal Survey of Local Governments, Public Elementary, and Secondary School Finances

PROTECTING STEALTH INEQUALITIES

Here, we provide a brief overview of what Baker and Corcoran (2012) referred to as *stealth inequalities* in a recent report for the Center for American Progress. Stealth inequalities in state aid formulas result from the tug of war over the finite pot of available state aid for schools. In short, state aid stealth inequalities are those cases where local public school districts receive state aid they otherwise shouldn't if adopting the state aid framework proposed previously—that state aid is intended to offset (a) local ability to pay for programs and services and (b) variations in student needs and/or regional costs of providing equitable and adequate programs and services. Some stealth inequalities are remnants of the past that remain untouchable in political debate. Others may be newly or recently introduced.

Among the common culprits Baker and Corcoran identified are the provision of minimum aid, or adjustments to state aid formulas that guarantee that all districts, regardless of their local taxable wealth or need, get something in state aid. Such provisions exist in one form or another in each state Baker and Corcoran explored in Table 7.3. Similarly, several states provide components of state aid "outside the formula," or in block grants that go in equal amounts to wealthier and poorer districts. By "outside the formula" we mean grants that aren't subject to the wealth equalization adjustments. For example, a district might be identified as requiring an additional $2,000 per pupil in funding to provide for specific programming. That district might, under the general aid formula, raise the first 50 percent of any target amount through local taxes and receive the remainder in state aid, which in this case would result in $1,000 per pupil in aid. But, if we apply the $2,000 "outside the formula," then the district gets the full $2,000 as state aid, even if the district would have otherwise been considered wealthy enough to pay the first 90 percent. Outside-the-formula grants are often used for special education or other categorical funding. But, when portions of the aid formula are separated in this way, state legislators representing districts that would not gain from increases to the general aid formula may be more likely to lobby for increases to go into special aid formulas that benefit their constituents. That is, the formula becomes more politically parsed, permitting politically motivated changes to some components of the formula without altering others.

Finally, Baker and Corcoran uncovered some particularly problematic—from an equity standpoint—tax relief provisions. Bear in mind that general state aid equalization formulas such as the prototype laid out earlier are designed to ensure that all local jurisdictions can achieve target funding levels with equitable tax effort. That is, the basic design is to ensure some degree of tax equity—or in other words, tax relief—for those who might otherwise be disproportionately burdened by high taxes. Baker and Corcoran explain how in both Texas and New York, policies have been adopted effectively to buy down the tax rates of the wealthiest communities. In effect, these aid programs are inverse tax equity programs providing disproportionate relief to those communities with the greatest capacity to raise revenues on their own, locally.

Where total state aid is constrained by available tax revenue, then any state aid allocated to districts with greater capacity and less need is aid that cannot be allocated to districts with less capacity and greater need. Each state identified in the Stealth Inequalities table is a state identified as having regressive overall funding. That is, state and local revenues are systematically higher in lower-poverty districts. These stealth inequalities serve to exacerbate regressiveness in the "new normal" era.

Table 7.3 Stealth Inequalities in Select States

	Adjustments to state aid ratio (and minimum aid)		Un-equalized (or ad hoc) categorical aid		Tax relief provisions	
	Note	*Amount*	*Note*	*Amount*	*Note*	*Amount*
Illinois[1]	Alternative aid formulas including flat minimum[2]	Minimum = $218 per pupil plus hold harmless aid[3]	Mandatory (state formula) and discretionary (ISBE distributed) categorical grants			
New York[4]	Minimum foundation aid and other adjustments	Minimum = $500 per aid able pupil unit			New York State School Tax Relief program[5] (STAR)	
Pennsylvania	Minimum basic funding aid ratio[6]	15% of foundation target	Special education (Census based)[7]	$400+ per ADM		
North Carolina	Minimum aid through personnel ratio formula					
Missouri[8]	Hold harmless (Transition to SB287 from SB380)		Classroom Trust Fund	$435 per ADA	Proposition C (1982)	$786 to $818 per WADA (10% of state and local revenue)
Texas[9]	Available school fund	Approx. $250 per pupil minimum, $466 per pupil in 2010–11[10]	NIFA		Additional State Aid for Tax Reduction[11] (ASATR)	Fills gap between revenue at compressed rate and target revenue

[1] www.isbe.state.il.us/funding/pdf/gsa_overview.pdf

[2] The second formula is the "Alternate" formula. Districts qualifying for this formula have available local resources per pupil of at least 93 percent but less than 175 percent of the foundation level. The third formula is the "Flat Grant" formula. Districts qualifying for this formula have available local resources per pupil of at least 175 percent of the foundation level.

[3] A hold harmless provision is included in Section 18-8.05(J) of the School Code. If, for any district in 2007–2008, the formula yields less than the sum of the district's 1997–1998 General State Aid and 1997–1998 Hold Harmless, a separately appropriated grant will be made to hold those districts harmless to the 1997–1998 levels. Districts will be eligible (subject to appropriation) to receive Hold Harmless grants in all subsequent years if the amount of General State Aid the district receives is below the 1997–1998 levels described earlier. www.isbe.state.il.us/funding/html/gsa.htm

[4] New York State Education Department Primer on State Aid: www.oms.nysed.gov/faru/PDFDocuments/Primer11-12D.pdf

[5] New York State Department of Taxation and Finance, STAR: www.tax.ny.gov/pit/property/star/index.htm

[6] Pennsylvania Department of Education, Basic Education Funding History: www.portal.state.pa.us/portal/server.pt?open=514&objID=509059&mode=2

[7] Pennsylvania Department of Education, Special Education Funding History: www.portal.state.pa.us/portal/server.pt?open=514&objID=509062&mode=2

[8] Missouri Senate Bill 287: www.senate.mo.gov/07info/pdf-bill/intro/SB287.pdf

[9] Texas Association of School Boards, School Finance 101 (Overview of Foundation School Program): www.tasbo.org/files-public/publications/TEA/School_Finance_101.pdf

[10] Direct link for Texas "Available School Fund" one-page overview: www.tea.state.tx.us/WorkArea/linkit.aspx?LinkIdentifier=id&ItemID=2147499903&libID=2147499900

[11] Link to catalog of Texas school finance topics one-page overviews: www.tea.state.tx.us/index2.aspx?id=2147499540

DISTRACTIONS, DIVERSIONS, AND SMOKESCREENS

We conclude with a discussion of three themes in the current political rhetoric regarding school finance that we see as creating significant barriers to substantive reforms. Three arguments in particular are pervasive in the broader education reform debate, with implications for school funding equity and adequacy:

1. First, that through years of court challenges states have largely resolved funding inequities between local public school districts, but the major persistent problems that remain are inequities in local district budget allocations to schools.
2. Second, that adopting broad-based, school choice programs necessarily provides equitable opportunities for children via the liberty to choose among high-quality alternatives, thus negating concerns over equitable or adequate funding.
3. Third, that local public school districts are inefficient in their basic design and they invariably have more than enough money to do the job well, but the lack of appropriate incentives, not lack of money, causes their failure.

THE INTRADISTRICT DISTRACTION

An increasing volume of rhetoric around school finance rests on claims that states have largely met their obligations to resolve disparities between local public school districts. This premise is then extended to the contention that the bulk of remaining disparities are those that persist within school districts, because of irrational and unfair school district resource allocation practices between individual schools (see, for example, McClure et al., 2008; Public Impact et al., 2008). In short, because states have done their job to promote equity and adequacy of school funding, school district officials must now meet their corresponding obligations. This argument is also often attached to the remedy of weighted student funding (see Roza, 2006, pointing readers to the Fordham Institute's "Fund the Child" campaign).

Notably, no leading researchers in economics and school finance have joined this overwhelming shift in emphasis away from state-level concerns. Many have opted instead for a broad description of the funding problem that encompasses both within-district and between-district resource disparities (see, e.g., Bifulco, 2005; Downes, 2004; Duncombe & Johnston, 2004; Imazeki & Reschovsky, 2004; Rubenstein et al., 2007; Stiefel, Rubenstein, & Berne, 1998). Nonetheless, arguments favoring a devolution in focus from states to school districts have gained significant traction in policy debates, and they have the rhetorical advantage of providing state policy makers with an enticing, revenue-neutral policy solution (see Public Impact et al., 2008). If states have done their job, no more money is needed, nor must these policy makers consider painful movement of limited funding away from wealthier districts. Rather, districts must simply reshuffle what they have to achieve optimal distribution.

But, as Baker and Welner (2010) dissected in great detail, the increase in popularity of these political arguments is backed by little or no empirical evidence for the premise that states have already met their end of the bargain. Baker and Welner explain that studies of within-district disparities are largely confined to a few states or individual districts where school-site expenditure data have been available. Yet, notwithstanding that state school finance policies are idiosyncratic, studies from select locations have been extrapolated by prominent researchers and advocates to have broader implications for within-district and between-district disparities in other states.

Baker and Welner summarize that the *intradistrict distraction* consists of five interconnected issues:

1. The existence of within-district funding disparities.
2. The extent of any such within-district disparities.
3. The continuing existence of between-district disparities.
4. The extent of any such between-district disparities.
5. The relative causal importance of within-district and between-district disparities.

Our best reading of the extant literature tells us that numbers (1) and (3) should be noncontroversial: disparities do exist, but they vary tremendously by jurisdiction. As discussed earlier, the evidence regarding number (2) is very limited, which also means we can provide no answers regarding number (5). But it is number (4) that is most interestingly implicated by the recent policy push—the contention that we as a nation have made such progress on addressing between-district disparities that we can now turn our attention elsewhere. As such, a 50-state analysis of the current status of between-district funding inequities is warranted.

THE CHOICE DIVERSION: LIBERTY AS SUBSTITUTE FOR EQUALITY

A second issue complicating the debate over school funding equity and adequacy is the role of choice programs including public financing of charter school alternatives and, in some cases, publicly subsidized vouchers or tuition tax credits for private schools. Implicit in policy preferences for choice program expansion is the notion that more children should have the choice to attend higher-quality schooling options and that such options will emerge, as a function of the competitive marketplace for quality schooling with little attention to the level of funding provided. In other words, the liberty choice programs achieve serves as substitute for the provision of broad-based, equitable, and adequate financing. Studies purporting significant advantages achieved by students attending charter schools have invariably neglected to evaluate their access to financial resources, frequently downplaying the importance of money or relevance of equity traditionally conceived (Baker, Libby, & Wiley, 2012).

But these arguments are merely a diversion, sidestepping whether, when applied in practice, adequate alternatives are equitably distributed. One problem with this assertion is that variation in resources across private providers, as well as across charter schools, tends to be even greater than variation across traditional public schools (Baker, 2009; Baker et al., 2012). Further, higher-quality and lower-quality private and charter schools are not equitable distributed geographically and broadly available to all. At the extreme, in New Orleans following Hurricane Katrina where traditional district schools were largely wiped out, and where choice-based solutions were imposed during the recovery, entire sections of the city were left without secondary-level options and provided a sparse few elementary and middle-level options (Buras, 2011).

Baker, Libby, and Wiley (2012) show that in New York City, charter expansion has yielded vastly inequitable choices. Table 7.4 shows the demographics, spending, and class sizes of New York City charter schools, by their network affiliation, compared to district schools. Most New York City charter school networks serve far fewer children qualifying for free lunch (those with income levels less than 130 percent poverty level), far fewer

English language learners, and far fewer children with disabilities than same grade-level schools in the same borough of the city. These patterns of student sorting induce inequities across schools. But these schools also have widely varied access to financial resources despite being equitably funded by the city. Some charter networks are able to outspend demographically similar district schools by more than $5,000 per pupil and to provide class sizes that are four to six (or more) students smaller.

Table 7.4 Inequitable Charter Choices in New York City

Affiliation	Demographics Relative to District Schools in Same Borough at Same Grade Level			Resources Relative to District Schools at Same Grade Level & Demographics			
	% Free Lunch	% ELL	% Special Ed	Spending	Elem. Class Size	Grade 8 Math Class Size	Grade 8 ELA Class Size
BOE	Baseline	Baseline	Baseline	Baseline	Baseline	Baseline	Baseline
Achievement First	−13.80	−11.61	−4.38	$1,271	−2.39	−16.23	−5.16
Beginning with Children	−17.59	−13.02	−3.03	$630	0.29	−4.46	−3.13
Believe	−25.73	−7.53	1.31	$4,116	0.00	0.00	0.00
Democracy Prep	−2.17	−13.05	−3.67	$6,605	−1.62	−1.52	−1.82
Explore Schools	−19.40	−14.84	0.67	$814	−4.72	−2.90	−1.38
Green Dot	3.22	−4.08	−3.81	$757	0.00	0.00	0.00
Harlem Children's Zone	−11.92	−10.01	−3.17	$3,958	−6.18	−7.84	−11.90
Hyde Charter	3.43	−6.77	−3.65	−$178	−1.24	−0.34	0.67
Icahn	−21.37	−13.15	−12.19	$3,360	−6.88	−2.85	4.42
KIPP	−13.56	−9.67	−2.54	$5,359	0.08	−6.65	−4.46
Lighthouse Academies	−14.51	−11.30	−8.03	$1,589	−2.34	0.00	0.00
National Heritage Academy	15.60	−15.84	−7.97	$1,802	1.43	1.73	2.98
Public Prep	−15.41	−18.01	−8.03	$4,525	−1.51	0.00	0.00
Success Charter Network	−10.35	−16.54	−5.42	$2,072	−0.14	0.00	0.00
Uncommon Schools	−22.08	−11.84	−6.31	$4,091	−0.91	−8.89	−11.99
Victory Education Partners	−19.28	−13.74	−9.39	$3,348	−0.95	0.00	0.00
Village Academies	−1.03	−11.45	−4.74	$966	0.00	0.60	−5.97
Unaffiliated	−9.21	−9.93	−2.56	$2,265	−1.96	−4.60	−3.96

[1] Relative demographics determined by regressing demographic measure on school grade configuration dummy variable, dummy variable indicating geographic location, and year indicators, using data from 2008–2010.

[2] Relative spending determined by regressing spending measure on school grade configuration dummy variable, student demographic factors, and year indicators, using data from 2008–2010.

[3] Relative class size determined by regressing class size measure on school grade configuration dummy variable, student demographic factors, and year indicators, using data from 2008–2010.

Further, these charter alternatives are not evenly distributed across city neighbor-hoods, nor do they all have equal unfilled enrollment slots. They need not, nor can they, accept all comers. Thus, the premise that liberty via choice programs provides a viable substitute for equitable and adequate funding for traditional public systems is, in reality, a hollow promise.

THE NEW NORMAL AND THE EFFICIENCY SMOKESCREEN

Finally, an argument that reoccurs with some consistency in debates over the adequacy of education funding is that little or no proof exists that adding more money would likely have any measurable positive effects. This argument hinges on the oft repeated (and as frequently refuted[2]) phrase that "no systematic relationship between funding and outcomes" exists. This argument fails to excuse the facial inequity of permitting some children attending some schools to have twice or more the resources of others, especially where, as in New York State, higher-need children are the ones with systematically fewer resources.

The more recent extension of the "no systematic relationship" or "money doesn't matter" argument that has eased its way into political rhetoric and litigation regarding school spending is that all local public school districts already have more than enough money, even those with the least, and that if they simply used that money in the most efficient way, we could see that current spending is more than adequate. This assertion is echoed in the quotes at the outset of this chapter. The extension of this argument is that therefore, even cutting funding to these schools would not cause harm and does not compromise the adequacy of their funding, if they take advantage of these cuts to improve efficiency.

A version of this argument goes that if schools and districts paid teachers based on test scores they produce, and if schools and districts systematically dismissed ineffective teachers, productivity would increase dramatically and spending could decline. Further, that because improving teacher quality is argued to be more effective and less costly than smaller class sizes toward improving student outcomes, one could increase class sizes dramatically (double them[3]), recapture the salary and benefits funding of those laid off in the process, and use that money to pay excellent teachers more. Thus, educational adequacy can be achieved at much lower cost—a much lower cost than what is currently spent.

The most significant problem with this argument is that no empirical evidence exists to support it.[4] It is speculative, frequently based on the assertions that teacher workforce quality can be improved with no increase in average wages, simply by firing the 5 per-cent of teachers least effective at tweaking test scores each year and paying the rest based on the student test scores they produce, or that the funding wage increases required to substantially improve the teacher workforce is necessarily dramatically less costly than maintaining equally productive smaller class sizes.

As Baker and Welner (2012) point out in a recent article in *Educational Researcher*, the logical way to test these very assertions would be to permit or encourage some schools and districts to experiment with alternative compensation strategies and other "reforms," and to evaluate the cost-effectiveness or relative efficiency of these schools and districts. That is, do schools/districts that adopt these strategies land in a different location along the curve? Do they get the same outcomes with the same kids at much lower spending?

In fact, some schools and districts do experiment with different strategies and those schools carry their relevant share of weight in any statewide cost model.

Too often, however, such experimentation falls disproportionately on the state's neediest children, because the state lacks the political will to provide sufficient funding to districts serving those children. Pure speculation that some alternative educational delivery system would produce better outcomes at much lower expense is certainly no basis for making a judicial determination regarding constitutionality of existing funding. Experimentation is no substitute for adequacy.

Regarding this theory, a three-judge panel charged with hearing arguments over school funding adequacy in Kansas eloquently opined:

> Here, it is clearly apparent, and, actually, not arguably subject to dispute, that the state's assertion of a benign consequence of cutting school funding without a factual basis, either quantitatively or qualitatively, to justify the cuts is, but, at best, only based on an inference derived from defendant's experts that such costs may possibly not produce the best value that can be achieved from the level of spending provided. (*Gannon v. State of Kansas*, 2013)

Further, that:

> This is simply not only a weak and factually tenuous premise, but one that seems likely to produce, if accepted, what could not be otherwise than characterized as sanctioning an unconscionable result within the context of the education system. (*Gannon v. State of Kansas*, 2013)

And:

> Simply, school opportunities do not repeat themselves and when the opportunity for a formal education passes, then for most, it is most likely gone. (*Gannon v. State of Kansas*, 2013)

The judges went on to tackle the logical extension of the state's argument, noting that the state was effectively endorsing experimentation on children who have "no recourse from a failure of the experiment."

> If the position advanced here is the State's full position, it is experimenting with our children which have no recourse from a failure of the experiment. Here, the legislative experiment with cutting funding has impacted Kansas children's K-12 opportunity to learn for almost one-third of their K-12 educational experience (2009–10 through 2012–13). (*Gannon v. State of Kansas*, 2013)[5]

CONCLUSIONS AND IMPLICATIONS

While the majority of this chapter portrays a cynical perspective on the current landscape of school finance reform in the states, some evidence exists that we are turning the corner. In February 2013 the President's Advisory Commission on Educational Equity and Excellence released its recommendations. The charge of the commission was to provide "advice to the secretary of the U.S. Department of Education on the disparities in meaningful educational opportunities that give rise to the achievement gap, with a focus on systems of finance, and to recommend ways in which federal policies could address such disparities. The findings and recommendations of the commission do not represent the views of the department, and this document does not represent information approved or disseminated by the Department of Education."[6]

For the first time in decades, renewed national interest has surfaced in understanding disparities in school funding and state school finance policies and the implications of these disparities for the quality and equitable distribution of educational programs and services. The first major recommendation of the commission focused specifically on state school finance policies:

> The time has come for bold action by the states—and the federal government—to redesign and reform the funding of our nation's public schools. Achieving equity and excellence requires sufficient resources that are distributed based on student need, not zip code, and that are efficiently used.

Elaborating that:

> Accordingly, this commission believes the time has come for bold action by the states—and the federal government—to redesign and reform the funding of our nation's public schools. The deep inequities in school funding documented by another federal commission more than 40 years ago . . . remain entrenched across our nation's states and school districts at a time when more than 40 percent of all American public school children are enrolled in districts of concentrated student poverty.[7]

Implicit in the Commission's recommendations is that sustained and substantive school finance reforms matter—that equity of financial resources matters. Recent comprehensive reviews of research literature on state school finance reforms and school finance comport with this assertion. Baker and Welner (2011b) explain that overblown claims regarding the ineffectiveness and inefficiency of judicially imposed school finance reforms are largely based on anecdotal information and exaggerated interpretations of descriptive data, whereas more rigorous studies of sustained and substantive school finance reforms produce more nuanced and often positive findings. Baker explains:

> Sustained improvements to the level and distribution of funding across local public school districts can lead to improvements in the level and distribution of student outcomes. While money alone may not be the answer, more equitable and adequate allocation of financial inputs to schooling provide a necessary underlying condition for improving the equity and adequacy of outcomes. The available evidence suggests that appropriate combinations of more adequate funding with more accountability for its use may be most promising. (Baker, 2012, p. 18)

Regardless of the dominant rhetoric of the new normal period, money still matters. First, on average, even in large-scale studies across multiple contexts, aggregate measures of per-pupil spending are positively associated with improved and/or higher student outcomes. In some studies, the size of this effect is larger than in others. And, in some cases, additional funding appears to matter more for some students than others. Clearly, other factors moderate the influence of funding on student outcomes, such as how that money is spent. But, on balance, in direct tests of the relationship between financial resources and student outcomes, money matters.

Second, schooling resources that cost money, including class size reductions and increased teacher compensation, are positively associated with student outcomes. Again, in some cases and for some populations, these effects are larger than for others. On balance, though, ways to spend money exist that have a solid track record of success. Further, while there may exist alternative uses of financial resources that yield comparable or better returns in student outcomes, no clear evidence identifies what these alternatives might be.

Third, sustained improvements to the level and distribution of funding across local public school districts can lead to improvements in the level and distribution of student outcomes. While money alone may not be the answer, adequate and equitable distributions of financial inputs to schooling provide a necessary underlying condition for improving adequacy and equity of outcomes. That is, if the money isn't there, schools and districts simply don't have a "leverage option" that can support strategies that might improve student outcomes. If the money is there, they can use it productively; if it's not, they can't. But, even if they have the money, there's no guarantee that they will. Evidence from Massachusetts, in particular, suggests that appropriate combinations of more funding with more accountability may be most promising.

NOTES

1. Baker, Sciarra, and Farrie (2010, 2012). The report endeavored to resolve many of the empirical flaws with other commonly referenced reports such as *Education Week*'s Quality Counts and the Education Trust's Funding Gap reports. The report uses a three-year panel of national data on all school districts, estimating a statistical model to determine the extent that school districts with higher poverty concentration have more or less total state and local revenue per pupil when compared with districts having lower poverty concentrations. The model controls for economies of scale, population sparsity, and geographic variation in labor costs.
2. See Baker (2012) for a thorough critique of these arguments and their origins.
3. www.nytimes.com/2011/12/03/nyregion/bloombergs-remarks-on-teachers-draw-scrutiny.html?_r=0
4. For a critique of oft-cited reports making these assertions, see Baker & Welner (2012).
5. www.shawneecourt.org/DocumentCenter/View/457
6. www2.ed.gov/about/bdscomm/list/eec/equity-excellence-commission-report.pdf
7. www2.ed.gov/about/bdscomm/list/eec/equity-excellence-commission-report.pdf

REFERENCES

Baker, B. D. (2009). Private schooling in the US: Expenditures, supply, and policy implications. Boulder and Tempe, AZ: Education and the Public Interest Center & Education Policy Research Unit.

Baker, B. D. (2012). Revisiting the age-old question: Does money matter in education?. Albert Shanker Institute.

Baker, B. D., & Corcoran, S. P. (2012). *The stealth inequities of school funding: How state and local school finance systems perpetuate inequitable student spending.* Center for American Progress.

Baker, B., & Green, P. (2008). Conceptions of equity and adequacy in school finance. In H. F. Ladd & E. Fiske (Eds.), *Handbook of research in education finance and policy* (pp. 203–221). New York: Routledge.

Baker, B. D., Libby, K., & Wiley, K. (2012). *Spending by the major charter management organizations: Comparing charter school and local public district financial resources in New York, Ohio, and Texas.* National Education Policy Center.

Baker, B. D., Sciarra, D. G., & Farrie, D. (2010). *Is school funding fair?: A national report card.* Newark, NJ: Education Law Center. http://schoolfundingfairness.org/National_Report_Card.pdf.

Baker, B. D., Sciarra, D. G., & Farrie, D. (2012). *Is school funding fair?: A national report card.* Newark, NJ: Education Law Center. http://schoolfundingfairness.org/National_Report_Card_2012.pdf.

Baker, B. D., Taylor, L., & Vedlitz, A. (2005). *Measuring educational adequacy in public schools* (Report prepared for the Texas Legislature Joint Committee on Public School Finance, The Texas School Finance Project).

Baker, B., & Welner, K. G. (2010). Premature celebrations: The persistence of inter-district funding disparities. *Education Policy Analysis Archives, 18,* 9.

Baker, B. D., & Welner, K. G. (2011a). *Productivity research, the U.S. Department of Education, and high-quality evidence.* Boulder, CO: National Education Policy Center. Retrieved from http://nepc.colorado.edu/publication/productivity-research.

Baker, B. D., & Welner, K. G. (2011b). School finance and courts: Does reform matter, and how can we tell? *Teachers College Record, 113*(11), 2374–2414.

Baker, B., & Welner, K. G. (2012). Evidence and rigor: Scrutinizing the rhetorical embrace of evidence-based decision making. *Educational Researcher, 41*(3), 98–101.

Bifulco, R. (2005). District-level black-white funding disparities in the United States 1987 to 2002. *Journal of Education Finance, 31*(2) 172–194.

Buras, K. L. (2011). Race, charter schools, and conscious capitalism: On the spatial politics of whiteness as property (and the unconscionable assault on black New Orleans). *Harvard Educational Review, 81*(2), 296–331.

Clune, W. H. (1994). The shift from equity to adequacy in school finance. *Educational Policy, 8*(4), 376–394.

Cuomo, A. (2011). State of the State. Albany, NY. www.governor.ny.gov/sl2/stateofthestate2011transcript.

Deslatte, A. (2011, October 11). Scott: Anthropology and journalism don't pay, and neither do capes. Orlando, FL: *Orlando Sentinel.*

Downes, T. A. (2004). School finance reform and school quality: Lessons from Vermont. In J. Yinger (Ed.), *Helping children left behind: State aid and the pursuit of educational equity.* Cambridge, MA: MIT Press.

Duncan, A. (2010, November 17). The new normal: Doing more with less—Secretary Arne Duncan's remarks at the American Enterprise Institute. Washington, DC: www.ed.gov/news/speeches/new-normal-doing-more-less-secretary-arne-duncans-remarks-american-enterprise-institut.

Duncombe, W. D., & Johnston, J. (2004). *Helping children left behind: State aid and the pursuit of educational equity.* Cambridge, MA: MIT Press.

Freeman, J. (2010, April 17). New Jersey's "failed experiment": The new governor is on a mission to make his state competitive again in attracting people and capital. New York: *Wall Street Journal.* http://online.wsj.com/article/SB10001424052702303348504575184120546772244.html.

Gates, W. (2011). Flip the curve: Student achievement vs. school budgets. *Huffington Post.* www.huffingtonpost.com/bill-gates/bill-gates-school-performance_b_829771.html.

Gist, D. (2010). R.I. formula funds children, not systems. *National Journal.* http://education.nationaljournal.com/2010/06/a-funding-formula-for-success.php.

Imazeki, J., & Reschovsky, A. (2004). School finance reform in Texas: A never ending story. In J. Yinger (Ed.), *Helping children left behind: State aid and the pursuit of educational equity* (pp. 251–281). Cambridge, MA: MIT Press.

McClure, P., Wiener, R., Roza, M., & Hill, M. (2008). *Ensuring equal opportunity in public education: How local school district funding policies hurt disadvantaged students and what federal policy can do about it.* Washington, DC: Center for American Progress. Retrieved December 20, 2009 from www.americanprogress.org/issues/2008/06/pdf/comparability.pdf.

Public Impact; The University of Dayton, School of Education and Allied Professions; and Thomas B. Fordham Institute. (2008, March). *Fund the child: Bringing equity, autonomy and portability to Ohio school finance. How sound an investment?* Washington, DC: Thomas B. Fordham Institute. Retrieved December 20, 2009 from www.edexcellence.net/doc/fund_the_child_ohio_031208.pdf.

New York State Education Department (NYSED) (2011a). Fiscal analysis & research unit. Primer on state aid 2011–2012. www.oms.nysed.gov/faru/PDFDocuments/Primer11–12D.pdf.

New York State Education Department (NYSED) (2011b). Fiscal analysis & research unit. Successful schools analysis technical report. www.oms.nysed.gov/faru/documents/technical_final.doc.

Oliff, P., Mai, C., & Leachman, M. (2012) New school year brings more cuts in state funding for schools. Washington, DC: Center on Budget and Policy Priorities. www.cbpp.org/cms/?fa=view&id=3825 Accessed May 24, 2014.

Rhode Island Department of Education (RIDE) Division of School Finance (2010). www.ride.ri.gov/Finance/Funding/FundingFormula/Docs/H8094Aaa_FINAL_6_10_10.pdf.

Roza, M. (2006). How districts short change low income and minority students. In *Funding Gaps 2006.* Washington, DC: The Education Trust.

Rubenstein, R., Schwartz, A. E., Stiefel, L., & Bel Hadj Amor, H. (2007). From districts to schools: The distribution of resources across schools in big city school districts. *Economics of Education Review, 26*(5), 532–545.

Stiefel, L, Rubenstein, R., and Berne, R. (1998). Intra-district equity in four large cities: Data, methods and results. *Journal of Education Finance, 23*(4), 447–467.

U.S. Department of Education (2013). For each and every child—A strategy for education equity and excellence, Washington, DC. www2.ed.gov/about/bdscomm/list/eec/equity-excellence-commission-report.pdf.

Wong, K. K. (2013). The design of the Rhode Island school funding formula: Developing new strategies on equity and accountability. *Peabody Journal of Education, 88*(1), 37–47.

8

FEDERAL EDUCATION POLICY FROM REAGAN TO OBAMA
Convergence, Divergence, and "Control"
Lance D. Fusarelli and Bonnie C. Fusarelli

> A revolution is taking place. It's not easy to see, and those experiencing it have yet to fathom its full depth and impact. That revolution is the reshaping of power and authority relationships at all levels of the educational governance and policy system. (Conley, 2003, p. 1)

The revolution Conley described in 2003 has been an incremental but steady one. Changes in governance and policy over the past decade when examined individually are relatively small in scope. However, when taken as a whole, the full impact of education policy changes since 1980 has created a new order and era in American education.

Education policy setting in the United States is no longer the sole purview of some 14,000 elected local school boards. Regional and local differences are quickly being subsumed by national interests in such matters as equality of opportunity and educational excellence (Fowler, 2012). At the local, state, and national levels, a government's policies are only as effective as their design and implementation permit, and even effective implementation is heavily influenced by the character of the relationship that exists between branches and levels of government. Thus, over the past decade the tension between competing values and debates about how best to structure the governance of education have gained increasing prominence in politics at the national level. Debates about the proper governance of public education often seem to revolve around the tension between the competing values of democracy and efficiency or more precisely between centralized or decentralized approaches (Boyd & Johnson, 2003). Education reformers have discovered over the past 30 years that, unfortunately, by themselves neither centralized nor decentralized approaches to government can guarantee either democracy or efficiency in the educational system.

Education reform initiatives are often reactions to external shocks to the system. Consequently, the history of the educational system and its reforms run parallel to major events in U.S. history. This chapter examines this history and the federalization of education policy from the Reagan administration through the Obama administration. We begin with a review of landmark events and argue that the rather loosely coupled, fragmented educational system in the United States has become in the past three decades more tightly coupled, as a succession of "education presidents" has sought to put their stamp on the educational system. Hess and McGuinn (2002) calculated that between 1960 (Kennedy) and 1976 (Carter), education was in the bottom third (usually last) of public concerns; from 1980 (Reagan) through 2000 (Bush), education ranked in the middle to upper third and ranked first of 11 issues important to voters in 2000. In accordance with this increased prominence, initiatives undertaken by these presidents have significantly affected education in state and local school districts throughout the country (Conley, 2003; DeBray, 2006; McGuinn, 2006).

THE REAGAN ADMINISTRATION

The early years of the Reagan administration ushered in powerful social and cultural forces that produced a wave of conservative reforms, which, at least in education, have been enduring and pervasive. Reagan's election reflected frustration with recession, stagflation, and limited economic growth. Evidence of our lack of international economic competitiveness was found in multiple international comparisons of student performance, such as TIMMS and now PISA, in which U.S. students generally fare poorly compared to those in other developed (and several underdeveloped) countries. Concerned by this lack of economic competitiveness, big business became a major player in pushing for system-wide, school-based accountability by linking reform to international economic competition (Jackson & Cibulka, 1992). Conley observes that the impact of such assessments is substantial. With intensive media coverage, "the audience for these reports has shifted from statisticians and academics to policy makers and the general public" (2003, p. 2).

Around this same time (early 1980s), educational researchers Elmore and McLaughlin (1981) found that it was "difficult if not impossible for state or federal government programs to garner the interest, effort, and commitment of local educators to the higher level government's objectives" (as cited in Odden, 1991, p. 2). Research on local education change processes also concluded that it was difficult to get new programs that were created outside the local system implemented (Sarason, 1982) unless there was a mutual adaptation process in which local educators could adapt, change, and mold the program to meet their unique needs and circumstances (McLaughlin, 1976). In sum, the educational research of the era concluded that local response was inherently at odds with state (or federal) program initiatives (Odden, 1991, p. 2).

Indeed Boyd (1987) argued that the top-down nature of state and federal education reforms rendered them unlikely to accomplish their goals of improving local education practice and that without the input of local educators, these movements were doomed to fail. Critics also voiced concern that the progress made since the 1960s on equity might be lost in the hard drive toward educational excellence. They argued that external efforts to improve local education systems simply would not work.

However, other indicators provided some hope that external efforts might not be dashed by resistance among street-level implementers (Odden, 1991). Research on the mutual adaptation process indicated that programs ultimately are implemented but not always as intended. By the late 1980s, consensus was building among researchers that state and federal initiatives do affect local practice. As Odden puts it, "the system is a bit more tightly coupled than previously thought" (1991, p. 4).

President Reagan was able to capitalize on these trends to sell the idea that states should solve their educational problem themselves. Reagan and Secretary of Education

William J. Bennett used their offices as bully pulpits from which to sermonize about what needed to be done to improve America's schools (Boyd, 1988). By powerful use of rhetoric and symbols, the Reagan administration was able to reshape the semantics and agenda of American education policy (Clark, & Astuto, 1986; Jung & Kirst, 1986).

Clark and Astuto assert that the Reagan administration brought about "significant and enduring changes in federal educational policy" (1986, p. 4). The push for greater accountability and school choice in the Reagan administration established the antecedents for later initiatives by President G. W. Bush, including passage of No Child Left Behind (NCLB) in 2002. Many of the reform proposals centered around the values of excellence and choice, and emphasized higher standards, competition, merit pay, and deregulation.

Reflecting the concerns of policy makers, multiple blue ribbon commissions were created and reports generated during this period, the most influential of which was *A Nation at Risk* from the National Commission on Excellence in Education (1983). With its militaristic rhetoric and political symbolism, "*A Nation at Risk* was galvanizing as political manifesto" and helped spur momentum for educational reform (Mazzoni, 1995, p. 54). The report included provocative language in the opening pages: "The educational foundations of our society are presently being eroded by a rising tide of mediocrity that threatens our very future as a Nation and a people" and again later in the document, "If an unfriendly foreign power had attempted to impose on America the mediocre educational performance that exists today, we might well have viewed it as an act of war."

This report and others like it, coupled with the "Toyota Problem" of declining U.S. international economic competitiveness, fueled widespread public concern about the condition of education in the United States and gave President Reagan a policy window (Kingdon, 2010) through which to initiate educational reform. Federal involvement in education was no longer framed as an emergency measure (e.g., address the crisis and get out); rather it shifted and was reframed as a necessary continuing federal function to preserve the common welfare.

A Nation at Risk clarified the connection between improving schooling and improving the economy, and for the first time schooling became a "hot and profitable political issue, one linked to the creation of jobs" (Boyd, 1988, p. 302). This marked a watershed moment in which the quality of education became "a major political issue in state and national elections" (Schoen & Fusarelli, 2008, p. 189). Mazzoni noted that, "The invocation of crisis, a repeated theme in commission reports and pulpit pronouncements, infused urgency into the cause . . . these pressures create[d] political incentives for state officials to risk the hazards of policy leadership" and undertake educational reform (p. 55).

Importantly, the changes in approach to government that were ushered in with Reagan's election went beyond simply a knee-jerk response to immediate crises (real or politically contrived). Much of the underlying conflict was centered on differing definitions of community and differing visions for America's future (one that embraced one national community and the other that saw America as a collection of multiple interdependent communities).

Over the previous century, the Democratic Party and its progressive and collectivist impulses that stretched from the New Deal to the Great Society had sought to push Americans out of their local, group, and ethnic loyalties to a greater American citizenship (Wills, 1985). However, as Schambra explains, faith in a national community had withered because the federal government "while advertising itself as an engine of unity, became a divisive force, a hammer pounding local communities . . . against the traditional prerogatives of locality and neighborhood to define and preserve their own way of life. . . . Local communities were told their children could no longer pray in school and often must be bused away from neighborhood schools" (Schambra, as cited in Wills, 1985, p. 80).

Reagan, on the other hand, embraced the "small republic renaissance." He called for "an end to giantism, for a return to the human scale . . . the scale of the local fraternal lodge, the church organization, the block club, the farm bureau" (Schambra, as cited in Wills, 1985, p. 80). Reagan did not see community as the Democrats did as a single national community. Reagan perceived community as a community of communities, tying his vision to an older Jeffersonian idea (Wills, 1985), and his approach to education policy reflects those beliefs. In many respects, his successor, George H. W. Bush, with his "thousand points of light" social policy, shared Reagan's ideal of community, while differing somewhat in the need to create an interconnected web of organizations bringing those points together.

The irony of the Reagan administration's education policy is that his rhetoric of decentralization and devolution (he repeatedly threatened to abolish the newly created U.S. Department of Education as a cabinet-level agency) did not match his actions as president (funding for the USDOE increased significantly during his administration). The blue ribbon panels and committees he created, with its corresponding obsession with international comparisons and competitiveness (what Spring [2010] refers to as the human capital paradigm), set in motion forces that later manifest themselves in efforts to federalize education. In education, Reagan talked locally but acted nationally, even globally. This theme continues and gradually expands under his successor, George H. W. Bush.

THE GEORGE H. W. BUSH ADMINISTRATION

Convening an education summit in Charlottesville, Virginia in 1989, President George H. W. Bush worked collaboratively with the nation's governors to establish broad performance goals for education, including voluntary national standards that were opposed by members of his own party (Rudalevige, 2003). To strengthen these ties, he appointed former Tennessee governor Lamar Alexander as secretary of education and Colorado Governor Ray Romer as chair of the National Education Goals Panel. Bush's education plan, America 2000, called for the creation of voluntary national standards and testing of students in five core areas—English, math, science, history, and geography—with testing to be administered in grades four, eight, and 12; school and district report cards, as well as school vouchers, were included in the plan (NYSED Archives). Republican disagreement with such standards ultimately led to the demise of Bush's America 2000 education plan; after passing both houses of Congress (albeit with tepid support), "the conference bill for America 2000 died in the Senate because of a filibuster by conservative Republicans opposed to any significant expansion of the federal role in education" (McDonnell, 2005, p. 28).

Hess and McGuinn point out that, "Although Bush did not call for any substantive increase in federal involvement in education, his efforts marked a significant break with Republican tradition and were attacked by congressional Republicans for threatening to nationalize education" (2002, p. 84). Conley asserts that this collaboration was significant because governors "are notoriously suspicious of federal intervention into state policy arenas" (2003, p. 24). In his view, "the act of creating [education] goals at a national level opened the door to a much more activist federal role in education policy," which has been expanded in succeeding administrations (p. 24). Hess and McGuinn point out that Bush's endorsement of national standards "represented the first step on a slippery slope toward nationalizing curricula and schooling" (2002, p. 86). It also "moved the federal agenda progressively closer to the mainstream instructional program within schools" (McDonnell, 2005, p. 28).

Although some political scientists and education policy scholars assert that President Bush's push for voluntary national standards was tepid and incremental, the forces President Bush set in motion—a type of accelerated wave, if you will—paved the way for the far more dramatic federalization of education that was to come under the leadership of Presidents Clinton, George W. Bush, and Barack Obama. Bringing the nation's governors together, many of whom were expressly interested in engaging in systemic educational reform, reflects an oft-overlooked success of the George H. W. Bush administration in education reform. Bush recognized the political realities of the period, recognized that national standards were coming and were in the nation's competitive best interest, and believed that the power of governors could be harnessed to promulgate those standards and reforms. It is no accident, Conley points out, that one of the leading governors who attended the summit and who was pushing education standards was Bill Clinton.

THE CLINTON ADMINISTRATION

Contrary to expectations, Bill Clinton's election did not produce a dramatic liberal shift in educational policy to the left, away from the conservative movement of the Reagan administration (Fowler, 1995). Much like his Republican predecessor, Clinton's presidency embraced the values of efficiency, excellence, and choice in education, while asserting that national standards, testing, and choice could serve as vehicles to promote those values in public schools. President Clinton's Goals 2000 education program was remarkably similar to that of his predecessor, George H. W. Bush; even the titles—America 2000/Goals 2000—were similar (Scribner, Reyes, & Fusarelli, 1995). Finn and Hess noted that "few outside the Beltway could spot major differences" in the two plans (2004, p. 37). The legislation pushed states to enact higher standards and encouraged them to create testing regimes to meet those standards. President Clinton also led efforts to invest in pre-K education initiatives, creating early Head Start for children ages zero to three and increasing significantly funding for Head Start.

Clinton's popularity as president presented an ideal opportunity to set new directions in educational policy. Instead, Clinton continued largely along the lines set by his Republican predecessors. Clinton emphasized choice as a goal of educational policy when he endorsed the charter school movement. In fact, he repeatedly touted the virtues of competition and choice within the public school system. He also endorsed performance-based accountability and standards-based reform. Rudalevige points out that "the notion of 'adequate yearly progress' that later became the linchpin of accountability in No Child Left Behind" was incorporated into the 1994 reauthorization of the Elementary and Secondary Education Act—the Improving America's Schools Act (IASA) (2003, p. 64). However, states were given wide latitude in determining what counts as "adequate" and did not set a deadline for annual yearly progress (AYP) to move students to academic proficiency (DeBray, McDermott, & Wohlstetter, 2005).

IASA insisted that all children be held to the same high academic standards and the Clinton administration's use of Title I funds as leverage for the adoption of standards and accountability reforms "was an outgrowth of the movement for state-level accountability policies" (McDermott & DeBray-Pelot, 2009, p. 208). With the provision of $7 billion in Title I funds, states "had to adopt curriculum standards and align assessments with those standards. These assessments were to be given three times between grades 3 and 12" (Firestone, 2012, pp. 9–10). However, Clinton was unwilling to attach significant consequences (such as withholding federal funding) to states that failed to create rigorous systems of standards and testing (Rudalevige, 2003). In fact, "Many states did not even comply with the IASA requirements for state assessments based on curriculum standards" (McDermott & DeBray-Pelot, 2009, p. 198). Reflecting the push and pull of federalism, as well as the prominence of more pressing domestic priorities such as health care reform, President Clinton was unwilling to spend the political capital necessary to "encourage" state policy makers to adopt rigorous systems of standards and assessment. However, his Republican successor, George W. Bush, cleverly used the traditional liberal value of educational equity as a rhetorical flag around which to rally advocates for school reform and improvement and was thus able to expand significantly the scope of federal control over education.

THE GEORGE W. BUSH ADMINISTRATION

Continuing the theme of higher standards and accountability begun under Reagan and continued through Clinton, President George W. Bush sought systemically to improve education by opening up the public education system (through expanded public school choice and contracting out educational services), making it more transparent (school report cards, a form of public accountability), incentivizing public employees (merit pay and performance bonuses), and closely monitoring quality inputs (the mandate for highly qualified teachers) and outcomes (performance reporting by student subgroup). In a divergence from the Clinton administration, education was Bush's top domestic policy priority and he "promoted a more forceful role for the federal government" in education (Finn & Hess, 2004, p. 38; Marschall & McKee, 2002). Building on his experience in education reform as governor of Texas, Bush "envisioned a strong national role in education policy ... [and] had to lobby to eliminate language calling for the abolition of the Department of Education from the 2000 Republican platform" (Rudalevige, 2003, p. 65).

Befitting reauthorization of the Elementary and Secondary Education Act of 1965 (ESEA), NCLB ushered in a host of new federal mandates and directives on local education, including mandatory statewide testing in grades three through eight in reading and math, school report cards reporting results by student subgroup, and greater accountability for student performance by teachers and school leaders (Fusarelli, 2004). AYP became the benchmark against which schools were measured, even if it was problematic and ill defined.

NCLB required identification of schools in need of improvement and imposed requirements of public school choice, the provision of supplemental educational services, and school reconstitution (Fusarelli, 2004). Districts were required to identify low-performing schools and develop comprehensive school improvement plans—a first for federal government involvement in local education (Herrington & Orland, 1992).

According to Boyd, "NCLB's requirement that students in 'failing schools' be given the option of obtaining supplemental services or transferring to successful schools links NCLB's standards-based accountability to market-based reforms" (2003, p. 10). Extending the theme of market-based accountability and in a divergence from the Clinton administration, President Bush signed the nation's first federal voucher law, the DC School Choice Incentive Act of 2003, which provided scholarships to up to 2,000 students from low-income families to attend private schools.

Despite the uneven effectiveness of components of President Bush's signature legislation, NCLB represents "a significant shift in federal education policy away from the federal government being primarily a source of funding for low-income students to being a major force in shaping the goals and outcomes of education" (Fusarelli, 2004, p. 71). It "significantly extended federal power over states' assessment and accountability policies" (McDermott & DeBray-Pelot, 2009). Finn and Hess note that NCLB "puts federal bureaucrats in charge of approving state standards and accountability plans; sets a single nationwide timetable for boosting achievement; and prescribes specific remedies for underperforming schools" (2004, p. 39). Conley asserts that, "In one fell swoop, the American educational system became federalized to an unprecedented degree" (2003, p. 28). Although state policy makers had already created accountability systems, NCLB created much momentum and pressure on states to implement performance-based accountability systems based on student performance (Hanushek & Raymond, 2005). Referring to it as "Great Society redux," Finn and Hess assert that NCLB "marks a radical break with conservative tradition, initiating a massive shift of education authority from states to Washington" (2004, p. 53). To apply a football metaphor, President Bush took the ball and ran with it, carrying federal control over education much farther than his Republican or Democratic predecessors.

THE OBAMA ADMINISTRATION

The election of Barack Obama brought the promise of a further increased role of the federal government in economic and social affairs (Bowling & Pickerill, 2013), as well as in education. Possibly no greater evidence exists of the increasing influence of the federal government on the daily operation of public schools than the Obama administration's Race to the Top (RTTT) program and its central curriculum reform initiative, the Common Core State Standards (CCSS). As the following sections will discuss, the Obama administration has demonstrated remarkable political skill in using an economic crisis and an economic stimulus package to advance its domestic policy goals, particularly with respect to education reform (McDonnell & Weatherford, 2011).

Race to the Top
The economic crisis that began in 2008 was unlike other fiscal downturns in recent history. Consequently, policies were crafted and enacted in a unique policy environment. The ways the federal, state, and local governments responded to the fiscal crisis revealed the complex interplay between the economic environment and educational political processes and outcomes and provides further insight about the intricate interconnectedness of the three levels of government. The Obama administration decided to use this critical time to beget major shifts in politics and schooling, viewing this period as an occasion for opportunity, and engaging in the bold and ambitious work of reinventing educational

institutions (Fusarelli & Young, 2011). In the words of Rahm Emanuel, President Obama's chief of staff, "You never want a serious crisis to go to waste" (Seib, 2008, p. 1).

The Obama administration's American Recovery & Reinvestment Act of 2009 (ARRA) or Stimulus Package provided approximately $100 billion for education (nearly twice the annual budget of the U.S. Department of Education) and opened a policy window through which to advance school reform and improvement in early learning, K-12, and postsecondary education. However, about $75 billion of the $80 billion designated for K-12 schools was funneled through formula-based programs, including the Individuals with Disabilities Act (IDEA) and Title 1, leaving $5 billion of ARRA for competitive grants. Included in this category are what became the administration's most potent reform levers, the RTTT state competition and the Investing in Innovation (i3) Fund (McDonnell & Weatherford, 2011). These initiatives addressed many of the same goals as NCLB, but in the form of a competitive grant process. The significant budget shortfalls faced by governors and state legislators made the relatively small federal carrot appear much larger than it was and difficult to resist.

Secretary of Education Arne Duncan was given unparalleled discretion in allocating the funds. As a *New York Times* article noted, "the $100 billion in emergency aid for public schools and colleges in the economic stimulus bill could transform Arne Duncan into an exceptional figure in the history of federal education policy: a secretary of education loaded with money and power to spend large chunks of it as he sees fit" (Dillon, 2009 as cited in McDonnell & Weatherford, 2011). In an effort to incentivize states to undertake substantive educational reform, the Obama administration chose to use competitive grants as a carrot to spur reform, rather than the seldom-used federal stick of sanctions contained in NCLB (McGuinn, 2012).

The criteria for the RTTT grants competition allowed the administration to specify its reform goals while also giving it considerable leverage over the conditions imposed on states applying for the funds. State applications were to be judged on 19 criteria that included the lifting of all caps on the expansion of charter schools and the requirement that applicant states could not have any laws barring the use of student achievement data in evaluating teachers and principals (McDonnell & Weatherford, 2011). One of the most contentious requirements was that states seeking RTTT funding were required to adopt new CCSS.

These requirements marked a significant departure from past practice of using a formula grant process to allocate federal funds. RTTT proposals were to be evaluated based on alignment with four administration reform priorities: 1) Adopting standards and assessments that prepare students to succeed in college and the workplace and to compete in the global economy and provide a common basis for school and student performance measurement; 2) Building data systems that measure student growth and success, and inform teachers and principals about how they can use these data to improve the teaching process; 3) Improving teacher effectiveness through recruiting, developing, rewarding, and retaining effective teachers and principals, especially where they are needed most; and 4) Turning around our lowest-achieving schools (targeting the bottom 5%).

The use of *specific* reform strategies as a condition for competitive stimulus grant funding sparked unprecedented changes in state laws to conform to the RTTT requirements. As McDonnell and Weatherford explain:

With absolutely no assurance that they would receive any Race to the Top funding, 17 states changed their laws to allow student test scores to be taken into account in evaluating teachers, 13 removed caps on the number of charter schools that can be established in their state, 48 agreed to consider adopting common academic standards, and 34 of those states formally approved the new standards within a few months of their publication. After two rounds of competition among 47 applicants, 11 states and the District of Columbia were awarded $4 billion in Race to the Top funding.[1] Yet the changes in state policies prompted by the competition extend beyond just the winners. The willingness of state officials to change laws to conform with federal priorities stemmed largely from a desire to obtain additional funding under tight fiscal conditions. Nevertheless, in a number of states, officials saw Race to the Top as an opportunity to move their own reform agendas. (2011, p. 312)

Only two states (Delaware and Tennessee) were awarded grants in the first round of the competition; only 10 states received awards in the second round (46 states and the District of Columbia applied for the competitive grants in rounds one and two) (McGuinn, 2012). States such as North Carolina, which lost in round one of the competition, had invested heavily in the application process and revised their applications for the second round. North Carolina and many other round two winners reworked their proposals to more closely align with the RTTT reform priorities. The large competitive grants in a time of economic crisis "generated a substantial amount of state policy change in a short period of time, particularly for a program of its relatively small size . . . [and] has had a sizable impact on the intensity and character of school reform discourse across the country" (McGuinn, 2012, pp. 137–138). Such changes would have been politically contentious and slow to occur in more stable economic times.

The RTTT grant initiative continues a chain of federal-level education reforms stemming from ESEA. RTTT has the potential to "rewrite" American federalism as it relates to public education, if federal lawmakers keep education as a priority item on the domestic policy agenda and if they are willing to continue the carrot and stick approach to governance.

Already, the heavy federal demands of RTTT have led to pushback by some school districts and states. In Ohio, 80 school districts and charter schools have backed out of the grant program in part because the cost of compliance was greater than the benefit of the funding (Binkley, 2013). Texas Governor Rick Perry objected to the idea of a national curriculum and pointed out that the offered federal funds would only be sufficient to operate schools for one day and were not worth the cost of compliance (Vergari, 2011). In Texas, the federal carrot is much too small to entice compliance. In addition, policy makers in several states have also complained that the administration's priorities underemphasize improvement in rural education, which in many states still constitutes a sizable number of schools (Vergari, 2011) (approximately 30% of schools in the United States are rural schools).

In addition, some districts assert that new teacher evaluation systems mandated under RTTT, in which half of a teacher's performance evaluation is tied to student growth, violate provisions contained in collective bargaining agreements with teachers (Binkley, 2013). An address by Secretary of Education Arne Duncan to members of the American Educational Research Association in April 2013 drew a mix of applause and boos from members. One critic called RTTT "No Child Left Behind on steroids" and claimed that it was "marginalizing and suffocating educators" (Lum, 2013, p. 1). Two aspects of the RTTT requirements draw the most criticism: CCSS and changes in the evaluation of teachers.

Common Core

Nearly all states have adopted CCSS in English/language arts (46 states) and math (45 states) and it represents a sweeping curriculum reform effort of unprecedented scale (Porter, 2013; Ujifusa, 2013). Though technically not a "national curriculum," CCSS serves as a guiding framework for states to use in developing curriculum and realigning testing (McCullen, 2013). Led by the National Governors Association and the Council of Chief State School Officers, the movement has the strong support of the Obama administration as well as some conservative think tanks such as the Thomas B. Fordham Foundation.

Long recognized as a major educational problem in a relatively affluent society with high mobility, the common core reflects an effort to standardize what students are learning and when, as well as to bring states to the same level of standards. To encourage states to adopt Common Core, the federal government, in its RTTT competition, awarded 40 of a possible 500 points (8% of the total) "if states documented that they were implementing standards that were internationally benchmarked and would prepare students for college and career" (McCullen, 2013, p. 3). Through RTTT, "states were incentivized to create uniform goals" (Bowling & Pickerill, 2013, p. 327). McGuinn asserts that one of the most important accomplishments of RTTT is the impetus it gave for "the adoption of common academic standards and assessments" (2012, p. 144).

However, despite widespread adoption, resistance has begun to spring up in several states. Critics contend that it amounts to a de facto national curriculum, the new standards are actually lower than existing standards in many states, and there is little evidence that the common core will improve student learning. Alabama withdrew from "the two consortia developing tests aligned with the common core" (Ujifusa, 2013, p. 1). In Kentucky, state schools chief Terry Holliday reported that the state "saw drops in proficiency rates of between 20 percent and 30 percent in language arts and math" (No Child Left Behind Hearing, 2013, p. 2). In Indiana, lawmakers are seeking to pause implementation of the common core, arguing that the mandated standards are lower in some key areas than the state's own standards. Opponents of the delay worry that failure to fully implement the common core means the state will fall behind because textbook publishers and standardized test makers "are moving quickly to adapt to the new standards" (Elliott, 2013, p. 2).

CCSS is the first curriculum reform of its kind to emanate from the national level, be filtered through state and district levels, and ultimately to be enacted by individual educators in the classroom. Because implementation is where the proverbial rubber hits the road, the success of the Common Core roll-out will be largely contingent on the practices of the classroom teacher. As Cooper, Fusarelli, and Randall note, "Policies, no matter how well designed, must be implemented successfully to achieve their intended effects" (2003, pp. 83–84). As with much education policy, regardless of the level at which it is initiated, school reforms are enacted by teachers and administrators at the school level. It is at this level that reform policy inevitably succeeds or fails to achieve its goals. Only time will tell the impact of school-level dynamics on the implementation of Common Core.

Teacher Evaluation

The Obama administration's education reform initiatives rely on the use of goals, rewards, and sanctions to pull and prod the system and the people in it toward better results. The reform strategies generally rest on the following: externally set standards, externally mandated assessments, and externally imposed rewards, sanctions, or interventions.

They shift power from those within a school or district to outside powerbrokers such as governors, state education agencies, state boards of education, and federal education officials. The underlying theory is behaviorist: that the system isn't capable of reforming itself because it lacks clear goals and standards, feedback loops concerning its actual performance, and the ability or will to reward its members' successes and intervene in (or discipline, or terminate/fire) their failures. This theory of action is most evident in Obama's position on teacher evaluation.

President Obama and Secretary Duncan have been vocal in their efforts to "underwrite federal efforts to experiment with teacher pay plans that deviate from traditional salary scales," including merit pay linked to gains in student achievement (Hoff, 2008, p. 2). This traditionally conservative idea is indicative of just how much ideological convergence has occurred in education at the national and state levels in the past three decades (Fusarelli, 2002a; Rudalevige, 2003).

President Obama has embraced the notion of performance-based accountability and believes teacher performance should be tied, in part, to student achievement (Lewis & Fusarelli, 2010). McGuinn observes that RTTT's focus on teacher accountability "has had a major impact on the relationship between the Democratic Party and the two major teachers' unions" (2012, p. 141). He states, "Obama and Duncan changed the politics around teacher accountability by repeatedly highlighting the deficiencies in our teacher-evaluation and tenure systems" (p. 145). RTTT has weakened the power of the National Education Association (NEA) and the American Federation of Teachers (AFT), who have been forced to compromise on some of their positions because they are misaligned with the Obama administration's priorities. Even traditional sacred cows such as salary schedules and teacher tenure have now become bargaining options rather than absolutes. When your traditional Democratic allies begin to desert you, you have no choice but to compromise (because the Republican Party is often outright hostile to unions).

Much like Reagan and his pit bull Secretary of Education William Bennett, Obama and Duncan have used the bully pulpit to keep the media, legislators (particularly state legislators), and the public focused on substantive reform in teacher evaluation systems (McGuinn, 2012). Because of RTTT, six states abolished laws that created firewalls prohibiting student achievement data from being used in teacher evaluation. In the competition to receive a RTTT grant, 11 states "enacted legislation that requires student-achievement data to be used in teacher evaluation or tenure decisions" (McGuinn, 2012, p. 146). Still, as McGuinn points out, many states have a long way to go in their efforts to substantively reform the teacher evaluation process.

EDUCATION REFORM UNDER PRESIDENT OBAMA, PART II

The reelection of President Obama afforded the president with an opportunity to make a lasting imprint on education policy. Significantly, the first budget he put forth contained funding for a major expansion of prekindergarten and early childhood education programs, grants for high school improvement, and a new $1 billion RTTT competition for higher education to improve student outcomes without raising tuition (Hoff, 2008; Klein, 2013). These initiatives are further evidence of the expansion of federal authority over education, expanding its scope of influence into pre-K and postsecondary education in potentially significant ways.

The focus on pre-K reflects federal recognition of significant gaps in access to high-quality preschool programs, particularly for those from low-income and middle-income families. Secretary of Education Arne Duncan called it "the largest expansion of educational opportunity in the 21st century" (Klein, 2013, p. 1). Of course, the proposal would require states to gradually contribute to the program to pay for its cost; the expected state share would be 10 percent in the first year of the expanded program and gradually increase over a decade to 75 percent. Regardless of whether states ever come close to assuming this cost-sharing burden, federal policy makers will have succeeded in pushing greater access to preschool education.

Significantly, states would be required to meet several "quality standards for their programs in order to tap the federal funds" (Klein, 2013, p. 2), including "state-level standards for early learning, qualified teachers, and assessment systems for early learning providers" (Samuels, 2013, p. 2). This has raised the specter of the federal government requiring highly qualified teachers in every preschool classroom. House member Todd Rokita (R-IN), who serves as chair of the House subcommittee overseeing K-12 policy, voiced concern that the administration's proposal could amount to "an alarming expansion of government power" (Klein, 2013, p. 3).

Waivers to NCLB

The Obama administration has come under fire for watering down key provisions of NCLB by granting more than 34 states and the District of Columbia waivers from its stringent test-based annual goals (McNeil, 2013). Of these, 19 states receiving waivers from NCLB's strict testing requirements were low performers on the National Assessment of Education Progress (NAEP) (Chubb & Clark, 2013). Kati Haycock, president of the Education Trust, who worked for the Obama administration reviewing states' waiver applications, asserted that the waivers allow states to shortchange underprivileged students by relaxing requirements to close the achievement gap. In prepared testimony, she stated, "This is very definitely a step backward from the civil rights commitment embedded in" NCLB (No Child Left Behind Hearing, 2013, p. 1).

The Obama administration contends that the waivers grant states more freedom to decide how best to address the achievement gap, while critics contend that the waivers are granted in exchange for agreement on other parts of the administration's education agenda, a view with which Firestone (2012) concurs, when he observed, "When ESEA bogged down in the partisan wrangling that had generally overcome Washington, the administration used its authority to authorize waivers to states to move the agenda forward" (p. 14). The precursor for these waivers may be found in the Education Flexibility Partnership Act signed by President Clinton in 1999, which granted state waivers of many requirements of federal education programs in exchange for results-based accountability, although oversight and enforcement were largely lacking. However, Conley (2003) is dismissive of federal waivers, asserting that in practice, little substantive relief is granted, making the waiver largely symbolic. This situation may be analogous to periodic efforts by state legislators toward decentralization, which Malen and Muncey (2000) argue give the appearance of relinquishing power, yet retaining state authority in the form of regulations, rules, mandates, and sanctions.

In a detailed comparative analysis of the state achievement gap, Chubb and Clark found that states that simply agree "to replace NCLB's requirements with alternatives specified by the Department" are more likely to be granted waivers "regardless of its track record" (2013, p. 10). Chubb and Clark also note, however, that states must "explain how they will execute the [alternate] options to which they commit," so just complying with the administration's agenda is insufficient to be granted a waiver (p. 10). Still, states who fail to narrow the achievement gap will continue to receive federal money; in effect, the small federal stick is being returned to the woodshed while the carrot remains. Haycock observed that the waivers do not require states to provide options for children who attend persistently failing schools (No Child Left Behind Hearing, 2013).

MORE CONVERGENCE THAN DIVERGENCE; MIXED EFFORTS AT "CONTROL"

As the preceding history of federal education reform from President Reagan through President Obama has shown, federal education policy appears to be converging along some basic approaches to reform, including greater accountability, performance evaluation (including merit pay), standards and assessment, and expanded school choice. This policy convergence on education is best illustrated by the significant bipartisan consensus on the passage of NCLB "when the parties readily agreed on substantially increased federal spending, modestly enhanced public choice, and the framework of a national accountability system" (Hess & McGuinn, 2002, p. 92). Reflecting these reforms, presidents from both political parties have played a role in reshaping the rhetoric of school reform, which has blurred the lines between the public and private spheres (Fusarelli & Young, 2011; Miron, 2008). Reforms that would have been unthinkable even a decade ago, such as the elimination of teacher tenure, are now firmly on the table, supported (albeit with varying degrees of enthusiasm) by both Democrats and Republicans.

In their analysis of President Reagan's educational initiatives, Clark and Astuto predicted that Reagan's theme of devolution and decentralization would likely "continue under successor administrations—Republican or Democratic" because of broad public support for the reforms, continued decentralization and growing state control over education, the very limited range of education reforms that are seriously considered and debated in Washington, weakened influence of Congress and the professional associations, and strong leadership in the Department of Education (1986, p. 12). In several important respects, Clark and Astuto's prediction proved erroneous, in part because of the conflicting requirements inherent in the reforms, which are discussed in detail later in this chapter.

For example, Finn and Hess saw significant similarities between the education platforms of Texas Governor George W. Bush and Vice President Al Gore and asserted, "The similarity of the Democratic and Republican positions resulted from both teams' acceptance of the same analysis of what ailed American K-12 education—and how to cure it. This diagnosis hearkens back to the celebrated 1983 report *A Nation at Risk* and the Washington-driven remedies urged in its aftermath by George H. W. Bush and Bill Clinton" (2004, p. 37). This elite ideological convergence in education policy among federal lawmakers is significant and may have lasting impact on education reform, particularly insofar as it redefines the "new normal." For example, many teachers, particularly those with less than a decade of experience, know nothing other than standards-based accountability and testing regimes. As a result, reforms that in the past would have brought about vociferous opposition among teachers are now taken for granted, if not fully supported.

Changing Institutional Environment

The past three decades have changed the institutional context of education policy making, "with greater emphasis on monitoring organizational performance" (Fusarelli, 2002b, p. 565). Education in the United States is becoming more tightly coupled. In part, the national movement to more tightly couple the educational system, exemplified in NCLB's emphasis on testing, performance reporting, and accountability while simultaneously opening the system up through expanded school choice, reflects growing dissatisfaction with the condition of education and with the slow pace of educational reform (Fusarelli & Johnson, 2004). A succession of presidents has sought to speed things up by working to more tightly couple education policy making.

In a society with increasingly high mobility and international competition for jobs, significant differences in educational standards, expectations, and outcomes within and between states are not only nonsensical but are harmful to students and to economic growth. In our increasingly "flat world," individuals must be prepared to remain competitive in a global market where historical and geographical divisions are becoming increasingly irrelevant (Friedman, 2005). Hirschland and Steinmo assert that "strong national policies on behalf of educational provision have been required to make right the great inefficiencies and inequities promulgated by this very localism" (2003, p. 345). A number of national organizations have played key roles in helping to nationalize education policy, including the National Governors Association, Education Commission of the States, and the Council of Chief State School Officers, which have raised the visibility of interstate differences in educational attainment and standards and which facilitate the coordination of state-level reform (CCSSO, 2008). As noted earlier, several presidents have utilized these national organizations to spur reform and improvement and to further their education policy agendas.

Institutional theorists observe that as public expectations and demands increase, so too will government develop and expand to meet those expectations (Thomas & Meyer, 1984). As evidence, they point to the fact that "the jurisdiction of the state in the West has tended to expand over time, as more and more aspects of social life have been incorporated into the general welfare function that is the essence of the Western state" (Thomas & Meyer, 1984, p. 468). With such expansion comes the likelihood of bureaucratic domination "justified by ever broader notions of justice and progress that go beyond the boundaries of any individual state," which in turn leads to greater uniformity in standards, processes, and expectations (Spring, 2002; Thomas & Meyer, 1984, p. 470).

This uniformity is the product of three distinct, yet interrelated isomorphic processes: (1) coercive isomorphism: the creation of mandates, regulations, rewards, and punishments (for example, the development of high-stakes accountability systems); (2) normative isomorphism: professional standards, certification, and accreditation (for example, changes in state standards for school leaders have had a dramatic impact on preparation programs); and (3) mimetic isomorphism: the federal and state governments model, copy, and build on successful reforms (DiMaggio & Powell, 1991). Collectively, these isomorphic processes produce greater uniformity and homogeneity, which leads to a more tightly coupled system, despite the limitations imposed by constitutional design (Fusarelli, 2002b, 2009). While not inconsequential, the limits imposed on U.S. presidents and lawmakers with respect to education policy can be overcome through creative use of federal carrots and, to a lesser extent, sticks—particularly when presidents effectively utilize the bully pulpit and existing national organizations to advance their policy agenda.

EFFECTS OF INCREASED FEDERAL INVOLVEMENT
IN EDUCATION

Despite a "theology of localism," educational historians and politics of education scholars have observed that local control over education has slowly eroded over the past four decades, as the federal and state governments exert ever-greater control over education (Institute for Educational Leadership, 2001, p. 2; Fusarelli & Cooper, 2010).[2] Despite a host of criticism and despite Common Core, federal involvement in education, with its heavy emphasis on testing, standards, and accountability, has, in the view of critics, narrowed the curriculum, focused attention to tested subjects, and encouraged teachers to teach to the test (English & Steffy, 2001; Jones, Jones, & Hargrove, 2003). Although the new Common Core standards are meant to encourage the teaching of higher-order thinking skills, ultimately, testing drives what and how teachers teach, particularly when teacher performance is tied to student growth on standardized assessments.

Encouraged by the federal government, states have developed rewards and consequences for students (in the form of promotion and exit exams), for teachers (in the form of merit pay and performance tied to student growth), and for school leaders (in the form of school performance evaluations). Such initiatives "represent top-down strategies to improve student achievement through tightened centralized control" (Fusarelli & Fusarelli, 2003, p. 170).

The almost unquestioning adoption of such reforms reflects the infusion of the ideals and practices of the New Public Management in education, which critiques the traditional, bureaucratic public administration paradigm and replaces it with tools adopted from the private sector, including outcomes-based accountability, benchmarking, contracting out of public services, vouchers, merit pay, and performance bonuses, among others (Peters, 2001; Terry, 2003). Scholars studying public administration have noted that the newer breed of Democrats, exemplified in former President Clinton, Al Gore, and President Obama, accept this paradigm and advocate for its application (Terry, 2003). This market-driven New Public Management paradigm emerged in the 1980s and 1990s and has become a dominant approach in public management (Terry, 1998). Fusarelli and Johnson cite the incorporation of outcomes-based accountability provisions into NCLB as "another example of the New Public Management applied to education" (2004, p. 120).

As Bill Boyd noted in an address at the American Educational Research Association in 2007, we have witnessed a significant paradigm shift from local control and the separation of education and politics in the 1960s to the paradigm that education is too important to be left solely to professionals; from one of local control (almost no federal control) over education to NCLB and now RTTT; from disconnected goals and curricula to systemic alignment, national standards, and testing. As Boyd noted, Title VI of ESEA stated that nothing in the act gave the federal government authority to exercise any direction, supervision, or control over education, and yet, when ESEA was reauthorized as NCLB in 2001, it violated every pledge in Title VI of the original legislation.

Today, the basic tenets of federal control (much less state control) are rarely questioned. Conley points out that the federal government "now feels free to examine educational functioning, effectiveness, and methods" (through such practices as tying federal funds to research-based best practices) (2003, p. 24). Despite recognized constitutional limitations of federal authority over education, NCLB is significant because it "moved the federal role closer to the instructional core of local schools and classrooms" (McDonnell, 2005, p. 21). The language written into NCLB ostensibly to protect local and state control over curriculum, standards, governance, and accountability conflicts with many of the pronouncements, rules, and regulations coming from the USDOE. The result is largely empty, symbolic rhetoric about local control. As scholars of federalism have noted, once a government exercises influence or control over a policy domain, little incentive exists to cede that control and this analysis of federal education initiatives from Presidents Reagan through Obama offers little hope they will do so.

Although the Obama administration recognizes the limits of its power "to force states and local districts to do things that they do not want to do," administration officials also firmly believe in "the need to use federal power to close racial and socioeconomic achievement gaps, and their belief that certain kinds of policy changes [such as merit pay, performance-based accountability systems, common standards, and school choice] could generate major improvement" in education across the country (McGuinn, 2012, p. 140).

Performance reporting is reshaping educational politics and creating new intra-organizational dynamics between federal, state, and local policy makers—producing greater impetus for organizational change (Fusarelli, 2002b). The utter pervasiveness of performance-based accountability in education distinguishes this era from previous ones (Linn, 2000); nearly a decade and a half later, that trenchant observation continues to ring true. At the federal and state levels, and among members of both political parties, performance-based accountability has been embraced as a best practice to improve education (Lewis & Fusarelli, 2010; National Governors Association, 1999).

Although an argument could be made that significant differences exist in the educational platforms of Republican and Democratic presidents—for example, both Reagan and George W. Bush supported voucher initiatives, while Clinton and Obama opposed them (although the DC voucher system remains in place as President Obama has chosen not to fight that fight)—these differences are on fairly marginal, fringe issues. Presidents Reagan and Bush knew they would be unable to get voucher bills through Congress. Although Reagan gave lip service to vouchers, he invested "very little political capital" in the effort, a stance also adopted by his Republican successor, George H. W. Bush (Cibulka, 1996, p. 382). Fusarelli observed, "With the exception of disagreement on fringe issues, there has been an emerging (even astonishing) degree of ideological consensus among Republican and Democratic presidents about national education goals and reforms" (2002a, p. 158).

THE FEDERAL ROLE: BOTH LEADER AND FOLLOWER

Although federal involvement in educational reform has increased significantly (and in important ways) in the past three decades, it is important to note that many of these reforms have built on state-level initiatives (Fusarelli & Cooper, 2010). For example, when Tennessee Governor Lamar Alexander led the National Governors Association (NGA) in the mid-1980s, the NGA studied educational reform in the states and released a major report, *A Time for Results,* many of whose recommendations were incorporated into the education platform of George H. W. Bush (Beyle, 1996). The report included recommendations for merit pay, teacher retention, school report cards, identification and state takeover of failing schools, and school choice (Alexander, 1986). Alexander later served as secretary of education in the Bush administration. The expansion of federal control over education has been enabled through the efforts of key Southern governors (Alexander,

Clinton, and G. W. Bush)—all of whom when moved to a national stage utilized their experience to promote education reform across state boundaries (McDonnell, 2005).

As Mazzoni points out, state policy makers "had long been active on education issues . . . [and] did not need the federal government to cede them that terrain" (1995, p. 55). The federal government did not discover the achievement gap nor was it the initiator of reforms such as higher standards, testing, and accountability (Hunt, 2002). Former North Carolina Governor James Hunt, who has a distinguished reputation as a leader in state-level education reform, pointed out that none of the reforms discussed earlier originated with federal officials, nor were federal officials the first to be concerned about placing a highly qualified teacher in every classroom (Hunt, 2002). Firestone (2012) observed that, "Much of the federal regulation of state government was to demand of everyone what had become common practice" (p. 29). However, "frequently, Congress takes [education reform] models from a few states' laws and imposes them on all states as mandates or grant conditions" (McDermott & DeBray-Pelot, 2009, p. 194). In this way, increased federal control is significant because it is less tolerant of major state-to-state differences in education policy and reform. While the federal government may not always lead the way, it increasingly pushes laggard states to catch up to those leading its reform agenda.

Federal officials use their position to issue challenges and generate ideas and momentum for education reform, often creating policies consistent with and that extend emerging state-level reforms, including curriculum frameworks and standards, school report cards (including disaggregation of data to the student level), expanded testing, performance-based accountability measures, and school choice (Conley, 2003; Doyle, Cooper, & Trachtman, 1991; Goertz, 1996; Wong, 2004). Throughout the 1990s, "states continued to increase the links between tests and consequences" (Firestone, 2012, p. 9). NCLB built on "reform policies and programs in place in a number of states, while extending, strengthening, and prodding others to engage in systemic, standards-based reform to improve educational outcomes for all students" (Fusarelli, 2005, p. 128). Vergari observed that "increased federal control has further reinforced state reform initiatives and power" (2011, p. 15). McDermott and DeBray-Pelot (2009) reach a similar conclusion when they note that federal programs such as IASA and NCLB, which dramatically expand federal authority, were made possible in part by the earlier efforts of state policy makers to extend *their* power over education at the local level.

Several decades ago, Iannaccone made a similar observation when he noted that federal intervention has "enlarged the scope of education and lifted the sights of educators, in spite of their initial opposition, to articulation of new values" (1975, pp. 139–140, cited in Mosher, 1977). In the case of RTTT, the initiative "has had a significant impact on the national policy discourse around education and pushed many states to propose or enact important policy changes, particularly around charter schools and teacher-evaluation processes" (McGuinn, 2012, p. 136). Cooper and Fusarelli (2009) observe that federal initiatives, from ESEA to NCLB (to now RTTT), often spur state activism and reform, particularly insofar as they empower state-level policy makers to engage in systemic reform and to develop and refine statewide testing and performance-based accountability systems. Manna (2006) refers to this phenomenon as "borrowing strength," whereby federal policy makers promote their policy priorities by building on and extending state-level reform initiatives, a view with which Firestone (2012) concurs. We believe the federal and state governments borrow strength from each other, as initiatives or reforms undertaken at one level of government often spur extensions or expansions of related initiatives in the other.

CONCLUSION

Despite the growing federal influence over education documented in this chapter, an influence that is disproportionate to its actual fiscal contribution to education, some significant limits to federal authority remain that mitigate, to some extent, its influence. McGuinn (2012) provides an excellent summary of the challenges faced in implementing RTTT, including state and federal capacity gaps. State department of education funding is a popular source of cuts during difficult budget times; further, most state departments of education, as well as the U.S. Department of Education, are woefully understaffed. Despite a massive expansion in the number of federal rules and regulations pertaining to education since passage of ESEA, staffing levels at the USDOE are 44 percent below the level of staffing in various agencies responsible for education when the department was created (Vergari, 2011). Monitoring compliance and providing technical assistance is difficult under such constraints. Since passage of ESEA, states have been able, within limits, to "resist and reshape federal education policy in accordance with their perceived interests" (Vergari, 2011, p. 16).

Given the well-documented difficulties of implementing federal programs (Odden, 1991), particularly education programs that encounter state and local opposition, and the relatively small carrot of federal funds available in the federal toolkit, policy makers at all levels recognize the limits to federal power (although those limits appear not to have stopped federal officials from trying to extend them). In the case of RTTT, "there are likely to be significant differences between what states originally pledge to secure RTTT funds and what actually happens" (Vergari, 2011, p. 25). This has led some scholars to view the increased federal role not so much as a revolution as an evolution reflecting the push and pull of politics and policy making (McDonnell, 2005; Vergari, 2011). McDonnell sees an "almost linear development from the ideas embodied in America 2000 to IASA and on to NCLB" (2005, p. 35).

McDermott and DeBray-Pelot view it as an incremental revolution—that changes in "the federal definitions of adequate yearly progress and corrective action" contained in NCLB appeared to be incremental, technical changes but actually "produced a revolutionary extension of federal power over education policy" (2009, p. 194). They observe that the evolution of policies "from the fairly broad regulation of IASA to the strict mandates of NCLB shows how incremental change can produce a revolution in intergovernmental relations" (p. 200). In effect, states must "ask federal permission before enacting certain kinds of policies over which they would previously have had sole authority" (p. 208).

If future presidents expand the use of competitive grants in ESEA, using RTTT as the model, then this much larger pot of money could be used to leverage even more substantive reform, increasing the federal influence dramatically, preventing RTTT fade, and blocking political opposition from sabotaging reform efforts (Klein, 2013; McGuinn, 2012). McGuinn believes that "RTTT's competitive grants program represents a new approach to using federal funds to drive school reform" (2012, p. 153). Several other trends suggest continued federal activism in education reform. International tests such as TIMMS and PISA are becoming more sophisticated and the international comparisons that result from such tests further reinforce the idea that education is a boundary-spanning national imperative, too important to be left to local policy makers. Local problems may require local solutions, but national problems require national solutions, even if the authority to do so is not explicitly granted in the Constitution.[3]

Conley believes that "the cumulative effect of these [federal education reform] policies is to insert the federal government into local schools in an ever-widening circle—formally and directly, informally and indirectly—in ways that exert influence over education practices. When combined with state policies that also seek to appropriate the local policy agenda, the available 'policy space' within which local schools operate is significantly restricted" (2003, p. 3). Given the growth and expansion of federal power and authority in domestic policy, especially in education as highlighted in this chapter, available evidence suggests that "the limitations imposed by constitutional design can be overcome" (Fusarelli, 2009, p. 263). At the national level, we believe that increased federal activism in education reform is making the politics of education even more exciting, as it has led to the creation of new political alliances and for some rather unlikely bedfellows. Further research is needed to determine how these new federal initiatives will impact reform and improvement in schooling in the United States.

NOTES

1. The 11 states are Delaware, Florida, Georgia, Hawaii, Maryland, Massachusetts, New York, North Carolina, Ohio, Rhode Island, and Tennessee.
2. Much like belief in Santa Claus, this belief in local control continues to exert a fairly powerful hold on local policy makers and serves as a counterstory to reform efforts at the state and federal levels, despite much evidence to the contrary.
3. Education is not alone in this respect. The scope of federal authority in virtually all policy domains far exceeds what all but a few of the Founding Fathers could have possibly envisioned.

REFERENCES

Alexander, L. (1986). Time for results: An overview. *Phi Delta Kappan, 68*(3), 202–204.

Beyle, T. L. (1996). Being governor. In C. E. Van Horn (Ed.), *The state of the states* (3rd ed., pp. 77–107). Washington, DC: Congressional Quarterly Press.

Binkley, C. (2013, March 10). Race to top grants not worth costs, officials say. *The Columbus Dispatch*.

Bowling, C. J., & Pickerill, M. (2013). Fragmented federalism: The state of American federalism 2012–13. *Publius, 43*(3), 315–346.

Boyd, W. L. (1988). How to reform schools without half trying: Secrets of the Reagan Administration. *Educational Administration Quarterly, 24*(3), 299–309.

Boyd, W. L. (2003). Public education's crisis of performance and legitimacy: Introduction and overview of the yearbook. In W. L. Boyd & D. Miretzky (Eds.), *American educational governance on trial: Change and challenges* (pp. 1–19). Chicago, IL: National Society for the Study of Education.

Boyd, W. L. (2007, April 12). *Insurmountable obstacles? The evolution of education policy and politics in the United States, 1950 to 2007*. Presentation at the annual meeting of the American Educational Research Association. Chicago, IL.

Boyd, W. L. (1987). Public education's last hurrah?: Schizophrenia, amnesia, and ignorance in school politics. *Educational Evaluation and Policy Analysis, 9*(2), 85–100.

Boyd, W. L., & Johnson, B. C. (2003). Intergovernmental relations in education. *The Encyclopedia of Education* (Vol. 2).

Chubb, J., & Clark, C. (2013). *The new state achievement gap: How federal waivers could make it worse—or better*. Washington, DC: Education Sector.

Clark, D. L., & Astuto, T. A. (1986). The significance and permanence of changes in federal education policy. *Educational Researcher, 15*(8), 4–13.

Conley, D. T. (2003). *Who governs our schools?* New York, NY: Teachers College Press.

Cooper, B. S., & Fusarelli, B. C. (2010). Setting the stage: Where state power and education meet. In B. C. Fusarelli & B. S. Cooper (eds.), *The rising state: How state power is transforming our nation's schools* (pp. 1–6). Albany, NY: State University of New York Press.

Cooper, B. S., Fusarelli, L. D., & Randall, E. V. (2003). *Better policies, better schools: Theories and applications.* Upper Saddle River, NJ: Pearson.

Council of Chief State School Officers (2008). *Educational leadership policy standards.* Washington, DC: Author.

DeBray, E. H. (2006). *Politics, ideology, and education: Federal policy during the Clinton and Bush administrations.* New York: Teachers College Press.

DeBray, E. H., McDermott, K. A., & Wohlstetter, P. (2005). Introduction to the special issue on federalism reconsidered: The case of the No Child Left Behind Act. *Peabody Journal of Education, 80*(2), 1–18.

Dillon, S. (2009, February 17). For education chief, stimulus means power, money and risk. *New York Times.* Retrieved from www.nytimes.com.prox.lib.ncsu.edu

DiMaggio, P. J., & Powell, W. W. (Eds.). (1991). *The new institutionalism in organizational analysis.* Chicago, IL: University of Chicago Press.

Doyle, D. P., Cooper, B. S., & Trachtman, R. (1991). *Taking charge: State action on school reform in the 1980s.* Indianapolis, IN: Hudson Institute.

Elliott, S. (2013, April 27). Lawmakers expand school voucher program, pause Common Core. *The Indianapolis Star*, pp. 1–2. (online version: IndyStar.com).

Elmore, R. F. and McLaughlin, M. W. (1981) Strategic choice in federal policy: The compliance-assistance tradeoff. In A. Lieberman and M. W. McLaughlin (eds.), *Policymaking in Education, National Society for the Study of Education, 81st Yearbook.* Chicago: University of Chicago Press.

English, F. W., & Steffy, B. E. (2001). *Deep curriculum alignment.* Lanham, MD: Scarecrow Press.

Finn, C. E. Jr., & Hess, F. M. (2004). On leaving no child behind. *The Public Interest, 157,* 35–56.

Firestone, W. A. (2012). *The irony of control in educational accountability.* Paper presented at the Annual Meeting of the Pennsylvania Educational Research Association, Philadelphia, PA, October 4.

Fowler, F. C. (1995). The neoliberal value shift and its implications for federal education policy under Clinton. *Educational Administration Quarterly, 31*(1), 38–60.

Fowler, F. C. (2012). *Policy studies for educational leaders: An introduction* (4th ed.). Upper Saddle River, NJ: Pearson.

Friedman, T. L. (2005). *The world is flat.* New York, NY: Farrar, Straus and Giroux.

Fusarelli, B. C., & Cooper, B. S. (Eds.). (2010). *The rising state: How state power is transforming our nation's schools.* Albany, NY: State University of New York Press.

Fusarelli, L. D. (2002a). The political economy of gubernatorial elections: Implications for education policy. *Educational Policy, 16*(1), 139–160.

Fusarelli, L. D. (2002b). Tightly coupled policy in loosely coupled systems: Institutional capacity and organizational change. *Journal of Educational Administration, 40*(6), 561–575.

Fusarelli, L. D. (2004). The potential impact of the No Child Left Behind Act on equity and diversity in American education. *Educational Policy, 18*(1), 71–94.

Fusarelli, L. D. (2005). Gubernatorial reactions to No Child Left Behind: Politics, pressure, and education reform. *Peabody Journal of Education, 80*(2), 121–137.

Fusarelli, L. D. (2007). Restricted choice, limited options: Implementing choice and supplemental educational services in No Child Left Behind. *Educational Policy, 21*(1), 132–154.

Fusarelli, L. D. (2009). Improvement or interference? Reenvisioning the "state" in education reform. In B. C. Fusarelli and B. S. Cooper (Eds.), *The rising state: How state power is transforming our nation's schools* (pp. 243–270). Albany, NY: State University of New York Press.

Fusarelli, B. C., & Cooper, B. S. (2009). *The rising state: How state power is transforming the nation's schools.* Albany, NY: State University of New York Press.

Fusarelli, B. C., & Fusarelli, L. D. (2003). Systemic reform and organizational change. *Planning and Changing, 34*(3&4), 169–177.

Fusarelli, L. D., & Johnson, B. C. (2004). Educational governance and the new public management. *Public Administration and Management: An Interactive Journal, 9*(2), 118–127.

Fusarelli, B. C., & Young, T. (2011). Preserving the "public" in public education. *The Journal of Thought, 46*(1&2), 85–96.

Goertz, M. E. (1996). State education policy in the 1990s. In C. E. Van Horn (Ed.), *The state of the states* (3rd ed., pp. 179–208). Washington, DC: Congressional Quarterly Press.

Hanushek, E. A., & Raymond, M. E. (2005). Does school accountability lead to improved performance? *Journal of Policy Analysis and Management, 24*(2), 297–327.

Herrington, C. D., & Orland, M. E. (1992). Politics and federal aid to urban school systems: The case of chapter one. In J. G. Cibulka, R. J. Reed, & K. K. Wong (Eds.), *The politics of urban education in the United States* (pp. 167–179). Washington, DC: Falmer Press.

Hess, F. M., & McGuinn, P. J. (2002). Seeking the mantle of "opportunity": Presidential politics and the education metaphor, 1964–2000. *Educational Policy, 16*(1), 72–95.

Hirschland, M. J., & Steinmo, S. (2003). Correcting the record: Understanding the history of federal intervention and failure in securing U.S. educational reform. *Educational Policy, 17*(3), 343–364.

Hoff, D. J. (2008, November 4). Obama elected 44th president. *Education Week* (online version).

Hunt, J. B., Jr. (2002). Leadership in education: A view from the states. *Phi Delta Kappan, 83*(9), 714–720.

Iannaccone, L. (1975). *Education policy systems.* Fort Lauderdale, FL: Nova University.

Institute for Educational Leadership. (2001). *Leadership for student learning: Recognizing the state's role in public education.* Washington, DC: Author.

Jackson, B. L., & Cibulka, J. G. (1992). Leadership turnover and business mobilization: The changing political ecology of urban school systems. In J. G. Cibulka, R. J. Reed, & K. K. Wong (Eds.), *The politics of urban education in the United States* (pp. 71–86). Washington, DC: Falmer Press.

Jones, M. G., Jones, B. D., & Hargrove, T. Y. (2003). *The unintended consequences of high-stakes testing.* Lanham, MD: Rowman & Littlefield.

Jung, R. & Kirst, M. (1986). Beyond mutual adaptation and into the bully pulpit: Recent research on the federal role in education. *Educational Administration Quarterly, 22*(3), pp. 80–109.

Kingdon, J. W. (2010). *Agendas, alternatives, and public policies* (2nd ed.). New York, NY: Pearson.

Klein, A. (2013, April 10). Obama budget would invest in pre-K, high school overhaul. *Education Week* (online version).

Lewis, W. D., & Fusarelli, L. D. (2010). Leading schools in an era of change: Toward a "new" culture of accountability? In S. D. Horsford (Ed.), *New perspectives in educational leadership: Exploring social, political, and community contexts and meaning* (pp. 111–125). New York, NY: Peter Lang.

Linn, R. L. (2000). Assessments and accountability. *Educational Researcher, 29*(2), 4–14.

Lum, L. (2013, May 1). Race to the top initiative getting mixed reviews on the road. *Diverse Issues in Higher Education,* pp. 1–3 (online version: http://diverseeducation.com/article/53035/)

Malen, B., & Muncey, D. (2000). Creating "a new set of givens?" The impact of state activism on school autonomy. In N. D. Theobald & B. Malen (Eds.), *Balancing local control and state responsibility for K-12 education* (pp. 199–244). Larchmont, NY: Eye on Education.

Manna, P. (2006). *School's in: Federalism and the national education agenda.* Washington, DC: Georgetown University Press.

Marschall, M. J., & McKee, R. J. (2002). From campaign promises to presidential policy: Education reform in the 2000 election. *Educational Policy, 16*(1), 96–117.

Mazzoni, T. L. (1995). State policy-making and school reform: Influences and influential. In J. D. Scribner & D. H. Layton (Eds.), *The study of educational politics* (pp. 53–73). London: Falmer Press.

McCullen, C. (2013, June 7). Join the distinguished "corps" of advocates supporting common core. *The Friday Report, 15*(44), 1–4. Raleigh: Public School Forum of North Carolina.

McDermott, K. A., & DeBray-Pelot, E. (2009). The incremental revolution: Nationalizing education accountability policy. In B. C. Fusarelli & B. S. Cooper (Eds.), *The rising state: How state power is transforming our nation's schools* (pp. 193–212). Albany, NY: State University of New York Press.

McDonnell, L. M. (2005). No Child Left Behind and the federal role in education: Evolution or revolution? *Peabody Journal of Education, 80*(2): 19–38.

McDonnell, L. M., & Weatherford, M. S. (2011). Crafting an education reform agenda through economic stimulus policy. *Peabody Journal of Education, 86*: 304-318.

McGuinn, P. J. (2006). *No child left behind and the transformation of federal education policy, 1965–2005.* Lawrence, KS: University Press of Kansas.

McGuinn, P. (2012). Stimulating reform: Race to the top, competitive grants and the Obama education agenda. *Educational Policy, 26*(1), 136–159.

McLaughlin, M. W. (1976, January). Evaluating innovations: The case for a new paradigm. *Journal of Career Development, 2*(3), 78–90.

McNeil, M. (2013, March 12). Details trickling out on latest NCLB waiver bids. *Education Week* (online version).

Miron, G. J. (2008). The shifting notion of "publicness" in public education. In B. S. Cooper, J. G. Cibulka, & L. D. Fusarelli (Eds.), *Handbook of education politics and policy* (pp. 338–349). New York, NY: Routledge.

Mosher, E. K. (1977). Education and American federalism: Intergovernmental and national policy influences. In J. D. Scribner (Ed.), *The politics of education* (pp. 94–123). Chicago, IL: University of Chicago Press.

National Commission on Excellence in Education. (1983). *A nation at risk.* Washington, DC: U.S. Government Printing Office.

National Governors Association. (1999). *Focusing on results: Toward an education accountability system.* Washington, DC: Author.

New York State Education Department Archives. States' impact on federal education policy. Federal education policy and the states: 1945–2009. Available at: www.archives.nysed.gov/edpolicy/research/res_essay_bush_ghw_amer2000.shtml.

"No child left behind hearing features waiver attack by Obama ally." (2013, February 7). *Huffington Post.*

Odden, A. (Ed.). (1991). *Education policy implementation.* Albany, NY: State University of New York Press.

Peters, B. G. (2001). *The future of governing* (2nd ed.). Lawrence, KS: University Press of Kansas.

Porter, R. (2013). *Understanding common core implementation: How educators intuit, interpret, and begin to integrate curriculum reform.* Unpublished doctoral dissertation. North Carolina State University.

Reyes, P., Scribner, J. D., & Fusarelli, L. D. (1999). Delta forces: The changing fabric of American society and education. In J. Murphy & K. Seashore Louis (Eds.), *Handbook of research on educational administration* (2nd ed., pp. 183–201). San Francisco, CA: Jossey-Bass.

Rudalevige, A. (2003). The politics of No Child Left Behind. *Education Next, 3*(4), 63–69.

Samuels, C. A. (2013, February 26). States size up Obama pre-K proposal. *Education Week* (online version).

Sarason, S. B. (1982). *Culture of the school and the problem of change* (2nd ed.). Boston, MA: Allyn & Bacon.

Schoen, L., & Fusarelli, L. D. (2008). Innovation, NCLB, and the fear factor. *Educational Policy, 22*(1), 181–203.

Scribner, J. D., Reyes, P., & Fusarelli, L. D. (1995). Educational politics and policy: And the game goes on. In J. D. Scribner & D. H. Layton (Eds.), *The study of educational politics* (pp. 210–212). London: Falmer Press.

Seib, G. F. (2008, November 21). In crisis, opportunity for Obama. *The Wall Street Journal,* http://online.wsj.com/news/articles/SB122721278056345271.

Spring, J. (2002). *Conflict of interests: The politics of American education* (4th ed.). Boston, MA: McGraw-Hill.

Spring, J. (2010). *The politics of American education.* New York, NY: Routledge.

Terry, L. D. (1998). Administrative leadership, neo-managerialism, and the public management movement. *Public Administration Review, 58*(3), 194–200.

Terry, L. D. (2003). *Leadership of public bureaucracies* (2nd ed.). Armonk, NY: M. E. Sharpe.

Thomas, G. M., & Meyer, J. W. (1984). The expansion of the state. *Annual Review of Sociology, 10,* 461–482.

Ujifusa, A. (2013, February 4). Pressure mounts in some states against common core. *Education Week* (online version).

Vergari, S. (2011). The limits of federal activism in education policy. *Educational Policy, 26*(1), 15–34.

Wills, G. (1985). *Reagan's America: Innovations at home.* New York, NY: Penguin.

Wong, K. K. (2004). The politics of education. In V. Gray & R. L. Hanson (Eds.), *Politics in the American states* (8th ed., pp. 357–388). Washington, DC: Congressional Quarterly Press.

9

FEDERALISM, EQUITY, AND ACCOUNTABILITY IN EDUCATION

Kenneth K. Wong

Public education is closely connected to the challenge of income inequality, racial/ethnic disparities, and the urban environment in our society. In the nation's largest central city school districts, more than 60 percent of the students are eligible for free or reduced-price school lunch programs, a sign of poverty. African American students constitute about one-third of the enrollment in large central cities as compared to about 15 percent nationwide. The nation's growing Latino population experiences significant school dropout problems. Schools that have a higher concentration of minority and low-income students are less likely to recruit qualified teachers, offer rigorous curricula, and maintain high academic performance.

The pervasive impact of poverty and racial/ethnic inequality in public schools raises a fundamental tension in our federal system of government. Given our decentralized system of governance, what is the role of government in addressing social redistributive needs? Decentralization is clearly prevalent in public education, where power and decisions are dispersed among 50 states and 15,000 local districts. Historically, state and local governments paid limited attention to the educational needs of disadvantaged students, whose parents were often not well organized and whose neighborhoods were less likely to be economically vibrant. States and districts tended to marginalize schooling opportunities for segments of at-risk populations.

The tension between decentralization and inequity constitutes a central concern in the discipline of political science. On the one hand, the U.S. Constitution recognizes the rights of the states to handle their own affairs, including public education. On the other hand, there is pressing public responsibility to address the needs of those who are less fortunate. An understanding of how the government manages this tension between local control and social responsibility lies in the distribution of power and functions between layers of government. The way we govern public education, allocate resources, and organize the delivery of services from one level to the other as well as across a diverse country constitute a natural setting for conducting research on intergovernmental relations in educational policy. This chapter will examine the evolution of the federal role in addressing income and racial/ethnic disparities in public schools. Particular attention will be given to evolving theories of intergovernmental relations, including patterns of conflict and cooperation between the federal and the local governments in education policy.

FROM DUAL FEDERALISM TO MARBLE CAKE FEDERALISM

The role of the government in addressing the needs of disadvantaged students occupies a prominent place in the study of education policy. The governmental responsibility has undergone major changes as American federalism evolved with the passage of time. While the federal government has assumed new responsibilities to promote equal educational opportunity, state and local governments continue to play a dominant role in governing, funding, and managing public schools.

Historically, the federal government has taken a permissive role in education that is consistent with what political scientist Morton Grodzins characterized as "layer cake" federalism. Article I, Section 8 of the U.S. Constitution specifies the "enumerated powers" that Congress enjoys and the Tenth Amendment grants state autonomy in virtually all domestic affairs, including education. Sovereignty for the states was not dependent on the federal government but instead came from the states' citizenry. Consistent with this view, in *The Federalist Papers,* which were first published during 1787 and 1788, James Madison suggested a line of demarcation between the federal government and the states (Hamilton, Madison, & Jay, 1961). He wrote, "The federal and state governments are in fact but different agents and trustees for the people, constituted with different powers, and designed for different purposes" (No. 46, p. 296). The dual structure was further maintained by local customs, practice, and belief. It came as no surprise that in his description of American democracy in the mid-19th century, Alexis de Tocqueville opened his seminal treatise by referring to the local governments' "rights of individuality." Observing the state-local relations in the New England townships, de Tocqueville wrote, "Thus it is true that the tax is voted by the legislature, but it is the township that apportions and collects it; the existence of a school is imposed, but the township builds it, pays for it, and directs it" (2000, p. 63). Public education was primarily an obligation internal to the state. The division of power within the federal system was so strong that it continued to preserve state control over its internal affairs, including the *de jure* segregation of schools, many decades following the Civil War.

Federal involvement in education sharply increased during the Great Society era of the 1960s and the 1970s. Several events converged to shift the federal role from permissiveness to engagement. During the immediate post–World War II period, Congress enacted the GI Bill to enable veterans to receive a college education of their choice. The Cold War competition saw the passage of the National Defense Education Act (NDEA) in 1958 shortly after the Soviet Union's satellite, *Sputnik,* successfully orbited the earth. At the same time, the 1954 landmark Supreme Court ruling on *Brown v. Board of Education* and the congressional enactment of the 1964 Civil Rights Act sharpened federal attention to the needs of disadvantaged students. Consequently, the federal government adopted a major antipoverty education program in 1965, Title I of the 1965 Elementary and Secondary Education Act (ESEA).

The ESEA, arguably the most important federal program in public schools in the past four decades, signaled the end of dual federalism and strengthened the notion of "marble cake" federalism where the national and subnational governments share responsibilities in the domestic arena. Prior to the 1965 law, there was political deadlock on the role of federal government in Congress. The states outside of the South were opposed to allocating federal funds to segregated school systems. Whereas some lawmakers refused to aid parochial schools, others wanted to preserve local autonomy from federal regulations. Political stalemates were reinforced through bargaining behind closed doors among the few powerful committee chairmen (Sundquist, 1968).

The eventual passage of ESEA and other social programs marked the creation of a complex intergovernmental policy system that is unique in American history. To avoid centralization of administrative power at the national level, Congress increased its intergovernmental transfers to finance state and local activities. During the presidency of Lyndon Johnson, categorical (or single purpose) programs, including Title I, increased from 160 to 380. By the end of the Jimmy Carter administration, there were approximately 500 federally funded categorical programs. Particularly important was the redistributive focus of many of these categorical programs that were designed to promote racial desegregation, protect the educational rights of the handicapped, assist English language learners, and provide supplemental resources to children from at-risk backgrounds. Despite several revisions and extensions, ESEA Title I, for example, continues to adhere to its original intent "to provide financial assistance . . . to local educational agencies serving areas with concentrations of children from low-income families to expand and improve their educational programs . . . which contribute particularly to meeting the special educational needs of educationally deprived children."

The literature on federalism has looked at structural sources in explaining why antipoverty policy is more likely to come from the national government. The federal government enjoys a broader revenue base in which taxes are primarily raised on the ability-to-pay principle, and it represents a constituency with diverse demands, including views that are not often supported by the majority (Peterson, Rabe, & Wong, 1986; Wong, 1999). In other words, it has both the fiscal capacity and the political justification (often facilitated by organized interest groups) to take a more active redistributive role.

Federal engagement in redistributive policy is evident in its contribution to the overall education spending. Federal aid to programs for special-needs students showed persistent growth in real-dollar terms. Between 1996 and 2005, these programs amounted to more than 60 percent of the total federal spending in elementary and secondary schools (Wong, 1999; Wong & Sunderman, 2007). The Title I program for the education for the disadvantaged increased from $8.9 billion to $14.6 billion in 2005 constant dollars. Federal aid in special education grew by more than two times, while the school lunch program increased its funding from $9.8 billion in 1996 to $12.2 billion in 2005. Head Start also jumped by 50 percent in real-dollar terms during this period.

This trend of growing federal involvement in programs for the disadvantaged continues in the Obama administration. Congress appropriated $98.2 billion to support education in the American Recovery and Reinvestment Act (ARRA) in 2009. ARRA provided additional funds to several major categorical programs for a two-year period, including $10 billion for Title I, $12.2 billion for IDEA, $650 million for technology, and $100 million for impact aid construction.

Further, federal redistributive grants have taken on several institutional characteristics that resemble a policy framework:

- Grants-in-aid arrangement: where federal government provides the dollars and sets the programmatic framework, but the delivery of services is up to the state and local agencies.

- Categorical or single-purpose grants: where well-defined eligible students are the intended beneficiaries; only they would receive the services.
- Supplementary and nonsupplanting guidelines: they are designed to guard against any local tendency to shift federal resources away from the disadvantaged.
- Bipartisan support: special-needs programs are often connected to well-entrenched political interests. For example, the free and reduced-price lunch program has received political support from the agricultural business.
- Incentives for local government to meet antipoverty objectives: federal funds are widely distributed to ensure broad political support. The territorial impact of federal grants has contributed partly to the popularity of Title I in Congress over time. For example, in the 1990s, the federal grant provided supplemental resources to 64 percent of all the schools in the nation, covering virtually every congressional district. Clearly, big city districts were not the only beneficiaries of compensatory education funds. Indeed, more than 20 percent of federal aid went to districts with fewer than 2,500 students. Districts with enrollments between 2,500 and 25,000 received almost 45 percent of the funds. Because there are Title I programs in almost every congressional district, partisan conflict has generally been limited during the appropriations process.

THE NEW POLITICS OF PERFORMANCE-BASED FEDERALISM

While redistributive grants-in-aid have gained bipartisan support, this policy arrangement faced its most serious political challenge in the mid-1990s. The 1994 midterm elections produced the first Republican majority in Congress in 40 years. The new congressional leadership claimed a public mandate to shrink the federal role in social programs and to shift programmatic authority to state and local governments. House Speaker Newt Gingrich tended to undermine long-term institutional practices in decision making. He depicted the federal government as the major cause of poverty, the federal bureaucracy as the major source of waste of taxpayers' dollars, and the private sector as the solution to social inequality.

Political confrontation between Congress and the president became highly visible in education policy during 1995. The Republican leadership, for example, proposed to cut significantly major redistributive programs, including Title I and bilingual education. To demonstrate its control over governmental appropriations, the Republican leadership shut down all federal agencies when the budget expired. In the end, however, the retrenchment tactics backfired. Within two years, education policy regained bipartisan support in the Republican Congress.

While federal redistributive education policy seemed to have survived a serious political challenge in the mid-1990s, its effectiveness was increasingly called into question in a broadened climate of outcome-based accountability. The passage of the Improving America's Schools Act in 1994 signaled the beginning of federal efforts to address accountability in its antipoverty programs. This legislation aimed at reducing program isolation of at-risk students from their peers, created incentives for whole school reform, and required districts and states to use their system-wide standards to assess the performance of at-risk students.

As the U.S. Congress enacted the No Child Left Behind Act (NCLB) of 2001, federal involvement expanded on educational accountability for all children. The federal law requires annual testing of students at the elementary grades in core subject areas, mandates the hiring of "highly qualified teachers" in classrooms, and grants state and local agencies substantial authority in taking "corrective actions" to turn around failing schools. Further, the law provides school choice to parents to take their children out of failing schools. Equally significant in terms of federal intervention is the legislative intent in closing the achievement gaps among racial/ethnic subgroups as well as income, English language learners (ELL), and special education subgroups. During the initial phase of NCLB, the federal government increased its allocation by $1.7 billion to a total of almost $11 billion in the Title I program, in addition to more than $900 million for early reading initiatives.

The expansion of the federal role occurred under an unusual set of political conditions in the post–September 11 climate where the presidency gained broad public support. From a governing perspective, the passage of NCLB may be characterized as a "regime change," where well-entrenched political interests set aside their traditional policy positions to support the new policy (McGuinn, 2006). Proponents of state power were ready to set aside their beliefs in state and local control and to endorse a visibly stronger federal presence in education. Advocates of accountability pushed for a fairly comprehensive set of accountability measures, including annual testing of students in core subject areas with consequences. Political interests across the board were supportive of disaggregated reporting on achievement. Federal expectations on academic proficiency now apply to all students, schools, and districts, regardless of whether they receive federal Title I funds. The federal government has elevated education performance to the top of the nation's policy agenda.

The unusual convergence of political interests in 2001 allowed NCLB to craft a new framework on the federal role: to promote proficiency across all student groups, including those who come from disadvantaged backgrounds. In terms of academic performance, the federal government holds states, districts, and schools accountable for a comprehensive set of standards, including annual academic progress, teacher quality, and achievement gaps. To determine if a school meets adequate yearly progress (AYP) in NCLB, student achievement is aggregated by grade and by subject area for each school. All students in grades 3 through 8 and one additional grade in high school are tested annually in mathematics, reading/English language arts, and, in selected grades, science. The school-level report includes the percentage of students proficient in each of the core content areas, student participation in testing, attendance rates, and graduation rates.

Equally prominent is the equity focus in NCLB. Depending on their socioeconomic characteristics, schools are required to report the academic proficiency of students in the following subgroups: economically disadvantaged students, students from major racial and ethnic groups, students with disabilities, and limited English proficiency (LEP) students. In this regard, NCLB has made the achievement gap within a school more transparent for accountability purposes. Schools that persistently fail to meet AYP are subject to a gradation of intervention, including school closure and conversion to charter school.

PERSPECTIVES ON POLICY IMPLEMENTATION: CONFLICT AND ACCOMMODATION

While the redistributive goals have relied on federal funding, state and local agencies have shown mixed support. Since the implementation of federally funded redistributive services since the 1960s, there have been three perspectives to understanding intergovernmental management of these issues.

The first generation of implementation studies was conducted mostly in the late 1960s and 1970s, which coincided with a period of policy formation. These studies covered a wide range of policy topics—from compensatory education and busing programs to integration to job training and employment programs in economically depressed communities. Given the "new-ness" of federal antipoverty policy, it came as no surprise that many first-generation studies were highly critical of how federal programs operated. For example, a 1969 study conducted by the NAACP Legal Defense Fund found that federal Title I funds were being used for "general school purposes; to initiate system-wide programs; to buy books and supplies for all school children in the system; to pay general overhead and operating expenses; [and] to meet new teacher contracts which call for higher salaries" (see Wong, 1999). Similarly, Jerome Murphy's (1971) analysis of the Title I program in Massachusetts found state and local interests competing against the federal antipoverty intent.

In short, as analysts examined the initial development of the intergovernmental administrative structure in implementing antipoverty programs, they often found confusion, conflict, and failure to meet national social objectives. In other words, federal resources set aside for the at-risk populations often failed to go to the intended beneficiaries. These first-generation studies no doubt raised important political and policy issues—whether the federal government can use grants to overcome structural obstacles that are embedded in constitutional tradition of state rights and local control. Consequently, throughout the 1970s, Congress adopted an exceedingly well-defined set of regulations to make sure that the intended beneficiaries receive the services.

A second perspective on intergovernmental relations emerges as the federal grants-in-aid system matures. As the federal government increasingly clarifies its antipoverty intent, state and local agencies seem more ready to meet programmatic standards. Based on a comparative analysis of federal roles in education, health care, and housing and community development, Peterson, Rabe, and Wong (1986) documented various patterns of state and local response to federal expectations. This study observes two major implementation patterns. While intergovernmental cooperation remains strong in activities pertaining to economic growth, conflict often occurred in redistributive programs. The lack of full federal funding to meet mandated standards can also be a source of intergovernmental contention. The federal government, for example, promised to provide 40 percent of the funds for special education; but in reality, its funding level seldom went over 25 percent of the program cost. Local and state agencies were also reluctant to change their practices in light of the federal focus. Interestingly, Peterson, Rabe, and Wong (1988) observed that intergovernmental tension became increasingly manageable with the passage of time. Professional exchange and identity across intergovernmental levels were instrumental in resolving program conflict and facilitating communication.

This second perspective tends to address some of the methodological concerns that are often associated with the first-generation implementation studies. First, these studies differentiated socially redistributive objectives from other purposes in federal programs. Having made explicit the differences in national purposes, these studies considered intergovernmental conflict as a function of social redistribution goals. Second, in conducting case studies, researchers often collected information from multiple years of the implementation process. This longitudinal view enabled policy analysts to denote cycles of political compromise and programmatic accommodation within the complex intergovernmental system. Further, researchers used comparative cases that involved multiple schools, districts, or states. Often, these studies specified the broader institutional context within which federal programs operated.

A third perspective has emerged to focus on accountability and innovation. Just as the intergovernmental system began to institutionalize its operational routines, as studies in the second-generation implementation observed, public pressure for greater academic accountability has created new tension in our federalist education system. States and districts have moved toward standards-based reform since the 1990s. For example, by 2001, only three states did not adopt academic content standards in the four subject areas. In 29 states, mathematics and English assessments were closely aligned to the content standards at various grade levels (Manna, 2006). A growing number of states have passed charter school legislation, which enabled almost 5,000 charter schools to provide schooling choice to 2.5 million students across the nation. With the passage of NCLB, performance-based accountability has gained national prominence. The Obama administration continued to advance performance-based accountability by encouraging states and districts to adopt innovative practices, including college readiness, teacher evaluation, and school restructuring.

IMPLEMENTATION REALITY IN PERFORMANCE-BASED FEDERALISM

The federal accountability agenda, as articulated in NCLB, has created tension in the intergovernmental policy system. As Manna (2010) puts it, there is a significant gap between the theory of accountability based on the federal intent and the practice of accountability at the state and local levels. The literature on the implementation of NCLB has suggested several key challenges in aligning the federal reform agenda with our current intergovernmental system of education governance (see, for example, Cohen & Moffitt, 2009; Hess & Finn, 2007; Hess & Petrilli, 2006).

First, federalism allows for varying degrees of policy specification in meeting the federal expectations. Federalism is not designed to support a uniform set of accountability measures across the 50 states and the District of Columbia. Clearly, states defined their own set of proficiency standards and measures in meeting AYP (Wong & Nicotera, 2007). Broadly speaking, states have chosen several methods to ensure that students reach proficiency: equal yearly goals, steady stair-step, and accelerating curve (Wong & Nicotera, 2007). In the equal yearly goals approach, the percentage of students meeting proficiency increases in equal increments every year until the 2014 deadline for 100 percent proficiency. Annual equal increments are calculated by subtracting the starting point proficiency from 100 and then dividing by 12. The steady stair-step approach requires that the percentage of students meeting proficiency will increase incrementally every two or three years to meet the 2014 deadline.

In the third approach, states create an accelerating curve for improvement where the percentage of students meeting proficiency will increase slowly in the initial years with greater gains occurring closer to the 2014 deadline. Within each state, the decision-making process allowed multiple stakeholders to weigh in on the rigor, scope, timing, and cost of student academic assessment. Consequently, state assessments vary widely in terms of the level of rigor, as indicated by the substantial gap between student proficiency in the state test and the performance in NAEP in many states.

Second, political negotiations among key stakeholders within a state tended to slow the pace of initial implementation in NCLB, which came as no surprise to observers of education reform. Four out of five states were not ready to meet the federal requirement on placing highly qualified teachers in the classroom. The annual testing requirement, a core concept in the new accountability system, faced major resistance. Virginia, Connecticut, Utah, Michigan, and several other states registered their opposition with legislative and legal actions. In a 2011 study conducted by the Center for American Progress, state education commissioners pointed out that strong accountability and innovative practices were the exceptions in state education agencies (Brown et al., 2011).

Third, the federal agenda encountered social constraints. The extent to which a district or a school meets AYP is affected by the number and size of students in the subgroups, including low-income students, English language learners, students with disabilities, and racial and ethnic minorities. In their analysis of this issue in California, Kim and Sunderman (2005) found that the percentage of schools meeting AYP declines as the number of subgroups rise in these schools. While 78 percent of the schools with only one subgroup met the reading AYP in 2003, only 25 percent of the schools with six subgroups were able to do so. When the authors considered the AYP data in Virginia, they found that 85 percent of the schools that met both the state and federal proficiency standards had two or fewer subgroups. Only 15 percent of the schools that met the AYP had three or more subgroups.

Faced with state power and differences in the socioeconomic characteristics of student enrollment across states, the federal government loosened up the standards in meeting the AYP by allowing for a "safe harbor" provision. Under this guideline, a subgroup is deemed as "meeting" AYP if the percentage of students in the "below basic proficiency" level is reduced by 10 percent from the previous year. In Philadelphia, a large urban school district with 266 schools, for example, of the 158 schools that made AYP in 2010, 37 percent of them met the proficiency standards by achieving the safe harbor target.

The "safe harbor" flexibility, however, may not have provided sufficient incentives to avert irregularities in student assessment practices at the local level. Recent reports on test cheating in Atlanta, Philadelphia, and other urban districts have called for a stronger state role in monitoring student testing. In Philadelphia, data on the 2009 test results were shelved by the state education agency for two years. Until a local news article exposed the problems in about 30 schools, the district was not formally notified by the state of any testing problems. These findings on cheating led to a closer working relationship between the state and the district on test administration and monitoring.

Fourth, the federal agenda on accountability may not have aligned effectively with the federal system of formula-based grant allocation. NCLB did not fundamentally alter the categorical grants-in-aid system. Categorical funding continued to grow during the first decade of the 21st century. Federal grants are largely allocated by formula, based on well-defined eligible students and only they would receive the services (Peterson et al., 1986). Federal guidelines on nonsupplanting and maintenance of fiscal efforts have ensured that federal resources are not diverted away from the eligible beneficiaries. Even during the current retrenchment, these federal fiscal requirements have not been relaxed. In providing matching funds and enacting their own redistributive initiatives, state agencies further complicate the intergovernmental categorical system by creating "underfunded" and "unfunded mandates"(Shelly, 2011).

The federal government was able to take only incremental steps in aligning its formula-based allocation to support its ambitious goal of improving persistently low-achieving schools. A key federal strategy was to reallocate existing Title I funds roughly proportional to the problems of student achievement. More specifically, NCLB calls for a set of progressively intensive "corrective actions" when districts and schools fail to make AYP for consecutive years. These sanctions require low-performing districts and schools to use their Title I funds differently. The sanctions begin with the relatively modest requirement for a school-improvement plan, including options for families in schools not making adequate yearly progress to transfer to another public or charter school, and the implementation of Title I-funded supplemental educational or tutorial services after school. In other words, sanctions in the first years of academic failure are not designed to change the structure or governance of the low-performing school. Following four consecutive years of failure, NCLB allows for more intensive sanctions. These include state-driven interventions that alter school governance and hiring decisions, such as school or district takeovers and replacement of personnel in poorly performing schools. Only in the most drastic restructuring are federal resources integrated with local and state funding to support the federal objectives.

Finally, federal reform generates new conflicts on the management and delivery of educational services. NCLB encourages a broader set of providers, including for-profit organizations and charter management organizations, to manage low-performing schools. Not surprisingly, local districts were generally protective of their control over supplemental education services (SES) and were slow in supporting parents to transfer their children from low-performing schools. In his study of California, for example, Betts (2007) observed that school choice, as stipulated by NCLB, was largely underutilized throughout the state. Reasons for limited local implementation included the delay in making data available to parents, failure of districts to communicate the choice program clearly to parents, an inadequate number of seats in better-performing schools, and lack of parental interest in moving their children outside of the neighborhood schools.

The California case also showed that participation rates for SES were low, though not nearly as low as for the transfer option. State agencies attributed implementation difficulties to several reasons. There was a general lack of information about state-approved providers for SES and districts received complaints about SES providers from participating parents and schools. Districts were tardy in providing parents with information about SES. Some districts did not allow nondistrict providers to work on district property. Finally, like school choice, one of the greatest impediments to participation in SES was the substance and form of communications sent by districts to parents.

In short, the federal role has shifted the policy focus from inputs to outcomes, opened service delivery to diverse providers, and required local and state agencies to publicly report on student performance. There are, to be sure, intergovernmental conflict over annual testing, federal intervention in persistently low-performing schools, and the cost in meeting the new federal mandates. Efforts to manage the federal goals in both accountability and equity have continued during the Obama administration.

OBAMA'S FOCUS ON INSTITUTIONAL INNOVATION: INCENTIVIZE STATES TO BUILD CAPACITY

The Obama administration had broadened NCLB accountability by creating new competitive funding streams to promote institutional innovation at the state and local levels. Under federal direction, states and districts competed in the Race to the Top, i3 grants, and other federal funding sources to "transform" their current policy and practices in educator accountability, charter schools, and turning around low-performing schools. These innovative initiatives, defined and promoted by the U.S. Department of Education, sought support from key state and local actors—including governors, state commissioners, mayors, unions, and networks of diverse providers, among others.

Building on the NCLB framework on "corrective actions," the Obama administration continues the push for more direct district intervention in persistently low-performing schools. In his proposal to reauthorize the federal law in elementary and secondary education, Secretary Duncan argued for four strategies to "turn around" the nation's lowest-performing 5 percent of schools (or approximately 5,000 schools). The federal government committed $5 billion during 2010–2012 to support these efforts. The four strategies tightened the approaches that were established under NCLB, allowing for fewer district options. More specifically, the Duncan strategies included:

- *Turnaround school* under a new principal who can recruit at least half of the new teachers from the outside,
- *Transformation school* that strengthens professional support, teacher evaluation, and capacity building,
- *Restart school* that will reopen as either a charter school or under management by organizations outside of the district, and
- *School closure* that results in moving all the students to other higher-performing schools.

In making its first school improvement grants (SIG) to support school turnarounds, the Obama administration allocated $3 billion in federal funds to more than 730 schools in 44 states in December 2010. Of these schools, an overwhelming number of them (71%) had chosen the "transformation" option while very few decided to use either "restart" (5%) or "school closure" (3%). The remaining 21 percent opted for the "turnaround" option where the principal and a majority of the teaching staff were replaced (Klein, 2011). Equally important, only 16.5 percent of the students in all the SIG schools were white, as compared to 44 percent African American and 34 percent Hispanic. The choices made by the SIG awardees seem to suggest a leaning toward a more incremental approach to school improvement. This tension between the federal push for innovation and local realities is likely to persist. In anticipation of the local inertia toward incremental organizational changes, the Obama administration created the Office of School Turnaround in late 2011 to monitor and support local efforts to raise school performance.

Further, Obama's February 2012 proposal to reauthorize ESEA aimed at stronger program coordination. Specially, the administration proposed to consolidate 38 major programs into 11 broad initiatives. Departing from the categorical arrangements, these new programs were designed to allocate federal funding through competitive applications, focus on what works, and allow for greater local discretion in implementation. Under this plan, "expanding educational options" was proposed to consolidate five programs, including charter school grants, credit enhancement for charter school facilities, parental information and resource centers, smaller learning communities, and voluntary public school choice. "Teacher and leader pathways" would include school leadership, Teach for America, teacher quality partnership, teachers for a competitive tomorrow, and transition to teaching. The "teacher and leader innovation fund" would consolidate the teacher incentive fund and advanced credentialing.

The Obama proposal to reauthorize ESEA maintained the federal redistributive focus, providing federal funding support for high-need students, including English language learners, migrant students, Native Americans, and homeless children. Equally important, the Obama administration sent a strong signal on its priority to promote college and career readiness in its ESEA reauthorization proposal. Title I, Part A of ESEA would be renamed as the College- and Career-Ready Students program (this is currently entitled Title I Grants to Local Education Agencies). Of the $14.8 billion requested for Title I, portions of the federal fund were proposed to be set aside to support local capacity to meet the challenge of readiness. For example, $300 million would be set aside as incentives for high-poverty Title I schools that make significant achievement growth. A competitive grant of $350 million was proposed to support early learning from birth to prekindergarten. State and local turnaround efforts would receive $600 million in federal Title I funds. While $500 million would be devoted to reward highly effective teachers and principals, $835 million would be set aside for competitive efforts to improve instruction in STEM (Science, Technology, Engineering, and Mathematics) and literacy in high-need schools.

Equally important is Obama's strong guidance on local and state institutional reform through competitive grants such as the Race to the Top. Departing from formula-based categorical allocations, the Obama administration invited states to submit their best ideas on system transformation and school innovation for the national competition for the Race to the Top program. Delaware and Tennessee were selected as the first two awardees of the first round of Race to the Top competition in April 2010. The competition resulted in awards to a total of 19 states and Washington, DC.

The first two winning applications submitted by Delaware and Tennessee shared several features in their approach on transforming public education. First, teacher accountability was prominent. Student achievement became a "cornerstone" of a new teacher assessment system, according to the Tennessee education commissioner. Delaware proposed to use the annual evaluation results to remove teachers who were rated as "ineffective" for consecutive years. Second, a system of support was proposed to enhance professional capacity. Delaware planned to hire 35 data coaches to train teachers in using data for instructional improvement. The state also planned to hire 15 "development" coaches to support principals and teachers in the highest-need schools. Third, external partners, such as Mass Insight Education and Research Institute, were brought in. Fourth, the two states were successful in gaining approval from key stakeholders on the reform agenda in the long term. During the application, Tennessee Governor Phil Bredesen was able to gain the endorsement on the application from all the gubernatorial candidates. To ensure institutional commitment, the two states set up administrative offices to oversee program implementation. Tennessee opened an "achievement school district" office and Delaware set up a project management division to monitor the implementation of the reform initiatives. Finally, the two states showed their support for expanding innovation. Tennessee recently passed legislation that increased the number of charter schools and broadened student eligibility in school choice. In short, the Race to the Top competition seemed to have leveraged significant efforts to redesign the state education policy system.

Finally, the Obama administration invites state applications for waivers in meeting the original NCLB goals of attaining 100 percent student proficiency by 2014. In the first cycle of application in November 2011, 11 states formally sought alternative ways to implement their accountability systems in exchange for fulfilling a new set of federal assurances. By early August 2012, 33 states and the District of Columbia received federal approval on their NCLB waivers. For example, the new Nevada system of accountability, which received federal approval in August 2012, plans to use student achievement growth and other measures to differentiate schools that are in need of particular support and intervention. Nevada's state superintendent of public instruction touted the significance of the waiver approval: "This next generation accountability system is a central lever in statewide efforts to substantially elevate student performance. This system was built through robust collaboration with key partners, together with whom we will re-engineer Nevada's educational system to realize true college and career readiness for all students" (Whaley, 2012). Indeed, an analysis of the waiver applications suggests that these states tend to adopt common core standards, use multiple indicators to measure annual student progress, use differentiated actions to intervene in low performance, and stay away from using school choice or supplemental education services as a key strategy to raise student performance (Riddle, 2011).

COMPETING IDEAS ON THE FEDERAL PRIORITIES

As NCLB passed the ten-year mark, student performance remained uneven across districts and states. According to a six-year trend study conducted by the Center for Education Policy, schools that failed their state-specified AYP standards jumped from 29 percent to 48 percent of all the schools in the nation between 2006 and 2011 (Usher, 2011). In this context, it is not surprising that the Obama blueprint on reauthorizing ESEA is viewed critically by political leaders and a wide range of stake-holding organizations. This section will use a few examples to illustrate the scope of competing ideas on the future of federal involvement in K-12 education.

Market-based Perspective: The Koret Task Force. In a critical reassessment of the federal role, the Hoover Institution's Koret Task Force proposed to prioritize federal resources on four functions. These functions are informed by a synthesis of two understandings on social and institutional behaviors, namely fiscal federalism that considers the dynamics of competition of governmental services at the local level and individuals' strong preference for choice. The functions include (1) knowledge creation with a focus on what works research. Compared to the 40 percent spent on research in health and human services, the Education Department allocated merely 1 percent for this purpose. The other functions include (2) enforcing civil rights; (3) providing financial support for high-need students; and (4) actively promoting competition among service providers, mainly though charter schools and choice programs.

The Koret Task Force offered some details on how the federal government should enable states to endorse school choice system-wide. Federal Title I and IDEA categorical funding will be turned into "backpack funding" so children can move with their federal funds to their chosen charter schools. Participating charter schools would be required to meet the state requirements on data collection. In prioritizing the support for charter schools and choice programs, the Koret Task Force recommended the elimination of several highly visible federal programs, including Head Start, curriculum development, and the Teacher Incentive Fund or the Teacher and Leader Innovation Fund, among others.

To be sure, the federal government has been supporting charter schools since the Clinton presidency. The Obama administration has not slowed down federal funding for charter start-ups. What is different about the Koret proposal is its scale. The proposal aims at replacing the federal accountability system, as articulated in NCLB, with a state-wide choice-based competitive system. From this perspective, the choice architecture that relies on competition constitutes a stronger accountability system. Low-performing charter schools, for example, would be eliminated by parental exits. At the same time, choice-based accountability does not necessarily eliminate the need for a top-down monitoring and sanctioning system to meet the quality assurance standards.

State Interest and Civil Rights Concerns. In early 2012, a coalition of key state and local governmental groups submitted to Congress its collective view on the reauthorization of ESEA. These groups included the National Governors Association, the National Conference of State Legislatures, Council of State Governments, National Association of Counties, and National School Boards Association. The coalition emphasized the importance of federal-state-local partnership in implementing school reforms. To ensure local and state commitment, the coalition urged Congress to remove "those restrictive and unnecessary federal policies that limit innovation" (NCSL, 2011). The current regulatory federal role was seen as hindering state and local leadership to promote their own school reforms.

Given their concerns on federal regulations, state and local governmental organizations sought greater flexibility in using federal funds to meet their specific academic needs. For example, the coalition viewed the federal threshold for maintenance of effort as "not realistic" in the current fiscal environment. The proposal pointed out that the maintenance of efforts requirements "could severely curtail state and local authorities' ability to control the use of their own state and local tax funds" (NCSL, 2011). Seeing this requirement as a symptom of federal regulatory excessiveness, the coalition called for a major overhaul on all the federal "paperwork requirements" and the federal "waiver process." A reduction in federal regulation was seen as a necessary condition to sustain state and local reform.

While state and local governments looked for greater flexibility, civil rights groups saw the need for federal direction to prevent public education from returning "to an earlier time when states could choose to ignore disparities for children of color, low-income students, ELLs, and students with disabilities" (The Education Trust, 2012). On January 24, 2012, 38 civil rights, disability, business, and education organizations submitted a joint statement to the U.S. House Committee on Education and the Workforce, opposing the draft ESEA reauthorization legislation known as the Student Success Act. Unlike the proposed legislation, the civil rights groups were strongly in favor of federal requirements on performance accountability of groups of students, such as racial and income groups. Using these performance disparity data, federal funds would support efforts to close the achievement gap.

Overall, the civil rights coalition saw "safeguarding equal educational opportunity" as a primary federal responsibility. From this perspective, the federal redistributive role was seen as a higher priority than balancing the power dynamics in the federal-state partnership. In an April 2011 joint statement, the civil rights leaders explicitly stated that "ESEA is a civil rights law" (NAACP, 2011). Civil rights leaders faulted NCLB for not providing the "mechanism to address the continued racial and ethnic isolation of students and the dramatic increase of, and disparities in, counter-productive school discipline practices." Likewise, civil rights supporters were concerned that federal accountability to protect the disadvantaged would be undermined by competitive grants, such as Race to the Top. Consequently, civil rights leaders recommended the federal government guide "targeted, tailored intervention options" for school improvement. For example, federal interventions were seen as necessary to address dozens of high schools that persistently maintained a very low graduation rate, often referred to as "dropout factories." Equally important was their proposal to eliminate systemic barriers to student success, including teacher preparation and data transparency.

Education Concerns as National Security Threat. An effort to approach K-12 reform from the perspective of collective interest came from the Council on Foreign Relations' Independent Task Force on K-12 education. This task force tried to frame the education challenges from a national security perspective. Whether such a frame will lessen partisan disagreements and form the basis for a new common commitment remains to be seen.

In March 2012, the Council on Foreign Relations Independent Task Force issued its report on the future of K-12 education, entitled "U.S. Education Reform and National Security." The task force was co-chaired by Joel Klein, former chancellor of New York City Schools, and Condoleezza Rice, U.S. secretary of state during the Bush administration. The report opened with the sobering warning that "a weak education system" threatens national security. The framing is reminiscent of the 1983 report *A Nation at Risk* (see Wong & Guthrie, 2004).

The American workforce is seen as inadequately prepared to ensure U.S. security in an increasingly complex global political economy. The report stated the importance of all students developing "a strong academic foundation in literacy and numeracy, as well as a sense of global awareness and a strong understanding of their nation's democratic values and practices." These foundational skills constitute the necessary building blocks for the nation to make continuing progress in technology, diplomacy, economic growth, and military readiness (p. 14). Consequently, the task force makes three major recommendations. First, the task force called for an expansion of the Common Core State Standards to include teaching and assessment of skills that pertain to the long-term security of the nation. Among these critical skills are science, technology, foreign languages, civic awareness, and problem solving (pp. 44–45). Second, the report supports school choice for high-need students who attend failing schools. Students who exercise the choice option will be given "equitable" resource support. Third, a "national security readiness audit," coordinated nationally, will be implemented to engage the public and to hold school and public officials accountable for meeting the academic standards.

Particularly interesting is the recommendation for a "national security readiness audit." The challenge is in its implementation. If these audits are not part of the "high-stakes" accountability system, school leaders and teachers are less likely to pay attention to them. To ensure public attention, proponents of the recommendations from the Council on Foreign Relations need to work with the education policy community and Congress to make sure that the task force's recommendations become part of the reauthorization bill.

CAN THE FEDERAL GOVERNMENT ADDRESS BOTH EQUITY AND ACCOUNTABILITY?

The implementation experience on NCLB during the Bush and the Obama administrations, as well as various competing ideas, form a useful basis for rethinking the role of federal government in K-12 education. Despite recommendations by some members of Congress to eliminate the Department of Education, federal involvement in K-12 is not likely to be phased out entirely. The key challenge lies in improving policy coherence in the intergovernmental system. This concluding section proposes several ways to sharpen the federal role that align accountability and equity.

First, the federal goal on accountability can be effectively promoted with a focus on equity. In our federal system, the federal government is uniquely positioned to address equity issues. As the fiscal federalism literature shows, competition for economic growth at the local and state levels tends to constrain their focus on redistribution. There has been bipartisan support for high-need students. About 60 percent of the federal K-12 dollars were allocated for redistributive purpose during a period when partisan control has shifted in both the executive and the legislative branches. This bipartisan agreement on the redistributive role of the federal government is not likely to be significantly diminished in the near future.

Given federal commitment to redistributive needs, how can the accountability agenda be strengthened? To align accountability with equity, the federal government needs critically to reassess categorical federalism, where outdated funding arrangements are constraining local and state action to find new ways to improve student achievement. Greater regulatory flexibility and other incentives that combine with clear and transparent outcome measures will allow for a more differentiated approach to support school improvement. Higher-performing schools and districts must be given more autonomy from federal and state regulations. Schools that are in the middle can benefit from specific support strategies. Persistently low-performing schools need to be restructured, closed, or restarted as charter schools. In this regard, instead of launching charter systems across the nation, as proposed by the market-based reformers, it may be more appropriate to make available the charter system option to persistently low-performing districts. The Recovery School District in New Orleans, and similar quasi-state agencies in other states, seem to provide promising examples for pursuing the choice approach.

Further, presidential leadership can improve policy coherence on issues that affect education and children. Considering education policies in other advanced industrialized democracies, the United States may consider a more holistic approach that pertains from *cradle to workforce*. On economic policy, the president receives expert advice from the Council of Economic Advisors. In education and affairs related to children and youth adults, policy coherence is impeded by institutional fragmentation. Currently, federal appropriations in key education and related services are managed by more than a dozen federal agencies. In addition to the Department of Education, these agencies include Agriculture, Defense, Health and Human Services, Homeland Security, Interior, Justice, Labor, Veteran Affairs, Appalachian Regional Commission, National Endowment for the Arts, National Endowment for the Humanities, and National Science Foundation. To coordinate policy across agencies, the White House can establish a Council on Education and Children's Affairs to provide timely policy advice and facilitate timely decisions. The council can enhance federal priorities and mobilize civic support.

A "cradle to workforce" approach may be necessary to improve strategic coordination in an increasingly resource-constrained policy environment. Strong coordination to support the development of the human capita pipeline has gained political support at the state level. For example, in Oregon, the governor-appointed education secretary replaced the elected school superintendent's office with an education investment board overseeing the education domain. In Rhode Island, the legislature in 2012 approved the consolidation of the K-12 board and the higher education board into a single governing board.

Finally, school reform will benefit from federal investment to promote long-term research on major educational challenges. In this regard, a functional division of research support may be considered. Given their primary responsibility over education, states have the incentives to fund program evaluation and technical assistance. Findings from these projects can be used promptly to improve strategies to raise school and student performance. An example is school leadership development initiatives. Because states, districts, and schools benefit directly from more effective school leaders, they are ready to use their own resources to support this type of research and development. They can also use firsthand information to make policy adjustment and reprioritize their resources.

In contrast, federal investment is needed in long-term research in which findings can be generalized to guide policy changes across states and districts. First, this federal role includes an investment in data infrastructure that is reliable and sustainable, including the creation and maintenance of longitudinal student and teacher data systems across the 50 states. Second, the federal government needs to address issues at scale, especially those that are consistent with social justice and national security that go beyond a particular region of the country. For example, federal research is needed to track graduation experience and postsecondary and workforce outcomes of minority and low-income students who have been exposed to certain reform initiatives. Another example is the effectiveness of charter schools in inner-city neighborhoods through an experimental design that controls for student self-selection. Yet another example is school turnaround initiatives in large cities and rural communities on student learning over several years. Third, federal investment in long-term research can stimulate matching funds from states and private foundations. Federal impact on research activities is enhanced when nonfederal sources are leveraged. In short, the federal agenda on equity and accountability can forge new public-private partnership in research and development activities.

In the long term, the critical challenges lie in the commitment of our intergovernmental system fully to address income and racial/ethnic disparity, particularly in urban and isolated rural communities. Toward this end, a functional, federally funded policy system will continue to play an instrumental role in mediating the tension between decentralized governance and social redistribution.

REFERENCES

Betts, Julian (2007). California: Does the Golden State deserve a gold star? In F. M. Hess & C. E. Finn Jr. (Eds.), *No remedy left behind: Lessons from a half-decade of NCLB* (pp. 121–152). Washington, DC: American Enterprise Institute Press.

Brown, C., Hess, F. M., Lautzenheiser, D. K., & Owen, I. (2011). *State education agencies as agents of change.* Washington, DC: Center for American Progress.

Cohen, David, & Moffitt, Susan (2009). *The ordeal of equality.* Cambridge, MA: Harvard University Press.

Council on Foreign Relations (2012). *U.S. education reform and national security.* Washington, DC: Brookings Institution Press.

de Tocqueville, A. (2000). *Democracy in America.* (H. Mansfield & D. Winthrop, Trans., Ed.). Chicago, IL: University of Chicago Press.

Hamilton, A., Madison, J., & Jay, J. (1961). *The Federalist papers.* New York: Mentor Press.

Hess, Frederick, & Finn, Chester Jr. (Eds.). (2007) *No remedy left behind.* Washington, DC: American Enterprise Institute Press.

Hess, Frederick, & Petrilli, Michael (2006). *No Child Left Behind primer.* New York: Peter Lang Publishing.

Kim, James, & Sunderman, Gail (2005). Measuring academic proficiency under No Child Left Behind: Implications for educational equity. *Educational Researcher, 34*(8), 3–13.

Klein, Alyson (2011). Turnaround-Program data seen as promising though preliminary. *Education Week,* January 11. Retrieved from www.edweek.org/ew/articles/2011/01/12/15turnaround-2.h30.html?qs=school+ turnaround.

Manna, Paul (2006). *School's in: Federalism and the national education agenda.* Washington, DC: Georgetown University Press.

Manna, Paul (2010). *Collision course.* Washington, DC: Congressional Quarterly Press.

McGuinn, Patrick (2006). *No Child Left Behind and the transformation of federal education policy, 1965–2005.* Lawrence: University Press of Kansas.

Murphy, J. (1971). Title I of ESEA: The politics of implementing federal education reform. *Harvard Educational Review, 41*(1), 36–63.

NAACP Legal Defense and Educational Fund, Inc. (2011). *Accountability principles for ESEA reauthorization: A joint statement of civil rights leaders.* Washington, DC: NAACP Legal Defense and Educational Fund, Inc.

National Conference of State Legislatures (NCSL) (2011). *State & local governance coalition letter to Congress calling on reauthorization of the Elementary and Secondary Education Act.* Denver and Washington, DC: NCSL.

Orfield, G. (1969). *The reconstruction of Southern education: The schools and the 1964 Civil Rights Act.* New York: Wiley.

Peterson, P. E., Rabe, B. G., & Wong, K. K. (1986). *When federalism works.* Washington, DC: Brookings Institution Press.

Peterson, P. E., Rabe, B. G., & Wong, K. K. (1988). The evolution of the compensatory education program. In D. P. Doyle & B. S. Cooper (Eds.), *Federal aid to the disadvantaged: What future for Chapter 1?* (pp. 33–60). Philadelphia, PA: Falmer Press.

Riddle, Wayne (2011). *Major accountability themes of initial state applications for NCLB waivers.* Washington, DC: Center for Education Policy.

Shelly, Bryan (2011). *Money, mandates, and local control in American public education.* Ann Arbor: University of Michigan Press.

Sundquist, J. (1968). *Politics and policy.* Washington, DC: Brookings Institution Press.

The Education Trust (2012). *Letter to the Honorable John Kline: Undersigned by 38 Organizations.* Washington, DC: The Education Trust.

U.S. Department of Education (2010). *A blueprint for reform: The reauthorization of the Elementary and Secondary Education Act.* Washington, DC: USDOE.

U.S. Department of Education (2012). *Reauthorization of the Elementary and Secondary Education Act: Administration's 2012 Budget Request.* Washington, DC: USDOE.

Usher, Alexandra (2011). *AYP Results for 2010–11.* Washington, DC: Center for Education Policy.

Whaley, Sean (2012, August 8). Feds approve Nevada waiver from No Child Left Behind. *The Record Courier.* Retrieved from www.recordcourier.com/article/20120808/NEWS/120809916/1062&ParentProfile=1049.

Wong, K. K. (1999). *Funding public schools: Politics and policy.* Lawrence: University Press of Kansas.

Wong, Kenneth, & Guthrie, James (Eds.). (2004). A 20-year reappraisal of A Nation At Risk. *Peabody Journal of Education.*

Wong, Kenneth, & Nicotera, Anna (2007). *Successful schools and educational accountability,* Boston, MA: Pearson Education.

Wong, Kenneth, & Sunderman, Gail (2007). Education accountability as a presidential priority: No Child Left Behind and the Bush presidency. *Publius, 37,* 333–350.

Part II

Interest Groups, Activists, Entrepreneurs, and
Education Reform

10

BINDERS OF WOMEN AND THE BLINDERS OF MEN

Feminism and the Politics of Education

Catherine Marshall, Lois Andre-Bechely, and Brooke Midkiff

Feminism and education politics highlight hot-button controversies like single-sex schooling; school violence; bullying and sexual harassment; and simmering issues of women in superintendencies; women educators' health plans including birth control; and universities violating Title IX. But these are the surface of deeper questions of equity, representation, and curricular priorities. Societal and economic shifts leave schools to teach and embrace the whole child, with frayed safety nets allowing many children to slip through the cracks. Mothers, still the primary caregivers in this country, and women, still the primary educators, are feeling less supported, and even attacked, by the governments that they were taught to trust.

News headlines continue to force public discussion of personal, private, and silenced issues, bullying and sexual harassment in the lives of women but also of boys and men: for example, the long-time cover-ups of sexual abuse by Catholic priests and Boy Scout troop leaders and the Penn State football coach. The nation grieved, and remarked on inadequacies of family and mental health supports after the slaughter of six-year-old boys and girls at Sandy Hook Elementary School. Clearly, these recent events are quandaries for women and for men as they see that our daughters and sons are at risk in an educational system that continues to perform poorly on addressing social injustices. So the politics of education needs to embrace a new theoretical construct, a new way of unpacking how it is that our schools come to be as they are, and how they often, systematically, disadvantage girls and women—who become future workers, mothers, and educators.

In this chapter we demonstrate the ways feminist theory can help uncover and address educational problems that affect us all. We examine the role that women play in various political arenas, and how that is situated within a postfeminist era as women struggle against a wave of backlash against women's struggle for equality. We raise questions about whether there's a war against women, about men in power being blind to women's realities, why some women appear to comply with institutional and political realities that continue to limit their choices, whether grassroots activism and the activism of women's groups hold potential for altering dominant agenda setting. Importantly, we show how feminist insights offer alternative policy directions. Former Massachusetts Governor Mitt Romney's approach, keeping "binders full of women" he could tap for state positions, doesn't solve deeper gender issues. When talented and accomplished women are only names in binders, their potential for alternative framing of politics and priorities goes to waste.

We begin with a vignette to illuminate women's realities. Sofia's story, while fictitious, will serve, throughout this chapter, to help ground discussion of the gains and losses in women's struggle for equality, to show how gender, power, and politics operate in educational arenas, and to search for new directions using feminist insights.[1]

Sofia's Realities

When last we saw her, Sofia had completed high school, despite becoming a single mother at age 17. At age 26, she was taking community college classes toward her lifelong dream to be a teacher. Since the bilingual program at her daughter's school was cut, Sofia has been teaching her daughter, Lily, Spanish at home in her spare time.

But today, she was fuming from an argument with her father. He kept telling her try harder, take more community college classes, "seas como una dulce abeja" (be as sweet as a honeybee) so she will get a good husband. But she'd done all of that. She was still in her $15/hour job as a teacher's aide and courses cut at the community college were ones she needed to transfer to the local state college to get her BA and teaching certification. And here she was, listening to the teachers where she worked, griping about how the governor was attacking their union and about how firefighters got respect but not teachers. The flare-up in the teachers' lounge made her wonder whether the issues they were debating were really anti-women, not anti-teachers. In the lounge, Cecile, an idealistic young teacher, was ranting, trying to rally protests, petitions, and marches against the city council eliminating birth control and abortions from city workers' health plans (although Trudy, the union rep, and other teachers told her to calm down if she wanted to keep her job).

Later, when Sofia went to pick up Lily from school, the principal dropped the news that they needed "more parental involvement" and help with copying and materials because of the cutbacks in funding. She asked herself what the hell had happened to the supports and resources she thought she would have for herself and her daughter. Sofia tried to figure out whether there was any way to turn these setbacks around. Trudy thought they'd get changed by using the vote and getting more politicians who showed loyalty to the interests of women, children, and educators. Cecile said petitions and protests were more effective. Who could afford to take time off for protest marches? And why would her father think a husband would be the answer?

Sadly, Sofia's scenario remains an area of silence, the opportunities not made available to Sofia, a problem that is not named (Fine, 1992). This chapter wonders, along with Sofia, whether women's needs and realities will be addressed in the structures of our education and political systems.

TEMPERATURE CHECK: WOMEN'S STATUS
IN PUBLIC ARENAS

The Intersection of Gender, Politics, and Power in Educational Arenas

Histories of education teach us that early systems of public education were established by men, mostly for boys (Spring, 2006; Tyack, 1974; Tyack & Cuban, 1995). Women assumed household roles constructed around a gendered division of labor with child raising and nurturance as home-based work (Biklen, 1995; Cutler, 2000; Griffith & Smith, 2005).

Women in Teaching

When public schooling began in the mid-19th century, women were recruited into the teaching force as the guardians of morality, bringing their habits of neatness, order, and thrift to the expanding profession (Spring, 2006). Teachers' contracts suggested they not be seen in public with men, and female teachers were paid less than male teachers. Patriarchy was the foundation for the politics, policies, and goals of schooling, underwriting the long-observed practice of privilege for males and keeping females attuned to domestic life.

By the late 19th and early 20th centuries, teachers were ready to form their own unions. The National Education Association (NEA) was chartered in 1857 as a national policy-making organization, born with huge controversies conflating curriculum policies and the administrator-teacher, male-female divides. The American Federation of Teachers (AFT), established in Chicago in 1897, was more workers' rights oriented, and took up as its first struggle adequate pensions for female grade school teachers (Spring, 2006). The teachers' unions had to address the economic needs of teachers, especially when women (mostly primary school teachers) were paid sometimes half of what male (mostly secondary teachers) earned. The NEA was especially active in the pursuit of a single-salary scale and in the defense of married women teachers (Urban, 2001).

Union political activism for specifically feminist issues has focused more on maternity leaves and pensions than on nonsexist curriculum, gay, lesbian, bisexual, transgendered, and queer (GLBTQ) rights, abortion, or the Equal Rights Amendment (C. Marshall, 2002). Still, with almost twice as many female as male members, the NEA has exhibited the most evidence of action-oriented recommendations on issues such as litigation for women's rights, providing training to eliminate sex stereotyping, building coalitions with minority women, lobbying for strong enforcement of Title IX, and creating information systems on women's employment status (Krenkel, 1975). Bascia (1998) reminds us that "union affiliation . . . could help alleviate some of the gaps, blind spots, and omissions inherent to women's subordinate positions in the educational system" (p. 561). While teachers' unions were once a powerful voice in American politics, the start of the 21st century has brought the dismantling of this source of protection for women. What happens to "teachers" is what happens to women. When the federal No Child Left Behind Act (NCLB) (2002) and subsequent government accountability and evaluation policies target teachers' performance, these laws target women primarily. Teacher politics has not been very effective at curbing the intensity of accountability and assessment mandates that focus blame on teachers for students' low performance. Therefore, the demise of teachers' unions' power is a blow to women, particularly as they have less protection within a patriarchal profession where teachers are mostly women and administrative positions continue to be disproportionately filled by men (Marshall & Young, 2013).

Women in School Administration

The construction of educational administration as a "masculinist" enterprise (Blackmore, 1993) is a classic illustration of the dynamics of power and knowledge. Within professional educational cultures, definitions of the attributes, norms, methods of accessing, and dominant modes of language and knowledges that constitute the "good administrator" have allowed men—and the women who will accept male values, life choices, and behaviors—to be seen as viable leaders legitimized to make policy for education (Blount, 1998; McFadden, 2004; Tyack & Hansot, 1988). The research on women in school leadership confirms that these "male traits" are a current issue, not just history. The high school principalship is viewed as a masculine role (Pounder & Merrill, 2001). Leadership career systems were constructed for traditional married males who had full-time domestic support freeing them from family responsibilities. The time demands of principalships force educators, especially women, to choose between family and careers in leadership (Mahitivanichcha & Rorrer, 2006).

In the micropolitics of middle and elementary schools, gender and power dynamics propel men (but not women) into leadership careers, with public sentiment preferring "strong" male leaders. This is unfortunate because many women school superintendents and school board members exhibit more inclusive, facilitative leadership, emphasizing "power-with" more than "power-over" styles (Brunner, 1997; Mountford & Brunner, 2010). Men are seen as good role models in schools where so many of the teachers are female (Lee, Smith, & Cioci, 1993). In their male-dominated position, women leaders often deny or remain silent about gender bias, any sense of being different, and their own ambition and desire for power (Chase, 1995; Dobie & Hummel, 2001; Marshall, 1993). Tallerico (2000), Brunner (1999), and Grogan (1996) have each documented in their work on the superintendency poignant experiences of countless female administrators feeling excluded and denigrated, watching their male colleagues getting credit for less effort than theirs.

Women's choices, given this hegemonic masculinity, are: (1) avoidance; (2) emphasized femininity; and (3) strategic combinations of compliance, resistance, and cooperation (Connell, 1987). Each trait requires expenditures of energy in everyday social contestations, adapting within the gender dynamics so that gender issues, usually, are pushed under the rug. The professional whose enactment of gender roles veers even slightly from the norm is at risk micropolitically. Their status and power are easily undermined with a mere glance or an off-hand remark. This hidden curriculum message is accentuated for GLBTQ educators when administrator associations shy away from GLBTQ issues (Marshall & Ward, 2004). Educators learn that activism for feminist and GLBTQ causes can jeopardize their career mobility (Fraynd & Capper, 2003; Harbeck, 1997; Jones, 2005; Legrand, 2005; Lugg, 2003a, 2003b).

As women do gain power positions, they pass through gatekeepers who are predominantly male. Gatekeepers' and foundations' assumptions and actions assume that access to leadership is gender neutral and all about individual achievement (Chase, 1995; Chase & Bell, 1990; Grogan, 2000; Marshall & Young, 2013). Such masculinist practices can only serve to limit the likelihood and ability of women superintendents proffering alternative modes of leadership and expanded or reframed agendas for school policies. Professions such as law, education, and management enact a cultural process of masculinization, and "indeed, to be (or to aspire to be) a professional is 'to do' gender [in a way that complies] with behavioral and interactional norms that celebrate and sustain a masculine vision of what it is to be a professional" (Bolton & Muzio, 2008).

The percentage of female superintendents has increased substantially, rising from approximately 13 percent in 2000 to 24 percent in 2010 (Kowalski et al., 2011). Given the labor pool, that 75 percent of all teachers are women (National Center for Education Statistics, 2012), one would expect a corresponding percentage of women to move up the career ladder into principalships and superintendencies. Yet only 29 percent of secondary principals are female. Typically the path to superintendent goes through secondary principalship, not elementary principalships (Mahitivanichcha & Rorrer, 2006). Even though women's representation in graduate programs in educational leadership has increased significantly, the number of women, particularly women of color, who are employed as secondary principals and superintendents is disproportionate to the number certified to hold these positions (Hodgkinson & Montenegro, 1999; Shakeshaft, 1998).

Similarly, the number of women in higher education who hold administrative positions is not representative of the number of women in academia.[2] This disproportionality between the number of women in the professional workforce and the number of women in upper leadership positions is found across many arenas beyond education such as law, business, and academia where women make up at least half or more of the workforce but only occupy 14 percent to 17 percent of the top leadership positions (Mahitivanichcha & Rorrer, 2006).

Additionally, even as more women have entered into the uppermost position in K-12 education, many superintendents are exiting the system. The American Association of School Administrators reports that only about half of superintendents surveyed in 2010 indicated that they planned to still be a superintendent in five years, suggesting that a large turnover is in store (Kowalski et al., 2011). In big city school districts, women who have worked their way up through school and central office administrative positions, with hopes of becoming superintendents, may not be the ones to land those jobs. Outside organizations are investing in leadership programs based on business executive training to develop superintendents to lead urban public schools. One such organization, the Broad Superintendents Academy, admits business executives and military leaders in addition to people with backgrounds in education with the goal that graduates will go on to become superintendents (Marshall & Young, 2013).

Women on School Boards

In the mid-19th century a few states and localities allowed women to vote in school board elections, even before women's suffrage (Flexner, 1975). This activity was seen as an appropriate political role for women because it was tied to mothers' work. Once women began serving on school boards, political scientists explored gender issues, finding differences not only in women's role orientations but also discovering that their feminine role predispositions faded with active participation. Bers (1978) found that for Illinois school boards, women were drawn to these positions because they were nonpartisan and did not require huge time expenditures or travel. School boards historically have been more open to women's involvement, and the number of women serving on school boards is increasing. The National School Boards Association reports that approximately 56 percent of board members are male, and 44 percent female (Hess & Meeks, 2010).[3]

However, Donahue (1999) found that the women elected to the local school boards were less likely to represent the interests of their own gender. She found that, given the logistics (difficulty) of getting to local meetings, feminist interest groups are generally not present at board meetings, so school policy makers are not regularly faced with organized advocacy and monitoring of their actions in regards to gender issues. Separate studies found that a higher percentage of female school board members is associated with increased favor for programs such as sex education and bilingual education, indicating that female politicians are more likely than their male colleagues to favor programs addressing social justice (Cook & Wilcox, 2009; Hess & Leal, 1999; Klein, 1984; Mueller, 1988).

Local and state school boards could address equity and gender issues. For example, the practice of tracking creates inequity and unequal educational opportunities for poor and underserved minority students. Datnow (1998) captured how gender politics among teachers can impede de-tracking efforts aimed at more equitable opportunities for students. Gender issues—for example, Latina girls discouraged from applying to universities by well-intentioned but misinformed and overloaded high school counselors (most of whom are women)—shape and determine the educational opportunities to which women and girls like Sofia and her daughter have access. School boards' focusing on gender, or reframing policy with the needs and voices of women and girls highlighted, seems unlikely. By their very nature, school boards must respond to local values and culture. Board members' politics, and the outcomes of their decisions, are more visible in local communities, a reason to avoid, ignore, or dismiss the most challenging gender issues. Moreover, state and federal legislation has all educators bound to an accountability-focused political context in which they must prove their professional worth; gender issues stand little chance of being addressed.

Seeing Gender and Power Dynamics in Education Policies

Throughout U.S. history, most education policy for educator employment, the structure of schools, and curriculum were constructed with no or only minimal discussion of gender. Controversies around gender issues were there, but were often played out as if everything were gender neutral, as if gender policies did not disadvantage females (Tyack & Hansot, 1988). For example, 19th-century traditionalists wanted sharp boundaries between the sexes and worried that mixed-sex schooling would masculinize girls. Later, when Ella Flagg Young pressured Dewey's progressives to encompass power and gender dynamics in curriculum reform (Maher, 1999), the feminist challenge, promoting different values and women having power, was quashed. The progressive era's concerns over the feminization of schooling, over educated girls eschewing marriage for careers, and over boys dropping out, were resolved without feminist critique. The "answers" came from reframing schooling to be more technical, and implementing work-oriented curriculum tracking, embedding substantial public funding in budgets for varsity sports as attractions for boys, and promoting the GI Bill, which catapulted many men into college and then into public-sector careers, including education.

Not until the feminist movement of the 1960s and 1970s did gender reach explicit and formal policy agendas. Gender equity activists and scholars pointed out overt educational barriers such as sex differences in course enrollments and subtle barriers such as sex stereotyping by school counselors.

In 1972, as part of the Elementary and Secondary Education Act (ESEA), Congress added Title IX, prohibiting sex discrimination in scholarships, housing, facilities, and access to courses, and in athletics, admissions, recruitment, wages, and financial assistance. Also in ESEA, the Women's Educational Equity Act Program (WEEA) was passed in 1974 to fund development of curriculum materials, evaluation, preservice and in-service training for teachers, and generally to promote women's equal educational opportunity. However, resources for WEEA have been below $3 million per year since 2003, with low resources steadily rendering WEEA essentially rhetorical only (Funding Status—Women's Educational Equity, 2011).

Title IX: The Jolt from Above

The passage of Title IX came as a surprise in this historically embedded patriarchal structure in employment, leadership, and curriculum. It came from above, in federal legislation, as a logical extension of civil rights activism and feminist groups' demands to end sex stereotyping and unequal access and outcomes for girls.

Title IX was groundbreaking as the first federal policy for gender equity—a mandate requiring schools to create equitable practices. The WEEA was capacity-building legislation to provide federal funds for implementing gender equity. However, long-embedded patriarchal assumptions constituted a gender regime that, to a large extent, has resisted this jolt to the system, as we will show.

Vocational education eventually addressed gender issues in the Carl Perkins Vocational Education Act (in 1984, then reauthorized in 2006), supporting school counseling that eliminates sex biases in vocational and technical education.

Reauthorization, adequate staffing, and funding for these provisions have always been a difficult political struggle for feminists and advocacy coalitions. Stromquist (1997) delineates among "gender sensitive policies" those that are: (1) coercive, meant to eliminate discrimination with punishments such as withdrawal of contracts and fines; (2) supportive, intended to fund and monitor institutions' gender equity work; and (3) constructive, designed to create new behaviors and knowledge with curriculum changes, educator retraining, and research. Title IX, and the other policies like those listed earlier, incorporate aspects of each of these elements in an effort to equalize educational opportunities.

The passage, implementation, evaluation, and reformulation of gender policies are understudied and are continuously contentious. For example, few have studied the cultural forces protecting traditions of male sports programs against implementation of Title IX played out in the *Grove City v. Bell* decision that protected universities from any forceful penalties for non-implementation of sex equity. Few have studied incidents like when a coach, protesting that his girls' basketball team got less money than the boys' team, was fired in retaliation. Importantly, the National School Boards Association fought his lawsuit for equity for girls' athletics (Henderson, 2004)!

Women's Outcomes: Education and Employment

One need only watch female Olympians to see the most obvious accomplishments of gender politics and policy. Statistics on girls and women demonstrate progress in the United States in that over the past 40 years of Title IX, women (ages 25–64 in the labor force) have seen significant increases in educational attainment. While in 1970, only 11 percent of women held college degrees, in 2010, 36 percent of women held college degrees (Bureau of Labor Statistics, 2011a). In fact, differences in educational attainment have altered so much over the past few decades that female attainment is now greater than male attainment at each education level (National Center for Education Statistics, 2012). Additionally, the number of female athletes has risen proportionally from 2004–2010 by a "14 percentage point increase in the proportion of female student athletes in Division I, a 21 percentage point increase for women in Division II, and a 14 percentage point increase for women in Division III" (Bracken & Irick, 2012). Additionally, the overall proportion of bachelor's degrees in science, technology, engineering, and mathematics (STEM) awarded to women has increased dramatically over the past four decades, primarily in biology (Hill & American Association of University Women, 2010).[4]

However, these accomplishments are not reflected in career outcomes. For example, though women increasingly complete college, their subsequent employment outcomes still do not match those of men. One year after graduating, men were more likely than women to be working full time and "even when controlling for undergraduate field of study, men earned higher average annual salaries than women in at least one-half of the fields examined" (Peter & Horn, 2005). The Riley report acknowledges that women's unequal pay, sexual harassment, sports scholarships, and gender bias are continuing challenges. The American Association of University Women (AAUW) Foundation in *How Schools Shortchange Girls* (1995) and *Gender Gaps: Where Schools Still Fail Our Children* (1999) documented some progress toward equitable treatment for boys and girls and identified remaining concerns. *Gender Gaps* (1999) highlighted intra-gender issues and included special issues surrounding Hispanic girls' leaving school. It also probes the paradox of girls underperforming on standardized tests, especially on the advanced and highly selective tests used for scholarships and advanced placement in math and sciences.

Following up on gender disparities in schools, the AAUW's report *Why So Few? Women in Science, Technology, Engineering, and Mathematics* (2010) uncovered social and environmental barriers that block girls' and women's participation in these fields. Gender disparities follow college women into the workforce and the AAUW's *Graduating to a Pay Gap: The Earnings of Women and Men One Year after College Graduation* (2012) highlights the significance of women's higher college loan debt. A decade ago, the AAUW led efforts in researching sexual harassment in schools with its report, *Hostile Hallways: Bullying, Teasing and Sexual Harassment in School* (2001). Its newest report, *Crossing the Line: Sexual Harassment at School* (2011), continues to document the prevalence and negative impact sexual harassment has on students' education. The AAUW and other groups' commitment to research and advocacy for girls and women's equitable education serves to monitor law and policy and to pick up where governments fail to press gender issues.

Still, stereotyped vocational and cultural patterns persist; in 2009–2010, females earned the smallest percentages of bachelor's degrees relative to males in the fields of engineering and engineering technologies as well as computer and information sciences and support services (National Center for Education Statistics, 2012). Furthermore, women's representation in computer science has been declining for the past decade (Hill & American Association of University Women, 2010). The impact of disparate access comes to bear in the economic situation for women who are directed into traditionally female jobs. For example, the average weekly earnings of child care workers is $364, and for elementary and middle school teachers $891, compared to the average weekly earnings of computer programmers, which is $1,182, and computer software engineers, which is $1,311 (Bureau of Labor Statistics, 2011b). At the same time, boys' advantages do not propel them ahead in schooling: graduation rates at four-year institutions are higher for women students than men students, a trend that is unchanged in public and private nonprofit postsecondary institutions (National Center for Education Statistics, 2012).

Women in Public Arenas beyond Education

The women's movement of the '60s and '70s advocated for the election of more women to public office, arguing that our governments did not sufficiently represent women's experiences, perspectives, and concerns. As more women assumed roles as elected public officials, feminists hoped that in addition to representing women, more issues of interest to women would be addressed. However, increased representation by numbers did not always translate into an increase in substantive representation on the issues (Carroll, 2001). Today, women are a majority of the population and they are affected by most legislation. Women are engaged with commerce, transportation, the environment, and so forth. The disparity in women's representation in state legislatures and Congress has serious implications for how women's issues will be addressed by the state and national governments.

> "In 1989, there were two women in the Senate. By 1992, the 'Year of the Woman,' that number had grown to seven. Twenty years later, we're at 20. That means we are electing less than two-thirds of a woman a year. At this rate, it will take roughly 46 years to achieve equal representation in the Senate."

As long as women are unequally represented in government, they will not have equal access to the degrees of liberty men have long enjoyed. According to the latest U.S. Census data, 50.8 percent of the population is women. However, only 20 percent of representatives in the House and Senate are female, even after the record-breaking election of women in the 2012 election. The underrepresentation of women in elected positions is not only an indicator of a stall in the women's liberation movement, but it is also an artifice of a patriarchal society whose time has passed.

Women in State Governments

State education politics determines most testing, curriculum, facilities, and personnel policy and budgets, and more governors regularly dub themselves "the education governor" (Marshall, Mitchell, & Wirt, 1989). Therefore, any proposals to address gender issues will encounter state political systems and actors. For the 2013 legislative session, women made up 24.1 percent of state legislators nationwide, a number only slightly higher than the percentage of female members of Congress (Women in State Legislatures 2013, 2013).

Sanbonmatsu (2002) found that the incentive structure for women being recruited to state legislatures is different in the Republican and Democratic Parties; thus, to understand women running and holding such offices, one must disaggregate by political party. Carroll notes that women who are most likely to work on women's rights legislation in state legislatures are "Democrats, liberals, self-identified feminists, and African

American . . . [and that] women who are Republicans, moderates, and conservatives, non-feminists, and white are more likely to work on women's rights legislation than men who share their characteristics" (2001, p. 18). Sanbonmatsu and Dolan (2009) found that while all female candidates were affected by gender stereotype threats, Republican candidates were more likely to encounter it.

Women's groups and organizations can help connect women legislators to the concerns and problems that other women face (Carroll, 2001). Women who seek powerful political positions—and who recognize women's rights issues and are, indeed, empowered by affiliation with women's groups—can support women's insights for policy reframing and women's leadership. In her study of a local chapter of the National Women's Political Caucus, A. Marshall (2002) found that the caucus promoted women candidates in part on the basis of their community organization leadership. Women's community credentials (e.g., Parent Teacher Student Associations, rape crisis centers, legal aid societies, community protests, symphony fundraising) enhanced their candidacy, demonstrating the ways political agendas are expanded when women candidates can bring grassroots and women's issues to visibility. Carroll (2001) found that women legislators worked on women's rights issues more when they belonged to women's organizations outside of their role as an elected official. In fact, Reingold and Harrell (2009) conclude that while gender does strongly impact women's political involvement, it is female candidates within women's preferred party that more strongly impact women' political involvement.

Title IX: Revisited

Modeled after Title VI of the 1964 Civil Rights Act, discrimination with respect to sex was prohibited in federally assisted programs. The struggle has continued, though, for more than 40 years, as Title IX has little enforcement and WEEA was defunded in subsequent federal budgets. So implementation of Title IX only affected educators when activists parents or women's groups' lobbying, working with a few congressional allies, found ways to monitor, sue, assess, and promote sex equity.

Women in National Government

Who promotes gender and education issues at the national level? Currently, five of the nation's 50 governors are women, and women make up 17.4 percent of mayors of cities with more than 30,000 people (Center for American Women and Politics, 2013). Additionally, there are currently six women in cabinet-level positions in federal government, and three women on the U.S. Supreme Court (Center for American Women and Politics, 2013), including Justice Sonia Sotomayor, who is also the first Hispanic Supreme Court member. Hence, it could be argued that women have made progress in winning elections and obtaining positions in high-profile and national public office. Despite these significant gains, though, women are still disproportionately underrepresented in political office.

Because inequalities in the educational system have a resultant impact on women's empowerment and earnings, education became a target of the women's movement

(Gladstone, 2001) and its advocacy at the federal level. Exit polls from the 2012 elections indicate that women, more so than men, ranked education as very important (Center for American Women and Politics, 2013), although it is not a change in issues of concern to women. Gladstone (2001) chronicled the women's issues addressed in Congress from 1832 to 1998. Fifteen key pieces of federal legislation were identified by Gladstone, from the 92nd Congress through the 103rd Congress, which impacted women and girls, but none more so than Title IX of the Educational Amendments of 1972. The list of women's issues range from civil rights to child care and child support to housing and education, indicating that a wide range of educational legislation and programs on women's educational equity concerns, specifically, were considered in Congress over the years (Cross, 2004). Women's participation in Congress has been critical to advancing these kinds of issues. Dodson (2006) presented a collection of case studies that demonstrate women's presence not only reshapes the agenda, but also can slowly begin to regender the political institution itself.

The War on Women: A Black Swan?

The phrase "war on women" reentered the public domain during the election cycle of 2012. Originally coined by Susan Faludi (1992) to define a media-based backlash against the women's movement of the 1970s through the 1990s, the term resurfaced throughout the national and state elections of 2012 as the war on women became synonymous with Republican Party candidates' efforts to restrict reproductive rights through limits on abortion, such as mandatory ultrasounds, limits on birth control, and reduced funding for Planned Parenthood. The term expanded in American discourse to include issues such as rape, domestic violence, and equal pay. The Republican National Committee has repeatedly denied the existence of a war on women (Edwards, 2012). However, women within the party have questioned this position—for example, Republican Senator Lisa Murkowski publicly challenged the party to "go home and talk to your wife and your daughters" to verify whether there is a current war on women (Johnson, 2012).

In May 2012, only a third of women believed there was actually a large-scale effort to limit reproductive rights; less than half the women polled indicated that they had taken any action in response to any information they had heard or received regarding reproductive health (Kaiser Family Foundation, 2012). Based on public opinion at the time, whether there was a war on women in reality and whether women would mobilize against it seemed a moot point—certainly not a game changer in the state and national elections to be held later that year. These data and trends indicated the improbability of the women's issue being of critical import during the election. However, in hindsight, it appears as a Black Swan event in American politics and for the feminist movement.[5]

Up until November 7, 2012, by all indications, women voters were focused on the economy above all other issues, with no consensus on whether a war on women was even real. Then came November 8, 2012: Republican party handlers were seeing that women had, indeed, turned out to vote their interests and a Black Swan event had clearly occurred.

The war on women drew reactions from a number of women's groups and in fact, the group UniteWomen.org was founded specifically in response to the war on women (About Us: UniteWomen.org, 2012). Additionally, the renowned women's political group Emily's List compiled, published, and disseminated to its members a day-by-day calendar of Republican acts against women (The War on Women: Day by Day, 2012). The National Women's Law Center also rallied women voters around protecting reproductive rights (Why Women Should Vote: To Make Sure Women Can Make Their Own Reproductive Health Care Decisions, 2012).

Based on polling done in May, no one expected these efforts to make a substantial impact; however, as election results poured in, it became increasingly clear that women's votes were high impact. Women's votes were critical in the U.S. Senate races that determined majority control as well as in the presidential race (Center for American Women and Politics, 2013b). "In the two U.S. Senate races where Republican candidates made controversial comments about rape, women's votes played important roles in the victories of the Democratic candidates. In Indiana, a majority of women voted for Democrat Joe Donnelly, while a majority often cast ballots for Republican Richard Mourdock" (Center for American Women and Politics, 2013b). Similarly, in the presidential election, "Obama also won a majority of women's votes, with Romney winning a majority of men's, in critical battleground states such as Ohio, Florida, Virginia, Wisconsin, Iowa, Nevada, and New Hampshire" (Carroll, 2012).

Was the war on women real or was it constructed by the Democratic Party as a political tactic or by the media as simply a red herring? Nonetheless, the perceived war on women, thought to be low on the list of causal inputs for election results, turned out to be crucial in the 2012 election. Perhaps women as mothers, as teachers, as college students, and as feminists are amassing power. Or, perhaps, women have always found alternative modes of political activism to effect change within the political system.

WOMEN'S MOBILIZATION: TRADITIONAL POLITICS, TO GRASSROOTS, TO SOCIAL MEDIA

Women's Voices, Representation, Citizenship, and Democracy

The notion of the gender gap as a political phenomenon to be reckoned with in politics came after the 1980 presidential election when decidedly more men voted for Ronald Reagan than did women. Women's power, as a voting bloc, aided the victory of Barack Obama in the 2008 and 2012 presidential elections.

So is politics still a man's world? Yes, if males and females receive different cues about political engagement (other than voting). But political scientists have noted that even after accounting for gender differences in education and income, a significant difference emerges between women and men in political interest, efficacy, and information. Suggestions as to why this is so have been explored: women's lack of aggressiveness, taste for conflict, and access to resources like civics skills and money. Does this mean that women are not interested in power, voice, and political position? Burrell reminds us that:

> Women have utilized a host of political persuasion techniques. . . . They have formed social movements, grassroots organizations, and national associations. They have marched, protested, boycotted, lobbied, filed lawsuits, and run for political leadership positions. Women have been especially active in their local communities, leading organizations to make their communities safer places for their children and improving educational systems. (Burrell, 2004, pp. 162–163)

Burrell predicts that if the political process and policy-making center on issues of particular concern to women, they will provide enhanced and enriched organizational and political lives.

Feminist scholars point out the need to focus politics and policy making in education debate and research on how politics and schooling practices valorize male privilege, allow violence and harassment, and trivialize emotion, relationships, and caring. Early efforts to address the gender dynamics of schooling resulted in some progress; still, the gender regime in society plays out in schools and in educational bureaucracies.

Sofia sensed that her father was trying to understand that people in schools were not always able to keep bad things from happening. One day he told her about how the men in the barbershop were moaning about poor Penn State getting penalized just because of what happened in the shower and HE was the one saying "what about those young boys!" Sofia told him she too knew the pressure to keep quiet and just go along—to avoid being seen as someone who was unappreciative of what the school system provides. Still, Sofia was left wondering whether her father, and men like him, could have blinders about the realities and unmet needs of women and girls. She wished she knew more about how to make politics work for her and Lily, and for making schools into places that made great efforts to prevent harm.

As women's participation in politics is changing, women are becoming more engaged, gaining voice and power to speak and act on behalf of their communities, their children, and themselves. Women's issues, once relegated to the private sphere, are being made public, although institutions continue to use their power to define issues and make policy that affects women differently from the way it does men.

As noted earlier (in "Women in Public Arenas"), "first wave" and "second wave" feminism have been labels for women's political activism. Now, "feminist" is an oft-disowned label. No matter what the label, women's activism has always incorporated (1) challenges to patriarchal and institutional powers that oppress women, and (2) demands that the values and needs of women and families be met. This is true, whether it was in the early 1900s with six-foot-tall Carrie Nation, who demolished saloons so that husbands could not spend their paychecks on drink rather than food; Margaret Sanger, who was outlawed for giving birth control information to women who could not feed the children they already had; or in the 1960s consciousness-raising groups of women who talked together about the range of oppressions they observed in their private and public lives.

The women's suffrage movement—first wave feminism—empowered women (mostly middle class, white) to challenge politics and policies that denied them the right to vote, and to keep property and children in marriage and divorce. The second wave of feminism came during the 1960s, when liberal feminists worked together on issues of economics and education, developing strategies for lobbying for legislation and administrative regulations, and building political networks for accomplishing reforms. Women's rights groups became professionalized foundations and interest group lobbies, influencing legislation at national and state levels, conducting research, creating programs, and raising money to promote selected women candidates. Long-standing groups that have been successful in such work include the League of Women Voters, the National Organization for Women (NOW), the Women's Political Caucus, the Women's Equity Action League, and the AAUW.

Title IX: Coalitions

Coalitions of women's groups, along with women's professional associations and the Women's Caucus of Congress, have actively monitored Title IX. The National Coalition for Women and Girls in Education coordinated efforts for educational equity and published the report *Title IX at 40* (NCWGE, 2012). The report reminds readers that Title IX is about more than athletics and protects all students, boys and girls, males and females, from sexual harassment. Title IX protects girls' and women's rights to equity in STEM, career, and technical education, as well as the rights of pregnant and parenting students, but does not upend patriarchal assumptions. Seeing Hillary Clinton and other strong women in high positions does not fix the situation of a child who is experiencing bullying or sexual harassment, or the teacher who can't help wondering whether tight accountability policies aren't attacks on vulnerable women, or the aspiring superintendent with the doctorate in education who sees generals and admirals selected instead of her.

Coalitions, Grassroots Organizing, and Advocacy

Coalition groups function politically in different ways. Some groups focused on specific issues, some focused locally, and others focused on broader social and national agendas. While well-known groups like NOW worked for the Equal Rights Amendment (ERA), the women's liberation movement's approaches were rooted in peace, civil rights, and freedom movements. They included less formal groups with shared values, and engaged in consciousness raising, festivals, arts, and: networking that was more radical and concerned with economic, class, and race oppressions. Payne's (1990) study of African American women in Mississippi during the civil rights movement found that while the men were more public and engaged in confrontation and negotiation, the women were the organizers, mobilizing social networks, coordinating activities, and doing the everyday work on which the civil rights movement depended.

Grassroots organizing, activism, and advocacy involve actions that women have always been good at, for example, working behind the scenes supporting and sustaining social movements. Whether using the collective power of activist networks to obtain more responsive policies or forming alliances and coalitions to support more broadbased initiatives around common interests to effect change (Warren, 2011), the impact of women's participation in efforts to confront vested power interests underlies many changes in law and policy and societal beliefs.

Many of the advocacy and professional groups work on gender issues but operate in coordination with other activist anti-oppression groups. The National Coalition for Women and Girls in Education's collaborations are often effective in defending Title IX coordinators' work, stemming the tide of undermining Title IX's mandates for athletic compliance, and pushing forward other equity objectives (e.g., conditions of employment of students, staff, and faculty, females in science and engineering, sexual harassment, and student admissions). The coalition was, for example, the first to coordinate the protest against the Department of Education's assertion that a survey of schoolgirls, used as the basis for Title IX implementation, was adequate for assessing girls' interest in sports. Coalitions, similarly, exert continual political pressure to monitor the enforcement of prohibitions against sexual harassment (AAUW, 2009).

Women's community activism helps build broader social movements, and the lessons learned guide "fighting against state disinvestment; violence against women; homophobia; racial, ethnic, and gender discrimination; and class oppression" (Naples, 1998a, p. 346). Naples (1998b) explains that a variety of social identities and constructions of community, as well as a diversity of personal and political concerns, politicize women and draw them into local political battles. Morgen and Bookman report that legislative reforms, for the most part, emerged from grassroots activity and that most of "the reforms benefiting working-class women have emerged from battles waged in extra-electoral terrains—the office, the factory, the hospital, the church, or the streets" (1988, p. 4).

Women, as bereaved mothers, have organized and initiated in nontraditional ways. Mothers Against Drunk Driving (MADD) forced tightened legislation and driver education programs. The famous "Mothers of the Plaza de Mayo," who congregated with signs and pictures of their disappeared children who were tortured by the Argentinean military for their political beliefs, are examples of women's solidarity and demonstrations of how motherhood and caring can be the basis for political movement, rejecting a culture of politics that expects private and sad passivity (Bouvard, 1994; Elshtain, 1981).

Grassroots activism also emerges in education. Luttrell (1988) studied a multiracial coalition of working-class women who demanded equal educational opportunities for white, black, and Hispanic children in an urban high school. Mothers Alone Working, as a group of black and white poor women, focused on children, especially daughters, and worked for nonsexist curricula and daycare. The Pat Robinson Group, affiliated with Freedoms Schools, worked on tutoring children rather than working through public schools and focused on childcare, birth control, and teenage pregnancy. More willing to indict capitalism and patriarchy, these black and poor women recognized that men were making all domestic and international political and economic decisions. For these women, their childbearing and motherhood were part of the agenda (Baxandall, 2001).

Mothers of children with special education needs were among the first to master the roles of activists and advocates for equity, inclusion, and educational opportunity for students with disabilities. Nespor and Hicks (2010) studied mothers who became advocates for parents with disabled children and learned to work the layers of the educational institutional complex, to decipher dominant professional discourses that held schools and districts harmless, and to challenge rulings that denied or limited resources for disabled students—wizards, as the authors referred to them. Women and mothers have had no choice but to take up grassroots activism as an alternative to dominant power structures and political interests. These studies of grassroots and community-based organizing, encompassing widened strategies, values, voices, and needs, and even wizardry, illustrate well the marrying of feminism and politics.

New Forms of Women's Organizing: The Internet and Social Media

Politics, however, is increasingly affected by technology and social media, which affects the advocacy and activist work of feminists. The development of the Internet brought the potential for diverse voices to access social media in more liberating and equalizing formats. In the 1990s, feminist organizations began using information technologies and the Internet to ensure online visibility and to further their own causes and activities (Irving & English, 2011). As Internet technology expanded into the private sector and to women as caregivers and homemakers, feminists were concerned about the ways feminine stereotypes were dominant in marketing Internet content to women (Royal, 2008). At the same time, the Internet released women from having to choose a single feminist identity because the technology platform allowed women to explore different versions of feminism and engage in a broader range of women's issues (Vogt & Chen, 2001).

Women's activist organizations incorporated information technologies and social media into their outreach and action agendas; however, mobilizing women into collective action posed a challenge as women constitute a large and diverse group. In their research, Goss and Heaney (2010) describe two actions in which that challenge was met: the Million Mom March on Washington, DC against gun violence and the antiwar movement of Code Pink: Women for Peace. Goss and Heaney show how the success of these two women's organizations, Million Mom and Code Pink, was a result of hybrid inter-constituency and inter-institutional coordination. Both organizations included smart use of the Internet to reach women from different generations and activist traditions and engage their member-activists in real time, directing them to rallies, forums, protests, and congressional hearings and between venues depending on the relevance to different member audiences. Goss and Heaney state that while different in many ways, the Million Mom March and Code Pink reflected "a long-standing tradition of American women organizing against what they saw as a muscular militarism deeply embedded within U.S. culture and politics" (2010, p. 28).

The Internet and other forms of social media are not without inherent inequities and inequalities as U.S. women who are poor or immigrants, whose primary language is not English, and who live in underserved and under-resourced communities are unable to participate in technological innovation. For many of the world's women suffering the most from oppression and abuse, the Internet is inaccessible (Vogt & Chen, 2001). Yet social media and information technologies like the Internet can instantly deliver news of women's oppression and women organizing for change. On the same day, people the world over learned about Malala Yousafzai, the young 15-year-old Pakistani girl shot in the head by Taliban supporters because she advocated for girls' education. People were abhorred and they mobilized in Pakistan and elsewhere for the right of all children to be educated, regardless of their sex.

The discipline of political science historically focuses on voting, campaigning, and office holding and often fails to encompass the political activities of community organizers and social movements that challenge basic power structures. Feminist politics, however, is closely connected to community organizing and social movement coalitions that address basic human needs like health care, low-cost housing, welfare, access to education, battered women's shelters, and women's banks (A. Marshall, 2002). Women have earned their political gains at the kitchen table, in schools, and in the streets.

FATHER: "How can this happen—this loco 20 year old can take an AK 37 and gun down a school full of little kids! There ought to be laws! Aren't those men in Congress fathers too?"

SOFIA: "At my work today, my teacher friend, Cecile, got a bunch of us together. She thinks we could get lots of parents, and even state legislators, to really take a hard look at gun laws, and at violence issues generally. When the macho boys pick on the smaller boys, those are small acts of violence. Plus, Cecile's saying things like, 'it may be more about whether that kid's mother had to handle him all by herself, sort of like Lily's principal thinks I should be able to handle everything Lily needs when they keep cutting the special programs. Cecile asked us all to come to a meeting Friday night. I know you say Cecile, and Trudy too, are feministas, but come with me, 'Apa.' [laughing] I'll protect you."

Sofia is learning that social, political, and educational institutions are slow at recognizing her needs and sometimes appear blind to the need for change. She hears of various ways to have a voice in the political system but worries about the downside of seeming radical. Also, she wonders if getting political means being seen as a troublemaker or a flaming feminist, or even losing her job. What theories and lines of research provide insight into the challenges of women like Sofia?

Powering Up Feminism in Education Politics and Offering Alternatives
Women's issues are men's issues too. Feminist theory and advocacy can underpin powerful politics. Feminism challenges the power of patriarchy and feminists and critical scholars challenge the politics and policies that patriarchy supports. Education scholars can use feminist theoretical insights, perspectives, or motivation for investigating, formulating, and reframing political issues. Feminist theory and research can "power up" alternatives that address the needs of a Sofia, or of a striving female school administrator.

The Integration of Feminist Theory into Education Politics
"A specifically feminist discourse can suggest reformulation of some of the most central terms of political life: reason, power, community, freedom" (Ferguson, 1984, p. 55). If, simply stated, feminist perspectives start with a focus on women and girls (recognizing that this will still bring in men's and boys' issues), then what are the various ways feminists have actually provided new questions and new knowledge and what are the big challenges raised by feminist perspectives in education politics? In education, feminists have used varied traditions and methodologies to extend their influence and impact across a wide range of issues (Marshall & Young, 2006; Tong, 1989). Feminist research seeks to discover lost women and silenced issues (Harding, 1987), and to get beyond shallow, token, "add women and stir" responses in research, programs, and practices.

Liberal feminists support Title IX policy logic, but the lack of enforcement highlights the *limits* of liberal theory.

Liberal feminists focus on the divergent routes girls and boys take in education and careers and expose the consequences of sex stereotyping and gender differentiation in our instructional and curricular practices (Arnot & Weiler, 1993). This, however, was insufficient for changing institutions with patriarchal and masculinist leadership historically embedded.

The Concept of the Gender Regime

A gender order is maintained through education's socializing functions as well as other institutions like the family, the media, and even interactions on the street (Connell, 1987). Males and females learn their proper sex roles, ensuing behaviors, and choices and feel the punishments of veering from them. Theories of children's socialization and development presume to know the outcomes of social practices. "They assume that the forces that operate on children will produce adults that are conveniently masculine and feminine, or else 'deviant' if the process slips or fails" (Thorne, 1993, p. 3). Children react to others through social group categorization, a practice that can mark "who people are and what their relationships are with other people . . . [as they are] inducted into intergroup relations that may be politically important in their environments" (Sapiro, 2004, p. 14). The rise of social media will only exacerbate this tendency. With gender identities and sexualities now part of the political arena, both boys and girls learn about gender politics, influencing their adult political and policy preferences. Thus politics is the location where the gender regime is constructed and maintained through the power dynamics operating in educational contexts.

Trudy was recruiting her, saying, "Sofia, I've got a better way for you to help bring about change. Here's how to join Emily's List and then help us get more women elected. I heard you've been hangin' out with that Cecile. But you can really only get heard by getting in with the people who have power." Papa, too, was wary about doing anything that might jeopardize the status they'd obtained as immigrants. He said often, "oh niña calladita de ve mas bonita" (a girl who sits quietly looks so much prettier) and encouraged her to be like her Mama, happy with staying home, raising kids, and not wanting to challenge every word out of a man's mouth. Sofia wanted to be a great role model for her daughter. What advice should Sofia give Lily about how to navigate her sexuality, speaking up when she sees boys getting more access to math and computers than the girls, and, for her future, about career goals? How could Sofia and Lily find the power within themselves to be strong about what would really make their lives better? Would showing Lily a news story about Justice Sotomayor be enough to offset the messages telling her that her future was more connected to dispensing food than to dispensing justice?

Power and Politics Dynamics in Defining Women's Issues

Radical or "power and politics" feminists have focused on a critique of the patriarchal state and its power to regulate the lives and bodies of women and girls—as teachers, mothers, daughters, and students (Connell, 1987). Feminists moved beyond Marxist insights that acknowledged the interplay of market economies and class as they affected boys' education and life choices (MacLeod, 1987; Willis, 1977). Scholars like Weiler

(1988), Weis (1993), and Fine (1993) investigated how economic systems combined with patriarchal traditions channel and limit females' futures.

Such insights can power up the teacher trying to articulate her objections to the dominant views on accountability; she could identify alternative language and challenge the dominant discourse. Similarly, educators and parents question how tracking is creating the dropout problem and a pipeline to prison. They would find the critique of the tight connections between goals of schooling and powerful economic forces. This critique helps reframe assumptions that diplomas automatically lead to jobs and social mobility. It forces formulations of alternative assumptions of the worth and content of schooling. The critique has the potential to strip naked the patriarchy and the class-based and race-based structures embedded in institutions and the economy.

Feminist critical policy analysis focuses on the power dynamics in framing dominant policy discourse and agendas (and repressing or silencing others) (C. Marshall, 1997a). Those with power can simply label feminist issues, voices, and knowledges as marginal or irrelevant.

"Outing" Areas of Silence and Nonevents

Sometimes feminist research entails analysis of nonevents; that is, issues that have been rendered invisible, muted, and inconsequential because they mask hidden power dynamics (C. Marshall, 1997a, 1997b). For example, Smulyan (2000) found that, in studying women school principals and hearing what was clearly a gendered construction of roles, the participants spoke as if everything were gender neutral. Such a gender-neutral story enables principals to function in an individualistic, male-dominated power dynamic.

Researchers operating out of feminist and critical frameworks, such as C. Marshall (1997a, 1997b), Stromquist (1997), Young (2003), Connell (1987), Laible (1997), Ah Nee-Benham and Heck (1998), and Knight (2002a), often develop research agendas aimed at empowerment from repressive and oppressive structures. Thus, "integrating feminist and critical theory into [research and] policy analysis will add critical issues and ways of framing questions about power, justice and the state" (C. Marshall, 1997a, p. 2) and encourage designs that explore the margins, areas of silence (Pillow, 2004), taboo topics (Lugg, 1998), nonevents (Andre-Bechely, 2005), what is not said, and, in the case of policy, what is not addressed or decided.

Without feminists' voices, the politics in the preparation, recruitment, and retention of teachers is often conducted as if there were no gender issues; and thus women's and girls' issues are easily relegated to the margins. Without feminists' insights, gender issues remain hidden in institutions, and the power to shape values and preferences through institutional discourses goes unchallenged. Young's (2003) aptly named chapter, "Troubling Policy Discourse: Gender, Constructions, and the Leadership Crisis," is an example. She uses feminist critical policy analysis to demonstrate how, in the very construction of the policy issue of a "shortage," women and minorities are considered in shallow ways. The crisis was framed and defined as a need to identify "strong leaders," with little sense that these were stereotyping code words that reduced women's access. Thus, gender was made a nonissue. Andre-Bechely (2005) similarly notes in her research on school choice how gender issues go unnoticed when implementing school choice policy. She found that mothers do the majority of "choice work," and mothers, often unknowingly, become complicit in the inequities and inequalities that will be experienced by other mothers' children who have less opportunity for choice. Dyrness (2011) tells of the community organizing work of Latina mothers to get a new school in their underserved immigrant neighborhood, showing how a city, a university partner, and a community organization validated the mothers' political agendas and voices. These examples illustrate how feminist critiques can bring forth otherwise ignored gender issues and "nonevents" in educational institutions, politics, and policy making. Feminism provides tools for analysis of discourse so that teachers, parents, students, and others who are often silenced, as community activists, can more clearly deconstruct and then challenge policies that marginalize, repress, and sustain inequality. Teachers, feeling blamed for all societal ills, critiquing accountability and antiunion rhetoric, can mobilize not just as teachers, but as women and as workers in an economy that budgets for war and banks more than for children and families.

> Title IX never incorporated insights from "women's ways" or "power and politics" feminist insights. So schools missed the possibilities of incorporating women's values and realities. They missed the chance to challenge the low status of women's work, for example, childcare, nurturance, teaching. Schools missed recognizing that equity means more than getting more women in chemistry classes, that schooling cannot get female chemists equal pay in a sexist economy.

"Outing" Incongruities in Differentiation and Valuation
of Public and Private Spheres

Another strand of feminism—labeled variously as women's ways, socialist, maternal, and "difference" feminism—focuses on ways to hear and represent women's different life trajectories, values, ways of knowing, and ethics. Recommendations for relationship building, caring, community, and nonhierarchical, facilitative, collaborative leadership emerged from the work of difference feminists (Brunner, 1999; Gilligan, 1982; Noddings, 1992; Tong, 1989).

Further, feminist scholars critique the false separations of private sphere and public sphere and placing emotion, caring, relationship, children, and sexuality as private, and the concern mostly of women. Showing how these assumptions that the public sphere—business, politics, war, property, law—is mostly for men lays the foundation for undoing all such false dichotomies: assumptions that politics in the public arena should be dominated by rational white males, but sex, relationships, and sexual orientation, and the need to be seen as a whole person were private-sphere matters, full of emotion.

Unmanageable and scary challenges of women's power, emotion, sexuality, messy children, and the dilemmas that ensue when failures in institutions like the church, family, and economy result in poor, hungry, and ill-prepared children on the doorsteps of schoolhouses are areas of silence. Such fearful issues tempt political actors to push these issues aside or to assert that they are private issues. The public spheres of politics, bureaucracies, and economic life are structured around myths of logical, dispassionate, gentlemanly discourse and rational action (Blackmore, 1993). Personal relationships, emotions, and caring must not interfere; they are part of family and social lives, which are to be kept separate. These assumptions are still used when uncomfortable issues emerge and blinders are more comfortable.

With schools incorporating these insights, then we would see serious consideration of curricula instilling peace, collaboration, community building, and relationship building, and leaders selected for their abilities to create caring, facilitative administration. Parents and educators can demand that governmental agencies, schools and universities, and faith-based congregations do more than token interventions to protect children from harm and injustice.

"Outing" Sexuality

In education, uncomfortable issues range from school boards' decisions about how to implement sex education or sexual harassment policies (Laible, 1997), to schooling for pregnant and parenting girls (Pillow, 2004), to professional standards boards' blindness to the need for dealing with specific gender and sexuality issues.[6] Such an avoidance is particularly troubling given research that shows how some preservice teachers "deny, dismiss, or discount women's oppression and distance themselves from feminism " (Titus, 2000, p. 26). Sexuality issues, seemingly taboo, are evaded in education politics and policy. Feminist and queer theories frame new issues for education politics, moving them from the margins of the private spheres to the education politics questions of curriculum, educator recruitment and retention, counseling, and employee and student rights. Children repress the hurt from bullying and being called dyke, fag, and worse. Few educators are trained to intervene. Similarly, educators seldom have preparation for dealing with adolescents' need for sex education and birth control or with pregnancies.

Gender power dynamics define societally accepted sexualities as schools' youth cultures, influenced by social media, and professional and organizational cultures allow exclusion, bullying, discrediting, and silencing of gays and lesbians and those whose identities are different from stereotyped males and females (Blount, 2005; Friend, 1993; Lugg, 2003a, 2003b; Shakeshaft, 1995). Educators remain silent on heterosexism and homophobia, as they fear backlash (Friend, 1993). Their silence makes schools unsafe for gay and lesbian students; they may drop out, abuse drugs and alcohol, or commit suicide (SPEAK: Suicide Prevention Education Awareness for Kids, 2013). Children do not see gay/lesbian role models while they are developing same-sex affectional and sexual orientations. Conflicts arise in curricular decisions about recognizing sexual orientation of famous characters in history or literature. GLBTQ students and their allies politick for space and budgets for student activities in schools, but ideological groups and parent groups try to restrict schools (Leck, 2000).

> By force of Title IX or because incidents no longer are swept under the rug, school boards are searching for remedies and formulating policies against peer bullying and sexual harassment, and thus having to recognize the sometimes brutal and sometimes more subtle realities of sexual domination.

Sex, gender, and sexual orientation rear up in human resource and hiring practices, as in the awkward groping to find out women applicants' family planning methods and intentions while avoiding illegal direct questions. They appear by avoidance, when men in power may avoid unspoken discomforts with being sponsors and mentors to aspiring women, and, conversely, when women victims of sexual harassment simply keep quiet rather than be labeled as troublemakers. Educators can demand that politicians and school programming take off blinders and invest in sex education and pregnant and parenting teens, and recognize adolescents' yearning for caring and connection, shown in their texting and in their focus on peers more than on physics.

Recent Expansions in Epistemology: Intersectionality and Agency

Feminist research has expanded the conversation within feminism to debate and discuss social constructions and critical epistemological issues. Instead of simply documenting women's realities (which is in and of itself an important accomplishment), feminist research has also worked to expand narrow understandings and deconstruct distorted assumptions about women, their experiences, and their work. Feminist scholars of education policy and politics have incorporated critical and poststructural perspectives into their theoretical and methodological frameworks to challenge embedded ideology and deconstruct/dismantle taken-for-granted Truth. Feminist critical analysis points out the politics in defining what counts as knowledge and knowing. Politics of knowledge, with a feminist critique, then, focuses on the power behind agenda framing and discourse, and beyond the confined assumptions of what belongs in the public sphere.

In most feminist research, gender and sexism are given positions of prominence. Some feminist researchers, however, stress caution with this practice, arguing that by focusing on gender, their colleagues are providing more visibility and power to what is essentially a social construction—not real but a fabrication or a construct created within cultural and historical discursive practices. Harding argues: "It is important to remember that in a certain sense there are no 'women' or 'men' in the world—there is no 'gender'— but only women, men, and gender constructed through particular historical struggles over just what races, classes, sexualities, cultures, religious groups, and so forth, will have access to resources and power" (1991, p. 151). Fuss (1989) adds that a focus on "women" as a group is essentializing.

> Title IX did nothing to examine how interactions and curricula in schools construct children's identities or to focus on agency and empowerment.

Feminisms that incorporate the social construction of identity recognize the fallacies of labels. First, seeing nationality, ethnicity, age, religion, sexual orientation, and race-, class-, and gender-based labels as socially constructed highlights the fallacious demarcations. People are constantly creating themselves and also responding to societal constructions of themselves. Further, it highlights how the intersecting and interrelated labels can be used in systems of oppression and subordination. Simplistic labels—when applied within power dynamics—facilitate categorization, dichotomizing, and controlling. The power to name can be used as a power tool. The application of labels—dropout, Hispanic, Muslim, senior citizen, mother, housemaid, bitch, whiner, troublemaker, bubbly, buxom, football star, hottie, stud, dyke, polack, trailer trash—contains assumed life trajectories and takes away individuals' power and agency in defining themselves. But by seeing reality as socially constructed, fluid, and evolving, every person has power to define herself. She has agency and she fits within no labels (not even the label "she")—thus incorporating a wide range of possibilities.

Peer cultures and education professions limit choices, often through micropolitical interactions. For men as well as for women, they deny or repress expression of emotion, nurturing and relational values, desires for hobbies and joy, and family roles that veer from the stereotypes. Unchallenged by any viable messages from educators or school practices, the schoolgirl feels pressure to starve herself and to construct her identity in ways that promote her, in the peer culture, to the higher status of desirable female. The male teacher feels pressure that to be a man means ascension to community politics, leadership, and administration. Men's studies are, in part, a movement (albeit marginal) to make these pressures visible and to point to what is lost. For example, in schools' hypermasculine curriculum and sports agendas, schools embrace a history of curriculum and military recruiting that valorizes the history of great men and generals, and entices boys into fighting and dying.

Further expansions of the feminist critique have brought forth epistemologies that come from women's own historically embedded experiences with oppression. For example, postcolonial women and women of color are defining and using endarkened feminist epistemologies (Dillard, 2000), black feminist epistemology (Collins, 1991), and Chicana feminist epistemology (Mendez-Morse, 2004), which have informed educational studies on issues such as teachers' unions (C. Marshall, 2002), Chicana student resistance (Bernal, 1998), teacher education (Knight, 2002b), mothers and school choice (Andre-Bechely, 2005), and women in school leadership as exemplified by Sanders-Lawson, Smith-Campbell, and Benham (2006). School leadership that incorporated such critical insights would reframe assumptions about how to attract minorities into education careers and how to create culturally sensitive pedagogies, a constant concern now labeled "the achievement gap." Further, feminists' agendas on women's liberation and gender equity politics could include the interlocking, interrelated, and historically embedded issues of class, race, and ethnicity (Collins, 1991; López, 2003; Wing, 1997).

Feminist scholars take aim at the fallacy, even damage, of such binaries and then expand theory and research on humans' identities, relationships, and sexuality. Social constructions of identity happen within "subjective, diverse and contradictory human experiences . . . and shifting gender relations" (Arnot, 2009, p. 45). Identity, then, is a dynamic occurring within power dynamics, be they school playgrounds, sex education classes, internships, or board meetings. With school policies and politics that encompassed the intersectionality of developing identities, then, educators could cast a wider net for managing, for example, the school dynamics that divide boys and girls, sex education, GLBTQ challenges, sexual harassment (Laible, 1997), and teen pregnancy (Pillow, 2004) instead of the automatic labeling of male/female, black/white, and so forth. Women and educators can feel the empowering sense of agency as they define themselves, rather than being defined by any one label.

Reframing

Feminist theories do reframe questions, while valorizing women's heretofore silenced voices, values, and realities. Seemingly radical (labeled unconventional, off the wall, weird, irrelevant, etc.) research questions and designs are sometimes required, and they challenge those in positions of power (in academia, in government, and in social institutions). Reframed questions contradict commonsense beliefs about essential gender differences. Reframed questions and knowledges are resisted, as they embed explanations with critiques of cultural and societal gender relations; and because they often emphasize the continuous pattern of inequity in which males are privileged, attaining more resources, positions of power, and wealth no matter their educational or social accomplishments. Indeed, such critical feminist reframing uncomfortably uncovers "the ideological messages and educational practices that reproduce male and female identities" (Stromquist, 1997, p. 38), and the complex mix of class, race, gender, sexuality, and school experiences.

As can be seen, each of these different feminist perspectives foreshadows different issues for the study of education politics and policy. Revolutionary research questions of yesterday may not be so revolutionary today. Reframed questions on the rights of gays and lesbians who are married and are parents and teachers and administrators are acceptable today. Feminist perspectives frame future research that examines oppressive male-dominant institutions such as the industrial-military complex, foreign nations that allow victimization of women and girls, universities' weak interventions against sexual abuse (ranging from date rape to Penn State), and the ways that social studies and ROTC support assumptions that war is glorious and that guns and violence are natural, and that can ignite new understanding of the political consequences of ignoring gender relations.

CURRENT POLITICAL DIRECTIONS:
IN RESEARCH AND IN REALITIES

Women Changing and Being Changed by Politics

Gains have been made as a result of feminist challenges to patriarchal politics and policy making. Women have assumed leadership roles, but this, in itself, is not enough. Kelly and Duerst-Lahti point out:

> Gender and gender power are critical concepts with related analytical tools that need to be incorporated into political and policy studies. Arguably, studies that ignore their implications simply represent faulty scholarship. . . . Considering public leadership and governance in terms of gender and gender power is necessary because so many of the masculinist ideological "givens" both visibly and invisibly support and reinforce the polity. Arrangements are such that men and masculinity continue to be advantaged even when women move into public leadership posts. (1995, pp. 270–271)

This final section reflects on the vulnerabilities but also on the promising directions, given the status of feminist influences on educational politics.

Feminists' Nation at Risk
Women Are Coopted, Spread Too Thin

As women move into higher levels of educational administration and politics, they must often suppress any feminist leanings and work more like men. Unless women leaders are active in local women's and community organizations, they may not have enough insight or strategies for promoting women's concerns about education-related issues and in laws and policies. In local community organizations and coalitions, poor and working-class white women and women of color can be noisy and effective activists; but in traditional political arenas, they must work skillfully within established power relations. Women in politics are faced with a quandary of issues, and women in power will be spread very thin as they try to represent women's concerns and the many issues affecting women's rights and the rights of children and youth. Gender issues in education may be near the bottom of their advocacy list when women are elected to public office.

Women Antifeminists

Redistributive policies bring backlash. Anita Bryant and Phyllis Schlafly portraying feminists as lesbians and as anti-marriage—with Bryant saying, "all I could do is weep for America" in her "Save the Children" campaign against GLBTQ educators—and more such attacks undermined educators with feminist leanings (Blount, 2000, p. 96). People who have privileges, often from inherited social capital, do not like to be told that their status should be questioned. Politicians can scare publics with fears of the erosion of family and increased child neglect when they fight against education policies that would equalize and liberalize male and female career choices and girls' empowerment.

Politicians' rhetoric about the traditional family, valuing of freedom to choose how parents run the home, the private sphere, and how parents educate their children, for example, home schooling, are ways of protecting the private sphere from governmental intrusions and are used to buttress the backlash (Kirp, Yudof, & Franks, 1986) and to hide business interests in private schooling and online degrees. This is especially ironic when, at the same time, politicians promote legislation to restrict and regulate women's reproductive choice, right down to requiring vaginal speculum sonograms for women seeking abortions.

Fear, Loss, and Backlash

Progress toward reducing the barriers that inhibit girls' and women's education and careers has created societal fear that gets translated into political action, programs, and policies. Education school boards and committees, reflecting these fears, then focus on boys' falling back, especially African American boys, and respond in ways such as refusing approval of charter schools for girls. Perhaps the most telling acts are the revisions of NCLB in 2006, allowing public school districts to create gender-segregated schools without providing a rationale. In fact, "a school district can offer an all-boys elementary school without having to offer an all-girls elementary school" legally (NASSPE: Legal status of single-sex education, 2011). Affirmative action is redistributive policy, aimed at undoing traditional privileges for white males, the wealthier, and the well connected. Policy goals that seek to reduce all institutional racism and sexism—thus giving women and minorities equal access to education programs and jobs—create a backlash.[7] As affirmative action is contorted into political rhetoric and court petitions, it is presented as an evil special preference for people just because of their gender or skin color.

The result of this kind of backlash was seen in the George W. Bush administration's recommended reductions in budgets, and even elimination of programs, aimed at gender equity in education. Under his administration, the federal Office of Civil Rights refused to examine the underrepresentation of girls and women in nontraditional fields in vocational education and higher education, saying that statistical disparities may simply be the result of individuals' career choices (National Women's Law Center, 2004).

Gender stereotypes limit choices for men as well as for women and feminist scholarship has explicated these dynamics. This research is generally ignored by politics of education scholars. Still, some men have become attuned to feminist issues, especially when they have daughters and strong wives. But when they think about and act on behalf of the women in their lives, men are more likely to understand the limited liberal feminist agendas, supporting equality of access and rights. Blindness to gender results in a loss of what otherwise can be discussions about educational purpose, politics, and leadership with women's insights.[8] As men take a more active role in childrearing as fathers and partners, sharing joint custody in divorce, they likely will be drawn to feminist issues and political action, creating new alliances. Still, feminisms that assert the values of women's perspectives and that challenge the structures of institutions and politics perpetuating male privilege (e.g., marriage, senates, school administration) remain more difficult for most men to embrace.

Worrying about Title IX's effects, Sommer (2006), resident scholar in the American Enterprise Institute, said: "It is now boys who are on the wrong side of the gender gap . . . and government meddling could seriously reduce opportunities for men . . . and we could see men's interest in math, physics, technology, and engineering capped at the level of female interest."

Politically, groups like Eagle Forum promote anti–Title IX agendas with rhetoric about the ruination of men's sports and the undermining of American womanhood and family values.

Derision and Disdain for Women as Educators and Leaders

Hillary Rodham Clinton's appearance and assertiveness are closely scrutinized as she and other powerful women know they will lose their power the moment they can be given a derisive label (e.g., bitch, witch, dyke). Some politicians gain votes using rhetoric that veils a fear of women's power while simultaneously promoting policies that rein it in. The rhetoric and framing of issues are never blatantly antiwoman but hide behind other education policy logics, as seen in:

- Adopting probusiness groups' mantras of the "right to work for less," thus turning the public against teacher unions. Workers lose benefits and mention of family needs, especially child care, birth control, and abortion in health plans, accompanies loss of ability to get pay raises. Weakened teachers' unions lose political clout in local, state, and national election campaigns.
- Focusing on the needs of the workforce in the development of curricula in schools and community colleges, and reducing resources and faculty for university programs in women's studies and gender studies.
- Sponsoring generals, admirals, and CEOs into paid fellowships to train as educational leaders who will run urban school districts and command high salaries with excessive contract buy-outs should they fail to accomplish significant change.
- Using parental choice and competitiveness-leads-to-quality logics to justify charter schools, privatization, vouchers, and tightening accountability and performance evaluations of teachers, leaders, and professors increases managerial surveillance.

• Disinvesting in funding public education and public social services, forcing austerity and limited availability of services for families historically the most underrepresented and underserved.

These policy trends have a negative effect on the power, voice, and leadership of women dedicated to education who have never before been placed under such scrutiny, subject to such derision (Marshall & Young, 2013). Consequently, it is no surprise to feminists that a war on women can lead to a Black Swan event in electoral politics. Nor is it a surprise that there is still too little research on gender and education reform or the impact of these trends on the future of girls and boys.

Marginalization of Gender in Educational Research and Reform

In state and district accountability reports required by NCLB, the differences along student subgroups' testing performance that are least discussed, compared, and analyzed are those between boys and girls. Federal agencies' grants and data collection deemphasize gender disparities in education, career earnings, and outcomes.

The liberal feminist agenda, while bringing small gains for mostly white and middle-class women, was not able to address the needs of many poor women and women of color. What Collins has called "matrices of domination" had not been challenged (Collins, 1991). Token gender equity policies have been formulated—and, as long as they merely add the category women to rights that are already on the books (i.e., voting, equal pay), and as long as they can be kept low budget and can be evaded—then symbolic action has been taken. No serious system changing and no state intrusion into gender relations and no disruption to institutions would be needed. However, sexual dynamics in education were untouched; and educators' training and the male-dominated hierarchy of schools were unchanged in most educational institutions. Further, the hidden curriculum reinforced by media and other societal forces continues to influence hypermasculinity for boys and to create sex-symbol images in adolescent girls' aspirations (ranging from Barbie images to peer culture pressures for unprotected sex). It becomes clear that class and race issues that intertwine with gender were untouched—despite laws eliminating sex stereotyping in coursework and career counseling—as the life patterns of males and females continued to follow class, race, and gender channelings (Gaine & George, 1999).

Feminist Nation at Promise in Education Politics

When a senator tells her colleagues to "go home and talk to your wife and your daughters" before they vote on issues, she is using great insider-outsider strategies, as well as the time-tested strategy of bringing the issue home. The particular focus on gender and the finer focus on feminist insights offer promise. Keeping that focus on women highlights the way that gendered social norms are unequally constructed. And as long as women as a group still live in uneven and oppressed conditions, we must use gender and categories like "women" for strategic purposes (Kristeva, 1980).

Beyond "Binders of Women": Promising Political Strategies and Agendas for Research and Action

From 1960s feminism to present-day feminism, the dominant political stories for women were about the Equal Rights Amendment, affirmative action, and the increasing number of women elected to public office. Feminists want more. Otherwise there is the assumption that you can just add women and stir, or that you can just keep binders of women, to give the look of equity.

But the grassroots mobilizing, the women's movement, and peace, social justice, environmental, and other causes led to coalitions at national and international women's ways of knowing and valuing, of sexuality, race, ethnicity, and class, Now they are more than subtexts brought by feminists and social movement activists, now, finally, catapulted to politicians' agendas by violent shootings and horrors of sexual assaults.

In the micropolitical and macropolitical arenas of education, feminist educators and many parents have continuously challenged school practices that reify sex stereotyping and those that enshrine competition, violence, and war. Today women's right to control their bodies, to have access to equal job opportunity, to expand women's studies, for GLBTQ rights, and the sex/power dynamics affecting all genders' identities, the violence and disrespect for individuals, communities, nations, and the environment—all are now part of a much-expanded and public feminist agenda for action and research. Feminist insights now can be used to push nuanced research on a range of specific issues by focusing on what happens in classrooms, in politics, and in policy:

- Examining how teachers are trained regarding gender equity;
- Reexamining the challenges faced by pregnant and parenting teens;
- Revising curriculum to incorporate intersectionality so that race, gender, sexual orientation, ethnicity, country of origin, and so forth are no longer false divisions;
- Critiquing the emphasis on competition and performance on standardized tests;
- Revealing barriers to collaborative pedagogy and empowerment curricula in schools;
- Attending to the participation and achievement of girls in advanced placement mathematics and science courses and any continuing barriers for women entering STEM careers;
- Critiquing the reification of masculinist leadership as women ascend to top educational leadership positions and organizational blindness to women's leadership qualifications, aspirations, and opportunities;
- Demanding substantive review of sexual harassment and awareness of date or acquaintance rape;
- Validating the voices of marginalized populations (including teachers) in narratives about what schools are for and how schools' accomplishments can be assessed;
- Focusing on schools' roles in early childhood development and as socializing agents with our economy revoking the myth of mother-at-home;
- Critiquing the rush to technology and online schooling that eliminates connection, collaboration, and relationship building;
- Auditing of public expenditure for scandal-ridden varsity sports; and
- Examining all policies and budgets with a gender analysis so that any potential gender effects can be critiqued.

Title IX politics, women's coalitions, mothers' politicking to pressure superintendents, the very question of how men continue to control education professions although women have always outnumbered them—these were (and still are) ripe issues, which politics scholars have ignored (Marshall, 1997a, 1997b). Plus, too many studies within the realm of education politics and policy (e.g., teachers' unions, leadership, drop-outs, teacher education) are often researched with *no* nod to the feminist critique.

Politics of education scholars can use this chapter to generate synaptic connections between mainstream politics and gender. These might start with identifying how women's groups' advocacy ranges from politically liberal yet narrowly designed and change-based policies to racial and class-encompassing polices that dislodge the ways bureaucratic hierarchies de-skill, de-professionalize, de-motivate, and disempower women and men who are excluded from opportunity structures (Ferguson, 1984; Kanter, 1977).

Struggles, challenging issues, and scholarship still lie ahead. This chapter shows what can happen when feminism is married with politics. When research on education politics is informed by feminism, look at what we get. We learn that women have always "been there" in social movements because women are more often involved in grassroots coalitions, frequently including women of color and women who are poor or working class. We show scholars and women identifying new avenues for feminist politics and pointing to new directions in educational leadership, policy, and public office.[9]

Thus, education politics must incorporate feminism. Education scholars who have cast a blind eye to challenges to the powerful patriarchal (and paternalistic) discourses embedded in educational politics and policy have conducted faulty analyses. Feminist insights offer ways to act powerfully, to articulate one's own realities, and to know it can be useful to "look awry" (Visweswaran, 1994, p. 80). We have attempted to do just that in this chapter, asking our readers to "look awry" for new answers and better solutions to gender inequalities and inequities still pervasive in our educational institutions.

This chapter could not cover higher education or global issues, but we stress that feminism and politics must be viewed in their connections between Pre-K-12, higher education, and life chances, and be viewed globally—feminism is a worldwide movement and global politics impacts us all. We need only extend analysis of Sofia's story into global economic policy and politics, and this becomes evident.

Sofia was having fun and feeling powerful, seeing big names like Hillary Clinton standing up to attacks, and hanging out with local women's and Latinas' groups who picketed with signs protesting against gun violence, against the defunding of Planned Parenthood, against being labeled "welfare queens." She was forming friendships at kitchen table coalitions with other moms who wanted reinstatement of the Spanish classes. She wanted to urge Cecile and Trudy to think about becoming school leaders, so that they could be on the inner circles and use that as leverage to introduce new ways of seeing issues from the eyes of women—the mothers, teachers, daughters, and sisters who do so much of the work in schools. She was drawn to news stories about the treatment of girls and women globally and they got her fired up. She found herself thinking about her daughter, Lily, and thinking feminist!

NOTES

1. The story of Sofia as a child and young woman was presented in a chapter in the first edition of the *Handbook of Education Politics and Policy* by Marshall and Andre-Bechely (2008). Sofia is the daughter of Mexican immigrants and, although born in the United States, was sent to live with relatives in Mexico for three years while her father established a business with Sofia's brothers. Sofia returned to the United States when she was 12 and has lived here since.

2. The wage gap takes on a new form within the academy; 32.2 percent of women faculty members are in a non-tenure track position, compared to only 19 percent of men faculty members (Report of the Committee on Economic Status, 2011, Table 11). Of those on the tenure track, moving through the ranks proves to be a persistent problem—22.9 percent of male, tenure-track faculty are ranked as full professors compared to only 9 percent of female, tenure-track faculty (Report of the Committee on the Economic Status of the Profession, 2011, Table 12).

3. Minority representation on school boards is increasing, although it is still persistently low with, on average, only 12.3 percent African American and 3.1 percent Hispanic school board members (Hess & Meeks, 2010). Minorities are better represented on school boards in large urban districts, and similarly it is also in smaller districts where school boards are predominantly male (Hess & Meeks, 2010).

4. "The numbers of master's degrees earned by Black and Hispanic students more than doubled from 1999–2000 to 2009–10 (increasing by 109 percent and 125 percent, respectively)" (National Center for Education Statistics, 2012).

5. Black swan theory was introduced by Taleb (2004) first in the context of financial markets as a way of understanding the randomness within market fluctuations, and has been further explained as a conceptual theory for social sciences by Taleb in *The Black Swan: The Impact of the Highly Improbable Fragility* (2010). Taleb's general criteria for determining if an event constitutes a Black Swan are: it is an outlier, existing beyond the bounds of regular expectations; it creates an extreme impact; and in hindsight, human nature prompts us to make it "explainable and predictable" (Taleb, 2010, Kindle Locations pp. 302–305). A Black Swan event is not predictable based on historical trend data; the event has a substantial impact; and the event seems rationally predictable only after it occurs. The 2012 presidential election illustrates how the *war on women* is just such an event.
   The paradox of a Black Swan is that it is perceived as expected only after it happens. Taleb offers a poignant example of this paradoxical characteristic of positionality: "Consider a turkey that is fed every day. Every single feeding will firm up the bird's belief that it is the general rule of life to be fed every day by friendly members of the human race 'looking out for its best interests,' as a politician would say. On the afternoon of the Wednesday before Thanksgiving, something unexpected will happen to the turkey. It will incur a revision of belief" (2010, Kindle Locations pp. 1236–1237). The caretaker of the turkey did not find the events of the Wednesday before Thanksgiving to be unexpected, but the turkey did because no previous trends indicated such an abrupt change that would have immediate and severe consequences for the turkey.

6. Review the National Board for Professional Teaching Standards (NBPST) and the standards of the National Council for Accreditation of Teacher Education (NCATE).

7. The AAUW (Corbett, Hill, & St. Rose, 2008) found no evidence of the popularized "boys crisis" in education.

8. Feuerstein (2006) has written of how he came to the realization that men can learn much by learning women's perspectives. Elliott's (2008) study of five feminist fathers explored how their experiences brought new definitions of masculinity and an expanded sense of feminism.

9. Many influential and prominent feminists who marry politics and feminism are from foreign countries such as Britain, Australia, and Canada (Arnot, 2002; Blackmore, 1999; Connell, 1987; David, 1993; Middleton, 1993; Taylor, 1997; Yates, 1997) and from other disciplines (Dietz, 1992; Elshtain, 1981; Fraser, 1989; Hawkesworth, 1994; Pateman & Gross, 1987; Smith, 1990). In the United States, many of our most respected feminist scholars have "made it" only by ensuring that they are well known for work other than their feminist work. Scholars like Marshall and Gerstl-Pepin (2005), Grogan (1996), and Weiler (1988) have been seen as valuable and credible for, respectively, their expertise in state politics and qualitative methodology, on the superintendency, and on the history of teaching.

REFERENCES

AAUW Public Policy and Government Relations Department. (2009). *AAUW's position on Title IX and sexual harassment*. American Association of University Women. Retrieved from www.aauw.org/resource/aauws-position-on-title-ix-and-sexual-harassment/.

About Us: UniteWomen.org. (2012). UniteWomen.org. Retrieved from www.unitewomen.org/?page_id=193.

Ah Nee-Benham, M. K. P., & Heck, R. H. (1998). *Culture and educational policy in Hawai'i: The silencing of native voices*. Mahwah, NJ: Lawrence Erlbaum Associates.

Andre-Bechely, L. N. (2005). *Could it be otherwise? Parents and the inequities of public school choice*. New York: Routledge.

Arnot, M. (2002). *Reproducing gender?: Essays on educational theory and feminist politics*. New York: RoutledgeFalmer.

Arnot, M. (2009). *Educating the gendered citizen: Sociological engagements with national and global political agendas*. London; New York: Routledge.

Arnot, M., & Weiler, K. (1993). *Feminism and social justice in education: International perspectives*. London; New York: Falmer Press.

Bascia, N. (1998). Women teachers, union affiliation, and the future of North American teacher unionism. *Teaching and Teacher Education, 14*(5), 551–563. doi:10.1016/S0742-051X(98)00005-5

Baxandall, R. (2001). Re-visioning the women's liberation movement's narrative: Early second wave African American feminists. *Feminist Studies, 27*(1), 225–245.

Bernal, D. D. (1998). Grassroots leadership reconceptualized: Chicana oral histories and the 1968 East Los Angeles school blowouts. *Frontiers: A Journal of Women Studies, 19*(2), 113–142.

Bers, T. H. (1978). Local political elites: Men and women on boards of education. *The Western Political Quarterly, 31*(3), 381–391. doi:10.2307/447738

Biklen, S. K. (1995). *School work: Gender and the cultural construction of teaching*. New York: Teachers College Press.

Blackmore, J. (1993). In the shadow of men: The historical construction of educational administration as a masculinist enterprise. In J. Blackmore & J. Kenway (Eds.), *Gender matters in educational administration and policy: A feminist introduction* (pp. 27–38). Washington, DC: Falmer Press.

Blackmore, J. (1999). *Troubling women: Feminism, leadership, and educational change*. Philadelphia: Open University Press.

Blount, J. M. (1998). *Destined to rule the schools: Women and the superintendency, 1873–1995*. Albany: State University of New York Press.

Blount, J. M. (2000). Spinsters, bachelors, and other gender transgressors in school employment, 1850–1990. *Review of Educational Research, 70*(1), 83–101.

Blount, J. M. (2005). *Fit to teach: Same-sex desire, gender, and school work in the twentieth century*. Albany: State University of New York Press.

Bolton, S., & Muzio, D. (2008). The paradoxical processes of feminization in the professions: The case of established, aspiring and semi-professions. *Work, Employment & Society, 22*(2), 281–299.

Bouvard, M. G. (1994). *Revolutionizing motherhood: The mothers of the Plaza de Mayo*. Wilmington, DE: Scholarly Resources, Inc.

Bracken, N. M., & Irick, E. (2012). *Gender equity 2004–2010* (No. 2004–10 NCAA) (pp. 1–100). Indianapolis: National Collegiate Athletic Association.

Brunner, C. C. (1997). Exercising power. *School Administrator, 54*(6), 6–9.

Brunner, C. C. (Ed.). (1999). *Sacred dreams: Women and the superintendency*. Albany: State University of New York Press.

Bureau of Labor Statistics. (2011a). *Women's earnings and employment by occupation*. Washington, DC: U.S. Department of Labor. Retrieved from www.bls.gov/spotlight/2011/women/data.htm#ces_industry.

Bureau of Labor Statistics. (2011b). *Educational attainment of women in the labor force, 1970–2010*. Washington, DC: U.S. Department of Labor. Retrieved from www.bls.gov/opub/ted/2011/ted_20111229.htm.

Burrell, B. C. (2004). *Women and political participation: A reference handbook*. Santa Barbara, CA: ABC-CLIO.

Carroll, S. (2001). Representing women: Women state legislators as agents of policy-related change. In S. J. Carroll (Ed.), *The impact of women in public office* (pp. 3–21). Bloomington: Indiana University Press.

Carroll, S. (2012, November 9). Election shows what women want. *CNN Election Center*. Retrieved from www.cnn.com/2012/11/08/opinion/carroll-women-election.

Center for American Women and Politics. (2013a). Retrieved February 24, 2013 from www.cawp.rutgers.edu/.

Chase, S. E. (1995). *Ambiguous empowerment: The work narratives of women school superintendents*. Amherst: University of Massachusetts Press.

Chase, S. E., & Bell, C. S. (1990). Ideology, discourse, and gender: How gatekeepers talk about women school superintendents. *Social Problems, 37*, 163.

Collins, P. H. (1991). *Black feminist thought: Knowledge, consciousness, and the politics of empowerment*. New York: Routledge.

Connell, R. (1987). *Gender and power: Society, the person, and sexual politics*. Cambridge, UK: Polity Press in association with B. Blackwell.

Cook, E. A., & Wilcox, C. (2009). Feminism and the gender gap: A second look. *The Journal of Politics, 53*(04), 1111.

Corbett, C., & Hill, C. (2012). *Graduating to a pay gap: The earnings of women and men one year after college graduation*. Washington, DC: American Association of University Women.

Corbett, C., Hill, C., & St. Rose, A. (2008). *Where the girls are: The facts about gender equity in education executive summary.* Washington, DC: American Association of University Women. Retrieved from www.aauw.org/resource/where-the-girls-are-the-facts-about-gender-equity-in-education-executive-summary/.

Cross, C. T. (2004). *Political education: National policy comes of age.* New York: Teachers College Press.

Cutler, W. W. (2000). *Parents and schools: The 150-year struggle for control in American education.* Chicago, IL: University of Chicago Press.

Datnow, A. (1998). *The gender politics of educational change.* London; Washington, DC: Falmer Press.

David, M. E. (1993). *Parents, gender, and education reform.* Cambridge, MA: Polity Press.

Dietz, M. (1992). Feminism and theories of citizenship. In C. Mouffe (Ed.), *Dimensions of radical democracy: pluralism, citizenship, community* (pp. 63–85). Brooklyn, NY: Verso Books.

Dillard, C. B. (2000). The substance of things hoped for, the evidence of things not seen: Examining an endarkened feminist epistemology in educational research and leadership. *International Journal of Qualitative Studies in Education, 13*(6), 661–681.

Dobie, D. F., & Hummel, B. (2001). Successful women superintendents in a gender-biased profession. *Equity & Excellence in Education, 34*(2), 22–28.

Dodson, D. L. (2006). *The impact of women in Congress.* Oxford; New York: Oxford University Press.

Donahue, J. C. (1999). The nonrepresentation of gender. *Women & Politics, 20*(3), 65–81.

Dyrness, A. (2011). *Mothers united: An immigrant struggle for socially just education.* Minneapolis, MN: University of Minnesota Press.

Edwards, D. (2012, April 5). RNC chair: GOP "war on women" fictional like "war on caterpillars." *The Raw Story.* Retrieved from www.rawstory.com/rs/2012/04/05/rnc-chair-gop-war-on-women-fictional-like-war-on-caterpillars/.

Elliott, C. M. (2008). *Raising change: Fathering as a feminist experience* (dissertation). California Institute of Integral Studies, San Francisco, CA.

Elshtain, J. B. (1981). *Public man, private woman: Women in social and political thought.* Princeton, NJ: Princeton University Press.

Faludi, S. (1992). *Backlash: The undeclared war against American women.* New York: Anchor Books.

Feuerstein, A. (2006). School administration and the changing face of masculinity. *Journal of School Leadership, 16*(1), 4.

Ferguson, K. E. (1984). *The feminist case against bureaucracy.* Philadelphia, PA: Temple University Press.

Fine, M. (1992). Silencing and nurturing voice in an improbable context: Urban adolescents in public school. In *Disruptive voices: The possibilities of feminist research* (pp. 115–138). Ann Arbor: University of Michigan Press.

Fine, M. (1993). Sexuality, schooling, and adolescent females: The missing discourse of desire. In L. Weis & M. Fine (Eds.), *Beyond silenced voices: Class, race, and gender in United States schools* (pp. 29–54). Albany: State University of New York Press.

Flexner, E. (1975). *Century of struggle: The woman's rights movement in the United States* (Rev. ed.). Cambridge, MA: Belknap Press of Harvard University Press.

Fraser, N. (1989). *Unruly practices: power, discourse, and gender in contemporary social theory.* Minneapolis: University of Minnesota Press.

Fraynd, D. J., & Capper, C. A. (2003). "Do you have any idea who you just hired?!?" A study of open and closeted sexual minority K-12 administrators. *Journal of School Leadership, 13*(1), 86–124.

Friend, R. (1993). Choices, not closets: Heterosexism and homophobia in schools. In L. Weis & M. Fine (Eds.), *Beyond silenced voices: Class, race, and gender in United States schools* (pp. 209–235). Albany: State University of New York Press.

Funding Status—Women's Educational Equity. (2011, November 2). *U.S. Department of Education.* Retrieved February 7, 2013 from www2.ed.gov/programs/equity/funding.html.

Fuss, D. (1989). *Essentially speaking: Feminism, nature & difference.* New York: Routledge.

Gaine, C., & George, R. (1999). *Gender, "race", and class in schooling: A new introduction.* Philadelphia, PA: Falmer Press.

Gilligan, C. (1982). *In a different voice: Psychological theory and women's development.* Cambridge, MA: Harvard University Press.

Gladstone, L. (2001). Women's issues in Congress: Selected legislation 1832–1998. In J. V. Lewis (Ed.), *Women and women's issues in Congress: 1832–2000* (pp. 11–106). Huntington, NY: Nova Science Publishers.

Goss, K. A., & Heaney, M. T. (2010). Organizing women as women: Hybridity and grassroots collective action in the 21st Century. *Perspectives on Politics, 8*(01), 27.

Griffith, A. I., & Smith, D. E. (2005). *Mothering for schooling* (1st ed.). New York: RoutledgeFalmer.

Grogan, M. (1996). *Voices of women aspiring to the superintendency.* Albany: State University of New York Press.

Grogan, M. (2000). The short tenure of a woman superintendent: A clash of gender and politics. *Journal of School Leadership, 10*(2), 104–130.

Harbeck, K. M. (1997). *Gay and lesbian educators: Personal freedoms, public constraints.* Malden, MA: Amethyst.

Harding, S. G. (Ed.). (1987). *Feminism and methodology: Social science issues.* Bloomington: Indiana University Press.

Harding, S. G. (1991). *Whose science? Whose knowledge?: Thinking from women's lives.* Ithaca, NY: Cornell University Press.

Hawkesworth, M. (1994). Policy studies within a feminist frame. *Policy Sciences, 27*(2), 97–118.

Henderson, S. (2004, December 1). Coach tries high court press. *The News & Observer,* p. 5A. Raleigh, NC.

Hess, F. M., & Leal, D. L. (1999). Politics and sex-related programs in urban schooling. *Urban Affairs Review, 35*(1), 24–43.

Hess, F. M., & Meeks, O. (2010). *School boards circa 2010: Governance in the accountability era* (pp. 1–38). The National School Boards Association.

Hill, C., & American Association of University Women. (2010). *Why so few?: Women in science, technology, engineering, and mathematics.* Washington, DC: American Association of University Women.

Hill, C., & Kearl, H. (2011). *Crossing the line: Sexual harassment at school.* Washington, DC: American Association of University Women.

Hodgkinson, H. L., & Montenegro, X. (1999). *The US school superintendent: The invisible CEO.* ERIC.

Irving, C. J., & English, L. M. (2011). Community in cyberspace: Gender, social movement learning, and the Internet. *Adult Education Quarterly, 61*(3), 262–278.

Johnson, L. (2012). Lisa Murkowski: It makes no sense to make this attack on women. *The Huffington Post.* Retrieved from www.huffingtonpost.com/2012/04/05/lisa-murkowski-war-on-women_n_1406923.html.

Jones, G. H. (2005). *Site-based voices: Dilemmas of educators who engage in activism against student-to-student sexual harassment* (Dissertation). University of North Carolina at Chapel Hill.

Kaiser Family Foundation. (2012). *Kaiser Health Tracking Poll—May 2012* (No. 8315). Retrieved from www.kff.org/kaiserpolls/8315.cfm.

Kanter, R. M. (1977). *Men and women of the corporation.* New York: Basic Books.

Kelly, R. M., & Duerst-Lahti, G. (1995). Toward gender awareness and gender balance in leadership and governance. In G. Duerst-Lahti & R. M. Kelly (Eds.), *Gender, power, leadership and governance* (pp. 260–271). Ann Arbor: University of Michigan Press.

Kirp, D. L., Yudof, M. G., & Franks, M. S. (1986). *Gender justice.* Chicago, IL: University of Chicago Press.

Klein, E. (1984). *Gender politics: From consciousness to mass politics.* Cambridge, MA: Harvard University Press.

Knight, M. G. (2002a). (In)(Di)Visible identities of youth: College preparation programs from a feminist standpoint. In W. G. Tierney & L. S. Hagedorn (Eds.), *Increasing access to college: Extending possibilities for all students* (pp. 123–144). Albany: State University of New York Press.

Knight, M. G. (2002b). The intersections of race, class, and gender in the teacher preparation of an African American social justice educator. *Equity & Excellence in Education, 35*(3), 212–224.

Kowalski, T. J., McCord, R. S., Petersen, G. J., Young, I. P., & Ellerson, N. M. (2011). *The American school superintendent: 2010 decennial study.* Lanham, MD: Rowman & Littlefield Education.

Krenkel, N. (1975). Activities of women's committees in a sample of professional associations. *Educational Researcher, 4*(9), 25–28.

Kristeva, J. (1980). Woman can never be defined. In E. Marks & I. De Courtivron (Eds.), *New French feminisms: An anthology* (pp. 137–141). Amherst: University of Massachusetts Press.

Laible, J. (1997). Feminist analysis of sexual harassment policy: A critique of the ideal of community. In Catherine Marshall (Ed.), *Feminist critical policy analysis I: A perspective from primary and secondary schooling* (pp. 201–215). Washington, DC: Falmer Press.

Leck, G. M. (2000). Heterosexual or homosexual? Reconsidering binary narratives on sexual identities in urban schools. *Education and Urban Society, 32*(3), 324–348.

Lee, V. E., Smith, J. B., & Cioci, M. (1993). Teachers and principals: Gender-related perceptions of leadership and power in secondary schools. *Educational Evaluation and Policy Analysis, 15*(2), 153–180.

Legrand, W. H. (2005). *Activism for LGBT rights: How participation affects the lives of activist educators* (3190482). University of North Carolina at Chapel Hill. Retrieved from Dissertations & Theses @ University of North Carolina at Chapel Hill; ProQuest Dissertations & Theses (PQDT). (305393453).

López, N. (2003). *Hopeful girls, troubled boys: Race and gender disparity in urban education.* New York: Routledge.

Lugg, C. A. (1998). The religious right and public education: The paranoid politics of homophobia. *Educational Policy, 12*(3), 267–283.

Lugg, C. A. (2003a). Sissies, faggots, lezzies, and dykes: Gender, sexual orientation, and a new politics of education? *Educational Administration Quarterly, 39*(1), 95–134.

Lugg, C. A. (2003b). Our straitlaced administrators: The law, lesbian, gay, bisexual, and transgendered educational administrators, and the assimilationist imperative. *Journal of School Leadership, 13*(1), 51–85.

Luttrell, W. (1988). The Edison School struggle: The reshaping of working-class education and women's consciousness. In *Women and the politics of empowerment* (pp. 136–156). Philadelphia, PA: Temple University Press.

MacLeod, J. (1987). *Ain't no makin' it: Leveled aspirations in a low-income neighborhood.* Boulder, CO: Westview Press.

Maher, F. (1999). Progressive education and feminist pedagogies: Issues in gender, power and authority. *The Teachers College Record, 101*(1), 35–59.

Mahitivanichcha, K., & Rorrer, A. K. (2006). Women's choices within market constraints: Re-visioning access to and participation in the superintendency. *Educational Administration Quarterly, 42*(4), 483–517.

Marshall, A. (2002). Organizing across the divide: Local feminist activism, everyday life, and the election of women to public office. *Social Science Quarterly, 83*(3), 707–725.

Marshall, C. (1993). Politics of denial: Gender and race issues in administration. In Catherine Marshall (Ed.), *The new politics of race and gender: The 1992 yearbook of the Politics of Education Association* (pp. 168–174). Washington, DC: Falmer Press.

Marshall, C. (1997a). Dismantling and reconstructing policy analysis. In Catherine Marshall (Ed.), *Feminist critical policy analysis I: A perspective from primary and secondary schooling* (pp. 1–39). Washington, DC: Falmer Press.

Marshall, C. (Ed.). (1997b). *Feminist critical policy analysis I: A perspective from primary and secondary schooling.* London; Washington, DC: Falmer Press.

Marshall, C. (2002). Teacher unions and gender equity policy for education. *Educational Policy, 16*(5), 707–730.

Marshall, C., & Gerstl-Pepin, C. I. (2005). *Re-framing educational politics for social justice.* Boston, MA: Pearson/Allyn & Bacon.

Marshall, C., Mitchell, D. E., & Wirt, F. M. (1989). *Culture and education policy in the American states.* New York: Falmer Press.

Marshall, C., & Rossman, G. B. (2011). *Designing qualitative research* (5th ed.). Los Angeles, CA: Sage Publications.

Marshall, C., & Ward, M. (2004). "Yes, but . . . ": Education leaders discuss social justice. *Journal of School Leadership, 14*(5), 530–563.

Marshall, C., & Young, M. (2006). Gender and methodology. In C. Skelton, B. Francis, & L. Smulyn (Eds.), *The SAGE handbook of gender and education* (pp. 63–78). Thousand Oaks, CA: Sage Publications.

Marshall, C., & Young, M. (2013). Policy inroads undermining women in education. *International Journal of Leadership in Education, 16*(2), 205–219.

McFadden, A. H. (2004). *The social construction of educational leadership: Southern Appalachian ceilings.* New York: P. Lang.

Mendez-Morse, S. (2004). Constructing mentors: Latina educational leaders' role models and mentors. *Educational Administration Quarterly, 40*(4), 561–590.

Middleton, S. (1993). *Educating feminists: Life histories and pedagogy.* New York: Teachers College Press.

Morgen, S., & Bookman, A. (1988). Rethinking women and politics: An introductory essay. In A. Bookman & S. Morgen (Eds.), *Women and the politics of empowerment* (pp. 3–32). Philadelphia, PA: Temple University Press.

Mountford, M., & Brunner, C. C. (2010). Gendered behavior patterns in school board governance. *Teachers College Record, 112*(8), 2067–2117.

Mueller, C. M. (Ed.). (1988). *The politics of the gender gap: The social construction of political influence.* Newbury Park, CA: Sage Publications.

Naples, N. A. (1998a). *Grassroots warriors: Activist mothering, community work, and the war on poverty.* New York: Routledge.

Naples, N. A. (1998b). Women's community activism: Exploring the dynamics of politicization and diversity. In N. A. Naples (Ed.), *Community activism and feminist politics: Organizing across race, class, and gender* (pp. 32–349). New York: Routledge.

NASSPE: Legal status of single-sex education. (2011). Retrieved February 25, 2013 from www.singlesexschools.org/policy-legalstatus.htm.

National Center for Education Statistics. (2012). *The condition of education 2012* (No. NCES 2012–047). Retrieved from http://nces.ed.gov/programs/coe/indicator_dcd.asp.

National Coalition for Women and Girls in Education (NCWGE). (2012). *Title IX at 40: Working to ensure gender equity in education.* Washington, DC: NCWGE.

National Women's Law Center. (2004). *Slip-sliding away: The erosion of hard-won gains for women under the Bush administration and an agenda for moving forward.* Washington, DC: National Women's Law Center. Retrieved from www.nwlc.org/resource/slip-sliding-away-erosion-hard-won-gains-women-under-bush-administration-and-agenda-moving-.

Nespor, J., & Hicks, D. (2010). Wizards and witches: Parent advocates and contention in special education in the USA. *Journal of Education Policy, 25*(3), 309–334.

No Child Left Behind Act of 2001. 115 Stat.1425, 20 U.S.C. 6301 et seq. (2002).

Noddings, N. (1992). *The challenge to care in schools: An alternative approach to education.* New York: Teachers College Press.

Oakes, J., & Wells, A. S. (1996). *Beyond the technicalities of school reform: Policy lessons from detracking schools.* UCLA Graduate School of Education & Information Studies.

Pateman, C., & Gross, E. (Eds.). (1987). *Feminist challenges: Social and political theory.* Boston, MA: Northeastern University Press.

Payne, C. (1990). Men led, but women organized: Movement participation of women in the Mississippi Delta. In V. L. Crawford, J. A. Rouse, & B. Woods (Eds.), *Women in the civil rights movement: Trailblazers and torchbearers, 1941–1965* (pp. 1–11). Brooklyn, NY: Carson Publishing, Inc.

Peter, K., & Horn, L. (2005). *Gender differences in participation and completion of undergraduate education and how they have changed over time (NCES 2005–169).* Washington, DC: U.S. Department of Education, National Center for Education Statistics. Retrieved from http://nces.ed.gov/pubsearch/pubsinfo.asp?pubid = 2005169.

Pillow, W. S. (2004). *Unfit subjects: Educational policy and the teen mother.* New York: RoutledgeFalmer.

Pounder, D. G., & Merrill, R. J. (2001). Job desirability of the high school principalship: A job choice theory perspective. *Educational Administration Quarterly, 37*(1), 27–57.

Reingold, B., & Harrell, J. (2009). The impact of descriptive representation on women's political engagement: Does party matter? *Political Research Quarterly, 63*(2), 280–294.

Royal, C. (2008). Framing the Internet: A comparison of gendered spaces. *Social Science Computer Review, 26*(2), 152–169.

Sanbonmatsu, K. (2002). Political parties and the recruitment of women to state legislatures. *Journal of Politics, 64*(3), 791–809.

Sanbonmatsu, K., & Dolan, K. (2009). Do gender stereotypes transcend party? *Political Research Quarterly, 62*(3), 485–494.

Sanders-Lawson, R., Smith-Campbell, S., & Benham, M. K. P. (2006). Holistic visioning for social justice: Black women theorizing practice. In C. Marshall & M. Oliva (Eds.), *Leadership for social justice: Making revolutions in education* (pp. 31–63). Boston, MA: Pearson/Allyn & Bacon.

Sapiro, V. (1981). Research frontier essay: When are interests interesting? The problem of political representation of women. *The American Political Science Review, 75*(3), 701–716.

Sapiro, V. (2004). Not your parents' political socialization: Introduction for a new generation. *Annual Review of Political Science, 7*, 1–23.

Shakeshaft, C. (1995). Peer harassment in schools. *Journal for a Just and Caring Education, 1*(1), 30–44.

Shakeshaft, C. (1998). Wild patience and bad fit: Assessing the impact of affirmative action on women in school administration. *Educational Researcher, 27*(9), 10–12.

Smith, D. E. (1990). *Texts, facts, and femininity: Exploring the relations of ruling.* London; New York: Routledge.

Smulyan, L. (2000). *Balancing acts: Women principals at work.* Albany: State University of New York Press.

Sommer, C. H. (2006). Title IX shouldn't be used as an academic weapon. *USA Today Magazine.* Retrieved from www.usatoday.com.

SPEAK: Suicide Prevention Education Awareness for Kids. (2013). *Www.speakforthem.org.* Retrieved February 7, 2013 from www.speakforthem.org/facts.html.

Spring, J. H. (2006). *American education* (12th ed.). Boston, MA: McGraw Hill Higher Education.

Stromquist, N. P. (1997). State policies and gender equity: Comparative perspectives. In B. J. Bank & P. M. Hall (Eds.), *Gender, equity, and schooling: Policy and practice* (pp. 31–62). New York: Garland.

Taleb, N. N. (2004). *Fooled by randomness: The hidden role of chance in life and in the markets* (2nd ed.). New York: Thomson/Texere.

Taleb, N. N. (2010). *The black swan: The impact of the highly improbable fragility [Kindle Edition]* (2nd ed.). Random House Digital, Inc.

Tallerico, M. (2000). Gaining access to the superintendency: Headhunting, gender, and color. *Educational Administration Quarterly, 36*(1), 18–43.

Taylor, S. (1997). Critical policy analysis: Exploring contexts, texts and consequences. *Discourse: Studies in the Cultural Politics of Education, 18*(1), 23–35.

The War on Women: Day by Day. (2012). Emily's List. Retrieved from http://emilyslist.org/waronwomen.

Thorne, B. (1993). *Gender play: Girls and boys in school.* New Brunswick, NJ: Rutgers University Press.

Titus, J. J. (2000). Engaging student resistance to feminism: "How is this stuff going to make us better teachers?" *Gender and Education, 12*(1), 21–37.

Tong, R. (1989). *Feminist thought: A comprehensive introduction.* Boulder, CO: Westview Press.

Tyack, D. (1974). *The one best system: A history of American urban education.* Cambridge, MA: Harvard University Press.

Tyack, D., & Cuban, L. (1995). *Tinkering toward utopia: A century of public school reform.* Cambridge, MA: Harvard University Press.

Tyack, D., & Hansot, E. (1988). Silence and policy talk: Historical puzzles about gender and education. *Educational Researcher, 17*(3), 33–41.

Urban, W. J. (2001). Courting the woman teacher: The National Education Association, 1917–1970. *History of Education Quarterly, 41*(2), 139–166.

Visweswaran, K. (1994). *Fictions of feminist ethnography.* Minneapolis: University of Minnesota Press.

Vogt, C., & Chen, P. (2001). Feminisms and the Internet. *Peace Review, 13*(3), 371–374.

Warren, M. R. (2011). Community organizing for education reform. In M. Orr & J. Rogers (Eds.), *Public engagement for public education: Joining forces to revitalize democracy and equalize schools* (pp. 139–172). Stanford, CA: Stanford University Press.

Weiler, K. (1988). *Women teaching for change: Gender, class & power.* South Hadley, MA: Bergin & Garvey Publishers.

Weis, L. (1993). White male working-class youth: An exploration of relative privilege and loss. In L. Weis & M. Fine (Eds.), *Beyond silenced voices: Class, race, and gender in United States schools* (pp. 237–258). Albany: State University of New York Press.

Wellesley College, & American Association of University Women. (1995). *How schools shortchange girls: The AAUW report: A study of major findings on girls and education* (1st trade pbk. ed.). New York: Marlowe & Co.

Why women should vote: To make sure women can make their own reproductive health care decisions. (2012, June 26). National Women's Law Center. Retrieved from www.nwlc.org/resource/why-women-should-vote-make-sure-women-can-make-their-own-reproductive-health-care-decisions.

Willis, P. E. (1977). *Learning to labor: How working class kids get working class jobs.* New York: Columbia University Press.

Wing, A. K. (1997). Introduction. In A. K. Wing (Ed.), *Critical race feminism: A reader* (pp. 1–6). New York: New York University Press.

Women in State Legislatures 2013. (2013, February 13). *National Conference of State Legislatures.* Retrieved from www.ncsl.org/legislatures-elections/wln/women-in-state-legislatures-for-2013.aspx.

Working the ruins: Feminist poststructural theory and methods in education. (2000). New York: Routledge.

Yates, L. (1997). Gender, ethnicity and the inclusive curriculum: An episode in the policy framing of Australian education. In Catherine Marshall (Ed.), *Feminist critical policy analysis I: A perspective from primary and secondary schooling* (pp. 43–53). London; Washington, DC: Falmer Press.

Young, M. (2003). Troubling policy discourse: Gender, constructions, and the leadership crisis. In M. D. Young & L. Skrla (Eds.), *Reconsidering feminist research in educational leadership* (pp. 265–298). Albany: State University of New York Press.

11

RELIGIOUS FAITH AND POLICY IN PUBLIC EDUCATION

A Political and Historical Analysis of the Christian Right in American Schooling

Nathan R. Myers and James G. Cibulka

One of the most remarked-upon phenomena in American politics is the growing influence of the Christian right. In this chapter we examine the Christian right's political influence on K-12 education. We pose several questions. First, is the political influence of religious groups on education a new development in American history? We shall argue that religious influences on public education were prevalent in both the 19th and 20th centuries. Although religious influences on public education were muted after World War II, during the 1970s religious groups reemerged as important political actors. We suggest that this historical interpretation sheds light on the significance of the Christian right as a political movement and its potential for transforming K-12 education. Accordingly, in the first section of this chapter we undertake an historical survey of the ways conservative religious groups from the mid-19th century forward have attempted to affect federal, state, and local policy.

We then pose a second question. How similar or different is the Christian right to its forbears in American history in terms of beliefs, internal strains, and its attitudes toward use of the political process to achieve its goals? To answer this question we draw an analytical distinction between the characteristics that we identify in the "old" fundamentalist political right, and the "new" Christian fundamentalism. This chapter explores what resemblance and distinctiveness the older fundamentalism bears to the newer form and what this means for K-12 education.

Third, we pose the question of how influential the Christian right has been on education issues, particularly in the context of the range of issues around which it has mobilized. Finally, given the characteristics of the movement and our assessment of its influence, we entertain some alternative scenarios for the future role of the Christian right as a political force shaping the politics of K-12 education.

METHODS

To investigate the issues surrounding political involvement of the Christian right, various primary and secondary sources were consulted. Documentary materials were reviewed at Baylor University's Oral History Institute. A total of 16 interviews with scholars (3), organizational directors (8), and activists (6) have been completed for this study. The interviews followed the traditions of elite interviewing (Dexter, 1970). We utilized a semi-structured format to gain a participant's perspective on: overall aims of the Christian right; educational agenda of the Christian right; internal cohesiveness of the Christian right; the external party politics of the Christian right; tactics; and the historical involvement of the Christian right.

Interviewees were encouraged to add other observations on the intersection of faith, politics, and education. Other primary materials utilized here include court cases, Christian right newsletters, and national and organizational newspapers. Individuals whose identity appears in previous published materials or collected oral histories will be named; however, the participants of source-protected interviews will be identified by their category (Scholar, Activist, Organizational director) and by the area of the country in which they work (Midwest, East, South, West).

After each interview, audiotapes were transcribed and coded. Initially, the coding scheme followed the topics from the interview schedule. The strategy of analytic induction through the "constant comparative method" was employed to identify clear cleavages among the respondents and to find theoretical explanations (Glaser & Strauss, 1999).

From the original seven topics, six clear themes were emergent from the interviews. The main themes were *family and sexuality as core concerns; splits on peripheral issues including education; the split on education between those who advocate free market reforms and those who wish to "save" the public schools; cooperation across denominational lines; competing interests in the Republican Party; and recent changes in the tactics and leadership of the Christian right.* In interpreting these themes, an attempt is made to connect the history of Christian fundamentalism to its present and future.

Historical Perspective

Virtually all of the politics of education scholarship views the intersection of faith and politics as a relatively recent phenomenon that either rose out of the Christian right movement of the 1970s or at the earliest, out of the fundamentalism and culture wars brought to the fore by the 1925 Scopes trial (e.g., Corbett & Corbett, 1999; Deckman, 2004; Diamond, 1995; Herberg, 1955). For example, Diamond traced the beginning of the religious right's political involvement to the 1930s but argued that the Christian right didn't become an indispensable part of the larger conservative movement until the 1970s and 1980s when it demonstrated "a rich network of organizational resources, including interdenominational parachurch ministries and an unparalleled religious broadcasting industry" (Diamond, 1995, pp. 92–93). Deckman documented conservative Christian involvement on local school boards beginning with the evolution battles of the 1920s but concluded that the Christian right only became a political force during the late 1970s and 1980s (Deckman, 2004, pp. 2–3). Lugg's insightful analysis of conservatism and American school policy traced one strand of today's conservatism to the social traditionalism of the 1950s (1966, pp. 13–16).

Historians such as Marty and Justice, however, trace the political involvement of fundamentalist (and progressive) religious groups to the 19th century. According to Marty, conservative Protestants consistently used the political process to maintain the control they enjoyed until after World War II (2004, p. 9). Justice (2005) shows that Protestants were heavily involved in the politics of the public school movement of the 1870s, many times resorting to anti-Catholic rhetoric and nativist attacks to ensure that public funds were not funneled to support parochial schools. In short, works by historians, political scientists, and others have demonstrated that the roots of religion in politics, particularly the role of Christian fundamentalists, are much deeper than the early to mid-20th century.

Although the participation of religious groups in American politics is a time-honored tradition, a distinct change in the type and pattern of participation occurred around World War II. Thus, our analysis distinguishes *old fundamentalism* and *new fundamentalism*. In the aftermath of World War II, a series of events marked the decline of the white Protestant domination of America. Protestant elites reconstituted *new fundamentalism* to reclaim the institutional control lost in American life by the 1960s and 1970s, including public education. The *new fundamentalism* bore some resemblance to the older form, but also important differences. In short, the current Christian right movement is a resurgence of an older strain of religious politics in America, which in education has reinvigorated old debates about religion in public schools, public aid to parochial schools, and so on.

Old Fundamentalism

Historians of religious movements in the United States have commented on the essentially Protestant character of 19th-century America, its politics, and its institutions (Dobson, Hindson, & Falwell, 1981; Marsden, 2006; Marty, 1993, 2004). As early as the 1830s, Christian evangelist Charles Finney wrote that Christians were "found to exert their influence to secure a legislation that is in accordance with the law of God" (Marsden, 2006, p. 87). Nineteenth-century Christian fundamentalists disagreed on a host of theological issues as well as on the political and moral issues of the day. Prior to the Civil War, these disagreements were largely sectional in nature. The best example in this regard is the abolitionist movement prior to the Civil War. While the abolition of slavery was supported from the Northern evangelical center of Oberlin College, Southern evangelicals and fundamentalists took more moderate views on abolition and, in some cases, even laid out theological defenses of slavery (Blue, 2004). Even in the aftermath of the Civil War, nonessential issues such as prohibition and anti-Masonry divided fundamentalists (Falwell et al., 1981; Isaac, 1965).

After 1870, a more national coalition of Northern and Southern fundamentalists emerged that united around the themes of antimodernism and anti-Catholicism. However, race would remain a divisive issue within the ranks of the old fundamentalists, as we have described them. In 1873, a professor at the Evangelical Alliance warned that "infidel bugles are sounding in front of us, Papal bugles are sounding behind us" (Marsden, 2006, p. 17). Their establishment fights against Darwinism and Catholicism would occupy the political efforts of the old fundamentalists for the remainder of the 1800s, the most visible battleground involving public schools. During the 1870s, "Bible wars" raged over whether local school boards would continue to be dominated by King James' Bible-toting Protestants with their theology of grace, or by Catholics who wanted to ensure their children were properly catechized and who used the Douay-Rheims Bible. Thus, in the late 19th century, fundamentalist Protestants engaged in politics for the purpose of protecting their own hegemony in American institutions such as the public school.

The decline of fundamentalism as an important political force was precipitated by several important factors including the decline of antimodernism as a political issue, and the onset of a common foreign threat in communism. During the 1930s, anti-Catholicism was taking its last gasps as a unifying force among fundamentalists when conservative religious leaders such as J. Frank Norris campaigned against presidential candidate Al Smith on the basis of his Catholic religion (Norris, 1963). Whereas the old fundamentalists became effectively united in the aftermath of the Civil War, after World War II the old issues did not unite them politically as they once had. From World War II until the 1970s fundamentalists such as Billy Graham and even Jerry Falwell tended to confine their political involvement to participation in mainstream partisan politics rather than in advocating distinct fundamentalist platforms, while other fundamentalists favored nonparticipation altogether.

New Fundamentalism

With the election of Jimmy Carter in 1976, an evangelical Christian was elected to the presidency who publicly talked about his faith; 1976 was labeled by *Time Magazine* as the year of the evangelical (Wuthnow, 1989). Carter was one of the first successful presidential candidates to make his personal faith a campaign issue, and by doing so attempted to capture a portion of the electorate that identified as Christian and conservative. The inclusive and prochoice Democratic Party was an odd fit, however, for conservative Christians who, after years of political division and nonparticipation, increasingly became united around two themes—family and sexuality.

Several tactics were key to the rise of "new fundamentalism." First, the rise of numerous Christian right organizations beginning in the late 1970s provided an organizational base for the new movement. The involvement of conservative, traditional Catholics such as Phyllis Schlafly, Richard Viguerie, and Paul Weyrich signaled a broadening of the Christian right's religious bases, as well as its appeal to Northerners as well as Southerners. Second, the use of the Christian media, together with the utilization of direct mail strategies, proved to be powerful organizing tools (Gallup & Castelli, 1989). Television evangelists such as Pat Robertson and Jerry Falwell built political movements by tapping their physical and television congregations. Ultimately, televangelists served an important function in helping to "guide evangelical laity toward increased political activity on the conservative and Republican side" (Heclo & McClay, 2003). In addition to religious broadcasting, direct mail strategies came to be very important to the new fundamentalist movement. With the aid of Richard Viguerie, fundamentalists and their allies would wage very successful "voter education" campaigns on a host of issues from abortion and school prayer to the Equal Rights Amendment (Marsden, 2006).

By 1980, Ronald Reagan was able to articulate an agenda that spoke to these two uniting themes, family and sexuality. Reagan campaigned on "values" issues such as restricting access to abortion, antifederalism, tax credits for private schooling, and welfare reform. In response to Republican overtures, conservative Christians organized behind Republican issues and candidates. Conservative Christians pioneered such techniques as targeted mail distribution lists and utilized a vast media empire of religious television, radio, and print mediums. This increase in political activity on the part of conservative Christians can be considered the beginnings of the new fundamentalism.

In sum, important similarities and differences emerged between the circumstances and goals of new fundamentalism versus old fundamentalism. The main difference is in the movements' respective goals. Whereas old fundamentalism basically sought to protect Protestant status and privilege, new fundamentalism seeks to reclaim some measure of status and privilege in public life. Another important difference is that where old fundamentalism was bipartisan, and sought to influence Democratic and Republican views on issues ranging from the teaching of Darwinism to legislation against liquor, new fundamentalism is closely identified with the Republican Party.

The similarities between the two movements are also instructive. Both old and new fundamentalism were united on a core set of issues that were considered central to their faith identities. Also, outside of these core issues, fundamentalist consensus in both eras began to fray on issues that were considered more peripheral such as anti-Masonry for the old fundamentalists or educational politics for the new fundamentalists.

Analyzing the Political Power of the Christian Right

In this section we analyze the political power of the contemporary Christian right. A number of forces explain why the political power of this group has grown; at the same time constraining factors also deserve attention. First, we focus on the internal coherence and strains in the Christian right movement, and then on the linkage between the movement and the national Republican Party.

THE INTERNAL COHERENCE AND STRAINS IN THE CHRISTIAN RIGHT

A major finding from our interviews has been that the Christian right is animated by two central themes: (1) the attempt to restore to American life the sanctity of family and (2) appropriate rules of sexual conduct and belief, both of which are rooted in the conviction that Christian morality has been replaced by secular values. This common starting point is a powerful cohesive force that brings together Americans from different ethnic, social, cultural, and religious traditions. At the same time, like most social movements, the Christian right is not a unitary movement with only one perspective. There are diverse strands within the Christian right. The Christian right is best seen as a collection of similar, but sometimes competing interests who must form coalitions to garner sufficient influence. A close reading of the history of the Christian right demonstrates differences among the erstwhile Christian Coalition, Southern Baptists, Eagle Forum, James Dobson's Focus on the Family, the National Right to Life Committee, Tony Perkins' Family Research Council, and other groups.

These differences are reflected in different denominational traditions—Protestants, Catholics, Jews, and the many subgroups within them—as well as in different goals. Christian Reconstructionists, for example, believe that Jesus will not return until a theocratic state is built, while dispensationalists interpret disasters as divine intervention and punishment for our errant ways (Phillips, 2006). Obviously, not all evangelical Christians share these extreme views, but the Christian right accommodates a wide range of specific doctrines. Religious denominations and sects historically have tended to be fractious, yet, since the 1970s, the Christian right has been able to put some of its denominational differences aside to work together on areas of common concern (Smidt, 2013).

During the early and middle 2000s, a loosely organized movement within Christian churches known as the Emergent Church (EC) movement began within the Christian right. While still a minority viewpoint within the Christian right, this movement is suspicious of ecclesiastical structures and authorities other than the Bible. Although the EC movement also hopes to transform the political arena, its methods are quite different from others in the new fundamentalist movement. Christians in the EC movement eschew overt political maneuvering in favor of pursuing communal ideas of justice (Gibbs & Bolger, 2005). While the EC movement exists within the spectrum of new fundamentalism and the Christian right, it is at this point poorly organized and not a dominant force within new fundamentalism. The forces of the EC movement, however, bear watching for its potential to change the ways that the Christian right interacts with politics.

Despite this heterogeneity, our research has underscored the powerful centrifugal forces binding the Christian right together around core issues. The cross-denominational character of the movement was reflected in interviews with individuals who had varying levels of involvement with the Christian right. The key idea here, best summed up by a religious historian, is that "Catholics, Protestants, Evangelicals . . . Pentecostals, fundamentalists and so on have been able to set their theological differences to the side to come together on what they have in common" (Scholar 1, Midwest). This phenomenon was noted by nearly all of the interviewees, including those with more of a direct working relationship to the Christian right.

One organizational director, describing her own involvement with the beginnings of the movement during the 1970s and 1980s, shared that one characteristic of the Christian right was to get "people of different denominations to come out of the churches and join the battle against the equal rights amendment and for the first time that put Baptists and Catholics and Jews and Mormons in the same room. They had never been in the same room. . . . They were brought up to be suspicious of each other. I built a real ecumenical movement where nobody felt theologically threatened. . . . Where they could work together in politics for a goal they shared" (Organizational Director 3, Midwest).

James T. Draper, former president of the Southern Baptist Sunday School Board, echoes this theme by describing his working relationship with other religious conservatives during the 1980s: "There have been a lot of things in the last twenty-five or thirty years—pornography—another issue where reaching across denominational lines you could join hands." Draper described one colleague as "pure Pentecostal," noting that he didn't "agree with his theology—not at all—but I can stand with him and pray for our country" (Draper, 1997, p. 27).

This cooperation continues to define the work of the Christian right. One activist who is also a pastor of a mega-church from the Midwest who has been active in building bridges between his own evangelical congregation and Pentecostals and others described his work in these terms: "I gathered with Pentecostals and . . . a whole room full of leaders [we] do not have a congruent theological template. You don't have to be my twin to be my brother. And he's my brother" (Activist 1, Midwest). Thus, the movement's ability to work across theological and denominational divides is a key finding.

At the same time, the Christian right's political unity depends on issues related to the broader themes of sexuality and family. One academic observer of the Christian right is demonstrative of this idea: "the galvanizing thing is abortion and gays" (Scholar 1, Midwest). In addition to abortion and homosexuality, other interviewees gave responses that the Christian right rallied around anti-stem cell research and traditional marriage and partnership arrangements. Another religious scholar commented: "Abortion . . . is the glue that can hold Catholics and Pentecostals and fundamentalists and other sorts of evangelicals together. And then the gay marriage is important. . . . It is happening so fast, the Christian right feels like the wheels are coming off civilization and it just ratchets up the sense of concern about this issue" (Scholar 2, West).

Activists and organizational directors were also adamant that the coherence of the Christian right depends on these kinds of issues. The director of a large Southern Christian right voter education organization framed it this way: "They [abortion and homosexual rights] are so foundational for evangelicals' beliefs, the structure of family . . . that everything else is secondary . . . if you support abortion on demand and increase homosexual rights, you're tearing apart the basic structure of what God put together in the family." An organizational director of a progressive policy organization from the Midwest, who describes the organization as actively opposing the Christian right, also described abortion and same-sex marriage as "hot button issues" under which every other issue was secondary (Organizational Director 5, Midwest).

When specific issues cannot be interpreted in terms of their relationship to either sexuality or family, the Christian right tends to fray into less formidable groups and individuals whose political stances may be unpredictable. Hence, the issues of the Christian right are actually divided into two camps: central issues (related to sexuality and family) and peripheral issues. Examples of peripheral issues include economic/trade policies, taxes, environmental issues, and, we would argue, education.

While public schooling is important to many Christian conservatives, it is peripheral unless it can be tied explicitly to threats to the traditional family and sexuality. Organizations on the Christian right have diverse aims for effecting change in public schooling. Generally speaking, the educational divide between Christian conservatives relates to their willingness to accept market-based school reforms (e.g., vouchers, charter schools) versus those who prefer reforming the public schools. Our interviewees exemplified this basic divide. One Midwest activist promoting vouchers at the state level opined that "you guys in public education want to teach survival of the fittest, you just don't want to practice it" (Activist 1, Midwest). Other activists and organizational directors felt that vouchers were not necessarily the best way for the Christian right to reform schools.

The non-voucher group tended to suggest increased engagement with the public schools. An organizational director from the South offered the philosophy that the Christian right should be establishing links with the public schools through after-school programs and mentoring programs. Other interviewees were intent on reforming the current public school system through the No Child Left Behind law and other policies that direct federal aid to religious groups (including social service areas outside public education). The split in educational perspective within the Christian right was demonstrated by a high-profile director of a national Christian right organization.

> The leadership class in this country have pulled their kids out of public schools and the people who are left don't have the money, the smarts, and the leadership quality to fight it. . . . [O]ne problem of why you don't get more action on my side, is that the people I talk to are giving all their money to put their kids through private schools. . . . Don't have time, money, and leadership left to fight [for] public schools. (Organizational Director 3, Midwest)

Since the 1980s, the power of the Christian right has been most obvious at the state level. While the array of new fundamentalist organizations constructed during the 1970s and 1980s is still in place, the strong leaders that once held sway over a group of politically motivated church members are increasingly aging, retired, or deceased. Within the conservative movement, once powerful groups such as the Eagle Forum, the Christian Coalition, and Focus on the Family have found that they can no longer exert direct political influence within their own conservative Christian community, let alone within the Republican Party.

Other groups, such as the Heritage Foundation and various state groups, remain quite powerful within the movement and the GOP. Evidence for this exists in the robust presence of speakers allied with new fundamentalism that continue to appear at Conservative Political Action Committee (CPAC) events. Recent CPAC speakers have included Sarah Palin, Marco Rubio, and Rick Santorum, important political figures who are sympathetic to the new fundamentalism positions.

Still other groups have increased in power. According to the director of a national organization that opposes the positions of the Christian right, the director of the Family Research Council, Tony Perkins, has "emerged as the most important figure in the Christian Right" (Interview, Barry Lynn, March 18, 2013). As the leadership of other Christian right political organizations has changed and aged, the Family Research Council has stepped into important roles of lobbying political figures, coordinating efforts between various state-based Christian right organizations, and serving as a disseminator of information to the array of Christian right groups.

The political activity of the Christian right is still focused on the state and local levels. School prayer continues to be a political issue. In 2011, the parents of a Texas high school student sued to block the Medina Valley Independent School District from sanctioning a prayer at the commencement ceremony (School Prayer Lawsuit Trial Postponed. *San Antonio Express News,* January 6, 2012). That court decision was legally challenged. Other recent lower court cases across the country, for example, have dealt with school vouchers and intelligent design.

One area where the Christian right continues to make progress is in the construction of an ever-expanding sector of evangelical higher education. Denominational colleges, once poorly funded and marginal within higher education, have become the recipient of major monetary gifts and are increasingly becoming deployed as a long-term weapon in the culture war. Liberty University is notable in this movement, listing a total enrollment of 74,000 students who are found online, at off-site centers, and on its main campus in Lynchburg, Virginia. With its religious-centered mission, Liberty University is also a routine stop for conservative Republican candidates (Virginia's Liberty University Transforms into an Evangelical Mega-University, *Washington Post,* March 4, 2013). Other notable institutions in the Christian right sphere of influence include Wheaton University in Illinois, Bob Jones University in South Carolina, and Oral Roberts University in Oklahoma, to name several.

THE CHRISTIAN RIGHT AND THE NATIONAL REPUBLICAN PARTY

Political alliances are made out of perceived self-interest, as is exemplified by the alliance forged between Christian conservatives and the Republican Party in the late 1970s. The national Republican Party saw the potential of broadening its electoral base to help it regain the White House after the Watergate scandal and the defeat of Gerald Ford as a one-term president in 1976. For Christian conservatives, the potential to influence national policy to advance their faith also had great appeal.

Republican strategists skillfully exploited the emergence of a more ideological brand of religious fundamentalism—what we have described as the new fundamentalism. While the presidency of Jimmy Carter, himself an evangelical, appealed to some new fundamentalists, Republican leaders such as Grover Norquist and Karl Rove assiduously cultivated Christian conservatives on a variety of issues (Hamburger & Wallsten, 2006). As a result, Christian conservatives emerged as a vocal constituency of the Republican Party beginning in the administration of Ronald Reagan. Prior to Reagan, the Republican Party had consisted mainly of three factions: libertarians, traditionalists, and cold warriors. After 1980, the party embraced two additional factions: the neoconservatives and the religious right. Christian conservatives supported Reagan in large numbers.

Subsequent Republican presidents continued to court Christian conservatives and to view them as a reliable voting bloc. When Republicans regained the White House in 2000 under George W. Bush, the new president's status as a "born again" Christian seemed to epitomize the symbiotic relationship between Christian conservatives and modern Republicanism. Indeed, the election of Bush as the 43rd president of the United States solidified and strengthened the alliance. About 75 percent of these voters supported Bush in the 2000 election (Hart, 2005). According to Green and Silk (2005), Bush also won the 2004 election because in the regions of the country where he captured the largest percentage of voters, the most important factor for these voters was "moral values" rather than the economy.

Despite the power of the Christian right during this period, the Republican Party remained, as it has been for decades, an uneasy alliance among competing factions, among whom Republican presidents had to broker (Hart, 2005). Businesspeople and neoconservatives, of course, do not necessarily share the same priorities as Christian conservatives and other social traditionalists in the party. Bush resolved the tension, much like Reagan, with largely symbolic support for Christian right issues, such as creation of the underperforming White House Office of Faith-Based and Community Initiatives and executive orders (Lichtman, 2008).

Beginning in 2008 a series of events further strained these factions in the Republican Party. Many conservatives had been unhappy with George Bush because they believed he embraced immigration and multiculturalism (Gerstle, 2010). When Barack Obama defeated John McCain in the 2008 presidential campaign, they became even more fearful, convinced that the country was being undermined by a progressive, socialist agenda.

President Obama's subsequent support for a large fiscal stimulus to respond to the worst national economic crisis since the Great Depression also alarmed many fiscally conservative Republicans, as did his decision to make health care reform his signature agenda. This constellation of aggravations galvanized a grassroots movement that came to be known as the "Tea Party." The Tea Party shared much in common with far-right movements of earlier decades, once described by Richard Hofstadter (1963) as the paranoid style of American politics. Fear of foreigners, attributions of conspiracy, fear of elites, and a host of other grievances animated Tea Party activists in ways reminiscent of the John Birch Society anticommunist crusaders in the 1950s and 1960s and Father Coughlin in the 1930s, among others. As a result, in the 2010 midterm elections congressional Republicans shifted sharply to the political right even compared to the first two years of the Obama presidency, as Tea Party members of Congress emphasized a sharply libertarian, antitax, small government agenda. Congressional Republicans continued to support social issues that concerned the Christian right, such as same-sex marriage, immigration, and abortion, but these issues were no longer the dominant focus of the Republican agenda. Indeed, the Tea Party in subtle ways usurped the priorities of the Christian right that had played so prominently in Republican Party politics since the Reagan years.[1]

By 2012, however, with the defeat of Mitt Romney as presidential candidate, the Tea Party's influence was waning. In the aftermath of the 2012 election, it became customary to blame the party's declining influence on its social agenda as being increasingly out of step with the mainstream American electorate. The party's narrow demographic base— heavily white, male, and older than the electoral coalition that Obama had constructed to regain the presidency—led to much soul searching among party leaders.

Yet the Tea Party's declining influence was not good news for the Christian right. The national Republican Party's internal civil war was unlikely to be resolved by returning to preeminence the family and sexuality themes that the Christian right has championed. The Republican Party's concern about broadening the party's electoral base by appealing to young people, Hispanics, and other new demographics also threatens the prominence of Christian evangelicals, whose demographic clout is also declining. By 2013 both the Tea Party and Christian conservatives were weakened, suggesting a continuing struggle for hegemony in the shifting Republican coalition.

On their side, Christian conservatives also have reason to question whether their alliance with the national Republican Party has yielded the results the group's leaders envisioned in the 1970s and 1980s. As the previous generation of leaders dies, those who replace them may not see the benefits of a national alliance with Republicans so clearly nor positively.

Certainly, from an objective point of view, few of the goals of the Christian right have been enshrined in public policy. On abortion, which is perhaps the group's signature issue, the U.S. Supreme Court has not overturned *Roe v. Wade* despite a more conservative court than when Reagan took office. Public opinion now supports same-sex marriage, reflected in the growing number of states that have legalized it. The U.S. Supreme Court struck down the federal Defense of Marriage Act on July 26, 2013. On the closely related issue of homosexual rights, Christian conservatives now find themselves at odds with both public opinion and new laws and court decisions protecting gay rights.

On education issues, the record of success in changing public policy at the national level has not been much better. The U.S. Supreme Court has not revisited its earlier decisions banning official state-sponsored school prayer or other school-sponsored activities in *Engel v. Vitale* (1962), nor overturned its prohibition of Bible readings in public schools (*Abington School District v. Schempp,* 1963). The long-standing effort to replace teaching of evolution in public schools with scientific creationism, later renamed creation science to remove overt biblical references, has not succeeded. The Supreme Court ruled in *Edwards v. Aguillard* (1987) that creation science violated the Establishment Clause of the First Amendment. A federal district court also held intelligent design unconstitutional in *Kitzmiller v. Dover* (2005).

Efforts to restrict teaching of sex education have met with some, although mixed, success. While Republicans in Congress and President Bush supported federal grants that promoted abstinence-only sex education programs, many states refused the aid, favoring comprehensive programs instead. In recent years federal funding for abstinence-only programs has dried up. Still, by one count more than a third of high school programs were reported to be abstinence only. Moreover, the Christian right has successfully narrowed the scope of many programs to exclude controversial issues such as sexual behavior and homosexuality. Many of these concessions have been won in state legislatures and on local school boards rather than at the federal level.

There also have been modest gains on issues of school choice and homeschooling, which are popular among many Christian evangelicals. All states now have laws accommodating homeschooling, and a small number of states support private school choice. Despite support for the latter by Presidents Reagan and Bush, however, federal policy has done little to promote a national program of vouchers. These issues remain largely at the margins of federal education policy, which in the administration of George W. Bush was dominated by No Child Left Behind with its focus on improving student achievement and more equitable outcomes across student subgroups.

Bush supported a choice provision in the bill, but accepted a much weaker compromise that allowed parents of children in schools that were low performing for at least three years to purchase tutorial services from nonschool-based providers. As governor of Texas in 1999, Bush had advocated vouchers but did not fight hard for them (DeBray, 2006). The growing strength of the Tea Party in Congress has made it even less likely that Republicans will support expansion of federal programs or regulations, even those that would support policies that Republicans favor. While the national Republican Party continues to need Christian conservative support as part of its base, it is more likely to expend its political capital on noneducation issues such as abortion.

When all of these developments are considered together, then, the Christian right has little to show for its alliance with the national Republican Party. Not surprisingly, federal education policy issues have gradually become less significant priorities for Christian conservatives. While the national Democratic Party remains even less attractive to them, it is likely that state and local activism will be seen as paying greater dividends.

The Future: Renewed Mobilization at State and Local Levels?

Two often-repeated themes from the interviews revolved around changes in the tactics and leadership of the Christian right. The best way to describe the changing tactics and leadership of the movement is to say that, in both senses, the movement is broadening out. A large cross-section of interviewees across all three categories believed that there has been a decentralizing of the movement away from its traditional leadership of national voter organizations and a renewed focus on grassroots activity in state and local organizations. State and local activism by the new right has a long tradition, even if it was overshadowed by a generation of new right leaders working at the national level. Phyllis Schlafly revived grassroots conservatism with her pro-family agenda, much of it propelled by evangelical Protestant denominations and the Mormon church (Lichtman, 2008).

One of the hallmarks of the Christian right since the mid-1980s has been the movement's ability to mobilize voters behind their two core issues and, in turn, to elect conservative Christian politicians to national public office, traditionally accomplished through massive voter education efforts, undertaken by organizations such as Jerry Falwell's Moral Majority or the Christian Coalition. George W. Bush, Tom DeLay, and Sam Brownback are examples of the kinds of national political powerbrokers the movement has been able to place in office. The failed presidential run of Pat Robertson in 1988 exemplified the basic top-down strategy that faith conservatives practiced during the 1980s and 1990s.

While the traditional Jerry Falwell/Pat Robertson types are still very important because of their media outlets and fundraising abilities, newer leadership is beginning to emerge alongside the old. One organizational director who has worked very closely with the Christian right had the opinion that:

> There are many evangelicals that are embarrassed by some of their leadership. And many who quietly speak complain about how they're portrayed and understood through the likes of D. James Kennedy, Jerry Falwell and Pat Robertson. . . . There's some public discussion within the community, but I think it's difficult for people to say publicly what they're thinking with some exceptions. Cal Thomas occasionally rings a warning bell; Joe LeConte at Heritage speaks pretty openly about problems with some of the leadership, so I think . . . that there are splits. (Organizational Director 2, East)

One of the best examples of the sorts of splits in leadership that have emerged comes from one of our interviews with an activist/organizational director of a Christian right voter organization in the Midwest. This individual has worked primarily through local churches to sponsor religiously oriented campaign events and other types of outreach. This movement claims to represent more than 400,000 voters in 2,100 churches. The significant point here is that this movement, and others like it in various places throughout the United States including Pennsylvania, Illinois, and Colorado, have flourished utilizing a model that seeks to build awareness through local and statewide partnerships and events, rather than by building a national organization. As one commentator put it, "You don't move anybody without getting pretty close to the individual . . . and in organized Christianity you get at the individual through their congregations . . . it's very inefficient to send cold mailings on a nice cause to 100,000 people, but if you get 8,000 churches and their pastors and leaders, you've got a lot going" (Scholar 1, Midwest).

Another scholarly observer of religion noted the localization of religious politics in this way:

> These organizations tend to be focused less on electing the next President, and more on State and local issues which are important to the Christian right. One notable arena of activity in this regard has been the recent anti-same sex marriage ballot initiatives. Advocates of this approach to political power see it as changing the culture. Some such as conservative commentator Cal Thomas now are saying you are more likely to change the politics by changing the culture than changing the culture by changing the politics first. (Scholar 2, West)

Some of the most important victories of the Christian right have been at state and local levels. The success of anti-same-sex marriage ballot initiatives is an example. Twelve states passed anti-same-sex-marriage amendments in 2004 and six more states brought a similar ballot issue before voters in 2006 (National Public Radio, 2006), although subsequently public opinion and political developments shifted in favor of same-sex marriage. Also, a variety of interest groups are structured at those levels rather than nationally. For example, Mel and Norma Gabler founded Educational Research Analysts in Longview, Texas, in 1963 to influence textbook content, particularly in the area of teaching evolution, and through their efforts indirectly influenced the content of textbooks nationwide owing to Texas' statewide textbook adoption system and its large size in the national market (Moore, 2002). More recently, the Tea Party has been very active on a variety of issues at both state and local levels (Skocpol & Williamson, 2012).

Arguably, a state and local approach to organizing would help Christian conservatives be more successful in winning seats on state and local school boards, and in changing educational policies. However, education issues may not be any more of a priority in state and local politics than they have been in the past. A detailed analysis of Christian right activity in 12 states where the Christian right has been especially active indicates that the movement has been preoccupied with other concerns, for example, right-to-life, antifeminism, and so on. An exception is Kansas, where the teaching of evolution has been a dominant issue at certain periods. Even in Kansas, though, Cigler, Joslyn, and Loomis (2003) argue, the Christian right's influence has been limited.

These state and local efforts have had an uneven impact (Green, Rozell, & Wilcox, 2003) across a range of issues. While the Christian right has enjoyed remarkable organizational success, its effects at state and local levels tend to mirror its dilemma nationally, with some mixed electoral successes but a noticeably lesser impact on policy (see Wilcox, 2010). The movement has gained influence in state Republican organizations and has been able to effect changes in party platforms and in some cases nominations, depending on the role of the primary election in various states. The study also showed limited success in ballot initiatives, except where the Christian right chooses to oppose initiatives with which it disagrees. If these cases are representative, they point to the complex outcomes that are likely to follow a shift toward mobilizing at state and local levels. So while a reasserted focus on state and local issues may be appealing to the Christian right, it is unclear that the strategy will yield better dividends for its members.

CONCLUSION

We have argued that the new fundamentalism of Christian conservatives found in contemporary America has a long history dating back to the 19th century. It is quite different from the old fundamentalism of the early 20th century that sought to preserve a separation of church and state and was suspicious of alliances with the state. The Christian right's current identification with the Republican Party, which until 2008 controlled the executive branch of the federal government, and the House of Representatives for much of the past 20 years, indicates how far this shift from old to new fundamentalism has taken Christian conservatives. We have also argued that the actual policy gains derived from this alliance, both in education and elsewhere, have been relatively modest for Christian conservatives, although profoundly beneficial to Republicans. Given the relatively marginal importance of K-12 education to Christian conservatives, compared with core issues of family and sexuality, their impact on educational politics has been equally marginal.

While one can only speculate about its influence in the future, we believe the answer to this question is twofold and can be thought of as a short-term view of the Christian right's prospects for success, versus a long-term view. The Christian right's ability to effect change on the politics of education seems to be better in the short term. Certainly, the Christian right has built strong organizational and media capacity with which to mobilize and educate voters. These important strategic advantages will remain. The Christian right has also shown resiliency, having been able to organize a decentralized network of state and local organizations and coalitions that work to complement the actions of more national organizations and leaders. As the older leadership of the Christian right (i.e., James Dobson, Pat Robertson) is aging or has passed, evidently a newer network of state and local activists will have to build and transform the conservative faith-based movement into a broader array of organizations with more decentralized centers of power.

Given some generational shifts toward greater tolerance on issues like gay rights, decentralization may signal changes in the coalitions that will emerge. This new leadership will face the challenge of broadening the Christian right's membership base to compensate for its aging demographics. How successfully it accomplishes this transition in leadership and membership may well determine how influential it will be within the national Republican Party. In fact, if these newer grassroots organizations are able to increase the overall level of voter and monetary support for conservative issues, the Christian right may become more indispensable to the Republican Party than is currently the case.

The long-term view of the Christian right's ability to affect politics and educational policy is far more equivocal. The character of religious fundamentalism in American politics has rendered it incapable of consistent and sustained involvement. Religious fundamentalism is a political force that has, throughout American history, alternated between dominating the national discourse and being barely noticeable. Between the 1870s and 1920s, religious fundamentalists captured the attention of many observers with their efforts to save the nation's public schools from Catholicism and modernism. After World War II, religious fundamentalists largely retreated from politics, abrogating leadership to radical-right activists. They left the structuring of public education in the form of the National Defense Education Act, and the array of equity-based educational legislation during the 1960s to others (Marsden, 2006; Marty, 2004). By the 1980s, the religious right again organized around perceived threats to the family and sexuality.

Although it is not in the purview of this chapter to explain fully the reasons for the high-tide/low-tide swings of religious influence in American politics, we believe that the role that fundamentalists have played in defining issues is very important in understanding this phenomenon. Throughout American history, fundamentalists have tended to practice reactive rather than proactive politics. Their political involvement has been predicated by outside events, rather than by any initial inward impetus to effect lasting change.

Because fundamentalists have never been issue generators, their political fortunes have usually been dictated by outside events. During the 1880s, large numbers of Catholics immigrating to America became a political force with which Protestants were forced to reckon. During the early 20th century, for example, the threat of Darwinist science prompted fundamentalists to lobby actively to ban evolution from the public schools. Later, fundamentalist concerns over issues such as the acceptance of same-sex partnerships prompted a new flurry of political activity.

Because fundamentalists have usually practiced reactive politics, their political involvement tends to die away once a new set of issues comes to dominate the political arena. For example, old fundamentalists' anti-Catholic political ideology was considerably weakened by the shared experience of Protestants and Catholics through two world wars and the common threat of communism after the 1940s. The threat of Darwinist science in the public schools lost political traction when, during the 1950s, public schools were mobilized to contribute to the nation's Cold War effort in producing students highly trained in math and science.

Once trends like modernism and the increasingly Catholic demographic of America gained widespread acceptance, fundamentalist political posturing on these issues was no longer relevant or powerful. The seasonal nature of outside events and political issues "can change rather quickly and considerably, and with these developments can come changes in the extent to which, as well as the ways in which, religion and politics become intertwined" (Smidt, 2013, p. 183). In this sense, fundamentalism can be seen as episodically fighting rear-guard actions against specific issues that represent broad trends in American culture (e.g., the acceptance of same-sex partnerships). When the issues that concern fundamentalists fade, or become subsumed by other concerns, history has shown their inability to transfer that political organization to new issues.

Christian conservatives desire to radically transform our politics and society. Given this worldview, the ability to compromise with political opponents also remains a challenge for many Christian conservatives, who believe that morality requires complete victory. The political discourse over abortion or same-sex rights is polarized partly by the Christian right's "all or nothing" approach. The American political system is built on accomplishing legislative and policy agendas through compromise, however, rather than by fiat. The structure of government in America—federalism, division of powers, a two-party system—all conspire to frustrate any interest that wishes to dominate or change the system and its laws. It is unlikely that the Christian right will ever achieve control or dominant influence in our federal system. Because religious utopians and millenialists cannot easily achieve their goals in such a fragmented political system, their capacity to persist in their political activism may be no greater in the future that it has been in America's past.

Yet there is a considerable disjuncture between trends that are observable in the short term—here the span of no more than recent decades—and the long-term regularities of a society and its political system. We have argued that although the short-term political prospects of the Christian right achieving many of its goals may seem reasonably good, the long-term prospects of its ascendant influence, if history is any guide, are far more doubtful. This trend is particularly true of educational issues, which remain at the margins of its core concerns and advocacies.

NOTE

1. The two wings of the party overlap but are not identical. While many Tea Party supporters also identify themselves as evangelicals and Christian conservatives, polling data after the 2010 elections revealed that Tea Party Republicans tended to be more antistatist and conservative on important racial and social issues (Dionne, 2012, p. 45). Many continued to support Medicare and Social Security, however, demonstrating the tensions within the Tea Party among different factions (Skocpol & Williamson, 2012).

REFERENCES

Abington School Dist. v. Schempp (1963), 374 U.S. 203, 222.

Blue, F. J. (2004). *No taint of compromise: Crusaders in anti-slavery politics.* Baton Rouge: Louisiana State University Press.

Cigler, A. J., Joslyn, M., & Loomis, B. A. (2003). The Kansas Christian right and the evolution of Republican politics. In J. C. Green, M. J. Rozell, & C. Wilcox (Eds.), *The Christian right in American politics: Marching to the millennium* (pp. 145–146). Washington, DC: Georgetown University Press.

Corbett, M., & Corbett, J. M. (1999). *Politics and religion in the United States.* New York: Garland.

DeBray, E. H. (2006). *Politics, ideology, and education: Federal policy during the Clinton and Bush administrations.* New York: Teachers College Press.

Deckman, M. M. (2004). *School board battles: The Christian right in local politics.* Washington, DC: Georgetown University Press.

Dexter, L. A. (1970). *Elite and specialized interviewing.* Evanston, IL: Northwestern University Press.

Diamond, S. (1995). *Roads to dominion: Right wing movements and political power in the United States.* New York: Guilford.

Dionne, E. J. (2012). *Our divided political heart.* New York: Bloomsbury.

Dobson, E., Hindson, E. E., & Falwell, J. (1981).*The fundamentalist phenomenon: The resurgence of conservative Christianity.* Garden City, NY: Doubleday.

Draper, J. T. (1997). *Oral memories of James T. Draper.* Unpublished oral history. Interviewed by Barry Hankins. Waco, TX: Institute for Oral History, Baylor University.

Edwards v. Aguillard (1987), 107 S. Ct. 2571, 2583.

Engel v. Vitale (1962), 370 U.S. 421, 424.

Epperson v. Arkansas (1968), 393 U.S. 97, 102.

Falwell, J., with Dobson, E., & Hinson, E. (1981). *The fundamentalist phenomenon: The resurgence of conservative Christianity.* Garden City, NY: Doubleday.

Gallup, G. Jr., & Castelli, J. (1989). *The people's religion: American faith in the '90s.* New York: Macmillan.

Gerstle, G. (2010). Minorities, multiculturalism, and the presidency of George W. Bush. In J. E. Zelizer (Ed.), *The presidency of George W. Bush: A first historical assessment* (pp. 249–359). Princeton, NJ: Princeton University Press.

Gibbs, E. & Bolger, R. K. (2005). Emerging churches: Creating community in postmodern cultures. Grand Rapids, MI: Baker.

Glaser, B. G., & Strauss, A. (1999). *The discovery of grounded theory: Strategies for qualitative research.* Hawthorne, NY: Aldine de Gruyter.

Green, J. C., Rozell, M. J., & Wilcox, C. (Eds.). (2003). *The Christian right in American politics: Marching to the millennium.* Washington, DC: Georgetown University Press.

Green, J. C., & Silk, M. (2005, Spring).*Why moral values did count. Religion in the News, 8(1).* Hartford, CT: The Leonard E. Greenberg Center for the Study of Religion in Public Life, Trinity College. Retrieved February 26, 2008, from www.trincoll.edu/depts./csrp/RINVol8No1/WhyMoral%.

Hamburger, T., & Wallsten, P. (2006). *One party country: The Republican plan for dominance in the 21st century.* Hoboken, NJ: Wiley.

Hart, J. (2005). *The making of the American conservative mind: National Review and its times.* Wilmington, DE: Intercollegiate Studies Institute.

Heclo, H., & McClay, W. M. (Eds.). (2003). *Religion returns to the public square: Faith and policy in America.* Washington, DC: Woodrow Wilson Center Press.

Herberger, W. (1955). *Protestant Catholic, Jew: An essay in American religious sociology.* Garden City, NY: Doubleday.

Hofstadter, R. (1963). *The paranoid style in American politics.* New York: Alfred A. Knopf.

Isaac, P. E. (1965). *Prohibition and politics: Turbulent decades in Tennessee, 1885–1921.* Knoxville: University of Tennessee Press.

Justice, B. (2005, Summer). Thomas Nast and the public school of the 1870s. *History of Education Quarterly, 45(2),* 171–206.

Kitzmiller v. Dover Area School District (2005), 440 F. Supp.2d707 (M.D Pa).

Larson, E. J. (2003). *Trial and error: The American controversy over creation and evolution.* New York: Oxford University Press.

Lichtman, A. J. (2008). *White protestant nation: The rise of the American conservative movement.* New York: Atlantic Monthly Press.

Lugg, C. (1996). *For God and country: Conservatism and American school policy.* New York: Peter Lang.

Marsden, G. M. (2006). *Fundamentalism and American culture.* New York: Oxford University Press.

Marty, M. (Ed.). (1993). *Modern American Protestantism and its world: Historical articles on Protestantism in American religious life.* Munich: K. G. Saur Press.

Marty, M. (2004). *The Protestant voice in American pluralism.* Athens: University of Georgia Press.

McLean v. Arkansas Board of Education, 529 F. Supp. 1255, 1274 (E.D. Ark. 1982).

Moore, R. (2002). *Evolution in the classroom.* Santa Barbara, CA: ABC-CLIO.

National Public Radio. (2006). *Marriage plays starring role in politics . . . Again.* February 15, 2006.

Norris, J. F. (1963). *John Franklin Norris collection, 1928–1952* [microform]. Nashville, TN: Historical Commission, Southern Baptist Convention (Microfilm housed in the Texas Collection at Baylor University, Waco, TX).

Phillips, K. (1969). *The emerging Republican majority.* New Rochelle, NY: Arlington House.

Phillips, K. (2006). *American theocracy: The peril and politics of radical religion, oil, and borrowed money in the 21st century.* New York: Viking.

Russell, C. A. (1993). William Jennings Bryan: Statesman-fundamentalist. In M. Marty (Ed.), *Modern American Protestantism and its world: Historical articles on Protestantism in American religious life* (pp. 69–97). Munich: K. G. Saur Press.

Skocpol, T., & Williamson, V. (2012).*The Tea Party and the remaking of Republican conservatism.* London: Oxford University Press.

Smidt, C. E. (2013). *American evangelicals today.* Lanham, MD: Rowman & Littlefield.

Wilcox, C. (2010). *Onward Christian soldiers: The Christian right in American politics.* Boulder, CO: Westview.

Wuthnow, R. (1989). *The struggle for America's soul: Evangelicals, liberals, and secularism.* Grand Rapids, MI: Eerdmans.

12

RESPECTING RELIGION AND CULTURE IN SCHOOLS
An International Overview
Charles L. Glenn

Educational freedom—recognized by international law as a fundamental human right—is consistent with rival social policies, those seeking to promote autonomous development of individuals as well as those concerned about the perpetuation of freely chosen communities within civil society. What freedom cannot be reconciled with is a state monopoly on the formation of the loyalties of youth and their perspective on how and to what ends to live their lives. Totalitarian regimes seek to achieve such a monopoly (see Glenn, 1995a); but pluralistic democracies recognize that no freedom is more basic than that of seeking to shape the beliefs and convictions of one's children.

Every Western democracy has faced two often-related challenges as it seeks to respect the rights of parents while providing universal schooling for common citizenship. One involves groups of parents who want their children to have schooling based on a religious worldview or if, as in Greece, the public schools are explicitly religious, on a different worldview than that of public schools. Sometimes these parents have religious views that were once prevalent in the schools but have been eroded away by secularization, as in the case of American evangelicals; in other cases they belong to minority or immigrant groups who are concerned to preserve their distinctive norms and beliefs.

The extent to which a nation's system of schooling respects the rights of its religious minority groups provides a good indication of whether it can be considered free, just, and democratic. Protection of the rights of minorities in the educational system, and conflict over the exercise of these rights, is a fundamental challenge for state policies and for the process of decision making in any society.

The other challenge is to show respect for the minority cultures that are important to many families, whether of "indigenous" minority groups (such as First Nations in Canada) or of immigrant groups, though the former warrant higher protection under international standards. These cultures, however, are seldom altogether distinct from religious traditions.

RELIGIOUS FREEDOM IN SCHOOLING

In the past, conflict often centered on the right to operate, to choose, and to receive public support for schools with a religious character; the Dutch speak of a 70-year *schoolstrijd* (school struggle) ending only with the *Pacificatie* (pacification) of 1917 that provided for equal funding of religious schools while guaranteeing the integrity of their *richting* or worldview. Across Europe and in the Americas, conflicts over the place of religion in education characterized the period from 1790 to 1914 when modern educational systems took shape, and such conflicts have occasionally resurfaced in more recent decades. The great exception to the temporary eclipse of religion as a source of conflict was the massive mobilization of parents of pupils in Catholic schools, in 1984, against governmental attempts in France and Spain to increase controls over these schools; it is hard to know to what extent religious motivations as such played a role in this widespread resistance.

The general armistice in conflicts over religion and education did not mean that the rights of religious minorities were in all cases adequately protected in the education sphere. In some countries, notably the United States and Italy, those parents who wish to ensure that their children receive an education informed by their religious convictions must pay for private schooling in addition to the taxes that they pay to support unused public schools; parents with insufficient resources are as a result unable to exercise educational freedom. In both countries, there are recent state/regional experiments with tuition vouchers and other forms of subsidy through parents to get around constitutional barriers.

In other countries, government supports some religious alternatives but not others. In some cases, religious instruction—usually voluntary—is provided within the context of the public school program, but may be available only to one or two faith communities in an increasingly diverse society.

Countries with written constitutions, at least among Western democracies, commonly provide an explicit commitment to freedom of religion within an essentially secular state. Modern states, aside from those still under communist rule, are seldom defined as "atheist" or in any sense hostile to religion. On the other hand, apart from the Islamic world, it is unusual for a state to have a religious character or to extend official recognition to a single religion; among the largely symbolic exceptions are the United Kingdom and the Scandinavian countries. Characteristically, a modern state is *secular* without being secularizing, supporting and interacting with all religions represented among its citizens without extending preferential treatment to any.

ROLE OF THE STATE

The state plays only a limited role in the religious sphere, in Western societies, but creates space for religious groups such as churches to be active in accordance with their own self-defined aims and aspirations and to advance and promote their values and beliefs in a spirit of respect for the rights of others. Although it seems likely that this owes more to historical developments and the balance of political forces than to the working out of a theory, it is often justified in the name of "subsidiarity," one of the founding principles of the European Union (Lenaerts, 1994).

This right to schooling based on religious perspective was thus, to a greater or lesser extent, achieved in the Western democracies, though in this respect the United States has lagged behind. Conflicts in most countries since the Second World War were more likely to center around demands on the part of cultural minorities, as in the conflict in France over mother tongue instruction in Corsican and in Breton, but in recent years there has been a revival of conflict over religion as a result of the increasing Muslim participation in public affairs.

MINORITY CULTURES IN SCHOOLING

Beginning in the 1960s for three decades, conflicts over education in Europe were more likely to arise from cultural than from religious differences, or from religious differences understood by elites to be essentially cultural. This perception was no doubt related to the secularist conviction that religion was essentially a phenomenon of the past, combined with the stark contrast between the customs of many of the families who followed the labor immigration of the postwar period and those prevalent in the host societies. As Talal Asad has observed, the general approach to Islam in Europe has mostly revolved around the question as to "whether Muslim communities can really adjust to Europe," rather than "whether the institutions and ideologies of Europe can adjust to a modern world of which culturally diverse immigrants are an integral part" (Mavelli, 2012, p. 2). Thus we have members of the European elite, like the founding editor of the influential French periodical *Le Nouvel Observateur,* proclaiming that "France is the site of an exciting venture, . . . that of transforming Islam through its contact with French civilization" (quoted by Scott, 2007, p. 81). This assumes, as Talal Asad has put it, that "people's historical experience is inessential to them, that it can be shed at will, [which] makes it possible to argue more strongly for the Enlightenment's claim to universality. Muslims, as members of the abstract category 'humans,' can be assimilated . . . once they have divested themselves of what many of them regard (mistakenly) as essential to themselves" (Asad, 2003, p. 169). That presumed "inessential" is, from the perspective of secularist elites, Islam or any other deeply held religious beliefs.

The 1970s and 1980s in Western Europe were a period of intense concern about minority cultures, stimulated above all by the family reunification following the end of labor recruitment from Turkey and North Africa. While the "guest workers" had been in a sense invisible, the arrival of their wives and children seemed to transform many urban neighborhoods in a highly visible (and audible) way. Many in elite circles welcomed what they called the new multicultural society; Paul Scheffer comments sardonically that "those who didn't live in the neighbourhoods where migrants settled were the warmest advocates of the multicultural society, while those who did live in them steadily moved out" (Scheffer, 2010, p. 29). By the 1990s, however, there were increasing concerns about whether these "new Europeans" could ever fit in—ironically, just as the generation strongly marked by the cultures of their homelands was passing from the scene.

The political changes in Eastern Europe since 1989 have allowed cultural conflicts to emerge that were largely—though not entirely—suppressed under the former communist regimes. Minority rights have been at issue in many of the political debates and (unfortunately) even in armed conflict and ethnic cleansing in the Balkans. Freedom of education proved an essential element in the resolution of ethnic conflicts in the former Yugoslavia, though not always with happy results, especially in Bosnia and Herzegovina (Kreso, 2012).

Policies for education have inevitably been among the issues requiring resolution within a framework of international law and—as European institutions develop—within that of common European law. Crucial to the resolution of the issues in the Balkans, for example, was reliance on to "the right to establish private institutions" (*Document of the Copenhagen Meeting of the Conference on the Human Dimension of the CSCE*, Copenhagen, June 29, 1990). In particular, to become a member of the European Union a country was required to demonstrate that it had stable institutions that guaranteed democracy, the rule of law, and human rights. Protection of the rights of minorities was defined as an essential aspect of the definition of a democratic regime (Capotorti, 1991; McKean, 1985; Rodley, 1995, p. 48).

The minimum standard of protection for the rights of minorities are those rights recognized by the various international covenants and United Nations resolutions as well as, for Europe, the instruments by the Organisation for Security and Cooperation in Europe, the Council of Europe, and the European Union.

Against this background governments and educational institutions are expected to make appropriate efforts to guarantee the right to an appropriate education of minorities. When assessing whether the protection of minorities in a particular country meets legal standards, one cannot escape the need to investigate the position of minorities in the education system. Not only are education rights the touchstone *par excellence,* the statutory situation and the situation on the ground reflect possible ethnic and cultural tensions within a country. Refinement of education law, on the other hand, can prevent or resolve tensions that arise around schools.

No sustainable peace in a society is possible without just treatment of the educational concerns of cultural minorities. Comparative constitutional law and political science have taught us that, at vital moments in their national history, many countries have had to put energy into regulations to resolve education conflicts. This is no less true for the new democracies within and outside Europe (De Groof & Bray, 1996, p. 371; see also De Groof, 1994, p. 166).

In reply to a world of overlapping ethnic/cultural loyalties, it is not generally possible for any group or individual to seek to be isolated from encounter with and influence by other groups. As distinguished sociologist Nathan Glazer concluded, "we are all multiculturalists now." Our educational systems have been obliged to take the pluralistic nature of contemporary societies into account. On the other hand, England's Commission for Racial Equality published an article in 2001 arguing that "multiculturalism has helped to segregate communities far more effectively than racism" (quoted by Modood, 2007, pp. 10–11).

ETHNICITY

One of the most thoughtful critics of the use of culture as a primary source of identity is intellectual historian David Hollinger, who calls for a "postethnic perspective [that] recognizes that most individuals live in many circles simultaneously and that the actual living of any individual life entails a shifting division of labor between the several 'we's' of which the individual is part" (2005, p. 3). Hollinger is concerned to be clear that he "reacts not against commitment but against prescribed affiliations on the basis of descent." He points out that an "individual who has every right to protection against discrimination on the basis of his or her involuntary classification as a member of a historically disadvantaged color group may have no interest whatsoever in the culture popularly associated with that group," and that public policies (as in school curriculum) presuming that a particular culture defines an individual fail to recognize the freedom that we all have to incorporate or reject that potential identity and the life orientations associated with it. "The multiculturalism of the 1990s carried the deeply anti-individualistic expectation that individuals would naturally accept the cultural, social, and political habits popularly ascribed to their communities of descent, rather than form their own associations to the extent that their life-circumstances permitted choices" (Hollinger, 2005, pp. 106, 117, 180, 220).

Ethnic diversity—and conflicts related to it—is of course no new phenomenon in the United States, Canada, and Australia, nations built up largely by immigration over the course of the 19th and early 20th centuries, nor in India, Indonesia, South Africa, and other multiethnic countries. While immigration is a highly relevant factor in Western European societies at present, the reaction to that immigration is shaped in part by pre-existing assumptions about the significance of language and cultural diversity, and public policies shaped by those assumptions. These assumptions are based in large part on how the society has dealt with the presence, in its midst, of language minority groups who are *not* immigrants but have a claim to belonging that is equal to that of the majority. The situation of Moroccan immigrants to Belgium, for example, cannot be understood apart from the history of conflict and precarious settlements over the use of French and Dutch and the cultural demands of the Flemish and Walloon communities.

The right of "indigenous" cultural minority groups to maintain elements of distinctiveness has generally been recognized in national and international law. The situation of immigrants, by contrast, is governed by the terms under which they are admitted to a country, and by international standards for the treatment of refugees and asylum seekers. It is also affected, of course, by the extent to which the majority population of a society perceives the immigrants as culturally distinct and even unassimilable. That this is a growing problem in Western Europe with respect to its Muslim minority is evidenced by recent elections in several countries and by the strong sales of alarmist polemics.

THE IMMIGRANT CHALLENGE

Immigrants present a pressing challenge to educational systems in most Western nations, but it is a different sort of challenge than that presented by indigenous groups who wish to have their distinctiveness taken into account. If there is more than one historical community occupying a given territory and sharing a distinct language and culture in a given state, a country is considered a "multinational" state. Of 132 sovereign states worldwide with a population exceeding one million, it is reported, only 12 can be considered ethnically homogeneous.

While indigenous minority groups often enjoy cultural and linguistic rights today, these differences have in the past been the target of policies seeking to create national unity on the basis of cultural homogeneity. Substituting a national language for the local dialects of indigenous regional groups was a major motivation in the development of state-sponsored schooling over the course of the late 18th and 19th centuries in France and elsewhere in Europe (see Weber, 1976).

Even though the distribution of speakers of a common language has frequently been the basis for defining the territorial extent of a nation-in-the-making, there are few nations of any size that do not include indigenous language minority groups concentrated (although not always representing the majority of inhabitants) in areas with which their language has traditionally been associated. In some cases they are the remnants of indigenous conquered peoples, like the Welsh, Bretons, and Basques in Western Europe. In other cases, they are groups whose minority status is the result of the untidy process of nation building and frontier drawing, like French speakers in Switzerland, German speakers in France, Italy, and Denmark, Danish speakers in Germany, Finnish speakers in Sweden, and Swedish speakers in Finland. The European Union recognizes 34 "minority languages" that are spoken by about 40 million of its inhabitants.

A special case is represented by those indigenous groups who are not only linguistically and culturally distinct but also socially marginalized by their relatively brief contact with modernity as well as by the actions and attitudes of the majority, such as native North Americans (Indians, Inuit, Hawaiians), Maori in New Zealand, Australian native peoples, Saami in Scandinavia, and, in a rather different sense, Roma (Gypsy) peoples in much of Europe. The situations of these peoples present complex issues that go well beyond our present scope (see Glenn, 1996, chapter 3).

Speakers of indigenous minority languages are almost invariably able to speak and understand the "national" language, but choose to be bilingual, maintaining as best they can the language of their group as well. The prognosis for the survival of the languages of American Indians into the next generation is not favorable, despite extensive efforts and federal government funding (see Glenn, 2011, chapter 13: "Continued Decline of Indian Languages"). Continuing to use Frisian in the province of Friesland is essentially a free choice, supported by public recognition and schooling, but everyone can also speak Dutch (Jonkman, 1991). Exceptional are those cases—native North Americans, Belgium, Quebec, and Switzerland are the most notable examples—in which bilingualism may even be discouraged to some extent out of a concern that it will lead to language shift; different languages have official status in distinct sections of the country.

In the emergence of nation-states in Central Europe and the Balkans, and more recently in the former Soviet Union, language has frequently served as the basis for defining who is and who is not a member of the nation. Throughout the 19th century, the gradual unification of Germany and the struggle for independence by Greeks and Czechs, by Irishmen and Poles, by Hungarians and Finns, from the multinational empires that ruled them were accompanied in every case by a strong emphasis on a distinctive language. Frequently this entailed transforming a language that had been used primarily by peasants into a vehicle for literature and for political discussion.

The administrative separation of Norway from Denmark in 1807 was followed by the definition of a distinctive Norwegian language; more recently, Greenlandish has replaced Danish as the official language of Greenland.

Other nations have set out to revive, for all purposes of civic and economic life, languages that were approaching extinction or were used only for religious purposes and to make them symbols and unifying vehicles of national life. The most successful examples of such policies are the revival of Hebrew in Israel and the standardization of Bahasa Indonesia as a common language for a nation of more than 500 ethnic groups and languages. Ireland's efforts, though persistent, have not been able to achieve widespread use of Irish in the face of a general preference for the use of English. Its popularity for political reasons did not outlive the independence struggle, and "the meanings assigned to the language in the nationalist rhetoric, before and after the establishment of the state, no longer carry the same power to mobilize public action. . . . [There is] a widening gap between the symbolic significance attached to Irish as an official emblem of national identity, and its use as a richly expressive vernacular in everyday life. Many people have learnt to associate Irish with feelings of guilt that they do not speak what national elites told them was their own mother tongue.... Irish today, as one hundred years ago, appears to be in serious danger of disappearing as a community language" (An Coiste Comhairleach Pleanála, 1988, xvi–xviii).

The European Parliament approved, in October 1987, a resolution to promote the "lesser-used languages" of its member states through allowing their use for education (Gorter, 1991, p. 57).

This is not the place to review all of the controversial situations in the European Union, much less worldwide, with respect to indigenous minority languages and cultures. Experience has shown that the solution to such open or smoldering conflicts has been found in education laws that create a balance between the cultural and educational rights of minorities and the duty of the state to work out standards that apply to both state and private schools and that ensure that every young person has the language and other competencies that will lead to economic opportunities and civic participation. There is a corresponding duty of loyalty toward the country on the part of minority groups (Brett, 1991, 1993, p. 159; Hillgruber & Jestaedt, 1994, p. 95).

If the linguistic—and related cultural—situation is complex in Western Europe and North America, it is even more so in Russia, South Africa, and the Balkans. There are more than 100 national and ethnic groups in Russia, for example; Russian legislation has attempted to reach a balance between the "unity of the federal, cultural and educational area" according to article 2 of the Basic Law on Education and the principles of pluralism, decentralization, and cooperative government. To this end, 40 percent of the school curriculum may be dedicated to subjects that are specific to the various regions. The law of October 23, 1991, On the Languages of the Peoples of the Russian Federation, stipulates that "with its multinational population, the traditional norm of language coexistence is the official use of two or several languages."

Similar complexity exists in South Africa; indeed, the last deadlock in the discussions preparing the new constitution were linked to education. There are 11 official languages, though not all of them can be employed as a medium of instruction throughout the country. The drafters of the constitution were strongly influenced by a minority group rights report concluding that segregated education along lines of mother tongues led mostly to bad results, whereas some use of the mother tongue as part of a goal of bilingualism or multilingualism and integration can lead to good educational results (see De Groof, Malherbe, & Sachs, 2000).

Why should politics respect the demand of minorities for protection of their culture and promote the diversity of cultures in education? Respecting minority cultural rights enlarges the freedom of individuals because for most, even with the extreme individualism often associated with modernity, freedom is intimately linked with and dependent on culture. Through access to a heritage culture, which may include understanding the history and language associated with that culture, individuals can enjoy a range of meaningful options (Kymlicka 1996, pp. 75–106). Education should therefore give access to information about cultures, and the possibility of exploring a particular culture in depth, but without falling into the trap of assuming that a student with a particular ethnic background necessarily has an affinity for its culture. Olivier Roy argues, for example, that those Muslim youth in Western Europe whom he describes as "neofundamentalists" have made a clear break with the cultures of the homelands from which their parents came. "Today's religious revival—whether under fundamentalist or spiritualistic forms—develops by decoupling itself from any cultural reference. It thrives on the loss of cultural identity: the young radicals are indeed perfectly 'Westernized'" (Roy, 2007, p. xi).

For a minority culture to survive and develop in the modern world, given the pressures toward the creation of a single common culture in each country, the public institutions, especially the schools, of the dominant culture must be reformed so as to provide some recognition or accommodation of the heritage of different ethnic groups as well as to make it possible for them, to the extent that they so choose, to maintain their cultural heritage, including the use of a minority language.

It is important to note, of course, that it is a characteristic of liberal democracies that individuals are not compelled to maintain a cultural heritage, a minority language, or their links with an ethnic group. Ethnic identity is—or should be—a matter of individual choice in a free society. For many members of minority groups, whether indigenous or immigrant, the effort to maintain the use of a second language besides that necessary for participation in the wider society is too great. In general, "stable societal bilingualism (diglossia) depends on institutionally protected functional sociolinguistic compartmentalization, so no ethnocultural collectivity can maintain two cultures on a stable basis past three generations if they are implemented in the same social functions (family, friendship, work, education, religion, etc.)" (Fishman, 1989, p. 193). In other words, most people maintain active use of a language only to the extent that they are essentially monolingual in that language in at least one essential dimension of their lives; if both languages are used in the home, for example, the minority language will gradually be used less over several generations. Immigrant families characteristically find—often to their dismay—that their children are unwilling to make the effort to use the language of their parents, though they continue to understand it, and that the third generation seldom even understands the language of their grandparents.

For some or many members of minority groups, the ties to a heritage culture are too strong to give up and a free society does not require that they make such a sacrifice. Access to one's culture should be treated as something that many individuals will want and that public policy will facilitate. Leaving one's culture should be seen as voluntarily renouncing a right to which one is entitled.

The evidence is clear that many individuals do value their cultural membership. Far from displacing national identities, globalization has gone hand in hand with an increased sense of nationhood. The creation of European institutions has strengthened national and subnational identities in many countries. The fact that Europe has become more pluralistic has not diminished the intensity of people's desire to live and work in their own cultures. Europe has experienced, in some quarters, a sharp rise in nationalist sentiment as well as demands for regional autonomy, most notably but not exclusively in Spain, Italy, Belgium, and Great Britain (Schade, 2000).

Belief in the necessary connection between a language and membership in a national community can lead to intolerance of other languages. To the extent that a common language functions as an expression of a common nationality, the status of minority languages is always liable to be called into question. Conflict over language policy (such as the unsuccessful efforts to declare English the "official" language of the United States, as French is the official language of France and Dutch of Flanders in Belgium) does not reflect xenophobia so much as it does conflicting ideas about what it means to be a full member of the society. Can societal membership appropriately be mediated through associations and communities that communicate among themselves in a language incomprehensible to the wider society, or are such mediating structures inimical to national unity and the rights of individuals?

Ethnic groups and their institutions, some argue, are an important aspect of the civil society; they are mediating structures that may reduce the *anomie* attendant on modernization and a mass society and perform an important function in the relation between individuals and the nation as a whole. To the extent that such groups depend on the maintenance across generations of a distinctive language, compulsory schooling can be either a fundamental threat or a valuable support to their continuing existence, depending on the policy that the school adopts toward the use of that language.

The bonds of language and culture are strong for most people because of the importance of cultural membership for their identity. Cultural membership has a "high social profile," in the sense that it affects how others perceive and respond to us. If a culture is not generally respected, then the dignity and self-respect of its members will also be threatened.

Liberal democracies, precisely because they allow individuals great freedom to choose their identity and lifestyle, are profoundly corrosive of cultural distinctiveness; they have, in French debates, been described as *ethnophage* or *ethnocidaire* (Schnapper, 1992, p. 18). For a minority culture to survive and develop in the modern world, given the pressures toward the creation of a single common culture in each country, requires "institutional pluralism" that provides recognition and accommodation of the heritage of different groups. Minority languages are especially threatened, in some countries, because the children of immigrant parents have overwhelming incentives to learn English as their second language in place of the language of their ancestors, though they may feel a fair amount of guilt associated with the failure to become proficient in a language that they perceive emotionally as an important aspect of identity. They or their parents may conclude (or be persuaded) that their efforts would be better spent on other aspects of the curriculum than maintenance of their heritage language. It was reported, for example, that although Turkish pupils in Berlin could opt to substitute their ancestral language for English as the first "foreign" language studied, very few did so because English is required for secondary education and for much employment (Fase, 1987, p. 113).

SCHOOL PRACTICES

School practices to promote understanding of and respect for the diverse cultures represented within a society are subject to the same cautions that apply to similar efforts in relation to religious diversity. Use of artifacts and customs from the ancestral homeland, for example, may be confusing and even embarrassing for pupils who experience their culture as something dynamic and constantly evolving in the host society. Contrary to the common practice of encouraging children to celebrate their ethnic distinctiveness, an exhaustive review of 30 years of research on the education of language minority pupils concludes that "to increase positive intergroup contact, the salience of group characteristics should be minimized, and a superordinate group with which students from different cultural and language groups can become identified should be constructed" (August & Hakuta, 1997, p. 94). In other words, well-meaning efforts to persuade the children in a class to identify how they differ "culturally" because of their differing ancestry are likely to be counterproductive.

On the other hand, minorities have successfully challenged the model that assumed that they should abandon all aspects of their heritage, and educators should be responsive to their concerns, while placing the primary emphasis on teaching the skills and knowledge necessary for successful participation in the larger society. As an influential African American educator has pointed out, "success in institutions—schools, workplaces, and so on—is predicated upon acquisition of the culture of those who are in power . . . children from other kinds of families operate within perfectly wonderful and viable cultures but not cultures that carry the codes or rules of power . . . schools must provide these children the content that other families from a different cultural orientation provide at home" (Delpit, 1995, pp. 25, 30).

Similarly, West Indian sociologist Maureen Stone, working with Afro-Caribbean families in England, concluded that, rather than seeking to promote minority cultures, schools should concentrate on providing minority children with access to successful participation in the mainstream of society. She insists that "the community, parents and children are sufficient guardians of the black cultural inheritance. Schools have to be about something else." After all, "if you really want to reduce educational and racial inequality, the best way is by providing your pupils with the skills and knowledge they need to make their own way in the society in which they live" (Stone, 1985, p. 6).

The purpose of ensuring that the curriculum reflects cultural pluralism, then, is not somehow to make minority pupils feel good about themselves—that is best achieved by making them fully competent in the academic material—but to strengthen the instructional program so that it does justice to social realities and provides an adequate education to all pupils, those of the majority as well as those of various minority groups. Whatever makes the curriculum richer and schools more effective will be of special value to pupils who do not come to school already possessing a foundation in the common knowledge, the "cultural capital," essential to success in a particular society's schools (Hirsch). That this can also have the effect of showing respect for pupils (and their families) with other traditions is consistent with what we should expect from an educational system in the 21st century.

SEPARATE MINORITY INSTITUTIONS

Perhaps the most controversial demand of some minority groups is to be provided the resources to support their own separate institutions, to ensure the full and free development of their cultures as the best response to some disadvantage or barrier in the decision-making process that makes it impossible for the group's views and interests to be effectively represented. In the United States, for example, there have been occasional proposals to carve out distinct political enclaves in which black voters would be self-governing. Such demands play into the hands of those members of the majority who would be delighted to isolate the minority.

A variation on this theme is the argument that only minority-run schools can educate minority children adequately. Those who support ethnically separate schooling do so in general on the basis of the contention that this is the most—perhaps the only—effective and principled way to educate minority pupils (see Glenn, 1995b).

The most widespread form of schooling organized by minority communities is supplemental schools serving the children and grandchildren of immigrants. There were 4,893 part-time "ethnic schools" identified in an American survey in the late 1970s, "maintained, by and large, by ethnic communities that are competently English-speaking" but for whom "language maintenance" is viewed as a moral necessity. Similarly, supplemental schooling has been organized by ethnic communities of immigrant origin in Western Europe, Canada, and Australia, seeking to maintain a connection with the homeland and its language among pupils who are unlikely to return. In England, "a survey of three local authorities in 1981 suggested that between 26 percent and 41 percent of linguistic minority pupils were attending supplementary schools and that most schools were established after 1975" (McLean, 1985, p. 327). More recently, however, the publicly funded programs, common in most Western nations in the 1980s (see Glenn, 1996 for a country-by-country survey), to maintain the heritage languages and cultures of immigrant children have largely been eliminated, and leaders of several European nations have announced that "multiculturalism" has been a failure.

As provisions in educational systems for maintenance of the languages and cultures of immigrant groups have faded, they have been replaced to a considerable extent by demand for recognition of the religious concerns of those groups. The earlier concern has come to seem less relevant as the second and even third generations of children from immigrant groups enter the schools, often with a very limited knowledge of their heritage languages and thoroughly acculturated to the host society by exposure to media from their earliest years. On the other hand, for at least some of the younger generation of Muslims—so identified by the surrounding culture whatever the actual state of their belief and practice—Islam has become an important source of identity and a basis for demands on government.

RETURN OF RELIGION AS AN ISSUE FOR SCHOOLING

It was only as the second and third generations deriving from immigration from predominantly Muslim countries came to maturity, largely abandoning their ancestral cultures but turning to Islam in ways that, for many of them, was more fervent than the practice of their parents, that religion reemerged as the predominant source of conflict over schooling. Muslim identity has become more important, for many, than it ever was in their homelands; in the words of one young Turk:

> since I came to the Netherlands I feel more drawn to Islam than ever before. We're discriminated against by the Dutch as Turkish Muslims . . . they look on us as inferior. But we have the strength of our religion. We're not at all afraid, not of anyone, only of Allah. We have the greatest religion. One Turk can, with his religion, take on 50,000 Dutchmen. . . . I think that we migrants will bring the true Islam back to Turkey through our experiences here. (Quoted by Sunier, 1994, p. 19)

While conventional wisdom has it that Western societies have become less "religious" in recent decades, as measured by declining church attendance, there has also been a movement in the opposite direction, both in the form of rapidly growing Islamic and Protestant Pentecostal movements (Kepel, 1987, 1991, 1994; Martin, 1990) and also in a diminution of the mutual mistrust between secular and religious leaders that marked much of the 19th and 20th centuries (see McLeod, 2000). The renewed visibility of religion was a worldwide phenomenon, seen in the explosive growth of Pentecostalism in Latin America, Africa, and Asia, and revivals—not to be confused with Islamism—in countries with a Muslim majority. "In the 1970s and 1980s, Muslim societies were swept by a resurgence of personal piety and public observance. Attendance at Friday mosque services swelled . . . women donned head coverings (*hijab*) and men sported facial hair" (Hefner, 2007, p. 32). Olivier Roy describes "the sudden emergence in all Western monotheistic religions of new forms of religiosity, all of them communitarian (but of a purely religious community), exclusive (a clear dividing line separates the saved from the damned), and inclusive (all aspects of life must be placed by the believer under the aegis of religion)" (Roy, 2007, p. 6).

The structuring of public life on a religious basis by Muslim immigrants is a reversal of the secularization and privatization of religion that have characterized Western European societies, and immigrants to them, for the past 100 years. Like Pentecostal and Evangelical Christianity among Latino immigrants in the United States, Islam has come to be extremely important for many immigrants in Western Europe, including some whose religious practice in the homeland may have been perfunctory; it is "the religion of marginalized immigrants whose inclusion has been a failure. . . . Religion works to construct a community and an identity which make it possible to endure the failure of inclusion and to give a positive meaning to marginality and to a dependence upon social services" (Dubet & Lapeyronnie, 1992, p. 95).

In particular, it is a means by which immigrants and their children can reject a dominant culture that appears (if only by neglect) to be rejecting them, and assert continuities when much in their lives is changing. More than "ethnic" values and traditions, and far more than minority languages, religion is seen as the essential element of connectedness with the family and the community. Thus sub-Saharan African ethnic groups in France are countering what they perceive as the inevitable loss of their languages by a strong emphasis on Islam as a cultural marker and a basis for identity. Within a growing number of families from Senegal, for example, "[l]earning the 'language of origin' is more or less abandoned and communication is carried on in the language of the child: French. In fact, the Muslim identity is given more positive emphasis [*valorisée*] than is the ethnic identity, often perceived as negative" (Timera, 1989, p. 22).

José Casanova has urged that there are advantages to conceiving identity in terms of religion rather than race or ethnicity (Casanova, 2007, p. 72). Religious identity can be abandoned or given a variety of meanings and applications based on the individual's choice, while minority racial/ethnic identity carries meanings that to a large extent are imposed on it by the majority; it is commonly used as a basis for discrimination, even if in fact, as Hollinger points out, the individual discriminated against may attach very little significance to her racial/ethnic identity.

In fact, what is occurring at the present time is a mixing together of what had been distinct conflicts over religion and culture, as education systems seek to accommodate Muslim pupils and their families for whom culture and religion are intertwined. This has changed the nature of the debates and the policy dynamic in significant ways. Respecting languages and cultures could be seen as a commendable choice, expressed in curricular and program modifications, but respecting religious conviction carries a weightier legal significance, and one that inevitably occurs within the accommodations that each society has made to religious diversity in the past. These accommodations vary widely, even within the European Union, between, say, the extreme pluralism of Dutch schooling and the strongly Catholic character of schooling in Spain until recent decades.

While it is characteristic of almost all national education systems in non-Muslim societies today that they avoid privileging a single religious perspective (see Glenn & De Groof, 2012, for profiles of 65 systems), there are significant differences in how this "neutrality" is exercised.

Strict separation seeks to exclude religious themes, motivations, and organizations from everything that government touches on. Because government has extended its helping hand (or its grasp, if the reader prefers) into more spheres of social and cultural life over recent decades, the logic of strict separation is to treat religion as an aspect of private life with no public consequences. Underlying this objective, as reflected in the reasons advanced by many of the advocates of its exclusion from public life, is a belief that religion is a dangerous and divisive force.

For some strict separationists, the solution is not so much a "naked public square" as one in which an alternative belief system—"secularism" (*laïcisme*)—is formally established. A characteristic articulation of this goal is John Dewey's little book *A Common Faith* (1934) or, more recently, Louis Legrand's *L'école unique: à quelles conditions?* (1981). Such "secular perspectives and belief structures represent a point of view, a worldview as much as various religious perspectives and beliefs do." Given the force and coherence of the secularist perspective, government policies are scarcely neutral if they accord it a privileged position through funding institutions and programs that promote it while handicapping faith-based perspectives by excluding them from the ever-enlarging sphere of government activity (Monsma & Soper, 1997, p. 46).

But exclusion of religious speech and motivations, of religious organizations and programs, from equal participation in the "public square" and in public funding is not neutral in its effects. "If, to receive the normal benefits of public policies that similar, secularly-based organizations are receiving, a religious nonprofit organization must downplay or give up certain of its religious practices, public policy is interfering with its free exercise of religion" (Monsma, 1996, p. 126).

Strict neutrality, by contrast, insists that government should not be in the business of making distinctions between religious and secular speech and other activities, and should confine itself to ensuring that neutral rules are enforced on each. Strict neutrality seeks not to influence either positively or negatively the choices that people make "for or against any particular religious or secular system of belief. It should neither advantage nor burden religion" (Monsma & Soper, 1997, p. 10).

Applying this principle consistently to education would require, as legal scholar Stephen Carter put it, that "if neutrality means that the government cannot take steps to treat religious schools better than other schools, it surely means as well that the government cannot take steps to treat religious schools worse" (Carter, 1993, p. 200).

Positive neutrality rests on a pluralist understanding of the political and social order that recognizes the important role of faith communities and associations alongside other forms of voluntary organization in maintaining society and in transmitting the habits and values that sustain it. A pluralist political order integrates such communities and associations "into the life of the body politic." Neutrality toward religion is not, from this perspective, an end in itself but a means to ensure fair play among individuals and groups, whatever their views, so long as they abide by the ground rules that make society possible (Monsma, 1993, pp. 176, 200).

IS THE PUBLIC SCHOOL NEUTRAL?

An underlying issue is what is meant by the *neutrality of the state school*. To employ the categories introduced earlier, *strict separation* would exclude all mention or acknowledgment of religion from state schools, *strict neutrality* would have the curriculum include, as appropriate, a neutral description of different religious traditions and their role in history and contemporary society, while *positive neutrality* would make room within the curriculum for the presentation of religious beliefs to willing participants as "assumptions that are, for the time being, unquestioned" (Thiessen, 1993, p. 130).

There is yet another possibility, however: that the state school itself may take on an ideological character, expressing and communicating a specific view of the world (Braster). Is it conceivable, in fact, that a real education, worthy of the name, could fail to be based on, and to convey, such a worldview? Can we conceive of the neutrality of the state school as simply a vacuum of perspective and commitments, or is the reality that there is always a "message" that is being communicated to pupils, even if it is a message of relativism and indifference, the "imposition of a specific form of materialism"? (Coleman & White, 2001, p. ix). Is there not a danger that, as a thoroughly secular legal scholar put it:

> the prevailing orthodoxy in most public schools is a negative one. There is order, but there is no community. Many schools are not simply moral vacuums, they are culturally confusing and devoid of significant shared values. . . . For many students, acculturation in public schools is learning to abandon home or subculture values; to relate to others through roles and rules rather than as whole persons and community members; and to deny meanings, feelings, and intellect. (Arons, 1986, p. 71)

The common practice (apart from the United States and Italy) of subsidizing independent schools with a religious character does not absolve the state from the obligation to respect in its own schools the religious and philosophical convictions of parents. Although in the state schools the "transmission of ideas" should take place in an "objective, critical, and pluralistic way," this does not prevent the establishment of religious instruction as part of the program, In that case, however, an alternative choice must be offered to parents and pupils.

The situation of culture and religion, especially in Western Europe, has undergone significant changes over the past two decades, as the generation of immigrants tied to their cultures of origin is replaced by their children and grandchildren, who do not necessarily identify with that culture or speak the language associated with it. For many of the second and third generations, forms of transcultural religious belief and practice (what Olivier Roy calls neofundamentalist Islam in Europe, Pentecostalism in North America and elsewhere) create new identities that cannot be addressed by any sort of multicultural curriculum.

> The neofundamentalist enterprise, by defining the community of believers not in sociological and cultural terms but as a voluntary association, has de facto constructed a space "other" than that of the surrounding society, thereby separating the religious from the social. The rule applies to only the believer . . . the believer lives his religion in a space shared with the nonbeliever, but he inhabits that space in a different way (Roy, 2007, p. 82).

Among Muslims in both Europe and North America there is a significant (though probably not a majority) interest in faith-based schools, and demands, as a matter of equity, for public funding of such schools. This reflects dissatisfaction not only with the secular message delivered by public schools, but also with the various efforts to provide teaching about religion within those schools. Spokesmen commonly insist—as Catholic school advocates have long insisted—that religion should be not a curriculum topic but the underlying ethos of a school.

One sign of the new self-confidence of Muslims in Western Europe is the demand for Islamic schools, which has been accommodated with public funding in the Netherlands, England, and other countries where there is already provision of schools of other religious traditions. These schools have been funded on the basis of religious freedom, rather than of ethnic separatism. Despite the reluctance of public authorities, Dutch law permitted a publicly funded Islamic school (sponsored initially by a Protestant school association) to get off the ground with 100 pupils in late 1988. The leaders insisted that it was "a Dutch elementary school on an Islamic basis," and noted that all five teachers were Dutch, supplemented by a Moroccan and a Turkish teacher to provide supplemental language and culture lessons. The lesson plan was that of other Dutch schools, except that the required periods of religious (or humanistic) instruction were devoted to Islam. Dutch was the language of instruction except for the periods of religion and of supplemental language and culture. The Moroccan chairman of the school's trustees pointed out that non-Muslim pupils were welcome and would be treated with the same respect that Muslim pupils have experienced in Catholic and Protestant schools; apparently no irony was intended.

In 1988 the Islamic Foundation for Education in The Netherlands (ISNO) was founded, in part as a less highly traditional alternative, and in 1989 it opened schools in Amsterdam, The Hague, and Rotterdam. The chairman said "our children will become more Dutch all the time, but they need to know where they stand, they need to have their own *zuil* [sector of society] and not be counted in with the Catholics or Protestants." Another board member said, "it is precisely our policy to make sure that our children can make good progress in the society right away. We are trying to convey Islam in a Dutch form" (Teunissen, 1990).

About 50 Islamic schools are functioning at present in the Netherlands and, despite serious concerns about the quality of the instruction and management of some (*Onderwijsraad*, Table 7: Percentage scholen primair onderwijs zwak en zeer zwak, 2009–2011, and Table 8: Percentage scholen voortgezet onderwijs zwak en zeer zwak, 2009–2011), no evidence indicates that they are tending to alienate their pupils from Dutch society.

The concern of the Islamic and Hindu schools was less with language than with providing children with an alternative to the *values* of Dutch society and thus of Dutch schools; they sought to provide an alternative schooling that was more consistent with the beliefs of immigrant parents, while equipping pupils to participate fully in the Dutch economy. A study of Turkish immigrants found that they had concerns not only with the norms and values presented in Dutch schools, but even more with the fact that teachers took no responsibility for overseeing the relationships between boys and girls; they deplored what they perceived as a lack of discipline and respect for adults. "It is thus not so much the content of education as the manner in which it is provided that determines the image [immigrants hold] of Dutch education" (Willems & Cottaar, 1990, p. 19). Similarly, a study of Surinamese parents found many concerned that their children were imitating the behavior of Dutch children (Koot, Tjon-a-ten, & Uniken Venema, 1990, p. 61).

Groups in the Muslim and Hindu communities in the Netherlands were seeking to reinforce their ability to socialize their children in their own values, to protect and isolate them in some respects from the acids of modernity. The fact that different models of Hindu schooling (Schwencke, 1994) as of Islamic schooling emerged reflected the fact that within each community there were those who chose to stay at arm's length from the host society, while others sought to occupy a middle position between two cultures. The call for Hindu and Islamic schools was in either case not related to ethnic nationalism or to a "myth of return," but to the universal desire of parents to have a major say in the raising of their children. The optimistic scenario for these schools was that

> this institutional segregation must lead later to societal integration. Through separate establishment schools can strengthen the cultural distinctiveness and self-worth of pupils. The schools make pupils conscious of their culture and their position in The Netherlands. . . . As their identity is strengthened, they will be better able—as individuals and as a group—to protect themselves from domination and discrimination. More [Islamic] schools should therefore be established. Self-organization can contribute to a considerable extent to the maintenance of culture and to better school achievement. (Teunissen, 1990, p. 54)

It should be noted that the new schools (now numbering about 50) serving the Muslim immigrant community in the Netherlands are *Islamic* rather than Turkish or Moroccan, and one proposed school in Utrecht was turned down because it would be explicitly Turkish. Even though all the pupils could turn out to be of one ethnic origin, this was the case with only one of six Islamic schools studied in 1990. That in The Hague, for example, enrolled 20 Turkish, 99 Moroccan, seven Tunisian, and six Pakistani pupils; four of the nine teachers were Dutch, and another four (somewhat curiously) Surinamese, while of the nine only two were Muslim. Indeed, in none of this sample of six Islamic schools was a majority of the faculty Muslim, though all teachers and pupils were expected to abide by Islamic behavioral standards, including modest dress and some form of head covering for women; non-Muslim pupils, if any, would not be required to take part in religious observances (Shadid & van Koningsveld, 1990, pp. 19–20). Under Dutch educational law and policy, a school could not be established on the basis of language or ethnicity, but religion is a privileged basis for school selection, enjoying protection as a right of conscience (Rath, Groenendijk, & Penninx, 1992, p. 32).

Whether or not public funding is provided, government oversight seeks to balance between the need to avoid promotion of racial segregation and the desire to encourage initiatives by minority communities. In practice, institutional autonomy is be seen as a condition that is capable of being modified, redefined, and with new requirements enforced as a price of its continuation. It is conditioned by the principles of accountability, performance assessment, and financial audit.

The emergence of new religiously separate schools is a considerable shock for those secularists who had confidently assumed that these were a phenomenon of a less enlightened age and would soon pass from the scene. A thoughtful account of the new political activism of Muslims in Western Europe notes how "European debates revert to the same syllogism, again and again. If they have not abandoned their faith, Muslims are religious fundamentalists. Since choice is meaningless among fundamentalists, only victims or bullies are Muslims" (Klausen, 2005, p. 209). This is clearly not an appropriate basis for respect toward or the integration into European society of millions of individuals of the second and third generations deriving from immigration whose primary identity is not as Moroccans or Turks but as Muslims, whether they attend the mosque or not (Laurence & Vaisse, 2006, pp. 95, 167).

As might be expected, there has been ongoing controversy and dire warnings about the possible effects of separate schooling on the basis of an Islamic (as contrasted with a Catholic, Protestant, or humanistic) worldview, and there have been a number of official studies asking whether in fact these schools are having harmful results. The current view on the part of the body that advises the Dutch government on education policy questions is that problems exist with the quality of some of these schools, attributable in part to the lack of sophistication of their boards, but that they have not been guilty of preventing the second and third generations from adapting to Dutch life. In fact, the Onderwijsraad has pointed out:

> Freedom of choice for parents is not only of great value for individuals, but also for society as a whole. In a context of similar views [within a school] there is often a strong internal social cohesion, promoting the social capital which binds people together. School directors report in the *Jaarboekje 2011* how important it is to give people the chance to build bridges from their own identity to those of others. (Onderwijsraad, 2012, p. 63)

There are other cases, in Western Europe, in which separate schooling has been developed to resist the encroachments of a majority culture perceived as being so attractive to the younger generation that they are at risk of losing their connection with their cultural heritage and ethnic community. As Muslim immigrants have become more settled in Western Europe and have abandoned any projects of return to their countries of origin, they have developed the resources and the organizational capacity to begin to educate their children separately. Conflicts of culture and of intention between immigrant Muslim groups and the host societies have led them in some cases to seek to segregate their children from those of the majority.

Legitimate concerns are expressed about whether religiously separate schools will prevent integration into the host society; this is precisely the charge that was brought against Catholic schools in the United States during the 19th century, only to be disproved by the salient role that such schools played in the transition of language, culture, and loyalty. Of course one cannot guarantee that the same process will occur with Islamic schools in Western societies, but there is no intrinsic reason to believe that it will not. After all, most Muslim parents want their children to learn what they need to be successful in the host society, without surrendering to aspects of popular culture that they find offensive—and who can say that they are wrong?

POLICY SOLUTIONS?

Just as resistance to religiously separate schools was motivated in part by legitimate—though, in the event greatly exaggerated—concerns that they would promote and perpetuate social divisions, so the criticism of introducing elements of minority cultures into the curriculum sometimes warns that it will get in the way of acquisition of those elements of the common culture of the host society that are necessary for academic and career success and for citizenship.

Of course, both cases included less worthy motivations as well, hostility to minority religions (or, sometimes, to all religion) on the one hand, and dismissal of the value of minority cultures on the other. Recognition of the existence of such denigrating attitudes, however, should not cause us to dismiss the legitimate concerns.

Policy makers are challenged with finding the right balance between respecting the right of voluntary communities formed around shared religious convictions to nurture their children in those convictions, and ensuring that those children grow into citizens capable of cooperating and deliberating with fellow citizens nurtured in other convictions, or none.

Christopher Shannon has pointed out that the "path to meaningful diversity lies not in the refinement of abstract, neutral, universal principles that affirm the dignity of all faiths and value systems, but in the fostering of alternative local institutions rooted in very particular faith and value systems . . . the public school system remains in the vanguard of promoting false universalisms" (2001, p. 134). The goal of secular liberalism was to segregate religion into the private sphere, a sphere that shrinks all the time as government takes on more functions previously carried out by families and voluntary associations, including religious communities. But it can be argued that

the alternative to the present segregation of religion is not integration but separation. Such separation marks a retreat only from the Enlightenment ideology of liberal universalism, not from participation in the political institutions that are, admittedly, the legacy of this ideology. . . . The fostering of local institutions, rooted in distinct, particular traditions, promises the most meaningful alternative to both the religious intolerance of the past and the secular intolerance of the present (Shannon, 2001, p. 136).

In country after country, often reluctantly, policy makers are seeking to develop appropriate frameworks of institutional pluralism to accommodate the cultural and religious diversity of their societies and the resurgence of civil society networks. The educational policy challenge of our times is to find the appropriate balance among (1) the freedom of families to choose schools that match their goals for their children, (2) the autonomy of educators to create distinctive schools in which to exercise their professionalism without undue bureaucratic restrictions, and (3) the appropriate government oversight to ensure that every young person receives an education preparing him or her for engaged and effective citizenship.

REFERENCES

Some of this material appeared previously in the author's introductory chapters to Glenn & De Groof, 2012, volume 1.

An Coiste Comhairleach Pleanála [The Advisory Planning Committee]. (1988). *The Irish language in a changing society.* Dublin: Bord na Gaeilge.

Arons, S. (1986). *Compelling belief: The culture of American schooling.* Amherst: University of Massachusetts Press.

Asad, T. (2003). *Formations of the secular: Christianity, Islam, Modernity.* Stanford, CA: Stanford University Press.

August, D., & Hakuta, Kenji (Eds.). (1997). *Improving schooling for language-minority children: A research agenda.* Washington, DC: National Research Council.

Braster, J. F. A. (1996). *De identiteit van het openbaar onderwijs,* Groningen: Wolters-Noordhoff.

Brett, R. (1991). *The development of the human dimension mechanism of the Conference on Security and Co-operation in Europe (CSCE),* Papers in the Theory and Practice of Human Rights. Colchester.

Brett, R. (1993). The human dimension mechanism of the CSCE and the CSCE response to minorities. In M. R. Lucas (Ed.), *The CSCE in the 1990s: Constructing European security and co-operation.* Baden-Baden.

Capotorti, F. (1991). *Study of the rights of persons belonging to ethnic, religious and linguistic minorities.* New York: United Nations.

Carter, S. L. (1993). *The culture of disbelief: How American law and politics trivialize religious devotion.* New York: Basic Books.

Casanova, J. (2007). Immigration and the new religious pluralism: A European Union/United States comparison. In T. Banchoff (Ed.), *Democracy and the new religious pluralism* (pp. 59–84). New York: Oxford University Press.

Coleman, E. B., & White, K. (Eds.). (2011). Introduction. In *Religious tolerance, education and the curriculum* (pp. 1–4). Rotterdam: Sense Publishers.

De Groof, J. (1994). The overall shape of education law: Status of comparative and supra-national education law. In Jan de Groof (Ed.), *Subsidiarity and education: Aspects of comparative educational law.* Leuven, Belgium: Acco.

De Groof, J., & Bray, E. (Eds.). (1996). *Education under the new constitution in South Africa.* Leuven, Belgium: Acco.

De Groof, J., Malherbe, R., & Sachs, A. (Eds.). (2000). *Constitutional implementation in South Africa.* Ghent, Belgium.

Delpit, L. (1995). *Other people's children: Cultural conflict in the classroom.* New York: New Press.

Dubet, F., & Lapeyronnie, D. (1992). *Les quartiers d'éxil.* Paris: Éditions du Seuil.

Fase, W. (1987). *Voorbij de grenzen van onderwijs in eigen taal en cultuur: Meertaligheid op school in zes landen verkend,* The Hague: Instituut voor Onderzoek van het Onderwijs.

Fishman, J. A. (1989). *Language and ethnicity in minority sociolinguistic perspective.* Clevedon, UK: Multilingual Matters.

Glazer, N. (1997). *We are all multiculturalists now.* Cambridge, MA: Harvard University Press.

Glenn, C. L. (1995a). *Educational freedom in Eastern Europe* (2nd ed.). Washington, DC: Cato Institute.

Glenn, C. L. (1995b). Minority schools on purpose. In E. Flaxman & A. H. Passow (Eds.), *Changing populations, changing schools: 94th yearbook of the National Society for the Study of Education,* Part II. Chicago, IL: National Society for the Study of Education.

Glenn, C. L. (1996). *Educating immigrant children: Schools and language minorities in 12 nations* (with Ester J. de Jong). New York: Garland Publishing.

Glenn, C. L. (2011). *Native American/First Nations schooling: From the colonial period to the present.* New York and London: Palgrave Macmillan.

Glenn, C. L., & De Groof, J. (Eds.). (2012). *Balancing freedom, autonomy, and accountability in education, volumes (1–4).* Nijmegen, Netherlands: Wolf Legal Publishing.

Gorter, D. (1991). Lesser used languages in primary education in the European community. In Koen Jaspaert & Sjaak Kroon (Eds.), *Ethnic minority languages and education.* Amsterdam/Lisse: Swets and Zeitlinger.

Hefner, R. W. (2007). Introduction: The culture, politics, and future of Muslim education. In Robert Hefner & Muhammad Qasim Zaman (Eds.), *Schooling Islam: The culture and politics of modern Muslim education.* Princeton, NJ: Princeton University Press.

Hillgruber, C., & M. Jestaedt. (1994). *Die Europäische Menschenrechtenkonvention und der nationaler Minderheiten.* Cologne.

Hirsch, E. D., Jr. (1996). *The schools we need . . . and why we don't have them.* New York: Doubleday.

Hollinger, D. A. (2005). *Postethnic America: Beyond multiculturalism.* Tenth Anniversary Edition. New York: Basic Books.

Jonkman, R. J. (1991). Triangulation and trilingualism. In Kjell Herberts & Christer Laurén (Eds.), *Papers from the Sixth Nordic Conference on Bilingualism.* Clevedon, UK: Multilingual Matters.

Kepel, G. (1987). *Les banlieues de l'Islam.* Paris: Éditions du Seuil.

Kepel, G. (1991). *La revanche de Dieu.* Paris: Éditions du Seuil.

Kepel, G. (1994). *A l'ouest d'Allah.* Paris: Éditions du Seuil.

Klausen, J. (2005). *The Islamic challenge: Politics and religion in Western Europe.* Oxford, England: Oxford University Press.

Kohn, H. (1967). *The idea of nationalism,* New York: Collier Books.

Koot, W., Tjon-a-ten, V., & Venema, P. U. (1985). *Surinaamse kinderen op school.* Muiderberg: Dick Coutinho.

Kreso, A. P. (2012). Bosnia and Herzegovina. In C. L. Glenn & J. De Groof (Eds.), *Balancing freedom, autonomy, and accountability in education* (vol. 4). Nijmegen: Wolf Legal Publishing.

Kymlicka, W. (1996). *Multicultural citizenship: A liberal theory of minority rights.* New York: Oxford University Press.

Laurence, J., & Vaisse, J. (2006). *Integrating Islam: Political and religious challenges in contemporary France.* Washington, DC: Brookings Institution Press.

Legrand, L. (1981). *L'école unique: à quelles conditions?* Paris: Scarabée.

Lenaerts, K. (1994). Subsidiarity and community competence in the field of education. In J. De Groof (Ed.), *Subsidiarity and education. Aspects of comparative educational law.* Leuven: Acco.

Martin, D. (1990). *Tongues of fire.* Oxford: Blackwell.

Mavelli, L. (2012). *Europe's encounter with Islam: The secular and the postsecular.* London: Routledge.

McKean, W. A. (1985). *Equality and discrimination under international law.* Oxford, England: Oxford University Press.

McLean, M. (1985). Private supplementary schools and the ethnic challenge to state education in Britain. In C. Brock & W. Tulasiewicz (Eds.), *Cultural identity and educational policy.* London: Croom Helm.

McLeod, H. (2000). *Secularization in Western Europe, (1848–1914).* New York: St. Martin's Press.

Modood, T. (2007). *Multiculturalism: A civic idea.* Cambridge, UK: Polity.

Monsma, S. V. (1993). *Positive neutrality: Letting religious freedom ring,* Westport, CT: Greenwood Press.

Monsma, S. V. (1996). *When sacred and secular mix,* Lanham, MD: Rowman & Littlefield.

Monsma, S. V., & Soper, Christopher J. (1997). *The challenge of pluralism: Church and state in five democracies,* Lanham, MD: Rowan & Littlefield.

Onderwijsraad. (2012). *Artikel (23 Grondwet in maatschappelijk perspectief: Nieuwe richtingen aan de vrijheid van onderwijs.* Den Haag.

Rath, J., Groenendijk, K., & Penninx, R. (1992). Nederland en de islam. Een programma van onderzoek. *Migrantenstudies, 8*(1).

Rodley, N. S. (1995). Conceptual problems in the protection of minorities: International developments, *Human Rights Quarterly, 17*(1), 48–71.

Roy, O. (2007). *Secularism confronts Islam.* Translated by George Holoch. New York: Columbia University Press.

Schade, A. (2000). A research topic in education law and policy: The development of regionalism and federalism in Europe and their impact on educational policy and administration. *European Journal for Education Law and Policy, 4*(1).

Scheffer, P. (2010). *The open society and its immigrants: A story of avoidance, conflict and accommodation.* Dissertation, University of Tilburg.

Schnapper, D. (1992). *L'Europe des immigrés.* Paris: François Bourin.

Scott, J. W. (2007). *The politics of the veil.* Princeton, NJ: Princeton University Press.

Schwencke, H. J. (1994). Schoolstrijd in Den Haag. Veranderingen in de religiuze cultuur van Surinaamse Hindoes in Nederland. *Migrantenstudies, 10*(2).

Shadid, W., & van Koningsveld, P. S. (1990). Islamitische basisscholen in Nederland. *Samenwijs, 1*(1), September.

Shannon, C. (2001). *A world made safe for differences: Cold War intellectuals and the politics of identity.* Lanham, MD: Rowman & Littlefield.

Stone, M. (1985). *The education of the black child: The myth of multiracial education.* London: Fontana Press.

Sunier, T. (1994). Islam en etniciteit onder jonge leden van Turkse islamistische organisaties in Nederland. *Migrantenstudies, 10*(1).

Teunissen, J. (1990). Basisscholen op islamitische en hindoeïstische grondslag. *Migrantenstudies, 6*(2).

Thiessen, E. J. (1993). *Teaching for commitment: Liberal education, indoctrination, and Christian nurture.* Montreal: McGill-Queen's University Press.

Timera, M. (1989). Identité communautaire et project éducatif chez les immigrés Sonikés en France. *Migrants-formation, 7*(6).

Weber, E. (1976). *Peasants into Frenchmen.* Stanford, CA: Stanford University Press.

Willems, W., & Cottaar, A. (1990). Ethnocentrisme en het beeld van minderheden over Nederland. *Migrantenstudies, 6*(3).

13

THE POLITICS OF ENTREPRENEURSHIP
AND INNOVATION

Michael Q. McShane and Frederick M. Hess

Our schools today confront challenges that our education system is not equipped to answer. Erected haphazardly over the course of two centuries, our system of schooling has been configured to process large numbers of students for lives in an industrial nation. Given the realities of globalization and the demands of a knowledge economy, a system that may have worked passably well 35 years ago is no longer adequate. Moreover, there is no evidence that our education system can be reconfigured commensurate with a new mission. In fact, decades of earnest efforts to reform public schools through conventional means have shown remarkably little ability to substantively alter routines or results (Hess, 1999).

There is widespread agreement that America's system of K-12 schooling needs to do better. A recent report by the National Center for Education Statistics (Stillwell & Sable, 2013) detailed the glaring shortfall in graduation rates in the United States, especially for children of color. While the average graduation rate for the class of 2010 nationwide was 78.3 percent, the District of Columbia posted a rate of 59.9 percent, Mississippi posted a rate of 63.8 percent, and Nevada, the lowest performer, posted a rate of only 57.8 percent. Disaggregating data by race shows even poorer performance for African American students. Nationwide, only 66.1 percent of African American students graduate from high school. States from Michigan (59.2%), to Nebraska (57.6%), to Nevada (46.7%) posted abysmal rates. The story is similar for Hispanic students, who while posting a national average of 71.4 percent, saw much lower rates in Connecticut (55.5%), New York (60.7%), and Utah (60.6%). Failing to graduate high school is an almost insurmountable barrier in the information economy of today and tomorrow.

Established, mature organizations are not particularly inclined to be agile or adaptive to changing circumstances (Downs, 1967). Public school officials, enmeshed in a public bureaucracy, governed by elected representatives, and scrutinized by anxious parents and civic leaders, have traditionally been averse to risk or disruptive change. Licensure requirements prevent nontraditional aspirants from becoming teachers or school leaders. Financing systems, charter school laws, and existing regulations make it arduous and fiscally perilous to open new schools. State law and collective bargaining thwart efforts

to reward the best and hardest-working educators. Teachers, principals, and district officials work in an environment where excellence is rarely rewarded, where those who do
more or devise new approaches are often stymied by rules or routines, and where keeping one's head down and following procedure are the surest paths to professional success
(Hess 2010, 2013).

Many thinkers have called for an infusion of entrepreneurship into education in an
attempt to change this state of affairs (Christensen & Horn, 2008; Hess, 2006, 2010; Hill,
2003, 2004). They believe that the underlying motivations and orientation of entrepreneurs have the potential to provide the "disruptive change" that the education system
needs to turn around some of these frightening indicators. Over the course of this chapter, we set out to describe entrepreneurship and its role in driving innovation. We will
describe the role that it can play in education, but give hearing to those who believe that
it has no place in a public institutions like schools. We will describe current barriers that
exist and map a way forward for leaders so inclined as to try and promote innovation
through leveraging entrepreneurship. In doing so we hope to explain current and past
trends in entrepreneurship and sketch out some possible opportunities for entrepreneurs to drive innovation in the future.

ENTREPRENEURSHIP AND INNOVATION

"Entrepreneurship" and "innovation" are loaded terms. Many see the language of business
as threatening to the world of education, with proponents of entrepreneurship attempting to "marketize" a democratic system that supplies a public good (Ravitch, 2011). But
in order to determine whether these ideas are something to be feared or embraced, it is
essential to understand what they mean. Over the next several pages we hope to lay out
how these ideas work in education, explaining both what they are, and what they are not.

Entrepreneurship

Entrepreneurship can be hard to define. More than two centuries ago, French economist
J. B. Say suggested that "the entrepreneur shifts economic resources out of an area of
lower and into an area of higher productivity and greater yield" (cited in Drucker, 1985).
Entrepreneurs do so by rethinking the fundamental assumptions about what works and
what is possible. Established organizations, left to their own devices, tend to stand pat.
In particular, bureaucracies tend to privilege the status quo, as protecting funding, manpower, and turf becomes much more important than breaking new ground and risking
their established position (Downs, 1967).

Entrepreneurs, by contrast, drive what Schumpeter (1975) titled "creative destruction," the development of new enterprises to emerge, challenge, and eventually replace
the old. Promoting entrepreneurship requires luring smart, motivated people to work
under pressure, solve problems in a variety of ways, and be held accountable for their
demonstrated results.

Rather than accept the condition of an industry or sector as a given, entrepreneurs
rethink fundamental assumptions about what works or what is possible. Business scholars W. Chan Kim and Renee Mauborgne have noted that entrepreneurial individuals
often ask some variation on four questions: "Which of the factors that our industry takes
for granted should be eliminated? Which factors should be reduced well below the industry's standard? Which factors should be raised well above the industry's standard? Which

factors should be created that the industry has never offered?" (1999, p. 200). This may mean harnessing a new innovation, but it might also mean making use of tools, ideas, or approaches that are underused or overlooked.

When it comes to understanding just what skills and traits an entrepreneur requires, there is cause to be wary of sweeping generalizations. But successful entrepreneurs do generally exhibit a broad set of common traits. Bryan Hassel, codirector of consulting firm Public Impact, has identified six key traits that these individuals tend to share:

- *A Need for Achievement* and a tendency to set high goals and pursue them relentlessly, with clear metrics for success.
- *An Urgent Approach to Problem Solving* in which they relentlessly seek out solutions, trying and discarding failed strategies.
- *An Internal Locus of Control* in which they deem themselves as responsible for the outcomes of their actions and are unwilling to make excuses for failure.
- *A Tolerance for Ambiguity* and a powerful ability to flexibly adapt as conditions warrant.
- *A Preference for Strategic Influencing.* Though they may have strong interpersonal skills, they focus less on cultivating long-term relationships and more on using personal relationships to address immediate organizational needs.
- *A Bias for Action through Organization Building.* As Smith and Petersen have written, "[Entrepreneurs'] sense of urgency and drive to achieve leads them to take action by creating new organizations that will make their vision a reality" (as quoted in Hess, 2010).

Education, as noted earlier, appears to be ripe for entrepreneurial innovation. There is potential in education for entrepreneurs to meet the currently unmet needs of students. They can seek to teach children who have been ill-served, improve the quality of educators and school leaders, provide more effective tools, and deliver services in more useful and accessible ways. As such, these entrepreneurial types can be grouped into three broad categories: *school builders, talent providers,* and *tool builders and service providers.*

The best-known educational entrepreneurs are those who launch new schools and new networks of schools. These *school builders* include a variety of charter management organizations and "mom and pop" efforts and include such well-known ventures as the National Heritage Academies, High Tech High School, and the Knowledge Is Power Program (KIPP) schools. These schools each have a hallmark innovation. For the National Heritage Academies, their efficient use of space (they design all of their schools exactly the same to save money on architecture and engineering costs) allows them to decrease their operating costs significantly. High Tech High School integrates technology in the curriculum and takes advantage of its co-location with a local community college, and KIPP is known for pioneering the "no excuses" discipline system that allows for instruction with fewer behavioral disruptions. Another great example is the Green Dot Public schools, a network of charter schools founded by novelist and political activist Steve Barr. Barr's innovation was something he calls the "thin contract," a more flexible, less bureaucratic alternative to the conventional labor agreement. Green Dot now enrolls more than 10,000 students in 18 schools across Los Angeles.

A second group of organizations are *talent providers.* These entrepreneurs focus on improving the quality of instruction and leadership by finding more promising ways to recruit, develop, and support teachers and school leaders. Teach for America (TFA) is an example of an entrepreneurial talent provider. Founded in 1989 by Wendy Kopp to recruit and prepare bright college graduates for two years of teaching in high-need classrooms, TFA used alternative credentialing to develop innovative processes to prepare teachers, including stringent criteria for candidate selection and a dramatically shortened, six-week preparation experience.

A third set of entrepreneurial ventures is composed of *tool builders and service providers*—entrepreneurs who provide distance learning, instructional devices, data systems, curricula, educational programs, or other services that leverage technology or research. Entrepreneurial tool builders and service providers take many forms, but those supplying new technology to change instruction have grabbed an outsized share of attention (Moe & Chubb, 2009). Teacher-generated lesson aggregators like Better Lesson, LearnZillion, and Mastery Connect provide a platform through which teachers can interact and share lessons and assessments with one another. Online video repositories like the Khan Academy have provided resources for teachers to incorporate new methods into their pedagogy. Management software providers like QuickSchools and Class Dojo have provided timesaving attendance and grade tracking programs that have streamlined managerial processes.

Innovation

Innovation is separate from, and often a by-product of, entrepreneurship. Innovation is the continual improvement of organizations, institutions, and products over time. Sometimes conflated with research and development, innovation is the product of research and development, paired with management and a response to market conditions that develops and continually refines a final product. It became a centerpiece of the education conversation with the publication of Harvard business professor Clayton Christensen's best-selling *Disrupting Class: How Innovation Will Change the Way the World Learns* (2008). In that work, he argues for what he terms "disruptive innovation" in education, using a term he coined in his 2003 book *The Innovator's Solution.*

Disruptive innovation goes beyond the incremental improvement of products and processes. It alters fundamental assumptions about organization, governance, and the delivery of products. It allows organizations to do more with fewer people, to more effectively serve customers, and to pioneer new and improved models of production and service.

One illustration of disruptive innovation in education can be glimpsed at the School of One, a New York City program for teaching math in grades 6 through 8. Rather than employ a conventional curricular scope and sequence for an entire class, the School of One unpacks each grade level's math objectives into its component parts. It uses pretests; brief, near-daily unit assessments; a slew of instructional modalities (large group, small group, online tutoring, computer-assisted, and so on); and an organizing algorithm to customize scope and sequence to each student's individual learning needs. Students skip over objectives they've already mastered and learn different objectives using the instructional approaches deemed most appropriate for them. They spend more on certain learning objectives when they need to and race ahead when they are able. By combining all the math courses at the school into a common, flexible enterprise, it becomes possible for teachers to differentiate instruction, share instructional responsibilities, and collaborate in ways that are usually impractical.

Disruptive innovations, however, often clash with entrenched interests and are stifled before they are able to make meaningful change. The system responds to the threat of disruption by thwarting it. It's easy to hail innovations so long as they are small and peripheral. Matters change when innovators become threatening or when their innovations expand and begin to threaten jobs, accepted arrangements, or assumptions about how work should be done. Moves to replace police with traffic lights, automate library collections and filing, or franchise restaurants all met with resistance due to cultural norms, fearful workers, threatened firms, or public officials hesitant about disruption.

Every meaningful disruptive innovation inevitably encounters this kind of resistance. In the public sector, where public officials are more attuned to passionate constituencies than to the diffuse, long-term benefits that innovations often provide, resistance to the "threat" posed by innovations can be intense. This is particularly true in schooling, where sensitivity to inequities and the vulnerability of the student population is acute (Payne, 2008). The result is that we have reams of highly regarded educational innovations—including specialty schools that span the nation—that have not made much of a systemic difference (charter schools today enroll less than 5 percent of all students across the country). Programs are tolerated and even accepted—so long as they remain small, isolated, "one-offs" that know their place and take care not to explicitly criticize the larger system. When such programs begin to rapidly expand, publicly indict the performance of their peer institutions, seek to change public policy governing pay or school governance, or advertise an intention of becoming large-scale providers, the reception grows chillier.

"Innovation" versus Innovation

As a result of this pressure, most "innovations" touted in education circles—ranging from efforts to promote block scheduling to new mentoring programs and from "themed" high schools to new instructional approaches—have been anything but disruptive. Rather, they have been new wrinkles on a variety of practices, dressed up with new names and new justifications. They have often taken the shape of school district A embracing an "innovative" approach already in use in district B, even as district C is unfurling as its "innovative" new approach the very program that district A is abandoning. This constant searching, swapping, and recycling has been termed "policy churn."

In short, not all innovations are created equal. Determining if a venture is a real, disruptive innovation depends on the degree to which it *promotes new efficiencies, addresses unmet needs, performs consistently at high levels, and is scalable enough to reach large numbers of students.*

It is not enough for an entrepreneurial venture simply to be good. To really be worthwhile, in addition to meeting one of the three criteria listed earlier, there's an imperative that it be able to *replicate* and to *grow*. This is where the ambition enters in. Even though it's immensely challenging to successfully launch even a single school or provide a boutique service, the real standard is far more demanding. It's not merely whether an innovation might plausibly be scaled, but whether it can be used to deliver transformative benefits to a broad swath of children, families, or educators.

Significant innovations need also to be *cost-effective*. Entrepreneurs who succeed by adopting a "more, better" strategy can make a useful contribution, but their impact is inevitably limited. Schools that rely on scant talent, big philanthropy, or extraordinary support from other sources are guaranteed to start hitting a ceiling when those resources grow scarce. The most compelling entrepreneurial ventures are those that find ways to deliver average or above average results for less money and with less manpower. For example, technological advances that can allow high-quality teachers to deliver more personalized instruction to more students or that remove some of the clerical burden from administrators can make schooling both more effective and more efficient.

Simply put, the most significant innovations will be those that are cost-effective and can be replicated at scale. These solutions have the power to transform schooling. In practice, though, would-be reformers and philanthropists have tended to favor exciting boutique ventures even when those are difficult to scale. For example, whether we are looking at small high schools, magnet schools, site-based management, or block scheduling, early sites had the advantage of opting in to the program, access to extra money designed to get the program off of the ground, and researchers at the test site eager to help make sure the program was a success. Later sites did not get any of those benefits. When innovations like these are taken to scale, it becomes apparent that the success of the small-scale test wasn't the innovative wrinkle, but the wrinkle in concert with resources, support, and buy-in. To our mind, that is not real or innovative success, it is just saying that you need to spend more and have more support and buy-in for programs to work, knowing full well that those things tend to be hard to scale. Disruptive innovations are those that can scale without all of that scaffolding.

When it comes to evaluating innovations the central question is, how innately replicable is the core innovation? Computer simulations, Web-based tutorials, or tightly scripted programs may be much easier to replicate than a school, service, or product that depends heavily on talent. Instructional or school models, on the other hand, have many more variables and are much more dependent on the quality of the instructors and classroom culture—which means consistent quality requires finding thousands of teachers as committed and skilled as the first handful.

CHALLENGES TO THE ENTREPRENEURIAL VISION

Now, it's a mistake to wax rhapsodic about the entrepreneurial process. The expectation is not that the typical venture will improve on the status quo, only that some will do so. This, as astute observers of the education sector will note, raises serious and important questions about uniformity of access guaranteed by many state constitutions. In fact, in 2006, the Florida State Supreme Court ruled against the state's school voucher program, directly arguing that it contradicted language in the state constitution that required "a uniform, efficient, safe, secure and high quality system of free public schools that allows students to obtain a high quality education."

It is true that opening space for innovation and entrepreneurship runs the risk of having a nonuniform system of education. But, it is also true that the current education system is far from uniform in its provision of education. The *de jure* uniformity of current state laws and policies has not led to *de facto* uniformity. If you need evidence, just drive from Houston to Austin to San Antonio and stop at schools along the way. Any pretense of uniformity will quickly drop away.

The entrepreneurial premise makes transparent a fiction we prefer not to acknowledge: that all students are receiving an adequate education. While this is a difficult reality to come to grips with, it is reality. A possible solution to this vexing problem would be to give more people the opportunity to do right by students. If you're weighing that prospect against a utopian status quo, it is clearly an unacceptable trade, but we know the status quo isn't like that. Against the real status quo, it's a challenging and morally pregnant question of how to weigh the trade-offs. Some ideas won't pan out and many ventures will fail. In fact, management scholars have estimated that 60 percent of all product development efforts are abandoned before they ever reach the market, and nearly half of those that do reach the market fail (Christensen & Raynor, 2003). The entrepreneur, however, accepts that the path of improvement is neither straight nor self-evident. Entrepreneurs have the flexibility and incentive to seek out new solutions, make judicious use of available data, and adapt as obstacles and opportunities dictate. While the plight of any given venture is uncertain, the entrepreneurial process itself ensures that potentially good ideas are constantly surfaced and then sifted. Given the lack of an omniscient planner to foresee what will work, entrepreneurs become the engines of progress.

There are also voices of concern that entrepreneurship and innovation might undermine the fundamental, democratic nature of public schooling. University of Wisconsin professor Michael Apple, for example, has argued for years that opening up education to markets will reinforce traditional, negative hierarchies of class and race (Apple, 1996, 2001). NYU professor Diane Ravitch, in her best-selling opus decrying what she sees as disturbing trends in public schooling, *The Death and Life of the Great American School System,* argues that "our schools will not improve if we expect them to act like private profit-seeking enterprises. Schools are not businesses; they are a public good" (2011, p. 227). Ravitch and the many others who share her views argue that public schools are foundations of our American democracy, and decentralizing their management threatens to undermine that ideal. Rather than relying on the watchful eye of our elected leaders, she argues, "removing public oversight will leave the education of our children to the whim of entrepreneurs and financiers . . . Education is too important to relinquish to the vagaries of the market and the good intentions of amateurs" (p. 222).

Others argue that the system should be reformed from within, not from without. A leading voice against such external actors has been Alex Molnar, professor of education policy at Arizona State University. He argues that including entrepreneurs, especially those who are motivated to earn a profit, raises serious questions about "possible tradeoffs between profits and the best interests of children, evidence that EMOs and supplemental services firms have rarely been held accountable for achieving promised academic results; and recurring allegations of questionable relationships among politicians and policymakers and for-profit companies" (2006, p. 115). Rather than risk that, he argues, greater investment in the human capital and institutional infrastructure is the answer, not external entrepreneurs.

However, as Paul Hill, former director of the Center on Reinventing Public Education at the University of Washington, has argued, the entrepreneurial assumption is consistent with the American ethos. As he notes, "Defining democracy as centralized deliberation leading to uniform coercive results is surely perverse. When controlled by policy, public education is defined by the relative strength of interest groups and their ability to control how issues are resolved in election, legislatures and courts." Hill argues we need "a Jeffersonian version of democracy," which "expects arrangements to be temporary, and institutions to be re-thought fundamentally as times and needs change" (as quoted in Hess, 2006, p. 6).

John Chubb and Terry Moe (1990) offer a related argument. In the first two chapters of their landmark work *Politics, Markets, and America's Schools* they make the point that in politically governed bureaucracies each successive majority wedges its preferences into the fabric of the organization. Over time, as new people come in, more rules and regulations are added, increasing layers of rigidity. This is particularly a problem in schools, they argue, because schools are ultimately about street-level discretion for educators. Teachers are closest to their students and need the most freedom to meet their students' diverse needs. Rigidity, no matter how well intentioned, is terrible for them as over time it creates policies and procedures that strangle school autonomy, preventing school leaders from making good decisions. For Chubb and Moe, the entrepreneurial presumption is central because it lets people build newly autonomous ways to serve kids.

IMPEDIMENTS TO INNOVATION

Those skeptical of entrepreneurial involvement in education have set up barriers to prevent it. But, it should be noted, barriers are not intrinsically bad. Insofar as laws, regulations, and political structures protect children and foster rather than impede successful processes, they are actually extremely important; it is only once they become stifling to positive behavior that they become a problem. One way to think about this is that the rules, regulations, and contracts that govern schools *evolve* over time. Many of these structures are perfectly reasonable for a given point in time, but, as years roll by, they can become ill suited to the needs of schools.

So the question is: How do you modify them?

Chubb and Moe argue that changing these policies and procedures is incredibly difficult to do because anyone interested in change needs both a majority to enact their policies and the ability to navigate the byzantine path that such proposals must take. That path is littered with veto points that make it much easier for policy makers to say no than yes.

Private-sector ventures have a clear solution to this; they fail. Failing organizations get replaced by organizations that have fewer old constraints, use new models and new technology, and are built around the changing labor force. But that is hard to do in contemporary education policy. Given that we're talking about the current policy context, we can examine those impediments and how they play out with respect to new ventures.

Barriers to innovation generally fall into two categories, informal and formal. Informal barriers are the *political realities, attitudes,* and *beliefs* that are change averse. Formal barriers are the *laws, rules,* and *regulations* that mandate particular behavior, from staffing ratios to funding formulae. Both offer their unique contributions to preventing change and both lead to what McGuinn argues is the trifecta of impediments to entrepreneurship: "barriers to entry, lack of access to financial capital, and lack of human capital" (2006, pp. 65–66).

Politics

As Niccolo Machiavelli argued 500 years ago, people who get hurt by changes seek to resist them, and people who may benefit from changes don't pay attention until after the fact. The politics of education are dominated by a few major players, particularly teachers' unions, which have grown up under a certain set of rules. They see the threats of disruption and the benefits of not allowing entrepreneurship to upend the world they know, so they tend to be skeptical and hostile to these types of changes. They have a lot of cards to play.

The K-12 public school system spends more than $600 billion per year and employs more than 6 million people, or almost 4 percent of the entire U.S. labor force (U.S. Department of Education, 2013). As a result, political constituencies of various stakeholders in the process, from teachers to administrators to parents to taxpayers, work to advance their interests. Many have a material interest in preserving the status quo, as allowing for technology to replace labor or schools to alter the way they assign teachers could result in the loss of jobs.

For decades, interest groups, school boards, and state-level legislatures involved in education as well as state and local education agencies have formed what political scientists label an "iron triangle"—a nearly impenetrable sub-government in public education that has resisted innovation (Maranto & McShane, 2012). The largest interest group—teachers' unions—makes up one corner of this triangle. It has long been an important power base of the Democratic Party. In fact, at the 2008 Democratic National Convention, around one-tenth of the 4,400 delegates were members of a teachers' union (Goldstein, 2008). In the past five years, the American Federation of Teachers (AFT) and the National Education Association (NEA) have spent more than $330 million to influence elections, overwhelmingly to support Democrats (Mundy, 2012). If these two groups were combined, they would represent the single largest donor to American political campaigns (Center for Responsive Politics, 2012).

School board elections—the primary democratic check on the education bureaucracy—are ripe for co-opting by interest groups interested in excluding entrepreneurs from entering the school system. As Terry Moe (2011) points out in his book *Special Interest: Teachers Unions and America's Public Schools,* most school board elections are off-cycle and nonpartisan, resulting in an extremely low turnout and voters without easy cues to separate the candidates. This would allow organized interest groups to seize control of elections and elect candidates more friendly to their agenda. Not surprisingly, Moe's empirical analysis found that teachers' unions are more likely to win higher salaries in elections held off-cycle than in elections held on-cycle.

In these off-cycle elections, and in the larger elections of state-level legislators, teachers' unions are most often the largest spenders on campaign contributions. In the attempt to oust the Republican governor of Wisconsin, Scott Walker, teachers' unions contributed more than $1 million (Butrymowicz, 2012). Walker had worked to limit the scope of collective bargaining, scrubbing away many of the formal barriers to innovative personnel management that we outlined earlier in this chapter. While not ultimately successful, they drastically altered the tenor of the election. The unions were more successful when attempting to oust DC schools chancellor Michelle Rhee, who had pioneered innovations in teacher recruitment and evaluation. Teachers' unions spent $1 million in the Washington, DC, mayor's election; and those figures only count direct contribution to campaigns, not lobbyists, independent radio or television commercials, flyers, phone banks, teams to knock on doors, or any number of other ways that unions can contribute to elections *in kind* (Smith, 2010).

Attitudes, Beliefs, and Habits
But almost equally as detrimental are the attitudes, beliefs, and habits of teachers and administrators as well as the American public writ large about how schools are supposed to operate. One need only to talk to school and system leaders or school board members, observe education leadership courses, or read texts by education leadership icons

to understand that the primary levers of leadership are expected to be culture, capacity building, coaching, and consensus (Hess, 2013). Educational employees face extensive procedural requirements adopted to ensure that educators are conforming to the wishes of lawmakers.

Given substantial penalties for violating statutes or offending elected lawmakers, and the lack of rewards for effective performance, public servants have incentives to hew to legal and procedural requirements—even if they deem such measures to be inefficient or flawed. Employees who respect rules and procedures tend to prosper, while entrepreneurial individuals who violate norms or offend powerful constituencies have difficulty gaining authority. It is not that bureaucracies are devoid of entrepreneurial personalities, but that these individuals are discouraged and find their professional progress impeded. Altering this reality requires deliberate steps to change policy and culture (Downs, 1967).

On the part of the body politic, a large barrier to innovation is what education historians David Tyack and Larry Cuban (1995) call the idea of the "real school." They argue that people in America have an idea of what a "real school" looks like, and it looks a lot like the school that they attended. Physically, it is a building with classrooms—connected by hallways full of lockers—filled with 20–30 students sitting in desks or at tables looking forward to a teacher in the front of the room writing on a blackboard or whiteboard. The students are arranged in age-grouped grades and progress from subject to subject and room to room at relatively standardized intervals along with their peers. Pedagogically, the methods, tools, and organization of schools are the same methods, tools, and organization that the schools they attended utilized. This powerful conception governs a great deal of public opinion regarding innovative changes in the American education system.

Formal Barriers

Born out of these political and cultural factors, formal barriers include the laws, rules, and regulations that mandate particular behavior on the part of school operators. These barriers inevitably exist because public schools spend public dollars and hire public employees to serve the public's children. For better or worse, schools are going to be governed by public policies. Whether made by legislators or bureaucrats, and in Washington or locally, those policies sketch what educators can and can't do, how money is to be spent, how performance will be judged, who can be hired, and much else (Hess, 2013).

Federal Laws and Regulations

Federal law is the source of many real and rumored obstacles, with policies adopted as far back as the 1960s having congealed into regulations that can feel unmovable. As Federal Education Group attorneys Melissa Junge and Sheara Krvaric have noted, "it is hard to overemphasize the number of federal compliance requirements that apply to states and districts. The Office of the Inspector General once estimated that Title I alone contained 588 discrete compliance requirements, and even this number does not provide a full picture" (2012, p. 4). The most common sources of noncompliance are requirements governing *time and effort* and *supplement not supplant*.

Federal law requires personnel paid with federal funds to keep *time and effort* records that track the time they spend on federal programs. The idea that staff paid with federal funds should be doing what they're supposed to makes obvious sense, but the practical result tends to erect bars and make it tougher to spend dollars wisely. The problem? Staff supported by multiple funding sources—such as those in a comprehensive early literacy program or school improvement efforts—become a bookkeeping nightmare. So districts tend to run programs in silos, just to be safe. As a result, smart efforts to weave together extra formative assessment, reading instruction, after-school coaching, ELL instruction, and the like are frequently not pursued, just because allocating and documenting the costs and personnel can seem so intimidating.

Rules governing *supplement not supplant* apply to the largest federal K-12 programs, including Title I and IDEA. They require that states, districts, and schools use federal funds to provide eligible students with *extra* services, staff, programs, or materials they would not normally receive. Like time and effort, supplement not supplant is sensible in theory. The problem is that districts and schools have to prove that each expenditure is an "extra" they would not have paid for, absent federal funds. The result: auditors tell districts they can't use Title I funds for things like an additional section of ninth-grade English to boost literacy skills or attendance incentive programs at schools with high absenteeism. Why? Because it's not clear that these things are extras. It's easier to spend federal funds on clear extras—like field trips—than on educational programs. This then shapes the use of state and local funds because, as Krvaric and Junge explain, "The easiest way to show that something is 'extra' is to build a budget in layers; in other words, to first budget costs supported by state and local funds, and then budget federal costs" (quoted in Hess, 2013, p. 89).

Layers of Governance

Because 90 percent of school spending in the United States is supported by state and local funds, most policy is made at the state and local levels. State policy is generally the result of a three-part process. First, the legislature typically enacts broad policies, governing things like accountability, teacher evaluation, and the school calendar. Second, the finer details of such policies are generally determined by the state board of education. Third, the state education agency (SEA) then crafts the rules and regulations required to put those policies into effect. Most major federal education programs are also "state-administered," meaning the SEA ensures that districts comply with federal requirements. In doing so, SEAs can layer on additional requirements—sometimes creating confusion about what's permissible.

Local policy is in the hands of the school board in each of the nation's 14,000-odd districts. Boards are much maligned for failing to provide strong leadership, being heavily influenced by the demands of employee groups, wading into micromanagement, and being prone to petty bickering. In a few districts, mostly located in urban areas, boards are appointed by mayors. These boards are less subject to the failings noted earlier, but mayor-appointed boards have raised their own concerns, most notably a lack of transparency. A particular challenge for elected boards is the difficulty they have sticking to one course or agenda. An even bigger challenge may be that board members, whether elected or appointed, have little appetite for conflict or negative publicity, and thus typically boast a feeble track record when it comes to negotiating firmly, pushing back on the federal government, or standing up to aggrieved employees or community members (Rich & Henig, 2003).

All the laws, rules, and regulations made by federal officials, the SEA, and the school board trickle down in complex and uncertain ways. The press to comply with federal, state, and district policies overwhelms most superintendents and leads them to organize their district as a series of silos. Meanwhile, crucial district functions like human resources, information technology, and finance are charged with merely keeping the trains running.

As a result of these rules and regulations, rather than acting as engines to drive change, state and local-level education officials are occupied with compliance with various mandates drafted by federal and state officials. Navigating the web of often conflicting policies is a herculean task for school and district leaders, and leaves time for little else.

Collective Bargaining Agreements

An example of this is embodied in the biggest frustration that most school and district leaders wrestle with—the teachers' contract. Because of what's in it, what they think is in it, and what might be in it, would-be innovators routinely find themselves stymied when it comes to problems involving teacher assignment, compensation, hiring, professional development, instructional time, and much else. States like West Virginia and Pennsylvania, for example, mandate seniority as the sole determinant when making layoffs, leaving districts with no wiggle room.[1] Six states require charter schools to operate in accord with all the provisions in the local district's collective bargaining agreements (Price, 2009).

These contracts routinely spell out procedures for evaluating teachers, allowances for preparation time, regulations on the use of substitute teachers, stipends for overseeing extracurricular activities, protocol for disciplining students, the extent and nature of professional development, and much else. Collective bargaining agreements (CBAs) are also cluttered with more idiosyncratic provisions. In Chicago, the contract specifies, "In all schools where an intercom is used, an oral signal shall be given to indicate the intercom is beginning to be put into operation, or a light shall be installed on each outlet to indicate when the intercom is in operation."[2] The Orange County, Florida, contract promises, "Each school shall provide . . . head lice shampoo when not provided by Workers Compensation."[3]

Officials hoping to create innovative staffing arrangements or calendars may run headlong into many of the barriers articulated in CBAs. However, as Hess and Loup (2008) note, collective bargaining agreements are far less restrictive than is widely believed. Leaders may have more freedom than they think when it comes to navigating these formal barriers.

FOSTERING ENTREPRENEURSHIP

Whether entrepreneurs should be driving innovation is a question over which there is legitimate debate. However, regardless of where one comes down on the issue, it is useful to understand what policies might or might not do to spur entrepreneurship.

Primarily, policy makers can engage in three types of activities to promote entrepreneurship and innovation in education—removing formal impediments, altering funding streams, and providing legitimacy to nascent efforts.

Removing Formal Impediments

Policy plays a significant role in both promoting and hindering innovation and entrepreneurship. As outlined by Drew University political scientist Pat McGuinn, reforms to the policies that insulate the system from innovation tend to take one of three forms. Some "attempt to reform existing public schools from the inside by fostering public entrepreneurship" (2006, p. 65). These reforms, like altering regulations of teacher and principal licensure or granting flexibility in collective bargaining agreements, try to move the system as it is toward one that promotes more innovation. Other types of reforms, like charter schools, "encourage the creation of new schools that operate within the public system but which utilize greater regulatory flexibility to institute different instructional governance approaches" (p. 65). The third kind relies on "embracing private entrepreneurs—either by contracting public school operations to private companies or by allowing students to use public funds to pay for private school tuition" (p. 65).

The government can also strip away the statutory impediments that stifle innovation. As Junge and Krvaric (2012) outline, *supplement not supplant* could be replaced by regulations that simply ensure that districts do not skirt their responsibilities by relying on federal Title I dollars. Such a policy might require states to have a funding formula that ensures funding for an adequate level of education before Title I dollars are taken into account. This would prevent schools and districts from having to do a "cost by cost" justification for every decision that they make, a hurdle that makes innovation all the more challenging.

Altering Funding Streams

Public spending dominates the K-12 school sector. The federal government provides funding streams like Title I (supplementary funds for schools with larger percentages of poor students) to states and districts; states and localities fund school systems; and the expenditures wind up almost entirely driven by state or district officials. But the vast majority of this spending is dedicated to salaries, benefits, school operations, and other routine line items. Vanishingly little is available for research, development, or new ventures. In fact, researchers have calculated that up to 70 percent of district money is formulaically allocated as soon as it arrives in the central office and never even appears in school budgets (Roza & Miles, 2002).

Given that public spending dominates K-12 schooling, successful ventures need access to those dollars if they are to ever achieve substantial scale. The logic is straightforward; with philanthropies contributing perhaps $3 billion a year to K-12 education, and taxpayers providing more than $600 billion, it is not feasible for new ventures to thrive otherwise. And, outside of the limited funding it provides for charter school facilities, the government channels little funding to entrepreneurial ventures. One such program that does exist is the U.S. Department of Education's Credit Enhancement for Charter School Facilities program, which provides several million dollars in grants intended to boost the credit of charter schools so that they can tap into private-sector capital to acquire, construct, renovate, or lease facilities (USDoE, 2008). Another is the State Charter School Facilities Incentive Grants Program, which provides about $10 million to $15 million a year in grants to help fund programs that provide charter school facilities (USDoE, 2009).

A possible model of government investment is the Vermont Sustainable Jobs Fund, established in 1995 by the state legislature as a nonprofit, public-private 501(c)3 organization to invest in market-based solutions to environmental challenges. It offers grants and technical assistance to Vermont entrepreneurs with promising business models in sustainable agriculture, forestry, and renewable energy. From 1997 to 2006, the VSJF received more than $2 million in state funds and leveraged an additional $4.7 million from other state, federal, and philanthropic sources. By coordinating funding and nonfinancial support, it seeks to help the ventures it supports survive their initial phases until they are able to tap private investment (Traver, 2004).

Providing Legitimacy to Nascent Efforts

Entrepreneurs are often seen as dubious and threatening outsiders. Policy makers can level the playing field for these individuals and organizations by recognizing and providing legitimacy to their efforts.

To borrow from Harvard's Jal Mehta and Johns Hopkins' Steven Teles (2012), policy makers can play a large role in encouraging "jurisdictional challenge." Under today's system, professional educators have "jurisdiction" over the public school system. They control the training of teachers at schools of education, the certification and licensure of teachers and administrators at the state level, the agendas of local and state political leaders, and the operation of schools themselves. The government and the public have given them what William and Mary political scientist Paul Manna (2006) refers to as "license" and "capacity": both the freedom to act and the ability to do so. As a result, actors in the space have been insulated from competition, as they have held a "jurisdictional monopoly." But, as Mehta and Teles point out, that does not have to be the case.

Policy makers have the ability to recognize and empower actors not currently in the system to challenge the position of existing interests. Mehta and Teles outline six tools that policy makers have to do just that (2012, pp. 200–202):

1. Subsidy
2. Adding or removing regulatory barriers
3. Shaping perceptions of costs and benefits
4. Shaping perceptions of moral legitimacy
5. Funding or hampering demonstrations of alternative systems
6. Investing in human capital

Through subsidies, policy makers can support alternative education models, like charter schools or private schools via school vouchers or tuition tax credits. In a way, this is the most direct way that the government can support alternative endeavors, by paying for them. This allows capital to flow to innovative organizations and encourages new actors to enter the market to access this capital.

Policy makers can also remove barriers to entrance by empowering alternative pipelines of tools and talent. In teacher preparation, this is accomplished by granting organizations like Teach for America or The New Teacher Project credentialing authority for new teachers. For tool providers, it can involve streaming state, district, and school procurement processes that make it easier for the developers to get their products in the hands of teachers.

The government can alter perceptions of the cost of public schools, and the benefits of alternative models. The recurring refrain regarding new ventures tends to be that they "drain money from public schools" and move it into untried and unproven ventures. If the government rebrands those decisions simply as money following the child into the school parents think is best, or a strategic investment in an up and coming technology, it can do a great deal to help burgeoning ventures.

The bully pulpit is a similarly valuable tool. Leaders can give up and coming ventures moral legitimacy, the very license that public schools currently have to serve students, by touting their accomplishments and explicitly including them in groups that are helping improve education in the state. A visit by a mayor or governor to a charter school or a prominent school board member testing out a new piece of technology for the public can reassure teachers and principals, as well as the community, that these efforts are good and should be supported.

Leaders are also served well by piloting programs and allowing them to be rigorously studied. The parlance of the social sciences refers to these as "demonstration projects" in which a new innovation is tried out and studied before being taken to scale. Now, it should be noted that, as stated before, these "hot house" conditions often turn out innovations that end up not being scalable, but the tacit admission on the part of leaders that such new ways of thinking and working are legitimate and worthy of study can help add to their cache with teachers, principals, and the broader community.

Finally, all of these ventures need employees. By investing in human capital, particularly in training programs that encourage entrepreneurial and innovative thinking, today's leaders can develop tomorrow's entrepreneurs. We may not know today what tools or organizations will be effective tomorrow, but by developing a crop of smart and open-minded educators, programmers, and leaders, policy makers can spark the process that discovers them in the future.

SEPARATING THE WHEAT FROM THE CHAFF

The process of fostering entrepreneurship in education does lead to important questions regarding the introduction and culling of effective innovations. Fundamentally we must wrestle with the question: What role should the government play to encourage innovation but at the same time protect children? When posed this question, those who support entrepreneurship tend to offer one of three general responses:

1. *It is too hard to judge what schools or products will be successful or helpful, so we should let the market work.*
2. *We should allow for entrepreneurship as long as it hits unbelievably clear performance benchmarks.*
3. *We need to find a middle ground that offers different kinds of accountability, different levels of freedom, and varying levels of evidence to prove efficacy.*

Depending on the response, a variety of programs are developed. On the end of the spectrum that supports entrepreneurship only if it hits benchmarks is the belief that it is too risky to allow for too much freedom because it is a threat to uniform and appropriate education. This tends to develop products that are really nondisruptive "innovations," like targeted remediation programs for districts from private vendors that are for the sole purpose of hitting a particular proficiency threshold on state reading and math exams. These programs might meet their specific goal, but it is unlikely that they will generate a rethinking of the fundamental processes of education.

More toward the middle of the spectrum are policies that grant more freedom but still have some metrics or guidelines for performance. This is best embodied by charter schools. These schools have more freedom than programs selected to hit specific targets, but still have to meet certain performance metrics or risk getting their charters revoked. Here, the opportunity for innovation is greater, but is kept in check by whatever standards for success the authorizing body has in place. In general, this has prevented much of the radical rethinking of educational processes, that is, most charter schools look the same as traditional public schools. However, there are promising examples, like those listed before, that rethink facilities (National Heritage Academies), technologies (High Tech High, School of One, and several others), discipline (KIPP and other "no excuses" schools), and teacher contracts (Green Dot).

Further down the path to the free market are programs that have simply to report performance metrics but are not held to them. School voucher and tuition tax credit programs that simply require the reporting of student test scores and other variables of interest are an example of this type of policy. These rely on market signals for accountability, but standardize the information available to consumers.

The fullest realization of the free market vision include programs with few if any reporting or accountability provisions. In many localities prekindergarten programs have these few regulations, as do supplementary education services provided as a result of NCLB sanctions. Here, consumers are by and large on their own and parents (in the case of pre-K) and schools (in the case of SES providers) are free to pick from a variety of options but do not have standardized metrics by which to judge them.

These visions all have their trade-offs. Programs with more certainty for minimum conditions driven by stronger accountability give less room to color outside the lines. Those with weaker quality control provisions run the risk of wide variances in the quality of services. Where your opinion falls on that spectrum is generally a function of your appetite for risk, comfort with the process of creative destruction, and faith in the winnowing process of the wisdom of crowds.

CONCLUSION

The assumption that entrepreneurial activity will improve education is controversial. It is contested by professional educators and education scholars who believe that the entrepreneurial premise is counterproductive and misguided. These authorities hold that the potential benefits of entrepreneurial activity are outweighed by its attendant risks, and pale beside the advantages of coordinated efforts to improve the current system of educators, training, and resources. They argue that reform should be administered through public bureaucracies that draw on the guidance of designated, professionally sanctioned experts.

There are various ways to marry a faith in professional authority with a call for entrepreneurship. For instance, entrepreneurial ventures frequently consult with professional authorities or make heavy use of ideas or strategies devised by recognized experts. The larger truth, however, is that the two perspectives are rooted in fundamentally distinct worldviews. One is skeptical of bureaucratic processes, the capacity of formal structures to support creative problem solving, the value of conventional expertise, and consensus; the other view places its trust in educational authorities and their corpus of knowledge.

The paradox of entrepreneurship is that it forthrightly accepts the risk that some ventures and ideas will fail so as to address a larger risk—the likelihood that systems will otherwise find themselves mired in a staid mediocrity. Entrepreneurship is frustrating to education specialists because it doesn't pose any hard and fast educational "solutions" to the problems it identifies. The entrepreneurial promise doesn't come with particular brain-based theories of learning or pat guidance on instruction—rather, it seeks to extract excellence by keeping the field open to fresh ideas, whether they be a skillful application of an old model or an effort to leverage new knowledge, management practices, or technology. This process is no doubt uncertain, but possesses great potential for positive change.

In the end, entrepreneurship is not about quick solutions to today's problems. In K-12 schooling, where all parties are quick to declare grandiose aims and then demand immediate solutions, such a stance approaches apostasy. Nonetheless, the greatest educational risk we confront today lies not in nurturing the nascent entrepreneurial sector but in continuing to cling to an inadequate and increasingly anachronistic status quo. Risk is the price of progress. Failed ideas, providers, and schools are indeed a high price to pay. It is only worth paying when compared to the alternative, to stagnation and the ceaseless, pointless tinkering that have for so long been the face of school reform.

NOTES

1. Layoff procedures for public school districts are governed by the Pennsylvania Public School Code of 1949. Section 1125.1 of the Pennsylvania Public School Code of 1949.
2. *Agreement between the Board of Education of the City of Chicago and the Chicago Teachers Union, Local No. 1, American Federation of Teachers, AFL-CIO July 1, 2007–July 30, 2012*, Section 44–17, www.nctq.org/docs/4. pdf.
3. *Contract between The School Board of Orange County, Florida and the Orange County Classroom Teachers Association 2010–2011*, Article VI, Section V, pp. 28–29, www.nctq.org/docs/CTA_Contract_2010–11_ FINAL_updated.pdf.

REFERENCES

Apple, Michael (1996). *Cultural politics and education.* New York: Teachers College Press.
Apple, Michael (2001). *Educating the "right" way: Markets, standards, god, and inequality.* New York: RoutledgeFalmer.
Butrymowicz, Sarah (2012). Following the money: Where are teachers' unions spending the most? *The Hechinger Report,* July 5.
Center for Responsive Politics (2012). Top all-time donors, 1989–2012. August 6. www.opensecrets.org/orgs/list. php?order=A (accessed August 29, 2012).
Christensen, Clayton M., & Horn, Michael B. (2008). *Disrupting class: How disruptive innovation will change the way the world learns.* New York: McGraw-Hill.
Christensen, Clayton M., & Raynor, Peter (2003). *The innovator's solution: Creating and sustaining successful growth.* Boston, MA: Harvard Business School.
Chubb, John, & Moe, Terry (1990). *Politics, markets, and America's schools.* Washington, DC: Brookings Institution Press.
Downs, Anthony (1967). *Inside bureaucracy.* New York: Waveland
Drucker, Peter F. (1985). *Innovation and entrepreneurship.* New York: HarperBusiness.
Goldstein, Dana (2008). The democratic education divide. *The American Prospect.* http://prospect.org/article.
Hess, Frederick M. (1999). *Spinning wheels: The politics of urban school reform.* Washington, DC: Brookings Institution Press.
Hess, Frederick M. (2006). *Educational entrepreneurship: Realities, challenges, possibilities.* Cambridge, MA: Harvard Education Press.
Hess, Frederick M. (2010). *Education unbound.* Alexandria, VA: ASCD.
Hess, Frederick M. (2013). *Cage-busting leadership.* Cambridge, MA: Harvard Education Press.
Hess, Frederick M., & Loup, Coby (2008). *The leadership limbo: Teacher labor agreements in America's fifty largest school districts.* Washington, DC: The Thomas B. Fordham Institute.
Hill, Paul T. (2003). Entrepreneurship in K-12 public education. In Marilyn L. Kourilsky & William B. Walstad (Eds.), *Social entrepreneurship.* Dublin: Senate Hall.
Hill, Paul T. (2004). *Making school reform work: New partnerships for real change.* Washington, DC: Brookings Institution Press.

Jacob, Brian, & Lefgren, Lars (2005). Principals as agents: Student performance measurement in education. *NBER Working Paper No. 11463.*

Junge, Melissa, & Krvaric, Sheara (2012). *How the supplement-not-supplant requirement can work against the policy goals of Title I.* Washington, DC: Center for American Progress and American Enterprise Institute White Paper.

Kim, W. Chan, & Mauborgne, Renee (1999). Value innovation. *Harvard Business Review on Breakthrough Thinking.* Boston, MA: Harvard Business School.

Manna, Paul (2006). *School's in: Federalism and the national education agenda.* Washington, DC: Georgetown University Press.

Maranto, Robert, & McShane, Michael Q. (2012). *President Obama and education reform, the personal and the political.* New York: Palgrave Macmillan.

McGuinn, Patrick (2006). The policy landscape. In Frederick M. Hess (Ed.), *Educational entrepreneurship: Realities, challenges, possibilities.* Cambridge, MA: Harvard Education Press.

Mehta, Jal, & Teles, Steven (2012). Jurisdictional politics. In Frederick M. Hess and Andrew P. Kelly (Eds.), *Carrots, sticks, and the bully pulpit.* Cambridge, MA: Harvard Education Press.

Moe, Terry M. (2011). *Special interest: Teachers unions and America's public schools.* Washington, DC: Brookings Institution Press.

Moe, Terry M., & Chubb, John E. (2009). *Liberating learning: Technology, politics, and the future of American education.* Hoboken, NJ: Jossey-Bass.

Molnar, Alex (2006). For-profit K-12 education: Through the glass darkly. In Fredrick M. Hess (Ed.), *Educational entrepreneurship: Realities, challenges, possibilities.* Cambridge, MA: Harvard Education Press.

Mundy, Alicia (2012, July 12). Teachers unions give broadly. *Wall Street Journal,* http://online.wsj.com/news/articles/SB10001424052702303644004577520841038165770.

National Center for Education Statistics. (2011). *Digest of education statistics.* Washington, DC: US Government Printing Office.

Payne, Charles (2008). *So much reform, so little change.* Cambridge, MA: Harvard Education Press.

Pennington, Hillary (2006). *Expanding learning time in high schools.* Washington, DC: Center for American Progress.

Price, Mitch (2009). *Teacher union contracts and high school reform.* Seattle: University of Washington, Center on Reinventing Public Education.

Ravitch, Diane (2011). *The death and life of the great American school system: How testing and choice are undermining education.* New York: Basic Books.

Rich, Wilbur, & Henig, Jeffery (Eds.). (2003) *Mayors in the middle: Politics, race, and mayoral control of urban schools.* Princeton, NJ: Princeton University Press.

Roza, Marguerite, & Miles, Karen Hawley (2002). *A new look at inequities in school funding: A presentation on the resource variations within districts.* Seattle, WA: Center on Reinventing Public Education.

Schumpeter, Joseph (1975). *Capitalism, socialism, and democracy.* New York: Harper.

Smith, Ben (2010, September 15). Teachers unions helped unseat Fenty. *Politico.*

Stillwell, R., & Sable, J. (2013). *Public school graduates and dropouts from the Common Core of Data: School Year 2009–10: First Look (Provisional Data)* (NCES 2013–309). U.S. Department of Education. Washington, DC: National Center for Education Statistics.

Traver, Tim (2004). New approach to economic development in Vermont. *Business, 26*(2) (March/April).

Tyack, David, & Cuban, Larry (1995). *Tinkering toward utopia: A century of public school reform.* Cambridge, MA: Harvard.

U.S. Department of Education, Office of Communications and Outreach. (USDoE) (2008). *Guide to U.S. Department of Education Programs.* Washington, DC. www.ed.gov/programs/gtep/gtep.pdf.

U.S. Department of Education (USDoE). (2009). State charter school facilities incentive grants. www.ed.gov/programs/statecharter/gtepstatecharter.pdf.

U.S. Department of Education (USDoE). (2013). Common Core of data—total staff (district) http://nces.ed.gov/ccd/data_resources.asp.

14

THE IDEOLOGICAL AND POLITICAL LANDSCAPE
OF SCHOOL CHOICE ADVOCACY

Janelle Scott, Christopher Lubienski, and Elizabeth DeBray

INTRODUCTION

In 2002, under the *Zelman v. Simmons-Harris* ruling, the U.S. Supreme Court upheld the constitutionality of the Cleveland, Ohio school voucher program. In the wake of the ruling, school choice advocates expected a rapid expansion of vouchers across the country, while opponents feared such a scenario. Advocates and opponents worked to realize voucher expansion, to stave off voucher legislation, and to undo existing laws. The advocacy efforts around vouchers reveal a complex interplay of ideology, advocacy, and policy networks. Though a nationwide expansion of publicly funded vouchers has of yet failed to happen, other school choice policies have become more common, though in some ways, as contested as vouchers, and as such, the terrain of school choice advocacy has been altered since *Zelman*.

In the intervening years, educational policy has undergone important transformations. With the election of President Obama in 2008, and the midterm electoral victories of Tea Party candidates in 2010, educational policies reflect a greater emphasis on the use of choice and competition to drive educational improvements. This emphasis is reflected in the federal Race to the Top (RTTT) and the Investing in Innovation fund (i3), which make the adoption of choice and other market reforms like merit pay for teachers a requirement for substantial grants. And intermediary organizations have helped to shape the research evidence used to demonstrate that these approaches are effective, though the research base remains largely unsettled around questions of effectiveness (U.S. Department of Education, 2010). As intermediary organizations advocate for expansion of choice programs, their promotion of research use has created what some have termed an "echo chamber" amongst policy makers, creating a new common sense about best approaches to school reforms (Lubienski & Garn, 2010).

While these policies remain controversial, important multipartisan support for these efforts in key locales has also emerged, and we see various school choice policies being taken up by Democrats, Independents, and Republicans alike. In the meantime, public education groups, teachers' unions, grassroots organizations, and state and national civil rights organizations have often opposed the adoption and implementation of these reforms.

For the first edition of this collection, our chapter was grounded in an examination of advocacy networks in the post-*Zelman* climate (DeBray-Pelot, Lubienski, & Scott, 2007). Since then, we have been examining the role of intermediaries and research use within the advocacy landscape of school reforms we term "incentivst" in nature. These policies use incentives to motivate teacher, school leader, or student behavior and include charter schools, merit pay for teachers, student pay-for-performance plans, and vouchers.[1]

Drawing from 2007 research and our more recent data, this chapter examines the ideological and political landscape of school choice interest groups. We are especially interested in the rise of educational intermediaries—groups that work between schools and government to advocate for particular policies. Nongovernmental organizations have long been involved in schooling; this sector includes for-profit vendors of textbooks and professional development to nonprofit school reform groups or research consortia. Researchers have made important strides in examining the sociological aspects of these interactions between intermediaries and school districts (Coburn, 2005; Daly & Finnigan, 2009).

The political and institutional landscape of the more recent rise of an active intermediary sector around research production and promotion for policy utilization, however, is less well understood (Lubienski, Scott, & DeBray, 2011). For example, educational think tanks and foundations have taken a particularly active role in advancing school choice reforms, though their preference appears to be for market-based reforms like vouchers and charter schools rather than more traditionally equity-minded choice forms like magnet schools or interdistrict and intradistrict student assignment plans (Reckhow, 2013; Scott, 2009; Scott & Jabbar, 2013).

We examined organizational position statements and conducted interviews with national-level advocacy groups and representatives of intermediary organizations working in states and school districts. From our analysis of these data, we discuss the confluence and conflicts of different ideologies and advocacy. Our guiding focus in this analysis is on the institutional and organizational landscape primarily around the advocacy of and opposition to school choice, and the politics of research utilization on school choice reforms. While vouchers feature prominently, we consider a range of school choice policy alternatives as an interrelated set of options in the policy menu. These considerations raise additional and equally compelling questions regarding the ideological motivations behind different forms of school choice, the particular programs that certain groups are likely to support or oppose, and the strategies—including the alliances and coalitions—employed around school choice policy. We aim to better understand the politics of policy making using school choice as a case, and we build on and extend existing thinking on school choice issues, and education policy more generally.

Overview of the Chapter

We begin our analysis with a discussion of our framework and methods. We expand on Carl's (1994) study of school choice advocacy to demonstrate that the shifting left-right ideological distinctions that he noted have further eroded, even as they have remained in many ways constant. We also employ Schattschneider's (1935) theory that new policies bring with them new politics. And finally, we are informed by Sabatier and Jenkins-Smith's (1999) notion of advocacy coalitions emerging from seemingly disparate groups in the service of realizing a particular policy goal.

What follows from the discussion of our framework is examination of ideologies and how they translate into school choice policy. Next, we consider the idea of policy networks, with particular attention to the growing role of think tanks in policy making, including their interrelationships, and relationships with policy-making elements within the government. As we show, this accelerating phenomenon goes beyond traditional left-right categories, but involves multiple coalitions and schisms cutting across ideology, issues, and political expediency. The power of this sector is particularly well illustrated by the issue of school choice being framed as a "new civil right" for minority and disadvantaged communities. We then consider the different strategies that are being adopted, and are likely to be adopted, around school choice advocacy and opposition. These strategies are not only national or federal issues, but are also played out in state and local arenas as well. We end with a concluding discussion of the implications of recent changes in the institutional landscape around school choice, and highlight the importance of an advocacy coalition framework for future research in educational policy making.

FRAMEWORK AND METHODS

In 1994, in an illuminating analysis in *Comparative Education Review,* Jim Carl examined national policies with regard to school choice in England and the United States. This analysis focused on the confluence of different and somewhat contradictory ideologies around market mechanisms in education, particularly under the banner of "parental choice." Most notably, neoliberals saw parental choice as a way to encourage diversity of options and increases in school effectiveness—essentially using market forces to address public policy problems, and to roll back ineffective government bureaucracies. On the other hand, neoconservatives interested in using the power of government to promote particular values saw choice as a way to reassert the primacy of parents in areas such as education. This "New Right" coalition encompassed some strange bedfellows, policy elites who otherwise tended not to agree on many policy strategies or objectives. What has emerged can perhaps best be understood as a "advocacy-coalition" network in which groups who disagree on other aspects of social policy come together in support of achieving wide-scale school choice adoption nationally and in the states.

Much has happened in the "school choice wars" in the United States since Carl first wrote about new coalitions, and this chapter updates Carl's analysis with an emphasis on the politics of school choice advocacy and the role research plays in this advocacy. For example, since Carl's 1994 publication, Republicans, generally more amenable to school choice policies, subsequently took control of Congress, the White House, and the Supreme Court, in addition to numerous state governments. The charter school movement has expanded to all but a handful of states, although political considerations have shaped many different varieties of these ideally independent schools. To an even greater degree, homeschooling has emerged as perhaps the most dramatic example of parents taking control of their children's education, with well over a million children now educated at home. Furthermore, policy makers used charter schools and portable vouchers to address the Gulf Coast destruction left in the wake of Hurricane Katrina in 2005. New Orleans has been made over as a portfolio of schools that are largely operated by private charter school management organizations and overseen by an appointed body called the Recovery School District. Reformers have touted this model as the best hope for struggling urban school districts (Bulkley, Henig, & Levin, 2010).

At the federal level, school choice continues to find favor in national policies. The No Child Left Behind Act of 2001 has become the most substantial federal education policy in a generation, embracing school choice, charter schools, and private provision of educational services as remedies for school underperformance. And the Obama administration has incentivized states to adopt or expand charter schools to be eligible for monies out of the RTTT fund. Perhaps most significant for school voucher policies, the U.S. Supreme Court ruled in 2002 on the constitutionality of using publicly funded vouchers to attend religious schools. The majority on the Court held that the Cleveland voucher program did not violate the Establishment Clause of the First Amendment, because parents, not the state, now possessed the authority to choose from a range of secular and religious schools.

Voucher plans have not expanded as rapidly as advocates might have hoped following the *Zelman* ruling. Since 2002, several state courts have struck down voucher programs under the more prohibitive language typical of most state constitutions, which often forbid public funding for religious schools. Meanwhile, since 2010, states like Louisiana and Indiana have proceeded with implementing and expanding voucher plans, with Indiana's law undergoing a successful legal challenge to its constitutionality. Meanwhile, voters have typically voted against state referenda to alter state constitutions or otherwise endorse voucher programs.

Other choice arrangements such as charter schools emanate from a combination of legislative action and advocacy from a range of intermediary organizations seeking to persuade policy makers to adopt charter school laws with their preferred provisions. In addition, voucher programs have often been limited to a particular area or means-tested population in order to demonstrate their effectiveness to policy makers. Moreover, much of the research providing support for, and ammunition against, choice programs has been heavily contested. Together, these issues raise questions about the potential role of litigation, federal legislation, voter initiatives, targeted or universal programs, and research evidence in advancing the choice agenda in the foreseeable future. Moreover, the continued contestation about the effectiveness of choice plans points to the importance of advocacy and coalition efforts to support or defeat the further expansion of school choice through policy initiatives, legislation, and local reform efforts.

New advocates and intermediary organizations have emerged to push (and oppose) the school choice policy agenda since the *Zelman* ruling. Philanthropies have become prominent in state and federal policy making by seeding organizations and reforms before policy makers enact or fund them, thereby establishing a policy environment external to the confines of government that can then be taken up formally by policy makers (Scott, 2009). The Broad and Gates Foundations are leading philanthropies in this new terrain. Advocacy organizations like Democrats for Educational Reform, Stand for Children, and Michelle Rhee's StudentsFirst organization have become involved in electoral politics, investing resources into the campaigns and endorsing state and national candidates favorable to school choice. And teachers' unions, along with public school associations and civil rights groups—the traditional opponents of market-based policies—also continue to advocate for their curtailment.

Because we are interested in describing and defining this institutional landscape of school choice advocacy that has emerged since Carl's work, *Zelman,* and the Obama administration, we consider the ideologies of organizations, their coalitions, strategies, and effectiveness. We are especially interested in the ideological impetus for various stances on school choice policies, especially as school choice forms have dramatically expanded, and in many ways, become institutionalized at all levels of government. As we will discuss, one interesting development in the institutional landscape of school choice interest group politics is that school choice advocates and opponents have become more specific about school choice preferences. While some support charter schools, they are reticent about vouchers or privatization, for example. This policy joins a still emerging literature on school choice since Carl's work (see Kirst, 2006 for a discussion of advocacy and charter schools, and Henig, 2013 for a discussion of more recent advocacy politics), and shines a critical light on our understanding of school choice politics and policy and the likely future permutations.

Methods

We report findings from our 2005–2006 research on national-level advocacy post-*Zelman*, and in our research on intermediary organizations and research utilization in the case of incentive-based reforms (2011–2014). Our data consist of through position papers and interviews conducted with leaders of interest groups, intermediary organization representatives from foundations, advocacy groups, civil rights organizations, teachers' unions, and think tanks at national, state, and local levels. Finally, we have collected hundreds of documents and catalogued relevant legislation. The organizations studied encompass a wide-ranging political spectrum: mainstream think tanks; free market advocates; education advocacy organizations; traditional civil rights groups; and "new" civil rights groups. A number of "education establishment" groups (i.e., the teachers' unions and the school board associations) are also included in the sample. In creating the sample, we attempted to be inclusive in our understanding of the broad range of organizations weighing in on the issue of school choice. For the research utilization study, we collected data in Denver, New Orleans, New York City, and with national policy makers' and intermediary organizations in Washington, DC.

In open-ended interviews, we asked questions designed to elicit information about where groups' representatives placed their organization's efforts within the broader movement for school choice. Examples of questions asked include: 1) "What groups support your organization?" 2) "What does your membership base look like?" 3) "Did the 2002 *Zelman* decision (U.S. Supreme Court ruling on the constitutionality of Cleveland's voucher program) alter your organization's overall agenda or strategy in terms of state and local-level efforts?" 4) "If your organization is partnering with others, what form does the partnership take?" 5) "What segments of the public is your organization trying to reach?" 6) "What is your organization's mission and what activities are you pursuing to realize it?" 7) We asked policy makers to discuss the ways evidence on school choice factored into their decisions to adopt, reject, or modify school choice policies. 8) We also asked intermediary organization representatives to describe the processes by which they disseminated research findings to policy makers, and how they used research evidence to bolster their advocacy of particular reforms. 9) Finally, we asked policy makers and legislative staff to discuss the processes by which they utilized research, and the extent to which this research informed their policy decisions.

The data led to the identification of the major coalitions favoring and opposing education privatization, school choice, and incentive-based reforms. We mapped the actors and groups that comprise these coalitions at three levels: national/federal, state, and local. A coding frame for interviews and documents identified three variables: (1) the groups' articulation of their major ideologies and beliefs; (2) their lobbying activities for and against specific local, state, and federal initiatives; (3) the strategic coordination of various interest groups, intermediaries, and think tanks *within* coalitions. We also examined documents to provide verification of the interviewees' statements and to supplement our understanding of their organizations. In the next section, we outline some of the ideological boundaries and contours of this topic.

IDEOLOGY

In the late 1980s and early 1990s, scholars of education began to emphasize the need to look beyond the usual left-right dichotomies in understanding the politics of education reform. Focusing particularly on issues of school choice, privatization, governance, and decentralization, researchers noted the significance of the "New Right" alliance between neoliberals and neoconservatives. As Carl (1994) pointed out, neoliberal market boosters with libertarian tendencies to roll back the state found common cause with neoconservative groups interested in using the power of the state to enforce particular values—through the idea of parental choice of schools. And progressives aligned themselves with this agenda in the hopes that it would give parents more power in recalcitrant school districts.

This insight provided the theoretical illumination for understanding the seemingly odd combinations of ideologies on topics associated with markets and school choice, specifically in paradoxical issues of centralization and decentralization, equity and individual rights, and innovation and best practices. However, times have changed. While some of these alliances persist, the landscape of education policy has evolved significantly. Still, even though the institutional landscape and ideological climate may look different now, ideology itself continues to play a significant role in shaping that landscape.

In fact, it appears that, now more than ever, school choice is an ideological issue, because policy debates, while referring to research when convenient, are still largely contested on ideological grounds and boundaries. For instance, without attempting to be too controversial, we believe that it would be fair to note that, after two decades of charter schools and voucher programs, primary outcomes are still heavily contested and, even in the most favorable light, rather modest, especially in view of initial optimism about the potential of these reforms. For instance, evaluations of voucher programs in Milwaukee, Cleveland, Dayton, New York City, and the District of Columbia have found a negligible to moderate impact on achievement (Belfield, 2006; Greene, Howell, & Peterson, 1997; Greene, Peterson, & Du, 1998, 1999; Howell et al., 2001; Metcalf et al., 2003; Rouse, 1998; Witte, 2000), but have been heavily contested on methodological grounds (Krueger & Zhu, 2004; Peterson & Howell, 2003; Witte, 1996).

Similar debates have occurred around charter school programs and other forms of choice (Hoxby, 2004a, 2004b, 2005; Lubienski & Lubienski, 2006; Miron, Urschel, & Saxton, 2011; Nelson, Rosenberg, & Van Meter, 2004; Reardon, 2009). Other predicted outcomes from choice, such as greater innovations in teaching and learning, are also somewhat less than originally anticipated (Lubienski, 2003). Consequently, in lieu of a substantial and compelling evidentiary basis, the policy debates have a decidedly ideological essence (Levin & Belfield, 2004).

This central role of ideology is further highlighted by something that Carl pointed out in his 1994 essay: choice advocacy tends to come more from policy elites than from grassroots organizing, even as policy elites have attempted to organize parents and grassroots organizations to support their preferred reforms. Although some community groups are active in advancing this issue, most gains for the choice movement have advanced from legislative and judicial action, while the most significant failures for choice have been at the hands of voters. While some groups attempt to represent wider communities, they tend to receive their primary support from private foundations or government funding. This dynamic may reflect apathy, rather than antipathy, on the broader public on this issue; but it also suggests the opportunity for ideology—rather than evidence—to shape the debate. Consider, for instance, the admonitions of Republican pollster Frank Luntz, who advises GOP policy makers not based on the research on choice outcomes themselves, but instead on research regarding how the language of school choice plays with the broader public. For example, policy makers are warned not to use the word "voucher" because of negative connotations, but instead to talk about "opportunity scholarships," to focus on the role of the parents, and to frame the issue as "the civil rights issue of our generation" (Luntz, 1998).

And yet, while the debates may appear at first glance to be matters of beliefs of Democrats and Republicans, the actions of ideological interest groups around the issue suggest something much more complex. Many liberals support choice on equity grounds, arguing that choice extends options to disadvantaged communities, that encourages empowerment in such communities, and that can lead to a greater range of education options better suited to meeting the needs of diverse learners. On the other hand, some conservatives are wary of choice, concerned about the possibility of identity politics and the erosion of civic values that are supposed to be fostered through a system of common schools.

The roles played by a growing number of ideological interest groups, both supporting and opposing the measures, have increased. Unions, administrators, and school boards have united against vouchers, which in Texas and Florida was strong enough to cause several Republican lawmakers to vote with Democrats to defeat a voucher proposal (Dillon, 2005; Pogrebin, 2006). Conservative think tanks, such as the Alliance for School Choice, have taken an active role in drafting and sponsoring legislation. In Georgia, groups have assisted the Georgia Alliance for Choices in Education with a lawsuit challenging the property tax-based system of funding schools (Donsky, 2005).

Indeed, the wide range of policy alternatives now available to choice advocates may in fact illuminate some of the more nuanced ideological schisms inherent in the broader alliance of interest groups supporting school choice. Charter school laws are already present in four out of every five states, and have become a flashpoint for state-level debates about expanding these options—as opposed to promoting private-sector choice through vouchers and tuition tax credits. The charter movement represented the marriage of market-oriented neoliberals working from a series of state-level think tanks and progressive reformers committed to creating options within a public system. Yet indications are emerging that this alliance is showing strains over the question of expanding choice beyond the "public" system through the adoption of universal voucher programs or online schooling platforms, and further deregulating quasi-independent schools.

While many state and local civil rights organizations have created educational options for their constituencies through the charter route, some religious organizations are growing increasingly concerned about the exodus of students from church-based schools to tuition-free charter schools in some regions (Lubienski, 2005). Likewise, supported by a strong network of state and local organizations, the homeschooling movement has continued to grow exponentially (Cooper & Sureau, 2007), often at the expense of both public and private schools; and the libertarian wing of this movement is quite suspicious of charter schools and voucher plans as potential threats to co-opt the movement.

On the federal level, the Republican Party's long-standing endorsement of federal legislation for vouchers and tuition tax credits for private schools—reflecting an ideology of local control and a preference for market solutions—has not yet translated into the necessary support among Republican lawmakers in Congress, even after the *Zelman* decision. Instead, both Democrats and Republicans in Congress settled on the legislative compromise of public school choice (including charter status) as a sanction for failing schools in No Child Left Behind (DeBray, 2006). In 2003, during the 108th Congress, a pilot voucher program for the District of Columbia was passed after an almost ten-year battle, only to expire in 2009, get reinstated in 2011, and now faces an uncertain future with funding only guaranteed through 2013. NCLB further established a friendly terrain for interest groups supporting vouchers in two important ways. First, the law expanded parental choice and encouraged organizational autonomy in cases where schools are said to be failing—two important precedents for the next ESEA reauthorization. Second, the triumph of the testing regime provides crucial information, in the form of standard metrics, from which parents are to judge relative strengths and weaknesses of schools.

Next, we discuss the ways policy networks have expanded in number and in influence, and the ways their advocacy has translated into school choice policy.

POLICY NETWORKS

Overview

Since Carl's 1994 writing, the policy networks among administration aides, think tanks, and interest groups, and Capitol Hill have expanded considerably and have become more ideologically complex. In particular, the financial base of conservative think tanks accelerated in growth during the 1990s and continues (Smith, 1991), so that by the time of the *Zelman* decision, these institutions were poised to push for vouchers. Another major institutional change occurred in 1994 that would alter the policy networks with respect to vouchers: the switch of both houses of Congress to Republican control.

This shift created the conditions whereby the conservative think tanks had the receptive ear of the new Republican majority, many of whom held to the long-standing GOP platform goal of creating federal voucher programs. As will be discussed further in the section on strategies, the robustness of the national think tank sector has also enabled new linkages to state and local-level activists. For instance, the foundations often support local-level voucher and charter demonstration projects or underwrite legal challenges, while other associations' missions are to mobilize inner-city poor and minority parents.

Meanwhile, the traditional coalitions opposing school choice have not significantly altered over the past decade, with civil rights groups, teachers' unions and administrators' groups, and other public school advocates banding together to battle various proposals. Notably, in 2001, the House Committee on Education and the Workforce rejected amendments to add voucher provisions to No Child Left Behind, the reason being an opposing coalition of moderate Republicans and Democrats. However, several legislative victories for vouchers in Congress since 2004—the District of Columbia pilot program and the Hurricane Emergency Relief Act—reveal the defensive position in which this long-standing coalition finds itself. In addition, state legislatures have passed voucher legislation; Louisiana, Indiana, and Arizona passed or expanded voucher laws in 2011 and 2012. Policy makers also continue to expand tuition tax credits, or "neo-vouchers" (Welner, 2008) across the country.

Proliferation of Think Tanks

The "war of ideas" for school vouchers and tuition tax credits by conservative think tanks has intensified from the mid-1990s forward, and is best understood as part of the overall proliferation of these institutions. As three reports for the National Commission on Responsive Philanthropy documented (Covington, 1997; Callahan, 1999; Krehely, House, & Kernan, 2004), the 1990s was a period of unprecedented spending by conservative think tanks. Andrew Rich writes: "As the ranks of think-tanks generally exploded during the 1980s and 90s, the rate of formation of conservative think tanks (2.6 per year) was twice that of liberal ones (1.3 each per year)" (2004, p. 20). Rich (2005) has also found that conservative foundations spend far more aggressively on public policy institutes and general organizational operating support than do their left-leaning counterparts.

In the realm of education policy, conservative foundations such as Bradley gave their funds to think tanks to support work on public policy institutes, whereas left-leaning foundations, such as Charles Stewart Mott, while investing comparatively more money, earmarked it for programmatic research. According to Rich, this financial edge for conservative think tanks' policy institutes is critical in their successfully influencing policy makers and the public on the merits of conservative philosophy, such as privatization.

However, another distinction between liberal and conservative think tanks is the differing views of the role of the researcher. Rich notes: "For many of the mainline foundations and the foundations that are more clearly progressive, the primary concern when it comes to funding think tanks is in funding rigorous research that strives to be neutral. For them, think tanks and policy institutes should be homes to the disinterested expert" (2005, p. 23). By contrast, foundations on the right are far less stringent in their demands that the research they fund be "unbiased," and are far more comfortable with blurring boundaries between research and advocacy (Rich, 2004).

The pattern of a "revolving door" between the federal government and think tanks, identified by both Carl (1994) and Spring (2005), has continued. This movement between government and intermediary organizations was active during both the Clinton and Bush administrations and persists under the Obama presidency. Former Clinton education advisor Andrew Rotherham, a strong charter school supporter, served as director of the 21st Century Schools Project at the Progressive Policy Institute (associated with the Democratic Leadership Council) and has now founded "Education Sector." Political appointees in the Bush administration included privatization advocates Nina Shokraii Rees of both Heritage and the Institute for Justice and Michael Petrilli of the Thomas B. Fordham Foundation. The latter two worked in a new administrative division within the Department of Education in the Office for Innovation and Improvement, which encourages choice and charters, and disseminates information to parents about their options for choice under No Child Left Behind.

Bush Administration's Funding of Groups

Another post-*Zelman* federal policy shift was the Bush administration's funding of parental choice initiatives above and beyond the realm of congressional authorization.

Every year in office, the president's budget proposal included the Choice Incentive Fund, which allocated $75 million for a five-city pilot voucher project like the one implemented in the District of Columbia schools.

In light of this lack of congressional support, President Bush's first education secretary, Roderick Paige, used the Fund for Innovation in Education (FIE), a discretionary pot of money, to provide $77 million to groups promoting parental options, including privatization. Grantees included the Black Alliance for Educational Options (BAEO), Hispanic CREO, the Education Leaders' Council, the Center for Education Reform, K12 (a group headed up by former Secretary of Education William Bennett), and the Greater Educational Opportunities (GEO) Foundation, an Indianapolis-based group. The federal grants were made for the express purpose of educating parents about their public school choice and supplemental services options under NCLB (People For the American Way, 2003).

Additionally, funds were given to the Education Leaders Council to support the American Board for the Certification of Teacher Excellence (ABCTE), an alternative teacher certification initiative. All of the intermediary organizations have a pro-voucher or privatization ideology, a report by People For the American Way (2003) notes, and there is little or no way to assess whether the federal dollars were actually spent on the implementation of NCLB or on promotion of their own agendas. This dynamic led the groups opposing vouchers to call for greater congressional accountability and oversight over the way FIE monies were being spent.

BAEO engages in activities such as advertising, state-level political organizing (i.e., providing support to legislators), and coordinating with churches located in primarily minority communities. Hispanic CREO, which is supported by the Bradley, Walton, and Daniel Foundations, supports a range of choices for parents, from public and magnet and charter schools to homeschools and private schools. Said Maite Arce of CREO of their relationship with the Office for Innovation and Improvement within the federal Education Department:

> We work with them to inform parents, they give us a tremendous amount of information, and we make sure that we deliver it in a very culturally appropriate way. . . . We have distributed so many materials from that office. They have participated in our conferences and our workshops. So at the local level, for instance, we had representatives come and do talks for parents. (M. Arce, personal communication, November 18, 2005)

The nexus Arce described reflects the niche her group fills in the prochoice spectrum of groups—and the extent to which NCLB's choice and supplemental services provisions have created a venue for governmental officials to use these groups in the service of their policy agenda. As is discussed later, the combination of noncongressional funding for groups' activities with the enacted provisions of NCLB have created both a voice and mission for the "new civil rights" organizations. These new civil rights groups tend to define school choice as the singular civil rights issue as opposed to more established civil rights organizations that embrace a broad-based social policy agenda to achieve civil rights including education, housing, employment, and voting rights.

To illustrate the alliances and ideological commitments of the school choice policy networks, we offer an outline of their associations in the next section.

GENERAL OUTLINE OF ALLIANCES AND DIVISIONS

Alliances and Divisions

While Carl discussed the emergence of a New Right coalition in support of school choice, our data show that the choice advocacy landscape has become more complex ideologically. Advocacy coalitions in support of school choice now encompass left and centrist groups as well as those from the New Right. Traditional public school supporters maintain their alliances with traditional civil rights organizations, but "new" civil rights groups have emerged, and these new education advocacy groups are aligned with centrist, left, and right school choice supporters. Tables 14.1 and 14.2 present a description of some school choice advocacy groups by political ideology, school choice stance, and name. We are mindful, however, that the coalition of supporters is loosely configured, and not all school choice supporters align themselves around the same school choice policies.

Several salient differences from Carl's 1994 analysis emerge from this alignment of interests: First, the coalition supporting the priorities of the New Democratic consensus of support for charter schools and public school choice has expanded. The Clinton administration's strong support of both types of choice in the 1994 Improving America's Schools Act provided a framework that would be expanded under NCLB. The 21st Century Schools Project of the Progressive Policy Institute listed one of its key principles as follows: "Governments must at once demand more from our public schools through meaningful standards and accountability for results, and also must support greater innovation and diversity among schools through choice and competition" (quoted in Spring, 2005, p. 81).

The National Alliance for Public Charter Schools (NAPCS, formally known as the Charter School Leaders Council) was founded in 2004 to serve as a national umbrella group and source of policy advocacy for state and local charter advocates. NAPCS represents a wide range of interests favorable to the issue, including the Center for Education Reform, the Progressive Policy Institute, and BAEO. It takes on several responsibilities, including advocacy and communication to state lawmakers, cultivating a more diverse leadership pool for charter schools, developing the capacity of state-level organizations, and educating the public on charter schools. Funders include the Walton Family, Gates, Annie E. Casey, Pisces, and Fordham Foundations. These backers reflect a diverse set of positions on choice in general, so the NAPCS focuses only on charter schools (despite internal sympathy on vouchers) because there is not a consensus in these groups on more controversial proposals such as vouchers.

Table 14.1 Alliances in Opposition to Market-Based School Choice

Ideology/Political Stance	Organizations
Public School Advocates	National Education Association, American Federation of Teachers, American Association of School Administrators, National School Boards Association, Council of Chief State School Officers, National Association of State Boards of Education, National Alliance of Black School Educators, Parents Across America
Traditional Civil Rights	NAACP, National Urban League, Mexican American Legal Defense and Education Fund, ACORN

Table 14.2 Alliances Promoting Market-Based School Choice

Ideology/Political Stance	Organizations
Libertarian	Cato, Alliance for Justice
Centrist/New Democratic	Progressive Policy Institute, National Alliance for Public Charter Schools, Education Sector, Democrats for Education Reform, Stand for Children
Center/Left	Center for American Progress, Teach For America
Neoconservative	Heritage, Fordham, Olin, Hudson, Manhattan Institute, Brookings, American Enterprise Institute, Walton Family Foundation
Neoliberal	Center for Education Reform, Bradley, Friedman, Walton, Daniel Foundations, Broad, Pisces, Fisher Family, NewSchools Venture Fund
States' Rights	American Legislative Exchange Council, Alliance for Justice
"New" Civil Rights	Black Alliance for Educational Options, Hispanic CREO, Institute for Justice, Parent Revolution

Second, the category of civil rights organizations now requires delineation between traditional bodies, such as the NAACP and the Mexican American Legal Defense and Education Fund, and "new" civil rights groups. Indeed, the emergence of "new" civil rights organizations raises questions about the nature and scope of civil rights in the current policy era. Whereas traditional civil rights groups have ideologies informed by liberal-progressive ideology, "new" civil rights organizations are more likely to hold conservative or neoliberal value systems. Still, these groups are similar in their quest for racial equality and individuals aligned with these groups may not wholly embrace the ideological tenets that define the organizations. This ideological complexity allows for members of new and traditional civil rights organization members to work in opposition *and* in coalition with each other.

Opposition Coalitions: The Education Establishment and Civil Liberties/Church-State Groups

At the federal level, the major coalition opposing vouchers is the National Coalition for Public Education (NCPE), founded in the 1970s. NCPE is comprised of 60 groups that work in unison whenever the threat of enactment arises. It operates to support the public school system and vocally expresses opposition to vouchers. Susan Nogan, an NEA staff member working on school choice issues, said: "Members of the coalition share information on bills that have been introduced or are being drafted, evaluate the threat level, and develop a coordinated advocacy effort" (S. Nogan, personal communication, October 2005). The major association lobbyists' lists of choice-related issues have expanded their scope to cover tuition tax credits, supplemental services, charter schools, and for-profit and nonprofit charter management organizations (CMOs).

The NEA's 2005–2006 resolutions, for instance, include statements of opposition to privatization and subcontracting programs that "[have] the potential to reduce the resources that otherwise would be available to achieve and/or maintain a system of quality public education, or the potential to otherwise negatively impact on public education" or that "allow public funds to be used for religious education or other religious purposes, or that otherwise weakens the separation between church and state" (NEA, 2005–2006 Resolutions). Said Nogan of the National Education Association's role: "NEA unequivocally opposes vouchers and related programs that divert tax money to private schools. This is a core organizational value on which we do not compromise" (personal communication, October 12, 2005).

A second anti-voucher coalition is run by the education task force of the Leadership Conference on Civil Rights. Civil liberties groups, such as People For the American Way, and the United Church of Christ, closely coordinate their efforts. And a third is a local, DC-based coalition against the District's voucher program. The NAACP played an active role in the DC opposition effort, as it had been billed as a measure to uplift black students (T. House, personal communication, October 11, 2005). Furthermore, the NAACP has officially opposed vouchers since at least 1992, and has affirmed this opposition at several annual meetings.

In view of the changing legislative and judicial context, it is worthwhile to consider how coalitions are responding to specific policies. The *Zelman* decision, according to Tanya House of People For the American Way, altered political, but not policy, strategies. The policy issue is redistribution and discrimination:

> The redistribution of funding is there, the indirect funding. The question is whether there was direct funding and that according to that case, this was not the direct funding of the private school system. So legally, we're faced with that issue. But from a public policy standpoint, we still have the same argument and that hasn't changed, and we continue to use that argument. It's something that's consistent across the board when it comes to these voucher programs. (T. House, personal communication, October 11, 2005)

That is, while the decision may have given legal legitimacy to vouchers in the hands of parents, it has not altered the core goal of fighting vouchers to promote public schools.

During the 2005 Hurricane Relief Act debate, for instance, the various groups in the coalition drew attention to the policy question of relative distribution of aid to public versus private schools. American Federation of Teachers lobbyist Kristor Cowan wrote in a letter to U.S. senators before the bill's passage that the union was "deeply concerned that because of a flawed funding methodology, nonpublic schools would receive a disproportionate share" of aid (Davis, 2005).

In Congress, the partisan divisions on vouchers remained strong during the initial committee consideration. In the House of Representatives, the measure that would have given money directly to private schools was defeated in the Committee on Education and the Workforce. Chairman John Boehner (R-OH) stated that "House Democrats and the education establishment" were standing in the way of meaningful relief, while George Miller (D-CA) called the proposal "ill conceived" and "ideological" (Washington Partners, 2005). Yet the proposal gained the support of moderates from both parties, many of whom viewed it as a one-time enactment of aid. Senator Kennedy was persuaded by the Catholic Educators' Conference that opposing aid unfairly punished students.

Among the national lobbyists interviewed, there was not great concern that the *Zelman* decision's wake had brought about an onslaught of public support for state-level voucher measures. They cited the 35 states that had their own language prohibiting the use of public dollars for religious organizations. Said Susan Nogan of the NEA about lobbyist efforts:

> I think the folks who promote vouchers as a "silver bullet" misinform the public. The more the public learns about vouchers, the less they like them. In every ballot initiative

in the past thirty years, once the people are informed, they vote down vouchers by a 2 to 1 margin. (S. Nogan, personal communication, October 12, 2005)

Thus, an unchanged core belief in the voucher-opposing coalitions is that there is shallow support for vouchers among the public, as evidenced by state ballot initiatives, and that the key to public opposition is to provide information.

Tension between Civil Rights Organizations and Rhetoric

The rhetoric on vouchers from the Bush administration has been cast in the language of civil rights. The president referred to the *Zelman* decision as the most important for education since *Brown v. Board of Education*. Former Secretary of Education Rod Paige wrote in a *Washington Post* editorial the day after the *Zelman* ruling:

> With *Brown*, education became a civil rights issue, and the decision introduced a civil rights revolution that continues to this day. *Zelman v. Simmons-Harris* holds the same potential. It recasts the education debates in this country, encouraging a new civil rights revolution and ushering in a "new birth of freedom" for parents and their children everywhere in America. (Paige, 2002, p. A29)

While the Institute for Justice promulgated the *Brown* comparison as a way to give vouchers a compelling theme and appealing public image beyond the church-state debates, some African American civil rights leaders have also likened the fight for vouchers to the fight for equality in *Brown*. As New York University Professor Joseph Viteritti wrote in the opening to his 1999 book *Choosing Equality*: "Some black leaders . . . see choice as a civil-rights issue, a mechanism to provide poor families with the same opportunities enjoyed by the middle class—indeed, as fulfillment of the promise made in *Brown v Board of Education:* to make education available to all 'on equal terms'" (2002, p. 32).

The stance of teacher unions against vouchers has been so strong that until recent efforts by intermediary organizations like Democrats for Education Reform and Stand For Children to unseat Democratic incumbents who did not support school choice, all but the most conservative congressional Democrats have responded to this electoral pressure in their districts by siding with the position of teachers' unions and civil rights groups on school choice. Terry Moe has argued that this picture would be destined to change if national civil rights leadership were to switch sides:

> For many Democrats, just as for many activists in the civil rights movement, opposition to targeted voucher programs has put them in an uncomfortable position: their own constituents are often disadvantaged and strong supporters of vouchers. At the mass level, vouchers could very easily be a Democratic issue, but Democratic politicians have not been able to treat it that way. Were it not for the unions, many Democrats, especially those representing inner-city areas, would simply line up with their own constituents. (2001, p. 387)

In predicting such a shift, however, Moe makes the assumption that national civil rights leaders would abandon their core rationale for rejecting vouchers: that they drain scarce state and federal dollars from the public schools. Given the likelihood of continued cuts to social programs, it is unlikely that either Democratic members of Congress or national civil rights leaders will readily change their votes, or their public stances, on vouchers. We have witnessed more support for other forms of market-based school choice from Democrats, including charter schools, merit pay for teachers, and so-called parent trigger laws, which allow parents to take over a low-performing school and enact a range of "turnaround" options including charter management organizations.

Two national organizations, BAEO and Hispanic CREO, both founded in the late 1990s, represent this divergence in the community of interest groups representing minority students. Parting ways with the National Urban League, the NAACP, the NAACP's Legal Defense Fund, and the Mexican American Legal Defense and Education Fund, these organizations' focus is on empowering minority and mostly urban parents by increasing the breadth of educational options. Our interviews with leaders of BAEO and Hispanic CREO revealed that the two organizations differ in terms of how they view their political missions and civil rights orientations. They also reveal that school choice is the central advocacy issue of concern to these groups, as opposed to the broader social policy platforms of established civil rights groups such as the NAACP.

The driving idea of BAEO is the radical alteration of urban schools as a means to educate African American students. Lawrence Patrick described an initial meeting convened in Milwaukee by choice activist and BAEO founder Howard Fuller:

> [Fuller argued] that we must change the power arrangements that exist within public education, if we're going to bring about lasting and significant change. So the mantra that came out of that meeting was that the centerpiece of any serious education reform effort must be parental choice. It's not that parental choice is some nice add-on, but it's both necessary . . . it's central from a social justice standpoint, but it's also central from a tactical standpoint, that even if you don't get excited about the social justice argument and that's not your main reason to do it, if you want your changes to stick and you if want your reforms to be permanent or lasting, you've got to change the power arrangements. (L. Patrick, personal communication, September 12, 2005)

Patrick was one of the attendees at the "Meeting of 50," a gathering of African American leaders convened by Howard Fuller in Washington, DC in 1999 that led to BAEO's founding. He described the group: "We all had a very strong sense of urgency and a real commitment to taking radical steps. So, in other words, we were not interested in re-hashing what's already been done. In this group, you had a lot of very seasoned veterans and warriors, people who had been through multiple battles trying to fix the schools. . . . This was a group that was at a point where we were ready to look at sort of taking it up a notch to the next level" (L. Patrick, personal communication, September 12, 2005).

The two organizations represent a contrast in the extent to which their leadership employs the language of the civil rights movement. BAEO seeks to train the next generation of leaders who can take up the fight, out-strategize its opponents, and in Patrick's words, bring about "total disruption of the status quo."

The League of United Latin American Citizens (LULAC) does not support vouchers so Hispanic CREO does not partner with them at the national level. However, the organizations sometimes collaborate via the Local Affiliate program with LULAC, as well as with the Mexican American Legal Defense and Education Fund (MALDEF), which have not taken a stance on vouchers overall (preferring to judge plans individually), but which opposed the Bush administration's efforts to use Title I to create a national voucher program.

Staff members for BAEO and Hispanic CREO say that *Zelman* did not alter the organizations' missions or their core beliefs. Said Lawrence Patrick of BAEO: "It affirmed our belief that parental choice is constitutional, and not only that, but that it's really interwoven in the fabric of America. I think when you read the opinion of the court, that individual parents . . . by recognizing that, it reaffirmed what we've been saying, it's been set aside for the individual child. But it did add strength to their cause" (L. Patrick, personal communication, September 12, 2005). Maite Arce of Hispanic CREO agrees: "It further emphasized what the past Supreme Court rulings have: that vouchers are constitutional and it added strength to our cause. It didn't necessarily alter our strategy, it just gave it further strength" (M. Arce, personal communication, November 18, 2005).

Hispanic CREO's grassroots are focused in five key states: Texas, Florida, Arizona, Colorado, and New Jersey. The group has a director of parental involvement who trains parents to work on the ground on advocacy. Arce explains that the group does not work in the national policy arena yet, but is indirectly involved in state-level policy. It supports policy initiatives at the state level in several ways. One is through information, data, and statistics. It has built a very large network of parents, so when new state-level initiatives surface, Hispanic CREO plays a publicity role, contacting the local media and organizing parent rallies in Washington, DC.

In conclusion, the realignment of "old line" civil rights groups toward voucher advocacy predicted by Moe is not even close to being in evidence. To the contrary, LULAC and the NAACP both still strongly oppose vouchers, while MALDEF remains neutral. In Congress, while New Democrats such as Mary Landrieu (D-LA), and Joseph Lieberman (D-CT) voted in favor of pilot voucher programs, there is almost no evidence that urban poor and minority constituents have exerted political pressure on, let alone changed, the anti-voucher positions of their representatives in Congress, such as Chakah Fattah (D-PA), Major Owens (D-NY), or John Conyers (D-MI). This lack of realignment has not stopped choice advocates' efforts, however. In the following section, we examine some of their strategies for expanding choice, which include targeted programs, NCLB provisions, and the reauthorization of the Elementary and Secondary Education Act, which at this writing had been delayed for some time.

STRATEGIES FOR CHOICE

Targeted Programs

As mentioned earlier, the passage in Congress of both the pilot voucher program for the District of Columbia in 2004 and the Hurricane Education Recovery Act in 2005 were significant departures from the logjams of the past. The political circumstances that produced each piece of legislation differ markedly. Both programs, however, reflect what Terry Moe predicted in 2001: enactment of limited programs for troubled urban systems and/or students—which, once enacted, gains constituents and beneficiaries—could feasibly become the immediate strategy of federal voucher legislation proponents. Voting for the enactment of targeted programs entails relatively little electoral risk for either senators or representatives, whose constituents are generally unaffected.

The DC pilot program provides a voucher worth up to $7,500 per student, based on financial need. As many as 1,700 students, all of whom must be eligible for the federal school lunch program, may participate each year. Nina Rees, formerly of the Department of Education's Office of Innovation and Improvement, explained that the District met all five conditions that movement strategists desire when seeking fertile ground for voucher programs: "a legislative and an executive branch controlled by supporters, local political champions for education or urban renewal, local business support, a weakened teacher union, and grassroots backing" (Hsu, 2006, p. 222).

The Hurricane Recovery bill was enacted under somewhat exceptional circumstances—a "crisis"—and public opinion that supported congressional action to help the displaced students nationally was such that it became very hard for even liberal Democrats to oppose. The commonality, viewed through the lens of the advocacy coalition framework, is the coalition's core strategy of moving incrementally with the institutional innovations, in this case, targeted programs, believed to further its longer-term goal of enacting broader programs.

The opposing coalitions—which have remained cohesive since at least the 1980s—were unsuccessful in preventing the enactment of the hurricane relief bill permitting federal dollars to flow directly to schools, partly because the context of a national crisis diminished the usual partisan divisions. In our view, this program is apt to be very difficult to eliminate or weaken if Congress remains under Republican control in the near future. As Clint Bolick of the Alliance for School Choice said: "More generally in the voucher wars, we hope this will prove to be a milestone . . . the word 'never' has been replaced by the word 'rarely,' and 'rarely' is a step on the road to 'sometimes'" (quoted in Robelen & Davis, 2006, p. 22).

NCLB

Supplemental services and public school choice in NCLB are both topics for strategizing for expansion to privatization for the pro-voucher coalition. Think tanks such as the Fordham Institute, the Heritage Foundation, and the Center for Education Reform have proposed that the next reauthorization go beyond the public school choice provisions to include private school choice and interdistrict choice. However, to the education establishment, the view has prevailed that NCLB was designed to pave the way for vouchers and privatization, by causing widespread discrediting of public schools through high failure rates and underfunding. In the meantime charter school management organizations have been advocating for the bulk of federal charter school expenditures to go to those CMOs that have a demonstrated record of effectiveness, thereby opening the possibility for intra-charter school competition between independent charter schools and those part of CMO networks or franchises. These new policy directions are setting the stage for the new political battles we will likely see into 2014 and beyond.

The Fordham Institute's early strategy shows the direction that other neoconservative think tanks may tack in the upcoming reauthorization. Referring to the lack of satisfactory schools for students in urban areas to transfer to, the Fordham Institute's leadership wrote in a memo to the board on NCLB strategy:

> Our goal is to correct these injustices. Private school choice should be on the table, as should inter-district choice. Excellent charter schools should be replicated. Our allies in the school choice movement should be motivated to help on these fronts—though unfortunately few have been engaged in the NCLB discussion to date. Making any progress on this front will require heavy lifting. (Fordham Institute, 2005)

The Fordham Institute, Heritage, ALEC, and the Institute for Justice have continued to work together as a coalition around choice. Looking toward the presidential campaign proposals, they may try to get to candidates such as George Allen or Rudy Giuliani to start to plant some ideas. In 2007, they were the standard bearers (M. Petrilli, personal communication, October 28, 2005). In addition, state-level advocacy is a focus. For example, the conservative American Legislative Exchange Council (ALEC) is a member organization of state legislators. Its education division helps to draft model legislation for its members for an array of issues, including school finance, alternative teacher certification, parent trigger laws, and especially school choice. ALEC also holds school choice academies where it provides media training, guidance for introducing school choice bills, and testimonials by families whose lives are positively affected by school choice. Lori Drummer, a staff member, shared that ALEC is focusing on smaller, concentrated school choice programs, such as those targeted to children with special needs, which maps on to the possible expansion of supplemental service provisions under NCLB (personal communication, March 3, 2006).

Officials in the Bush Education Department indicated that over time, NCLB's supplemental educational services provisions could become part of a larger choice strategy. In July 2002, for instance, Undersecretary of Education Eugene Hickok stated that the Supreme Court ruling "does not have a significant impact in terms of where we are" with the new education bill. But he added: "Somewhere down the road, I think it might as school choice and supplemental services become a bigger part of the puzzle" (quoted in Sweeney, 2002, p. 15). The supplemental services provisions have become a battleground because the regulations stripped out the nonreligious discrimination requirements. The NEA has retained a very firm stance against privatization of supplemental services. It has insisted if a private entity is to receive federal funds for tutoring, then it needs to be accessible to all students in need, but these regulations are difficult to enforce federally.

CONCLUSIONS

The alignment of conservative think tanks, policy networks, foundation funding, and federal policy has strengthened since the 2002 *Zelman* decision and with the election of President Obama in 2008 and his reelection in 2012. We find that school choice advocacy is lively outside the Beltway, and transcends easy left-right ideological markers. For example, added to this conservative coalition in Washington, DC are "new" civil rights groups such as Hispanic CREO and BAEO who share the commitment to school choice. More recently newer intermediary organizations have emerged, and are engaged not only in promoting school choice, but also in producing and disseminating research evidence on its effects, and are also active in endorsing and providing support for candidates in national, state, and local elections. New Democrats are also advocates of particular school choice forms, such as charter schools; and venture philanthropies have emerged as powerful, often de facto policy makers, particularly in California. In many ways, this revitalized school choice coalition is driving the expansion of charter schools and CMOs in particular urban school districts. Yet the school choice policies policy makers are adopting are also yoked to a broader effort to incentivize better school performance through merit pay, pay-for-performance, and other rewards, making the study of the politics of school choice that much more complex.

As school choice politics become increasingly complicated and layered on other market-based reforms, we find that advocates and opponents are focusing on the details of particular policy initiatives. They are attempting to answer particular policy questions: How can more states adopt voucher legislation? How can we increase the caps on charter schools? As voucher programs expand, what are the implications for charter school management organizations, private and religious schools, and how does this alter advocacy-coalition networks that had been fairly tightly aligned over the past two decades? How can school choice be used as a remedy in school finance litigation? As Schattschneider (1935) implied, these new school choice policies bring with them new politics. These are the areas of concern on the institutional landscape as charter school, virtual schooling, homeschooling, and voucher advocates make decisions about when and where to align around the expansion of school choice policies.

NOTE

1. With support from the William T. Grant Foundation, we are conducting a three-year study (2011–2014) to understand the processes by which intermediaries are serving a research brokering, production, and advocacy role in three school districts and in Washington, DC.

REFERENCES

Belfield, C. R. (2006). *The evidence on education vouchers: An application to the Cleveland scholarship and tutoring program* (Occasional Paper No. 112). New York: National Center for the Study of Privatization in Education.

Bulkley, K., Henig, J., & Levin, H. (Eds.) (2010). *Politics, governance, and the new portfolio models for urban school reform* (pp. 277–304). Cambridge, MA: Harvard Education Press.

Callahan, D. (1999). *$1 billion for ideas: Conservative think-tanks in the 1990s.* Washington, DC: National Committee for Responsive Philanthropy.

Carl, J. (1994). Parental choice as national policy in England and the United States. *Comparative Education Review, 38*(3), 294–322.

Coburn, C. (2005). The role of nonsystem actors in the relationship between policy and practice: The case of reading instruction in California. *Educational Evaluation and Policy Analysis. 27*(1), 23–52.

Cooper, B., & Sureau, J. (2007). The politics of homeschooling: New developments, new challenges. *Educational Policy, 21*(1), 110–131.

Covington, S. (1997). *Moving a public policy agenda: The strategic philanthropy of conservative foundations.* Washington, DC: National Committee for Responsive Philanthropy.

Daly, A., & Finnigan, K. (2009). A bridge between worlds: Understanding network structure to understand change strategy. *The Journal of Educational Change.* Available online at: www.springerlink.com/1040n 7231740m232/.

Davis, M. (2005, December 23). Federal aid goes to public, private schools hit by Hurricanes Katrina and Rita. *Education Week* (online edition).

DeBray, E. (2006). *Politics, ideology and education: Federal policy during the Clinton and Bush administrations.* New York: Teachers College Press.

DeBray-Pelot, E., Lubienski, C., & Scott, J. (2007). The institutional landscape of interest groups and school choice. *Peabody Journal of Education, 82*(2–3), 204–230.

Dillon, S. (2005, July 13). For parents seeking a choice, charter schools prove more popular than vouchers. *The New York Times*, A23.

Donsky, P. (2005, January 28). Fed-up father joins suit for better schools. *The Atlanta Journal-Constitution*, D1.

Fordham Institute (2005). Memorandum to the board of trustees on No Child Left Behind strategy. Washington, DC: Author.

Greene, J. P., Howell, W. G., & Peterson, P. E. (1997). *An evaluation of the Cleveland scholarship program* (Occasional Papers). Program on Education Policy and Governance, Harvard University.

Greene, J. P., Peterson, P. E., & Du, J. (1998). School choice in Milwaukee: A randomized experiment. In P. E. Peterson & B. C. Hassel (Eds.), *Learning from school choice* (pp. 335–356). Washington, DC: Brookings Institution Press.

Greene, J. P., Peterson, P. E., & Du, J. (1999). Effectiveness of school choice: The Milwaukee experiment. *Education and Urban Society, 31*(2), 190–213.

Greenhouse, L. (2002, July 14). Win the debate, not just the case. *The New York Times,* Week in Review, p. 4.

Hall, T. (2003). Congress and school vouchers. In R. Kahlenberg (Ed.), *Public school choice versus private school vouchers.* New York: Century Foundation Press.

Henig, J. (2013). *The end of exceptionalism: The changing politics of school reform.* Cambridge, MA: Harvard Education Press.

Howell, W. G., Wolf, P. J., Peterson, P. E., & Campbell, D. E. (2001). Effects of school vouchers on student test scores. In P. E. Peterson & D. E. Campbell (Eds.), *Charters, vouchers, and public education* (pp. 136–159). Washington, DC: Brookings Institution Press.

Hoxby, C. M. (2004a). *Achievement in charter school and regular public schools in the united states: Understanding the differences.* Cambridge, MA: Harvard University and National Bureau of Economic Research.

Hoxby, C. M. (2004b). *A straightforward comparison of charter schools and regular public schools in the United States.* Cambridge, MA: Department of Economics, Harvard University.

Hoxby, C. M. (2005). *Competition among public schools: A reply to Rothstein (2004)* (NBER Working Paper No. 11216). Cambridge, MA: National Bureau of Economic Research.

Hsu, S. (2006). How vouchers came to DC. In P. Peterson (Ed.), *Choice and competition in American education* (pp. 219–230). Lanham, MD: Rowman & Littlefield.

Kirst, M. (2006). *Politics of charter schools: Competing national advocacy coalitions meet local politics.* New York: National Center for the Study of Privatization in Education.

Krehely, J., House, M., & Kernan, E. (2004). *Axis of ideology: Spending by conservative think tanks.* Washington, DC: National Committee for Responsive Philanthropy.

Krueger, A. B., & Zhu, P. (2004). Another look at the New York City school voucher experiment. *American Behavioral Scientist, 47*(5), 658–698.

Levin, H. M., & Belfield, C. (2004). Vouchers and public policy: When ideology trumps evidence. *American Journal of Education, 111*(4).

Lubienski, C. (2003). Innovation in education markets: Theory and evidence on the impact of competition and choice in charter schools. *American Educational Research Journal, 40*(2), 395–443.

Lubienski, C. (2005). Public schools in marketized environments: Shifting incentives and unintended consequences of competition-based educational reforms. *American Journal of Education, 111*(4), 464–486.

Lubienski, C., & Garn, G. (2010). Evidence and ideology on consumer choices in education markets: An alternative analytical framework. *Current Issues in Education, 13*(3). Available at: http://cie.asu.edu/ojs/index.php/cieatasu/article/view/584.

Lubienski, C., Scott, J., & DeBray, E. (2011). The rise of intermediary organizations in knowledge production, advocacy, and educational policy. *Teachers College Record Online (Commentary).*

Lubienski, S. T., & Lubienski, C. (2006). School sector and academic achievement: A multi-level analysis of NAEP mathematics data. *American Educational Research Journal, 43*(4), 651–698.

Luntz, F. (1998). *Language of the 21st century* (updated ed.). Washington, DC: The Luntz Research Companies.

Metcalf, K., West, S. D., Legan, N. A., Paul, K. M., & Boone, W. J. (2003). *Evaluation of the Cleveland scholarship and tutoring program: Summary report 1998–2002.* Bloomington: Indiana University Press.

Miron, G., Urschel, J., & Saxton, N. (2011). *What makes KIPP work? A study of student characteristics, attrition, and school finance.* Kalamazoo: College of Education and Human Development, Study Group on Educational Management Organizations, Western Michigan University.

Moe, T. (2001). *Schools, vouchers, and the American public.* Washington, DC: Brookings Institution Press.

National Education Association (2005). 2005–2006 NEA Resolutions. Available online, www.nea.org/annualmeeting/raaction/resolutions.html.

Nelson, F. H., Rosenberg, B., & Van Meter, N. (2004). *Charter school achievement on the 2003 national assessment of educational progress.* Washington, DC: American Federation of Teachers.

Paige, R. (2002, June 28). A win for America's children. *The Washington Post,* p. A29.

People for the American Way. (2003). Funding a movement: U.S. Department of Education pours millions into groups advocating school vouchers and education privatization. (Press Release, November 18, 2003).

Peterson, P. E., & Howell, W. G. (2003). *Efficiency, bias, and classification schemes: Estimating private-school impacts on test scores in the New York City voucher experiment.* Cambridge, MA: Program on Education Policy and Governance, Harvard University.

Pogrebin, R. (2006, May 12). Breaking ranks over education, GOP lawmakers deal a setback to Governor Bush in Florida. *New York Times,* p. A1.

Reckhow, S. (2013). Follow the money: How foundation dollars change public school politics. New York: Oxford University Press.Reardon, S. F. (2009) *Review of "How New York City's Charter Schools Affect Achievement."*

Boulder and Tempe, AZ: Education and the Public Interest Center & Education Policy Research Unit. Retrieved from http://epicpolicy.org/thinktank/review-How-New-York-City-Charter

Rich, A. (2004). *Think tanks, public policy, and the politics of expertise.* Cambridge, UK: Cambridge University Press.

Rich, A. (2005). War of ideas: Why mainstream and liberal foundations and the think tanks they support are losing in the war of ideas in American politics. *Stanford Social Innovation Review,* Spring 2005.

Robelen, E., & Davis, M. (2006, January 11). Hurricane aid is on the way to districts, private schools. *Education Week* 25:18, p. 1.

Rouse, C. (1998). *Schools and student achievement: More evidence from the Milwaukee parental choice program.* Princeton University and the National Bureau of Economic Research.

Sabatier, P., & Jenkins-Smith, H. (1999). The advocacy coalition framework: An assessment. In P. Sabatier (Ed.), *Theories of the policy process* (pp. 117–166). Boulder, CO: Westview.

Schattschneider, E. E. (1935). *Politics, pressures, and the tariff.* New York: Prentice Hall.

Scott, J. (2009). The politics of venture philanthropy in school choice policy and advocacy. *Educational Policy,* 23(1), 106–136.

Scott, J., & Jabbar, H. (2013). Money and measures: Foundations as knowledge brokers. In D. Anagnostopoulos, S. Rutledge, & R. Jacobsen (Eds.), *The infrastructure of accountability: Mapping data use and its consequences across the American education system.* Cambridge, MA: Harvard Education Press.

Smith, J. A. (1991). *The idea brokers: Think tanks and the rise of the new policy elite.* New York: Free Press.

Spring, J. (2005). *Political agendas for education from the religious right to the Green Party.* Mahwah, NJ: Lawrence Erlbaum Associates.

Sweeney, J. (2002, July). Voucher case expected to have little impact on federal programs. *Title I Report.*

U.S. Department of Education. (2010). *Research behind the Obama administration's proposal for reauthorizing the Elementary and Secondary Education Act (ESEA).* Washington, DC: U.S. Department of Education.

Viteritti, J. (1999). *Choosing equality: School choice, the constitution, and civil society.* Washington, DC: Brookings Institution Press.

Viteritti, J. (2002). Vouchers on trial. *Education Next 2:2,* 25–33.

Washington Partners (2005, November). *NCLB Insider* 1:1. Washington, DC: Author.

Welner, K. (2008). NeoVouchers: The emergence of tuition tax credits for private schooling. Lanham: Rowman & Littlefield.

Witte, J. F. (1996). *Reply to Greene, Peterson and Du: "the effectiveness of school choice in Milwaukee: A secondary analysis of data from the program's evaluation."* Madison, WI: Department of Political Science and The Robert La Follette Institute of Public Affairs, University of Wisconsin–Madison.

Witte, J. F. (2000). *The market approach to education: An analysis of America's first voucher program.* Princeton, NJ: Princeton University Press.

15

THE COLLECTIVE POLITICS OF TEACHER UNIONISM
Bruce S. Cooper

INTRODUCTION

Teacher unions in the United States have been growing in number, size, and political power since the 1970s. For as states began passing public-sector bargaining laws, teachers and other public employees (e.g., policemen, firemen, and civil servants) were empowered to form unions, to engage in collective bargaining, to grieve controversial management decisions, and even to strike (although still considered illegal in most states with bargaining laws).

However, in Wisconsin recently, the politics appeared to have shifted, as Republican governor Scott Walker and the legislature moved to prevent all public employees in the state from unionizing and bargaining for salaries, benefits, and conditions of employment. Wisconsin politics was typical, somewhat, as the Republicans—dominating the state house of representatives—voted in 2011 to end collective bargaining, a new law quickly signed by conservative Governor Scott Walker.

In no time, the teacher associations sued the state, and the local court ruled that banning bargaining "violates the school and local employees' constitutional rights to free speech, free association and equal representation" (Davey, 2012, p. 1). Even Michigan, historically perhaps one of the most active states for industrial union policies and programs, has recently passed two laws that cut back on the rights of workers and their unions.

As Davey (2012, p. 1) explained, "The two bills, approved by the Michigan House of Representatives over the shouts of thousands of angry union protesters who gathered on the lawn outside the Capitol building, and signed hours later by Gov. Rick Snyder, will—among other things—bar both public and private sector workers from being required to pay fees as a condition of their employment" (Cooper & Sureau, 2008). The Michigan Senate passed the legislation shortly thereafter.

The political reactions were grand in scope, as "Democrats around the nation, including President Obama," denounced the measures. "You know, these so-called right-to-work laws, they don't have to do with economics," said Mr. Obama during a visit to a truck factory outside Detroit. "They have everything to do with politics. What they're really talking about is giving you the right to work for less money" (Davey, 2012, p. 1).

Thus, politics, teachers, and their unions go together in ways that few could have predicted four decades ago when public school teachers—as one of the nation's largest public employee groups—gained state-level rights to unionize and to bargain collectively in the larger, more urbanized industrialized states (Cooper & Bussey, 1982; Kerchner, Koppich, & Weeres, 1997; Lieberman, 1997; Loveless, 2000; Porgursky, 2003).

Today, teachers' unions negotiate with school boards for their members' salaries, benefits, and conditions of employment in all but 12 states (or bargain, as in the case of Hawaii, with the *state* board of education because the state of Hawaii has no local school districts or local school boards).

In a biennial survey of state lawmakers, legislators generally ranked their state's teacher union as the most active and effective lobbying entity in the state capital, outpacing the business community, trial lawyers, doctors, utilities, bankers, environmentalists, and the state's AFL-CIO.

These labor relations laws have helped to create strong political coalitions, not only among the 4.5 million teachers in the United States, but also for teachers and other unionized public and private-sector employee groups, who were also granted the right to bargain collectively. And unionization has placed teachers—through their unions—at the heart of the politics of education in the United States, as they are often the largest, most active, and well-organized public interest group. These unions also have a key role to play politics full time and in all political arenas: nationally, state by state, and locally—even school by school.

Thus, while private-sector unions now have declined in membership to only about 12 percent of the labor force in the United States, the percentage of U.S. teachers who are members of their local, state, and national unions (often either the National Education Association [NEA] or the American Federation of Teachers [AFT]), now includes close to 80 percent of all the teachers in the nation (Wilson, 2012, p. 67).

Kaboolian and Sutherland make just that point, explaining that "public education has, by every measure, the highest density of membership and coverage by collective bargaining of any industry, public or private" (2005, p. 15). Ironically, just as *public*-sector workers have unionized in growing numbers under state labor laws (see Burton & Thomason, 1988; Edwards, 1989; Zax & Ichniowski, 1990), *private*-sector unionization peaked in 1955 with 54 percent of all employees in unions and has since hit bottom in the first decade of the 21st century, now with only 12 percent of employees in industry and manufacturing as members of a union.

The transformation of businesses and commerce—from a blue collar/mass production to white collar/service society, with a movement of many factory jobs overseas—has nearly depleted the ranks of the AFL-CIO and related unions, just as the public sector and its many unions are growing and expanding. Looking across the national landscape, we see teachers' unions as fundamental units of political organization and collective action in public education and public enterprise, with some 51 million students and national spending of nearly $600 billion in 2013.

These national unions are structured to be influential in the nation's capital. Both the independent NEA, with about 3.4 million members, and the AFT, with 1.1 million members nationally—an affiliate of the major labor federation, the AFL-CIO—are powerful national voices and political forces for teachers in particular and education in general.

These affiliated teachers' associations are likewise primary lobbying groups in Washington, DC, as well as in the 50 state capitals, where key educational policies are made. As Fossum explains, "Because education laws and funding methods vary by state and most bargaining occurs at the local school board level, state-level services are mostly devoted to lobbying and assisting negotiations" (1992, p. 477).

Locally, these teacher associations are usually collectively bargaining with school boards for salaries, benefits, and working conditions: for example, class periods to be taught, course loads, and in- and out-of-classroom job responsibilities, and days of professional development required. In fact, at the local level, teachers and their unions are the largest, best-organized political voice in many communities—turning out in large numbers for local school board elections—and in tracking the issues in education that affect their members. As Moe discussed:

> As individuals, then, district employees have strong incentives to get involved in school-board politics and to take action in trying to elect candidates who will promote their occupational interests. . . . In school board elections, the incentives of the teacher unions are strong and clear. If they can wield clout at the polls, they can determine who sits on local school boards—and in so doing, they can literally choose the very "management" with whom they will be bargaining. (2006, p. 60)

However, little research has been done on just how union leaders socialize and involve teachers' union members in the goals and operation of these bargaining units. Ben Pogodzinski found some limits on the ability of unions to bring new members into their associations. As the research found, "although union leaders' attempts to socialize new teachers into the union—and their local context . . . it was limited in scope and duration" (2012, p. 197). While "informal relationships with colleagues" did help to build union support, Pogodzinski determined that these teacher interactions were few, informal, and not very effective in building a strong union culture so that unionism could grow and survive in the teaching profession.

Thus, of all the agencies in the nation, teachers' unions are those closest to all four levels of school politics (i.e., federal, state, local, and school site) that have a prevailing interest in and influence on education politics and policy. Also, teacher unions are becoming more committed to "organizing around teaching and learning quality," putting the NEA and AFT into the education quality business. Both associations have endorsed "peer reviews, higher training standards for teachers, and teacher work schedules that treat professional development as part of a teacher's job, not as an add-on option" (Kerchner & Koppich, 2000, p. 283; Moe, 2000).

Yet Kerchner and Koppich also assert that these unions' concerns for quality are actually a form of "accidental policy making." For even though teacher unions were not created to be organizations of academic quality, they are now in a powerful political position to press for school reform and improvement.

This chapter analyzes the politics of teachers' unions around four different and sometimes conflicting needs and politics of public school teachers:

1—**The Politics of Worker Rights and Class Conflict:** Analysis begins with those political forces in the 1970s that led to the passage of public employment relations labor legislation in 36 states. These public employment laws enabled teachers' unions to be recognized as official spokes-groups for teachers, and required school boards to engage in "good faith" collective bargaining. This political action is reminiscent of the early U.S. labor movement (see Dougherty & Oberer, 1967; Kerchner & Mitchell, 1986, 1988; Lieberman & Moscow, 1966), when workers banded together, fighting to change those labor laws governing employment (see Eaton, 1975).

2—**The Politics of Professional Standing:** Running counter to the collective bargaining impulse among teachers is a century-long interest and drive for teachers to be seen and treated as professionals. Even though Lortie (1969, 1975) and Etzioni (1968) considered teaching a so-called semiprofession, teachers have always yearned to be held in higher esteem, as "real" professionals, such as physicians, lawyers, and engineers (Ballou & Podgursky, 1997, 2000).

So while the teachers' associations worked to gain union rights, they also wanted all teachers to be: (a) given improved occupational status; (b) consulted and involved in making education decisions affecting their students and classrooms; and (c) treated with respect and well paid as professionals. The politics of professional status may explain teachers being placed on committees at the state and local levels to assist in setting educational policies (see Boyd, Plank, & Sykes, 2000). Mitchell and Kerchner (1983) called this second generation of teacher union activity "professional unionism," including those political actions to seek higher standards and more resources for students and their teachers and schools.

3—**The Politics of Institutional Improvement:** While the first two political domains in this chapter—unionization and professionalism—focus on the role status of teachers, the next two concentrate on the political motivations and collective political behaviors of teachers' unions as active lobbying associations. The NEA and the AFT now represent nearly 90 percent of U.S. public school teachers, and have taken active roles in national, state, and local policy making. We also see unions being recognized as spokes-groups for teachers and for the overall improvement of U.S. public education (see Fuller, Mitchell, & Hartman, 2000).

Even (or perhaps particularly) in states *without* teacher unions, as in the South, teachers are likewise strong, if not the strongest, public-sector lobbyists for more tax resources and better curricula and teaching standards—a key political role. The politics of institutional improvement places the once troublesome teachers and their unions at the center of the educational establishment, working as lobbyists for more and better education at the national, state, and local levels. Furthermore, both the NEA and AFT have become more involved in the promotion and conduct of research and development (R&D) activities, to benefit education in general and teachers in particular (see Urban, 1982; Vinovskis, 2000).

4—**Politics of Institutional Survival:** Finally, as U.S. public schools have come under closer public scrutiny, and federal and state policies have experimented with voucher programs (e.g., in Milwaukee, Cleveland, the State of Florida), charter schools (Weidner & Herrington, 2001; Nathan, 1995), and other forms of educational privatization, teachers' unions have taken ever-stronger political stands against diverting public school students, resources, and control away from the public school sector. Perhaps teachers' union leaders see what happened in the private sector: that as business changed from manufacturing to a service orientation, many industrial jobs moved overseas and union membership declined significantly. Ensuring the growth and survival of public education in its current form—and preserving the teachers' unions' role—have become critical priorities of teachers into the future.

Politics of Worker Rights and Class Conflict

Unions seek greater collective political power. Power to the workers! Teachers unite! Speaking up at public meetings, and even in a few cases resorting to sit-ins, illegal strikes, and other forms of civil disobedience, teachers have sought and received the right to negotiate collectively and obtained greater political clout in many states (Liotta, 2002). This form of active politics—similarly important to the history of the American labor movement in the 1920s and 1930s—meant that private-sector workers gained the right to form collective bargaining units and strike under the National Labor Relations Act (NLRA) of 1935, the Wagner Act, one of President Franklin D. Roosevelt's (1934–1946) first major and most radical forms of New Deal legislation (Lipset, 1959). The NLRA had a clear purpose of:

> Encouraging the practice and procedure of collective bargaining and by protecting the exercise by workers of full freedom of association, self-organization, and designation of representatives of their own choosing, for the purpose of negotiating the terms and conditions of their employment or other mutual aid or protection. (29 U.S.C., Sec. 151–169)

The argument was that recognizing industrial unions—and their right collectively to negotiate—would reduce "labor strife" and the chances of class warfare. The labor law would give employees greater voice and parity with management, using the bargaining table and collective strength to improve pay, working conditions, benefits, and the general health of employees (e.g., eliminating the ten-hour workday, the six-day workweek, and the use of children as workers in mines and sweatshops).

At least another 40 years would be required for teachers and other public employees to gain the legal right to unionize and bargain, not under a national labor relations law, but through state legislation that created different Public Employment Relations Acts (PERAs) eventually in all except 12 states, mostly in the antiunion South and far West: for example, Virginia, North Carolina, South Carolina, Georgia, Mississippi, Arkansas, Alabama, Tennessee, Kentucky, West Virginia, Texas, and Oklahoma have no public bargain laws.

The rise of teacher bargaining, described by Kerchner and Mitchell, involved in their words a transition from the "Meet-and-Confer Generation" to a second one called the "Good-faith Bargaining Generation." The political organizations of workers—private and public—were often greeted with fear and legal resistance, a radical departure from the view of teachers as public servants dedicated to helping children to being union activists. In Kerchner and Mitchell's words:

> Both law and social custom were hostile to combinations [unions] of employees. Up until the mid-nineteenth century, unions of all types were considered to be *illegal*

conspiracies, and as late as the second decade of the 20th century, they were prosecuted as violations of anti-trust laws. Combinations of teachers were even more suspect: teachers were public "servants" in an era when the word had clear class connections, and they [teachers] were women for whom work propriety was not forwarded in active voice. (1983, p. 5)

Furthermore, "meet-and-confer" sessions were not defined as "bargaining," but rather were a chance for teachers, administrators, and school board members to "talk about" common concerns. Requests for more pay were often "taken under advisement," and teachers' salaries and benefits were usually kept low.

Not until the late 1960s and 1970s did the politics of union-management relations in the public sector change, to support union formation, bargaining, mediation, arbitration, and in a few states, teacher strikes—all typical of processes for reducing class conflict between worker and manager. When Samuel Gompers, a British-born cigar maker who was a founder and president of the American Federation of Labor (AFL) from 1886 to his death in 1924, was asked: "What does labor want?," he responded quite simply, "More!—i.e., More pay, better benefits, and improved conditions of work" (Stone, 2002, p. 48).

Public Employees Follow

Almost 40 years later, in the absence of a national bargaining law for state and local *public* employees (except for some federal employees like postal workers who were already unionized), 36 states enacted various PERAs to allow teachers and other public-sector workers (e.g., police, fire, state, county, and municipal employees) to bargain, but rarely to strike legally.

The only exceptions to teacher bargaining rights were states in the more conservative, antilabor South where state legislatures, being less familiar with unionization, refused to pass a PERA, and often explicitly forbid local school boards from engaging in collective negotiations with teachers. Under the First Amendment and the "right to assemble," labor laws could not prevent teachers from forming unions. But what use are unions if they have no legal way "to bring management to the bargaining table?"

The formalized power of teachers' unions, and their right to exist and to bargain for pay and benefits, grew in part out of the larger U.S. labor movement. This politics of collective action has shaped teacher associations, creating greater unity and clout for teachers all across the nation. Each state, however, has its own labor laws (or none) affecting teachers, making for a complex political environment. For, as Fossum explains, "Because education laws and funding methods vary by state, and most bargaining occurs at the local school board level, state-level [union] services are mostly devoted to lobbying [the governors and state legislatures] and assisting in negotiations" (1992, p. 477).

The politics of union recognition and collective bargaining is among the most dramatic, as it requires: (1) legislation to protect the right of workers to bargain; (2) a realignment of political power; and (3) a decision to include the union and its members as equals partners at the bargaining table (Gordon et al., 1980). The politics of unionization sets the stage for the remaining political activities, including collective bargaining, strikes, political action, and a stronger, unified voice for teachers in the political arena.

Unions now seek, also, to redefine teachers as professionals (or at least "semiprofessionals"). These associations work to build and reorganize support for public education nationally, as the AFT and NEA have become key spokes-groups for American education. Further, for the sake of public school survival, unions may lobby and even advocate publicly for issues, including vouchers, charter schools, and entrepreneurial schools (e.g., the Edison Program) while networking with other public lobbying groups (Van Geel, 2003).

Teachers' Unions under Attack

While teacher unions are now almost 40 years old in some states, these unions are also under renewed political attack, as some states that have bargaining laws are working to end them. As Sean Cavanagh (2011) explained:

> Teachers unions find themselves on the defensive in states across the country, as governors and lawmakers press forward with proposals to target job protections and benefits that elected officials contend they can no longer afford educationally or financially. (online)

Today, we see a decline in the size and percentage of private-industrial sector employees in unions, while the public sector, including education unionization, has grown in most but not all states. As Graham Wilson explains:

> This increased strength in the public sector is far from being an unqualified blessing for unions. On the one hand public sector unions such as the NEA have the political advantage of having members and organization in most states and numerous Congressional districts, whereas the strength of old style private sector unions such as the UAW was always geographically concentrated. On the other hand, unions' shift into representing public sector workers has the disadvantage that union interests necessarily conflict with the short term interests of homeowners (hence property tax payers) in minimizing the costs of running local government services such as schools. (Arguably the long-term interests of citizens, in general, in a more educated and productive workforce are more congruent with teachers' interests.) (2012, p. 54)

Politics of Professional Standing

Running concurrently with—if not antithetically to—the collective politics of union recognition and power, teachers have also been striving for recognition as higher-status, more respected *professionals,* with the same kind of discretion and authority enjoyed by doctors, lawyers, accountants, and engineers, that is, being treated as "true" professionals. Dan Lortie (1969 1975 described teachers as "semiprofessionals"—having the trappings and qualities of the professions, but lacking (a) the status, (b) the arcane preparation and training, and (c) the skills and vital activities (e.g., performing medical operations, pleading before the Supreme Court, or building a bridge or viaduct) that are associated with the full "professionals."

Yet the teaching profession has made strides in discovering what teachers do and do well. As educators of children, our nation's most prized people, teachers' unions can talk and act like a professional through an essential association when arguing for standards, better pay and benefits, improved conditions of work, and other important educational and societal issues.

This semiprofessional status (see Etzioni, 1968; Lortie, 1969 1975) has long permitted easy access to the field of teaching (much like entry into nursing and social work, two other of the "semiprofessions"); but this ease of access also has limited professional and political status as K-12 educators. So the NEA, formed in 1854 by school principals and teachers, was sometimes dominated by school administrators, who served as its president and other officers.

This leadership often restricted the collective power of the teachers themselves, right up until the 1950s when the association changed its practices so that teachers were placed into leader positions and were more in control. Since then, teachers have sought recognition and respect, wanting to be consulted on important education policy issues. Thus, the "politics of professionalism" is complex and often hard to pursue.

However, what teachers may lack in professional status, they made up for in their important role and sheer numbers (3.7 million public school teachers in 2011), essential to keeping the 51 million-student public K-12 educational system running. For as Vinovskis explained, "few studies exist of the contributions of teachers unions to educational R&D, even though this topic is potentially of great interest to many educators and policy-makers" (2000, p. 211).

For just as the U.S. Congress would rarely consider changing major medical policies without first consulting the medical societies such as the American Medical Association (AMA) and the scientific research community, so too teacher groups are assuming a greater role in setting standards and determining the quality of education in the classroom. Kerchner and Mitchell posited three generations of union development, calling this one *professional unionism,* a unique attempt by teachers to protect themselves as employees while also taking responsibility for their action as professionals: Kerchner and Mitchell suggest:

> [A] new idea of teacher unionism—one we call professional unionism—is contrasted with industrial unionism, which has guided teacher unionization during the Second Generation . . . In addition to bargaining economic issues, *professional unions* need to negotiate frankly and openly about such issues as curriculum, teaching methods, student assignments, criteria for assessment of student achievement, and teachers responsibility for non-instructional duties. (1983, p. 18, emphases added)

More recently, unions have seen efforts to relate professionalism and teacher quality to pay levels and salary increments. Stone (2002) and Eberts and Stone (1984, 1986) have studied the effects of unionization on teachers' behavior and students' learning, thus bringing collective bargaining together with positive changes in pedagogy and results. Building in controls for students' socioeconomic status (SES), pretest scores, and other predictors, Eberts and Stone found significance in "that students in districts with a collective bargaining contract score roughly 1 percent higher on standardized mathematics examination toward the end of the year, or about 3.3 percent higher as a percentage of the average gain from the pre- to the post-test" (Stone, 2002, p. 57).

The politics of professionalism begins to make sense if and when unionization had some effect—negative or positive—on teachers, their work, and students' learning. While some critics argue that teachers' unions play a negative and distracting role in school reform (Hoxby, 1996), others like Stone (2002) found no effectiveness, not even a slight improvement, in districts where teachers are organized, vocal, and well remunerated. The teaching profession and its work are often a quieter, more subtle form of the "helping professions" than medicine and law; however, the politics of teachers' unions is more public and obvious in the halls of Congress, state legislatures, and certainly in local school board meetings.

Politics of Institutional Improvement

Once issues of the right to bargain as a union were settled, teachers could pursue the goals of building and improving education—using their numbers and authority to pursue the politics of institutional improvement. While unionization may have put some teachers in contention with their bosses (i.e., school boards, superintendents, and principals), the politics of institutional improvement also places the two main teachers' unions, the NEA and AFT, in close collaboration with the seven national associations, including organizations of superintendents, school boards, and so forth that support public education. Research has attempted to connect unions, teacher pay, and measures of student performance, to see to what degree teachers' unions support better pay with improved student outputs.

For example, West and Mykerezi, in the *Economics of Education Review,* sought to show just how teachers' unions reacted to connecting pay to student performance. The authors explained that:

> Private sector unions have also been shown to be opposed to output based performance pay (Brown, 1989). Within education, Ballou (2001) and Goldhaber et al. (2008) find a negative union impact on the incidence of "pay for excellence" and we assess that these plans are likely a combination of teacher input and student test score based rewards. Our results suggest that the negative union impact in previous studies may be primarily driven by union aversion to output based plans. Previous studies may underestimate the negative effect.
>
> This study clearly shows that future analysis of the union effect on performance pay plans and on the consequences of such plans must distinguish between input and output based rewards. We show that performance pay that rewards teacher efforts and credentials receives a union reaction similar to more traditional credentials like a master's degree. On the other hand, performance pay based on outputs is likely to be opposed. (West & Mykerezi, 2011, p. 101)

These education associations include the following: (1) the superintendents at the state and local levels (Council of Chief State School Officers and the American Association of School Administrators), (2) the national (and state) principals' associations (National Association of Elementary School Principals and the National Association of Secondary School Principals), (3) the governors of states (National Governors Association and the Education Commission of the States), and (4) the curriculum and teaching supervisors (Association of Supervision and Curriculum Development).

These organizations can and do influence the U.S. Congress and state legislatures to pass laws to benefit teachers (e.g., better pay, training support, better health and retirement benefits) and to support various liberal causes related to improved education. Teachers and other educators have now formed major, active voting blocs and have a strong voice in selecting their own democratically elected leaders, their local school boards.

Moe (2001) has found that teachers and their unions are key players in determining who gets elected to local school boards because overall turnout is often low and public interest diffuse, making teacher votes more significant. He further explains that teachers and other school board employees are vitally interested in these elections and are three times more likely to cast ballots in a local election than do average, less concerned citizens:

> But apathy stops at the schoolhouse door. One group of local citizens—teachers and other employees of the school district—has an intense interest in everything the district does: how much money it spends, how the money is allocated, how hiring and firing is handled, what work rules are adopted, how the curriculum is determined, which schools are to be opened and closed and much more. The livelihoods of these people are fully invested in the schools, and they have a far greater stake in the system than do any other members of the community. (Moe, 2006, p. 60)

Teachers are well organized, as their unions often sign up new members automatically (at their hiring) and collect union dues right out of teachers' paychecks. Teachers will usually vote as a bloc, giving them a strong voice in who gets elected and how school boards may vote on key issues. This form of organized, grassroots politics is effective and often essential to the relevance and authority of teachers' unions.

Summary. Under federal education legislation, now called No Child Left Behind (NCLB), government has brought politics into the schoolhouse and classroom, and directly to the child with reports on their adequate yearly progress (AYP) (Center on Education Policy, 2003; Conley, 2003). The unions are caught in the middle of the politics of learning standards, as debated in Congress, state legislatures, school boards, and local schools.

Here the politics reaches from the unions' support of NCLB, and other federal laws to help schools (Individuals with Disabilities Education Act [IDEA], science, and math), to the state, and to the local and classroom levels. So teachers serve on key committees that work in three areas: (1) teacher preparation and certification; (2) curriculum and learning standard setting; and (3) the testing and promotion (retention) of students.

These areas are truly the foundation, that is, the deep grassroots, in education politics because never before has the federal government so powerfully demanded universal education standards and testing results, forcing local school districts and their employees to come together in school politics and policy making.

The Politics of Institutional Survival

The most recent political motivation for teachers' unions is that of maintaining the public schools to benefit employees, as well as to battle against growing efforts to *privatize* education through vouchers, charter schools, and homeschooling (Cooper, 2005), and the general loss of power—as some states become Republican regimes (Center on Education Policy, 2003). The essential politics of teachers' union power rests on maintaining the size and hegemony of public education, and preventing the government from funding other nonpublic means for educating children.

Most threatening perhaps is the school voucher, a device (see Friedman, 1955) for privatizing payment through the direct funding of children's education. Under funding of this program, parents could then "cash in" vouchers for educational services in a choice among public, private, or even religious schools (legal now under a U.S. Supreme Court ruling, originating in Cleveland, under the *Zelman v. Simmons-Harris* (536 US 639, 2002) decision (see Russo & Mawdsley, 2006).

A Move to the Right: Cases of Michigan and Pennsylvania
Unions have long been identified with liberal, often Democratic Party politics. When the nation has moved to the right—and Republicans are gaining the majority in state and national politics—teachers' unions sometimes can find themselves on the outside looking in. Boyd, Plank, and Sykes, explaining about Michigan and Pennsylvania school politics, wrote:

> With the election of activist Republican governors in both Michigan and Pennsylvania in the 1990s, however, the power of the teachers unions began to decline precipitously. . . . Rather than being the protagonists of reform, they are bystanders at the reform parade. At times they are even the objects of reforms initiated by their political adversaries. (2000, p. 174)

Because teacher unions are at left of center in interest group politics, as teachers seek higher pay and benefits, it often means higher local property taxes, and more state subsidies, which the Republicans may resist. In Michigan, Governor John Engler signed legislation eliminating local property taxes—backing a proposal made, ironically, by a Democratic legislator—and increasing the number of charter schools that have now placed Michigan in the top ranks of states offering this form of privatization. While the Michigan Education Association (MEA), an affiliate of the NEA, and the Michigan Federation of Teachers (MFT), an AFT affiliate, fought hard to preserve the power of the union and the resources for teachers, their role diminished and their ability to support better teacher opportunities declined. As Boyd, Plank, and Sykes concluded:

> The unions' power to protect their members against take-backs is increasingly being challenged by local school boards. Moreover, their political power has eroded badly . . . They have played virtually no significant role in recent education policy debates, unsuccessfully opposing each of the state's innovations (Proposal A, charter schools, enhanced statewide testing programs) that the Governor John M. Engler administration had introduced. Political action to reverse past defeats or obtain new revenues for education is consequently unlikely to bear fruit. As one union leader acknowledged, "If [our members] knew how little the union can do in return for their [annual dues], they would be leaving the union in droves." (2000, p. 185)

Similar events had occurred in another urbanized state, Pennsylvania, where Republican Governor Tom Ridge curtailed the rights of public employees to strike. Here the two state unions, the Pennsylvania State Education Association (PSEA, that is NEA affiliated); and Pennsylvania Federation of Teachers (PaFT, affiliated with the national AFT), struggled to resist privatization, and marginalization, by Republican strategies for school reform.

Pennsylvania's unions were better off than their counterparts in Michigan, although the future of public education and teachers' unions is less sure or clear in their struggle to maintain the status quo. Although Governor Ridge never got his voucher bill passed, he was quite successful in increasing the number of charter schools in Pennsylvania, whereby Boyd, Plank, and Sykes conclude that, "Over the long haul, Ridge's chances of success in school choice seem to be increasing. The charter school law has no limit on the number of such schools that can be created. Polling data suggest that support for school choice is growing among African Americans, in part because of an increasing divide between public and private sector union members" (2000, p. 192; see also Aronowitz, 1999).

Structural Changes

Of late, teachers' unions have found the public system leaders, for whom they work, and with whom they bargain, threatened by politics to privatize education. In union political terms, this effort should come as no surprise because industrial unionism in the United States has diminished, dropping from 55 percent unionized private employees in 1955 to only 8 percent now. Jobs have changed or moved overseas, where labor is often cheaper, and mass production has grown. As the United States becomes a "postindustrial state," blue-collar unionism has likewise declined.

If U.S. education becomes a more privatized, post-public school system, teachers' unions would likely go the way of industrial unions, as the AFL-CIO has decreased in size, lost general support, and is now threatened with a break-up, as disenchanted member unions may seek to form a new national union. As one account indicated:

> Conservatives in politics and business are gleeful at the prospect, while many ordinary citizens merely shrug their shoulders. Only one out of nine American workers are represented by a trade union, down from more than 40% of the workforce 50 years ago, so the fragmentation of the AFL-CIO would seem to have little impact on the majority of Americans. (*Los Angeles Times*, June 12, 2006, p. 1)

For now, public school teachers are among the largest single group of unionized workers in the nation—status that rests on a large-scale, publicly supported education system, which will decline as schooling becomes more privatized and private. Already, 5.6 million children in the United States attend private, often religiously affiliated (nonunionized), schools or are homeschooled (Cooper, 2005; and another 400,000 U.S. children attend charter schools, where teachers are not often unionized).

In Brooklyn, New York, recently, however, a charter school teacher "charged that she was illegally fired for attempting to organize colleagues to seek higher wages" (*N.Y. Post*, June 28, 2006, p. 7). For at the Williamsburg Charter School, Nichole Byrne Lau's teacher's contract was not renewed after she had, apparently, distributed copies of the NYC public school teachers' pay scale, which were much higher, a good reason, she felt, to get her charter school colleagues to unionize. Sounds like the 1920s when "union troublemakers" were fired from companies, until the federal employment law (Wagner Act) protected that right.

So, when the AFT and the NEA oppose diverting public resources to private schools (e.g., vouchers or charters), it makes sense politically to resist because the total privatization of schools may mean the loss of union members and union power. A number of states are already funding private (nonunionized) schools through various voucher programs (e.g., Wisconsin, Ohio, Florida).

The AFT has issued two important reports (American Federation of Teachers, 1996, 2002) on charter schools, a moderate effort to privatize public education. While AFT leader Albert Shanker originally supported charter schools, he and the AFT changed their position when some of these schools witnessed a quiet attack on the public school "monopoly." As the AFT explained:

The justification for charter schools has moved from one that is based on education and innovation to one that is based on choice and competition. Yet charter schools provide a narrower range of services to a more homogeneous student body, and "competition" from charter schools has not brought about significant educational change in other public schools. (American Federation of Teachers, 2002, p. 7)

As we see from the level of involvement and concern about charter schools and what they symbolize, the politics in this last phase of our analysis is marked by increased identification with the educational enterprise, and a strong commitment to defending and maintaining public education. Teachers, and their unions, are working to keep public schools "public." They close ranks with other public school constituencies, for unions understand what privatization can do to public education—in similar ways to what the restructuring of the industrial sector did to the AFL-CIO and other industrial unions. This change in American education is likely, particularly in light of the legalization of voucher programs for religious schools (see Bernheim, 1937). As Kerchner and Cooper explained:

If schools are fundamentally restructured following the decision by the U.S. Supreme Court in the Cleveland voucher *Zelman* case (June 2002; see van Geel, 2003), or if the current federal tax credit policy passes Congress, then the large, hegemonic public school system could begin to become more private, smaller, and diverse. In this case, teachers unions will face the same problem that private-sector unions are confronting— how to unionize a restructured, entrepreneurial economy in which more and more companies are small and technological, and/or serviced oriented. (2003, p. 244)

Thus, some scholars see the restructuring of U.S. education coming in the future; and the role and politics of teachers' unions changing and perhaps diminishing as the "monopoly" of public schooling declines. Others believe, in contrast, that the future will hold a continued commitment to *public* schools, and with them, national support for teachers' unions and collective bargaining.

Kaboolian and Sutherland stated well the arguments about keeping unions, and maintaining public education, when they wrote:

The fantasy of union-free school districts, however, like many fantasies, rests on a false premise: on the one hand, a stereotype that union contracts stand in the way of education reform; and on the other hand, an administrators' paradise where labor markets and managerial discretion are unbridled and collective action by teachers is unknown.

Whatever ambiguity might shroud about past and current effects of collective bargaining, the future is more certain: collective bargaining and unionization aren't going to go away, and education reform wouldn't be any better off if unions did. (2005, pp. 14–15)

While criticizing the bureaucracy of unions, Meier contends that teachers' unions are essential in correcting injustices in education:

In correcting such inequities, strong unions—not just teacher unions—are the primary and steady vehicles; they are the only substantial counterparts to the power of organized greed. In a society where the income differential is steadily widening, the clamor about the decreasing academic gaps . . . won't be serious until there is an organized and "interested" power bloc whose members stand to gain, in the here and now, from greater equity. (2004, pp. 54–55)

An NEA-AFT Merger

It may also make sense for the two national teachers' unions to merge, much as the industrial labor movement created the American Federation of Labor-Congress of Industrial Organizations (AFL-CIO) in a major labor merger in 1955, to have one organization and a more unified presence. Undoubtedly, as the threat to public education grows and public funding decreases, the two major teachers' unions will likely overlook their historical and cultural differences and perhaps form one large, unified union. The politics of unity will replace the politics of contention (as the two unions have a history of "raiding" each other for members), in an effort to have a majority vote for a merger and national affiliation.

If, in 1999, as attempted, the AFT and NEA had successfully merged (see Fusarelli & Cooper, 1999; Cooper 2000), the new "American Teachers Association" [ATA]—or perhaps the "United Teachers Union" [UTU], or whatever it would be called—would have become the largest union of public employees in the nation.

Thus, the new national teachers' union, if one were created, could be virtually ubiquitous—as teachers work everywhere—in a middle-class political organization. At the 1999 National Meeting in the Dome Stadium in New Orleans, the representatives at the NEA Delegate Assembly voted against a national merger resolution proposed by Bob Chase, the NEA president, as the gulf between ideology and culture of the NEA and the AFT was still too wide (Cooper, 1999). However, local and state teacher associations are merging—as are some state NEA and AFT affiliates. Hence, the national NEA and AFT will probably try joining up again at the national level, creating the largest public-sector union in the country, and an even stronger supporter of public schools. Cooper explored the potential for a single union, as follows:

Clearly, the unification of the two national unions enhances their clout in the nation's capital. A corporate arrangement between the two well staffed, highly expert national offices will mean a stronger, more unified teachers' voice in pressing Congress, the White House, and the U.S. Department of Education. Lobbying should be effective, because few politicians or policy-makers will ignore an organization of 3 million strong, with members in every community in the country. (1998b, p. 58)

Similarly, Cooper and Liotta documented the emerging pressures for such unification:

Mergers have begun locally in recent years. Grassroots test cases in Minnesota, Wisconsin, Los Angeles, and San Francisco may well demonstrate the merit of mergers from the bottom up. When combined with continued perceived threats to public education posed by the privatization of education, teachers nationally may well decide to close ranks to enhance their collective voice, buttress their political power, and fight shoulder-to-shoulder to save jobs—and the public school system, as they know it. Hence, pressures for an NEA-AFT merger in the 21st century will come from both greater external pressures and more successful internal cooperative experiences—together convincing teachers that big mergers, big unions and big power are necessary to fight off serious threats to use privatization to restructure public schools. (2001, pp. 109–110)

The politics and power of a new merged union would enable it to take on larger issues, to influence local, state, and national elections, and to bring Big Politics and Big Unionism together as never before in education.

Unification of Political Power

Teachers' unions—critical players in the politico-financial world of schools—are not only the largest single education employee group, absorbing the greatest share of education resources in salaries and benefits (Cooper, 2003); but they also would form the most powerful national and state-level school lobbying groups, with strong links to political parties (usually the Democrats) and the policy-making process at local, state, and national levels. Wirt and Kirst explored these sentiments, arguing that teachers' unions were now the prominent political force in education: "The timid rabbits of 30 years ago are today's ravening tigers in the jungle of public school systems" (1997, p. 181; see also Kerchner & Cooper, 2003).

As Cooper explains in his chapter in *Conflicting Missions? Teachers Unions and Education Reform*:

In less than half a century teachers have risen from underpaid, undervalued "semi-professionals" to powerful voices in education, becoming key leaders within the larger labor movement and prime movers in regional and national politics. To a large degree, this emergence from obscurity to prominence and transition from exploited, sympathy-invoking martyrs to respected agents at the bargaining table and in the halls of government are the result of the unionization of teachers—a phenomenon in virtually every developed nation on earth. (2000, p. 240)

Although the efforts of teachers to form and join unions have accelerated since the 1970s, we find little agreement about the costs and benefits of unionization, or about the appropriate role of unions in the politics and economics of education into the future (Bacharach, Bamberger, & Sonnenstuhl, 2001). Johnson and Kardos stated:

As school reformers work intently to repair and rethink public education in the United States, there are conflicting calls to *eliminate or to expand* the influence of teachers unions. Those opposing collective bargaining and unions typically contend that teachers' contracts unduly regulate schools and unwisely constrain teachers' best professional efforts. Those endorsing a broader role for unions stress that teachers must play a key part in school improvements. (2000, p. 7, emphases added)

We also see that the preparation and training of teachers at colleges and universities are often separate from the initiation, support, and evaluations of teachers at the pre-school through 12th grade levels. Arthur Wise noted the problems with this difference—as seen from the more unified way doctors, lawyers, and engineers are educated and reviewed as professionals—when he wrote:

The National Association for the Accreditation of Teacher Education (NCATE) expectations in this area are now stronger and reflect the need to mesh the P-12 and the pre-service educator cultures. Teacher educators and teachers now jointly plan and implement the clinical education of teachers. This expectation brings teaching closer to the culture of shared experience and collegiality apparent in the established professions. (Wise, 2005, p. 330)

COMPETING, CONFUSING MODELS OF EDUCATION

Both models (nationalization-publicness and privatization) pose major challenges for unions, but in very different ways, making the unions vulnerable from all sides. Because the econo-politics of these two models—going nationally public, or locally private—virtually oppose one another, the teachers' unions' responses and results will be complex. They confront the paradox of whether education is a national, highly regulated public activity; or primarily a personal, local, private, and familial concern, with the government mainly subsidizing market "choices" among public, private, and even religious schools.

Wedding themselves to the "one best system" (Tyack, 1994), and reinforcing the more centralized, rule-bound hegemony of a federalized public education, private school controls, Tyack argued, would undermine the much-valued professional autonomy that teachers have long enjoyed. Meanwhile, standing by while the public system monopoly is dismantled—thus, substituting commercial and choice-based market models—could mean the overall reduction of public education and the rise of smaller, more diverse, and even faith-based private providers—reducing the size and influence of teachers' unions as we know them.

Furthermore, the teachers' unions' commitment to the public system is itself filled with irony. For while teacher unionization was once perceived as an attack on, and even a threat to, public schools, now teachers' unions have become the nation's staunchest defenders of the status quo in public education. As Kerchner and Cooper explain, "To challenge teacher unions, it is not now necessary to attack them directly; one need only to challenge the *institution* of public education as currently organized" (2003, p. 219). Teachers' unions, once a "critical voice for teachers in their struggle for dignity, respect and a little money, now find themselves the prime *defenders* of the institution they sought to criticize" (p. 220; emphases added).

Given the complexities facing education, we can identify four possible futures for teacher unions, including shifts, as follows: (1) from local to national controls, standards, tests, and accountability; (2) from the "single salary schedule" where all teachers receive the same remuneration, based on universal criteria of experience, education, and time spent in schools, to a more merit-drive system of compensation; (3) from a divided, mainly state and local union structure to the likelihood of merging the two national unions—the American Federation of Teachers and the National Education Association—into one mammoth organization; and (4) from the economics of a socialized, public school monopoly shifting perhaps to a competitive, privatized, mixed system of public, private, and even religious schools.

CONCLUSIONS

The politics of teacher unions has dramatically changed since the days of "meet-and-confer" when teachers organized themselves into associations, but had little collective power or authority over determining their pay and benefit levels and work lives, much less control over the conditions of education in the United States. Radical, class-driven politics, in some ways modeled on the labor movement of the 1920s and 1930s, placed teachers at odds with the establishment, that is, with their school boards, superintendents, and local citizens. These class-related politics—often pitting workers against management—led to a revolution, initiated by changing the laws while maintaining the school system as it was.

The next phases of the politics of teacher unionization saw a unification of teachers, with an increased level of vocal and political activism, and a growing sense of support for the system—from which teachers in a former generation had felt left out and had in some cases picketed and gone on strike against. Teachers' unions went from being system "outsiders" to becoming the major and largest spokes-groups *for* public education, defending the system against attacks and numerous attempts to reduce, diversify, and even privatize schools (Conley, 2003).

Kerchner and Koppich (2000) explain that teachers' unions can be treated as "the problem" or part of "the solution," as a major resource for improving the quality of education, or as the major roadblocks. Either way, teachers and their working conditions in the classroom cannot be ignored if education is to improve: Kerchner and Koppich found that:

> By ignoring labor relations policy, school reform has been tied to either an unsatisfactory present or an antiquated past. Few would argue, particularly those who favor the radical restructuring [e.g., privatization] of education, that the current system of school governance will deliver the education system that can educate the vast majority of American to high academic standards. (2000, p. 313)

Teachers have also retained their desire to be professionals, to be informed and involved in school reform, including the training of future teachers: for example, their testing and certification, as well as the educational standards, curriculum, alignment, and evaluations. Teachers' unions, with their large membership, can voice and devote resources to problems common to education, such as the shortage of qualified, experienced teachers in hard-to-fill jobs like math, science, and special education (Goodnough, 2003). New York City's United Federation of Teachers, the nation's largest local teachers' union with more than 84,000 members, has joined ranks with the local public school system (called the Department of Education, DOE), to offer a housing subsidy to new teachers as a recruiting incentive because finding a place to live in New York City is difficult and expensive, often making it tough to find new teaching staff. For example:

> The New York City Department of Education (DOE) and the United Federation of Teachers (UFT) today announced an agreement that will allow the Department to offer up to $15,000 in housing support to attract teachers of math, science or special education. Housing support will be available to certified middle and high school math and science teachers, as well as special education teachers in all grades, who have at least two years of experience, pass a rigorous selection process, and commit to teach in New York City for at least three years. Certified teachers who formerly taught in New York City are also eligible as long as they have been out of the system for at least two years. (New York Department of Education, 2006, online)

We see in the future a national politics of education, involving a couple national teacher associations or a single, merged national union (e.g., the new National Teachers Association, or whatever the new NEA-AFT group is called). We see Big Politics around Big Issues in education, involving a Big Teachers Union or two. While teachers individually may want greater autonomy and professional status, they may also have to sacrifice this local autonomy to a growing national movement to standardize and federalize education.

In the 1980s, as before, national changes in education usually occurred under liberal Democratic leadership, with President Lyndon B. Johnson as perhaps the best example. As Lorraine McDonnell noted years ago, teachers like it both ways: they want to be respected and treated like professionals, while understanding that improving the government-controlled public school system also requires centralized, politicized union organization at the state and national levels. As she explained:

> Professionalism assumes that because the members of a particular profession possess a specialized body of knowledge and have been judged competent to practice that profession, they should be free to decide how best to serve their individual clients. In other words, accountability should be based on norms and standards collectively defined and enforced by peers. In their pure forms, these values each suggest different modes of governance and accountability for education. (McDonnell, 1989, p. v)

The politics and control of education will continue to shift from the local school and school district to the state and national levels. Popular influence and parental choice may likely mean that the politics of education has changed, and that teacher unions have been passed over. But without the support of teachers, collectively as unions, professionals, and individuals, we see little chance of school reform and improvement taking hold. So while teachers have moved from lone practitioners to members of two (and later, perhaps one) of the nation's largest and best-organized unions (Ingersoll, 2003), we have yet to see the results.

Studies of teacher contracts have shown to what degree these arrangements could benefit both the teachers and the students. Strunk's work, for example, found that many leaders are concerned that all educators are at an advantage in their work:

> U.S. Secretary of Education Arne Duncan recently hosted a conference for union and district leaders to discuss ways the two sides might work together in pursuit of reform. AFT president Randi Weingarten released a new position paper on how teacher evaluation processes should be improved to better serve both students and teachers, which has been both criticized and praised by the media and policy analysts. The stage is set for unions and districts to come together to negotiate better collective bargaining agreements (CBA's) that serve to enhance administrators' abilities to implement necessary education reforms while still maintaining teachers' rights and professional working conditions. (Strunk, 2012, p. 21)

The Future of Unions: Some questions for future research and practice are: What form and direction might teachers' union politics take in years to come? How can these unions represent the needs of their membership while supporting the public school enterprise, and still striving to help teachers be treated like professionals in their classrooms? If in the next decade the NEA and AFT merge, will the new mega-union lobby effectively slow privatization and increase resources for public education?

And what may happen in those states with little or no legal support for teacher unions? In Wisconsin, recently, we saw what happens when the legislature and governor attempt to restrict the rights of teachers to bargain—or in Michigan for unions to charge membership fees to their members.

Former Wisconsin Supreme Court Justice Janine Gesky believes that higher courts will stay the Dane Country ruling that restricted the rights of public employees to bargain as a violation of the constitutional right of assembly. As Gesky said, "I would be shocked if it was not granted so that all these bargaining units don't have to deal with the fallout while it's in litigation." And Paul Secunda, a labor law professor at Marquette University, said that ending collective bargaining now would create "mass confusion."

How will teachers in the future balance the macropolitics of public school survival with the micropolitics of collective bargaining and policy making at the school district and now the school-site levels? Whatever the outcome, teachers' unions will continue to grow, merge, lobby, and fight as a key political force in American education.

The International Labour Organization (ILO) noted the progress that teachers had made across the world, stating:

Thus, governments generally accept the need to assure teachers of their status which is in accordance with, on the one hand, the essential role played by teachers in the progress of education, and on the other hand, the importance of their contribution to the development of humanity and society . . . which remuneration obviously plays a central role. However, important are moral and professional satisfaction, public esteem for teachers, their recognized role in society, and the opportunity to pursue a professional career. (1996, online)

The role and importance of teachers' unions in the United States have not changed a great deal in the past 30 years or so (Cooper & Bussey, 1982). One teachers' union, the American Federation of Teachers, states that its mission is to "represent the economic, social and professional interests of classroom teachers." In other words, the AFT works to improve the economic conditions of teachers by bargaining a positive contract for teachers, and by supporting legislation that would increase teachers' pay to the national average, which would improve the economic conditions of teachers and the lifestyles that their salaries support.

Thus, Richard Kahlenberg could not imagine "A World without Teacher Unions" when he wrote in *The American Prospect*: "Despite the myriad criticisms of teacher unions, their abolition would be a huge loss for supporters of public education—and for the American labor movement as a whole" (2007, p. 1).

REFERENCES

American Federation of Teachers. (1996). *Charter school laws: Do they measure up?* Washington, DC: Author.

American Federation of Teachers. (2002). *Do charter schools measure up? The charter school experiment after 10 years.* Washington, DC: Author.

Aronowitz, S. (1999, March 17). Testimony before the 106th Congress on impediments to union democracy: Public and private sector workers under the labor-management reporting and disclosure act. Washington, DC:

Subcommittee of Employer-Employee Relations of the Committee on Education and the Work Force, U.S. House of Representatives. Serial No. 106–11.

Bacharach, S. B., Bamberger, P. A., & Sonnenstuhl, W. J. (2001). *Mutual aid and union renewal: Cycles of logics of action.* Ithaca, NY: ILR Press of Cornell University.

Ballou, D., & Podgursky, M. (1997). *Teacher pay and teacher quality:* Kalamazoo, MI: W. E. Upjohn Institute.

Ballou, D., & Podgursky, M. (2000). Gaining control of professional licensing and advancement. In T. Loveless (Ed.), *Conflicting missions? Teachers unions and educational reform* (pp. 69–109). Washington, DC: Brookings Institution Press.

Bernheim, A. L. (1937). *Big business: Its growth and its place.* New York: Twentieth Century Fund.

Boyd, W. L., Plank, D. N., & Sykes, G. (2000). Teachers unions in hard times. In T. Loveless (Ed.), *Conflicting missions? Teachers unions and educational reform.* (pp. 174–210). Washington, DC: Brookings Institution Press.

Burton, Jr., J. F., & Thomason, T. (1988). The extent of collective bargaining in the public sector. In B. Aaron, J. M. Najita, & J. L. Stern (Eds.), *Public sector bargaining* (2nd ed.) (pp. 1–51). Washington, DC: Bureau of National Affairs.

Cavanagh, S. (2011, January 1). Teachers' unions on defensive as GOP lawmakers flex their muscles. *Education Week.* www.edweek.org/.

Center on Education Policy. (January 2003). *From the capital to the classroom: State and federal efforts to implement the No Child Left Behind law.* Washington, DC: Author.

Conley, D. T. (2003). *Who governs our schools? Changing roles and responsibilities.* New York: Teachers College Press.

Cooper, B. S. (1998a, March 11). Merging the teachers' unions: Opportunity amid complexity. Commentary. *Education Week, 52,* 34.

Cooper, B. S. (1998b, May/June). Toward a more perfect union: An NEA-AFT merger would create the nation's largest labor group. That's good and bad. *Teacher Magazine,* 55–58.

Cooper, B. S. (1999). Merging the AFT and the NEA. *Annual developments in education.* New York: Gale Publishing.

Cooper, B. S. (2000). An international perspective on teachers unions. In Tom Loveless (Ed.), *Conflicting missions? Teachers unions and education reform* (pp. 240–280). Washington, DC: Brookings Institution Press.

Cooper, B. S. (2005). *Home schooling in full view: A reader.* Charlotte, NC: InformationAge Publishing.

Cooper, B. S. (2003). Spending in urban public school systems—policies, problems and promises. In Faith E. Crampton & David C. Thompson (Eds.), *Saving America's school infrastructure.* Volume II in Series, Research in Education Fiscal Policy and Practice: Local, National, and Global Perspectives (pp. 103–125). Greenwich, CT: Information Age Publishing.

Cooper, B. S., & Bussey, J. (1982). *Collective bargaining, strikes and related costs in education.* Eugene: University of Oregon, ERIC Center for Education Management.

Cooper, B. S., & Liotta, M. (2001). Urban teachers unions face their future. *Education and Urban Society, 34*(1), 101–118.

Cooper, B. S., & Sureau, J. (2008). Teacher unions and the politics of fear in labor relations, *Education Policy, 22*(1), 86–105.

Davey, M. (2012). Michigan governor signs law limiting unions. *New York Times,* online: nytimes.com/2012/12/12/us/protesters-rally-over-michigan-union-limits-plan.html?

Dougherty, R. E., & Oberer, W. E. (1967). *Teachers, school boards, and collective bargaining: A changing of the guard.* Ithaca: New York State School of Industrial and Labor Relations, Cornell University.

Eaton, W. E. (1975). *The American Federation of Teachers, 1916–1961: A history of the movement.* Carbondale: Southern Illinois Press.

Eberts, R. W., & Stone, J. A. (1984). *Unions and public schools: The effect of collective bargaining on American education.* New York: Lexington Books.

Eberts, R. W., & Stone, J. A. (1986). Teacher unions and the costs of public education. *Economic Inquiry, 24,* 631–644.

Eberts, R. W., & Stone, J. A. (1987). Teachers' unions and the productivity of public schools. *Industrial and Labor Relations Review, 40,* 355–363.

Edwards, L. N. (1989). The future of public sector unions: Stagnation or growth. *American Economics Review, 79*(2), 161–165.

Etzioni, A. (Ed.). (1968). *The semi-professions and their organization.* Chicago, IL: The Free Press.

Fine, S. (1969). *Sit-Down: The General Motors strike of 1936–1937.* Ann Arbor: University of Michigan Press.

Fossum, J. A. (1992). *Labor relations: Development, structure, process.* (5th ed.). Chicago, IL: Richard D. Irwin.

Friedman, M. (1955). *Democracy and freedom.* Chicago, IL: University of Chicago Press.

Fuller, H. L., Mitchell, G. A., & Hartmann, M. E. (2000). Collective bargaining in Milwaukee Public Schools. In T. Loveless (Ed.), *Conflicting missions? Teachers unions and educational reform.* (pp. 110–149). Washington, DC: Brookings Institution Press.

Fusarelli, L. D., & Cooper, B. S. (1999). Why the NEA and AFT sought to merge—and failed. *School Business Affairs, 65*(4), 33–38.

Goodnough, A. (2003). Teachers' union president turns against schools plan: Says Bloomberg and Klein are out of touch. *The New York Times* (Sunday, Metro Section, May 11), p. 33.

Gordon, M. E., Philpot, J. W., Burt, R. E., Thompson, C. A., & Spiller, W. E. (1980). Commitment to the union: Development of a measure and an examination of its correlates, *Journal of Applied Psychology, 65,* 474–499.

Hartney, M., & Flavin, P. (2011). From the schoolhouse to the statehouse: Teacher union political activism and U.S. state education reform policy. *State Politics and Policy Quarterly, 11*(3), 251–264.

Hoxby, C. M. (1996). How teachers' unions affect education production, *Quarterly Journal of Economics, 111,* 671–718.

Ingersoll, R. M. (2003). *Who controls teachers' work? Power and accountability in America's schools.* Cambridge, MA: Harvard University Press.

International Labour Organization. (1996). *Teachers, educators and their organizations.* Paris: ILO. www.ilo.org/ipec/Action/Education

Johnson, S. M., & Kardos, S. M. (2000). Reform bargaining and its promise for school improvement. In T. Loveless (Ed.), *Conflicting missions? Teachers unions and educational reform* (pp. 7–46). Washington, DC: Brookings Institution Press.

Kaboolian, L., & Sutherland, P. (2005). *Win-win labor-management collaboration in education: Breakthrough practices to benefit students, teachers, and administrators:* Washington, DC: Education Week Press.

Kahlenberg, R. (2007, November 7). A world without teachers union. In *The American Prospect,* 1.

Kerchner, C. T., & Cooper, B. S. (2003). Ravening tigers under siege: Teacher union legitimacy and institutional turmoil. In W. L. Boyd & D. Miretzky (Eds.), *American educational governance on trial: Change and challenges.* 102nd Yearbook of the National Society for the Study of Education (pp. 219–248). Chicago, IL: University of Chicago Press.

Kerchner, C. T., & Koppich, J. E. (2000). Organizing around quality: The frontiers of teacher unionism. In Tom Loveless (Ed.), *Conflicting missions? Teachers unions and educational reform* (pp. 281–315). Washington, DC: Brookings Institution Press.

Kerchner, C. T., Koppich, J., & Weeres, J. (1997). *United mind workers: Unions and teaching in the knowledge society.* New York: Jossey-Bass.

Kerchner, C. T., & Mitchell, D. E. (1986). Teaching reform and union reform. *Elementary School Journal 4*(4), 449–470.

Kerchner, C. T., & Mitchell, D. E. (1988). *The changing idea of a teachers' union.* Philadelphia, PA: Falmer Press.

Lieberman, M. & Moskow, M. H. (1966). *Collective negotiations for teachers: An approach to school administration.* Chicago: Rand McNally Co.

Lieberman, M. (1997). *The teacher union: How the NEA and AFT sabotaged reform and hold students, parents, teachers, and taxpayers hostage to bureaucracy.* Chicago, IL: The Free Press.

Liotta, M. (2002). *The four great strikes of Yonkers teachers: Historical analysis of conflict and change in urban education.* Unpublished Dissertation, Fordham University, New York.

Lipset, S. M. (1959). *Union democracy: The internal politics of the International Typographers Union.* Glencoe, IL: Basic Books.

Lortie, D. C. (1969). The balance of control and autonomy in elementary school teaching. In Amitai Etzioni (Ed.), *The semi-professions and their organization* (pp. 21–54). Chicago, IL: The Free Press.

Lortie, D. C. (1975). *Schoolteacher: A sociological study.* Chicago, IL: University of Chicago Press.

Loveless, T. (Ed.). (2000). *Conflicting missions? Teachers unions and education reform.* Washington, DC: Brookings Institution Press.

Mauss, A. L. (1975). *Social problems as social movements.* New York: J. P. Lippincott.

McDonnell, L. (1989). *The dilemma of teacher policy* (JRE-03). Santa Monica, CA: RAND Corp.

Meier, D. (2004). On unions and education. *Dissent, 37,* 54–56.

Mitchell, D., & Kerchner, C. T. (1983). Labor relations and teaching policy. In Lee Shulman & Gary Sykes (Eds.). *Handbook of teaching and policy.* (pp. 214–238). New York: Longman.

Moe, T. M. (2000). Teachers unions and the public schools. In F. Wirt & M. W. Kirst (Eds.), *Schools in conflict: Political turbulence in American education* (pp. 176–189). San Francisco, CA: McCutchan.

Moe, T. M. (2001). A union by any other name. *Education Next, 1*(3), 40–45.

Moe, T. M. (2006). The union label on the ballot box. *Education Next, 6*(3), 59–66.

Nathan, J. (1995). *Charter schools: Creating hope and opportunity for American education.* San Francisco, CA: Jossey-Bass.

New York Department of Education. (2006). New York State's Revised Plan to Enhance Teacher Quality (2006). The University of the State of New York: The New York State Education Department Albany 12234 September 2006 Update (nclbnys@mail.nysed.gov).

Pogodzinski, B. (2012). The socialization of new teachers into teacher unions. *Labor Studies Journal, 37*(3), 183–202.

Porgursky, M. (2003). Fringe benefits: There is more to compensation than a teacher's salary. *Education Next: A Journal of Opinion and Research, 5*(3), 71–78.

Russo, C. J., & Mawdsley, R. D. (2006). Equal educational opportunities and parental choice: The Supreme Court upholds the Cleveland voucher program. *Education Law Reporter, 169*(2), 485–504.

Stone, J. A. (2002). Collective bargaining and public schools. In T. Loveless (Ed.), *Conflicting missions? Teachers unions and educational reform* (pp. 47–68). Washington, DC: Brookings Institution Press.

Strunk, K. O. (2012). Policy poison or promise: Exploring the dual nature of California school district collective bargaining agreements. *Educational Administration Quarterly, 20*(1), 1–42.

Tyack, D. B. (1994). *The one best system: A history of American urban education.* Cambridge, MA: Harvard University Press.

Urban, W. J. (1982). *Why teachers organized.* Detroit, MI: Wayne State University Press.

Van Geel, T. (2003). Vouchers, the Supreme Court, and the next political rounds. In W. L. Boyd & D. Miretsky (Eds.), *American education governance on trial.* Yearbook of the National Society for the Study of Education (pp. 136–154). Chicago, IL: University of Chicago Press and NSSE.

Vinovskis, M. A. (2000). Teachers unions and educational research and development. In Tom Loveless (Ed.), *Conflicting missions? Teachers unions and education reform* (pp. 240–280). Washington, DC: Brookings Institution Press.

Weidner, V. R., & Herrington, C. D. (2001). Are parents informed consumers? Evidence from the Florida McKay Scholarship Program. *Peabody Journal of Education, 81*(1), 27–56.

West, K. L., & Mykerezi, E. (2011). Teachers' unions and compensation: The impact of collective bargaining on salary schedules and performance pay schemes. *Economics of Education Review, 30,* 99–108.

Wilson, G. K. (2012). American unions in comparative perspective. *The Forum. Labor in American Politics, 10*(1), 54–69.

Wirt, F., & Kirst, M. (1997). *Schools in conflict.* Berkeley, CA: McCutchan.

Wise, A. E. (1988). The two conflicting trends in school reform: Legislated learning revisited. *Phi Delta Kappan 69*(5), 328–333.

Wise, A. E. (2005). Establish teaching as a profession: The essential role of professional accreditation. *Journal of Teacher Education, 56*(4), 318–331.

Zelman v. Simons-Harris 122 S. Ct 2460 (2000).

Zax, J. S., & Ichniowski, C. (1990). Bargaining laws and unionization in the local public sector. *Industrial and Labor Relations Review 4,* 447–462.

16

OUTLIERS

Political Forces in Gifted and Special Education

Frances R. Spielhagen, Elissa F. Brown, and Claire E. Hughes

Not every child has an equal talent or an equal ability or equal motivation;
but children have the equal right to develop their talent, their ability,
and their motivation. (John F. Kennedy)

INTRODUCTION

Nothing seems to polarize group value systems in education more than discussion of the needs of gifted students and students with special needs. According to Wirt and Kirst, politics is "a form of social conflict rooted in group differences over values about using public resources to meet private needs" (1997, p. 4). The imbedded value bias in American educational philosophy favors opportunities for all students over specialized education for exceptional students. Even terminology within the two groups is extraordinarily value-laden, where the term "gifted" is forbidden in terms of labeling in some educational contexts, and "person-first" language among students with disabilities remains a hot-button issue. Confusion over the identification of students, both gifted and special education, confounds the problem.

The very structure of our public school system has created groups of students whose needs have been ill served because they are different from what might be considered the norm. These groups remain on the periphery of educational policy and attempt to influence the larger educational landscape while maintaining the integrity of their educational purpose. Since the move away from the one-room schoolhouse model, schools have grouped by age, rather than abilities. Driven by Piaget's developmental principles, shaped by the factory model, and based on an agrarian calendar, public schools today isolate students who do not fit into their age-appropriate molds and expectations. As a result, the fields of special education and gifted education have emerged in response to pressure from advocates, have been shaped by legal mandates—and absence of legal mandates—and have struggled with the issue of equity. What is fair and right for students whose needs do not fall within the general education mainstream? And where is that line between the mainstream "box" and those who do fit within it? As a result, gifted education and special education have found themselves at times on the same side and at times in competition for scarce educational resources.

Table 16.1 displays how historical events have impacted special education and gifted education in different ways. While not all events will be addressed in depth, the chart serves as an advance organizer for the complex and intersecting forces that affect these two populations.

Table 16.1 Timeline of Major Events and Implications for Outlier Groups

Historical Time Frame	Events	Impacts on Gifted Education	Impacts on Special Education
Pre-1850s	Pre-Industrial Revolution One-room schoolhouse Agrarian society	Students progressed through conventional curriculum at individual pace; limited age/grade restrictions.	Nonvisible disabilities rarely identified—accommodated within the one-room schoolhouse or not identified; visible disabilities were served in institutions, almshouses, or prisons.
Late 1800s/ Early 1900s	Industrial Revolution Rise in Progressivism	Prescribed age-grade curricula established; courses like algebra were designated as "college preparatory" and moved to high school, creating a ceiling for rural students and those without resources to continue education.	Rise in public institutions to serve students with disabilities
1900–1950	IQ test developed Common Curriculum	Influx of immigrants into the cities; American dream of "education for all"; first major study of "gifted" students undertaken; GI Bill makes postsecondary education a goal for the common man.	Use of IQ test to sort students; poor and minorities identified as having disabilities to be served in separate schools and programs; CEC founded
1950s–1960s	*Brown v. Board of Education* *Sputnik* Johnson's Great Society Civil Rights Movement	First advocacy groups for gifted students; NAGC founded; *Sputnik* launches the space race and emphasis on math and science in U.S. schools; focus on equity of opportunity becomes a major political issue.	Birth of inclusion; separate is inherently unequal; special education becomes aligned with civil rights of low-income students and minorities because of the overrepresentation
1970s	Marland Report PL 94-142	U.S. Department of Education issues a broad definition of "giftedness"; "Office of Gifted and Talented" created, providing official status in the department; gifted students ultimately not included as a designated or protected group in PL 94-142.	PL94-142; Special education law enacted; funding issues begin as districts cannot pay for what federal government has required

(Continued)

Table 16.1 (Continued)

Historical Time Frame	Events	Impacts on Gifted Education	Impacts on Special Education
1980s	*A Nation at Risk* report published; Julian Stanley founded the Center for Talented Youth at Johns Hopkins University; Educational Consolidation and Improvement Act; Jacob Javits Gifted and Talented Students Act (1988)	Renewed emphasis on math and science in schools; national outreach to gifted children, especially among underserved populations; elimination of the federal Office of Gifted and Talented; block grants eliminated specific funding for gifted programs. Refocus of gifted education on a national level; funds for research and program development; creation of the National Research Centers on the Gifted and Talented.	Aspects of the law codified at state levels
1900s–2000s	"National Excellence: A Case for Developing America's Talent" (1993) Third International Math and Science Study (TIMSS) and PISA reports published NCLB enacted Standards movement "A Nation Deceived: How Schools Hold Back America's Brightest Students" (2004) Common Core State Standards adopted by 46 states (2011)	Focused attention on the "quiet crisis" of unmet potential among gifted students in the United States Students in the United States lag behind their counterparts in other developed nations; policy makers begin to examine implications for global competition. Federal legislation requires states to articulate standards and focus on moving students up to proficiency but not beyond proficiency. Report highlighted reasons why schools are reluctant to accelerate students beyond their grade level, restraining gifted students from making progress. Documents 50 years of research. Content standards set the stage for uniformity of English language arts and mathematics content across the country.	Person-first language became more pronounced; PL 94-142 rewritten as Individuals with Disabilities Education Act (IDEA); scheduled to be reviewed and modified every seven years Inclusion movement became more significant; SWD (Students with Disabilities) defined as a category in NCLB; pressure to achieve the same standards as general education Congressional political deadlock stalls modification of 2004 Individuals with Disabilities Education Improvement Act As this volume goes to press, the impact of the CCSS on these special groups is yet to be determined.

SETTING THE CONTEXT: THE 19TH CENTURY

Examining the purposes, histories, and educational efforts of these two groups can provide policy makers and educational leaders insight into the role that "equity" plays in the formation of the identity of these two groups. Historical and political events of the 19th and 20th centuries affected the general education community and all stakeholders in that community. Schooling had been simple in the early 19th century. Local schools in both rural and urban areas provided a "conventional" curriculum that was familiar to all who had attended school. Mastery of established and familiar content led to advancement through that curriculum. Students progressed individually, especially in rural one-room schools that grouped them in multi-age and multi-grade arrangements (Corn, 1999). Individual differences in learning were relatively easily accommodated, both within the school environment and in the culture and economy.

Many of the "disabilities" of today's schools, such as autism, learning disabilities, and attention-deficit disorder were not defined, identified, or served prior to the industrialization of America in the 1800s, simply because these nonvisible disabilities were more easily accommodated in an economy and culture that was rooted in a rural, agricultural mode where schooling itself was a luxury. A disability is defined by the context, and in preindustrial America, difficulty learning was not an especially relevant issue. Children with more visible or pronounced disabilities were either given an education in a private setting with tutors and/or private schools if their family were wealthy, or taken care of in almshouses, poorhouses, and even prisons if they were not (Osgood, 2008). This placement of students with visible and societally defined differences in institutions set the groundwork for the initiatives of special education in the 20th century.

As early as the 1860s, precocious students in St. Louis advanced frequently through an accelerated curriculum that provided more challenging work and prevented an attitude of laziness (Passow, 1979). Students who displayed exceptional talent advanced to secondary school upon completion of the curriculum, but often this advancement derived not only from achievement but also from the financial resources to pay the fees associated with secondary instruction (Newland, 1976). This economic reality ultimately tainted the political perceptions of acceleration and opportunity, a perception that, some would argue, exists today.

In 1856, school reformers across the country began to remove advanced subjects like algebra to the high school curriculum, to free elementary teachers from the burden of teaching those courses (Kaestle, 1983). "Normal School" training for elementary school teachers, almost universally female, did not include more complex subjects, like mathematics and foreign languages. Primarily male college students studied these advanced subjects and then later taught these courses in high schools and academies (Spring, 1994). As a result, a new standardized curriculum in elementary school, driven by the lack of qualified teachers, effectively truncated the academic experiences of gifted students before high school. Because most students did not require an advanced curriculum, the social efficiency model (Spring, 1994) of school management removed the possibility of a special curriculum for those who were outliers, those who might be regarded as gifted.

Cremin concluded that restructuring the curriculum by removing advanced subjects "restricted chances for the talented but less advantaged youth to taste the higher learning" (1980, p. 154). In terms of educating gifted and talented students, these reforms effectively created a ceiling on the achievement levels of some students before high school. Meanwhile, isolated pockets of resistance to this egalitarian reform occurred throughout the nation, as various school districts introduced tracking policies that provided for the selection of certain students to advance at a faster, more accelerated pace than their agemates. For example, in St. Louis, tracking allowed some students to complete the first eight grades in less than eight years and advance to high school (Colangelo & Davis, 2003). These reforms also laid the foundation for charges of elitism and racism that plagued gifted education in the later years of the 20th century.

In the latter 1800s and the early 20th century, several cultural, economic, and political shifts occurred, including the rise of humanism, growing technology, rise of factories, immigration, and the growing impact of governmental agencies designed to create and support a working class (Winzer, 2009). These movements led to an increasing divide between bureaucrats who sought to provide for those who were struggling academically and those who did not.

THE STRUGGLE INTENSIFIES: THE EARLY 20TH CENTURY

Between 1880 and 1920, the American high school struggled to define its identity. This struggle, beset by political issues of the time, set the stage for conflict over what constituted appropriate curriculum for all students. Was high school a college preparatory institution or simply an extension of elementary school? Which students should be able to study advanced courses? Which students needed additional remediation? By 1918, new child labor laws forced nearly all children and youth to remain in school, while waves of European immigrants, particularly in urban areas, changed the demographics of schools. Government as a humanistic method of ensuring equal opportunities became more prominent as a social movement, and public schools grew significantly. Education reformers grappled with skepticism about the capabilities of the new student population and the capacity of the schools to meet their needs (Powell, Farrar, & Cohen, 1985). As public schools grew, those students who could not learn in the same ways or at the same pace as other children were provided opportunities in publically funded institutions, beginning with the first public school in 1869 in Boston for children who were deaf and had hearing impairments.

After World War I, Americans embraced the progressive dream of education for all citizens. Getzels characterized this period as "the age of mediocrity" (1977, p. 264) in which educators focused on bringing everyone up to but not beyond a minimum standard. Compulsory education of all children forced educators to determine basic benchmarks to determine the effectiveness of that education. In 1918, the Commission on Reorganization of Secondary Schools mandated that schools (1) offer something of value for the various needs of their many diverse students; and (2) reexamine the conventional academic curriculum. These movements had both positive and negative aspects—promoting cultural common understanding but also promoting cultural conformism and racism (Kaestle, 1983). Through the rise of humanism and government involvement, the needs of those children who exhibited difficulties became a more public issue, while the needs of children who were excelling became less so.

As a result of this cultural shift toward progressivism and humanism, government became an instrument of change and caring (Strax, Strax, & Cooper, 2012). Because government involvement was inextricably linked to issues of poverty and race, disability issues became a by-product of government as well. This can be seen in the founding of the Council for Exceptional Children (CEC) organization in 1922, which brought together a number of separate disability advocates to collectively advocate for students with disabilities and impact government policy. This collective approach to advocacy, led by parents bound together by similar issues, proved a mighty force in later years.

Concerns about abilities of increased and diverse student populations dominated discussions of curriculum reform. Numerous nonacademic courses were added to the curriculum, "and often academic courses were modified or watered down to meet the needs of this new pupil population" (French, 1964, p. 161). Despite the fact that the new standard curriculum did not meet the needs of students with exceptional ability or talent, by 1920, "approximately two-thirds of all large cities had created some type of program for gifted students" (Colangelo & Davis, 2003, p. 6).

Terman's work in 1916 was a watershed moment in education, and significantly impacted the education of both students with disabilities (Gargiulo, 2011) and gifted students. Terman (1925) conducted his original studies on intelligence and introduced the term IQ into American consciousness. The newly developed Stanford-Binet intelligence tests opened the door to examination of diverse intellectual talent, based on specific tests and scores and simplistic, numerically derived labels. Suddenly, educators thought they had a way to quantify and, therefore, "know" about diverse ability in a simple, easily understood way.

This resulted in far-reaching consequences for students with high IQ scores. When Leta Hollingworth (1926), an early advocate of services for gifted students, was demonstrating the administration of the Stanford-Binet test to a class at Columbia University, one child achieved an IQ score of 187. Prior to this, all of her subjects had scores in the "mental retardation" range. Hollingworth (1942) was so intrigued at the child's abilities that from that point forward, Hollingworth devoted her professional career to the study of gifted students and advocacy for services for the gifted.

However, the use of a single test reduced the subjectivity of the child's experience, and the scientific approach advocated a particular form of instruction for a particular level of IQ. IQ tests and other measures of "moral and medical" abilities became significant sorting factors in education (Osgood, 2008). Students were provided either a highly functional curriculum that emphasized work-related skills, or advanced opportunities through a change in the pacing of the standard curriculum. Such instruction was more easily accomplished in separate schools and classes and such institutions flourished.

This process of creating separate schools and separate classes continued throughout both world wars. However, two of the more confounding factors to the success of this model were immigration and poverty (Osgood, 2005). While the Great Depression and World War II laid the foundation for equity-based reforms in education, Thompson (1976) maintained that those key political events in American history ultimately obscured the educational inadequacies of the progressive movement by polarizing the opportunities afforded to students according to their class in society. In the 1930s and 1940s, poor children left school to go to work or to war, whereas wealthy children went to private school or elite public high schools. Public schools became the domain of the middle class, who was largely satisfied with the curriculum—or had no financial means to complain. Public schools provided opportunity for those students, but actually offered little in the way of variation or advancement.

At the same time, special education became a "dumping ground" (Osgood, 2005, p. 133) for those students from non-majority backgrounds. The issue of special education became entwined with equal access issues of minorities, second language learners, and children from poverty. During this era, most of these institutions followed a medical model of treatment, in which the disability was the focus and children were provided instruction that sought to ameliorate the impacts of the disability. Disability was perceived as something to be "cured," or at least kept away from the mainstream of the population. However, during the 1940s, psychologists such as Goodwin Watson focused on the contributions that children with disabilities could make, as opposed to merely training them to be invisible (Osgood, 2005). This, perhaps, was the birth of the "disability as difference" movement and the emphasis on the child and his or her relationship to the environment.

1950s–1960s

Post World War II, the United States, as recent liberator of the Western world and newly ordained superpower, operated within a framework of nationalism and opportunity for all citizens. Soldiers returned to the United States with a sense of pride and power, fueled by the GI Bill, which made higher education attainable to the common man. No longer the province of the rich and privileged, college enrollment became a common goal among the Baby Boom generation, children of these soldiers. As a result, "college preparatory" classes became a hot commodity among the rank and file of students and were no longer reserved for the most capable or most likely to succeed. In the midst of this political euphoria, special courses for gifted students once more came under scrutiny as contradicting the American ideal of opportunity for everyone.

Who was to benefit from these expanded educational opportunities was clearly defined by *Brown v. Board of Education* in 1954. Perhaps no other court case has had the impact on special education of this case, in which the Supreme Court clearly stated that "separate educational facilities are inherently unequal" (*Brown v. Board of Education,* 347 US 483, 1954). The correlations between special education needs and race and ethnicity were, and continue to be, too clearly established to ignore (Harry & Klingner, 2014). A number of factors may contribute to disproportionality, including: test bias, poverty, special education processes, inequity in general education, issues of behavior management, and cultural mismatch/cultural reproduction (Skiba et al., 2008).

By connecting the rights of individuals with disabilities to the movement for equal rights for African Americans, advocates for children with disabilities began a march toward inclusion that continues to this day. In this respect, there are no swings in public policy between conflicting ideals that can be found in so many other educational movements. The implications of this case, and resultant laws, formalized the divide that exists between special education and gifted education. Although gifted education and special education have many similarities with their focus on individual differences, in *Brown v. Board of Education,* they found themselves on opposing sides of the educational debate of equity. Equity became synonymous with access in special education, while gifted education became aligned with national and competitive interests.

In 1957, the Soviet Union launched *Sputnik* I and the United States felt the threat of international competition for space and national defense. The unintended positive consequence of *Sputnik* for gifted education was the creation of the National Defense Education Act of 1958 making federal funding available for programs whose goals were developing mathematical and scientific talent. Gifted learners, in an era of a national external threat, were seen as a natural and precious resource, needing cultivation of human potential and public resources (Coleman, 1999).

Shortly after *Sputnik,* during the 1960s, both civil rights protection and the formalizing of the Elementary and Secondary Education Act (ESEA, 1965) were passed with an emphasis on protection of group rights, but not totally at the exclusion of individual rights. The passage of the Civil Rights Act in 1964 and the civil rights movement was the platform for educational access and opportunities for all children, yet the broad interpretation was a way to provide opportunities for people of color (Cross, 1999). Concurrent with the broader context of the civil rights movement, in educational circles, ESEA was passed. This act sought to target funds to students from low-income families as a way to prevent poverty from restricting academic access and achievement. ESEA reflected a larger political desire to erase the stigma of racial oppression, stimulated by *Brown* a few years earlier. By the end of the 1960s, legal challenges to segregation had promulgated throughout the South. In this political climate, earlier targeted services for the gifted were put on hold as these political events focused educational leaders on providing equitable and adequate services for all students.

1970s

The early 1970s brought back a swing to educational excellence and individual potential, because Americans were growing weary of the Vietnam War, an oil crisis, and growing domestic unrest as expressed through music and lifestyles. U.S. Commissioner of Education Sidney Marland issued a report to Congress (Marland, 1972). In his report, among other things, was evidence that a majority of school administrators stated that they had no gifted children in their schools, and that the identification of gifted students was impeded by cost, apathy, and hostility on the part of school personnel. Congress appropriated $290,000 earmarked for teacher training, research, and the development of a national office for gifted education. The attention and money, albeit small, created a ripple effect in the gifted community that can still be seen today in everything from entities such as the National Research Centers for Gifted and Talented (NRCGT) to many state and local definitions employing components of the Marland definition.

This momentary swing for educating the gifted was soon erased by the passage of Public Law 94-142 and the resultant mandated education of children with disabilities. Congress enacted the Education for All Handicapped Children Act (Public Law 94-142) in 1975 to support states and localities in protecting the rights and meeting the needs of infants, toddlers, children, and youth with disabilities and their families. PL 94-142, later renamed the Individuals with Disabilities Education Act (IDEA) in 1997, has essentially remained unchanged in the intervening years and does not include gifted students. Although some states afforded "special education" status to gifted students, it was solely at the discretion of local and state governments. If a ten-year-old student has the cognitive capacity of a six-year-old, then he is afforded an individualized education that requires extra funding. But if a six-year-old has the cognitive capacity of a ten-year-old he may or, more likely, may not receive any special accommodation. Virgil Ward (1981) addressed this philosophical contradiction and its effect on the education of gifted students. He urged that real equity in education would result in working with both groups of outliers, students with disabilities and gifted students.

PL 94-142 emphasized the need for labels and subsequent processes to receive treatment, rather than an educational response to individual differences. Some claim that the use of labels has been a significant issue in the marginalization of students in special education even more than they are by naming what are natural differences; however, the use of labels is directly tied to federal funding (Adelman, 1996). No longer could school systems ignore children with disabilities or place them in settings where instruction did not occur (Zigmond, 2001). Special education was legally defined by a relatively underfunded mandate that provided a significant level of protections and procedures designed to create access to programs, with little emphasis on the programs themselves.

Two elements defined in PL 94-142 provide perhaps the strongest sense of educational tension in special education. The inherent tension between "Least Restrictive Environment" (LRE), and "Free and Appropriate Public Education" (FAPE) are challenged and debated in the classrooms of every public school building. These two areas of tension are characterized by Strax, Strax, and Cooper (2012) as the competing perspectives of "Justice" and "Care." It is clearly understood that the linkages and relationship between overrepresentation of ethnic and culturally different groups are complex and challenging (Skiba et al., 2008). The "solution" however, is less complex, according to advocates who argue that LRE means full inclusion with no separate, hence unequal, educational settings.

This movement of deinstitutionalizing children and placing them squarely within the context and flow of the educational process has become a full-throated roar of advocacy, captured by Sapon-Shevin (2007) in her demand of inclusion as a moral right, not as education as something that is earned by the right behavior or the right academic background. She poses the argument that by excluding students with special needs, a sense of "otherness" is created, allowing certain populations to be considered "less than" and unworthy of education.

A significant issue raised by PL 94-142 is funding for special education. As Strax, Strax, and Cooper state, "the politics and financing of special education are intertwined and complexly related. Money reflects policies and programs, and programs are determined and expanded based on local, state, federal and private funding—all to meet the needs of our children in their development and improvement" (2012, p. 78). Approximately 21 percent of the federal educational budget pays for special education. However, because of the individual needs and the mandates and requirements of the law, a child with disabilities costs about 1.9 times more to educate, but only approximately 17 percent of a district's costs come from federal dollars (SEEP, 2004).

Because PL 94-142 did not address gifted students, the gifted community drew on advocates, rather than law, for assistance. Advocacy for gifted students has had limited success, both in attaining the services needed and in enlisting support from the larger public. Early advocates and theorists chronicle the struggle to bring issues surrounding gifted education to the forefront of American consciousness. Tannenbaum (1972) once compared the gifted child movement to a rocking chair, constantly moving but going nowhere. Proponents of gifted education have acknowledged the failure of advocates for gifted education to gain momentum. In a 50-year perspective of gifted education, Stanley, George, and Solano (1977) noted that modest changes in theory and research over the previous half century resulted in similarly modest gains for gifted students in that same time period.

Stanley ultimately founded the Center for Talented Youth at Johns Hopkins University and has come to be considered one of the giants of gifted education. However, despite his significant contribution to gifted education, his lament foreshadowed similar concerns by Passow (1986) and Gallagher (2002), who noted a quarter century later that, "The engines of educational change: *legislation, court decisions, administrative rule making* and *professional initiatives* have only lightly touched on the education of gifted students."

However, starting in the 1970s, hundreds of supplemental programs have targeted gifted students to augment the regular school experience. These supplemental programs are offered from universities, school systems, nonprofit and for-profit agencies, and private organizations. These programs take place after school, on Saturdays, during the summer, or online and serve as a form of advocacy, albeit through direct services to students. However, these programs also differ substantially from programs for students with special needs that are funded through mandated federal programs.

1980s–1990s

The decade of the 1980s was, for the most part, politically positive for gifted education. In 1983, the National Commission on Excellence in Education released a report on the state of American schools, entitled *A Nation at Risk*. It took the nation's educational system to task for losing ground to other nations, for employing low academic standards, and for losing academic focus. It reported that 50 percent of gifted students were not performing to their potential. The result of *A Nation at Risk* for gifted educators was a flurry of activity and positive attention, albeit briefly, including the development of new programs for gifted students, educational provisions for underprivileged gifted students, and less reliance on intelligence quotients as measures for giftedness (Tannenbaum, 1998). Expanded notions surfaced about the concept of intelligence during the mid-1980s (Gardner, 1983; Renzulli, 1986; Sternberg, 1985) as well as different curricular and programming models as catalysts to serve gifted students (Renzulli & Reis, 1985; VanTassel-Baska, 1988).

In 1988, the Jacob K. Javits Gifted and Talented Students Education Act was enacted. While the Javits Act provided limited monetary initiatives and a physical presence in Washington, DC, this one piece of legislation was Washington's only sign of interest in gifted education. Since 2004, however, Congress has steadily decreased funding for the program; and in 2011 under the pressure to address the growing budget deficit, policy makers eliminated the act and the contribution dropped to $0. The act had provided the only federal funding for programs targeting low-income gifted students for close to 25 years.

Even though the Javits Act was a national shot in the arm for gifted students, the irony was that at state and local levels, programming, funding, and philosophical support continued to battle itself out in classrooms, school board meetings, and school district offices. At one level, the federal legislation invigorated states to work on their own legislation and to formalize programming provisions, and yet the barriers Gallagher (1979, 1985, 1986a) perceived, such as insufficient funds, inadequately trained personnel, inadequate curriculum development, inadequate diagnostic techniques, lack of public interest, an inadequate legal base, insufficient physical space, and other limitations, still persisted at local and state levels.

Shortly after the enactment of the Javits Act, President George H. W. Bush and the states' governors convened and adopted the National Goals for Education, which called for ambitious goals for America's students to be achieved by the year 2000. These goals were directed at the entire school population, but gifted students were not explicitly mentioned. One of the goals, for example, was the "United States will be the first in the world in mathematics and science achievement." A few years later, the Third International Mathematics and Science Study (TIMSS) was conducted consisting of a randomized study of 41 nations comparing fourth, eighth, and 12th grade students in mathematics and science on a myriad of measures. It showed that our nation ranked in the middle and lower quadrants when compared to other nations.

In 1993 another national report commissioned by the U.S. Department of Education was issued. *National Excellence: A Case for Developing America's Talent* reflected a "quiet crisis in educating talented students" (p. 6) and brought to light problems in current schooling practices that were inhibiting the development of America's talented youth. One of the hallmarks of the National Excellence report was that it provided a broadened definitional blueprint stating that "Outstanding talents are present in children and youth from all cultural groups, across all economic strata, and in all areas of human endeavor" (p. 7), providing a metaphor for talent development and a template for excellence.

In contrast to gifted education, the 1980s were a relatively quiet time for special education as the PL 94-142 law became implemented at state and local levels. Numerous court cases clarified elements of the process and the IEP became a structured reflection of the outcomes of legal battles, rather an emerging, student-centered document.

2000 AND BEYOND: THE 21ST CENTURY

In January 2001, President George W. Bush passed the No Child Left Behind (NCLB) (2001) framework emphasizing that "too many of our neediest children are being left behind" despite the nearly $200 billion in federal spending since the passage of ESEA. The impact on both special education and gifted education has been significant. NCLB, and the related standards movement, are in direct opposition to a more open, more inclusive approach in which student differences are valued and appreciated (Osgood, 2008). NCLB, which reauthorized ESEA, focused attention on bringing students "up" to proficiency but said nothing about students who needed to go beyond proficiency or students who were far below proficiency because of the inherent challenges of their special needs.

At the same time as the standards movement gained influence, IDEA was reauthorized in 2004, bringing with it a new model of identification for students with learning disabilities that sought to not use the "discrepancy" model that defined disability as the difference between potential, as measured by an IQ test, and achievement. Instead, a "response to intervention" (RTI) model sought to identify disability in a more dynamic manner and focused on students' responses to focused, scientifically based instruction (Fuchs, Fuchs, & Compton, 2004). This instruction was integrally linked to the standards movement, tying the definition of disability to the use of standards-based instruction and the responsibility of teachers, rather than the exclusive use of tests and measures and the responsibility of psychologists. Gifted education has also looked at a similar model of identification by linking identification of needs to classroom performance, rather than to isolated measures (Coleman & Hughes, 2009).

There is a tension between teachers who focus only on students who can be brought up to proficiency and instruction driven by the Individualized Education Plan (IEP) (Booher-Jennings, 2006). In a small effort to combat this, students with disabilities were included as a subgroup in its accountability measures, but gifted students remained uncounted and unaccountable. Tomlinson stated that "the No Child Left Behind Act aims the nation's attention and resources at ensuring that non-proficient students move systematically toward proficiency. Schools have no incentive for schools to attend to the growth of students once they attain proficiency, or to spur students who are already proficient to greater achievement, and certainly not to inspire those who far exceed proficiency" (2002, p. 36). She continues with "it appears to be another missed opportunity."

While this deficiency in the law impacted all categories of students, arguably it harmed disadvantaged students disproportionately.

In 2004, a report funded by the Templeton Foundation entitled *A Nation Deceived: How schools hold back America's brightest students* (Colangelo, Assouline, & Gross, 2004) charged that America is ignoring excellence and holding back bright students. The report sought to change the conversation in schools about the benefits, research, and practices for employing acceleration as a defensible educational tool for gifted students. Even though acceleration as a viable option for students who are operating above grade level expectations has one of the largest empirical research bases for school-based options, philosophically and politically, educators and policy makers have been reluctant to employ forms of acceleration in practice, largely citing concerns about students' emotional maturity and lack of flexibility on the part of the school system (Spielhagen & Cooper, 2005).

At the end of the first decade of the 21st century, international comparisons focused policy makers on preparing students in the United States for international competition. The publication of the 2009 Program for International Assessment (PISA) test scores, published by the Organisation for Economic Co-operation and Development (OECD), revealed that 15-year-old students in the United States had fallen drastically behind their peers in the developed nations of the world (29th out of the top 30 in mathematics; 23rd out of the top 30 in science). Only 1.9 percent of U.S. students ranked comparatively at the 95th percentile on the highest (Level 6) proficiency level, below the average of 3 percent of the total sample of students from OECD member nations, and well below the top students in Korea, Japan, Switzerland, China, and Singapore. International comparisons like PISA have focused federal efforts on training for the much touted and heavily funded STEM (science, technology, engineering, and mathematics) programs that will enable students in the United States to engage in global competition.

THE ULTIMATE OUTLIERS

In addition to the perceived dichotomy between gifted education and special education, other classifications emerge that defy, contradict, and confound a simplistic understanding of the political forces affecting students in these two groups. Some students, by virtue of their personal characteristics, socioeconomic status, or both, constitute a group we call the "ultimate outliers." The political forces on their behalf cross group lines and challenge conventional thinking about meeting their needs.

Witness the "twice-exceptional child." While gifted education and special education may both be outliers in education with significant differences, the two fields sometimes merge in the same child, creating a need for the two fields to collaborate with each other. With the exception of the label of "Mental Retardation" or "Intellectual Disability," none of the other disability labels precludes the potential for advanced ability in specific areas or high-level intelligence. Gifted students who also have disabilities are caught in the double bind of special education and gifted education. If their disabilities are pronounced enough that they get services, they can be covered under special education. Thus, they can easily find themselves focusing exclusively on their areas of weakness.

However, the need to develop their area of talent is not similarly mandated. If their disabilities are mild, and their abilities are very pronounced, they might qualify for gifted services, if their state has such programs, but not receive assistance in their area of challenge and remain frustrated. However, if they have enough of a disability that they have to struggle, but gifted enough to still compensate adequately for their area of challenge, they may often go completely unnoticed as an "unmotivated" child and receive neither form of service. This "masking" interaction between superior abilities and areas of disability can create programming problems as well as educational intervention challenges. Organizations such as the Association for the Gifted Division of the CEC and the Special Populations Network of the National Association for Gifted Children recognize the overlapping agendas and interests that become necessary.

An additional group of "outliers" has also emerged, that is, gifted students in schools without financial resources for gifted programs and those who have been overlooked by traditional identification measures. Although the gifted movement progressed slowly, in the last quarter of the 20th century, specific private and public advocacy efforts bolstered support for special programs for underserved students of above average ability. Castellano (2003) and Castellano and Frazier (2011) have focused the attention of educators on identification of gifted students in growing Hispanic populations in the nation and currently serves as chair of the NAGC Diversity and Equity Committee.

Underrepresented students have caught the attention of the Jack Kent Cooke Foundation, a private, independent foundation founded in 2000, supporting the needs of exceptionally promising students. The foundation focuses in particular on exceptionally promising students with financial need. The Jack Kent Cooke Foundation's mission is to advance the education of exceptionally promising students who have financial need because the foundation believes that all exceptionally talented students who have financial need will excel academically when given the resources to develop their talents. In 2012 alone, the Jack Kent Cooke Foundation spent more than $20 million on grants and scholarships.

Identification of gifted and talented students in diverse populations has been challenging to schools that rely on traditional English-language-based tests of intellectual ability. Across the nation and particularly in urban areas like New York City, educational administrators have adopted the Naglieri Nonverbal Ability Test (NNAT2) to identify potentially gifted students. This test is administered in a group setting, available in paper-pencil or online formats, and claims to provide assessment, regardless of the student's primary language, education, culture, or socioeconomic background, addressing all the political issues surrounding the process of identifying for giftedness.

Finally, in 2012, the NAGC issued a comprehensive report of that national organization's stance regarding this group of outliers, that is, those who have been underrepresented in gifted programs because of low income. Olszewski-Kubilius and Clarenbach consider this report a call to action that "challenges the nation to move beyond its near singular focus of achieving minimum performance for all students, to identifying and developing talent of all students who are capable of high achievement, including our promising low-income and culturally and linguistically diverse students who too often languish in our schools" (2012, p. 3). This report captures once more the political dilemma facing educational policy makers at all levels. Do we educate everyone to the same standard or must we help each student progress to the maximum of his or her capacity? The proponents of any of the outlier groups believe the latter.

IMPLICATIONS

Based on the ebb and flow of the relationship, historical contexts, and politics between special education, general education, and gifted education the following implications are important to consider.

- Gifted education remains a state and local control issue. Systematic efforts in funding, and coherence of curricula, teacher preparation, program delivery, and accountability can be achieved to provide for the academic and social/emotional needs of gifted students.
- Outlier students (e.g., special education and gifted education) are an integral part of the overall system of education and therefore must be thoughtfully and strategically considered part and parcel of any educational efforts, initiatives, and priorities.
- Human capital is our country's greatest strength; we can no longer afford to ignore *some* students for the sake of *all* students.
- Advocacy for special education and gifted students remains an essential component in ensuring policies, regulations, program implementation, funding, and accountability. In special education, advocacy has garnered grassroots energy that has resulted in federal legislation. In gifted education, advocacy has largely remained localized and in many cases, the result of one person or a small group of people.
- Public perception about ability grouping because of academic and/or intellectual needs has never been politically correct. Yet ability grouping with regard to athletic ability (e.g., sports) is valued, financially supported, and covered extensively in the media.
- Education of outlier students (special education and gifted learners) is explicitly linked to political, social, and economic factors in society.
- The definition of "gifted" itself has been redefined and ill-defined throughout history. As a result, identification and services lack coherency and infrastructure and are subject to political whims.
- Traditionally underrepresented gifted populations, such as culturally diverse, English language learners, and low-income students, continue to be underrepresented and unrepresented in gifted programs and overrepresented in special education, despite years of research, advocacy, professional development, and some funding.
- Twice-exceptional students representing ability and disability are a largely untapped group of learners whose needs are not being identified or addressed in any systemic way.
- Supplementary programs for gifted students such as Saturday enrichment programs, summer academies, online learning options, and the like are thriving perhaps because of an underlying assumption that the general education program is not meeting nor cannot meet their academic and social/emotional needs.

Moreover two additional variables deserve further consideration:

- Teacher preparation, teacher training, differentiation of curricular and instructional approaches, documenting student growth, and resource allocation continue to be barriers in gifted and special education.

- Parents of special education and gifted students continue to push against a large educational bureaucracy for their children to be provided equitable opportunities for individual growth.

These are a few of the implications of working with outlier students, from inputs such as conceptual definitions and ways to identify, to process variables such as instruction, grouping, school, district, and state reform emphases, to outputs such as student growth and performance, and an educational system that embraces, nurtures, and develops the potential of all of its students.

CONCLUSION

Education has long struggled with acceptance and promotion of those individuals who do not fit within the "box" of society—whether they are children with disabilities who do not succeed within that context, or gifted children who supersede that context. Unfortunately, many policy makers and educators took equal treatment to mean the exact same instruction for children who are the same age, regardless of their general readiness or their ability to learn from it. Until recently, American society, grounded in a liberal philosophy of care, was the target "of an attempted rescue by a constantly expanding central government trying to keep its capitalistic society afloat through a growing welfare state" (Strax et al., 2012, p. 12). In the current neoliberal climate, those "outlier" elements of education are under attack (Smith & Max-Neef, 2011).

In recent years, researchers outside of the field of gifted education have become proponents of gifted education, citing the nation's rhetoric toward equity as a failure of the country to value its human capital. An incendiary report (Petrilli & Scull, 2011) from the Thomas B. Fordham Institute brought into sharp focus the decline in achievement among the top students in our nation, those with the potential and demonstrated capacity to excel in school and assume leadership roles in the United States and the global community. Quite simply, this report suggested that this nation's brightest students are the unintended victims of the lofty goals of NCLB. They are not making the much heralded "adequate yearly progress" that is supposed to characterize school success, but instead are losing ground when their performance is tracked over time. When compared to the top academic peers across the globe, there are fewer U.S. students in the highest percentiles of recent PISA results (Spielhagen, 2012).

Chester Finn, president of the Thomas B. Fordham Institute (2013), states that as a country, we all lose by focusing on who is gifted rather than on what we can do to nurture intellectual potential. "Collateral victims are a society and economy that thereby fail to make the most of this latent human capital." Finn goes on to state further that "It's not elitist to pour more resources into educating our brightest kids. In fact, the future of the country may depend on it." He posits seven explanations as to why education leaders and philanthropists fail to take an interest in gifted students (Finn, 2012).

- The country's nervousness about elitism.
- A widespread belief that "equity" should be solely about income, minority status, handicapping conditions, and historical disenfranchisement.
- A mistaken belief that high-ability youngsters will do fine, even if the education system makes no special provision for them.

- The definition of "gifted" itself has been ill-defined.
- The field of gifted education lacks convincing research as to what works.
- Whether because of elitism angst or a shortage of resources, the gifted education world has been meek when it comes to lobbying and special pleading.
- The wishful proposition that "differentiated instruction" would magically enable every teacher to succeed with every kid in a mixed classroom.

According to Gallagher (2000), the equity-excellence struggle for gifted students has been addressed on a piecemeal basis when and where the opportunities arise. Special education, on the other hand, has linked tightly to overall school reform, including initiatives in teacher efficacy, instructional approaches, and two significant movements that relate specifically to special education: co-teaching and differentiation. Co-teaching is a method in which two teachers are within the classroom, sharing planning, instruction, and assessment tasks (Murawski, 2010). Differentiation is the process of adapting the content, concepts, process, produce, and learning environment of a classroom, based on a student's readiness, interests, or learning profile (Tomlinson, 2005). Both of these approaches attempt to create a "radical and massive restructure of not only special education but of the entire public educational system" (Osgood, 2005, p. 195).

Smith notes that after 40 years of inclusive efforts, teachers and administrators are still resistant to including everyone as a moral and ethical right. He suggests that "it might be easier and more productive to simply start over: blow up education, particularly special education, as we currently understand it . . . and begin fresh with something that starts from a completely different place" (2010, pp. 221–222). By linking to overall school reform and promoting multiple approaches, special education has set itself the task to redesign and reconceptualize education itself. Rather than blowing up education as Smith posits, we should look inward and perhaps redefine our conceptions of equity and excellence as synonymous.

The evolutions of the fields of gifted education and special education have been impacted significantly by the ebbs and flows of public perceptions of equity and excellence and political and historical events. Our society has competing values for the desire to cultivate potential in individuals and yet not cultivate potential if it means pulling resources and attention from another individual. We believe that equity in education is about closing the achievement gap among different ethnicities and leaving no child behind at the expense of our talented youth and American's future international competitiveness. If policy makers are concerned about America's ability to remain internationally competitive with other advanced nations, we must maximize the academic potential of our top students. Over the past century legislation such as IDEA or NCLB has placed primary emphasis on moving lower-performing students up toward proficiency or safeguarding those with special needs, with no attention on moving proficient students or beyond proficient students toward levels of mastery and developing expertise. To understand these influences on the respective "outlier" student, it's important to consider the context of the time frame and events.

It is too early to determine whether the 21st century will prove to be any better for gifted and special education students but if the past or current trends are any indication, the equity-excellence struggle will continue as a dichotomy rather than as a coherent framework providing equal rights and access for outlier students to develop their unique talents and abilities.

REFERENCES

Adelman, H. S. (1996). Appreciating the classification dilemma. In W. Stainback & S. Stainback (Eds.), *Controversial issues confronting special education: Divergent perspectives,* 2nd ed. (pp. 96–111). Boston, MA: Allyn & Bacon.

Artiles, A. J., Kozleski, E. B., Trent, S. C., Osher, D., & Ortiz, A. (2010). Justifying and explaining disproportionality, 1968–2008: A critique of underlying values of culture. *Exceptional Children, 76*(3), 279–299.

Baker, B. A., & Friedman-Nimz, R. (2002). Is a federal mandate the answer? If so, what was the question? *Roeper Review, 25*(1), 5–10.

Benbow, C. (2006). *Studying the development of math/science talent for 35 years through SMPY: Implications for the flat world.* Keynote Address. National Research Symposium on Talent Development. Iowa City: The University of Iowa.

Benbow, C. P., & Stanley, J. C. (1996). Inequality in equity: How "equity" can lead to inequity for high potential students. *Psychology, Public Policy, and Law, 2,* 249–292.

Booher-Jennings, J. (2005). Below the bubble: Educational triage and the Texas accountability system. *American Educational Research Journal, 42*(2), 231–268.

Brown, E. F. (2001). Systemic reform: The impact of North Carolina's state-initiated policies on local gifted programs. Unpublished dissertation. UMI 3003489.

Castellano, J. A. (2003). *Special populations in gifted education: Working with diversified learners.* Boston, MA: Allyn and Bacon.

Castellano, J. A., & Frazier, A. D. (2011). *Special populations in gifted education: Understanding our most able students from diverse backgrounds.* Waco, TX: Prufrock Press.

Colangelo, N., Assouline, S., & Gross, M. (2004). *A nation deceived: How schools hold back America's brightest students.* The Templeton National Report on Acceleration. Iowa City: The University of Iowa Press.

Colangelo, N., & Davis, G. (2003). *Handbook of gifted education, 3rd edition.* New York: Allyn & Bacon.

Coleman, M. R. (1999). Back to the future: The top 10 events that have shaped gifted education in the last century. *Gifted Child Today Magazine, 22*(6), 16–18.

Coleman, M. R., & Hughes, C. E. (2009). Meeting the needs of gifted students within an RTI framework. *Gifted Child Today, 32*(3), 14–17.

Corn, A. (1999). Missed opportunities—but a new century is starting. *Gifted Child Today Magazine, 22*(6), 19–21.

Cremin, L. (1980). *American education: The national experience.* New York: Harper & Row.

Cross, C. (2010). Race, poverty, and special education. *Connect for Kids.*

Cross, T. (1999). Top ten list (plus or minus two) for the 20th century. *Gifted Child Today Magazine, 22*(6), 22–25.

Finn, C. E. (2012). www.theatlantic.com/national/archive/2012/12/gifted-students-have-special-needs-too/266544/.

Finn, C. E. (2013). www.edexcellence.net/commentary/education-gadfly-weekly/2013/january-17/playing-the-gifted-student-race-card.html.

French, W. (1964). *America's educational tradition: An interpretive history.* Boston, MA: D. C. Heath.

Fuchs, D., Fuchs, L. S., & Compton, D. L. (2004). Identifying reading disabilities by responsiveness-to-instruction: Specifying measures and criteria. *Learning Disability Quarterly, 27*(4), 216–227.

Gallagher, J. J. (1979). Issues in education for the gifted. In A. H. Passow (Ed.), *The gifted and the talented: Their education and development* (pp. 28–44). Chicago: University of Chicago Press.

Gallagher, J. J. (1985). *Teaching the gifted child* (3rd ed.). Boston, MA: Allyn & Bacon.

Gallagher, J. J. (1986a). A proposed federal role: Education of the gifted children. *Gifted Child Quarterly, 30*(1), 43–46.

Gallagher, J. J. (1986b). Equity vs. excellence: An educational drama. *Roeper Review, 8*(4), 233–235.

Gallagher, J. J. (2000). Unthinkable thoughts: Education of gifted students. *Gifted Child Quarterly, 44,* 5–12.

Gallagher, J. J. (2002). *Society's role in educating gifted students: The role of public policy.* Storrs, CT: The National Research Center on the Gifted and Talented.

Gallagher, J. J. (2004a). No child left behind and gifted education. *Roeper Review, 26*(3), 121–123.

Gallagher, J. J. (2004b). Public policy in gifted education. In S. Reis (Ed.), *Essential readings in gifted education, vol. 12.* Thousand Oaks, CA: Corwin Press.

Gallagher, J. J. (2006). *The twice exceptional dilemma.* Washington, DC: National Education Association.

Gallagher, J. J., & Weiss, P. (1979). *The education of gifted and talented children and youth.* Washington, DC: Council for Basic Education.

Gardner, H. (1983). *Frames of mind.* New York: Basic Books.

Gardner, J. (1961). *Excellence: Can we be equal and excellent too?* New York: Harper and Row.

Gargiulo, R. M. (2011). *Special education in contemporary society, 4th ed.,* Thousand Oaks, CA: Sage Publications.

Getzels, J. W. (1977). General discussion immediately after the Terman Memorial Symposium. In J. C. Stanley, W. C. George, & C. H. Solano (Eds.), *The gifted and the creative: A fifty-year perspective* (pp. 225–269). Baltimore, MD: Johns Hopkins University Press.

Harry, B., & Klingner, J. (2014). *Why are so many minority students in special education: Understanding race and disability in schools, 2nd ed.* New York: Teachers College Press.

Hollingworth, L. S. (1926). *Gifted children: Their nature and nurture.* New York: McGraw-Hill.

Hollingworth, L. S. (1942). *Children above 180 I.Q. Stanford-Binet.* New York: World Book Company.

Kaestle, C. (1983). *Pillars of the republic: Common schools and American society, 1780–1860.* New York: Hill & Wang.

Karnes, F. A., & Marquardt, R. G. (1991). *Gifted children and the law: Mediation, due process, and court cases.* Dayton, OH: Gifted Psychology Press.

Marland, S. P. (1972). *Education of the gifted and talented: Vol. 1.* Report to Congress of the United States by the U.S. Commissioner of Education. Washington, DC: U.S. Government Printing Office.

Murawski, W.W. (2010). *Collaborative teaching in elementary schools: Making the co-teaching marriage work.* Thousand Oaks, CA: Corwin Press.

Newland, T. E. (1976). *The gifted in historical perspective.* Englewood Cliffs, NJ: Prentice-Hall.

Olsewski-Kubilius, P., & Clarenbach, J. (2012). *Unlocking emergent talent: Supporting high achievement of low-income, high-ability students.* Washington, DC: National Association for Gifted Children.

Osgood, R. L. (2008) *The history of special education: A struggle for equality in American Public Schools.* Westport, CT: Praeger Press.

Osgood, R. (2005). *The history of inclusion in the United States.* Washington, DC: Gallaudet University Press.

Passow, A. H. (1979). *The gifted and the talented: Their education and development. The Seventy-eighth Yearbook of the National Society for the Study of Education, Part 1.* Ed. Chicago: University of Chicago Press.

Passow, A. H. (1986). Reflections on three decades of education of the gifted. *Roeper Review, 8*(4), 223–225.

Petrilli, M. J., & Scull, J. (2011, March). *American achievement in international perspective.* Washington, DC: Thomas B. Fordham Foundation.

Powell, A., Farrar, E., & Cohen, D. (1985). *The shopping mall high school: Winners and losers in the educational marketplace.* Boston, MA: Houghton Mifflin.

Renzulli, J. S. (1986). The three-ring conception of giftedness: A developmental model for creative productivity. In R. J. Sternberg & J. E. Davidson (Eds.), *Conceptions of giftedness* (pp. 246–279). New York: Cambridge University Press.

Renzulli, J. S., & Reis, S. M. (1985). *The schoolwide enrichment model: A comprehensive plan for educational excellence.* Mansfield Center, CT: Creative Learning Press.

Report by the National Association for Gifted Children and the Council of State Directors of Programs for the Gifted (NAGC). (2005). *State of the states.* Washington, DC: NAGC.

Sapon-Shevin, M. (2007). *Widening the circle: The power of inclusive classrooms.* Boston, L Beacon Press.

Skiba, R. J., Simmons, A.B., Ritter, S., Gibb, A.C., Rausch, M.K., Cuadrado, J., & Chung, C-G (2008). Achieving equity in special education: History, status, and current challenges. *Exceptional Children, 74*(3), 264–288.

Smith. P. B. & Max-Neef, M. (2011). *Economics unmasked: From power and greed to compassion and the common good.* Devon, UK: Green Books.

Smith, P. (2010). Future directions, policy, practice and research. In P. Smith (Ed.), *Whatever happened to inclusion?* (pp. 221–242). New York: Peter Lang.

Special Education Expenditure Project (SEEP). (2004). *What are we spending on special education services in the United States, 1999–2000? Report 1.* Report prepared for the Office of Special Education Programs, U.S. Department of Education. Available from http://csef.air.org/publications/seep/national/advrpt1.pdf

Spielhagen, F. (2012). Don't forget gifted students: High achievers are essential to global competition. *Commentary in Education Week, 31*(2), 28–29.

Spielhagen, F., & Cooper, B. (2005, April 13). The unkindest cut: Seven stupid arguments against programs for the gifted. *Education Week 24*(31), 47–48.

Spring, J. (1994). *The American school, 1642–1993* (3rd ed.) New York: McGraw-Hill.

Stanley, J. C., George, W. C., & Solano. C. H. (Eds.). (1977). *The gifted and the creative: A fifty-year perspective, 1925–1975.* Baltimore, MD: Johns Hopkins University Press.

STEAM, not STEM. Retrieved from http://steam-notstem.com/about/mission-statement/.

Sternberg, R. J. (1985). *Beyond IQ: A triarchic theory of intelligence.* New York: Cambridge University Press.

Strax, M., Strax, C., & Cooper, B. S. (2012). *Kids in the middle: The micropolitics of special education.* Lanham, MD: Rowman & Littlefield.

Tannenbaum, A. J. (1972). A backward and forward glance at the gifted. *The National Elementary Principal, 51,* 14–23.

Tannenbaum, A. J. (1998). Programs for the gifted: To be or not to be. *Journal for the Education of the Gifted, 21*(1), 3–36.

Tanner, D., & Tanner, L. (1990). *History of the school curriculum.* New York: Macmillan.

Terman, L. M. (1925). *The mental and physical traits of a thousand gifted children.* Stanford, CA: Stanford University Press.

Thompson, J. T. (1976). *Policymaking in American education: A framework for analysis.* Englewood Cliffs, NJ: Prentice-Hall.

Tomlinson, C. (1996). Good teaching for one and all: Does gifted education have an instructional identity? *Journal for the Education of the Gifted, 20*(2), 155–174.

Tomlinson, C. (2002, November 6). Proficiency is not enough. *Education Week 22*(10), 36, 38.

Tomlinson, C. (2005). Quality curriculum and instruction for highly able students. *Theory into Practice, 44*(2), 160–166.

U.S. Department of Education Office of Educational Research and Improvement (1994). *National Excellence: A case for developing America's talent.* Washington, DC: Author.

VanTassel-Baska, J. (1988).Curriculum for the gifted: Theory, research, and practice. In J. VanTassel-Baska et al. (Eds.), *Comprehensive curriculum for gifted learners* (pp. 1–19). Boston, MA: Allyn & Bacon.

VanTassel-Baska, J. (1998). *Excellence in educating gifted and talented learners* (3rd ed.). Denver, CO: Love.

Ward, V. (1981). *Differential education for gifted learners* (2nd ed.). Ventura County, CA: Office of the Superintendent of Schools.

Wirt, J., & Kirst, M. (1997). *The politics of American education.* Berkeley, CA: McCutcheon.

Wright, P. W. D., & Wright, P. D. (2006). *Wrightslaw: From emotions to advocacy* (2nd ed.). Hartfield, VA: Harbor House Law Press.

Zigmond, N. (2001). Special education at a crossroads. *Preventing School Failure, 45*(2), 70–74.

17

A NEW KIND OF INTEGRATED EDUCATION
Paul Green

In June 2007 a conservative majority of the Supreme Court declared in a 5 to 4 decision that school district policies intended to integrate school districts are unconstitutional. Chief Justice John Roberts wrote in his opinion that the Seattle, Washington and Louisville, Kentucky school districts could no longer assign students to schools based on their race. The Court's decision in *Meredith v. Jefferson County School Board* (2007), and its companion case, *Parents Involved in Community Schools v. Seattle School District No. 1* (2007), forced the school districts to rethink student assignment policies and confront challenging questions to genuine school integration. Is school integration simply to mix students of different colors to ensure equity or to promote familiarity among the races? Does integration produce concrete gains like greater academic achievement for all students? If so, is student assignment by race the most effective mechanism for attaining it?

This chapter explores how resistance from neighborhoods and school districts continues to define the politics of desegregation and the pursuit of integration. The courts' continued retreat from the resegregation of public schools portends a return to an *apartheid* system of schooling. As such, integration cannot be achieved absent holistic, communitywide, or "integrated" strategies. So any educational reform efforts must be framed by a reconfiguration of our collective understanding of the important role of education in sustaining our democracy, and our political will to affect the common good. This chapter will also map out additional types of integrative measures required of a pluralistic society and integrated community.

Educational Integration as Transformational Democracy
Few dispute that segregation has played a role in the shaping of social and educational opportunity in the United States. As segregation denies unfettered access to schools, parks, restaurants, and libraries, desegregation removes these legal and social barricades. Integration, on the other hand, is far more profound and inclusive than desegregation. Integration is the active acceptance of desegregation and the encouraged participation of all groups and communities in its institutions. Integration is genuine intergroup and interpersonal decision making. (De)segregation is a short-range goal while integration is

the primary goal of a true democracy (Green, 2008). So, as educational leaders and policy wonks pursue the important task of respecting the letter of the law, (i.e., compliance with desegregation decisions), they must also respect the spirit of the law (i.e., commitment to the democratic principles of integration).

The task of integration is essential not only to our democracy but also to those institutions intended to reproduce that democracy: our nation's public schools. The urgency of this matter looms large as the nation's public schools rapidly resegregate, and as the courts, states, and school districts abandon the limited desegregation efforts, accepting the colorblind rhetoric of school choice and accountability.

Genuine integration requires a broader meaning than desegregation. It is not assimilative but rather transformative. So, while desegregation assimilates poor youth and students of color into the mainstream, integration transforms the mainstream. It does not assume that poor youth of color and their communities benefit from white youth and their communities if they occupy the same classrooms, libraries, neighborhoods, parks, hospitals, or places of employment. On the contrary, it acknowledges that people and their cultures are dynamic, not static, and therefore are constantly evolving, and that every student and community benefits from an equal and just system of education. Integration pursues an inclusive milieu, placing value on the historical, intellectual, and cultural contributions of all its groups and communities. So integrated schools are creative and engaged environments well equipped to prepare all students in an evolving multiracial and multiethnic democracy.

Integrated communities and schools address the issues of academic achievement, opportunity, community, and relevancy at a systemic level (Powell, 2010, 2011). In doing so, institutions, communities ,and individuals are fundamentally changed to foster multiracial and ethnic social interaction and to provide equal opportunities for each and every student. Interdistrict desegregation or school consolidation can be an initial and temporary step in this structural transformation. A more holistic approach is needed. Regional versus local planning is also required to link housing, school, and employment, as well as political and cultural, opportunities to spread accountability throughout entire metropolitan areas. When these changes are made between districts and within schools, they often produce real learning for students. When districts and schools adopt a colorblind position to avoid conflict with the community, it often leads to resegregation and it inadvertently legitimizes educational policies and practices that disadvantage poor youth and students of color (Powell, 2009).

Instead, integrated districts and schools must employ pedagogical techniques that address the multitude of student learning styles and utilize materials fashioned by and about people of diverse racial and ethnic backgrounds. Additionally, integrated schools must build an inclusive, supportive atmosphere that motivates teachers, students, and administrators, while encouraging positive interactions in both the school and the community. This requires districts and schools reexamine accountability measures, tracking and discipline policies, curricula, and in some instances the entire school environment, including extracurricular activities. The goal of real integrated education is to reach beyond educating poor students of color as a means to assimilate and acculturate them. Integration as a strategy for developing an inclusive and multicultural environment no longer suffices. The most important need is to integrate the abilities, minds, and talents of all students and to prepare them to prosper in a culturally dynamic and pluralistic world (Powell, 1996).

INTERDISTRICT INITIATIVES: ESTABLISHING
EQUAL RACIAL GROUP REPRESENTATION

If genuine integration is to succeed, it requires equal racial group representation among students. When students of any one ethnic or racial group find themselves the sole minority within a social setting (e.g., school), they can often be excluded or even withdraw from learning. Conversely, when one race exists in a large percentage (more than 75%), it establishes the assumptions and norms of behavior that define school status and achievement. According to Bankston and Caldas, group status can have positive or negative effects on student achievement; depending on what "capital" the majority group brings (Bankston & Caldas, 1996). As a result, teachers may not respond to the learning and emotional needs of the minority students (Boger, 2010; Patchen, 1982).

Clearly, one important strategy of civic and community leaders and school officials is to identify the optimal school percentage of students of color and white students so that the benefits associated with a racially integrated school contribute most to the learning experiences and academic achievements of all students (Bankston & Caldas, 1996; Schofield, 2001; Wells et al., 2009). Students can maximize contact and friendship formation between and among group members (McConahay, 1981) and reduce in-group and out-group interactions detrimental to student learning. The rise in concentrated poverty in metropolitan areas and second language learners means school leaders and teachers build linguistic skills and acknowledge disparate income levels (Institute on Race and Poverty, 2002). While it is unrealistic to think that all schools can effectively address racial balance criteria, research clearly supports their necessity when structuring interdistrict, district, and school enrollment policies, practices, and procedures (McKenzie, 2000; Powell, 2007; Wells et al., 2009).

Metropolitan-Wide (De)segregation: What Works

A metropolitan-wide school desegregation plan is the most effective means of establishing equal racial group representation as well as achieving racial and economic equality. Desegregation plans that do not reach beyond the district boundaries are not likely to affect segregation. Because the nonwhite population is heavily concentrated in the older metropolitan areas while all-white developments are continuously constructed on the periphery of these neighborhoods, metropolitan-wide (interdistrict) desegregation policies are more enduring and stable (Frankenberg & Chungmei, 2002; Orfield, 2002; Orfield & Lee, 2007; Powell, 2002). And except in extremely large districts where 70 percent or more students are poor students of color, such as Chicago, Los Angeles, New York, Philadelphia, St. Louis, and New Orleans, regional desegregation policies can increase educational opportunities for these students (Orfield, 1996; Orfield & Lee, 2007; Orfield & Monfort, 1988). They have been far more effective in Southern states where less dense countywide school districts serve more racially diverse communities than school districts in the North (Frankenberg, 2005; Orfield & Yun, 1999).

When we look at metropolitan plans, Orfield notes that metropolitan areas like New York, Chicago, Los Angeles, and Atlanta are among the nation's most educationally integrated communities and the most rapidly growing metropolitan economies (Orfield & Lee, 2007; Orfield & Monfort, 1988; Wells et al., 2009). For example, in Raleigh, North Carolina, in the mid-70s, city and suburban school district boundaries were removed; inner-city magnet schools opened and 15 percent of primarily black students were bused to the suburbs. By the mid-80s, a racial balance was achieved, academic scores had increased among blacks, and neighborhoods remained stable. Durham, North Carolina chose another path. Because it did not follow Raleigh's lead, by the 1980s, its schools had become 90 percent black and mostly low income. Concomitantly, educational achievement also declined markedly. By the time Durham, North Carolina initiated integrative policies in the mid-90s, racial balance occurred, dropout rates decreased, and test scores improved (Report to McKnight Foundation, 1997).

Orfield cites further data supporting the value of interdistrict policies. For example, resources invested in segregated schools yield poorer results than similar resources invested in metro-wide integration plans. The struggle to desegregate, let alone integrate, Kansas City Missouri Public Schools is an example. A $1.4 billion court-ordered renovation of the city's deteriorated schools initiated the most comprehensive magnet school plan in the history of public education. The court-appointed monitoring committee reported few academic gains in achievement relative to the state resources expended to increase teacher and staff salaries and lower class sizes (Moran, 2005; Orfield & Thronson, 1993) Importantly, none of the states with the largest average size of school districts (metropolitan areas) reported more than one-third of its black students attending intensely segregated schools, while states with the highest levels of segregation for black students had relatively small school districts and fragmented district patterns (Orfield & Lee, 2007; Orfield & Monfort, 1988; Wells et al., 2009).

Mandatory metropolitan-wide plans have proven far more effective than voluntary desegregation or integration. For example, under St. Louis' voluntary metropolitan desegregation plan, many African American students continued to attend schools that were predominantly attended by poor students of color—even though the court emphasized that refusal to participate could result in interdistrict mergers (Levine & Eubanks, 1986; Wells, 1995, 1996). Whereas the number of students participating in interdistrict choice was poor as of 1993, only one-half of one percent of all public school children were attending interdistrict schools (Ryan & Heise, 2002). Conversely, segregation declined dramatically in Wilmington, Delaware and Charlotte-Mecklenburg, North Carolina once mandatory desegregation was ordered. (Orfield, 1986). According to a 1980 study, cities with metropolitan-wide school desegregation plans experienced decreased residential segregation (Report to McKnight Foundation, 2002).

Metropolitan-wide desegregation plans can involve either interdistrict transfers or district consolidation. Interdistrict transfers preserve city and suburban school districts but permit or require student transfers among these districts. For example, Indianapolis and St. Louis implemented interdistrict transfers. District consolidation merges urban and suburban districts into a metropolitan district. Because the division of areas into many separate school districts concentrates poverty and intensifies segregation, consolidation is preferred. Districts are politically manufactured boundaries of the state, and thus can be dissolved or consolidated by the state. Wilmington–New Castle County, Delaware and Louisville–Jefferson County, Kentucky are examples of district consolidation (Wells et al., 2009).

When district boundaries are redrawn within a metropolitan area, several approaches are possible. They can be redrawn into fewer, larger, more racially balanced districts. The suburban district can be merged with those in the inner city, or the entire metropolitan area can be consolidated into a city. Another strategy is to consolidate the entire metropolitan area into one district. For example, the closings of schools in Buffalo combined with school boundary assignments resulted in significant desegregation involving both minority and nonminority students (Levine & Eubanks, 1986; Orfield, 1996, 1997, 2002).

Many school districts in the South comprise both cities and the surrounding suburbs. These metropolitan districts are more racially stable, have higher achievement levels, and receive higher approval ratings among parents than urban districts. They also serve as examples of successful urban-suburban integration (Ryan & Heise, 2002). Even in districts where academic gaps remain, like Jefferson County public schools, progress in raising student achievement has occurred (Beyond Merger, 2002).

Busing is often required to ensure mandatory, metropolitan-wide desegregation efforts. Charlotte-Mecklenburg County was the first school system to desegregate its schools using busing. As a result, the average number of black children in the suburban tracts is closer to that in the city, and both areas continue to attract black and white families, thus providing a sound basis for further residential desegregation (Pearce, 1985).

If districts bus, a choice is required between one-way or two-way—urban or suburban— the latter being more effective. Children in central cities have often faced the burden of desegregating white schools. Instead, urban schools can be improved and communities regentrified and become more attractive to middle-class families (Orfield, 2007).

Unfortunately, opponents of busing, including minority groups, seek not only to reduce its use but also to retreat from desegregation. They claim that it promotes white flight, has not improved the lives or education of students of color, and hinders neighborhood schools, parental involvement, and community building (Orfield, 1997, 1999). Busing is not the only problem. Many students participate in busing for other reasons. State and school district policies "force" some suburban district students to bus for more than half an hour to attend suburban schools versus taking a five-minute ride to their "neighborhood" school in the nearby urban district. In so doing, some suburban communities choose to bus students for segregative purposes. (Shulman, Shulman, & Almonor, 1997; Wells et al., 2009).

Clearly, busing is but an interim solution toward integrated housing and schools. While most school desegregation plans do not include a housing component, one policy option is the exclusion of integrated neighborhoods from busing. Again, in the Charlotte-Mecklenburg school district, busing exemptions for integrated neighborhoods have been responsible for promoting residential desegregation (Boger, 2010; Boger & Orfield, 2005; Smrekar & Goldring, 2009). Similarly, in Louisville–Jefferson County, busing exemptions account for the lowest levels of residential segregation in 50 years. When busing began in Louisville in 1978, 23,000 students were bused for desegregation purposes. By 1992, only 8,200 students were bused (Kentucky Commission on Human Rights, 1993). In brief, the more housing is integrated, the less a school desegregation plan needs to rely on busing (Orfield, 2007; Powell, 2002).

One suggestion to increase support for busing is that the federal government pay for busing rather than local school districts (Stevens, 1990; Wolters, 1996). Other suggestions for improving community support for integration initiatives include making federal funds available to state education departments to develop metropolitan integration plans and providing competitive grants to researchers who engage in applied research on integration. These initiatives presume a federal government committed to integration (Stevens, 1990). However, we seem to fall short on political, legal, and policy levers to achieve mandatory, metropolitan desegregation. An acceptance of colorblindness, belief in choice, and a willingness to embrace accountability measures undergirds the waning value for federally mandated desegregation and the hostility by the courts toward even voluntary race-conscious remedies. For this reason, many are seeking to substitute income-driven solutions in place of race-based ones (Kahlenberg, 1996, 2011, 2012).

Class-Based Desegregation Efforts versus Race-Based Ones

Because persons of color are disproportionately numbered among the poor, proponents of income-based desegregation believe it can achieve racial diversity by restricting preferences to those who have to overcome economic disadvantage (Kahlenberg, 1996, 2007, 2012). Richard D. Kahlenberg, adopting the colorblind position, argues that defining education reform "through the lens of race" is an "increasingly frustrating uphill battle" (Kahlenberg, 2001, p. 4). Rather, he advocates the more "politically palatable" strategy of integrating students by economic status because the factors that drive the quality of a school, such as high expectations, active parental involvement, and motivated peers, "have much more to do with class than with race" (Kahlenberg, 2001, 2012). A fair measure of racial integration will emerge as a by-product, concludes Kahlenberg (2001, 2012).

Boger concurs, claiming that the class and test score student assignment policy employed in Wake County in Raleigh, North Carolina will integrate along racial lines because of the disproportionately high percentage of black African American children who reside in low-income families or who perform poorly on state standardized tests. Boger notes, however, that about 40 percent—and rising—of the country's poor students of color, namely in large urban school districts, will no longer be targeted for integration because they performed well on the states' standardized tests and are ineligible for free or reduced-price lunches (Boger, 2000, 2010; Clotfelter, Ladd, & Vigdor, 2005).

Orfield also points out, that while desegregation by class is a good idea, it does not provide the advantages of desegregation by race. According to Orfield, race functions in a related, but different, way to socioeconomic status. "Middle-class blacks and Latinos face discrimination on racial grounds, poor blacks and Latinos face dual discrimination, and even upper-class blacks tend to live in segregated patterns and experience differential treatment on the basis of race" (Orfield, 2001, p. 1). Orfield argues further that without something very specific like Chicago's Gautreaux housing remedy, addressing class without race will only meet with equal resistance, intensify white flight, and intensify housing segregation. Moreover, socioeconomic remedies are not enforceable by law, leaving persons of color without civil rights remedies (Orfield, 2001). In her analysis of strategies to integrate housing, Florence Wagman Roisman concurs that economic remedies absent racial remedies will fail. So, economic remedies alone will not solve racial problems, and additional remedies supplemented by economic remedies are required (Orfield & Lee, 2007; Roisman, 2001).

Early Integration Is Possible and Needed

Research tells us that racial attitudes are formed early and the sooner the student participates in the interdistrict efforts, the more likely genuine integration will be achieved (Cook, 1984; Crain & Mahard, 1984; Wells et al., 2009). Any delay due in part to community and parental fear only socializes more resistance in the higher grades, especially junior high (Hawley, 1981). The earlier the intervention and exposure to integrated communities, neighborhoods, and schools the better.

Real integration takes time and collective effort as a process rather than an event. Moreover, it is too early to decide that desegregation efforts in our communities and schools have failed or can never be transformed. Initial desegregation effort is strongly influenced by the positions taken by the community. When the community rallies to make whole true integration, schools and classrooms are positively affected. On the other hand, when the community is uncertain or opposes the efforts, schools and classrooms are negatively affected. Hostile contacts and intolerance increase. Time must pass before these effects weaken. Furthermore, the immediate effects of integrative initiatives may differ from the long-term effects. For example, teaching the history of communities of color may at first lead to resistance and hostility; but over time, it can lead to more fruitful results. Last, because it is necessary to change housing integration and foster regional approaches alongside education efforts, time is essential.

IN-SCHOOL INITIATIVES

School sites tend to reflect the community they serve and therefore tend to be monocultural and assimilative. To promote real integration, it is vital to encourage community and school strategies to transform them into more pluralistic cultures. This requires structural, organizational, and procedural changes (Crowfoot & Chesler, 1981). Some scholars such as Schofield (1995a, 1995b) advocate a school-based governance to foster a more positive and localized sense of interracial collaboration by placing teachers, administrators, and staff in control of their own schools.

Leading, Planning, and Monitoring

Administrators who exhibit leadership, spirit, and foresight can more successfully foster true integration (Schofield, 1995a, 1995b). First, they can publicly support integrative efforts and pursue community partnerships to harness resources and positive public sentiment. Second, they can strategically plan any structural or procedural changes needed to affect integration (Crowfoot & Chesler, 1981). This includes active recruitment, hiring, and retention of racially diverse staff who are insistent on high performance and racial equality. It also includes involving teachers, students, and parents in planning (Hawley, 1981, 2007). Third, administrators can support the school personnel involved in integration efforts by providing extra funding, training, and expertise. Even bus drivers and custodians can be trained and supported in implementing integrative strategies and methods. And administrators can monitor and follow up on integrative efforts. This process might review not only student achievement, but race relations and student-staff interactions as well. Principals or staff unwilling to implement integrative strategies need to be removed (Crowfoot & Chesler, 1981).

TRANSFORMING STUDENT ASSESSMENT, PLACEMENT, AND EVALUATION

Vital to the implementation of integration is the transformation of the policies and practices of how school systems assess and place whites and students of color on differential paths with unequal outcomes (Carter, 2009; Gordon, 1999).

Taking Differential Circumstances of Students into Account

To start with, it is so important to explore the agency of students of color in the process of academic assessment and academic placement. John Ogbu's perspective on culture and agency among students of color is the theory of oppositional culture—for example, the argument that black resistance to assimilating to white culture on white terms has entailed rejecting the path of academic achievement or academic self-sabotage (Ainsworth-Darnell & Downey, 1998; Ogbu, 1978, 1991). This theory has been important for contesting social perceptions that differential achievement is related to race. But it has met with criticism both for the explanation and for inadequate attention to the power dynamics.

Prudence Carter questions Ogbu's theory that blacks see academic achievement as "white" and therefore do not wish to "act white" (Carter, 1999, 2009). Her survey and interviews with black and Latino students from high schools in Yonkers, New York reveal that acting white was not related to a set of beliefs about school or academic achievement. Rather, it referred to an attitude of superiority that some students of color associate with whites and students of color who perform well academically (Carter, 1999, 2009; Warikoo & Carter, 2009). According to her research, because many black and Latino students refuse to assimilate to majority modes of speech, dress, and attitudes, teachers label them as uneducable, unruly, and undesirable, thereby removing these students from important educational networks and resources vital to performing well academically (Carter, 1999, 2009; Warikoo & Carter, 2009). Also, because of the pretentious airs these students associate with whiteness and white social circles, many may actively avoid the higher-track classes or niches heavily populated with white students (Carter, 1999, 2009).

The differential teaching practices within affluent and poor districts and schools, and the often unspoken racial judgments that support them, as well as the cultural dynamics at play, indicate the need for conscious attention in pedagogy to counteract inequalities and to work proactively with students of color. Gordon argues that equitable education and social justice are intimately linked and require the development of conscious pedagogical praxis (Gordon, 1999). Whereas equality requires the "same" treatment, equity requires that treatment be "contextual," or appropriate to the needs of the particular social group (Gordon, 1999).

Substantive integration requires that students' differential circumstances be acknowledged, especially those denied access to "human capital" (e.g., physical health, educated parents, financial security, skills, social networks, access to mainstream institutions). Students of color need the institutional and pedagogical resources to meet their physical, mental, and emotional needs. Schools should provide for their intellectual development rather than focusing predominantly on the vocational, compensatory, or remedial that has characterized their curriculum to date (Gordon, 1999).

Need to Eliminate Ability Grouping and Tracking as Educational Policy and Practice

Because rising academic competition, rigid forms of ability grouping, and tracking most often draw negative attention to racial differences, undermine self-esteem, limit academic mobility, contribute to the continuing gaps in achievement between students, and compromise the quality of education of students assigned to lower tracks while doing little for those in higher tracks, integration requires that they be eliminated (Braddock & Slavin, 1993; Brewer & Reese, 1995; Heubert & Hauser, 1999; Oakes, 1992; Schofield & Sager, 1980). According to some, homogeneous ability grouping maximizes learning by challenging low achievers while eliminating boredom among high achievers. Oakes, however, has shown that most increases in learning were not from the homogeneity of the group, but rather from an enriched curriculum that benefits lower achievers if given adequate support (Oakes, 1992). One survey reported that half the schools surveyed have modified their use of ability grouping. Only 15 percent still use traditional tracking methods (Carry, Farris, & Carpenter, 1998).

Some schools have avoided the practice of ability grouping by eliminating low-level classes as a part of a detracking strategy (Oakes & Wells, 1998). It is necessary to encourage in their place competition between goals, rather than between fellow students, and to create heterogeneous groups. Other detracking strategies include cooperative learning, and individualized learning through personalized assignments, learning centers, and peer tutoring (Slavin, 1990). In these schools all students receive enriched curriculum and problem-solving techniques most often used in gifted and talented programs (Levin, 1987). Other schools have adopted nontraditional instructional strategies like eliminating textbooks and instead use field trips and group projects that encourage students' unique access to mathematical, engineering, and scientific concepts (Oakes & Wells, 1998).

If detracking is to succeed, changes in schools are important (Wheelock, 1992). Namely, six markers characterize the learning environments of most schools that are successfully detracked (Ascher, 1992). First, a culture of detracking and a commitment to inclusivity ensures that all students are given the opportunity to learn from the best curriculum and to learn together from each other. Second, community and family engagement that encourages parents to abandon competitive, individualistic ways of viewing education transforms learning into a holistic experience with curricula that challenges all students. Third, state and district support for professional development co-opts teacher commitment to detracking and provides incentives to achieve it (Cooper, 1997). Fourth, decentralized phase-in processes allow schools to detrack at a controlled pace and adjust accordingly. Fifth, rethinking the calculus of what constitutes learning for poor students of color reimagines areas of school life from playground to advanced placement courses. And sixth, support for detracking policies and practices exists at district, state, and federal levels.

Accountability Measures Redux

Sustainable integration means that standards and standardized testing be implemented to equalize educational opportunity and improve achievement, not to punish poor students of color who reside in neighborhoods of concentrated poverty and who attend inferior segregated schools. Instead, testing should be used in combination with other academic indicators of success, such as grades and teacher recommendations, to curtail arbitrary social promotions. Monitoring processes can be used to evaluate the effect of accountability measures on all students in general, and on students of color. State and district funding for resources and training should be available to schools before they are held accountable for systemic inequalities. As school districts vary in the inequalities (e.g., urban, suburban, rural) that shape their student enrollments, the type and kind of resources and training required between and among the districts and schools will vary. So the appropriate resources must be extended to the entire metropolitan community, as discussed later in this chapter.

Promoting Positive Interracial Contact among Students

Research tells us that race relations improve with increased interracial contact. In fact, studies show that racial prejudice can be reduced by bringing students together under conditions of equal status that emphasize common goals and deemphasize individual and intergroup competition (Allport, 1979; Cook, 1979; Patchen, 1982). The process of addressing perspectives different from their own also fosters the development of higher-level analytical skills among students. Opportunities for developing these cognitive capabilities do not necessarily exist in racially isolated schools (Lin & Bransford, 2001; Perry, 2001). And, according to Caldas and Bankston (1997), more diverse schools benefit disadvantaged students if they are structured in such a way that students interact equitably as peers.

Students, however, continue to use racial differences to self-select into distinct groups that limit opportunities for interracial contact. While students should be encouraged to celebrate difference, stigmas attached to differences are also used to stereotype or conversely to retaliate against being stereotyped. For example, students who do not speak English are shunned by middle-class white peers and teachers, while these ostracized students intentionally speak dialects of poor English in opposition to the status quo and to legitimize agency in a counterculture as a response to assimilative policies and educational practices supporting majority norms.

It is not surprising that researchers tend to focus on differences from a majority perspective rather than from a nonmajority one, leaving gaps in our understanding of the complexity of difference. This is troubling as minority communities have now become the majority in large metropolitan districts. Blalock (1986) suggests we positively exploit cultural differences "that are only of minor relevance with the school setting" such as native costumes, religious beliefs, and dietary customs. But differences such as familial norms and modes of communicating, he argues, might become too problematic to encourage because students tend to rely on them more as they select social networks and cliques (Blalock, 1986; Patchen, 1982). These bifurcations of minority differences, however, leave the norms of white students intact.

The social norms, funds of knowledge, and ways of communicating expressed by students of color hold the same worth as their "native costume." They are inextricably linked yet often devalued, distorted, and appropriated by the majority to maintain hegemonic supremacy. One example is the use of Native American tribal names and poorly costumed white males to promote collegiate and professional sports. Another example is the pedagogical tradition of dressing elementary school children in Native American costumes as a normative and harmless practice to explain the first Thanksgiving. It is normative to distort and appropriate the identities of marginalized communities and groups—and profit from it.

Sustained integration requires that communities proactively engage districts and demand that schools institutionalize respect for differences across the curriculum and throughout the pedagogical strategies that develop teacher learning strategies. The value of programs designed to improve race relations through classroom discussions is limited. One study shows no relationship between class discussions and various measures of prejudice among black students (Patchen, 1982; Schofield, 1989a, 2001; Slavin & Madden, 1979). As for white students, some programs have led to improved interracial interactions and attitudes, while others have had only short-term impact or no significant effects (Schofield & Sager, 1977). Rather, resegregation can be avoided by directing students' experiences into productive intergroup relations within cooperative social and educational environments (Schofield, 1989a, 1995a, 1995b). This requires careful instructional planning and productive interracial contact in communities and schools.

Leadership for Integration

Schools are more likely to promote positive interracial contact when school leaders are ideologically committed to it. For example, research shows that black, Hispanic, and white children were more likely to interact in the lunchroom and at recess when the principal valued such contact, than in schools in which the principal was less committed (Wellisch et al., 1976). School leader behavior can affect students' interactions in several ways. First, school leaders can set school policies that foster productive interracial contact. For example, school leaders would resist academic tracking or racially homogeneous classes despite state boards of elementary and secondary education, community, or teachers' requests (Schofield, 1977b, 1995a, 1995b, 2001). School leaders can also promote an instructional climate where teachers actively pursue pedagogical and instructional practices that encourage diverse cultural and social experiences. One study of a large number of schools showed that school leaders' racial views directly influenced those of the teachers (Forehand, 1976). Last, school leaders can foster a humane and disciplined school environment that minimizes interracial problems. One comparative study found that low levels of conflict in one school was the result of a skilled campaign on the part of the school leader working closely with his staff (Schofield, 2001; Schofield & Sagar, 1980). Importantly, when students are aware of and participate in student courts and student counseling solving procedures are in place, their attitudes toward their peers of a different race are more positive (Schofield, 2001; Schofield & Sagar, 1980).

Teacher attitudes, behaviors, and skills also provide a model for students. Positive relations and equal status among teachers are essential. Interracial teaching teams can be formed to model competence and positive racial relations (Crowfoot & Chesler, 1981). But students and teachers of different races sharing the same classroom do not necessarily ensure positive academic outcomes. (Schultz, Buck, & Niesz, 2000). Rather, the optimal environment exists when teachers remain free of stereotyping and refrain from making assumptions or judgments about the competence, probable success, or behavior patterns about both white students and students of color and are more likely to increase positive learning experiences between students (Crowfoot & Chesler, 1981).

Racial fairness among school leaders and teachers has been correlated to white students' racial attitudes and interracial contacts. This pattern is stronger among high school teachers and students than among elementary teachers (Schofield, 1995a, 1995b). And teachers who harbor prejudice against students of color often discourage minority group members from being friends with white students (Gerard, Jackson, & Conolley, 1975). Procedures can be initiated to uncover racism on the part of teachers, administrators, or other staff members and to confront it quickly (Crowfoot & Chesler, 1981). However, it is much easier to avoid negative stereotyping of students of color than it is to operationalize how white students are viewed as the norm by which the "others" are valued or stigmatized (Steele, 2010, 2011).

Since the 1970s many metropolitan school districts have become catchments for poor students and students of color. It vital that districts train school leaders and teachers to understand and value the different funds of knowledge, experiences, and backgrounds of a diverse classroom and then implement this knowledge to create a culture of engaged and active learning (Hatano & Miyaki, 1991; Moll, 1992). However, there is skewed evidence as to whether teachers' professional development improves interracial contacts in the schools. Professional development can communicate the commitment of school leaders to achieving a sustainable culture of integration. This discussion can transform school leaders and teacher behavior and beliefs. Care must be taken, however, not to reinforce negative stereotypes, behaviors, and expectations some teachers use when instructing students of color. Therefore, it is important to compel all teachers to examine white privilege and to "construct an ongoing process of learning from and connecting with people of color" (Sleeter, 1993, pp. 168–169).

In addition, progressive integration requires that school counselors model positive interracial contact and seek to improve the inclusive nature of the school's community. So, stereotyping and stigmatizing results in institutional tracking of students into certain programs is detrimental and hinders teachers', administrators', and parents' ability to take the needs and interests of all students into account in an equitable manner (Crowfoot & Chesler, 1981).

Classrooms as a Balancing Act

Although there is disagreement as to whether classrooms should numerically reflect the makeup of the school or grade, research shows that racially balanced classes are more likely to produce positive interracial attitudes and behaviors. A study of seventh and eighth grade students tracked in racially homogeneous classes revealed the students were more likely to eat lunch in same-race clusters than those who were in untracked, racially heterogeneous classes (Schofield & Sager, 1980). A follow-up study also found that the positive interracial behavior was undone once the detracted students were rigidly retraced the following year (Schofield & Sager, 1980). So detracting can be useful in the development of heterogeneous learning groups within the classroom and in the school environment (Oakes & Wells, 1996).

When students are allowed to select their own seats they typically sit with those of the same race and academic clique. School leaders and teachers can foster increased interracial contact using seating assignments rather than letting students resegregate themselves (Schofield, 1989b, 1995a). Another study has shown that elementary students of different races assigned to sit next to each other were more likely to develop personal relationships in informal settings like lunch rooms and playgrounds (Wellisch et al., 1976); this interaction is further facilitated by reassigning seats, as studies have found this increases the quality of student interactions made during the year (Schofield, 1995a).

Unfortunately, discouraging desegregation within classrooms is not sufficient. Instructional strategies that promote interracial group interactions between students while intensifying superordinate group identities encourage students to participate with out-group members in learning and social experiences that enable them to build trust and learn new forms of knowledge as individuals (Schofield, 1995b, 2001).

Erecting Smaller Schools and Classes

When fiscally possible, smaller schools and classrooms are vital to reducing desegregation and, more importantly, supporting integration. Research on school and class size makes clear that smaller classes minimize the scale of students' experiences and create a more personal sense of community—even among teachers (Bruner & Negrete, 1983). In smaller environments it is more likely that stereotypes are broken down, common values are identified and pursued, friendships are formed, and uncertainties and anxieties with which students and teachers deal are minimized (Hawley, 1981). Studies have also shown that all students, no matter their race, ethnicity, or gender learn better in small classes (Word, 1990).

Appropriate Teaching Strategies

Research also shows that a school culture driven from the bottom up and not the top down by instructional leader teachers immediately affects how students interact and how they perceive group differences in performance levels. In addition to the teaching techniques that enable detracking to succeed, several others factors can foster positive racial relations.

Effective teaching in racially and ethnically diverse classrooms reflects high expectations for every student, is academically rigorous, encourages critical and innovative thinking, uses the funds of knowledge of all students in the instruction, teaches subject matter in depth using a variety of examples for a strong factual base, and explicitly develops students' metacognitive skills (Bransford, Brown, & Cocking, 1999). When poor students and students of color come to school with fewer academic skills, these deficiencies can quickly result in self-sorting. However, when student performance is not made public through posting of grades, evidence suggests that friendship patterns are less likely to form along performance lines. Some suggest that "basing students' evaluation on improvement relative to curriculum goals as well as their absolute improvement" can also help to equalize students' status across racial and ethnic lines (Schofield, 1995a, p. 257). Rather than institutionalizing rewards that support the academic status quo, teachers can diminish competitiveness and reward cooperative interracial endeavors (Crowfoot & Chesler, 1981).

More importantly, evidence also suggests that when teachers use team learning projects that encourage students to cooperate in achieving a common goal, (Blalock, 1986) positive interracial contacts are increased and prejudices decreased (Aronson, 1978; Cohen, 1980; Hallihan & Aage, 1985; Slavin, 1985). Researchers have found that these intergroup projects also improve academic achievement (Johnson, 1979). One study of 51 desegregated high schools showed that programs involving cooperative learning among students of different tracks were most likely to lead to positive race relations (Slavin, 1979). One example is that interracial and interethnic learning groups can work in what is called the "jigsaw technique." Each of the members in the group can be given one part of a paragraph to master and to teach to the other students in the group until the material is mastered by all (Aronson & Bridgeman, 1979). This approach not only eliminates competition and brings about positive interracial contact, but is able to overcome the "interracial interaction disability" that makes true equal status among members of interracial groups difficult to achieve (Cohen, 1975).

Student committees and teams can be initiated to develop joint projects as well (Schofield, 1985b, 1995a, 1998). Teachers can also provide a broad range of classroom tasks so all students have expertise in some area. Students can be involved in the design of these tasks and other activities and can respond to different racial and cultural learning styles including linguistic and verbal/nonverbal preferences. Constant student feedback should also accompany their experiences in the classroom (Crowfoot & Chesler, 1981).

TRANSFORMING CURRICULA AND PROGRAMMING

Including the aforementioned changes, "equal status" among students can be achieved through the transformation of curricula to reflect the knowledge and experiences of all students, including local cultures and their roles in the school and community (Crowfoot & Chesler, 1981; Oakes & Wells, 1998). Although the demographics have changed dramatically in many schools, few school districts have made fundamental changes in organization and programs to address the differing needs of incoming student populations. Many states, districts, and schools continue using curricula that is biased and stereotypes nonwhite students (Ware & Ware, 1996).

According to Slavin and Madden (1979), however, the use of these materials does not necessarily relate to any measurable change in racial attitude or behavior in either blacks or whites. Nonetheless, inclusive racial texts are an integral part of the curricula because they are more accurate and because they dismantle the assumption that majority knowledge is normal. Successful multicultural programs also engage students with little interest in traditional curriculum and allow poor and low-achieving students of color to use their culturally specific knowledge (Oakes & Wells, 1998). Without them, an inclusion of all voices will rarely be accomplished.

It is equally important for curricula to explicitly address both past and present racism in the United States including current discussions of integration, affirmative action, welfare reform, and concentrated poverty. Students can also be encouraged to work within different racial communities themselves (Crowfoot & Chesler, 1981). Ideally, educators can maximize "the capacity of the curriculum to help all groups understand the meaning and impact of racial and ethnic status and to equip them with skills to address inequities" (Jackson, 1995, p. 445).

Creating Inclusive Spaces and Activities

Because dominant groups and their ideologies take over prime locations within schools or on school grounds, particular attention to spatial layouts that are not uniform in quality, convenience, or other aspects is essential. While students often divide into groups according to age—which can foster interracial contact—this is not guaranteed. Recess and lunch periods, patterns of facility use, and conditions of facilities are best monitored by school leaders to maximize interracial contacts (Blalock, 1986).

Another effective way school leaders and teachers can support interracial friendships and cooperative involvement is by promoting extracurricular activities that encourage equitable interracial contact (Patchen, 1982; Patchen & Davidson, 1977). Typically, participation in integrated athletic teams leads to positive intergroup attitudes and reduced prejudice (Braddock, Dawkins, & Wilson, 1995; Wahlberg, 1979). Winning athletic teams can also improve relations between blacks and whites who are not themselves athletes (Schofield, 1977b).

However, studies also suggest that strictly voluntary, unstructured activities lead to spatial segregation and very low levels of racial contact. Interracial contact is more likely to occur when activities are structured and made attractive to a diverse body of students and when adult supervisors are aware of the goal. Schools that consciously attempt to improve representation in activities beyond music and sports encourage students of color to participate and majority groups to be accepting.

For example, Schofield reported that to achieve greater racial balance one school administrator monitored club lists and actively recruited students, or groups of students who were friends, to diminish the fear of being the only participant from a racial group (Schofield, 1977a). The official also encouraged students who had dropped out to rejoin with some of their friends. Attempts were also made to distribute positions of status within school clubs and teams equally between whites and blacks. Similarly, in Minnesota, a recent settlement agreement in a class action discrimination suit brought by Latino/a parents resulted in local school officials acknowledging the need to increase Latino/a students' participation in extracurricular activities.

A productive atmosphere can also be fostered through the creation of special clubs or interracial committees comprised of principals, faculty, staff, and students representing the various racial groups within the school. These committees can adjudicate grievances and consider policies to promote racial harmony (McConahay, 1981). Mediation groups, such as those implemented successfully in schools in New Mexico and Poughkeepsie, are also helpful (Lam, 1989). The groups identify and clarify ethnic assumptions, intervene in ethnocentrism, avoid stereotypes, address the instructional issues, apply pressure for settlement, and ensure implementation of agreements (Coleman & Deutsch, 1995). Last, districts and schools must eliminate school symbols that stereotype, discriminate, or exclude. Instead, student initiatives can be fostered to institute multiracial, multicultural traditions and symbols such as flags, songs, and banners (Crowfoot & Chesler, 1981). These initiatives are driven by parental support.

Increasing Parental Involvement

Interracial parental involvement in shaping school integrative goals is essential to achieving true integration. Researchers have shown that parental stereotyping toward certain groups fosters similar attitudes among children (Patchen, 1982). Parental support of successful integration is crucial. Conversely, positive interactions between minority and majority groups are increased through parental involvement in instruction, school activities, and monitoring integrative efforts on buses, playgrounds, hallways, classrooms, and administrative meetings (Doherty et al., 1981). Parents can also plan in-school and communitywide multiethnic committees (Hawley & Evertson, 1993).

It is vital, however, that careful attention is paid to how parental involvement is solicited, supported, and structured. Low-income parents need added resources to become involved, including assistance with transportation and childcare. It is also essential to include parents of color in the structuring of involvement to avoid replicating dominant majority social knowledge and norms.

WHAT TRUE INTEGRATION REQUIRES OF US AS A LARGER COMMUNITY

Genuine integration of districts and schools from an educational standpoint is impossible without engaging and leveraging the entire community in support of integrative efforts. Education reform and its antecedents are often treated as a uni-linear variable with its own cause and effect by policy makers and by municipal, civic, and school leaders. On the contrary, education reform and its problems is tied to regional issues and community institutions like housing, yet rarely are these connections made explicit in educational research (Muhammad & Collins, 2007). For example, the influences of regional and local housing patterns on school desegregation let alone integration often are left unaddressed. The following sections will shed light on three aspects of this leveraging task: renewing legal strategies, adopting regional strategies that include housing elements, and transforming our public discourse on race and choice.

Legal and Social Strategies

The *Brown v. Board of Education* (1954) decision was the hope that the courts could eradicate segregation, increase desegregation, and foster real integration. The Supreme Court's retreat from desegregation and legitimizing inaction is mirrored now in a number of recent judicial decisions in K-12, higher education, employment discrimination, and voting rights. But rather than allowing the judiciary to turn its back on integration and civil rights, we must ensure its pursuit by renewing our legal strategies in the following ways.

Desegregation Cases and Federal Law

Kahlenberg claims that, from a legal standpoint, *Brown* has run its course and this has been made whole in the Court's recent opinions endorsing class rather than race-based desegregation. He asserts the Supreme Court's ruling, as well as rulings in the First and Fourth Circuits, have mandated that race neutrality is required in K-12 student assignments except where race is used as a remedy to past discrimination (Kahlenberg, 2001). Professors James Liebman and Kevin Brown disagree, provided we adopt new strategies for achieving Brown's unmet educational goals. (Brown, 1996, 2005; Liebman, 1990). As of 1990, almost 700 school districts, or 60 percent of our largest 150 nationwide, had formal desegregation plans, the majority of which were either court-ordered or mandated by a state or federal agency. Most of the court orders were at least 20 years old, and many far older (Armor, 1996). During the past decade, however, courts have been rapidly declaring that school districts have achieved unitary status, in part reversing the Court's mandate requiring states and school districts to eliminate racially segregated schools (Ware, 1999). As of 2000, the federal government monitored desegregation plans in only 440 school districts. (Catalogue of Federal Domestic Assistance, 2002).

In no uncertain terms, recent federal jurisprudence has undermined the positive shift in the racial makeup of districts or schools. Since *Washington v. Davis* (1976) to prove that a school policy or practice violates the 14th Amendment, litigants must demonstrate that the policy was enacted with the specific intent to discriminate against a class of students based on their race, ethnicity, or national origin. This is a difficult standard to meet. Private suits under Title VI can now be brought only for intentional discrimination. This raises the bar on the burden of proof required by litigants to acquire judicial standing.

In response, Liebman proposes a theoretical reorientation of the arguments in favor of desegregation, emphasizing the communal nature of our rights under the Equal Protection Clause. With this legal and social reorientation, argues Liebman, education reform is now considered less as a private right that desegregation dislocates, than as a common good that is fit for governmental and constitutional distribution. Considering the important role that education has always played in our democracy and given that, unlike public employment, the governmental influence (No Child Left Behind and Race to the Top Acts) now comprises a greater portion of public education, the courts should be more responsive to this ethical and legal shift.

> Rather than being portrayed or vilified . . . as the redistribution of resources from "innocent" whites to "unjustly enriched" blacks . . . [an effective remedy] . . . induces . . . empathy by making each person recognize the interests she potentially shares with all other persons. . . . Once advocates give up arguing that desegregation corrects imbalances in the distribution of private rights when it palpably does not, they are free to point out that the rearrangement of private rights that Brown incidentally does effect is relatively inconsequential and clearly worth the politically reconstructive candor. (Liebman, 1990, p. 1463).

Brown also advocates an understanding of education as a public good in his defense of racial preferences in student assignments. Although the Supreme Court subjects all racial classifications to strict scrutiny, Brown argues that desegregation efforts should be viewed in light of their socializing function, their role in inculcating "fundamental values necessary to the transmission of our democratic society." Because "education must both foster individual self-determination, but at the same time attempt to constrain the choices individuals make in order to allow others the same ability for self-determination" and because desegregation clearly furthers the values of tolerance of racial and ethnic diversity, it should survive strict scrutiny analysis when examined from a value-inculcating perspective (Brown, 1996).

While districts and schools have adopted Liebman and Brown's strategies, the courts on, the other hand, have not adopted their transformative approaches. Charles Boger (2000) also describes a way to circumvent a growing reliance on strict scrutiny by the courts by using socioeconomic status and academic skills in place of race when assigning students. Neither classification is "inherently suspect" and their use might result in some racial desegregation, he argues. Orfield and others, however, caution against relying solely on this approach.

FEDERAL SUITS

Federal suits can also be brought to secure limited English proficiency (LEP) rights (*Lau v. Nicholls*, 1974; *Idaho Migrant Council v. Board of Education*, 1981; *Gomez v. Illinois State Board of Education*, 1987; *U.S. v. Texas*, 1982; *Casteneda v. Pickard*, 1981). Unfortunately, this requirement now makes challenging high-stakes testing futile (Heubert & Hauser, 1999). However, according to Kevin G. Welner, the new standards and accountability legislation may actually expand potential liability to all school districts and even to states. While past challenges focused on the fairness of exit exams (as a violation of substantive due process) and sought a diploma as a remedy, future challenges might embrace the standards movement and contend that the plaintiffs' schooling itself is inequitable. Welner further argues that federal claims could support states' own adopted standards, and their clear obligation to provide all students with the adequate opportunity to learn the curriculum and be assessed by the state (Welner, 2001, 2006).

Similar challenges might be brought under the Bush administration's No Child Left Behind Act (Public Law 107–110, 2002). As a group of Harlem parents have claimed, under this act, school board, district, and state officials are obliged to provide resources to parents to transfer their children from low-performing schools or to provide "intervention" services for students currently in them (Campanile, 2002).

STATE LAW

Interestingly, opportunities exist for building true integration by challenging discriminatory policies or practices under state law. All state constitutions guarantee protections similar to those of the 14th Amendment. Importantly, state courts have the authority to interpret equal protections more broadly than the protections under the federal constitution. For example, the California Supreme Court has held that the state equal protection clauses allow actions based on racial disparate impact (*Jackson v. Pasadena*, 1963). In addition, all state constitutions recognize education as a function of the state. Some constitutions explicitly prohibit discrimination or the implementation of educational policies with discriminatory effects (*McDuffy v. School of Education,* 1989) and others guarantee a certain minimum level of education to all students. For example, California's constitution requires the state to provide a "thorough and efficient education."

State litigation has largely challenged the *equity* or a*dequacy* of the state's public school funding mechanisms. Equity suits assert that the constitution (through the 14th Amendment and/or the education clause) guarantees equality in school funding across districts. Adequacy suits assert that these provisions require the state to provide some minimum quality of education to all students and that this presumes a basic level of funding. As of late, courts in 43 states had considered the constitutionality of their public school funding systems (Durham, 2001). Twenty-six found them constitutional; (Durham, 2001) five states held that education is a right of all students and that inequitable education funding violates this right (Durham, 2001); six states held that, while education is a right, states need only to provide a minimally adequate level of funding, not an equally funded education (Durham, 2001).

Not surprising, remedies beyond funding formulas under adequacy suits vary greatly. In *McDuffy v. Secretary of Education* (1993), for example, the Massachusetts court defined educational adequacy. And in *Rose v. Council for Better Education* (1989), the court invalidated the entire public school system and gave sole responsibility for the implementation of a detailed instructional plan that included accountability to the state.

In *Sheff v. O'Neil* (1996), however, the state court required that the state remedy the extreme racial and ethnic isolation in the public schools that had resulted from voluntary interdistrict desegregation plans in New Haven, Connecticut. Affirmative responsibility was placed by the courts on the legislature to remedy segregation, regardless of whether it was *de jure* or *de facto*. A similar adequacy suit was also settled in Minnesota after Minneapolis' decade-long open enrollment plan resulted in de facto racial and socioeconomic segregation between the city and its surrounding suburbs (Ryan & Heise, 2002). As multiple remedies were sought, including requiring the state to adopt integrative housing policies, the settlement only required eight suburban districts collectively to make 500 seats available for low-income city students each year for four years. While limited in their ability to produce effective remedies, these types of adequacy suits still hold the most promise.

PURSUING REGIONALISM: REGIONAL GOVERNMENT AND REGIONAL STRATEGIES

While litigation provides relief from discriminatory policies, it rarely requires the systemic changes necessary to foster sustainable integration (Powell, 2010). Regionalism and legislative strategies can provide the greater potential for sustainable change. And while strategies of reinvestment in inner cities are important, if leaders seek to limit polarization, stabilize urban neighborhoods, and equalize educational opportunity in metropolitan areas, a regional approach to social and educational policy decisions must be undertaken (Orfield, 1997).

Regionalism offers municipal and civic policy makers a way to rethink metropolitan areas as centers of common good for all residents. Rather than seeing each part of the region as independent and responsible for its own governance, regionalism approaches the entire region as inseparable—an organic system of interdependent parts. In short, the whole prospers only when all parts function to support one another. Conversely, whenever one region faces dysfunction, the entire system is compromised and incapable of functioning.

Today, cities are often indistinguishable from the total metropolitan area. So the means to reverse patterns of racial and economic segregation means civic, municipal, and educational leaders must create effective, visionary metropolitan governments; or, if the metro area is too large, ensure that local governments are pursuing common policies that foster integration. Minnesota legislator Myron Orfield refers to this process of pursuing regionalism as "metropolitics" (Orfield, 1997).

Effective regional governments require the building of enduring political coalitions (Orfield, 1997). These coalitions are best formed between the urban core and the inner-ring suburbs. One example comes from business leaders like those in Chicago (who formed CHICAGO METROPOLIS 2020), who frame regionalism as the most effective strategy for maintaining economic viability. This argument persuades municipal and business elites, and those who have adopted a colorblind position, that the most cost-effective course is to pursue regional strategies to integrate.

A regionalist approach traditionally supports several policies, many of which deal with achieving equity in housing, including: (Rusk, 1993): (1) land use reform that sterns urban sprawl and provides adequate funding to older areas saddled with old infrastructures; (2) "fair share" housing policies that encourage, or better yet, require the construction and maintenance of low-income and moderate-income housing in all jurisdictions; (3) housing assistance policies to disperse low-income families to small-unit, scattered-site housing projects and to rent-subsidized private rental housing throughout a diversified metro housing market; (4) fair employment and fair housing policies that ensure full access by persons of color to the job and housing markets; (5) tax-sharing arrangements that will offset tax base disparities between the central city and its suburbs; (6) welfare reform that goes beyond the recent federal measures by focusing on job readiness and creation in core poverty neighborhoods as well as tackling transportation, child care, and health care; and (7) until affordable housing is available, lawsuits calling for mandatory metropolitan-wide desegregation and adequate education in the inner-ring schools.

Federal and state governments continue to play important roles in fostering reform through regional reform strategies (Rusk, 1993). The federal government can provide incentives to promote regionalism by providing municipal governments with bonuses in grants-in-aid formulas. State governments can facilitate city-county consolidation, require all local governments to have "fair share" affordable housing laws, utilize state aid as a revenue-equalizing mechanism, and require a minimum guaranteed income or minimum living wage.

Regionalism, unfortunately, often meets resistance from communities of color because it is perceived as having the ability to fragment their communities. As West (1993) argues, the dispersion of black professionals and entrepreneurs into predominantly white communities does little to change the culture and values of the white opportunity structure. Instead, the argument goes, deconcentration of persons of color results in both their assimilation into more affluent areas and the dilution of their culture and political power (Gunier, 1995) in areas where white flight and poverty persist.

Orfield (1997) argues that proponents of regionalism must carefully communicate to poor communities of color the hopelessness of the present course of action and the patterns of polarization it produces. Metropolitan efforts should not be alternatives to existing programs or competition for resources and power. Instead, they should be complementary efforts that reduce problems in the center cities to a manageable size and provide more resources for development through programs like tax revenue sharing. Furthermore, communities of color can be convinced that regional fair housing opportunities and metropolitan-wide desegregation efforts do not force their communities to disperse but give each person a *real* choice to remain or seek opportunity elsewhere. The difficulty of developing and sustaining a regional approach cannot be underestimated. Importantly, it must be undertaken or any attempts at truly integrating schools will fail and conditions throughout a metropolitan area worsen.

COMMUNITY COALITIONS

For regional strategies to work, community leaders must coordinate efforts among those fostering integration and those dealing with transportation, housing, tax policy, metropolitan planning, and antidiscrimination policies. They can also build relationships with influential foundations, institutes, corporations, and government agencies to increase support and resources of local programs. Interracial grassroots organizations can exert pressure on administrators to affect innovative changes and punish entropy in local schools. Active information groups or blue-ribbon committees can educate the public about sustainable integration and deter incomplete knowledge from resting in the hands of apathetic educators. Clergy can mobilize to support racial equality and interracial contact within their congregations and throughout the community. Local universities and businesses associations can adopt particular schools and provide a link to equal educational and employment opportunities. And collectively community members can work to neutralize those groups who resist (de)segregation much less integration (Crowfoot & Chesler, 1981; Green, 2008).

TRANSFORMING PUBLIC DISCOURSE ON RACE

The importance of eradicating "colorblindness" from our public discourse cannot be overemphasized. Oscar H. Gandy, Jr., makes clear in *Communication and Race: A Structural Perspective,* "There is little doubt that it is through communication that the structural influence of racism is maintained and power distributed" (1998, p. 3). It is necessary, therefore, for all citizens to challenge the narrative that racism no longer exists and that while battles have been or are being won (e.g., the "war on drugs," welfare reform, equal opportunity in employment, segregated housing and education), the war is not over.

One of the first steps in achieving this transformation of public discourse is to recognize race as a social construct (Goodman, Moses, & Jones, 2012). Research has proven that race has little scientific reality; it has a powerful social reality as it orders and affects our daily lived experiences. Early in its history white America designated in law, policy, and practice who is entitled to privilege, establishing systems of inequality with educational disparities as one example (Goodman et al., 2012).

The second step we must take in achieving this transformation of public discourse is to expose the institutional, structural, and systemic nature of racism. Laws and institutions need not be explicitly racist to disempower communities of color; they need only to perpetuate unequal historical conditions (Ford, 1995). In the context of education, while de jure segregation has disappeared, de facto (de)segregation and resegregation persist, fueled by residential segregation. So, while neutral on its face, the entire education system functions to maintain a culture of subordination for poor and communities of color. Unfortunately, this type of racism often goes unacknowledged in our public discourse, allowing whites to retain their unfettered access to resources and opportunities (Ford, 1995). For this reason municipal and civic leaders must transform the discourse and acknowledge publicly that institutional, structural, and systemic racism affects us all.

While this transformation is incremental, we have already witnessed elements of it. Racial profiling, for example, was not part of our national discourse until a massive public education campaign and coalition-building effort, undertaken largely by the ACLU, managed to shift legislatures into high gear over the past several years. Today, almost half of the states are considering data collection legislation in response to this anti-integration dilemma. We have also seen a shift in discourse surrounding welfare reform. During the Clinton administration, welfare reform in many states shifted away from federal entitlements to state-driven, work-first, time-limited programs with severe sanctions for noncompliant users. Since this change, we have seen a counterdiscourse emerge stressing the long-term goal of "poverty reduction" rather than the short-term goal of welfare roll reduction. Concomitantly, our inability to embrace genuine integration, as both policy and practice in our educational reform efforts, suggests we have not yet begun a transformation of public discourse when it comes to education.

CHOICE ENVISIONED AS A SOCIAL GOOD

Transforming school choice discourse requires policy wonks, education, and community leaders to view education as a social good, rather than a private commodity. As argued earlier, education is the site of the constitution of the self and the basis for the creation of a more equitable multiracial and multiethnic democracy. Because of the collective persistence of segregation and concentrated poverty, effective remedies cannot be furnished by purely individualistic solutions, such as letting students choose their schools one by one. The rights of our children to a truly integrated education cannot be fully achieved in isolation from what happens to other children. Rather, we need a coordinated systemic action that safeguards against white supremacy and forces choices that foster segregation (Gerwitz, 1986). This requires talking about how racism undermines real choice. When students and parents from communities of color meaningfully participate in the creation of school and educational goals and practices, all students and parents have a different set of choices (Gerwitz, 1986).

If we transform our discourse about choice, it may result in more educational decision making on the part of individuals. Again, while this has yet to happen, when it comes to integration in education, we have witnessed glimpses of it in other areas. In fact, choice discourse can even be couched in economic terms. The viability of the entire community, whether metropolitan or global, requires an educated citizenry, not a perpetual underclass. It is in our own self-interest, if you will, to choose what is good for the whole, rather than just for our individual selves.

CONCLUSION

The variety of initiatives required to build genuine integration in our communities and schools must encourage us. Rather, we must undertake a commitment to educate the public as to the urgency of this social good. And with the knowledge that segregation harms our children, as well as our democracy, we need to realize that we have not effectively (de)segregated our communities let alone our schools. So we can combat the colorblind position and the discourse of school choice and accountability measures by advocating a transformation of our educational system into a multiracial and multiethnic one. To achieve this transformation, however, we must first interrogate the discourse of individualism and see the humanistic connections between who we are and where we live and what we all want for our communities, our children, and our nation. That is, we must integrate our genuine lives with policies and practices of common good for all— and not just for the few. Only then will we begin to integrate our schools.

REFERENCES

Ainsworth-Darnell, J., & Downey, D. (1998). Assessing the oppositional culture explanation for racial/ethnic differences in school performance. *Sociological Review, 63,* 500–536.

Allport, G. W. (1979). *The nature of the prejudice.* New York: Perseus Books Publishing.

Armor, D. J. (1996, April 16). Testimony to the House of Representatives Committee on the Judiciary, Subcommittee on the Constitution. U.S. House of Representatives, Washington, DC.

Aronson, E. B. (1978). *The jigsaw classroom.* Oxford: UK: Sage Publishers.

Aronson, E. B. (1997). *The jigsaw classroom: Building cooperation in the classroom.* New York: NY: Longman Publishers.

Aronson, G. W., & Bridgeman, D. (1979). Jigsaw groups and the desegregated classroom: In pursuit of common goals, personality and social. *Psychology Bulletin, 5,* 438–446.

Ascher, C. (1992). *Successful detracking in middle and senior high schools.* New York: ERIC Clearinghouse on Urban Education, ED351426.

Bankston, C. L., & Caldas, S. J. (1996). Majority African American schools and social injustice: The influence of de facto segregation on academic achievement. *Social Forces, 72,* 535–555.

Beyond Merger. (2002). A competitive vision for the regional city of Louisville. www.brookings.edu/research/reports/2002/07/louisville.

Blalock, H. M. (1986). A model for racial contact in school. In J. Prager, D. Longshore, & M. Seeman (Eds.), *School desegregation research: New directions in situational analysis.* New York: Plenum Publishers.

Boger, J. C. (2000). Willful colorblindness: The new racial piety and the resegregation of public schools. *North Carolina Law Review, 78,* 1700–1720.

Boger, J. C. (2010, February). Common schooling in the 21st century: What future for American education. 20th Festival of Legal Learning, University of North Carolina Law School, Chapel Hill, NC.

Boger J. C., & Orfield, G. (Eds.). (2005). *School resegregation: Must the south turn back.* Chapel Hill, NC: University of North Carolina Press.

Braddock, J. H., Dawkins, M. P., & Wilson, G. (1995). Intercultural contact and race relations among youth. In A. W. Hawley & A. W. Jackson (Eds.), *Toward a common destiny: Improving race relations in America.* San Francisco, CA: Jossey-Bass Publishers.

Braddock, J. H., & Slavin, R. E. (1993). Why ability grouping must end: Achieving excellence and equity in American education. *Journal of Intergroup Relations, 20*(10), 51–64.

Bransford, J. D., Brown, A. L., & Cocking, R. R. (1999). *How people learn: Brain, mind, and experience, and school.* National Research Council, Washington, DC: National Academy Press.

Brewer, D. J., & Rees, D. I. (1995, November). Detracking America's schools: The reform without costs? *Phi Delta Kappan, 77*(3), 210–15.

Brown, K. (1996). Implications of the equal protection clause for the mandatory integration of public school students. *Connecticut Law Review, 29,* 999–1025.

Brown, K. (2005). *Race, law and education in the post-desegregation era.* Chapel Hill: North Carolina Academic Press.

Brown v. Board of Education of Topeka, Kansas (No II) 349 U.S. 294, 301 (1955).

Bruner, J. E., & Negrete, E. (1983). Analysis of teacher wage incentive programs for promoting staff stability in large urban school district. *The Urban Review, 15*(3), 139–149.

Burnett, G. (1995). Alternative to ability grouping: still unanswered questions, ERIC Clearinghouse on Urban Education, ERIC Clearinghouse on Urban Education, ED255591.

Caldas, J., & Bankston, C. L. (1997). Effect of school population on socioeconomic status on the individual. *Academic Journal of Educational Research, 90,* 225–269.

Campanile, C. (2002). Parents threaten suit over Harlem's failing Schools, *New York Post,* July 16, p. 12.

Carter, P. (1999). Low income black and Latino youths' mobility orientation: Aspirations, culture and resistance to "acting white." Unpublished manuscript, on file at Institute on Race and Poverty.

Carter, P. (2009, Summer). Equity and empathy: Toward racial and educational achievement in the Obama era. *Harvard Educational Review, 79*(2), 287–297.

Carry, N., Farris, E., & Carpenter, J. (1998). *Curricular differentiation in public high schools.* Washington, DC: Office of Educational Research and Improvement, U.S. Department of Education.

Casteneda v. Pickard, 648 D 2d. 989 (5th Cir. 1981).

Catalog of Federal Domestic Assistance, Desegregation of Public Education, http://aspe.os.dhhs.gov/efda/p16100. htm.

Clotfelter, C. T., Ladd, H. P., & Vigdor, J. L. (2005). Classroom level segregation and resegregation in North Carolina. In J. C. Boger & G. Orfield (Eds.), *School resegregation: Must the South turn back* (pp. 70–86). Chapel Hill, NC: University of North Carolina Press.

Cohen, E. D. (1975). The effects of desegregation on race relations. *Law and Contemporary Problems, 39,* 271–299.

Cohen, E. G. (1980). Design and redesign of the desegregation school: Power and conflict. In J. R. Stephens & J. R. Feagin (Eds.), *School desegregation: Past, present and future* (pp. 251–258). New York, NY: Plenum Press.

Coleman, P. T., & Deutch, M. (1995). In W. D. Hawley & A. W. Jackson (Eds.), *Toward A common destiny: Improving race and ethnic relations in America* (pp. 371–396). San Francisco, CA: Jossey-Bass.

Cook, S. W. (1979). Social science and school desegregation: Did we mislead the Supreme Court? *Personality and Social Psychology Bulletin, 5,* 410–437.

Cook, T. D. (1984). What have black children gained academically for school integration? Examination of the Meta-Analytic Evidence, ERIC Clearinghouse on Urban Education, ED241671.

Cooper, R. (1997). Report Number 12: Detracking in a racially mixed urban high school. Baltimore, MD and Washington, DC: Center for Research on the Education of Students Placed at Risk, Johns Hopkins and Howard University.

Crain, R. L., & Mahard, R. E. (1984). Research on minority achievement in desegregation schools. In Christine H. Rossell & Willis D. Hawley (Eds.), *The consequences of school desegregation* (pp. 100–125). Philadelphia, PA: Temple University Press.

Crowfoot, T., & Chesler. M. (1981). Implementing "attractive ideas": Problems and perspectives in effective school desegregation. In W. D. Hawley (Ed.), *Effective school desegregation: Equity, quality, and feasibility* (pp. 265–295). Beverly Hills, CA: Sage Publications.

Doherty. W., Caldwell, J., Russo, N. A., Mandell, V., & Longshore, D. (1981). Human relations study: Investigations of effective human relations strategies, Volume 2, Santa Monica, CA: System Development Corporation.

Durham, C. M. (2001). The judicial branch in state government: Parables of law, politics and power. *New York University Law Review, 76,* 1500–1625.

Ford, R. T. (1995). The boundaries of race and political geography in legal analysis, *Harvard Law Review, 107*(8), 1844–1921.

Forehand, G. A. (1976). *Conditions and processes of effective school desegregation.* Princeton, NJ: Educational Testing Service.

Frankenberg, E. (2005). The impact of school segregation on residential housing patterns: Mobile, Alabama and Charlotte, North Carolina. In J. C. Boger & G. Orfield (Eds.), *School resegregation: Must the South turn back.* Chapel Hill, NC: Carolina Academic Press. The Civil Rights Project, Cambridge, MA: Harvard University.

Frankenberg, E., & Chungmei, L. (2002). *Race in American public schools: Rapidly resegregating school districts.* UCLA: The Civil Rights Project/Proyecto Derechos Civiles. Retrieved from: http://escholarship.org/uc/item/1tz5k622

Gandy, O. H. (1998). *Communication and race: A structural perspective.* London: Arnold Publishers.

Gerard, H., Jackson, H. D., & Conolley, E. (1975). Social contact in the desegregated classroom. In H. Gerard & N. Miller (Eds.), *School desegregation: A long term study.* New York: Plenum Publishing.

Gerwitz, P. (1986). Choice in transition: Desegregation and the corrective ideal. *Columbia Law Review, 86,* 700–751.

Gomez v. Illinois State Board of Education, 811 D 2d. 1030 (7th Cir. 1987).

Goodman, A. H., Moses, Y. T., & Jones, J. L. (2012). *Race: Are we so different?* Malden, MA: Wiley-Blackwell Publishers.

Gordon, E. (1999). *Education and justice: A view from the back of the bus.* New York: Teachers College Press.

Green, P. (2008). The politics of (de)segregation. In B. Cooper, J. Cibulka, & L. Fusarelli (Eds.), *Handbook of education politics and policy.* New York: Routledge Publishers.

Guinier, L. (1995). More democracy. *University of Chicago Legal Forum, 1*(6), 1–15.

Guinier, L., & Torres, G. (2009). *The miner's canary: Enlisting race, resisting power, transforming democracy.* Cambridge, MA: Harvard University Press.

Hallihan, M. T., & Aage, S. (1985). Student diversity and instructional grouping. *Sociology of Education and Socialization, 5,* 59–81.

Hatano, G., & Miyaki, P. (1991). Commentaries: What does a cultural approach offer to research on learning? *Learning and Instruction, 1,* 237–281.

Hawley, W. D. (1981). *Effective school desegregation, equity, quality and feasibility.* Sage Focused Additions 42, Beverly Hills, CA: Sage Publications.

Hawley, W. D. (2007). From equal educational opportunity to diversity advantaged learning. *Journal of Negro Education, 76*(3), 250–262.

Hawley, W. D., & Evertson, C. M. (1993). Re-visioning the education of teachers. ERIC Clearinghouse on Urban Education, ED362495.

Heubert, J. P., & Hauser, R. M. (1999). *High stakes testing for tracking, promotion and graduation.* National Research Council, Washington, DC: National Academy Press.

Idaho Migrant Council v. Board of Education, 647 F 2d. 69 (9th Cir. 1981).

Institute on Race and Poverty, Executive summary of report to the McKnight Foundation, Examining the relationship between housing, education and persistent segregation, 20, June 1997. Minneapolis, MN: Author.

Institute on Race and Poverty, Draft for KRC Research—Data on Desegregation, Internal document (2002).

Jackson v. Pasadena City School District, 382 P. 2d 878)Cal 1963).

Jackson, A.W. (1995). Toward a common destiny: An agenda for future research. In W. D. Hawley and A. W. Jackson (Eds.), *Toward a common destiny: Improving race and ethnic relations in America* (pp. 440–455). San Francisco, CA: Jossey-Bass.

Johnson, D. W. (1979). Effects of cooperative, competitive and individualistic goals structures on achievement: A meta-analysis. *Psychological Bulletin, 89*(1), 47–62.

Kahlenberg, R. D. (1996). *The remedy: Class, race and affirmative action.* New York: Basic Books.

Kahlenberg, R. D. (2001, September/October). *Socioeconomic school integration, poverty and race.* Washington, DC: Research Action Council.

Kahlenberg, R. D. (2007). *Rescuing Brown v. Board of Education: Profiles of twelve school districts pursuing socioeconomic school integration.* New York: Century Foundation Press.

Kahlenberg, R. D. (2011). Socioeconomic school integration: Preliminary lessons from more than 80 districts. In Erica Frankenberg & Edward Debray (Eds.), *Integrating schools in a changing society* (pp. 167–187). Chapel Hill, NC: University of North Carolina Press.

Kahlenberg, R. D. (2012). *The future of school integration: Socioeconomic diversity as an education reform strategy.* New York, NY: The Century Foundation Press.

Kentucky Commission on Human Rights, Housing Segregation Lowest in Fifty Years (1993). Lexington, KY: Author.

Kurleander, M., & Yun, J. (2001). Is diversity a compelling educational interest? Evidence from Louisville. In Gary Orfield (Ed.), *Diversity challenged: Evidence on the impact of affirmative action* (pp. 111–142). Cambridge, MA: Harvard University.

Lam, J. A. (1989). The impact of conflict resolution programs on schools: A review and synthesis of the evidence. ERIC Clearinghouse on Urban Education, ED368535.

Lau v. Nicholls, 94 S. Ct. 786 (U.S. Cal. 1974).

Levine, D. U., & Eubanks, E. E. (1986, Spring). The promise and limits of regional desegregation plans for central city school districts, *Metropolitan Education, 1,* 36–51.

Levine, H. M. (1987). New schools for the disadvantaged. *Teacher Educational Quarterly, 13*(4), 60–83.

Liebman, J. S. (1990). Implementing *Brown* in the nineties: Reconstruction, liberal recollection, and litigatively enforced legislative reform. *Virginia Law Review, 76,* 285–375.

Lin, X., & Bransford, J. D. (2001). People knowledge: A missing ingredient in many of our educational designs. Unpublished manuscript, Vanderbilt University, Vanderbilt, TN.

McConahay, J. (1981). Reducing racial prejudice in desegregated school. In W. D. Hawley (Ed.), *Effective school desegregation: Equity, quality and feasibility* (pp. 311–356). Beverly Hills, CA: Sage Publications.

McDuffy v. Secretary of Education. 415 Mass 545 (1933).

McKenzie, E. (2000). The politics of school desegregation in Oak Park Illinois, Great Cities Institute Working Paper, University of Illinois, Chicago, IL.

Meredith v. Jefferson County Board of Education, 551 U.S. 05–915 (2007).

Moll. L. C. (1992). Funds of knowledge for teaching: Using a qualitative approach to connect homes and classroom, *Theory into Practice, 31*(1), 132–142.

Moran, P. W. (2005). *Race, law and the desegregation of public schools.* New York: LFB Scholarly Publishing.

Muhammad, D., & Collins, C. (2007, May/June). Race, wealth and the commons. *Poverty & Race, 16*(3), 1–15.

Oakes, J. (1992). Can tracking research inform practice?: Technical, normative and political considerations. *Educational Researcher, 4,* 12–21.

Oakes, J. W., & Wells, A. S. (1996). Beyond the technicalities of school reform: Policy lessons from detracking schools. Los Angeles, CA: Research for Democratic School Communities, University of California, Los Angeles Graduate School of Education and Information Studies.

Oakes, J., & Wells, A. S. (1998). Detracking for high student achievement. *Educational Leadership, 55,* 12–21.

Ogbu, J. (1978). *Minority education and caste. The American system in cross-cultural perspective.* New York: Academic Press.

Ogbu, J. (1991). Low performance as an adaptation: The case of blacks in Stockton, California. In Mark Gibson and John Ogbu (Eds.), *Minority status and schooling: A comparative study of immigrant and involuntary minorities.* New York: Garland Publishing.

Orfield, G. (1986). Status of school desegregation, 1968–1986. Council of Urban Boards of Education. Civil Rights Project. Cambridge, MA: Harvard University.

Orfield, G. (1996). Metropolitan school desegregation: Impacts on metropolitan society. *Minnesota Law Review, 80,* 825–845.

Orfield, G. (2001, September/October). Response to Richard d. Kahlenberg, socioeconomic school integration, Poverty and Race Research Action Council.

Orfield, G., & Lee, C. (2007). *Historic reversals, accelerating resegregation, and the need for new integration strategies.* Los Angeles: University of California, The Civil Rights Project/ Proyecto Derechos Civiles.

Orfield, G, & Monfort, F. (1988). *Racial change desegregation in large school districts: trends through the 1986–87 school year.* Harvard Civil Rights Project. Cambridge, MA: Harvard University Press.

Orfield, G., & Thronson, D. (1993). Dismantling desegregation: Uncertain gains, unexpected costs. *Emory Law Journal, 42,* 759–782.

Orfield, G., & Yun, J. T. (1999). *Resegregation in American schools.* Civil Rights Project, Harvard University, Cambridge, MA.

Orfield, M. (1997). *Metropolitics: A regional agenda for community and stability.* Washington, DC: Brookings Institution Press.

Orfield, M. (1999). Metropolitics: A regional agenda for community and stability. *Forum for Social Economics, 28*(2), 33–49.

Orfield, M. (2002). *Metropolitics: A regional agenda for community and stability.* Washington, DC: Brookings Institution Press.

Parents Involved in Community Schools v. Seattle School District No 1, 551 U.S. 05–908 (2007).

Patchen, M. (1982). *Black-white contact in schools: Its social and academic affects.* West Lafayette, IN: Purdue University.

Patchen, M., & Davidson, J. D. (1977). Determinants of students' interracial behavior and opinion change. *Sociology of Education, 501,* 55–75.

Pearce, D. (1985). *Metropolitan desegregation.* New York: Plenum Publishing.

Perry, P. (2001, February). White means never having to say you are ethnic: White youth and the construction of cultural identities. *Journal of Contemporary Ethnography, 30*(1), 56–91.

Powell, J. A. (1996, September/October). Is racial integration essential to achieving quality education for low-income minority students, in the short term? *Poverty and Race, 5,* 5.

Powell, J. A. (2002, August). Racism and metropolitan dynamics: The civil rights challenge of the 21st century. A briefing paper prepared the Ford Foundation. Institute on Race and Poverty, Research Education and Advocacy. Minneapolis, MN: University of Minnesota.

Powell, J. A. (2007). Expanding membership through inclusive education. In Erica Frankenberg & Gary Orfield (Eds.), *Lessons in integration: Realizing the promise of racial diversity in American schools.* (pp. 265–290). Charlottesville, VA: The University of Virginia Press.

Powell, J. A. (2009). Post racialism or targeted universalism? *University of Denver Law Review,* 785–830.

Powell, J. A. (2010). Regionalism and race. Kirwan Institute for the Study of Race and Ethnicity, The 20th Anniversary Issue, 17, 1.

Powell, J. A. (2011, June). Systems thinking, evaluation and racial justice. Kirwan Institute for the Study of Race. Minneapolis, MN: University of Minnesota Press, 1–55.

Public Law 107–110, 2002.

Reardon, S. F., Yun, J. T., & Kurleander, M. (2006). Implications of income-based school assignment policies for racial school segregation. *Educational Evaluation and Policy Analysis, 28*(1), 49–75.

Roisman, F. W. (2001). Opening the suburbs to racial integration: lessons for the 21st century. *New England Law Review, 65,* 50–85.

Rose v. Council for a Better Education, 790 S.W. 2d. 186 (Ky. 1989).

Rusk, D. (1993). *Cities without suburbs.* Baltimore, MD: Johns Hopkins University Press.

Ryan J. E., & Heise, M. (2002). The political economy of school choice. *Yale Law Review,* 2043–2067.

Schofield, J. W. (1977). *Social process and peer relations in a "nearly integrated" middle school.* Washington, DC: National Institute of Education.

Schofield, J. W. (1989a). *Review of research on school desegregation's impact on elementary and secondary school students.* ERIC Clearinghouse on Urban Education ED319825.

Schofield, J. W. (1989b). *Black and white in school: Trust, tension or tolerance?* New York: Teachers College Press.

Schofield, J. W. (1995a). Improving intergroup relations among students. In J. A. Banks (Ed.), *Handbook of research on multicultural education* (pp. 635–646). San Francisco, CA: Jossey-Bass.

Schofield, J. W. (1995b). Promoting positive intergroup relations in school settings. In W. D. Hawley and A. W. Jackson (Ed.), *Toward a common destiny: Improving race and ethnic relations in America* (pp. 257–290). San Francisco, CA: Jossey-Bass.

Schofield, J. W. (2001). Maximizing the benefits of student diversity: Lessons from school desegregation research. In G. Orfield (Ed.), *Diversity challenged: Evidence on the impact of affirmative action* (pp. 99–110). Cambridge, MA: Harvard Educational Review.

Schofield, J. W., & Sager, H. A. (1977). Peer interaction patterns in an integrated middle school. *Sociometry, 402,* 130–138.

Schofield, J. W., & Sager, H. A. (1980). Classroom interaction patterns among blacks and white boys and girls. *Journal of Educational Psychology, 75*(5), 722–732.

Schultz, K. P., Buck, P., & Niesz, T. (2000). Democratizing conversations, racialized talk in a post-desegregated middle school. *American Educational Research Journal, 37*(1), 33–65.

Sheff, v. O'Neil, 609 A 2d. 1072, 1076 (1996).

Shulman D. R., Shulman, J. G., & Almonor. J. M. (1997, August 2). NAACP still standing firm against school segregation. *Star Tribune,* Saturday, A19.

Slavin, R. E. (1979). Effects of biracial learning teams on cross-racial friendships. *Journal of Educational Psychology, 713,* 381–387.

Slavin, R. E. (1985). Using student team learning. Johns Hopkins Team Learning Project. Baltimore, MD: Johns Hopkins University.

Slavin, R. E. (1990). Achievement effects of ability grouping in secondary schools: A best evidence synthesis with discussion. *Review of Educational Research, 3,* 471–499.

Slavin, R. E. (1995). Cooperative learning and intergroup relations. In J. A. Banks (Ed.), *Handbook on multicultural education.* New York: Jossey-Bass.

Slavin, R. E., & Madden, N. A. (1979). School practices that improve race relations. *American Educational Research Journal, 162,* 162–180.

Sleeter, C. E. (1993). How white teachers construct race. In C. McCarthy & W. Crichlow (Eds.), *Race, identity and representation in education* (pp. 160–170). New York: Routledge Publishing.

Smrekar, C. E., & Goldring, E. B. (2009). *From the courtroom to the classroom: The shifting landscape of school desegregation.* Cambridge, MA: Harvard University Press.

Steele, C. (2010). *Whistling Vivaldi: And other clues how stereotypes affect us.* New York: W. W. Norton Publishers.

Steele, C. (2011). *Whistling Vivaldi: How stereotypes affect us and what we can do.* New York: W. W. Norton Publishers.

Stevens, L. (1990). The dilemma of metropolitan school desegregation, *Urban Education and Society, 23,* 65–85.

Student voices across the spectrum: Educational integration initiatives. Report to the Joyce Foundation, Institute on Race and Poverty, no. 16, 2000.

U.S. v. Texas, 680 F 2d. 356 (5th Cir 1982).

Wahlberg, H. J. (1979). Promoting student integration in city high schools: A research study and improvement guidelines for practitioners final report. ERIC Number: ED181160.

Ware, L., & Ware, M. L. (1996). *Plessy's legacy: Desegregating the Eurocentric curriculum. Georgia State University Law Review, 12*(4).

Ware, M. L. (1999). School desegregation in the new millennium: The racial balance standard is an inadequate approach to achieving equality in education. *St. Louis University Law Review, 18,* 465–486.

Warikoo, N., & Carter, P. (2009). Cultural explanations for racial and ethnic stratification in academic achievement: A call for a new and improved theory, *Review of Educational Research, 79*(1), 366–394.

Washington, v. Davis, 426 U.S. 229 (1976).

Wellisch, J. W., Marcus, J. A., MacQueen, A., & Suck, G. (1976). *An in-depth study of emergency school aid act.* Washington, DC: U.S. Office of Education.

Welner, K. G. (2001). Ability tracking : What role for the courts? *Education Law Reporter, 163.*

Welner, K. G. (2006). K-12 race-conscious student assignment policies: Law, social science and diversity. *Review of Educational Research, 76*(3), 349–382.

Wells, A. S. (1994). Perpetuation theory and the long term effects of school desegregation. *Review of Educational Research, 64*(4), 531–555.

Wells, A. S. (1995). Reexamining social science research on school desegregation: Long versus short-term effects. *Teachers College Record, 96*(4), 691–706.

Wells, A. S. (1996). African American students' view of choice. In B. Fuller, R. Elmore, & G. Orfield (Eds.), *Who chooses? Who loses? Culture institutions, and the unequal effects of school choice* (pp. 25–49). New York: Teachers College Press.

Wells, A. S., Baldrige, B. J., Draun, J., Grzesikowski, C., Lofton, R., Roda, A., Warner, M., & White, T. (2009, November). *Boundary crossing for diversity. Equity and achievement. Inter-district school desegregation and educational opportunity.* Charles Hamilton Institute for Race and Justice Report. Cambridge, MA: Harvard University Press.

West, C. (1993). *Keeping faith: Philosophy and race in America.* London: Routledge.

Wheelock, A. (1992). *Crossing the tracks: How "untracking" can save America's schools.* New York: The New Press.

Wolters, R. W. (1996). *Right turn: William Bradford Reynolds, the Reagan administration, and black civil rights.* New Brunswick, NJ: Transaction Publishers.

Word, E. R. (1990). The state of Tennessee's student/teacher achievement ratio star project: technical report 1985–1990. Tennessee State Department of Education and Tennessee State University, Nashville, TN.

18

INTEREST GROUPS REVISITED

Tamara Young, Catherine DiMartino, and Brian Boggs

INTEREST GROUPS REVISITED

In the first edition of the *Handbook of the Politics of Education,* Opfer, Young, and Fusarelli (2008) point out that the number of interest groups and the amount they spend on lobbying has increased dramatically over the past few decades. Yet, despite this proliferation of interest groups and their activity, Opfer and colleagues contend that interest groups remain an understudied subfield of the politics of education. They also find that the paucity of scholarship that examines interest groups in education policy typically utilizes an inclusive definition of interest groups, a characterization, according to Opfer and her colleagues, that largely relies on Thomas and Hrebenar's (1992) definition that considers an interest group as "any association of individuals, whether formally organized or not, that attempts to influence public policy" (as cited in Opfer et al., 2008, p. 197). Opfer and colleagues argue that this use of an inclusive definition conceals important conceptual problems related to our understanding and, hence, study of interest groups, notably organizational, activity, and distinctional ambiguity.

In addition to discussing the challenges to defining interest group, Opfer and colleagues describe how interest groups exert influence over the educational policy process. They point out that interest groups employ a wide range of lobbying tactics, and contexts play an important role in the likelihood of an interest group successfully exerting influence over educational policy. They reason that traditional educational associations, business groups, and conservative interest groups are the most influential interest groups in education policy. At the conclusion of their chapter on interest groups, Opfer and colleagues describe how interest groups shape educational policy through advocacy coalitions in policy subsystems and call for additional research on the role of policy entrepreneurs in the politics of education.

Our intention for this chapter is not to restate the conclusions in Opfer and colleagues' "Politics of interest: Interest groups and advocacy coalitions in American education" (2008). Rather, we endeavor to expand and complicate the arguments about interest groups made in the first edition in light of theoretical and empirical scholarship that was not incorporated by Opfer and colleagues. Juxtaposing this chapter alongside Opfer and colleagues' chapter, readers should not only have an understanding of key developments in an important subfield in the politics of education—interest groups—but also become aware of fruitful directions for future scholarship. This approach will allow us to expand our understanding of the factors that influence the composition of the educational policy interest group landscape at the local, state, and federal levels and bolster or limit the influence of interest groups in the educational policy process across a wide range of contexts.

Our review and commentary rely on important works from politics of education scholarship and the larger discipline of political science as well, for several reasons. First, the literature on the politics of education draws heavily on theories and methodologies emerging from the study of interest groups in other areas. Second, with the perpetual dearth of scholarship on interest groups in education (Opfer et al., 2008), we must extrapolate from research in other disciplines to understand the role of interest groups in education. Additionally, comparisons with findings from other policy sectors will allow us to discern the contextual variables that influence the activities of interest groups and mediate or moderate their impact on policy outcomes. Last, if politics of education scholars are to make a theoretical contribution to the larger literature on interest group politics, then we need to be acutely aware of the theoretical and methodological directions of the field in general.

In the sections that follow, we discuss the interest group landscape and entry and exit of interest groups from the pressure community (i.e., interest groups as a collective, also referred to as *interest group community* or *interest group system*). Then, we focus on lobbying and influence, articulating both recent theoretical and methodological developments that can advance our understanding of the influence of interest groups on the educational policy process. Next, we discuss the increasing influence of one particular type of interest group, philanthropists and their affiliated foundations. Last, we detail the advantages and disadvantages of different types of comparative research for providing insights about interest groups in the education policy community. Throughout this chapter, we intentionally consider Opfer and colleagues' (2008) conclusions and point out how our review and commentary expand or complicate their suppositions.

INTEREST GROUP LANDSCAPE: SIZE, COMPOSITION, AND LEVEL

Opfer and colleagues (2008) call attention to a substantial increase in the number of interest groups associated with education. Kay Schlozman's (2010) recent work bolsters their claim. What is most interesting, however, about Schlozman's findings is that much of the expansion in the interest group community has been attributed to the political mobilization of existing groups. Specifically, a snapshot of the pressure community in Washington, DC indicated that compared to 1981, the 2006 *Washington Representatives* directory lists 643 more interests in education which represented a relative increase of 612 percent—the second largest relative increase in share of lobbying organizations in Washington, DC. Close examination of the trends across sector show that in education, 76 percent of members of the pressure community had been in existence in 1981 but were outside of politics—apolitical; 16 percent were not yet in existence; and 8 percent were in existence and listed as members of the pressure community. These figures suggest that many education groups were mobilized into pressure politics during the 25-year period studied. Interestingly, in education, we know little about the composition of this expanded interest group community. Who are these organizations that have mobilized in the past 25 years and whose interest do they represent—that is, what is the shape of the pressure community? "Since organized interests are so important in informing public officials about the preferences and needs of stakeholders in political controversies about how policies affect their lives and fortunes, the shape of the pressure community matters crucially for the equal protection of citizen interests" (Schlozman, 2010, p. 449).

According to Schlozman (2010), even with the expansion of the number of organizations from 1981 to 2006, the kinds of interests that are represented across all sectors remain the same. Referencing E. E. Schattschneider's (1960) observation of the pressure community, Schlozman remarks of the shape of the pressure community: "as the heavenly chorus has gotten bigger, neither its accent nor the mix of voices has been transformed" (2010, p. 450). That is, when we look at interest groups across all sectors, the pressure system of American politics largely represents the interests of the upper class.

As it relates to education, we need to understand the shape of the interest group landscape to discern to what extent disadvantaged groups are represented in pressure politics. If we were to disaggregate the pressure community by sector and focus on education, would the accent and mix of voices that Schlozman (2010) identified be characteristic of the interest group community in education policy? Does this dramatic increase in the number of politically active interest groups mean that more interests are represented, or is the composition (ratio) of the interests largely the same as in previous decades, voicing primarily the interests of the upper class? Does *more* mean more of the same, or is more something altogether different? Because education has long been idyllically considered the great equalizer, despite the presence of a substantial volume of theoretical and empirical research that suggests otherwise, equity has been a key theme of research on the politics of education. We need to closely examine the composition of the interest group community to discern whether the voices of marginalized populations (based on economic status or affiliation with an identity group) are represented in different stages of the policy process.

In addition to looking at the mobilization of groups that represent the interests of marginalized populations, future research needs to consider state and local governments' participation in the pressure community. With the expansion of states' power over educational policy coupled with the federal government's increasing financial incentives, the establishment of a plethora of accountability policies (Jacobsen & Young, 2013), and an environment in the past few years that experienced dramatic fiscal cutbacks in the education sector (Young & Fusarelli, 2011), state and local governments (especially the large urban school districts) are certainly motivated to influence federal educational policy (cf. Schlozman, 2010). Two implications result from considering government actors as interest groups. First, to deem government actors as interest groups is to allow for the continued use of an inclusive definition of interest groups in educational research, which Opfer and colleagues address. Second, by considering state and local governments as interest groups, we are better able to understand the interaction between levels of government, that is, how federalism works in educational policy.

Last, given this increase in the centralization of educational policy at the state level as a result of policy changes resulting from No Child Left Behind (Jacobsen & Young, 2013; McDonnell, 2013), we should not only be concerned with the composition of the interest group universe at the federal level, but also pay close attention to the organized interests pressure community at the state level. Studying the extent to which Schattschneider's classic observation and Schlozman's (2010) conclusion about the voice and mix of the heavenly chorus characterize state level politics of education is tantamount to understanding the educational policy process and outcomes. If certain interests are not represented, theories on interest group formation and barriers to entry (e.g., free-rider and resource-constraint problems) may prove useful in explaining why groups choose not to mobilize despite having a collective concern.

INTEREST GROUP ENTRY AND EXIT

Opfer and colleagues define what is commonly meant when we use the term *interest group* and explain the challenges to defining interest groups. The definition commonly used by politics of education scholars largely focuses on the goals of interest groups. It ignores why interest groups mobilize, typically referred to as *interest group theory*. The most comprehensive attempt to explain interest group theory as it relates to education policy is Sipple, Miskel, Matheney, and Kearney's work that outlines five theories that can be used as frameworks to "examine and interpret the formation, agenda setting, and maintenance" of interest groups (1997, p. 442). The first of these theories, moving chronologically, is Truman's *disturbance theory* (1951). The premise of disturbance theory is that "humans are group oriented and that organizations commonly arise through the natural interaction of people with similar beliefs" (Sipple et al., 1997, p. 443). These naturally occurring similarities also drive how the agenda is set and organized. Given this natural sorting, there are always a variety of groups forming and sorting of different sizes in response to similarly held views, fostering pluralism and, as Sipple and colleagues argue, creating a natural balance to the formation of public policy.

The second theory, Olson's (1965) *by-product theory*, posits "individuals primarily act rationally on behalf of their own interests to maximize their own well-being" (Sipple et al., 1997, p. 443). From this perspective individuals are essentially, in economic terms, rational operators. This theory presumes that people generally act to promote their best interest. This means that their membership in the group will benefit them in some fashion and any "wider social benefits are rendered only as a by-product" or residual of increasing the membership's worth (Sipple et al., 1997, p. 445). Because membership is about personal gain, setting the agenda for an interest group can become challenging. Thus, interest group leaders and policy-oriented members set the formal external political agenda.

The third theory, *exchange theory* by Salisbury (1969), has many of the elements of by-product theory, but on a slightly different scale. Exchange theory holds that beyond personal gain, there may be political elements that pull members together—not all benefits have to be monetized. "If the proposed collective political benefit is sufficient and in agreement with their individual interests, individuals are apt to form and join organizations" (Sipple et al., 1997, p. 445). Exchange theory argues for a wider interpretation of what it means to gain from grouping collective interests together. Gain is about bettering one's or one's group's position and "members expect to succeed and garner the rewards of success, whether individual or collectively, economically or politically" (p. 445). Similar to by-product theory, exchange theory holds that agenda setting is driven by the politically and policy-minded contingent of the group—making leadership an important driving force for the interest group.

The fourth theory is Sabatier's *commitment theory* (1992), which holds that members of a special interest group are generally more dedicated to a cause than the general public. As Sipple and colleagues explain, "strong conviction to a topic motivates individuals to engage in political action and to exert the time, energy, and effort necessary to form an interest group" (1997, p. 443). Given the focus on dedication to the issue at hand, groups can be small and often the work of moving toward a goal and the bringing together of others are just as important as actually achieving the goal. The emphasis on dedication also means that oftentimes those who are most committed to the cause or issue set the agenda, and leadership in these organizations can take extreme positions.

The last approach to explaining interest group formation is *countervailing power theory*, posited by McFarland (1992). According to countervailing power theory, the reasons people join interest groups are completely different than the theories about commonality and economic and political gain. Instead, countervailing power theory assumes that groups form in response to other groups that have mobilized and are the prevailing voice on an issue, thereby "filling a void in the policy debate" (Sipple et al., 1997, p. 445). The same issue that brought the groups together also sets the agenda and drives the policy advocacy efforts of the group.

On the whole, these prominent interest group theories explain interest group formation and link their formation to group characteristics, such as size, leadership, extremism, and goals. What is clearly evident from Sipple and colleagues' (1997) summary of interest group theories is that these approaches all assume that the definition of an interest group is a formal organization comprised of individual members interested in political action (e.g., a teachers' union). These theories explaining group formation do not explain the decision of all of the other types of interest groups that fall under the inclusive definition of interest groups commonly used by scholars (cf. Opfer et al., 2008) to become politically active. If many interest groups active in educational policy are indeed more than associations representing individuals (such as institutions, like corporations and foundations; associations of institutions; and government entities), then we need interest group theories that explain their formation (i.e., what causes an interest group to devote resources to political action?), and the dimensions of these interest groups that impact their political activity and influence (e.g., leadership and agenda setting). Further, we need to know how these other types of interest groups interact with and impact formal education pressure groups comprised of individual members' teachers' unions. In brief, we need to expand the literature on certain aspects of interest groups, interest group theories (i.e., formation) as a case in point, to correspond to the increasingly inclusive definition of interest groups. Of course as Schlozman (2010) points out, once we include these institutions, associations of institutions, and governments as interest groups, then the concept of representation becomes more complicated. For example, whose interests does a large urban school district that lobbies represent: teachers, staff, administrators, influential families from upper-income neighborhoods, disadvantaged students, or contractors?

Furthermore, in the same way that we need to begin to shift our attention to understanding the formation of interest groups (broadly defined), we also need to improve what we know about interest groups' (broadly defined) decisions to desist political action—a topic Opfer and colleagues allude to when they describe a marching band that becomes politically active on one issue, gas tax for high occupancy vehicles, and then exits the pressure community after the legislature votes on the issue. Understanding the entry (formation) and exit of all types of interest groups will allow us to better depict the members of a pressure community and better discern whose interests are actually being represented in the educational policy process.

LOBBYING AND INFLUENCE: THEORETICAL AND METHODOLOGICAL CONSIDERATIONS

Opfer and colleagues' review of the literature on interest group lobbying echoed two persistent themes: (1) organized interests seek to influence policy and (2) certain contexts can diminish or preclude organized interests' ability to employ lobbying tactics to secure the enactment of favorable policies or prevent unfavorable legislation or regulation (Baumgartner & Leech, 1998; Lowery, 2007). Indeed, the empirical research on lobbying from both the transaction and neopluralist paradigms has failed to consistently demonstrate that lobbying results in influence over policy decisions (Lowery, 2007). Of this inconsistency in findings about lobbying and influence, Lowery commented:

> Our general expectation, perhaps based as much on a steady diet of journalistic horror stories as on the theoretical arguments of the transactions model, is that special interests routinely exercise undue influence. On the other hand, the large-n studies of the 1990s almost uniformly failed to find consistent evidence of extensive influence on the part of organized interests. Or rather, they failed to find evidence of significant influence where we might expect it to be most likely—when vast numbers of organizations engage in titanic battles over large, new issues, spending fortunes and employing hundreds of lobbyists to influence public officials. In contrast, our best evidence of influence arises from quite different settings—when only one or a handful of organizations lobby on narrow, technical issues of little concern to the public. (2007, p. 36)

This observation led Lowery to raise an important question: Given that the prospect of success is limited in certain conditions, which commonly surround the development of important policies, why do organized interests actively lobby in these situations? Challenging the underlying assumption of much of the scholarship on interest group lobbying that interest groups lobby for influence, Lowery concluded that interest group survival, and not immediate influence, is the principal purpose of interest group lobbying. According to Lowery, other goals are present but are "necessarily secondary considerations since failure to survive will preclude achieving any of them" (2007, p. 47). Lowery argued that in the same manner that Mayhew's (1974) theory of legislative behavior views electoral security as the most important goal of legislators, a theory of organized interest lobbying behavior must consider survival as the most important goal of organized interests. This goal of survival is most evident when we observe organizations actively lobbying in contexts that diminish, if not eliminate, the certainty or effectiveness of lobbying over an impending policy decision.

This focus on survival shifts our attention away from the pluralist, transactions, and neopluralist perspectives of lobbying to niche theory and resource dependence theory for explaining why organized interests lobby. According to Gray and Lowery's (1996) notion of niche theory, competition occurs among similar organizations seeking to sustain themselves. To compete in this competitive environment, organizations seek to become autonomous on five resource dimensions: membership (or patrons in the case of institutions), selective benefits to mobilize potential members, financial resources, access to the policy-making process on issues of concern, and proposed action by the government that creates something to lobby for (or against). By establishing a niche—some portion of each of these resources—organizations advance their efforts to survive. Contextual forces, such as public opinion, composition of the interest community, and other variables, increase or decrease an organization's realization of these resource dimensions, improving the certainty and effectiveness of lobbying (Lowery, 2007).

To counterbalance a key limitation of niche theory—a focus on similar organizations—the survival theory of lobbying encompasses resource dependency theory as well (Lowery, 2007). Resource dependency theory presumes that organizations interact with their environment to acquire the resources needed to survive. Including the resource dependence perspective as a component of the survival theory of lobbying allows for theory to take into account the influence of other actors in the political environment, such as the public and political elites, on an organization. The combination of these perspectives can lead us to construct hypotheses that explain lobbying in both favorable and unfavorable contexts.

Understanding that survival, and not immediate influence, is the primary motive of interest groups in certain contexts is an important initial step to accurately predicting political activity, and ultimately understanding policy actors' influence over policy (Lowery, 2007; Young, 2010). Important implications of this theory of lobbying need to be accounted for in our understanding of educational policy in a democratic society (Young, 2010). First, if all lobbying activity is not motivated by a desire to influence an immediate policy outcome, then lobbying activity is not an adequate indicator of pluralism—the distribution of influence among interest groups—in a policy community. As a result, scholars should consider only those interest groups who are truly seeking to influence an immediate policy decision when discerning what interests are truly represented and what interest groups are influential. Otherwise they run the risk of skewing, if not masking, the realities of influence over policy.

Second, the absence of influence despite lobbying should not always be regarded as evidence of a lack of influence. Rather, lack of influence may be attributed to either an organized interest's inability to exert influence or lack of interest as a result of their focus on other objectives that ensure survival. Simply, if immediate influence is not the goal of the lobbying activity for a particular organization, then influence should not be a measure of lobbying effectiveness for that organization (Lowery, 2007). Overall, if we allow Lowery's propositions to guide future research on interest group lobbying in education, then we must consider that interest groups have multiple goals (survival and immediate influence) and operate in different contexts (favorable and unfavorable) that influence their goals for lobbying. Additionally, we should presume that because lobbying behavior can reflect more than efforts to exert influence over an impending policy, lobbying may not be an adequate predictor of policy outcomes.

In contrast to Lowery's proposition that the theoretical underpinnings of much of the research on interest group lobbying and influence has led to conflicting findings about interest group influence, Leech (2010) contends that in addition to contextual factors (c.f. Baumgartner & Leech, 1998; Opfer et al., 2008; Smith, 1995), other methodological and theoretical shortcomings are responsible for the inconsistent findings about the effectiveness of interest group lobbying:

a. *Selecting on the dependent variable:* "Selecting only issues in which interest groups are known to have been influential or selecting only prominent cases" may lead to erroneous conclusions about the relationship between lobbying and influence (Leech, 2010, p. 541);

b. *Focusing on a single state of the process:* Focusing on policy outcomes "turns our attention away from the earlier stages of the policy process in which interest groups may have the most influence"; and "by looking only at the end state of the process, we risk assuming that the conditions present at the end stage are the conditions that result in interest group influence (Leech, 2010, p. 541);

c. *Wrong assumptions about what it is interest groups do:* "One of the most important roles for interest groups is their role as allies to government officials in policymaking process, providing information, strategy, and public support. . . . Studies that define lobbying only as attempts to pressure legislators to change their votes are liable to measure influence incorrectly because they overlook the tactics that interest groups use that are most likely to bring success: working together with like-minded allies within government, monitoring the policymaking environment, and working to build momentum for an issue to get it onto the policymaking agenda. . . . Provision of information remains a central component of interest group influence today" (Leech, 2010, pp. 546–547);

d. *Wrong assumptions about how policy works:* Because in many cases there are two opposing sides with a mix of different types of groups on each side (i.e., heterogeneous sides), "if the group that donated the most in campaign donations won, so would a group that did not have a PAC at all, since they shared the same side . . . any given group's resources correlating only weakly with the total resources of its side" (Leech, 2010, p. 548). So scholars would need to ensure that they have considered all interest groups on the competing sides to fully understand the nature of combined resources on policy outcomes. Second, because of the power of status quo, "getting an issue on the political agenda, lining up support, and working for passage are not done quickly for most interest groups. This means that before interest group success is observed, there will be many years of lack of success" (p. 548). Last, influence is conditional on countervailing pressure that "comes from many sources and not just other interest groups . . . [such as] the desires of elected officials, the policy beliefs of bureaucrats and judges, [and] the expected reaction of the general public" (p. 549).

Future studies on interest groups in educational policy need to take into account these limitations specified by Leech (2010). First, politics of education scholars should consider a wider range of issues. Opfer and colleagues (2008) reached a similar conclusion; however, this recommendation is perhaps more important now than in the past because the politics of education scholarship has become increasingly narrow, focusing on several prominent issues largely associated with the neoliberal and conservative agendas (e.g., charter schools, school choice, accountability policy, and merit pay). In doing so, we have skewed our understanding of interest group influence over education policy. Second, education researchers must expand our focus beyond any single stage of the policy process. Of particular interest in education policy would be including post-enactment lobbying activity, in particular influence over bureaucratic processes (see Godwin & Selden, 2002, as cited by Leech 2010). This is a particularly timely perspective to adopt because as states have contracted private organizations to implement a wide range of activities associated with accountability policies, the line between the private and public sector has increasingly become obscured. In these roles as government *insiders,* interest groups may be advancing regulatory rules and processes that advance their private interests in ways that are rarely investigated (cf. Anagnostopoulos, Rutledge, & Bali, 2013; DiMartino & Scott, 2013).

Third, politics of education scholars need to take a contextually rich, long-term perspective to explaining the relationship between interest group lobbying and influence or risk misestimating the power exerted by interest groups and mischaracterizing the policy process. The more nuanced our understanding of the contexts, the better able we are to discern when lobbying will most likely lead to influence over policy process and outcomes—a theme that Opfer and colleagues and Lowery advocate as well. Additionally, because creating substantial change in policy requires consistent advocacy and is a long-term enterprise process (Baumgartner & Leech, 1998; Leech, 2010), research on lobbying and influence that is short in duration may lead to erroneous conclusions about how influential an interest group is over a specific policy. Fortunately, Leech's call for studies that are long term and fully consider the extent to which issues have two sides supported by a coalition comprised of a mix of different types of groups with different resources resonates with some of the premises of Sabatier and Jenkins-Smith's (1993; 1999) advocacy coalition framework, which Opfer and colleagues explain has been employed in several studies of the politics of education.

VENTURE PHILANTHROPISTS AND FOUNDATIONS AS INFLUENTIAL INTEREST GROUPS

Opfer and colleagues conclude the chapter by suggesting key areas of research for scholars curious about interest group politics. Specifically, they write, "we suggest that while interest groups and advocacy coalitions will continue to be important in shaping educational politics and policy making, scholars should give more careful attention and devote more research to policy entrepreneurs" (2008, p. 209). The authors, citing Morken and Formicola, characterize these policy entrepreneurs as "activists who are independent, freewheeling, sensitive to marketing issues, and able to move with lightning speed and chutzpah"(1990, p. 209). They also note that "much policy making change in education, particularly education reform, comes from outside of traditional policy-making sub-systems" (p. 209). In fact, these scholars could not have been more prescient as the past ten years has seen a growth in educational advocacy by private-sector actors such as venture philanthropists and foundations.

Since the Progressive Era, society's elites have been involved in reforming and improving public education as well as other social causes through philanthropy. The early 20th century saw the rise of foundations, many of which were founded by wealthy industrialists such as Andrew Carnegie and Henry Ford. These industrialists, through their foundations, sought to improve public education by funding programs in colleges and universities, state education departments, and school districts. Over the past ten years, a new and very influential iteration of philanthropists has emerged. These philanthropists, referred to as *venture philanthropists* (Scott, 2009), sit on boards of their own foundations as well as of the foundations of their peers and have a very targeted approach to giving. Embracing market-based approaches to school reform and accountability, this coalition of foundations pushes a very specific reform agenda. The Bill and Melinda Gates Foundation, the Walton Family Foundation, and the Eli Broad Foundations are examples of these new actors. This move toward venture philanthropy has emerged from the current reformers' dissatisfaction with the historical record of traditional foundations' attempts to reform public education.

Despite spending large sums of money, traditional foundations have provided limited evidence of their effectiveness in affecting change within public education, especially in urban contexts (Scott, 2009). To increase their influence in public education, venture philanthropists differ from traditional philanthropists in distinct ways: they pool their resources, forming advocacy networks; they target funding toward districts bearing friendly policy climates, with a penchant for districts under mayoral control; they show a preference for funding private-sector organizations; and they fund think tanks to conduct supportive research on their policy issues and then leverage media outlets to burnish their message and gain public support.

In the hopes of leveraging more policy power and enacting sustained change, venture philanthropists have combined their resources to change the status quo within public education. Scott describes this phenomenon: "A number of relatively newly formed philanthropies are pouring large sums into education reform . . . functioning as de facto advocacy coalition, they often fund the same educational initiatives and organizations, gauge success according to similar outcome measures, and pursue similar goals for public education" (2009, p. 107). For example, the Bill and Melinda Gates Foundation, Broad Foundation, and Fisher Foundation joined together in providing significant financial support for the development and growth of charter schools in New York City. Here, it is important to note that mayoral control of schools exists in New York City, offering fertile ground, from the philanthropists' perspectives, for reform (Scott & DiMartino, 2010).

Targeted funding gives venture philanthropists a tremendous amount of influence in shaping the culture of partner organizations. Stipulations attached to receiving funds—whether they involve using the money to create a teacher evaluation system, enact a merit pay program, increase a cap on charter schools, or collect data on program effectiveness—act as powerful catalysts in shaping how and why organization make decisions. This effect becomes especially true during tough financial times when nonprofit organizations and school districts alike find themselves in need of external funding. Here, foundations—through their giving—have the power to advocate for and shape public policy (DiMartino & Scott, 2013; Reckhow, 2010, 2013; Scott, 2009). Unlike foundations of the past that gave to a disparate group of sometimes private-sector, but mostly public-sector, organizations, this new breed of philanthropists focuses their attention on funding private-sector organizations. Venture philanthropists hope that the outsider status of these organizations will make them more effective at leveraging educational change and fostering innovation (DiMartino, 2009; McDonald, McLaughlin, & Corcoran, 2000). Reckhow describes this change:

> Foundations have helped to set the terms of the national educational policy debate by defining which policy strategies are "real" reforms and which actors are "real" reformers. By concentrating their grant making on a new set of organizations, they have raised the prominence of these groups in relation to traditional stakeholders in education politics. Based on the foundations' selections, "real" reforms are not union leaders or schools of education or school board members; "real" reformers are new nonprofit organizations—Teach for America, KIPP, and New Leaders for New Schools. (2010, p. 301)

Foundation support, as this citation illustrates, empowers and emboldens organizations, while those that are not in their favor lose clout and influence, thus changing the educational policy landscape. Venture philanthropists also attempt to shape the hearts and minds of citizens through research and media. For example, the philanthropists through their foundations fund think tanks to conduct research, thereby influencing the type of research that takes place. Additionally, through various media outlets from blogs to movies such as *Waiting for Superman,* venture philanthropists have engaged the public directly in conversation about policy issues important to them. These deliberate actions create a well-orchestrated and very influential force within public education (Reckhow, 2013; Scott, 2009).

The formation of advocacy coalitions by venture philanthropists through their foundations changes the political dynamics of educational policy making. Their targeted giving and strategic use of research and the media have made them a powerful force in building coalitions around issues. These venture philanthropists and their foundations act as a potential check on well-established special interest groups in educations, such as teachers' unions, and circumvent boards of education by focusing on districts under mayoral control; all of these actions make them a formidable influence within public education.

COMPARATIVE RESEARCH ON INTEREST GROUPS

To improve our understanding of interest groups, especially to discern how variation in variables (political institutions, culture, stage of the process, etc.) influences characteristics of the education pressure community in general, or the specific activities of certain groups focused on an issue in particular, additional comparative research, a topic briefly highlighted by Opfer and colleagues (2008) is still needed. Generally, with the exception of studies that focus on multiple school districts or states, such as Young, Shepley, and Song's (2010) work on reading policy, most studies on interest groups are single-focus local or state-level studies. A key advantage to conducting comparative research is that it allows scholars to attend to interactions across localities, states, and the national government. Examining horizontal and vertical interactions allows us to explore policy diffusion across states or to and from different levels of government and expand our understanding of educational policy in a federal system (e.g., how national policy influences mobilization at the state level) and discern how organizations select different levels of government to accomplish their goals (Lowery & Gray, 2010). Comparative research on interest groups can allow us to examine how political institutions and other variables influence a variety of characteristics of organized interests (e.g., lobbying tactics, number of organized interests) as well (Lowery & Gray, 2010).

One particularly fruitful avenue that has received no attention in the research on interest groups engaged in educational policy is time series analyses. Time series analyses could be useful in examining variation of variables of interest over time at the state and local levels. Additionally, as Lowery and Gray (2010) explain, politics of education scholars should be particularly cautious about carrying out research on interest groups that involves comparisons with other nations because "it is quite difficult to formulate comparative theories capable of coping with the hard fact that variables that are meaningful in one political system are not always meaningful in another very different one" (2010, p. 495). Drawing on Sartori's notions of the *traveling problem* and *stretching,* Lowery and

Gray point out that "to cope with comparisons across widely distinct systems, scholars must define concepts at a higher level of abstraction" and in doing so, scholars end up with concepts that are "too vague and broad and are, as a consequence, no longer falsifiable" (p. 495). Lowery and Gray indicate that to make concept stretching viable, "we would need a true multilevel theory about how the several steps in the influence prediction production process are linked within separate national governments as a necessary precursor to accounting for variation across polities in causal relationships within each of the segments" (p. 494). However, this type of multilevel theory is likely to be difficult because of the types of variables that account for interest group patterns and behaviors.

CONCLUSION

Given the overview and commentary detailed in this chapter, we conclude that the state of the literature on interest groups in the politics of education remains woefully underdeveloped when we consider recent theoretical and methodological developments in political science, the sheer size of the number of education interest groups in the pressure community, the national, state, and local resources dedicated to public education in the United States, and the importance of education to maintaining a democracy. Although we have some understanding of the role of interest groups in the politics of education, what we do not know dwarfs our current state of knowledge. The research terrain is ripe with opportunities.

REFERENCES

Anagnostopoulos, D., Rutledge, S., & Bali, V. (2013). State education agencies, information systems, and the expansion of state power in the era of test-based accountability. *Educational Policy, 27*(2), 217–247.

Baumgartner, F. R., & Leech, B. L. (1998). *Basic interests.* Princeton, NJ: Princeton University Press.

DiMartino, C. (2009). *Public-private partnerships and the small schools movement: A new form of education management* (Doctoral dissertation). New York University, New York.

DiMartino, C., & Scott, J. (2013). Private sector contracting and democratic accountability. *Educational Policy, 27*(2), 307–333.

Godwin, K. R., & Selden, B. J. (2002). What corporations really want from government. In A. Cigler & B. Loomis (Eds.), *Interest group politics* (6th ed., pp. 205–224). Washington, DC: Congressional Quarterly Press.

Gray, V., & Lowery, D. (1996). A niche theory of interest representation. *Journal of Politics, 58*(1), 91–111.

Jacobsen, R., & Young, T. V. (2013). The new politics of accountability: Research in retrospect and prospect. *Educational Policy, 27*(2), 155–169.

Leech, B. L. (2010). Lobbying and influence. In L. S. Maisel & J. M. Berry (Eds.), *The Oxford handbook of American political parties and interest groups* (pp. 534–551). New York: Oxford University Press.

Lowery, D. (2007). Why do organized interests lobby? A multi-goal, multi-context theory of lobbying. *Polity, 39*(1), 29–54.

Lowery D., & Gray, V. (2010). The comparative advantage of state interest organization research. In L. S. Maisel & J. M. Berry (Eds.), *The Oxford handbook of American political parties and interest groups* (pp. 485–501). New York: Oxford University Press.

Mayhew, D. R. (1974). *Congress: The electoral connection.* New Haven, CT: Yale University Press.

McDonald, J., McLaughlin, M. W., & Corcoran, T. B. (2000). *Agents of reform: The role and function of intermediary organizations in the Annenberg Challenge.* Paper presented at the American Educational Research Association, New Orleans, LA.

McDonnell, L. M. (2013). Educational accountability and policy feedback. *Educational Policy, 27*(2), 170–189.

McFarland, A. S. (1992). Interest groups and the policy-making process: Sources of countervailing power in America. In M. P. Petracca (Ed.), *The politics of interest: Interest groups transformed* (pp. 58–79). Boulder, CO: Westview Press.

Olson, M. J. (1965). *The logic of collective action.* Cambridge, MA: Harvard University Press.

Opfer, V. D., Young, T. V., & Fusarelli, L. D. (2008). Politics of interest groups and advocacy coalitions in American education. In B. Cooper, J. Cibulka, & L. Fusarelli (Eds.), *Handbook of education politics and policy* (pp. 195–216). New York: Routledge.

Reckhow, S. (2010). Disseminating and legitimating a new approach: The role of foundations. In K. Bulkley, J. Henig, & H. M. Levin (Eds.), *Between public and private: Politics, governance and the new portfolio models for urban school reform* (pp. 277–306). Cambridge, MA: Harvard Education Press.

Reckhow, S. (2013). *Follow the money: How foundation dollars change public school politics.* New York: Oxford University Press.

Sabatier, P. A. (1992). Interest group membership and organization: Multiple theories. In M. P. Petracca (Ed.), *The politics of interest: Interest groups transformed* (pp. 99–129). Boulder, CO: Westview Press.

Sabatier, P. A. & Jenkins-Smith, H. (1993). *Policy change and learning: An advocacy coalition approach.* Boulder, CO: Westview Press.

Sabatier, P., & Jenkins-Smith, H. (1999). The advocacy coalition framework: An assessment. In P. Sabatier (Ed.), *Theories of the policy process* (pp. 117–166). Boulder, CO: Westview Press.

Salisbury, R. H. (1969). An exchange theory of interest groups. *Midwest Journal of Political Science, 13,* 1–32.

Sartori, G. (1970). Concept misinformation in comparative politics. *American Political Science Review, 64*(4), 1033–1053.

Schattscheneider, E. E. (1960). *The semi-sovereign people.* New York: Holt, Rinehart and Winston.

Schlozman, K. L. (2010). Who sings in the heavenly chorus? The shape of the organized interest system. In L. S. Maisel, J. M. Berry, & G. C. Edwards (Eds.), *The Oxford handbook of American political parties and interest groups* (pp. 425–450). New York: Oxford University Press.

Scott, J. (2009). The politics of venture philanthropy in charter school policy and advocacy. *Education Policy, 23*(1), 106–136.

Scott, J., & DiMartino, C. (2010). Hybridized, franchised, duplicated, and replicated: Charter schools and management organizations. In C. A. Lubienski & P. C. Weitzel (Eds.), *The charter school experiment: Expectations, evidence and implications* (pp. 171–196). Cambridge, MA: Harvard Education Press.

Sipple, J. W., Miskel, C., Matheney, T., & Kearney, C. (1997). The creation and development of an interest group: Life at the intersection of big business and education reform. *Educational Administration Quarterly, 33*(4), 440–473.

Smith, R. A. (1995). Interest group influence in the U.S. Congress. *Legislative Studies Quarterly 20*(1), 89–139.

Thomas C. S., & Hrebenar, R. J. (1992). Changing patterns of interest group activity. In M. P. Petracca (Ed.), *The politics of interest: Interest groups transformed* (pp. 150–174). Boulder, CO: Westview Press.

Truman, D. B. (1951). *The governmental process.* New York: Knopf.

Young, T. V. (2010, May). *Surviving in politics: Understanding why organized interests lobby when victory is unlikely.* Paper presented at the annual meeting of the American Educational Research Association, Denver, CO.

Young, T. V., & Fusarelli, B. C. (2011). The politics of education and equity in turbulent times. *Peabody Journal of Education, 86*(3), 211–214.

Young, T. V., Shepley, T. V., & Song, M. (2010). Agenda setting in state educational policy: An application of Kingdon's multiple streams model. *Educational Policy Analysis Archives, 18*(15). Retrieved from http://epaa.asu.edu/ojs/article/view/771.

CONTRIBUTORS

Thomas Alsbury is a professor of educational leadership at Seattle Pacific University, and currently codirects the national University Council for Educational Administration (UCEA) Center for Research on the Superintendency and District Governance. Alsbury is a frequent speaker and consultant on school board and superintendent issues nationally and abroad. His 2008 book *The Future of School Board Governance: Relevance* and Revelation earned Dr. Alsbury the UCEA Culbertson Award for significant contributions to educational leadership research.

Lois Andre-Bechely is a professor in the Charter College of Education at California State University, Los Angeles. She is the Director of the Ed.D. Program in Educational Leadership. Her research interests focus on educational policy implementation incorporating institutional ethnography as a method of inquiry.

Bruce D. Baker is a professor in the Graduate School of Education at Rutgers, The State University of New Jersey, where he teaches courses in school finance policy and district business management. His recent research focuses on state aid allocation policies and practices, with particular attention to the equity and adequacy of aid for special student populations. He is a past recipient of an NCES/AEFA new scholar's award and has received research funding from the Association for Institutional Research for studying variations in costs to baccalaureate degree attainment.

Brian Boggs is an educational policy doctoral candidate and graduate assistant with the Office of K-12 Outreach at Michigan State University and a lecturer in the Department of English at the University of Michigan-Flint. His research interests include organizational theory, policy making, and the history and politics of U.S. education.

Elissa F. Brown is the director of the Hunter College Center for Gifted Studies & Education and the program coordinator for the Advanced Certificate Program in Gifted Education. Before coming to Hunter, she was the North Carolina state director of teacher preparation programs.

James G. Cibulka is President, Council for the Accreditation of Educator Preparation. His career includes service as a public school teacher and administrator and a faculty member, department chair, doctoral program director, and associate dean at several universities. Most recently, he was dean of the College of Education at the University of Kentucky. He is a graduate of Harvard College and the University of Chicago. He is a past president of the Politics of Education Association and a recipient of the Association's Stephen K. Bailey Award for shaping the intellectual and research agendas of the field.

Lora Cohen-Vogel is the Robena and Walter E. Hussman, Jr. Associate Professor of Policy and Education Reform at the University of North Carolina at Chapel Hill. She studies the policy process, teacher quality, and the politics of school improvement. She serves as the coprincipal investigator of the National Center for Research and Development on Scaling Up Effective Schools.

Bruce S. Cooper is a professor (retired) at the Graduate School of Education at Fordham University, NYC. He earned his doctorate at the University of Chicago and has taught at Dartmouth College, the University of Pennsylvania, and the University of London Institute of Education. A former president of the Politics of Education Association (PEA), he has studied and published on topics of teacher and school administrator unionization, school finance, and teacher professionalism. His most recent books are *Intersections of Children's Health, Education, and Welfare* (Palgrave Macmillan, 2012) with Janet D. Mulvey, and *Moving Teachers from Isolation to Collaboration*, with Sharon Conley (Rowman & Littlefield, 2013).

Elizabeth DeBray is an associate professor in the Department of Lifelong Education, Administration, & Policy in the College of Education, University of Georgia. She received her Ed.D. from Harvard University. Her research interests are the politics of federal education policy, policy implementation, and interest group politics, including the role of intermediary organizations in disseminating research and information about education reforms.

Catherine DiMartino is an assistant professor in the Department of Teaching, Literacy, and Leadership at Hofstra University. Her research explores the role of public-private partnerships in public education, the implications of marketization and privatization for school leaders, and the politics of school choice.

Fritz Edelstein is a principal in Public Private Action. His work with clients utilizes his expertise and experience in strategic government, stakeholder and constituent relations at the federal, state and local levels; advocacy research and policy analysis; strategic planning and resource development; and outreach and public engagement. He created and produces "Fritzwire," the nation's leading email newsletter on education that provides timely education and related information. From February 2003 through December 2006, he was a Senior Advisor at the U.S. Conference of Mayors, where he directed the Conference's effort to increase and improve mayoral leadership and involvement in education. From 1975 to 2003, he held a variety of positions at the U.S. Department of Education. He has a B.A. from Washington University (St. Louis, MO) in political science; M.Ed from the University of Nebraska, Lincoln in elementary education; and a Ph.D. from the University of Nebraska, Lincoln in the politics of education.

Karen Febey is a senior report review officer for the Transportation Research Board, part of the National Research Council at the National Academies of Science in Washington, DC. She has a Ph.D. in evaluation studies from the Department of Educational Policy and Administration at the University of Minnesota.

Bonnie C. Fusarelli is a professor of educational leadership at North Carolina State University, a faculty research fellow at The Friday Institute for Educational Innovation, and an NC State University faculty scholar. She has received funding from the U.S. Department of Education, the National Science Foundation, the Bill and Melinda Gates Foundation, and the NC Department of Public Instruction. She currently serves as the director of the Northeast Leadership Academy, a Race to the Top–funded initiative to prepare innovative school leaders for rural schools (http://go.ncsu.edu/nela).

Lance D. Fusarelli is professor, associate department head, and director of graduate programs in the Department of Leadership, Policy, and Adult and Higher Education at North Carolina State University. He recently served as Visiting Professor in the Department of Public Policy at the University of North Carolina–Chapel Hill. He conducts research on federal education policy, the politics of education, child welfare and comparative social policy, and the superintendency.

Charles L. Glenn has been a professor of educational leadership and policy studies at Boston University since 1991. From 1970 to 1991, Glenn was the director of urban education and equity for the Massachusetts Department of Education, including administration of more than $200 million in state funds for magnet schools and desegregation, and initial responsibility for the nation's first state bilingual education mandate and the state law forbidding race, sex, and national-origin discrimination in education. He is the author of nine books in educational history or comparative policy, and author/editor of eight others.

Molly F. Gordon is a senior research analyst at the University of Chicago Consortium on Chicago School Research. Her research interests include how educators interpret and enact policies into practice, the process of organizational change and school improvement, and family and community engagement.

Paul Green is an associate professor in the Department of Ethnic Studies in the College of Humanities, Arts, and Social Sciences at the University of California, Riverside. His research focuses on educational politics, social policy, and law with particular interest in urban organizational politics and policy, historically black colleges and universities, and historically black Catholic schools and education.

Preston C. Green is the John and Carla Klein Professor of Urban Education at the University of Connecticut's Neag School of Education. He is also a professor of educational leadership and law at the University of Connecticut. Dr. Green has written four books and numerous articles and book chapters pertaining to educational law. He primarily focuses on the legal and policy issues pertaining to educational access and school choice. Dr. Green has a J.D. from Columbia University and an Ed.D. from Teachers College, Columbia University.

Frederick M. Hess is a resident scholar and the director of education policy studies at the American Enterprise Institute. His books include *Cage-Busting Leadership*, *The*

Same Thing Over and Over, Education Unbound, Common Sense School Reform, Revolution at the Margins, and *Spinning Wheels.* Hess serves as the executive editor of *Education Next,* on the review board for the Broad Prize in Urban Education, and on the boards of directors of the National Association of Charter School Authorizers and 4.0 SCHOOLS. He holds his M.A. and Ph.D. in government, and his M.Ed. in teaching and curriculum, from Harvard University.

Claire E. Hughes is an associate professor at the College of Coastal Georgia where she teaches in an integrated elementary/special education teacher preparation program. She has a doctorate in special education and gifted education from the College of William and Mary, and has been a visiting fellow at Oxford University in the area of autism. Her research areas include: twice-exceptional children, particularly children with high-functioning autism; cognitive interventions; and inclusive strategies. She is coeditor of *Excellence and Diversity in Gifted Education* (EDGE).

Christopher Lubienski is a professor of education policy at the University of Illinois, and the director of the Forum on the Future of Public Education. He is also a fellow with the National Education Policy Center at the University of Colorado and Sir Walter Murdoch Visiting Professor at Murdoch University in Western Australia. Lubienski recently published *The Charter School Experiment: Expectations, Evidence, and Implications* (with Peter Weitzel, Harvard Education Press). His most recent book is *The Public School Advantage: Why Public Schools Outperform Private Schools* (with Sarah Theule Lubienski, University of Chicago Press).

Betty Malen is a professor in the Department of Teaching and Learning, Policy and Leadership at the University of Maryland. Her research interests include the politics of education reform, intergovernmental relations, the political determinants and substantive effects of prominent education reforms (e.g., decentralization, high-stakes accountability, pay for performance initiatives); case study designs; and qualitative research methods.

Catherine Marshall is the R. Wendell Eaves Distinguished Professor of Educational Leadership and Policy at the University of North Carolina, Chapel Hill. Her ten books include *Designing Qualitative Research* (Sage), *Reframing Educational Politics for Social Justice* (Allyn & Bacon), *Feminist Critical Policy Analysis* (Falmer), *Leadership for Social Justice* (Allyn & Bacon), and *Activist Educator* (Routledge). She received the Politics of Education Association Stephen Bailey Award for "Shaping the Intellectual and Research Agendas of the Field," and the University Council for Educational Administration's Campbell Lifetime Achievement Award for contributions that changed the leadership field.

Martha McCarthy is Presidential Professor in the Department of Educational Leadership at Loyola Marymount University. McCarthy's research is in primarily educational law and policy, and the evolution and reform of leadership preparation programs. She currently is working on the seventh edition of *Public School Law: Teachers' and Students' Rights* (with Nelda Cambron-McCabe and Suzanne Eckes). She has received the Living Legend Award from the National Council of Professors of Educational Administration and the Roald Campbell Lifetime Achievement Award from the University Council for Educational Administration. McCarthy earned her B.A. in elementary education and her M.A. in instructional management and planning from the University of Kentucky. She earned her Ed.S. and Ph.D. in educational leadership from the University of Florida.

Michael K. McLendon is the Centennial Distinguished Professor of Education Policy and the associate dean at Southern Methodist University's Simmons School of Education and Human Development. He studies finance, governance, politics, and public policy for higher education. A primary strand of his research is directed toward understanding the factors influencing policy change at both the state and campus levels, with a particular focus on the role of political behavior in shaping the policy choices of states.

Michael Q. McShane is a research fellow in education policy studies at the American Enterprise Institute. He is coauthor of *President Obama and Education Reform: The Personal and the Political*, published by Palgrave Macmillan in 2012, and coeditor of *Common Core Meets the Reform Agenda*, published by Teachers College Press in 2013. He began his career as an inner city high school teacher in Montgomery, Alabama and earned his Ph.D. in education policy from the Department of Education Reform at the University of Arkansas.

Brooke Midkiff is a doctoral student at the University of North Carolina. She is pursuing a degree in policy, leadership, and school improvement. Her research interests are in gender issues in education including women and the politics of education, feminist critical policy analysis, and sex education policy.

Nate Myers is an associate professor of Education at Ashland University. His research has concentrated on the history of evangelicals and their impact on public policy in education.

Janelle Scott is an associate professor at the University of California at Berkeley in the Graduate School of Education and African American Studies Department. She earned a Ph.D. in education policy from the University of California at Los Angeles' Graduate School of Education and Information Studies, and a B.A. in political science from the University of California at Berkeley. Her research explores the relationship between education, policy, and equality of opportunity through three policy strands: 1) the racial politics of public education; 2) the politics of school choice, marketization, and privatization; and 3) the role of elite and community-based advocacy in shaping public education. She is the editor of *School Choice and Diversity: What the Evidence Says* (Teachers College Press, 2005).

Karen Seashore Louis is a Regents Professor and the Robert H. Beck Chair at the University of Minnesota. Her research focuses on school improvement and reform, leadership in school settings, and the politics of knowledge use in education. She is a fellow of the American Educational Research Association, and received the Campbell Lifetime Achievement Award from the University Council for Educational Administration.

Anchala Sobrin is a doctoral student in the Department of Educational Leadership, Administration, and Policy at Fordham University.

Frances R. Spielhagen is a professor of education and the director of the Center for Adolescent Research and Development at Mount Saint Mary College, Newburgh,

NY. Spielhagen is editor in chief of the *Middle Grades Research Journal*. Publications include *Unsolved Equations: The Algebra Solution to Mathematics Reform* (Teachers College Press, 2011), *Debating Single Sex Education* (Rowman & Littlefield, 2013), and *Adolescence in the 21st Century: Constants and Challenges* (Information Age Press, 2014).

Melissa Vincent Cochran has spent the past ten years working in education as a teacher, researcher, and teacher educator. She currently teaches humanities at High Tech High North County, a project-based learning charter school in San Marcos, California. She has worked as a lead mentor in High Tech High's Graduate School of Education and Leading Schools Program. Her research focuses on new teacher learning and how school contexts can better support innovative teaching practices in the classroom.

John Wachen is a doctoral student in the policy, leadership, and school improvement program at the University of North Carolina at Chapel Hill. He is a researcher at the National Center on Scaling Up Effective Schools.

Kenneth K. Wong is the Annenberg Chair for Education Policy and the director of the Urban Education Policy Program at Brown University. A political scientist by training, Wong has conducted extensive research in the politics of education, federalism, school finance, and urban school governance. His publications include *The Education Mayor* and *Successful Schools and Educational Accountability*.

Tamara Young is an associate professor in the Department of Leadership, Policy, and Adult and Higher Education at North Carolina State University. Her research focuses on the politics of education, educational policy, and implementation of education programs and policies.

INDEX

Note: Page numbers followed by *f* indicate figures, by *t* indicate a table on the corresponding page.

ability grouping and tracking 391–2

Abramson, Jerry 65, 70–1

accountability: achievement gaps 133; contemporary policy theory 86; curriculum 47; data collection and 124; for disadvantaged populations 224; dominant views on 249; federal government addressing of 224–5; low-performing schools 8; micropolitics of schools 25; policies for interest groups 419; principle-teacher interactions 15–16, 19–20; racial/ethnic inequality 211–12; standards-based accountability 64, 127–8, 130–1, 138–9; state accountability 134–5, 140; stronger efforts needed 6–7; in student assessments 392; teacher-teacher interactions 22; vulnerable women concerns over 244; *see also* federalism, equity, and accountability; performance-based accountability

achievement gaps: accountability for 133; closing of 71, 215, 223, 380; comparative analysis of 200–1, 204, 205; defined 253; educational opportunities 185; NCLB and 132, 200

adequacy: governmental decisions 108; modern era 170; objectives 173; school funding 168, 173, 180, 181, 183–6, 401; state aid formulas 168–9; state courts 159

Adequate Yearly Progress (AYP) 193, 215, 217–18, 352

advanced curriculum 368

advisory committees 5, 8, 51, 184

advocacy: feminism and 237–8; gifted and special education 107–8, 369–70, 373–4, 377, 378; organizations/coalitions 326, 411, 420–1; policy change and 88–110, 419–20; validity and 173–7; *see also* individual advocacy groups

advocacy coalition framework (ACF) 92, 96–9, 107–9

affirmative action 255, 257

AFL-CIO (American Federation of Labor and Congress of Industrial Organizations) 344, 354–6

African American students 211, 304, 336, 387

after-school programs: advocacy over 374; analysis of 97; Christian right and 273; development of 81; laws and regulations 314; managing and funding 68, 72; tutorial services 219

Alexander, Lamar 192, 204–5

Alliance for School Choice 328, 338

alternative organizational forms 5, 8, 11, 17

American Association of School Administrator's (AASA) 48, 235

American Association of University Women (AAUW) Foundation 238, 243

American Educational Research Association 203

American Federation of Teachers (AFT): charter schools 354; dropout prevention 71; influence of 312, 334; membership size 344; teacher-evaluation and tenure systems 199; union merger 356–7; unions, future of 361; women's status in public arenas 233

American Legislative Exchange Council (ALEC) 339

American Medical Association (AMA) 350

American Recovery & Reinvestment Act of 2009 (ARRA) 196, 213

American School Board Association 39

A Nation Deceived report 376

Annenberg Institute for School Reform 66

antifeminists 255, 279

anti–Vietnam War sentiment 153

applied social scientist role 40, 41

arena (delegate) governance 39

Arizona Christian School Tuition Organization v. Winn (2011) 159

Arizona State University 310
Asad, Talal 286
Asian students 125
Association for the Gifted Division of the CEC 377
at-risk students 6, 214
attention-deficit disorder 368
autism 368
avoiding/suppressing conflict 9–10, 12–13, 16–17, 22

Bahasa Indonesia language 289
Baker, Rick 76–7
Balfanz, Robert 71
Ballard, Greg 78
bargaining boards 43, 213
Basic Law on Education 289
Baumgartner, Frank 93–4
Baylor University's Oral History Institute 268
beliefs, hierarchical structure 96–8
Bennett, Barbara Byrd 81
Bennett, William 199
Bethel School District v. Fraser (1986) 149
bilingual education 214, 236, 427
Bill and Melinda Gates Foundation 51, 419–20
Black Alliance for Educational Options (BAEO)
    336–7, 339
Black Swan events 241–2, 257
Bloomberg, Michael 63, 71
Boehner, John 334
Bolick, Clint 338
"borrowing strength" phenomenon 205
Bosnia and Herzegovina 286
Boston Public Schools 63, 74
Boyd, Bill 203
Bredesen, Phil 221
Brizard, Jean-Claude 81
Broad Foundation 420
Brown, Jerry 65
Brown, Kevin 399–400
Brown v. Board of Education (1954) 151, 153, 335,
    371, 398
budgeting 5, 51, 94
Burger, Warren 150
Bush, George H. W. (administration) 192–3, 201, 374
Bush, George W. (administration): budget reduction
    recommendations 255; Christian right and 277;
    educating needy children 375; education policy
    194–5, 201; funding of groups 330–1; voucher
    initiatives 204; see also federal education policy
busing of students 216, 388
by-product theory 414

California Mayors' Education Roundtable 76
Campaign for Fiscal Equity v. State (2006) 174
capacity building 123, 220, 313
capitalism 245
Carl, Jim 324–8
Carl Perkins Vocational Education Act (1984) 237
Carnegie, Andrew 419
Carter, Jimmy 213, 270, 275

Carter, Prudence 391
Casanova, José 295
Catholic Educators' Conference 334
Catholicism 280, 297–8
Cavanagh, Sean 349
Cavanaugh, Jerome 74
Center for Education Policy 222
Center for Education Reform 332
Center for Talented Youth at Johns Hopkins
    University 373
Center on Budget and Policy Priorities 166
Center on Reinventing Public Education 310
centralization 121, 213, 327, 413
centrist groups 332
charter management organizations (CMOs) 333
charter schools: adequate yearly progress 219; as
    alternatives 8; approval for 77–8; choice of 13,
    82, 256, 323–9, 339–40; collective bargaining
    agreements 315; conversion to 215, 225;
    deregulation of 6; development and growth of 353,
    420; education scholarship 418; effectiveness of
    226; establishment of 63, 80, 99, 128; expansion
    of 196–7, 222; federal expenditures 338; financing
    for 181, 220, 304, 316–17; freedom with 318–19;
    innovation in 306, 316; legislation 102, 103, 106,
    131, 217, 221; like-minded groups and 17; parent
    involvement 11; policies 96, 205; reliance on 76;
    school board agendas 53; support for 193, 222–3,
    255, 330, 336; teacher unions and 354–5; technology
    impact 318; voucher programs 192, 274, 317, 330,
    340, 346, 349, 352
Chicago Public Schools 14, 63, 70, 81
Chicago regionalism 402
Chicana feminist epistemology 253
Children's Aid Society 71
choice diversion 181–3, 182t
Choosing Equality (Viteritti) 335
Christensen, Clayton 307
Christensen, Doug 131
Christian Coalition 271, 274, 277
Christian fundamentalism 267–9
Christian right: internal coherence 271–4; renewed
    mobilization of 277–9; Republican Party and 274–9,
    280; see also religious faith and policy in education
Christie, Chris 167
Chubb, John 310–11
Cicilline, David 78
civic engagement role 10, 41, 42
Civil Rights Act (1871) 152
Civil Rights Act (1964) 157, 212, 240, 371
civil rights groups 326, 333–4, 335–7
civil rights laws 156, 157, 223
civil rights movement 154, 244, 335, 336, 371–2
class-based desegregation efforts 389
class conflict 345–8
Class Dojo 307
class sizes 170, 181–3, 186, 387, 395
Cleveland Public Schools 76, 160, 325–6, 355
Clinton, Bill (administration) 193–4, 195, 201

Clinton, Hillary 244, 256, 259
closed political cultures 120
Code Pink: Women for Peace 246
coercive isomorphism, defined 202
Cold War effort 280
Coleman, Michael 63, 67–8, 76
collective bargaining agreements: limiting scope of 312; mayoral skill 69; teacher contracts 315–16; teacher evaluation systems 197, 304–5; teacher unions and 343–4, 346–8, 350, 355–61
college savings plans 86, 104
Colorado Supreme Court 160
Columbus Education Commission 68
Commission for Racial Equality 287
commitment theory 415
Committee on Education and the Workforce 334
Common Core of State Standards: capacity to meet 82; elimination of 127–8; establishment of 65, 87, 102; expansion of 224; federal education policy 195, 198; number of states adopting 119; political culture and 132
Communication and Race: A Structural Perspective (Gandy) 403
communication effectiveness 48, 55
community activism 12
community coalitions 403
community diversity 42, 245
community organizations 11, 240, 250, 254
community power struggles 49–50
conflict: avoiding/suppressing conflict 9–10, 12–13, 16–17, 22; class conflict 345–8; embracing of 23; expression of 17; management of 10–12, 19; mobilization of 12, 13; preempting of 17–18
Conservative Political Action Committee (CPAC) 274
Conyers, John 337
Copeland, Warren 76
cost-effective innovations 308–9
Council for Exceptional Children (CEC) 369
Council of Chief State School Officers (CCSSO) 65, 73, 110, 118, 198, 202
Council of Economic Advisors 225
Council of Europe 287
Council of State Governments 110
Council on Education and Children's Affairs 225
Council on Foreign Relations Independent Task Force 224
counter-aristocratic ideology 37–8
countervailing power theory 415
Cowan, Kristor 334
Cox Proportional Hazards model 103
Creating Essential Educational Opportunities for All Children Act (2005) 131
Credit Enhancement for Charter School Facilities program 316
Crew, Rudy 76
critical feminist reframing 254
Cuban, Larry 313
cultural pluralism 46, 293
Cuomo, Andrew 167

curriculum: accountability 47, 132; advanced curriculum 368; articulated content 6–7, 10; changes to 237; components 155; conventional curriculum 366–7; cultural pluralism in 293; decision-making forums 20; development 21, 130; early struggles over 369–70; education politics 239, 251; elimination of 135; hypermasculine curriculum 253; lack of demanding 51; media reinforcement 257; minority cultures in 300; neutrality and 296–8; reforms 195, 198, 258; responsibility for 44; standards 194, 204–5, 367; teacher influence on 17; teacher unions and 350–3, 359; transforming curricula and programming 396–8; *see also* Common Core of State Standards; No Child Left Behind Act; Race to the Top (RTTT) program

Daley, Richard 63, 69, 70, 74–5
Darwinist science 280
Dean, Karl 71, 81–2
Deasy, John 80
The Death and Life of the Great American School System (Ravitch) 310
decentralization/decentralism: detracking 392; faith and policy 277, 279–80; federalism 211, 226; federal policy and 189, 192, 200–1; ideology and 327; impact of 310; micropolitics 35; parameters of influence 5; participation increases through 121, 128; political culture 120, 129–30, 132; principles of 290; of social relations 120
decision making: competing interests by consolidating of 38; curriculum and 20; introduction 5; micropolitics of schools 24; multiple-streams framework 88–92; political culture and 129–30; public inclusion in 42–3; of school-board superintendent 43, 50–1
deep core beliefs 96–7
Defense of Marriage Act 276
democracy: competing values of 189; education and 52, 189; federalism and 212; liberal democracies 291–2, 338, 360; loss of 52; public school role in 37–8, 41, 42; redefined 310–11; transformational democracy 384–5; voter role in 45; women's mobilization and 242–4
Democratic Party: Christian right and 277; education priority with 126; national community 191; new fundamentalism and 270; teachers unions and 199; teacher unions 312, 353; war on women and 242
democratic statesman 40, 41
Democrats for Education Reform 325, 335
desegregation *see* educational integration
DeStefano, John 70, 78
de Tocqueville, Alexis 212
devil shift argument 97
Dewey, John 296
disadvantaged populations: educational needs of 211, 212–14, 215; ethnicity concerns 287; federal accountability over 224; gender differences 231, 236; minority institutions 293; politics over 94;

scholarship programs for 159; school choice and 324, 328, 335; site-based governance councils 10; teacher unions 349; *see also* gifted and special education students

Disrupting Class: How Innovation Will Change the Way the World Learns (Christensen) 307

disruptive innovation 307–9

disturbance theory 414

diversity: among immigrants 125; community diversity 42, 245; in data collection techniques 106; efficiency *vs.* 35; encouragement of 324; ethnic/cultural diversity 288, 290, 400; ideological diversity 46; racial diversity 389; religious diversity 292, 295, 301; support for 332

Dobson, James 271

Donnelly, Joe 241, 242

Draper, James T. 272

Duffy, Robert 65

Duncan, Arne 62, 70, 71, 166–7, 196, 200, 220, 360

Eagle Forum 271

economic competitiveness 101, 190–1

economic development 73–4, 76, 87, 106

Edelstein, Frederick (Fritz) 63

education: bilingual education 214, 236, 427; cost of 129; curriculum politics 239, 251; democracy and 52, 189; economic development 73–4; employment outcomes of women 237–9; for-profit education 8, 333; litigation 148, 153–6, 158; management of 8; market-based school reforms 99, 325; models of education 358; national security concerns and 224, 226; needs of disadvantaged populations 211, 212–14, 215; opportunities 185; sexual dynamics in 257; supplemental education services 219; *see also* charter schools; Common Core of State Standards; federal education policy; feminism and education politics; gifted and special education students; judicial impact on education politics and policies; political culture in education; public schools; religious faith and policy in education

Educational Commission of the States (ECS) 110

educational integration: ability grouping and tracking 391–2; cases and federal law 399–400; choice as social good 404; class-based desegregation efforts 389; in classrooms 395; class sizes 395; community coalitions 403; conclusions 404–5; desegregation cases 151; early integration 389–90; federal suits 400; inclusive spaces and activities 397–8; in-school initiatives 390; by larger communities 398–400; legal and social strategies 398–9; metropolitan-wide desegregation 386–9; overview 384; parental involvement 398; positive interracial contact 392–3; public discourse on race 403–4; racial groups, equal representation 386–90; regionalism 401–3; state laws 400–1; student assessments 390–6; teaching strategies for 396; as transformational democracy 384–5; transforming curricula and programming 396–8

educational leadership: business theory techniques 41; fellowships for 256; gender differences 258–9;

graduate programs in 235; policy makers and 367, 372, 385, 402; principal mistreatment of teachers 36

Educational Quality Accountability Act (1999) 130

Educational Research Analysts 278

Education Commission of the States (ECS) 107, 202

Education for All Handicapped Children Act 372

education governance 189

Education Law Center of New Jersey 170

education politics 239, 247–8, 251; *see also* federal education policy; feminism and education politics; judicial impact on education politics and policies

efficiency 183–4, 193

egalitarianism 120, 126, 128–9

Eldredge, Niles 92–3

Elementary and Secondary Education Act (ESEA): economic development and 73; federalism 212–13; federal policy 193–4, 197, 206; gender differences 236; gifted and special needs students 371–2; passage of 375; program cooperation under 220–1; reauthorization of 223, 329; school choice policies 337

Eli Broad Foundation 419

elite (trustee) governance 39

elitism 368, 379–80

Emanuel, Rahm 68, 70, 81

Emergent Church (EC) movement 271–2

empowering schools 5

end of course (EOC) exams 134

The End of Exceptionalism in American Education (Henig) 63

Engel v. Vitale (1962) 276

English language learners (ELLs) 158, 215, 223

entrepreneurship: altering funding systems through 316–17; challenges to 309–11; defined 305–7; formal impediments to 315–16; fostering of 315–18; innovation with 318–19; legitimacy with 317–18; overview 304–5; solutions and 90–1

environmentalism 154, 344

Equal Educational Opportunities Act (EEOA) 158

Equal Protection Clause 150–1, 159, 399

Equal Rights Amendment (ERA) 233, 244

equity: adequacy in modern era 170; educational equity 244–5, 250; educational experiences 22; educational legislation 280; educational policy 123, 128–9, 131, 133, 255, 257–8; equity politics 253; evaluation of 168; focus on 46; in funding 180–1, 185, 297; gender differences 231, 236, 240–1; gender equity 258; gifted and special needs students 365, 367, 370–2, 377, 379–80; ideology of 327; in integrated education 401–2; school finance 170; in state aid formulas 168–9; tax equity 178; teacher unions and 355–6; *see also* federalism, equity, and accountability

established interests 9–10, 12, 22–4

Establishment Clause 151, 159–60, 276, 325

ethnic/cultural diversity 288, 290, 400

ethnicity and religion 287–8

European Union 118, 285–6, 287, 295

Evangelical Christianity 294
event history data sets 109
Excellent Schools Act (1997) 128
exchange theory 414
existence proofs 3, 10, 17
Expanding Minds and Opportunities: Leveraging the Power of Afterschool and Summer Learning for Student Success (Peterson) 72
extended learning 72–3, 79

facilitative role of school boards 42–3
"fair share" housing policies 402
Faludi, Susan 241
Falwell, Jerry 277–8
Family Educational Rights and Privacy Act (FERPA) 153, 157
Family Research Council 271
Fattah, Chakah 337
federal education policy: Bush (George H. W.) administration 192–3; Bush (George W.) administration 194–5, 204; changing institutional environment 202; Clinton administration 193–4, 195; Common Core of State Standards Initiative 195, 198; conclusions 206–7; convergence *vs.* divergence 201–2; education reform under Obama administration 199–201; equity 123, 128–9, 131, 133, 255, 257–8; federal role 204–6; grassroots organizing/activism 99, 121; increased federal involvement 203–4; innovation and 313–14; local government issues 195; market-based school reforms 99, 325; merit pay 191, 194, 199, 203–4; No Child Left Behind waivers 200–1; Obama administration 65, 111, 193, 195–9, 204; overview 189–90; performance-based accountability 193, 195, 199, 204–5; Reagan administration 190–2, 204; teacher evaluation 198–9
federalism, equity, and accountability: competing ideas on 222–4; federal government addressing of 224–5; institutional innovation 219–22; marble cake federalism 212–14; overview 211–12; performance-based federalism 214–15, 217–19; policy implementation 215–17
feminism and education politics: antifeminists 255; challenges to patriarchal politics 254; critical policy analysis 249, 252; integration of 247–8; judicial impact 153; nation at promise 257–9; nation at risk 254–7; overview 231–2; reframing of feminist questions 236, 240, 247, 253–4; women's status in public arenas 233–42
Fenty, Adrian 63, 71
First Amendment 151, 159–60, 325, 348
Fischer, Greg 71
Fisher Foundation 420
Florida Supreme Court 160
Focus on the Family 271, 274
Ford, Gerald 274
Ford, Henry 419
Ford Foundation 72
Fordham Institute 338–9

formal arenas: patterns of politics 9–12, 16–18, 22–3; principle-teacher interactions 15–20; professional-patron transactions 8–9, 14–15
for-profit education 8, 333
Foster, Bob 82
Fourteenth Amendment 400
Free and Appropriate Public Education (FAPE) 373
Fuller, Howard 336
funding of groups 330–1
funding sources 137–8

Gabler, Mel and Norma 278
Gallup Poll information 107
Gandy, Oscar H., Jr. 403
garbage can decision making *see* multiple-streams framework
Gates, Bill 167
Gates Foundation's Postsecondary Success Strategy 138
gay, lesbian, bisexual, transgendered, and queer (GLBTQ): campaign against 235; rights 233, 234, 258; same-sex marriage 273, 276, 278; sexuality issues 251–2, 253
gender and power dynamics 236–7
gender differences: disadvantaged populations 231, 236; equity and 231, 236, 240–1
gender gap 242–4
gender regime concept 248–52
gender stereotypes 255–6
Georgia Alliance for Choices in Education 328
GI Bill 138, 371
gifted and special education students: conclusions 379–80; implications 378–9; introduction 365–7, 365t–367t; learning disabilities 368, 375; 1980s–1990s 374–5; 1950s–1960s 371–2; 1970s 372–4; 19th century 367–9; other classifications 376–7; 20th century 369–75; 21st century 375–6
Gingrich, Newt 214
Gist, Deborah 176–7
Glazer, Nathan 287
globalization 136, 291, 304
Gompers, Samuel 348
Good, Dan 68
Gordon, Eric 76
Gore, Al 201
Gould, Stephen Jay 92–3
governance: education governance 189; ideology and 327; instructional governance 316; layers of 314–15; *see also* school governance
Governing American Schools study 50
graduation rates: above national average 126; below national average 125, 224, 304; future research on 141; increases in 64, 71, 87; reports on 215; standards-based accountability 138–9; tracking of 226
grassroots organizing/activism: building public support through 130; in educational systems 40, 52; education policy 99, 121; impact of 231;

interracial organizations 403; religion and public education 275, 277, 280; school choice 337–8; in special education 378; for teacher unions 322, 328, 352, 356; for women candidates 240, 242–54, 258–9
Gray, Vincent 71
Great Depression 40, 275, 370
Great Recession 171–3, 172*f*
Great Society 191, 212
Green Dot 306
Greenlandish language 289
Grodzins, Morton 212

Harp, Toni 78
Harries, Garth 78
Harris, Daniel 78
Harris, Gene 68
Haslam, William 65
Hassel, Bryan 306
Hazelwood School District v. Kuhlmeier (1988) 149
Head Start program 193, 213, 222
Hebrew language 289
Henig, Jeff 63, 66
Heritage Foundation 274
Hickenlooper, John 65, 70
Hickok, Eugene 339
high-performing schools 6
high-stakes testing 400
High Tech High School 306
Hill, Paul 310
Hindu schools 298–9
Hispanic CREO 336–7, 339
historical school governance recycling 51–3
Holliday, Terry 198
Hollinger, David 287–8
Hollingworth, Leta 370
homeschooling movement 324, 328–9
Honaker, Reba 71–2
HOPE scholarship program 86
Hunt, James 205
Hurricane Emergency Relief Act (2005) 329, 334, 337–8

ideology: counter-aristocratic ideology 37–8; decentralization/decentralism 327; of equity 327; governance and 327; ideological diversity 46; in school choice advocacy 327–9
immigrant challenges 46, 125, 288–92, 295, 298
Improving America's Schools Act (IASA) 193–4
Indiana Supreme Court 160–1
individualistic political cultures 121
Individuals with Disabilities Act (IDEA) 157, 196, 213, 314
Industrial Revolution 39–40
inequitable charter choices in New York City 182*t*
informal arenas: patterns of politics 12–13, 18–19, 23; principle-teacher interactions 15–20; professional-patron transactions 8, 15
Ingraham v. Wright (1977) 157

innovation: attitudes, beliefs, and habits 312–13; collective bargaining agreements 315; defined 307–9; disruptive innovation 307–9; with entrepreneurship 318–19; federal laws and regulations 313–14; formal barriers to 313; impediments to 311–15; institutional innovation 219–22; layers of governance 314–15; overview 311; politics and 311–12
The Innovator's Solution (Christensen) 307
instability in school systems 47
Institute for Justice 335
institutional environment, changing 202
institutional improvement 346, 351–2
institutional innovation 219–22
institutional pluralism 292, 295
institutional survival 346–7, 352
institutional system differences 138
instructional governance 316
instructional leadership 21, 44, 47
intelligence quotient (IQ) 370
intentional discrimination 399
interest groups: comparative research on 421–2; conclusions 422; defined 411; entry and exit 414–16; lobbying and influence of 416–19; niche theory 416–17; overview 411–12; size, composition, and level 412–14; theory of 414; venture philanthropists 419–21; wrong assumptions about 418
internal determinants 100
the Internet and women's mobilization 246–7
interracial group interactions: grassroots organizing/activism 403; interethnic learning groups 395, 396–8; positive interracial contact 392–3; racial/ethnic inequality 211–12, 394, 403–4; racial groups, equal representation 386–90
interstate determinants 100
Inter-University Consortium for Political and Social Research 110
intradistrict distraction 180–1
intrastate determinants 100
Iowa Lighthouse Project 55
Islamic Foundation for Education in The Netherlands (ISNO) 298
Islamic schools 298–9
isomorphism 202
iterative role cycles 53–4

Jack Kent Cooke Foundation 377
Jackson, Frank 76
Jacob K. Javits Gifted and Talented Students Education Act 374
Jews 271, 272
Johns Hopkins University 373
Johnson, Kevin 63
Johnson, Lyndon B. 360
Johnston Public Schools (JPS) 135–6
Jones, Bryan 93–4
J.S. v. Blue Mountain School District (2012) 149
judicial impact on education politics and policies: criteria or tests 150–2; federal and state courts

158–61; final words on 161–2; historical trends in education litigation 153–6; judicial, legislative and executive exchanges 156–8; overview 148–53; reliance on precedent 149–50; sanctions and incentives 152–3

Kahlenberg, Richard D. 361, 389
Kansas Public Schools 184, 279
Hurricane Katrina 181
Kennedy, D. James 278
Kim, W. Chan 305
Kingdon, John 88–92, 105
Kitzmiller v. Dover (2005) 276
Klein, Joe 224
Knowledge Is Power Program (KIPP) schools 306
Koret Task Force 222–3

Landrieu, Mary 337
Latino immigrants 211, 295, 389, 391, 397
Lau v. Nichols (1974) 158
Layshock v. Hermitage School District (2012) 149
leadership: instructional leadership 21, 44, 47; leadership councils 15, 330; school-based leadership 8, 10; school leadership 35, 45, 220, 226, 234, 253; teacher leadership 15, 21; *see also* educational leadership
Leadership Conference on Civil Rights 334
League of United Latin American Citizens (LULAC) 336
League of Women Voters 243
learning disabilities 368, 375
Least Restrictive Environment (LRE) 373
legislative behavior theory 416
liberal democracies 291–2, 338, 360
liberal feminists 247–8, 257
licensure requirements for teachers 104, 138, 304–5, 316–17
Lieberman, Joseph 337
Liebman, James 399–400
like-minded staff 8, 15, 17, 21, 418
limited English proficiency (LEP) 158, 215, 400
Lindsay, John 74
lobbying and influence of interest groups 416–19
local government issues: advocacy 65–7, 70, 78, 81, 83; budgeting 94; common policies 402, 413; cost of services 349; federal education policy 195; federalism 211–12, 214, 223
local school council (LSC) sessions 10
Lortie, Dan 349
Los Angeles Unified School District (LAUSD) 67, 79–80
Louisiana Supreme Court 160
low-performing schools: economic development of 73; identification of 194; inner city schools 14; introduction 6, 8; mayoral engagement in 80; NCLB waivers 200, 219–20, 222–3; religion and education 277; restructuring of 225, 336; teacher blame 233; transferring away from 400; voucher program for 160
Luntz, Frank 328

McCain, John 275
McCrory, Pat 65, 126
McDuffy v. School of Education (1989) 401
McDuffy v. Secretary of Education (1993) 401
McGuinn, Pat 315
Machiavelli, Niccolo 311
McLin, Rhine 76
macropolitical agenda 93
Madison, James 212
Malloy, Dan 69
Malloy, Dannel 65
Manna, Paul 317
Maori peoples 289
marble cake federalism 212–13
market-based school reforms: acceptance of 273; accountability to 195; advocacy for 323; choice 332*t*, 333*t*; federal education policy on 99, 325; government investment in 316; support for 336, 419; *see also* charter schools
Marland, Sidney 372
Marxist insights 248
Mass Insight Education and Research Institute 221
Mauborgne, Renee 305
mayoral roles: conclusions 82–4; education and economic development 73–4; establishment of 66–70; expanding leadership and involvement 76–7; extended learning time opportunities 72–3; general trends 77–9; historical context 64–5; introduction 62–4; literature on 65–6; maturing of 74–6; perils and consequences 79–81; sustaining of involvement 81–2; wrap-around services 70–2
mayoral takeovers 51–2
Medina Valley Independent School District 274
"meet-and-confer" sessions 347–8
Mehta, Jal 317
Menino, Thomas 74–5
mentoring programs 15, 77, 131, 252, 273, 308
Meredith v. Jefferson County School Board (2007) 384
merit pay: advocacy and 322–3, 336, 339; control over 201; federal education policy on 191, 194, 199, 203–4; interest groups and 418, 420
merit-scholarship programs 86
metropolitan-wide desegregation 386–9, 403
Mexican American Legal Defense and Education Fund (MALDEF) 336, 337
Michigan Education Association (MEA) 353
Michigan Federation of Teachers (MFT) 353
Michigan Public Schools 353, 361
micropolitics of schools: introduction 4–5, 8, 11; in middle management 35–6; observations on 24–6
middle-class advantage 12–13, 24, 243, 335, 356, 370, 388
Military Tuition Assistance Program 137–8
Miller, George 334
Million Mom March on Washington, DC 246
mimetic isomorphism, defined 202
Minnesota Public Schools 397, 401–2
minority cultures in schooling 286–7
minority-run schools 293–4

models of education 358
Moe, Terry 310–12, 335, 337
Molnar, Alex 310
moralistic political cultures 121
Mormons 272
Morse v. Frederick (2007) 149
Mothers Against Drunk Driving (MADD) 245
Mothers of the Plaza de Mayo 245
Mott, Charles Stewart 330
Mourdock, Richard 242
multiculturalism 294
multicultural programs 397
multidimensional view of power 4
multiple-streams framework 88–92, 104–6
Murkowski, Lisa 241
Murphy, Jerome 216
Muslim minority 288
Muslims 294–5, 297–300

NAACP Legal Defense Fund 216
Naglieri Nonverbal Ability Test (NNAT2) 377
Nation, Carrie 243
National Alliance for Charter Schools 128
National Alliance for Public Charter Schools
 (NAPCS) 332
National Assessment of Education Progress
 (NAEP) 200, 217
National Assessment of State Progress 125
National Association for the Accreditation of Teacher
 Education (NCATE) 357–8
National Association for the Advancement of Colored
 People (NAACP) 334, 336
National Center for Education Statistics (NCES) 138,
 176, 304
National Center for Higher Education Management
 Systems (NCHEMS) 107
National Coalition for Public Education (NCPE) 333
National Coalition for Women and Girls in Education
 244–5
National Commission on Excellence in Education
 191, 374
National Conference of State Legislatures (NCSL)
 107, 110
National Defense Education Act (NDEA) 212, 280
National Education Association (NEA): advocacy
 and 333; as interest group 312; membership of
 344; politics of 349–50; public resources to private
 schools 354; union merger 356–7; women in
 teaching 233
National Education Goals Panel 192
National Federal Relations Network conference 52
National Governors Association (NGA): advocacy
 and 65, 73; Common Core standards 198; federal
 education policy 202, 204; policy making 110;
 political cultures 118
National Heritage Academies 306
National Institutes of Health 138
National Labor Relations Act (NLRA) 347
National League of Cities 66

National Organization for Women (NOW) 243, 244
National Report Card on School Funding Fairness
 170–1, 171*f*
National Research Centers for Gifted and Talented
 (NRCGT) 372
National Right to Life Committee 271
National Science Foundation 138
national security concerns and education 224, 226
National Urban League 336
National Women's Law Center 241–2
A Nation at Risk report 155, 191, 201, 224, 254, 374
Nebraska Public Schools: localism, maintenance of
 135–6; political culture 125–6, 129–32
Nebraska State Accountability Framework 131
Nebraska State Department of Education 130
neighborhood schools 192, 219, 388
neoliberals 324, 327, 328
neutrality in schooling 295, 296–300, 399
New Deal 191, 347
new fundamentalism 269–75, 279
Newsom, Gavin 65
New Teacher Project 317
New York school finance reforms 174–6, 175*f*, 176*f*
niche theory 416–17
Nickels, Greg 71
No Child Left Behind Act (NCLB): accountability
 and 214; achievement gaps and 132, 200;
 additional responsibilities from 155; adequate
 yearly progress notion 193, 215, 217–18, 352;
 advocacy and 69; challenges to 400; compliance
 with 158; corrective actions under 219, 220; goals
 of 379; historical context 64–5; identification
 of schools needing 194–5; implementation
 experience on 224–5; introduction 7; local control
 over 203–4; national educational agenda and 118,
 122; original goals of 221–2; overview 338–9;
 parental choice under 330; passage of 73, 126, 131,
 201, 215, 375; performance-based accountability
 217; performance-based federalism 217–19; policy
 changes resulting from 413–14; political culture
 141–2; reforming of 273; requirements 87, 205;
 sanctions and 319, 329; student assessments and
 135; substantial nature of 325; waivers/vouchers to
 200–1, 329
Nogan, Susan 334
nongovernmental organizations (NGOs) 81, 140, 323
normative isomorphism 202
Norquist, Grover 275
Norris, J. Frank 270
North Carolina Public Schools: political culture 124–5,
 126–9; state accountability 134–5
Norwegian language 289
"no systematic relationship" phrase 183
Nutter, Michael 68–9, 76, 79

Obama, Barack (administration): economic
 development 73–4; federal education policy 65,
 111, 193, 195–9, 204; institutional innovation,
 promotion of 219–22; political cultures 118;

programs for disadvantaged 213; Race to the Top (RTTT) program 195–7; teacher unions 343–4
Office of Civil Rights 255
Office of Innovation and Improvement 330, 338
Office of School Turnaround 220
Ogbu, John 390–1
Ohio Mayors' Education Roundtable 76
old fundamentalism 269–70
O'Neill, Beverly 82
open systems 133
Organisation for Economic Co-operation and Development (OECD) 376
Organisation for Security and Cooperation 287
outcome standards 174
outing concept in feminism 249–52
Owens, Major 337

parameters for influence 5–8
Parents Involved in Community Schools v. Seattle School District No. 1 (2007) 384
participatory reforms 10
patriarchal state: embedded patriarchal structure 237; feminist challenges to 247–9, 254, 259; gender differences 233; Title IX assumptions 244; women's liberation movement 239, 243
Patrick, Lawrence 336–7
Pat Robinson Group 245
patterns of politics: in formal arenas 9–12, 16–18, 22–3; in informal arenas 12–13, 18–19, 23
pay-for-performance plans 323
peer cultures 253
Pennsylvania Federation of Teachers (PaFT) 353
Pennsylvania State Education Association (PSEA) 353
performance-based accountability: federal education policy 193, 195, 199, 204–5; federalism 217; political cultures 139
performance-based federalism 214–15, 217–19
Perkins, Tony 271, 274
Peterson, Bart 77–8
Peterson, Terry K. 72
Petrilli, Michael 330
pluralism: community values pluralism 53; cultural pluralism 46, 293; in Dutch schooling 295; immigration and 46; institutional pluralism 292, 295; interest groups and 414; lobbying activity 417; political pluralism 55; principles of 290; social pluralism 55
pluralistic patterns of power: alternative organizational forms 8; cultural pluralism 46; new actors 8; policy content 5–8; principle-teacher interactions 15–20; professional-patron transactions 8–15; purpose and perspective 3–5; teacher-teacher interactions 20–4
Plusquellic, Donald 75
Plyler v. Doe (1982) 156
Policy Agendas Project 107
policy changes: advocacy 88–110, 419–20; advocacy coalition framework 96–9, 107–9; conclusions 111; contemporary policy theory 86; educational leadership 367, 372, 385, 402; faith and policy 277, 279–80; federalism 215–17; feminism and education politics 249, 252; future research 104–11; multiple-streams framework 88–92, 104–6; overview 86–8; pluralistic patterns of power 5–8; policy innovation and diffusion framework 99–104, 109–10, 111; punctuated equilibrium framework 92–6, 106–7; redistributive policy 213, 214, 216, 225, 255; resulting from NCLB 413–14; school choice advocacy 329–31; systemic policy level 88; theories of 88–104; *see also* federal education policy; religious faith and policy in education
policy conversion process 91
policy core beliefs 96–8, 108
policy innovation and diffusion framework (PID) 99–104; overview 99–104; policy changes 109, 111; political cultures 121, 140; spread of 95; theories of 88–92
policy stream, defined 89–90
policy subsystems 93–4, 96–9, 109, 411
political analysis 3–4
political culture in education: additional elements 128–9, 131–2; bottom-up view of 133–6; closed political cultures 120; Common Core of State Standards 132; concept of 120–2; data and methods 124; decentralization/decentralism 120, 129–30, 132; decision making 129–30; discussion over 139–42; educational policy 122–3; funding sources 137–8; future research directions 141–2; higher education concerns 136–9; illustrative cases of 123–33; individualistic political cultures 121; institutional system differences 138; introduction 118–20; moralistic political cultures 121; performance-based accountability 139; policy innovation and diffusion framework 121, 140; social justice 134–5; standards-based accountability 127–8, 130–1, 138–9; state characteristics 124–6; state comparisons 126–33; traditionalistic political cultures 121
political pluralism 55
political strategist role 40, 41, 54–5
political stream 90–1
Politics, Markets, and America's Schools (Chubb, Moe) 310–11
Populist Party 125
portable vouchers 324–5
positive interracial contact 392–3
positive neutrality in schooling 296, 297
post-enactment lobbying activity 418
power struggles 38, 49–50
prepaid tuition programs 86
preparatory strategies 18
President's Advisory Commission on Educational Equity and Excellence 184–5
principle-teacher interactions: formal/informal arenas 15–20; outcomes of 19–20; patterns of politics 16–19; sources of tension 15–16
private-sector unions 344
problem stream, defined 89–90

professional learning communities 20–1
professional-patron transactions: micropolitics of schools 24–6; outcomes 13–15; overview 8–9; patterns of politics 9–12; sources of tension 9
professional standing 346, 349–51
Program for International Assessment (PISA) 190, 206, 376, 379
Progressive Era 419
Progressive Policy Institute 330, 332
protective strategies 18
public discourse on race 403–4
public employees, bargaining law 348–9
Public Employment Relations Acts (PERAs) 347, 348
Public School Forum 126–7, 133
public schools: empowering schools 5; facilitative role of school boards 42–3; funding 168, 173, 180, 181, 183–6, 401; low-performing schools 8; micropolitics of accountability 25; role in democracy 37–8, 41, 42; school choice 337–8; *see also* after-school programs; education; educational integration; graduation rates; low-performing schools; micropolitics of schools; No Child Left Behind Act; Race to the Top (RTTT) program; school choice advocacy; school finance; school governance; superintendents and school boards; voucher programs; specific public schools
punctuated equilibrium (PE) framework 92–6, 93–6, 106–7
Purcell, Bill 71, 81–2

QuickSchools 307

Race to the Top (RTTT) program: charter schools and 325; competitive grants under 221; educational improvements and 322; federal education policy 195–7, 203, 205; requirements 82, 122
racial/ethnic inequality 211–12, 394, 399, 403–4
racial groups, equal representation 386–90
rapid diffusion 102
rationalism of social relations 120
Ravitch, Diane 310
Reagan, Ronald (administration) 190–2, 201, 204, 270, 277
redistributive policy 213, 214, 216, 225, 255
Reed, Stephen J. 75
Rees, Nina Shokraii 330, 338
reforms: curriculum 195, 198, 258; No Child Left Behind Act 273; under Obama administration 199–201; participatory reforms 10; scaling back of 12–13; social justice 336; *see also* market-based school reforms
reframing of feminist questions 236, 240, 247, 253–4
regime theory 64
regionalism 401–3
religion and culture in schools: ethnicity and 287–8, 291; immigrant challenges 288–92; minority cultures in schooling 286–7; neutrality in 296–300; overview 284; policy solutions 300–1; religious freedom 285; return of 294–6; role of the state 285–6; school practices 292–3; separate minority institutions 293–4
religious diversity 292, 295, 301
religious faith and policy in education: conclusions 279–81; historical perspective 268–9; methods 267–71; new fundamentalism 270–1; old fundamentalism 269–70; overview 267; *See also* Christian Right
religious freedom 285, 298
representative role by school board 43
Republican National Committee 241
Republican Party: Christian right and 274–9, 280; competing interests within 268; dominance in Nebraska 125; hostility toward unions 199; new fundamentalism in 271; private school endorsements 329; restriction of reproductive rights 241
resegregation 384–5, 393, 403
response to intervention (RTI) model 375
Rhee, Michelle 312
Rhode Island school finance reforms 176–7, 177*t*
Rice, Condoleezza 224
Ridge, Tom 353
Robe, Karl 275
Robertson, Pat 277–8
Roe v. Wade (1973) 276
Roisman, Florence Wagman 389
role incongruity 48–9
role negotiation 46–7
role shift ambiguity 54
Roma (Gypsy) peoples 289
Romer, Roy 79–80
Romney, Mitt 232, 276
Roosevelt, Franklin D. 347
Rose v. Council for Better Education (1989) 401
Rotherham, Andrew 330
Roy, Olivier 290–1

Saami peoples 289
same-sex marriage 273, 276, 278
San Antonio Independent School District v. Rodriguez (1973) 159, 161
Sanfer, Margaret 243
Schattschneider, E. E. 413
Scheffer, Paul 286
Schlozman, Kay 412–13
scholarship around policy innovation 66, 104, 259, 268
scholarships 86, 159, 418
School-based Teacher-led Assessment and Reporting System (STARS) 130
school choice advocacy: alliances and divisions 332–7; charter schools 13, 82, 256, 323–9, 339–40; choice diversion 181–3, 182*t*; civil rights groups and 326, 333–4, 335–7; conclusions 339–40; disadvantaged populations 324, 328, 335; educational integration 404; framework and methods 324–7; funding of groups 330–1; grassroots organizing/activism 337–8; ideology in 327–9; introduction 322–4; market-based school choice 332*t*, 333*t*; methods

326–7; opposition coalitions 333–5; overview 323–4; policy networks 329–31; strategies for choice 337–9; think tanks 330

school finance: choice diversion 181–3, 182*t*; conclusions and implications 184–6; equity and adequacy 170; fairness and effort 170–1, 171*f*; Great Recession and 171–3, 172*f*; intradistrict distraction 180–1; introduction 166–8; modern politics of 173; New York school finance reforms 174–6, 175*f*, 176*f*; protecting stealth inequalities 178–9, 179*t*; Rhode Island school finance reforms 176–7, 177*t*; state aid formulas 168–9, 169*f*; veneer of empirical validity 173–7, 175*f*, 176*f*, 177*t*

school governance: alterations to 219, 308, 359; centralization of 45; decision-making in 50; effectiveness of 48; historical recycling 51, 56; power of 9–11; roles in 42; structure of 37–8; superintendent's authority in 40

school improvement: bookkeeping nightmare 314; decentralization and 128; development of 6–7, 14, 194; direct intervention in 41; evolution of 124; grants for 199, 220; intervention options for 224; plan requirements for 219; principle-teacher interactions 15; reforms 5, 15, 44, 122; school board role in 42; support for 225; teacher unions and 357; teams 5

School Improvement and Accountability Act (1989) 127–8

school improvement grants (SIG) 190, 220

school leadership 35, 45, 220, 226, 234, 253

school-level budgeting 5

school practices: challenges to 258; gender differences 253; judicial opinions on 151, 154, 158; overview 292–3; racial disparities in 13

school vouchers 192, 274, 317, 330

Schwarzenegger, Arnold 76

scientific creationism 276

Scott, Rick 167

secondary beliefs 97–8, 108

Segarra, Pedro 78

segregation *see* educational integration

separate minority institutions 293–4

Serrano v. Priest (1971) 159

service providers 222, 306–7

sexual dynamics in education 257

sexual harassment claims 152

sexuality issues 251–2

Shannon, Christopher 301

Sheff v. O'Neil (1996) 401

site-based management councils 5, 15

Slay, Francis 63, 80

Smith, Al 270

Smith v. Robinson (1984) 157

social justice: development of 391; issues need addressing 226, 236; political culture and 134–5; reforms 336; school district culture 41; women's movement 258

social media and women's mobilization 246–7

social pluralism 55

socioeconomic status (SES) 52, 350

Southern Baptists 271

Southern Regional Education Board (SREB) 110

Soviet Union 371

special education *see* gifted and special education

Special Interest: Teachers Unions and America's Public Schools (Moe) 312

Special Populations Network of the National Association for Gifted Children 377

standards-based accountability 64, 127–8, 130–1, 138–9

Stand For Children 325, 335

Stanford-Binet test 370

state aid formulas 168–9, 169*f*

State Charter School Facilities Incentive Grants Program 316

state education agency (SEA) 314

State Higher Education Executive Officers Association (SHEEO) 107, 110

state takeovers 51, 53, 80, 204

status differences 15, 21

stealth inequalities 178–9, 179*t*

STEM (Science, Technology, Engineering, and Mathematics) 221, 238, 244, 376

Stone, Maureen 293

strict neutrality in schooling 296, 297

strict separation in schooling 296

student assessments: accountability in 392; adjustments to fit NCLB 135; educational integration 390–6; *see also* specific programs

StudentsFirst organization 325

Student Success Act 223

student tuition organizations (STOs) 159–60

superintendents and school boards: communicator role 55; conclusions 53–6; contemporary school board role 42–5; contemporary superintendent role 41–2; decision making 43, 50–1; demands on 46–7; future research directions 53; historical roles 38–41; historical school governance recycling 51–3; influences on 46; issues of representation 43–5; iterative role cycles 53–4; moving from roles to role 55–6; overview 37–8; power struggles 49–50; relationship between 47–51; role incongruity 48–9; role shift ambiguity 54; superintendent instability 46–7

supplemental education services (SES) 219

supplement not supplant rules 314, 316

systemic policy level 88

talent provider organizations 306

Tanya House of People For the American Way 334

Taveras, Angel 78

Teacher and Leader Innovation Fund 222

Teacher Incentive Fund 222

teacher-scholar role 38–9, 41, 52, 53–4

teachers/teaching: evaluation of 198–9; leadership by 15, 21; licensure requirements for 304–5; racial inequality by 394–5; strategies for educational integration 396; teaching status of women 233 teacher-teacher interactions: outcomes of 23–4; overview 20–1; patterns of politics 22–3; sources of tension 21–2

teacher unionism: under attack 349; conclusions 358–61; future of 360–1; institutional improvement 351–2; institutional survival 352; introduction 42, 343–58; models of education 358; professional standing and 349–51; structural changes in 354–6; unification of political power 357–8

Teach for America (TFA) 220, 307

Tea Party 275–6, 278

Teles, Steven 317

Templeton Foundation 376

"theology of localism" 203

think tanks: conservative think tanks 198, 328, 330, 339; educational think tanks 323; funding of 420, 421; in policy process 105, 176, 324, 329; proliferation of 330; school choice and 338; teacher unions 326

Third International Mathematics and Science Study (TIMSS) 374

Thomas B. Fordham Foundation 198, 379

three-tiered belief system 96

Time Collaborative 72

TIMMS test 190, 206

Title I: federal education policy and 194; federalism 212–16, 219, 221–2; laws and regulations 313; litigation and 152; school choice 337; supplement not supplant rules 314, 316

Title IX: coalitions 244; enforcement of 233; feminist support of 231, 247; gender differences 236–7, 240, 241; politics over 258–9; women's values and realities in 250; worry over effects of 256

tool builders 306–7

traditionalistic political cultures 121

Turkish immigrants 298

tutorial services 219, 307, 309, 339, 368

21st Century Schools Project 330

Tyack, David 313

union-management relations 348

United Federation of Teachers (UFT) 359

University of Washington 310

upper middle-class advantage 12–13

U.S. Conference of Mayors 51, 62–3, 66, 73

U.S. Constitution 148–9, 211

U.S. Department of Education: achievement gap 185; education labor force 312; federal education policy 206; funding streams 137–8, 166, 316; gifted and special education students 375; political culture 131; Supreme court decisions 153, 158

U.S. Department of Health, Education, and Welfare 158

U.S. Supreme Court 148–50, 153, 158, 240

venture philanthropists 419–21

Vermont Sustainable Jobs Fund 316

Vietnam War 154, 372

Villaraigosa, Antonio 63, 67, 80

Viteritti, Joseph 335

Voices III national study 48

voter turnout in school-board elections 45

voucher programs: charter schools and 192, 274, 317, 330, 340, 346, 349, 352; federal education policy 204; No Child Left Behind Act 200–1, 329; pilot legislation 337–8; portable vouchers 324–5; school vouchers 192, 274, 317, 330

Wagner Act 347

Walker, Jack 100

Walker, Scott 312, 343

Walton Family Foundation 419

Ward, Virgil 372

war on women 241–2

Warren, Earl 150

Washington v. Davis (1976) 399

Watergate scandal 274

Watson, Goodwin 370

web of rules 5–6

Welner, Kevin G. 400

Western Interstate Commission on Higher Education (WICHE) 110

White, Kevin 74

Williams, Creg 80

Wilson, Graham 349

Women's Educational Equity Act Program (WEEA) 236–7

Women's Equity Action League 243

women's liberation movement 239, 244

women's mobilization: coalitions, grassroots organizing, and advocacy 244–5; epistemological issues 252–4; feminism in education 247; feminist theory in education politics 247–8; gender regime concept 248–52; the Internet and social media 246–7; representation, citizenship, and democracy 242–4

Women's Political Caucus 243

women's status in public arenas: beyond education 239; current political directions 254–9; derision and disdain for 256–7; education and employment outcomes 237–9; gender and power dynamics 236–7; marginalization of 257; mobilization of 242–54; national governments 240–1; school administration 234–5; school boards 235–6; state governments 239–40; teaching status 233; war on women 241–2

Wong, Kenneth 63, 66

worker rights 347–8

Workforce Development Council 74

working-class women 245

World War I 369

World War II 370

wrap-around services 70–2

Young, Ella Flagg 236

Yousafzai, Malala 246

Zelman v. Simmons-Harris (2002) 335, 355